Social Security

Social Security:
A Documentary History

Larry W. DeWitt, Daniel Béland,
and Edward D. Berkowitz

CQ PRESS

A Division of Congressional Quarterly Inc.
Washington, D.C.

CQ Press
1255 22nd Street, NW, Suite 400
Washington, DC 20037

Phone: 202-729-1900; toll-free, 1-866-4CQ-PRESS (1-866-427-7737)

Web: www.cqpress.com

Cover design: Kimberly Glyder Design

Cover images: SSA History Archives

Composition: BMWW

♾ The paper used in this publication exceeds the requirements of the American National Standard for Information Sciences—Permanence of Paper for Printed Library Materials, ANSI Z39.48-1992.

Printed and bound in the United States of America

11   10   09   08   07   1   2   3   4   5

Library of Congress Cataloging-in-Publication Data

DeWitt, Larry, 1949–
  Social security : a documentary history / Larry DeWitt, Daniel Béland, and Edward D. Berkowitz.
    p. cm.
  ISBN 978-0-87289-502-7 (alk. paper)
  1. Social security—United States—History—Sources. I. Béland, Daniel.
II. Berkowitz, Edward D.   III. Title.

  HD7125.D495 2007
  368.4'300973—dc22   2007030363

Contents

5. ENLARGING THE PROGRAM AND INDEXING BENEFITS TO THE RATE OF INFLATION, 1966–1972   **255**

Documents

About the Authors

Larry W. DeWitt is the public historian at the U.S. Social Security Administration. A recognized authority on Social Security history, he is a member of the National Academy of Social Insurance and the Society for History in the Federal Government.

Daniel Béland is associate professor of sociology at the University of Calgary (Canada). A political sociologist analyzing politics and policy from a comparative and historical perspective, he is the author of *Social Security: History and Politics from the New Deal to the Privatization Debate* (2005), *States of Global Insecurity: Policy, Politics, and Society* (2007), and more than three dozen journal articles.

Edward D. Berkowitz is professor of history and public policy and public administration at George Washington University. He has written widely on the history of social welfare policy, including biographies of Robert Ball and Wilbur Cohen and histories of American disability policy and the U.S. welfare state. *Something Happened* (2006), his most recent book, chronicles the political and cultural history of the 1970s.

Preface

Social Security: A Documentary History uses primary documents to tell the story of the creation, growth, and retrenchment of the U.S. Social Security program. It focuses on the cash benefits programs under Title II of the Social Security Act of 1935—what is commonly referred to as Social Security.

This volume documents the legislative history, and thus development, of the Social Security program over the years. It is not a political or social history of Social Security or a survey of the academic literature about it. Rather, the documents are designed to serve as a ready reference tool to the laws enacted by Congress and signed by the president and to provide background materials to enable readers to understand and appreciate Social Security's legislative history.

The volume opens with an essay summarizing the major developments in the history of the program. The documents are extracts, but they are lengthy enough for readers to appreciate the full depth and complexity of the issues covered. They are arranged in chronological order for the most part, although in some instances policy development did not always allow for a strictly chronological sequence.

Brief introductions, and in some cases longer narratives, accompany each document, placing the documents in historical context, pointing to their significance, and explaining technical elements of Social Security policy. In addition, appendixes provide detailed information about various measures related to the development of the Social Security system.

Social Security: A Documentary History follows from the assumption that history matters. If one seeks to understand the development of the Social Security program and the genesis of its current challenges, it is essential to know the program's history. Viewing it through a historical lens reveals the key points of decision making that resulted in the program as it exists today. For instance, examination of the 1939 amendments, which created the family benefits that remain in place today, explains how the program's treatment of women came about. In a similar manner, the debate over the future of the program's finances stems from the consequences of decisions made over the course of the program's history—from the 1935 decision not to rely on general revenues (chapter one), to the congressional desire not to raise taxes in the 1940s (chapter four), to the major 1972 decision to index benefits to the rate of inflation (chapter six), to more recent political skirmishes over the program (chapters seven, eight, and nine). The selection of documents presented here illustrates how the Social Security program evolved over the course of the past seventy-plus years and offers insight into its future course as well.

A NOTE ABOUT SOURCES

There are three principal archival collections of documents related to the history of Social Security: the National Archives II in College Park, Maryland; the Social Security Administration (SSA) History Archives, located at SSA headquarters in Baltimore, Maryland; and the Social Security collection of the Wisconsin History Society on the campus of the University of Wisconsin, Madison. The SSA Historian's Office has published online guides to all three collections. These guides are accessible at www.ssa.gov/history/archives/archives.html.

ACKNOWLEDGMENTS

As in all documentary histories, our greatest debt is owed to the people who created the historical record. These include not only highly visible political leaders but also staff who worked in relative anonymity to analyze problems in Social Security and make policy. Beyond that fundamental debt, we also owe a great deal to each other. Each of the editors would therefore like to thank his fellow editors.

This project originated in a request by Doug Goldenberg-Hart of CQ Press to produce a Social Security reference book. We are grateful to him and the staff of CQ Press for bringing this book to print. We especially want to thank January Layman-Wood, the development editor on our project, for getting things started so well and for helping us integrate the numerous photographs into the text.

Authors sometimes think the role of editors is to throw obstacles in their path, but our copy editor, Kerry V. Kern, has proven this old idea wrong yet again. She has been a marvel of efficiency and helpfulness and her suggestions invariably improved the text and saved us from numerous small (and sometimes not so small) errors.

We want to note in particular that Marc Goldwein, while a student at Johns Hopkins University, conducted the research for Appendix B as part of an internship with the Social Security Administration's Historian's Office. Marc also made many important contributions to Chapter 9 on Social Security reform proposals, a topic on which he wrote his senior thesis at Johns Hopkins and on which he has developed an impressive expertise.

Each of us also has particular debts. Larry DeWitt would like to thank his wife, Gabriela, for tolerating the project and its many demands on family time over such an extended period and especially for being such a stable source of love and support in a very stressful period during the preparation of this book. Daniel Béland would like to thank his wife, Angela Kempf, who provided important and much-appreciated support and also helped in editing some of the introductory material in the various chapters. Ed Berkowitz would like to acknowledge academic colleagues with whom he has collaborated on pieces related to Social Security, including Kim McQuaid, Eric Kingson, Wendy Wolff, Daniel Fox, Richard Scotch, Richard Burkhauser, Chris Howard, and David Dean.

Finally, we want to make it clear that the selection of the documents and the historical commentary reflect the predilections of the authors and in no way represent the official viewpoints of our employers: the Social Security Administration, the University of Calgary, and the George Washington University.

Introduction: An Overview of the Social Security Program, 1935–2006

In size and scope, the Social Security program is the most expansive and important social welfare program in the United States. Some 48,445,900 Americans received Social Security benefits in 2005 (**Appendix E**), which meant that more Americans were on the Social Security rolls than the combined populations of California and New Jersey.

In that year, the program received more than $700 billion from payroll taxes and other sources and spent a little more than $500 billion on benefits (**Appendix D**). To put that in prospective, the program took in about as much revenue as the gross domestic product of the Netherlands.

The Social Security program is also the largest single function in the federal government's budget, accounting for nearly one-quarter of all expenditures.

THE CREATION OF SOCIAL SECURITY

Congress passed the Social Security Act in 1935. Ironically, a program now deemed by some too large to keep its promises was criticized at the time for not making enough promises. Critics worried that it would be too small and inconsequential to get fully implemented. What became America's most durable social program almost did not receive congressional approval.

In the simplest sense, Social Security relied on the idea of social insurance, which arrived first in the advanced industrial countries of Western Europe, such as Germany and England, and received attention in the United States during the Progressive Era at the beginning of the twentieth century (**Documents 1.1–1.5**). Under social insurance, the state forced workers to contribute to a fund from which they received benefits that cushioned them against the untoward contingencies of industrial life, such as being unable to keep up the pace of production in old age or suffering from a layoff that put them out of work. Most states passed workers' compensation programs, such as existed in Germany, during the Progressive Era. These laws required employers to insure themselves against the risk of costs imposed on employees by industrial accidents. Two of the key leaders of the movement to create Social Security—Secretary of Labor Frances Perkins (1933–1945) and Arthur Altmeyer, the second head of the Social Security Board and the long-time chief administrator of Social Security (1937–1953)—got their starts as workers' compensation administrators, in New York and Wisconsin respectively.

Apart from the example of workers' compensation, foreign precedent carried relatively little weight in the creation of Social Security, as domestic concerns dominated the policy debate. For one thing, neither workers nor unions nor employers placed much faith in the administrative competence of the federal government. Most unions, in particular, feared that the state held the interests of capital over those of labor. In the United States,

President Roosevelt signs the Social Security Act of 1935 in the Cabinet Room of the White House. Also shown, left to right: Rep. Robert Doughton (D-N.C.); Sen. Robert Wagner (D-N.Y.); Rep. John Dingell, Sr. (D-Mich.); Unknown man in bowtie; Secretary of Labor Frances Perkins; Senator Pat Harrison (D-Miss.); Rep. David L. Lewis (D-Md.).
Source: Library of Congress.

private collective bargaining over working conditions predominated over government laws and regulations.

Despite these feelings, Social Security—defined as retirement pensions for workers sixty-five years of age or older—made it to the U.S. public policy agenda. One reason was the continued agitation of Secretary Perkins within President Franklin Roosevelt's cabinet. Another reason was that the onset of the Depression in the 1930s highlighted the problem of old-age insecurity. In a time of mass unemployment, the plight of the elderly seemed especially poignant, even though the elderly, unlike other groups in the battered population, tended to have more assets, such as homes, than younger citizens. In partial response, an organized movement to assist the elderly poor gathered strength in the 1920s and resulted in the passage by 1935 of twenty-eight state old-age pension laws. Reformers such as Perkins criticized these laws for their stringent age limits (fourteen states limited aid to people over seventy), for their restrictions on eligible beneficiaries (some states required that the recipient must have lived in the state for more than ten years), and for the extremely low level of payments, which did not go beyond a dollar a day for the few people lucky enough to receive them.

Another reason for the emergence of federally administered old-age pensions was the presence of the Townsend Plan (**Documents 1.6 and 1.7**), which proposed to pay a sizable pension to any elderly U.S. citizen over age sixty. Precedents for this sort of proposal came from the extensive system of veterans payments that followed the Civil War and from the many schemes to inflate the money supply that flourished in the populist era at the end of the nineteenth century. Francis E. Townsend, a California medical doctor, wanted to put more money in the hands of the elderly and in that manner reinvigorate the economy. The popularity of the Townsend Plan created grassroots support for federal old-age pension legislation.

Despite being urged on by Perkins and pushed by the Townsend Plan, President Roosevelt did not rush to send an old-age pension law to Congress. Instead, he let Congress take the lead in this area and concentrated his energies on the more immediate problems of recovery. The president initially focused on emergency relief, not the longer-term reform of the labor market to require employers to pay old-age pensions or unemployment benefits. Like other progressive reformers, the president disapproved of schemes that imposed large costs on the federal budget and, in the manner of veterans' pensions, promised to saddle future generations with even larger expenditures.

Nonetheless, the president decided to act in the summer of 1934, just before his party's landslide victory in the congressional elections that fall. He created a cabinet level committee—the Committee on Economic Security (CES), which would be headed by Perkins—to study problems related to economic security and to come up with practical solutions in the form of legislation that he could present to the next Congress. This committee, assisted by workers drawn from the relevant government departments and a staff of outside consultants called to Washington, drew the blueprint for what became Social Security (**Documents 1.8–1.11**). The experts who did most of the work on old-age pensions were a professor of labor economics from Princeton (J. Douglas Brown), an expert on industrial pensions (Murray Latimer), and a California law school professor with a special interest in social welfare policy (Barbara Armstrong). Together this group worked through the complicated logistics of creating a viable old-age pension scheme.

The group considered such matters as how to design a program that would pass muster with the Supreme Court and not be declared unconstitutional, as had happened with key New Deal programs passed in 1933. The three experts also faced the question of how to provide for people already old and no longer able to make contributions. They wanted to finance old-age pensions in a way that did not strain the fiscal capabilities of workers, employers, or the federal budget and did not place a crushing burden on future generations. Finally, the group needed to decide what, if anything, the federal government should do about the state pensions already in place and, in general, how to respond to the advocates of the Townsend Plan.

The final plan took a pragmatic approach to the problems. State old-age assistance (welfare pensions) would be preserved, even strengthened, with federal matching funds and new federal requirements designed to make their administration more professional and less overtly political. That, it was hoped, would take care of those already old and unable to participate in a social insurance plan. Younger workers would be required to participate in a pension program financed by payroll taxes. Those near retirement would have their pensions subsidized by the other workers and ultimately by adding general revenues to the pool of payroll taxes collected from workers and their employers. To collect enough money to pay meaningful pensions and to solve the many administrative problems posed by such a scheme, the program would begin to collect payroll taxes at the beginning of 1937 and pay its first regular benefits in 1942.

President Roosevelt made a key adjustment to this plan before he presented it to Congress in January 1935 (**Document 1.12**). Thinking it improper to saddle future generations with expenditures accrued in the 1940s, he insisted that the program be entirely self-supporting. That is to say, it should pay pensions with money raised through payroll taxes rather than general revenues. Secretary of the Treasury Henry Morgenthau Jr. announced the change in his testimony to the House Ways and Means Committee in early February. Relying entirely on payroll taxes meant higher tax rates than originally envisioned, as much as 6 percent of taxable payroll by 1949.

Contrary to the expectations of the administration, passage of the Social Security Act was neither speedy nor free of controversy (**Documents 1.14–1.16**). At key points the bill threatened to become unraveled and postponed to a future session of Congress. Early in 1935 the president hoped to make the bill one of the first measures passed in the legislative session. Trouble developed almost immediately. Most members reacted with indifference to the multifaceted bill, with its provisions for welfare, old-age insurance, unemployment compensation, and public health, except for the section that allowed states to augment their old-age pension programs through federal assistance. The other parts of what was then called the Economic Security Act—with provisions for payroll taxes and promises of future, rather than immediate, benefits—offered little of short-term political value. Coverage restrictions, such as limiting old-age insurance to industrial and commercial workers, made Social Security appear irrelevant to the many members who came from agricultural districts. Rep. Allen Treadway of Massachusetts, the ranking Republican member of the Ways and Means Committee, called the old-age insurance program the "worst title in the bill."[1]

On March 20, 1935, the *New York Times* ran a story by reporter Louis Stark, who had already filed a series of unsympathetic reports on the legislation, under the headline: "Hopes Are Fading for the Social Security Bill." Stark wrote:

> The confusion that has arisen since hearings of the Ways and Means Committee on the omnibus bill, the apathy of members of Congress on the measure, and the split between the bill's adherents, serve to support the opinion of those who are convinced that President Roosevelt's elaborate plans for social security will probably result in the enactment of but one major measure—old-age assistance for indigent persons over 65 years of age.[2]

The next day the *Times* editorialized that the president's Social Security program was simply "too large" and that it should be broken up, with only the state old-age pensions passed and the rest carried over into the next year.[3]

During the crucial month of April 1935, the Ways and Means Committee passed what the *Times* described as a "drastically altered" bill, but it retained old-age insurance. Committee members worried about what would happen to the bill once on the floor for debate. They feared that the measure would be "Townsendized," split into separate measures, or changed to include lower tax rates.[4] Realizing he could lose a key piece of legislation, Roosevelt called the House leaders to the White House and urged them to pass the Social Security Act as a matter of personal loyalty to him. The members swallowed their doubts and passed the bill by a substantial 372–33 margin.[5]

Congress made significant changes in the administration's bill. Perhaps most importantly it scaled back the administration's proposal of nearly universal coverage to one that included only workers in commerce and industry (about 60 percent of the jobs in the economy). Among the groups excluded from coverage were federal employees, professionals (such as attorneys and doctors), the self-employed, domestic workers, and agricultural workers. Members of Congress and administration officials believed that the practical problems of collecting payroll taxes from these last two groups made their participation inadvisable. Although the final report of the CES supported the inclusion of domestic and agricultural workers, the Roosevelt administration subsequently asked the Ways and Means Committee to postpone temporarily their inclusion to the Social Security system (**Document 1.13**).

In retrospect, historians have attributed the exclusion of domestic and agricultural workers—occupations in which a disproportionate number of African Americans participated—to the politics of race. It remains a contested point. Little direct evidence demonstrates that racial prejudice or the mobilization of southern Democrats was the driving force behind the decision to exclude these workers from Social Security. The limited administrative capacity of the federal government is frequently cited as playing a part in the decision.[6]

House passage failed to end the legislative controversy. In the Senate, a dispute arose over whether employers who already provided their workers with pensions could opt out of the Social Security system. Sen. Bennett Champ Clark (D-Mo.), the sponsor of the amendment that came to bear his name, argued that many private plans had more liberal features than the new public plan, such as earlier retirement ages for women, disability protection, and increased pensions for married couples. The Clark Amendment passed the Senate and became a sticking point in the conference committee considering the bill. In the end, the Senate conferees agreed to withdraw the Clark Amendment for further discussion. Its passage would have changed the nature of Social Security by altering its status from compulsory to voluntary.

With this matter disposed of, but after further delays, President Franklin Roosevelt signed the Social Security Act into law on August 14, 1935.

THE FIRST CONTROVERSY OVER FUNDING

Even after the passage of the law, prospects did not improve for the Social Security program. The Republicans decided to make an issue of Social Security in the 1936 election (**Documents 2.1–2.3**). Plans for implementation of the law waited on the Supreme Court's decision on the act's constitutionality, which did not come until Justice Benjamin Cardozo's favorable opinion of May 1937 in *Helvering v. Davis* (**Document 2.4**). When the first payroll deductions began in January 1937, some workers found a note in their pay envelopes that equated the new Social Security taxes with theft (the notes were a joint project of the Republican National Committee and some employers). As late as May 1938 Social Security officials had to meet with a group of employers who questioned the point of providing workers with receipts for Social Security deductions. Most workers, the employers said, simply threw the receipts away, and some suspicious workers even wanted to visit the Social Security headquarters in Baltimore, Maryland, and make sure that their contributions had been credited to their accounts. For years, Social Security employees faced problems matching employers' contributions with the appropriate workers, and they were even tasked with tracking down covered employers and workers and making sure they were participating in the program. Some covered workers were unaware of the new law and some employers wanted to avoid new tax and paperwork responsibilities. Thus it was not uncommon in the early years of the program for compliance with existing coverage to be an ongoing administrative concern.

In the period between 1935 and 1939, Social Security's method of financing attracted the most criticism and dominated the program's politics. Sources as varied as the Republican Party, the Brookings Institution, the American Federation of Labor, the Chamber of Commerce, and the *New York Times* attacked the notion of the program collecting a surplus of funds in the early years of its operation and using the interest on that surplus to meet the debt that would accrue in its later years. The problem stemmed from President

Roosevelt's earlier decision to finance the program entirely through payroll taxes. In order not to impose crushing tax burdens on future generations, planners decided to spread the burden more evenly by building a reserve fund and using the interest on that fund to help meet the program's future shortfalls. Between 1937 and 1942, for example, workers and employers would contribute payroll taxes and the program would pay out nearly no benefits. Hence, Congress would appropriate most of the $511 million collected in 1937 into a reserve fund. In 1980, according to the original plans, payroll taxes would yield $2 billion—but benefits would cost $3.5 billion. The shortfall would be made up by interest from the reserve fund that, according to projections, would have contained $47 billion in 1980.[7]

The critics questioned the ability of the government to effect those sorts of savings when, in the 1930s, the federal budget was running a constant deficit. Any money that the government received it spent, which begged the question of how it could simultaneously save the money for the future. The predicted $47 billion represented an astonishing amount of money in the late 1930s. It was enough money to buy all the farms in the United States and still have $14 billion to spare. Commenting on the fantastic nature of the plan, the Republican Party stated in its 1936 platform that the "so-called reserve fund is no reserve at all, because the fund will contain nothing but the government's promise to pay, while the taxes collected in the guise of premiums will be wasted in reckless and extravagant political schemes."[8] On September 26, 1936, Republican presidential nominee and Kansas governor Alfred Landon blasted Social Security as "unjust, unworkable, stupidly drafted, and wastefully financed" (**Document 2.1**).

The attack on the reserve fund led to a Senate resolution condemning reserve financing and to a Senate Finance Committee hearing that resulted in the creation of the 1937–1938 Advisory Council on Social Security, composed of representatives of labor, management, and the public, to study the matter further and issue concrete recommendations (**Documents 2.5–2.10**).

The members of the 1937–1938 council debated important matters related to the future of Social Security. Some, such as Wisconsin professor Edwin Witte, defended the reserve method of financing as a means of restraining future tax increases and guaranteeing the government's future commitment to the Social Security program. Others, such as Provident Mutual Insurance Company actuary Albert Linton, attacked the reserve method of funding as putting too much temptation in the path of the government, which would—through the irresistible impulses of politics—use reserves to expand program benefits, leaving future generations with catastrophic costs and no means of paying for them.

The advisory council met for the first time in November 1937 and issued a report in 1938 that formed the basis for the 1939 amendments to the Social Security Act. In essence, the amendments ended the controversy over reserve financing by moving up the date for the start of regular benefit payments from 1942 to 1940 and expanding the range and generosity of the benefits through the creation of life insurance and family protection features. Because the amendments called for spending more money early in the life of the program, they cut down on the surpluses collected and effectively stopped the reserve controversy, at least until 1983 when different circumstances once again prompted the creation of a reserve fund to meet future contingencies (**Documents 2.12–2.15**). Once implemented, the 1939 amendments diminished the large reserves but also expanded benefits.

The form of the expanded benefits created a pattern that would define how the program approached sensitive matters related to women's labor force participation, divorce, and other controversial topics tied to family structure. In February 1938, for example, the advisory council took the first steps by approving a plan prepared by the Social Security Board to create a benefit for a contributor's wife and another benefit for a contributor's widow. By the terms of the plan, a married couple would receive 150 percent of the man's benefit and a beneficiary's widow would receive 75 percent of a single man's benefit. A few months later the council reviewed and approved a plan to extend benefits to a deceased worker's dependent children and to the mother who cared for the children. "A democratic society has an immeasurable stake in avoiding the growth of a habit of dependency in its youth. The method of survivors' insurance not only sustains the concept that a child is supported through the efforts of the parent but affords a vital sense of security to the family unit," the council wrote in its report.[9]

Beyond these generalities, a host of details—seemingly technical in nature but each of which represented value judgments that later observers would call into question—needed to be settled. The basic percentages—50 percent for a wife and 75 percent for a widow—contained the hidden assumptions that dependent wives, but not dependent husbands, deserved support; that married couples deserved more than single individuals; and that widows deserved less than single men. Each of these decisions—made first by the Social Security Board staff, then by the Advisory Council on Social Security, and then by Congress—was rooted in traditional ideas about gender and family roles. As gender-related labor force participation patterns changed, these decisions increasingly began to appear unjust and anachronistic. The family benefits locked in the world as perceived by Social Security policymakers in 1939, just before the rise in female labor force participation during the World War II and at the beginning of an era in which 60 percent of additions to the labor force would be female.[10]

In 1939 policymakers seldom confronted gender issues directly. For example, they chose to ignore the fact that women lived longer than men and instead made benefits for female workers the same as those for male workers. Wives and widows were to receive benefits, beginning at age sixty-five, despite the fact that men tended to marry younger women. As a result, full benefits for married couples were often delayed well beyond the man's sixty-fifth birthday. Policymakers reasoned that, if women workers had to wait until age sixty-five to receive benefits, then wives should wait as well. Widows without children in their care needed to wait until the normal retirement age until they could receive benefits, even if that meant years without regular wage support. The persistence of the Depression made policymakers extra careful in the design of benefits, so that, for example, a marriage had to last five years for a wife to become eligible for benefits. Similar considerations applied to widows for fear that women eager to secure support would make "deathbed marriages." Divorce, relatively rare in 1939 but the end result of nearly half of all marriages by 1975, further complicated the problem, as policymakers needed to decide what claim a divorced wife had on her husband's benefits.[11]

Although each of the many decisions could and would be reconsidered over the course of the program's history, the process inevitably took a great deal of time. The long process excluded whole generations from the liberalizing tendencies of incremental change. For example, a basic matter of gender equity remained unresolved until 1950. In that year, benefits were established for husbands and widowers, analogous to the benefits for wives and widows. Even then, more stringent conditions applied to men obtaining benefits from the wage records of their spouses than to women who claimed support on the basis of marriage or death of their spouses. In a similar manner, Congress awarded benefits to divorced wives in 1965 but with limiting conditions that were not fully eased until 1983. A divorced woman needed to have been married to her former husband for at least twenty years, she could not be married at the time she received the benefit, and she had to demonstrate financial dependence on her ex-husband. Over time, Congress lowered the age at which widows could receive benefits and raised the percentage of the basic benefit that widows received. A 1956 law, for example, set minimum ages for women's retirement benefits, widows' benefits, and wives' benefits at sixty-two.

Although pushed by women's rights groups in the 1980s, gender equity competed with many other concerns, such as the basic adequacy of benefits, benefits for people with disabilities, and reforms intended to ease recurrent financial crises. In general, the pattern created in 1939 remained with the program, giving married couples higher benefits than single individuals.

THE 1940S AND THE 1950 AMENDMENTS

Despite the 1939 amendments, Social Security did not gain great popularity. Instead, it remained a relatively neglected program (**Document 3.2**). During the World War II, programs more directly related to national service predominated over Social Security. In 1940, for example, even before the nation's entrance into the war, the United States spent more on veterans' payments and workers' compensation than it did on Old-Age and Survivors Insurance (OASI). Even in the area of old-age security, social insurance—a federal program—played a distinctly secondary role to welfare—a state and local program. By the end of the 1940s, more than 20 percent of the elderly received old-age assistance (welfare) benefits, and in a few states more than 50 percent received such payments. The average monthly welfare benefit was $42 in 1949, although there was considerable variance from state to state; the average Social Security benefit was $25.[12] As late as 1950, more than twice as many people were on state welfare rolls receiving old-age assistance as were receiving retirement benefits from the federal government under Social Security. In the more rural and agricultural states, the disparity was extreme.

The coverage issue proved particularly vexing for the Social Security program in the 1940s. Only about half the jobs in the economy were covered by the social insurance program as enacted in 1935. The push to expand coverage made little headway. The Advisory Council on Social Security of 1937–1938 recommended that coverage be extended to farm and domestic workers; employees of nonprofit organizations; and federal, state, and local government employees. President Roosevelt endorsed these measures at the beginning of 1939, but Congress declined the recommendations. "Doctor, when the first farmer with manure on his shoes comes to me and asks to be covered, I will be willing to consider it," crusty Ways and Means Chairman Robert Doughton (D-N.C.) told Social Security administrator Arthur Altmeyer.[13] Congress dropped the list of potential entrants to the Social Security system and replaced it with a much smaller one of its own. Merchant marines got coverage while key groups like farmers remained outside of the system. The administration concurred in these small changes, because survivors' benefits mattered more to it in 1939 than expanding coverage.[14]

The coverage issue did not reemerge until the end of the 1940s. In March 1948, Congress enacted legislation that exempted about 500,000 newspaper and magazine vendors from Social Security coverage.[15] Vetoing the bill, President Harry Truman told Congress, "This legislation . . . raises the fundamental question of whether or not we shall maintain the integrity of our social security system. . . . The security and welfare of our Nation demand an expansion of social security to cover the groups which are now excluded from the program."[16] Unimpressed, the Republican Congress easily overrode the veto (with the president receiving only 35 sustaining votes in both houses combined).

Quick on the heels of this effort, Congress enacted a second law exempting another 500,000 workers. This time the congressional Democrats and the administration mounted a full-court press against the change, turning the coverage question into a partisan issue in the 1948 election. The acting secretary of the Treasury, the Federal Security Agency administrator, and officials at the Social Security Administration (SSA) all issued formal statements of opposition to the legislation. The president vetoed the bill in June, just as he had done in the case of the newspaper vendors two months earlier, using much the same language.[17] But even with the political stakes raised, the Republican Congress once again overrode the president (but the political push upped the president's combined total to 89 sustaining votes). The decade ended as it had begun, with little congressional interest in widespread coverage extension.

If Congress tended to treat coverage extension in a rather cavalier manner during the 1940s, it paid far more attention to the financing issue. By the terms of the 1939 amendments, the tax rate increase scheduled to take place in 1940 was cancelled. Instead, the program was poised for an earlier start of more generous benefits and for regularly scheduled periodic rounds of tax rate increases. The tax rate was scheduled to triple by 1950, from its frozen 1939 rate of 2 percent to an eventual 6 percent of payroll. However, when the rate increase scheduled for 1943 loomed, Congress froze the rate for a second time. Congress repeated this pattern six more times during the decade. The Social Security tax rate, which had been scheduled to rise four times by 1949, stayed at its 1937 rate until 1950.

Favorable economic conditions eased financing problems. Wartime mobilization kept the unemployment rate low (thus assuring high flows of revenue to the Social Security system) and encouraged people to postpone retirement (thereby reducing benefit demands on the system). The result was a Social Security system unexpectedly flush with cash. Indeed, the actuarial projections used in the 1939 law anticipated a reserve of $2.6 billion by 1943; the actual reserve was more than $4.8 billion by that time. In such an environment, the short-range view that taxes were higher than they needed to be proved irresistible to members of Congress in both parties. Congress repeatedly took the popular step of postponing Social Security tax increases.

Flush with cash, the Social Security program nevertheless seemed stuck on a relatively low plateau, eclipsed by other programs and with few ardent supporters in Congress. The situation faced by Social Security advocates was a crisis of inactivity, although opponents of Social Security continued to worry that large surpluses in a healthy economy would eventually mean an expanded program. As things turned out, the fears of the opponents materialized with the expansion of the system in 1950.

The process that led to the 1950 amendments resembled that of 1939 (**Documents 3.6–3.11**). The Senate Finance Committee, under Republican control in the 80th Congress, once again appointed an advisory council, officially titled the Advisory Council on Social Security. Meeting in 1948, the council produced a report that had a lasting impact on the future of Social Security in the form of the 1950 amendments, which incorporated many of the council's suggestions.

The chief idea of the report centered on a perceived choice in the nation's approach to old-age security. It could either rely on welfare, which the council portrayed as demeaning since it required recipients to prove they were poor and induced a state of dependency, or on social insurance, which the council believed to be the superior alternative. As the council stated, "Our goal, so far as possible, is to prevent dependency through social insurance and thus greatly reduce the need for public assistance." In this formulation, social insurance reinforced "the interest of the individual in helping himself."[18] Contributory social insurance provided a worker (assumed to be male in the official rhetoric of the era) "with the best guarantee that he will receive the benefits promised and that they will not be conditioned on his accepting either scrutiny of his personal affairs or restrictions from which others are free."[19]

Looked at in this manner, the problem became how best to expand social insurance. Two obvious means presented themselves. One was to extend coverage to more workers so that, as the council put it, "the character of one's occupation should not force one to rely for basic protection on public assistance rather than insurance."[20] Another was to raise the benefit levels for everyone, so as to make Social Security as generous financially as welfare. The problems stemmed from accomplishing these goals while still preserving the much lauded contributory nature of social insurance. If someone who had worked in a previously excluded occupation, such as a small businessman or a farmer, were suddenly to be given Social Security benefits, then that person would have done nothing to earn his benefits. Even people near retirement age, brought into the Social Security system, would not have enough time to "earn" their benefits. Yet if the benefits were to be politically useful, they would have to be higher than those paid by state welfare authorities. Dealing with those questions required pragmatic adjustments to the system. The council's plan called for new groups to be brought into the Social Security system under terms that allowed them to qualify for benefits relatively quickly. The plan also relied on a change in the benefit formula so as to pay higher benefits for all current and future recipients.

On August 28, 1950, after considerable congressional scrutiny and debate, the recommendations of the advisory council became law. Through this law, the proponents of Social Security gained what they wanted: a greatly expanded Social Security program that paid substantially higher benefits. The proponents included labor unions, which had negotiated pensions for large industries (such as automobile and steel manufacturers) that factored in Social Security as part of those pensions. Higher Social Security benefits made it easier for employers to meet their pension obligations and encouraged them to offer higher pensions. The ranks of Social Security supporters also included liberal Democrats, who were boosted in the 1948 elections with President Truman's surprising reelection, the revival of Democratic control of Congress, and the election of Social Security supporters Paul Douglas of Illinois and Hubert Humphrey of Minnesota to the Senate. These factors helped change the congressional mood from indifference to a willingness to expand the system.

The 1950 amendments raised average benefits by 77 percent and broke the impasse over Social Security taxes. Congress agreed to raise the tax level to 3 percent, split as always between employers and employees, and to raise the taxable wage base (the amount of earnings on which taxes were paid) from $3,000 to $3,600. Once again, Congress, reaffirming the principle that the system should never have to depend on general revenues, included a schedule of future tax increases in the measure, with a maximum of 6.5 percent to be reached in 1970.

The 1950 law added a new feature to the tax and to program coverage. A majority of self-employed persons received Social Security coverage, at a tax rate of 2.25 percent of taxable payroll (measured through income tax returns). In other words, the self-employed paid more than industrial and commercial workers but less than the combined rate of these workers and their employers—just the sort of pragmatic political adjustment that figured prominently in the 1950 amendments. The change meant that the program no longer was limited to commercial and industrial employees. Eight million new workers came into the system and added to its political base. Arthur Altmeyer, who remained in charge of the program through the Roosevelt and Truman years, later termed the 1950 law "crucial" to Social Security's survival.[21] It meant that Social Security had finally attained parity with welfare. In February 1951, for the first time in the nation's history, more people received old-age insurance than received old-age assistance. In August 1951, also for the first time in the nation's history, the total amount of insurance payments exceeded the amount of old-age assistance payments.

EXPANSION IN THE 1950S

After 1950, the incremental engine of Social Security expansion kicked into high gear. The expansions of 1952 and 1954 set a pattern that persisted until the early 1970s, as new occupational groups came into the system and the average level of benefits was raised. In the 1952 amendments, policymakers took advantage of an expanding economy and a new attitude toward the program. During the 1940s, large surpluses developed in the Social Security trust fund, and Congress reacted by postponing tax increases against the backdrop of a nation channeling its savings into the war effort and a public indifference to a program that compared unfavorably with state welfare programs. What changed after 1950 was the indifference. Expansion of Social Security attracted a wider coalition of advocates because more people benefited from the program than had been the case in the 1940s. In that sense, the 1950 amendments paved the way for the expansions that were to follow.

Congress was not in the habit of making regular Social Security expansions and needed to learn how to go about it. Bureaucrats in the SSA proved to be willing tutors. In the spring of 1952, Robert M. Ball, head of the Division of Program Analysis, sought out the chief clerk of the House Committee on Ways and Means and pointed out that Social Security benefits could be raised without a tax increase. The technical reasons related to actuarial assumptions were of less interest to Chairman Doughton and his committee colleagues than the practical results: a 12.5 percent increase in benefits, passed in July, just in time for the 1952 presidential election. A new spirit of expansion entered Social Security politics. As Wilbur Cohen, another key official in the SSA, explained to a fellow advocate of expansion, the 1952 legislation "gets us away from the idea that OASI is a depression phenomenon and that it will be another 10 years before benefits can be increased."[22]

Although the program appeared to be gaining momentum, it faced a new test in 1953, with the arrival of Dwight Eisenhower, the first Republican president since Herbert Hoover, and the return of a Republican majority in Congress. The Republican position on Social Security remained uncertain at the beginning of the year. President Eisenhower included a line about expanding Social Security in his first State of the Union address delivered February 3, but he left out key details. His position on a contributory program, in which only those who paid social security taxes received benefits, remained unclear. Some thought he might recommend providing a benefit to all the elderly in the manner of the earlier Townsend proposal. The irony was that the suggestion for such a benefit came from the conservative, rather than the liberal, wing of the Republican Party. Conservatives believed that surpluses in the Social Security trust funds inevitably led to benefit expansions, as was the case in 1950 and 1952. Congress always took steps to cover future liabilities, such as by raising tax rates in the distant future. Conservatives placed little faith in Congress honoring those tax increases, however, a feeling reinforced by the experiences of the 1940s. Some conservatives, such as Albert Linton, an actuary and insurance executive with influence in Social Security policymaking circles, believed it would be better to provide universal coverage. That would reduce current surpluses and make it harder for liberals to raise benefit levels beyond the country's current capacity to pay for them. During the presidential campaign of 1952, neither Eisenhower nor Democratic nominee Adlai Stevenson discussed the program in this sort of detail. After the election, conservatives, such as Linton, came forward with tangible proposals.

In 1953 an intensive debate over Social Security took place in three separate forums. The first was an advisory group assembled by Oveta Culp Hobby, an Eisenhower appointee who became the first head of the Department of Health, Education, and Welfare (HEW). During the spring of 1953, this group formulated options for Hobby that she could use in her deliberations within the administration and with Congress. The second forum consisted of a special Ways and Means subcommittee convened by Carl Curtis (R-Neb.) that held hearings in November 1953 to consider whether the financing and coverage of the program, as constituted in 1953, made sense and deserved to be continued. The final and most important forum involved government officials from HEW, the SSA, and the White House meeting throughout the fall of 1953 to prepare legislative recommendations for Congress to consider in 1954.

In each of these forums, the proponents of Social Security prevailed. The "Hobby Lobby," as the group was known, began with a conservative cast. The secretary soon yielded to pressure generated by labor unions and liberal groups and expanded the membership to include proponents of expansion. The Social Security Administration lent its expertise to the effort, and in the end the group endorsed continuity, rather than radical reform. The congressional hearings failed to create a groundswell of public opinion in favor of radically revising the program. Instead, they provided yet another arena for staff members from the SSA, such as Robert Ball and former commissioner Altmeyer, to demonstrate their detailed knowledge of the program. These two forums influenced the outcome of the third, as the administration ended up proposing to expand Social Security coverage and increase benefits. The plans to blanket in all the elderly and constrain the program's ultimate growth were quietly laid aside. President Eisenhower explained to one critic of Social Security that "it would appear logical to build upon the system that has been in effect for almost twenty years, rather than embark upon the radical course of turning it completely upside down and running the very real danger that we would end up with no system at all."[23]

Congress, despite its Republican majority, acquiesced in the program expansion. A vote to expand Social Security, after all, meant following the administration's line. The bipartisan cooperation that prevailed in 1952, during the Korean emergency, extended to the peacetime era of 1954 and beyond. The result in 1954 was a major extension of coverage to include farm operators, a rise in the average level of benefits of 13 percent, a rise in the tax rate to 4 percent, and a rise in the level of wages on which workers and their employers paid taxes from $3,600 to $4,200.

Despite the harmony on the basic principles, Social Security politics maintained a partisan edge between 1950 and 1956. Although conservative Republicans, such as Sen. Robert Taft of Ohio, accepted the fact that Social Security benefits could be increased without unduly raising tax rates, they balked at creating new types of benefits. In the 1950s, the debate centered on disability benefits. Congress members who believed that Social Security costs could be controlled nonetheless worried that disability benefits were somehow different and could lead to prohibitive costs that would bankrupt the system. If, for example, people with physical infirmities were permitted to retire before the normal retirement age and still receive full benefits, then a surge in unemployment might produce a run on the rolls. General retirement patterns, a function of age, could be predicted with some certainty. Disability patterns, a function of perceived health status and the state of the economy, were by their very nature less certain and more volatile. A group of conservatives in the Senate, such as Taft and Harry Flood Byrd (D-Va.), formed an imposing block opposing the passage of disability insurance.

Historical circumstances allowed these opponents to be more than negative. In World War II, physicians like Howard Rusk and Henry Kessler dramatized the achievements of a new branch of medicine that they called rehabilitation medicine. Their national campaign on behalf of rehabilitation led to a general sentiment that in the postwar era, with all the medical and vocational advances in the United States, people with disabilities deserved to be rehabilitated. Instead of making these people dependent on government benefits, the government should mobilize public and private resources to restore their productivity. That was the more efficient, economic, and humane alternative. Hence, by the time serious discussion of disability insurance began in the 1950s, rehabilitation was posed as a viable alternative to disability insurance. It became the conservative counterproposal.

Proponents of disability insurance did not oppose rehabilitation. They made the more subtle and less satisfying argument that disability insurance and rehabilitation were both necessary. Those who could benefit from rehabilitation services should receive them; those who were too old or too sick to work should be given the dignified option of dropping out of the labor force and receiving benefits as a matter of right. But to argue for cash disability benefits was inevitably to question the ultimate effectiveness of rehabilitation and to attack an article of faith among conservatives.

In this intellectual setting, the debate over disability insurance played itself out between 1949 and 1956. In 1949 the House of Representatives included disability insurance in its version of what became the Social Security Amendments of 1950. Since the Senate chose to emphasize rehabilitation, rather than cash benefits, it did not include disability insurance in the bill that it passed in 1950. The House receded in conference, and as a compromise measure Congress adopted a new public assistance category: Aid to the Permanently and Totally Disabled.

In 1952 Rep. Robert Kean (R-N.J.) introduced an interim idea, known as a "disability freeze," that passed the House but not the Senate. Under this scheme, persons with a permanent disability could ask to have their wage record "frozen" with the result that should they survive to the normal retirement age they would receive regular Social Security benefits. The idea, although a compromise and at the outer edges of acceptability for Social Security advocates, generated a great deal of controversy. Representatives of insurance companies and the medical profession objected to what they characterized as the control over the practice of medicine that the measure gave to the federal government. Upon hearing of the freeze, the American Medical Association (AMA) dispatched telegrams to every member of Congress saying that the freeze amounted to socialized medicine. The AMA campaign scared off many Congress members from the 1952 Social Security bill and almost led to its defeat in the House. Representative Doughton, about to retire from Congress, managed to convince his colleagues to back the disability freeze as a special tribute to him. The Senate passed the Social Security bill but without the disability freeze. In the conference committee, the bizarre idea arose of putting the measure in the books but having it die before anyone could apply. Both houses of Congress could claim victory—in the House one of principle and in the Senate one of practice.

In the next two Congresses, disability insurance stood at the top of the Social Security agenda. When the Eisenhower administration arrived, Roswell Perkins, an assistant secretary in charge of legislation at the newly created Department of Health, Education, and Welfare, said that the new administration's philosophy was that "the first line of attack on disability should be rehabilitation, in order that people be restored to useful and productive lives."[24] The disability freeze idea nonetheless survived in the Eisenhower administration and became part of the Social Security Amendments of 1954 (**Documents 4.1–4.4**). Perkins, as well as many Republicans, thought of the freeze as a recruiting tool for the state agencies that ran vocational rehabilitation programs. Those who came to the SSA asking to be declared disabled would be put in touch with a rehabilitation counselor and set on a course of rehabilitation. The administration even toyed with the idea of using money from the Social Security trust fund to pay the costs of rehabilitation services. As Oveta Hobby told President Eisenhower in October 1953, "This provision would require only a very small investment of OASI funds, but no accountant can estimate the physical rewards, the sense of independence, pride, and usefulness and the relief from family strains, which accrue to one of the disabled when he returns to his old job or to a newly learned job suited to his limitations, and once more takes his place as a man among men."[25] The administration ultimately dropped the idea of using trust fund money but nonetheless backed the freeze.

The climactic battle over disability insurance occurred in 1956 (**Documents 4.5–4.9**). As usual, a host of Social Security matters claimed the attention of the 84th Congress, such as whether to permit women to retire before the customary age of sixty-five. The

House, the more liberal of the two bodies, included disability insurance in its version of a comprehensive Social Security bill. The real battle came in the more conservative Senate, where the Finance Committee, headed by Senator Byrd, refused to endorse the measure. The key fight moved to the Senate floor. Sen. Lyndon Johnson (D-Texas) and Nelson Cruikshank of the AFL-CIO pressured members to oppose the Finance Committee's recommendation and to support an amendment on the Senate floor. Wavering senators got the Johnson treatment and were told that support of disability insurance was an important party position. Union officials of the recently united AFL-CIO squared off against officials representing the interests of the AMA—an organization with influential members in every state. In the end, the measure passed by a one-vote margin.[26] In many respects, this vote was the closest in the history of the Social Security program. Thus, by the barest of margins, the OASI program became the OASDI (Old-Age, Survivors, and Disability Insurance) program.

The fight over disability benefits failed to derail the engine of Social Security expansion. In 1958 Congress resumed where it had left off in 1954 and passed a benefit increase of 7 percent. In addition, policymakers began to undo some of the restrictions they had placed on disability benefits in order to gain its passage in 1956. The disability legislation of that year started a program for people fifty years of age or older and contained no extra benefits for the dependents of people with disabilities on the Social Security rolls. In 1958 Congress amended disability insurance to allow payments to dependents and, in 1960, with little debate, removed the age restriction. In these regards, the program followed a course set by the proponents of Social Security expansion. As Arthur Altmeyer wrote to his friend Wilbur Cohen in 1956, "I think we should begin to press for dependents benefits for persons permanently and totally disabled, as well as for elimination of age 50. We have licked the opponents and their dupes and accomplices . . . on the basic proposition. Now, let's press our advantage."[27]

Although some of the restrictive provisions proved easy to undo, some remained in the law from its inception to the present day. In particular, the law created a complicated structure to make disability determinations. A person applied for benefits to the Social Security Administration but state agencies, acting under contract to the federal government, made the actual decisions to grant benefits. If, however, a person was denied benefits, he could have the decision reconsidered and, if still unsatisfied, eventually receive a hearing before an administrative law judge. If still dissatisfied, a person could press his claim to the federal courts. The structure allowed disability allowance rates to vary by state and encouraged a rejected applicant to appeal, since administrative law judges, in particular, often overturned the decisions of the state agencies. The complicated administrative setup made it hard to apply a consistent disability standard to every applicant. It also contributed to the volatility that plagued the program, with surges in the disability rolls in the 1970s and again in the 1990s. A system in which people worked through several layers of appeal in order to prove their inability to work did not encourage the process of rehabilitation. Although the law paid lip service to the ideal of rehabilitation, few applicants were, in fact, rehabilitated. Despite continued criticism of the state-federal disability determination system that began with extensive Ways and Means Committee hearings in 1959, the basic system remained in place.

CONTINUED PROGRAM LIBERALIZATION

As disability benefits were expanded at the end of the 1950s, Congress made other adjustments to the program, such as raising the widow's benefit from 75 percent to 82.5 percent of a basic benefit in 1961(**Documents 4.19–4.21**). Despite these signs of incremental expansion, the issue of health insurance for Social Security beneficiaries came to preoccupy policymakers between 1958 and 1965. Key votes on what came to be called Medicare occurred in 1960, 1962, and 1964. Medicare finally became law in 1965. That legislation unleashed a torrent of changes in the Social Security program, all in the direction of expansion. In particular, the law brought a general benefit increase of 7 percent and initiated a new program that allowed states to receive money from the Social Security trust funds to rehabilitate disabled workers.

With Medicare on the books and with the continuing prosperity of the 1960s, the process of Social Security benefit liberalization continued until 1972 (**Documents 5.1–5.8**). A ritual developed in which Rep. Wilbur Mills (D.-Ark.) initiated the increases in his role as head of the House Committee on Ways and Means, and Sen. Russell Long (D-La.), head of the Senate Finance Committee, affirmed the increases or proposed higher ones. Government officials, with the concurrence of President Johnson, oversaw the entire process, with the SSA actuaries helping to determine just how much of an increase the system could afford in a particular year. Disputes developed over related areas of social policy, also under the purview of Mills and Long, such as how to handle the precipitous rise in the welfare rates or contain the escalating costs of Medicare. Although these disputes sometimes delayed the enactment of comprehensive Social Security legislation, they never prevented benefit increases. Social Security proponents saw these benefit increases as contributing to the next program goal: to make Social Security a truly effective bulwark against poverty. Benefit increases of 13 percent in 1968 and 15 percent in 1969 fit this general pattern.

INDEXING BENEFITS TO THE RATE OF INFLATION

President Richard Nixon's administration could not afford to neglect the Social Security program. If the president did nothing, Congress would nonetheless continue to enact benefit increases. Nixon's novel response to this situation involved automatic cost-of-living adjustments (COLAs). Instead of waiting for Congress to pass a benefit increase, the elderly, disabled, and their dependents would be assured of benefits that were automatically adjusted to changes in the cost of living. In this manner Nixon hoped to take the credit for Social Security benefit increases away from Congress and claim some of the credit himself. In addition, he could argue—as many Republicans did—that the move would help to rationalize Social Security and replace the arbitrary system then in existence (**Documents 5.9–5.13**).

To obtain automatic cost-of-living adjustments, Nixon needed the approval of Wilbur Mills and the other congressional leaders who had profited from the old system. Not surprisingly, Mills proved resistant to the idea, effectively blocking it in 1969 and 1970. It was becoming clear, however, that the measure had some bipartisan appeal, even if Mills opposed it. Robert Ball, the commissioner of Social Security, sold Mills on a plan that permitted automatic cost-of-living adjustments but only if Congress failed to raise benefits in a discretionary manner. In other words, Congress would still have the freedom to pass a benefit increase on its own, but if for some reason Congress did not take action and if prices rose high enough to trigger an automatic benefit increase, then this increase would take effect. With this proviso, Mills acquiesced to automatic COLAs and played a key role in their enactment.

Because of disagreements between the House and the Senate, largely over the matter of welfare reform, the process took until the summer of 1972 to resolve. In the end, Congress acquiesced to cost-of-living adjustments on Mills's terms. As usual, the Democratic Congress outbid the Republicans on the level of Social Security benefits. Where Nixon hoped for a 5 percent increase, Mills and his colleagues legislated a 20 percent increase (**Document 5.10**). This large increase was considered affordable because—in keeping with the addition of automatic benefit increases and automatic increases in the wage base under the 1972 changes—the actuaries at Social Security changed their basic assumptions regarding future economic activity. In particular, they abandoned the notion that wages would remain steady in the future and instead factored a wage increase into their calculations. That produced a large future surplus in the actuarial reports that Congress in effect spent to fund the 20 percent increase. The president got his automatic cost-of-living adjustments but only at the expense of the 20 percent increase. President Nixon, a candidate for reelection, signed the new bill into law at the beginning of July 1972 (**Document 5.9**).

Congress, which still needed to resolve the matter of welfare reform, continued to work on comprehensive social policy legislation. In October Congress passed an omnibus law (**Document 5.12**). The bill contained the Medicare expansions and initiated an ambitious new federal program, known as Supplemental Security Income (SSI). SSI put a national minimum benefit standard in place for adult welfare beneficiaries (and, as it later worked out, many children as well) and allowed the federal government to take over the administration of previously state-administered welfare programs in aid of the disabled, blind, and elderly. The idea was to supplement the Social Security benefits of those who, even with Social Security, fell below an acceptable income standard. All in all, the two pieces of Social Security legislation in 1972 represented the apex of postwar social welfare legislation.

In 1973, as the Watergate scandal slowly engulfed the Nixon administration, the postwar system remained in place. To be sure the 20 percent benefit increase in 1972 and the shift in actuarial assumptions sapped some of the expansionary energy. Even the leaders of the SSA realized that a plateau had been reached with the 1972 legislation. "I just don't see anything in the way of a near-term future of the kind of quantum jump we have just had in these recent amendments," Social Security Commissioner Ball said at the time.[28] On another occasion, he remarked that Social Security had reached "the level of considerable stability."[29] Still, the automatic benefits were not scheduled to take effect until January 1975, and Congress decided to use its discretionary power to raise benefit levels in 1973.

As the year began, the *New York Times* reported that "the United States is in the midst of a new economic boom that may prove to be unrivaled in scope, power, and influence by any previous expansion in history."[30] That rosy report lent support to the notion that the United States could afford its expanded Social Security program. In Congress, the tax committees set about their work, almost as if the 20 percent increase had not happened. In June, for example, the Senate Finance Committee voted a 5.5 percent increase in benefits that would become effective at the beginning of 1974. The rationale was that no benefit increases were scheduled until January 1975 and, because of the high inflation rate, something needed to be done in the interim. Inflation, which would prove to be a major economic problem for the 1970s, appeared to be advancing at a record pace. In May, the Consumer Price Index stood 5.5 percent above its level of the previous year.[31] The House concurred in this analysis, and the Ways and Means Committee paved the way for a 5.6 percent increase that passed both houses at the end of June. The Nixon administration, which had hoped to contain the pressure for Social Security increases by acquiescing to the 1972 changes, worried about the effect of the new increases on the federal budget. The Ways and Means Committee made only a slight concession to the administration's concerns, deciding to postpone the effective date of the increase to June 1974.[32]

Congress felt justified in making these changes because the Social Security system, so far as the actuaries could tell, appeared to be relatively well financed. Each year the Board of Trustees of the Social Security trust funds made a report to Congress on the funds' fiscal health. The report issued on July 16, 1973, showed a small imbalance, expressed in the technical language of Social Security as –0.32 percent of taxable payroll. The trustees reported that the inflation rate made it likely that the first cost-of-living adjustment, were it to go into effect, might be 7 percent rather than the 5 percent that had been predicted earlier. The main problem, according to the trustees, was the rising disability rate, the reasons for which the trustees admitted were "not entirely clear."[33] Disability, with its sensitivity to the employment rate, would become a major problem of the 1970s. As early as 1974, the staff of the Ways and Means Committee reported that "chronic actuarial deficiencies have developed in the Disability Insurance system over the past ten years." Disability insurance became an often-cited example of a program that appeared to go out of control during the seventies.[34]

Disability was, however, a relatively minor component of the Social Security system, and rising disability rates could not derail the movement for Social Security's expansion. Not content with the benefit increase passed in June 1973, Congress reconsidered the matter at the end of the year, with the result that the President Nixon signed an 11 percent benefit increase at the beginning of 1974. This increase was to take effect in two stages. A 7 percent benefit increase would show up in the April benefit checks, and a 4 percent increase would take effect in July. With this new legislation, Congress quietly put aside the measure it had passed earlier in 1973. The only significant concession to those who favored a slower rate of Social Security growth came in the decision to postpone the first automatic cost-of-living adjustment increases until July 1975. Nixon, by now thoroughly embroiled in the Watergate scandal and in danger of losing his job, put a positive face on the developments. He praised the new bill as an "extremely important, far-reaching measure" and noted with pride that Social Security benefits had gone up 68.5 percent during his administration.[35]

THE SECOND FINANCING CONTROVERSY

Even as these events were taking place, key changes were occurring in the Social Security program that, by 1975, would transform the program and end the postwar era of Social Security expansion. President Nixon would leave office in August 1974, and the entire

Watergate incident would strengthen Congress at the expense of the executive. In the Social Security field, the tight collaboration between the executive branch in the form of the SSA and Congress in the form of the tax committees loosened. Early in 1973, as part of a second term purge of leftover officials from an earlier era, Ball resigned as Social Security commissioner and the agency's reputation for administrative competence began an almost immediate decline. The implementation of the Supplemental Security Income program proved to be a particular public relations disaster for the SSA, as the changeover from state to federal administration of the adult welfare categories failed to go smoothly. None of Ball's successors would enjoy anywhere near his long tenure in office.[36] An even more important factor in the transformation of Social Security's policymaking structure was the departure of Rep. Wilbur Mills from a central position of authority in 1975.

A newly reformed Congress dealt with Social Security in chastened economic circumstances. In June 1974, the trustees announced that the program was "underfinanced in the long range with a negative balance of about 3 percent of taxable payroll" (**Document 6.2**). The actuaries pointed to new demographic and economic factors that contributed to the problem. Looking at data from the 1970 census, they decided that their earlier estimates of fertility had been too optimistic, and it would be more rational to assume a fertility rate of 2.1 babies per woman, rather than a range of 2.3–2.8. A slower rate of population growth meant a higher future percentage of aged people in the population and a heavier future burden for Social Security. The performance of the economy also presented problems. Early in 1975 the Bureau of Labor Statistics reported that the Consumer Price Index was 12.2 percent higher at the end of 1974 than at the beginning, the worst performance in that category since 1946. In 1974 reflecting the inflation and the economy's sluggish performance—a deadly combination that came to be known as *stagflation*—real spendable earnings declined by 5.4 percent. The economic boom predicted in 1973 did not seem to be materializing, at just the time that the Social Security system was vulnerable to inflation (which raised benefit levels) and unemployment (which lowered tax collections). Not surprisingly, then, the actuaries noted in February 1975 that "rising inflation and unemployment are throwing the Social Security retirement system into deficit years earlier than expected." There was both a short-run and a long-run crisis. As early as 1976 system revenues might not be enough to cover system expenditures, with the result that the system would have to dip into its reserves. By the end of 1980 the reserves on hand would be dangerously low.[37]

Support for the Social Security system remained high, but the system faced a new vulnerability. In May 1975, President Gerald Ford received word from a top aide that "the reserve in the cash benefit funds will be impaired almost immediately and will be completely exhausted by the early 1980s."[38] The trustees report in May 1975 showed even worse results than before, with the worsening economy the main culprit (**Document 6.3**). In the middle of the 1970s, then, the program experienced an unprecedented degree of criticism.[39] As William Simon, Ford's conservative secretary of the Treasury, noted, "Once beyond controversy, Social Security has come under persistent attack in the news media for its inequities, its financial uncertainties and its complexity."[40]

Social Security survived its vulnerable period between 1975 and 1983 because of the many beneficiaries invested in its survival but also because it contained built-in legislative protection. As a result of the 1972 amendments, benefit levels were protected against inflation, without Congress having to do anything. President Ford tried to limit the benefit increase in 1975 to 5 percent as an anti-inflationary measure, but he got nowhere with the proposal. Because Congress had the luxury of doing nothing, the burden of the unpopular action fell squarely on the president. As a direct result of historical contingency and this prevailing political dynamic, benefit levels continued to go up with the inflation rate, which meant that they went up considerably in this period.[41]

Part of the problem stemmed from a feature of the 1972 law establishing automatic benefit increases, which came to be known—in somewhat of a misnomer—as "double-indexing." The benefit formula provided adjustments for both increases in prices and increases in wages whenever a general benefit increase was enacted. Thus the adjustments for prices and wages were "coupled" together in the benefit formula. The automatic COLAs would happen every year. As the economics of the 1970s produced disruptions in the historic relationship between prices and wages, this had an adverse effect on Social Security benefits. In a period of stagflation, overall program costs soared and initial benefit levels for future beneficiaries rose much higher than planned.[42] These unexpectedly high future benefits produced what even Social Security advocates conceded to be irrationally high replacement rates and unacceptably high program costs.

The Ford administration focused on the problem (**Documents 6.7–6.11**) and came up with a solution that involved, in the technical parlance of the program, a "neutral decoupling scheme with constant replacement rates."[43] In other words, the formula was to be changed to yield benefits that replaced the same percentage of real wages over time. If workers who retired in 1975 received 30 percent of their real wages in their social security benefits (which were then indexed for inflation during the worker's retirement), then those workers who retired in 2010 should receive a similar percentage.[44] On June 17, 1976, the White House released the Social Security Benefit Indexing Act. "Very simply stated," said SSA commissioner James Bruce Cardwell in briefing the press, "the President's proposal is intended to stabilize the replacement rates under a Social Security system that is indexed, as the present one is, for the cost of living for the retired person."[45]

President Jimmy Carter adopted a similar approach as Ford and decided to accompany the proposal on "decoupling" with legislation designed to solve Social Security's other financial problems. His advisers decided that an appropriate moment to announce such legislation would be soon after the May 1, 1977, release of the Social Security Trustees Report (**Document 6.5**). The president learned that the report would "almost certainly show both long and short term financing problems for the Social Security trust fund." If the administration moved quickly enough, it could soothe the public about the soundness of the system and give the president, rather than Congress, control over the solution.[46]

Carter's proposal relied on collecting more money for Social Security by raising the amount of the worker's earnings on which workers and their employers paid Social Security taxes. He also suggested gradually implementing a change in which employers paid Social Security taxes on the full wages of their employees, while raising the level for employees only a little. If the plan were put into effect, benefit levels would not rise beyond what was already planned because benefit levels were based on the level of wages on which employees paid taxes, but revenues to the system would increase because employers would pay more. In addition, the plan contained a feature that would add general revenues to the system, if the unemployment rate exceeded 6 percent. In other words, if the economy continued to cause the program trouble, then the federal government would add money both to maintain the system's solvency and to boost the economy through countercyclical spending.[47]

By the time the protracted legislative process concluded in December, the administration got neither its general revenue scheme nor a higher wage base for employers than for employees. Instead, Congress decided to add revenues to the system by raising the contribution and benefit base for employers and employees alike beginning in 1979 and to increase the combined tax rates for Social Security and Medicare, also beginning in 1979 (**Documents 6.12 and 6.16**).[48] Passage of the bill showed the lengths that Congress was willing to go to preserve the basic Social Security system. As President Carter's domestic affairs and policy assistant Stuart Eizenstat explained to the president in urging him to sign the bill, the legislation "moves the social security system out of a deficit situation in 1980 and maintains a current surplus until about the year 2030."[49]

While policymakers preserved the Social Security system in 1977, they also began to explore ways of changing it. The disability part of the program, in which projected costs exceeded projected revenues, came in for particular scrutiny. Critics pointed out that the high replacement rates offered by disability insurance created an incentive for people with impairments to leave the labor force and enter the disability rolls. The structure of the program favored younger over older workers and families with children over families that no longer had children in their care. Disabled workers were, by definition, younger than sixty-five and much more likely than elderly retirees to have children in their homes. Policymakers responded by proposing to change the formula for computing disability benefits in order to lower the percentage of a worker's wages that the disability benefits replaced. They also sought to put a cap on family benefits, so that no family could receive more than 150 percent of a disabled worker's benefits. These changes, developed first in the newly created Social Security Subcommittee of the House Ways and Means Committee and later endorsed by the Carter administration, occasioned a great deal of controversy.

The House debated the proposed changes in the disability program in the fall of 1979. Rep. Jake Pickle (D-Texas) defended the changes as necessary to control the costs of a runaway program. He also pointed to aspects of the legislation that provided work incentives to disabled workers, such as allowing people who left the rolls and went back to work to keep their Medicare benefits for an extended period of time. In this way, he and the other advocates of change reinvigorated the old debate between the rehabilitation and income maintenance approaches to disability. "Disability," said Pickle, "may be permanent but unemployability is not."[50] Rep. Claude Pepper (D-Fla.) countered that the people on the disability rolls were not chiselers and were too impaired to rejoin the labor force.[51] The Senate debate, conducted in December, picked up on these themes. Sen. Edward Kennedy (D-Mass.) said that lowering benefits would do little to prod people with disabilities to go back to work. "That is using buckshot to kill a mosquito," he said.[52] Sen. Robert Dole (R-Kan.) countered, "With a little imagination and creative thought handicapped persons can lead active lives and find employment suitable to their skills."[53] In the end the optimism over rehabilitation and the desire to contain the growth of disability benefits prevailed over arguments that the traditional system needed to be maintained. President Carter signed the legislation into law in the summer of 1980 (**Documents 8.1–8.7**).

As sometimes happens in public policy, the 1980 disability legislation produced unintended consequences. The culprit was an uncontroversial feature of the law that required states to reexamine each "non-permanently" disabled beneficiary at least once every three years. The idea was to prune from the rolls those who had recovered from their disabling condition and to make sure that people on the rolls really belonged there.

When the Reagan administration learned from the General Accounting Office and the SSA that perhaps 20 percent of those on the disability rolls did not meet the eligibility standards and that as much as $2 billion a year could be saved by removing them, it launched a major campaign to remove people from the rolls. The 1980 law provided legislative cover. As the campaign gathered momentum, the administration reviewed the cases of about 1.2 million disability beneficiaries and informed about 490,000 that they would lose their benefits.

The disability reviews unleashed an avalanche of protest. Newspapers ran stories about people on the verge of death or too disabled to move being taken off the rolls. Some of the people, learning their benefits were to be cut off, committed suicide. Others protested to their Congress members, who promptly launched investigations aimed at embarrassing the Reagan administration and exposing the injustices done to such groups as the mentally disabled. Many appealed their decisions and brought their cases back to the state agencies and administrative law judges who had put them on the rolls in the first place. Some of the states refused to process requests to reexamine disability beneficiaries, and some administrative law judges openly rebelled against dictates that they remove people from the rolls. The courts soon entered the battle and protected certain classes of beneficiaries from losing their benefits.

The fact that the disability determination system mixed together Social Security recipients and SSI recipients further complicated the situation: people on welfare because they were permanently disabled could be reduced to destitution if their benefits were taken away. In the end, Congress intervened and passed a disability reform law in 1984. The rehabilitation features of the 1980 law never took hold (**Documents 8.8–8.28**).

THE THIRD FINANCING CONTROVERSY AND THE 1983 AMENDMENTS

The controversy over disability benefits took place at the same time as a more fundamental controversy over Social Security financing. Jimmy Carter's advisers assured him that the 1977 amendments had "fixed" Social Security both in the short and long runs. The economic recession of the late 1970s soon undid the projections of program planners and once again pointed the way to a crisis. In 1980, for example, the benefit increase, as determined by the automatic indexing formula, was 14.3 percent, but wages went up only 9 percent and employment remained sluggish. The effect on Social Security was direct. From a high of $37.8 billion in 1974, the Old-Age and Survivors Insurance Trust Fund declined to a low of $19.7 billion in 1983. As the actuaries duly reported, there was the possibility that the program would not be able to meet its obligations and pay full benefits in 1983.

Once again, remarkably, Congress—which included a House under Democratic control—and the Reagan administration joined forces to "save" the program and preserve its basic structure. The administration began with an aggressive stance on Social Security, seeking, among other things, to reduce the size of early retirement benefits and to eliminate benefits that it considered frivolous, such as the minimum benefit and the so-called student benefit that went to college-aged dependents of Social Security beneficiaries. The minimum benefit, present in the program from the beginning, guaranteed that no Social Security benefit—no matter how low a person's wages or how little the individual participated in the labor force—could be lower than a certain specified amount. The eventual elimination of the student benefit and the minimum benefit in 1981 proved the willingness of Congress to entertain the prospect of at least some cuts in Social Security to reduce current expenditures. Broad opposition to cuts in early retirement benefits, without giving future beneficiaries advance warning well ahead of the fact and protecting the benefits of current retirees, indicated that deep cuts in Social Security would be politically difficult. At the same time, something needed to be done to keep the program solvent. Democrats tended to favor tax increases, Republicans benefit cuts. Interested in sharing the blame, each side hesitated to take action without the tacit approval of the other.

President Ronald Reagan and House Speaker Tip O'Neill (D-Mass.) decided to remove the issue from the glare of public scrutiny, at least until after the 1982 elections. At that time, both sides could reassess their situations and see if they could muster a working majority to make changes in Social Security. In December 1981, Reagan appointed a bipartisan commission, the National Commission on Social Security Reform, to propose solutions to Social Security problems.

Commission members tended to think of the problem in pragmatic political terms. They sought effective adjustments that could be made at the least political cost. As a consequence, they tended to frame the issue as how best to assure the program's survival rather than how to create a new system.

Each side regarded the other warily. Democrats, starved for a winning issue in the Reagan era, thought of Social Security as something they could use as a weapon against the Republicans. The Republicans, for their part, wanted to remove Social Security from the negative side of the political ledger. Neither side wanted to accrue the blame for making the system insolvent. As commission member Daniel Patrick Moynihan, the ebullient Democratic New York senator, put it, a default on Social Security would discredit the federal government. It would show that the government lied to the people, stole taxpayers' money, and, in the end, could not be trusted to handle fundamental issues.[54]

The commission held a number of ceremonial meetings, waiting to see how the 1982 elections turned out. The results gave the commission no easy outs. Neither party gained a victory decisive enough to provide a comfortable working majority in Congress to deal with the issue. The Democrats gained 26 seats in the House, but the Senate remained under Republican control. Since neither party had a working majority in both houses of Congress, neither could rely on Congress to handle the problem without fear of one side imposing unacceptable conditions on the other. Even liberal commission member Claude Pepper worried about fighting out the issue in Congress because he feared that President Reagan might allow things to deteriorate to the point where full benefits might not be paid on time. The president also remained wary of a confrontation with Congress because he thought that the longer the issue remained alive, the more benefit the Democrats would receive from it.

After the election, President Reagan and Speaker O'Neill used surrogates on the commission to negotiate a deal. In fashioning a compromise, Moynihan and Ball worked with Republicans Alan Greenspan, Senator Dole, and Rep. Barber Conable of New York, as well as several administration appointees, including White House Chief of Staff James Baker and Deputy Chief of Staff Richard Darman. As might be expected in this sort of close-range political bargaining, the two sides left the program largely intact. Instead of debating fundamental alternatives, they kept a running score sheet that listed the potential savings from each item—all the time hoping to roughly balance tax increases and benefit cuts. In the spirit of reaching a deal, the Democrats accepted a permanent six-month delay in the annual cost-of-living adjustment—in effect producing a 2 percent reduction in benefits. The Republicans acquiesced to small increases in Social Security taxes achieved by initiating already legislated payroll tax increases earlier than scheduled. In addition, the commission recommended that the self-employed pay essentially the same rate as the combined rate for workers and employers, a change that could be scored as a tax increase. Both sides agreed to the treatment of up to 50 percent of Social Security income as taxable income for middle- and upper-class beneficiaries and to the extension of coverage to new federal employees.

The 98th Congress that convened in 1983 honored the terms of the compromise. The only substantive changes it made to the agreed-upon settlement concerned Social Security's long-term deficit. Instead of putting a tax increase in the distant future into the law, Congress decided to raise the retirement age from sixty-five to sixty-seven in a phased in manner beginning in 2000 (**Documents 7.7–7.10**).

Politicians on both sides of the aisle celebrated the rescue of Social Security, and Ronald Reagan signed the 1983 Social Security Amendments with pomp and circumstance. The White House decided to hold the signing ceremony outside, despite unseasonably cold temperatures for April, and to treat the occasion as a high-profile event. In contrast to Carter, who signed the 1977 amendments with some reluctance, Reagan appeared to relish the passage of the amendments. The president claimed the bill as a great victory and as a "clear and dramatic demonstration that our system can still work when men and women of good will join together to make it work." He regarded the passage of the bill as concluding a "tumultuous debate about Social Security" that "has raged for more than two decades in this country." Now, according to the president, Social Security would be preserved, reaffirming "the commitment of our government to the performance and stability of Social Security" (**Document 7.10**).

THE FOURTH FINANCING CONTROVERSY—TOWARD THE PRESENT DAY

Conservatives believed that the episodes leading to the 1983 amendments illustrated the vulnerability of the system to crisis and the unwillingness of Congress to take steps to avert that crisis. Liberals pointed to the apparently robust shape of the Social Security trust funds as proof that the amendments had, in effect, solved the crisis. When the Committee on Economic Development issued a report with the unsettling title, "Social Security: From Crisis to Crisis," Robert Ball, Alan Greenspan, and actuary Robert Myers wrote an op-ed piece that argued, "We believe that it is highly probable that the social security system will be financially healthy over at least the next two decades." It would take double-digit unemployment and high inflation to throw the system out of whack and, once beyond the mid-1980s, even that would not be enough to disrupt it. Meanwhile, the surpluses kept accumulating. As Ball told the Joint Economic Committee in 1989, the trust funds were "building at an astonishing rate." By the end of 1989 the OASDI trust fund levels (the 1956 law had established a separate trust fund for disability) would reach $168.3 billion, and the system would continue to pay out less than it took in and grow, according to the experts, for the next forty years.[55]

In the face of this onslaught, conservatives began to rethink their strategy on Social Security (**Document 9.1**). Advocates in think tanks like the Cato Institute and the Heritage Foundation tried to make people aware of Social Security's long-term liabilities and its inability to provide windfall gains to later entrants into the system (such as the baby boom generation and its echo). They also touted governmentally sanctioned alternatives that relied on individual and private sector administration, such as individual retirement accounts (IRAs) and 401(k)s—a parallel private universe for Social Security, equivalent to the private health insurance on which most Americans relied.

When Social Security reform returned to the agenda in the 1990s, the conservatives were able to offer more fundamental alternatives than simply tinkering with the present system. This new debate about Social Security caught many program advocates by surprise, since many believed that the most important problems had been anticipated in and taken care of by the 1983 amendments. The retirement of the baby boomers, for example, was not unanticipated. To be sure, the ratio of workers to beneficiaries would fall in the future from about 3.3 in 1995 to 1.8 in 2070. That explained why the cost per individual, and hence the tax rate that each individual must bear, would rise in the future, but the declining ratios had already been figured into the 1983 calculations and nothing had happened in the interim to change those ratios. The sources of the shortfall of 2.17 percent of taxable payroll in 1995 lay elsewhere. For one thing, the mere passage of time made the estimates deteriorate. This was true because costs were rising faster near the end of the seventy-five-year estimating period than at the beginning, and so with each passing year one lower-cost year would drop out of the seventy-five-year projections at the near end and a higher-cost year would replace it at the far end. For another thing, disability rates continued to rise beyond expectations. The actuaries also made their assumptions about real wage growth more pessimistic and changed some of their methods of estimating costs. The result, despite favorable factors such as increased immigration and fertility rates, was a projected long-term deficit.[56]

Evidence that the latest Social Security controversy would be handled differently from previous ones came when an advisory council met in 1994 through 1996. This officially sanctioned group, of the sort that usually reinforced the conventional bureaucratic wisdom about Social Security, could not agree on a single recommendation and instead gave official sanction to privatization as one of three solutions to the Social Security financing problem. Senators Daniel Patrick Moynihan and John Breaux (D-La.) and Rep. Charles Stenholm (D-Texas) proposed that some of the Social Security tax money should be carved out and placed in a private account. Even liberal Social Security supporters proposed that some of the money in the surplus should be invested in the stock market rather than in government securities. Everyone wanted to catch the magic of the current bull market.

After some hesitation, President Bill Clinton rejected creating private accounts by "carving them out" of the system in what many viewed as "partial privatization." Instead, he talked about using some of the budget surplus to save Social Security and in 1999 advocated that private savings accounts be created alongside Social Security.

When George W. Bush came into office in 2001, he thought he could ride the crest of a building wave, solve the long-term financing problem, and point the way to a fundamental reform of Social Security. In 2000 candidate Bush said it was time for Democrats and Republicans to save Social Security together. He wanted to give younger workers the chance to put part of their payroll taxes into what he called "sound, responsible investments."[57] Then, when he got into office, he appointed the President's Commission to Strengthen Social Security, cochaired by none other than Democrat Moynihan, a man with a reputation for telling the hard truth in social policy.

This commission fell from the public eye after the tragedies of September 11, 2001, but nonetheless continued its work. Members of the commission agreed that its recommendations "must include individually controlled voluntary personal accounts."[58] With the exception of Moynihan, liberal Democrats made a point of staying away. Unlike the "Hobby Lobby" of 1953, Bush's commission would remain true to the conservative cause.

Interspersed with the political rhythms of the post-September 11 era, the president continued his initiative. In his 2004 State of the Union address Bush said, "We should make the Social Security system a source of ownership for the American people." That would be the grand theme of the social welfare system that Bush hoped would be his legacy to the American people.

Franklin Delano Roosevelt had developed in the New Deal a means of making the wage bargain more secure for a worker over the course of a lifetime. Lyndon Johnson had wanted to create the Great Society, which would become great by means of government investment in health care, education, and social services. Richard Nixon had wanted his New Federalism program to adjust the scale of social welfare to bring governmental activity closer to the people who received government services, and he wanted to create a rational system for the dispersal of social welfare benefits by making sure that the programs contained economic incentives for consumers to use their benefits wisely.

George W. Bush would create the "ownership society" in which, within broad government mandates and markets conditioned by government regulation, people assumed control over their own health care and retirement decisions, thus developing private initiatives toward a collective goal.

During the third presidential debate with Democratic candidate Sen. John Kerry of Massachusetts on October 13, 2004, President Bush once again talked about personal savings accounts that would bring much higher rates of return than current Social Security program, saving the program's finances and reinforcing individual responsibility.

After his 2004 reelection, President Bush brought the Social Security campaign to center stage, announcing that it would be an administration priority. If nothing were done, Bush argued, then the system would go broke. It was, he said, on an unsustainable course. The specter of a future collapse of the system thus set the stage for the great unveiling of the president's proposal on February 2 at the 2005 State of the Union address. According to President Bush, Social Security had been a great moral success in the past century, but something new would be required for the new millennium because the program was headed toward bankruptcy. The president followed up his speech with a full-scale publicity campaign. In addition to his substantive efforts, the president was not above a little political theater. On April 5, 2005, he visited the Treasury Department facility in Parkersburg, West Virginia, where the records of the Social Security Trust Funds are maintained. The president asked to see the trust fund surplus and was shown a ledger with bookkeeping entries. There was, according to the president, no Social Security surplus. This was to be taken as further evidence that the current program was unsustainable.

President Bush set off on a media blitz to speak to sixty groups in sixty days. But by May 20, 2005, the *Washington Post* reported that "on the 78th day of a 60-day roadshow, the president's nationwide Social Security tour, even to some of his own aides, has the feel of a past-its-prime Broadway production that has been held over while other, newer shows steal the spotlight."

The president faced serious technical and political obstacles and did not seem to be gaining any political traction. One obstacle, broadly stated, was how to move from one system to another. Benefits for people already receiving benefits needed to be preserved while simultaneously moving over to a private system—a difficult and costly transition problem. It would also be costly for a private system to replicate the benefits of the public one that already existed. Disability benefits would be difficult to finance in a private system, for example. The political problems began with the fact that there was no action-forcing event. The Democrats could oppose Bush and not propose an alternative, unlike the situation in 1983 when the immediacy of the financing crisis forced bipartisan action. It was difficult for Bush to pick up Democratic support, and most liberal groups refused to rally to his Social Security reform banner. The test case was the AARP, which worked closely with the president on changes in Medicare but led the opposition to Social Security reform, beginning an advertising campaign aimed at turning voters of various ages against the Bush plan. By the end of 2005, the conventional wisdom was that Bush's plan was dead.

Following the 2006 midterm elections, the Bush administration signaled it would make another attempt at comprehensive Social Security reform in the last two years of the Bush presidency. At the same time, leaders in Congress expressed a willingness to consider reforms, as long as they were not designed around Bush's original plan. Meanwhile, the shortfall in the program's long-range financing provided continuing pressure on all parties to find some common ground, producing a policy challenge that still confronts both the proponents and opponents of this major entitlement program.

Notes

1. Rep. Allen Treadway quoted in Eric Kingson and Edward D. Berkowitz, *Social Security and Medicare: A Policy Primer* (Westport, Conn.: Auburn House, 1993), 36.
2. Louis Stark, "Hopes Are Fading for Social Security Bill," *New York Times*, March 20, 1935, p. 4.
3. "Too Large a Program," *New York Times*, March 21, 1935, p. 22.
4. "Recast Social Security Bill Ready for House; 'Gag' Rule Sought," *New York Times*, April 3, 1935, p. 1.
5. "Parley at White House Decides on a Program to Speed Up Congress," *New York Times*, April 10, 1935, p. 1; Turner Catledge, "Filibuster Threat on Lynching Bill Hangs over Senate," *New York Times*, April 22, 1935, p. 1.
6. Gareth Davies and Martha Derthick, "Race and Social Welfare Policy: The Social Security Act of 1935," *Political Science Quarterly*, 112 (2) Summer 1997: 217–236.
7. "Cumulative Tax Collections, Benefit Payments, Net Excess of Tax Collections," (no date) and "Annual Appropriations, Benefit Payments and Reserves," File 025, RG 47, Records of the Social Security Board, National Archives, Washington, D.C.
8. See Theron F. Schlabach, *Edwin E. Witte: Cautious Reformer* (Madison: Wisconsin State Historical Society, 1969), pp. 158–159, and Edward Berkowitz, "The First Advisory Council and

the 1939 Amendments," in Berkowitz ed., *Social Security after Fifty: Successes and Failures* (Westport, Conn.: Greenwood Press, 1987), 55–78.

9. *Final Report of the Advisory Council on Social Security* (Washington, D.C.: Government Printing Office, 1938), 29.

10. Edward Berkowitz, "Family Benefits in Social Security: A Historical Commentary," in Melissa M. Favreault, Frank J. Sammartino, and C. Eugene Steuerle, eds., *Social Security and the Family: Addressing Unmet Needs in an Underfunded System* (Washington, D.C.: Urban Institute Press, 2002), 19–46.

11. Alice Kessler Harris, "Designing Women and Old Fools: The Construction of the Social Security Amendments of 1939," in Linda R. Kerber, Alice Kessler-Harris, and Kathryn Kish Sklar, eds., *U.S. History as Women's History: New Feminist Essays* (Chapel Hill: University of North Carolina Press, 1995), 95–97.

12. Edward Berkowitz, *America's Welfare State* (Baltimore, Md.: Johns Hopkins University Press, 1991), 56.

13. Arthur Altmeyer, *The Formative Years of Social Security* (Madison: University of Wisconsin Press, 1966), 103.

14. Altmeyer made a very diplomatic concession to the Ways and Means Committee during its consideration of the bill, telling the committee that the administration recognized their authority in these matters of public policy. See *Hearings Relative to the Social Security Act Amendments of 1939, Committee on Ways and Means, House of Representatives, Vol. 3* (Washington, D.C.: Government Printing Office, 1939), 2328–2329.

15. The bill passed both chambers without any recorded votes, which is an indirect indicator of no serious opposition.

16. *Congressional Record,* April 6, 1948, p. 4134.

17. *Congressional Record,* June 14, 1948, p. 8188.

18. Quoted in Berkowitz, *America's Welfare State,* p. 57.

19. Quoted in Edward Berkowitz, *Robert Ball and the Politics of Social Security* (Madison: University of Wisconsin Press, 2003), 70.

20. Ibid.

21. Altmeyer, *Formative Years,* 169.

22. Wilbur Cohen to Elizabeth Wickenden, August 1952, Correspondence Files, Elizabeth Wickenden Papers, Box 1, Wisconsin State Historical Society, Madison, Wisconsin.

23. President Dwight D. Eisenhower to Edward F. Hutton, October 7, 1953, Central Files, Box 848, File 156–C, Dwight D. Eisenhower Presidential Library, Abilene, Kansas.

24. Roswell Perkins to William Mitchell, August 12, 1954, Record Group 47, File 056.11, Box 38, Accession 64A–751, Washington National Records Center, Suitland, Maryland.

25. Oveta Culp Hobby to President Eisenhower, draft, October 15, 1953, Vol. 43, Nelson Rockefeller Papers, Rockefeller Archives, Pocantico, New York.

26. The actual vote was 47–45 on an amendment to add the disability program to the Senate bill. But with Vice President Nixon prepared to cast a no vote in the case of a tie, a switch of one vote would have defeated the amendment and would have prevented the disability provision from passing the Senate.

27. Arthur Altmeyer to Wilbur Cohen, October 8, 1956, Altmeyer Papers, Wisconsin State Historical Society, Madison, Wisconsin.

28. Robert Ball, "Transcript of Remarks at the National Conference," SSA Auditorium, November 20, 1972, Robert Ball Papers, Wisconsin State Historical Society, Madison, Wisconsin.

29. "Our New Social Security Program," Robert Ball speech before Commonwealth Club of California, January 5, 1973, Ball Papers; a twenty-eight minute audio clip of this speech is available at *www.ssa.gov/history/sounds/ball1ram.*

30. Thomas E. Mullaney, "Economic Upturn through Decade Appears Possible," *New York Times,* January 7, 1973, p. 177.

31. Eileen Shanahan, "Senate Panel Votes Increase in Pensions," *New York Times,* June 22, 1973, p. 10.

32. Richard L. Madden, "Social Security Increase Is Approved by Congress," *New York Times,* July 1, 1973, p. 1.

33. "1973 Annual Report of the Board of Trustees of the Federal Old-Age and Survivors Insurance and Disability Insurance Trust Funds," July 16, 1973, House Document 93–130 (Washington, D.C.: Government Printing Office, 1973), 32.

34. U.S. House of Representatives, Committee on Ways and Means, *Committee Staff Report on the Disability Insurance Program,* July 1974 (Washington, D.C.: Government Printing Office, 1974); Edward D. Berkowitz, *Disabled Policy: America's Programs for the Handicapped* (New York: Cambridge University Press, 1987).

35. "Senate Panel Votes 11% Rise in Pensions," *New York Times,* November 15, 1973, p. 29; "President Signs 11% Benefit Rise in Social Security," *New York Times,* January 4, 1974, p. 61.

36. Martha Derthick, *Agency under Stress: The Social Security Administration in American Government* (Washington, D.C.: Brookings Institution, 1990).

37. "1974 Annual Report of the Board of Trustees of the Federal Old-Age and Survivors Insurance and Disability Insurance Trust Funds," June 3, 1974, House Document 93–313 (Washington, D.C.: Government Printing Office, 1974), 35; Edwin L. Dale Jr., "Consumer Prices Rose 12.2% in '74, Worst Since '46," *New York Times,* January 22, 1974, p. 1; "U.S. Confirms Fear of an Early Deficit on Social Security," *New York Times,* February 25, 1975, p. 37.

38. James Cannon to President Ford, May 2, 1975, James Cannon Papers, Box 33, Gerald Ford Presidential Library, Ann Arbor, Michigan.

39. "1975 Annual Report of the Board of Trustees of the Federal Old-Age and Survivors Insurance and Disability Insurance Trust Funds," May 6, 1975, House Document 94–135 (Washington, D.C.: Government Printing Office, 1975); Edwin L. Dale Jr., "Social Security: Healthy but Facing Problems," *New York Times,* February 3, 1975, p. 23.

40. William Simon to the executive board, Economic Policy Board, Spencer Johnson Papers, Box 11, Gerald Ford Presidential Library, Ann Arbor, Michigan.

41. James Cannon to President Ford, May 2, 1975.

42. Rudolf G. Penner, *Social Security Financing Proposals* (Washington, D.C.: American Enterprise Institute, 1977), 6.

43. Bruce Cardwell and Bill Morrill, draft memorandum for President Ford, March 10, 1976, Spencer Johnson Papers, Box 11.

44. The administration accepted this idea, even in the face of an alternative suggestion from a Congressional Research Panel led by actuary and economist William Hsiao. Instead of indexing wages in the benefit formula, Hsiao advocated linking benefit increases to increases in the cost of living. This approach would stabilize benefits in relation to their purchasing power, rather than in relation to rises in the standard of living as reflected in rising average wages. Jim Cannon to President Ford, April 30, 1976, Cannon Papers, Box 10; Martha Derthick, *Policymaking for Social Security* (Washington, D.C.: Brookings Institution, 1977), 387–408.

45. "White House Fact Sheet, Social Security Indexing Act," June 11, 1976, Spencer Johnson Papers, Box 11; James Cardwell, "Transcript of Press Briefing," June 17, 1976, Spencer Johnson Papers, Box 11.

46. Stuart Eizenstat and Frank Raines to President Carter, April 29, 1977, Stuart Eizenstat Papers, Box 278, Jimmy Carter Library, Atlanta, Georgia; Stuart Eizenstat to Joseph Califano, March 18, 1977, Eizenstat Papers, Box 278; Michael Stern (Senate Finance Committee staff) to Stuart Eizenstat, April 8, 1977, Eizenstat Papers, Box 278; Joseph A. Califano Jr., *Governing America: An Insider's Report from the White House and the Cabinet* (New York: Simon and Schuster, 1981), 369.

47. Robert Ball, "Notes for File on Meeting with the President, May 4, 1977, on SS Financing," May 6, 1977, Ball Papers; John Snee and Mary Ross, "Social Security Amendments of 1977: Legislative History and Summary of Provisions," *Social Security Bulletin,* March 1978, p. 6.

48. Snee and Ross, "Social Security Amendments of 1977," p. 18; for the administration's view of the passage of the bill, see Califano, *Governing America,* 380–381.

49. Stuart Eizenstat and Frank Raines to President Ford, December 19, 1977, Eizenstat Papers, Box 277.

50. Statements of Rep. Jake Pickle, *Congressional Record,* September 6, 1979, pp. 7397ff.

51. Ibid., pp. 7408–7409.

52. Remarks of Sen. Edward Kennedy, *Congressional Record,* December 5, 1979, p. S17800.

53. Remarks of Senator Dole in Ibid., p. S17778.
54. Berkowitz, *America's Welfare State,* pp. 79–80.
55. Robert Ball to Honorable Gene Sperling, Director, National Economic Council, December 10, 1987, in Robert Ball, "Issues Related to the Future of Social Security: A Series of Memoranda by Robert M. Ball," Ball Papers; Alan Greenspan, Robert Myers, and Robert Ball, "Social Security: It's Almost Secure," February 1984, Ball Papers; Ball, "Confidential Note to Files—Conversation with Rick Foster, Office of the Actuary, SSA," February 17, 1984, Ball Papers; "Statement by Robert Ball before Joint Economic Committee," Hearing on Social Security Fund Surplus, June 16, 1989, Ball Papers.
56. "Appendix I: Developments since 1983," in *Report of the 1994–1996 Advisory Council on Social Security, Vol. I: Findings and Recommendations* (Washington, D.C.: Government Printing Office, 1997), 163–164.
57. See Daniel Béland, *Social Security: History and Politics from the New Deal to the Privatization Debate* (Lawrence: University Press of Kansas, 2005), 179.
58. Ibid., 180.

The Creation of
Social Security in America

By the time America adopted Social Security in 1935 there were already more than twenty nations around the world with operating social insurance systems of various types. The most influential of these models—and the one American theorists looked to the most—was the system of social insurance pioneered in Germany and designed principally by German chancellor Otto von Bismarck.

The first section of this chapter features three documents relating to the history of the German social insurance system: excerpts from two books recounting conversations with Bismarck about his views on social insurance and the first official American government recognition of the developments in Germany.

During the Progressive Era (1890–1917), old-age insurance never moved to the center of American policy debates, but it was part of the discussion, as illustrated in two documents excerpted here: a speech

The German Chancellor, Otto von Bismarck, in the late nineteenth century designed some of the earliest European social insurance programs, which served as partial models for American designers in the early twentieth century. Source: Library of Congress.

from Theodore Roosevelt's third-party campaign for president in 1912 and the work of social insurance theorist I. M. Rubinow.

The Great Depression (1929–1941) increased the agitation for government economic support of the elderly. One influential mass movement in this regard was the Townsend Plan, which is excerpted here, along with rebuttal from President Franklin D. Roosevelt's administration (1933–1945).

Roosevelt's message to Congress in 1934, and his subsequent creation of the Committee on Economic Security (CES), were the prelude to the legislative process that resulted in the Social Security Act of 1935. Using the CES report as a baseline, Congress held hearings and debates on the administration's proposals during 1935, resulting in enactment of the law in August. This sequence of policy development is traced in the documents in this chapter.

Document 1.1
Dr. Moritz Busch's Diaries, 1898

Chancellor Otto von Bismarck, who was the primary force behind the design of the German social insurance system, regarded social insurance as a limited reform designed to weaken support for socialism in Germany. This was a primary concern of American labor leaders, who initially distrusted the social insurance movement because they viewed it as having an antilabor pedigree.

Bismarck introduced his first social insurance bill in 1881. The health insurance package passed the Reichstag (parliament) in 1883, followed by the workmen's compensation proposals in 1884 and the old-age insurance plan in 1889.

One of Bismark's favorite tactics was to "plant" stories with journalists he thought would communicate his policy views favorably. One such long-term relationship was with journalist Moritz Busch, who published this account of Bismarck's views within months of Bismarck's death in 1898.

. . . On the 18th of January, 1881, I wrote to the Chief reminding him of my readiness to place myself at his disposal in case he wished to have any matter of importance discussed in the German or English press, and requesting information. On the 20th I received the following answer from the Imperial Chancellerie: "The Imperial Chancellor begs Dr. Moritz Busch to do him the honour to call upon him to-morrow, Friday, at 1 o'clock."

I went to the Chancellor's palace at the appointed time, and I remained with him for an hour and a half. The Prince sat at his writing-table with his face towards the door, and looked particularly well and hearty. He said: "So you have come for material, but there is not much to give you. One thing occurs to me, however. I should be very thankful to you if you would discuss my working-class insurance scheme in a friendly spirit. The Liberals do not show much disposition to take it up and their newspapers attack my proposals. The Government should not interfere in such matters—*laisser aller.* The question must be raised, however, and the present proposal is only the beginning. I have more in view. I grant that there may be room for improvement in many respects, and that some portions of the scheme are perhaps unpractical and should therefore be dropped. But a beginning must be made with the task of reconciling the labouring classes with the State. Whoever has a pension assured to him for his old age is much more contented and easier to manage than the man who has no such prospect. Compare a servant in a private house and one attached to a Government office or to the Court; the latter, because he looks forward to a pension, will put up with a great deal more and show much more zeal than the former. In France all sensible members of the poorer classes, when they are in a position to lay by anything, make a provision for the future by investing in securities. Something of the kind should be arranged for our workers. People call this State Socialism, and having done so think they have disposed of the question. It may be State Socialism, but it is necessary. What then are the present provisions for municipal assistance to the poor? Municipal Socialism?"

He paused for a moment, and then continued: "Large sums of money would be required for carrying such schemes into execution, at least a hundred million marks, or more probably two hundred. But I should not be frightened by even three hundred millions. Means must be provided to enable the State to act generously towards the poor. The contentment of the disinherited, of all those who have no possessions, is not too dearly purchased even at a very high figure. They must learn that the State benefits them also, that it not only demands, but also bestows. If the question is taken up by the State, which does not want to make any profit, or to secure dividends, the thing can be done."

He reflected again for a few seconds, and then said: "The tobacco monopoly might be applied in that way. The monopoly would thus permit of the creation of an entailed estate for the poor. You need not emphasize that point, however. The monopoly is only a last resource, the highest trump. You might say it would be possible to relieve the poor of their anxiety for the future, and to provide them with a small inheritance by taxing luxuries such as tobacco, beer, and brandy. The English, the Americans, and even the Russians have no monopoly, and yet they raise large sums through a heavy tax upon these articles of luxury. We, as the country which is most lightly taxed in this respect, can bear a considerable increase, and if the sums thus acquired are used for securing the future of our working population, uncertainty as to which is the chief cause of their hatred to the State, we thereby at the same time secure our own future, and that is a good investment for our money. We should thus avert a revolution, which might break out fifty or perhaps ten years hence, and which, even if it were only successful for a few months, would swallow up very much larger sums, both directly and indirectly, through disturbance of trade, than our preventive measures would cost. The Liberals recognise the reasonableness of the proposals—in their hearts; but they grudge the credit of them to the man who initiated them, and would like to take up the question themselves, and so win popularity. They will, perhaps, try to bury the scheme in Committee, as they have done other Bills. Something must, however, be done speedily, and possibly they may approve of the general lines of the scheme, as they are already thinking of the elections. . . ."

Source: Moritz Busch, *Bismarck: Some Secret Pages of His History, Being a Diary Kept during Twenty-Five Years' Official and Private Intercourse with the Great Chancellor,* vol. 2 (London: Macmillan, 1898), 257–259.

Document 1.2
Introduction of Social Insurance in the German Parliament, February and March 1881

In 1881 Bismarck formally proposed to the German parliament a program of social insurance against accidents in the workplace—the first in a series of measures implemented in that decade. The proposal was introduced in the annual speech to the Reichstag given by German king William I.

The first excerpt is from the text of the speech itself—which was delivered on February 1, 1881. The second is from a statement attached to the formal bill that was sent to the Reichstag in March 1881. The statement seeks to provide additional rationale for the proposed legislation.

The Speech from the Throne

. . . At the opening of the Reichstag in February 1879, the emperor, in reference to the [anti-socialist] law of October 21, 1878, gave expression to the hope that this House would not refuse its cooperation in the remedying of social ills by means of legislation. A remedy cannot alone be sought in the repression of socialistic excesses; there must be simultaneously the positive advancement of the welfare of the working classes. And here the care of those workpeople who are incapable of earning their livelihood is of the first importance. In the interest of these the emperor has caused a bill for the insurance of workpeople against the consequences of accident to be sent to the Bundesrat—a bill which, it is hoped, will meet a need felt both by workpeople and employers. His Majesty hopes that the measure will in principle receive the assent of the federal governments, and that it will be welcomed by the Reichstag as a complement of the legislation affording protection against social democratic movements. Past institutions intended to insure working people against the danger of falling into a condition of helplessness owing to the incapacity resulting from accident or age have proved inadequate, and their insufficiency has to no small extent contributed to cause the working classes to seek help by participating in social democratic movements. . . .

The Statement Attached to the Legislation

. . . That the State . . . should interest itself to a greater degree than hitherto in those of its members who need assistance, is not only a duty of humanity and Christianity—by which state institutions should be permeated—but a duty of state-preserving policy, whose aim should be to cultivate the conception—and that, too, amongst the nonpropertied classes, which form at once the most numerous and the least instructed part of the population— that the state is not merely a necessary but a beneficent institution. These classes must, by the evident and direct advantages which are secured to them by legislative measures, be led to regard the state not as an institution contrived for the protection of the better classes of society, but as one serving their own needs and interests. The apprehension that a socialis- tic element might be introduced into legislation if this end were followed should not check us. So far as that may be the case it will not be an innovation but the further development of the modern state idea, the result of Christian ethics, according to which the state should discharge, besides the defensive duty of protecting existing rights, the positive duty of pro- moting the welfare of all its members, and especially those who are weak and in need of help, by means of judicious institutions and the employment of those resources of the commu- nity which are at its disposal. In this sense the legal regulation of poor relief which the mod- ern state, in opposition to that of antiquity and of the Middle Ages, recognizes as a duty incumbent upon it, contains a socialistic element, and in truth the measures which may be adopted for improving the condition of the nonpropertied classes are only a development of the idea which lies at the basis of poor relief. Nor should the fear that legislation of this kind will not attain important results unless the resources of the Empire and of the individ- ual states be largely employed be a reason for holding back, for the value of measures affect- ing the future existence of society and the state should not be estimated according to the sacrifice of money which may be entailed. With a single measure, such as is at present pro- posed, it is of course impossible to remove entirely, or even to a considerable extent, the dif- ficulties which are contained in the social question. This is, in fact, but the first step in a direc- tion in which a difficult work, that will last for years, will have to be overcome gradually and cautiously, and the discharge of one task will only produce new ones. . . .

Source: William Harbutt Dawson, *Bismarck and State Socialism: An Exposition of the Social and Eco- nomic Legislation of Germany since 1870* (London: S. Sonnenschein & Co., 1891), 110–112.

Document 1.3
Ambassador Andrew White's Letter to the State Department, February 21, 1881

This letter from Andrew White, the American minister to Germany, is probably the first offi-cial recognition by a U.S. federal government agent of the emerging European movement for old-age social insurance.

It is noteworthy that this development, as expressed by Ambassador White, was not received favorably by the majority of Americans. This letter was written in the closing days of the Ruther-ford B. Hayes presidency (1877–1881), and it would be another twenty years before a presi-dent sympathetic to the idea of social insurance would come to office (that is, Theodore Roosevelt in 1901), and another thirty-four years after that before America would adopt a national social insurance program.

Legation of the United States
Berlin, 21 February 1881
Mr. White to the Secretary of State
Subject: The Opening of the Imperial Parliament (Reichstag)
Synopsis: Mr. White in sending a copy and translation of the Speech from the throne; describes the chief legislative measures mentioned therein, especially the project for the State Insurance of Workmen, a copy of which he also endorses, giving some indications of its prob-able effects.

Sir,

The opening of the Imperial Parliament (Reichstag) took place on the 15th inst. Very lit-tle interest was manifested in the ceremony itself, since neither the Emperor nor the Chan-cellor took part in it.

But upon the Speech from the Throne very general attention was concentrated. It was expected to contain a programme for a new system of dealing with taxation and labor throughout the Empire, of which the public has heard much for some time past. Intimations as to the immediate future of Europe, whether peaceful or war-like, were also looked for.

As to the general concerns of Europe, the speech was neither full nor clear, yet on the whole indicated expectations of peace.

As to the internal affairs of the Empire, public expectation was more than realized. Bills were announced of the greatest importance to the millions concerned, and of deep interest to all students of politics throughout the world.

For the idea which underlies and permeates them all is socialistic—the idea that the advancement of the laboring classes is to be left not merely or mainly to individual fore-sight or energy but to society as a whole, acting through its constituted authorities. These bills are presented with the express declaration that the Imperial government thus begins to redeem the promise made at the introduction of the law for the repression of socialist excesses in October 1878,—a promise to prepare measures for the relief of the working classes. On this point the speech lays stress in more than one passage.

These measures, which seem generally considered as only a first installment, involves relieving the working-classes of direct taxation, the creation of a system of Guilds or Trade

Corporations, a change in the laws regarding crimes committed during intoxication, but, above all, a system under which the State shall insure certain large classes of workmen throughout the Empire in view of disability or death, the premiums to be collected in stated proportions by government officials from employers, employed, and sundry local boards.

Of course, this cannot strictly be called the *beginning* of government upon the socialistic theory, since we have already seen here the absorption of the railways by the Prussian State, and various other measures clearly based on the theory that "that government is best which governs *most;*" but it is clearly the beginning of a new stage in the practical development of the theory, a development which I am assured, after talking with many of the most noted statesmen and thinkers of the Empire, will go on logically to embrace all workmen under a State insurance scheme, and which would seem to have no logical end short of that which the extreme socialists have advocated as the "Organization of Labor."

These projects will no doubt meet with much opposition and be considerably amended; but the expectation generally is that, in their main features, they will become law. It has been thought by many that Bavaria would declare against them; but the recent speech of the Bavarian Minister—President Lutz—seems to indicate ultimate acquiescence in the national insurance scheme by the second of the leading German States. With Prussia and Bavaria acting together, there is little indeed to be feared from the lesser governments.

Whatever may be the value of the other parts of the plan, that which proposes to remove taxation from the working classes will hardly gain universal applause, since the result is arrived at not by retrenchment either of military or civil expenditures but by substituting indirect for direct taxes.

It is not unlikely that there is some ground for the taunt that the Chancellor, in thus proposing a great plan for ameliorating the condition of the working classes, may have the coming elections in view. This is the last session during the continuance of the present Parliament. A new election is already on the horizon; and with the Liberal Party split into fractions, and the Central or Ultramontane Party, embittered by what all consider harsh and some perfidious treatment, the Chancellor may think it best to bid for the votes of the working classes in order to secure a majority in the next Parliament devoted to himself. But anyone who has studied at all thoughtfully the Chancellor's idea of government can hardly fail of the conclusion that these measures are the legitimate result of a certain theory which he has long cherished. Its germs lie in his character, and they have been developed not only by his own reasoning but by that of his most intimate advisors. This theory appears to be simply that the Empire must thrust its roots down among the working-classes; that it must draw support from their most cherished interests and hopes; and that all classes must be impressed more and more with the idea that provision both for their own present wants and for the future wants of their families depends, first of all, upon the stability of the central government.

I enclose a translation of the Imperial Speech, and of the national insurance bill; also the original text of the same in full, with annotations.

I have the honor to be, Sir, your obedient servant.

And. D. White

Source: Photographic copy of letter in the Social Security Administration History Archives, Revolving Files, Folder: "Social Security Antecedents."

Document 1.4
Progressive Party Campaign Material, August 1912

While old-age insurance was not the focus of American policy debate during the Progressive Era, European-style social insurance did have some powerful advocates, such as Theodore Roosevelt. In the presidential election of 1912, Roosevelt ran unsuccessfully as a third-party candidate representing the Progressive Party (which was nicknamed the Bull Moose Party). During this campaign, he advocated the adoption in America of social insurance programs similar to those already in operation in Europe. Roosevelt's speech to the Progressive Party's nominating convention in Chicago in August 1912 was a passionate call for social insurance and related labor reforms.

No Hope from the Old Party Machines

The prime need to-day is to face the fact that we are now in the midst of a great economic evolution. There is urgent necessity of applying both common sense and the highest ethical standard to this movement for better economic conditions among the mass of our people if we are to make it one of healthy evolution and not one of revolution. . . .

. . . Moreover, our needs are such that there should be coherent action among those responsible for the conduct of National affairs and those responsible for the conduct of State affairs; because our aim should be the same in both State and Nation; that is, to use the Government as an efficient agency for the practical betterment of social and economic conditions throughout this land. There are other important things to be done, but this is the most important thing. . . .

Social and Industrial Justice to the Wage-Workers

I especially challenge the attention of the people to the need of dealing in far-reaching fashion with our human resources, and therefore our labor power. . . .

In the last twenty years an increasing percentage of our people have come to depend on industry for their livelihood, so that today the wage-workers in industry rank in importance side by side with the tillers of the soil. As a people we cannot afford to let any group of citizens or any individual citizen live or labor under conditions which are injurious to the common welfare. Industry, therefore, must submit to such public regulation as will make it a means of life and health, not of death or inefficiency. We must protect the crushable elements at the base of our present industrial structure.

The first charge on the industrial statesmanship of the day is to prevent human waste. The dead weight of orphanage and depleted craftsmanship, of crippled workers and workers suffering from trade diseases, of casual labor, of insecure old age, and of household depletion due to industrial conditions are, like our depleted soils, our gashed mountain-sides and flooded river bottoms, so many strains upon the National structure, draining the reserve strength of all industries and showing beyond all peradventure the public element and public concern in industrial health. . . .

We stand for a living wage. Wages are subnormal if they fail to provide a living for those who devote their time and energy to industrial occupations. The monetary equivalent of a living wage varies according to local conditions, but must include enough to secure the elements of a normal standard of living—a standard high enough to make morality possible, to provide for education and recreation, to care for immature members of the family, to maintain the family during periods of sickness, and to permit of reasonable saving for old age. . . .

It is abnormal for any industry to throw back upon the community the human wreckage due to its wear and tear, and the hazards of sickness, accident, invalidism, involuntary unemployment, and old age should be provided for through insurance. This should be made a charge in whole or in part upon the industries the employer, the employee, and perhaps the people at large, to contribute severally in some degree. Wherever such standards are not met by given establishments, by given industries, are unprovided for by a legislature, or are balked by unenlightened courts, the workers are in jeopardy, the progressive employer is penalized, and the community pays a heavy cost in lessened efficiency and in misery. What Germany has done in the way of old age pensions or insurance should be studied by us, and the system adapted to our uses, with whatever modifications are rendered necessary by our different ways of life and habits of thought. . . .

Source: Social Security Administration History Archives, Revolving Files, Folder: "Roosevelt, Theodore."

Document 1.5
Isaac M. Rubinow's Book on Social Insurance, 1913

Isaac M. Rubinow, an M.D. with a Ph.D. from Columbia University, was an expert in economics and actuarial science, and his 1913 book, Social Insurance, *was probably the most influential early American work on the subject. According to former U.S. senator Paul Douglas, President Franklin Roosevelt was much influenced by Rubinow and considered him to be the "greatest single authority upon social security in the United States." In this excerpt from the book's first chapter, Rubinow educates America on the basic concepts of social insurance.*

Chapter 1: The Concept of Social Insurance

Insurance, the *Encyclopedia Britannica* says, "is a provision made by a group of persons, each singly in danger of some loss, the incidence of which cannot be foreseen, that when such loss shall occur to any of them, it shall be distributed over the whole group."

All insurance, therefore, is essentially a social function. Why, then, this emphasis upon "social insurance" and what features are necessary to distinguish it from other forms? The historical origin of the term within rather recent times from the older one "workingmen's insurance," is sufficiently significant. It emphasizes the fact that social insurance is the policy of organized society to furnish that protection to one part of the population, which some other part may need less, or, if needing, is able to purchase voluntarily through private insurance. That originally only the wage-workers were considered entitled to the protection of this policy, and that within recent times the sphere of this policy in several European countries was extended to include other social classes. . . .

The term "social insurance" is as yet very little understood by the vast majority of English-speaking nations. The first necessary step, therefore, is not so much a technical definition, as a description, or rather circumscription of the term, and the distinction between social and ordinary commercial insurance may be best emphasized by first indicating the characteristics common to both.

All insurance is a substitution of social, co-operative provision for individual provision. Technically, this substitution of social effort for individual effort, is known as the theory of distribution of losses and the subsequent elimination of risk. Highly technical as is the organization of this function of distribution in practice, its theory is singularly lucid and simple. . . .

This elementary principle must necessarily underlie all existing forms of insurance. There is an individual advantage in substituting a small definite money loss for the possibility of a very large financial loss, there is an evident gain in the freedom from anxiety, concerning the possibility of the larger loss, which is purchased for that price of the premium. . . .

. . . The distress that might follow the death or disability of the family's provider may be prevented by a payment of a corresponding premium. . . .

Thus, the social advantages of distribution of loss are equally applicable to all forms of insurance, to commercial insurance as well as social insurance; and having learned the underlying basis common to both, we are better prepared to study the essential differences, to define, at least in a general way, the proper domain of social insurance, and to justify the study of the latter, not at all as a branch of the insurance business, but as an essential part of social policy. . . . The situation is evidently quite different as between insurance of property, when a certain very small loss guarantees the possession of a very large amount of property, and insurance of the continuity of earning capacity which may be the only possession of the individual. It will be readily admitted that our standard of wages does not in the majority of cases yield a continuous surplus. In fact, investigations of the earnings and expenditures of wage-workers in all countries have proven beyond doubt that an annual surplus is a very unusual phenomenon in the life of the working class; the earnings at best are only large enough to cover the current expenditures. Under such conditions, every expenditure is a matter of serious financial importance for a wage-worker's family, as the satisfaction of every new want may be obtained only at the sacrifice of another want, perhaps equally important and pressing.

In the workingman's psychology, therefore, insurance of any kind is never a matter of choice between a danger and a slight discomfort, when the arguments for insurance are so overwhelming that they can be trusted of themselves to produce the necessary results. Rather is it a selection between a possible deprivation in the future and a certain serious loss in the present which the payment of the premium requires. While this represents a serious difficulty on one hand, another still more serious is the large variety of economic risks to which the modern wage-earners are exposed, thus multiplying the number of insurance premiums which they would have to pay to obtain the full benefit of the advantages of loss distribution. It is often stated as a truism that the measure of security of life is the measure of the progress of civilization. That might be true in a certain physical sense. . . . But, economically speaking, there has not been such increase in the security of obtaining means of livelihood as far as our working population is concerned.

Modern society is based upon a system of free labor. Under such system, the working ability of the wage-worker is his only means to support, and then only if it finds a ready market. Many wage-workers may have some property, but of capital, in the sense of revenue-bearing property, they have very little or none. The amount of property saved, if readily convertible into units of universal value—money (which is an exception rather than the rule), may influence the period of waiting time between stoppage of earning and actual distress; but in the vast majority of cases, interruption of the wage-worker's income soon leads to serious economical distress.

This leads up to the question—what are the usual causes of interruption of income in a wage-worker's family? . . .

In the vast majority of cases, the cause of absence of income is the inability to perform remunerative work. This factor again may be further analyzed. It is the result usually of one of the following three conditions:

1. Absence of a worker in the family.
2. Physical inability to perform labor, either because of illness or accidental injury or chronic invalidity, or the physical deterioration accompanying old age; or,
3. Finally, inability to find employment because of lack of adjustment between demand and supply in the labor market.

Sickness, accidents, invalidity, premature or normal old age, premature death, and finally unemployment,—such are the economic risks which stare in the face each and every workingman. Their economic consequences are very much more serious in his case, than in the middle classes deriving their income from property, business, or profession, where the continuity of income is not so closely dependent upon continuity of effort.

Not only are the various risks more numerous and more serious, but they are also more frequent in the case of the workman. Clearly, then, the premiums to protect against such possible losses upon the now familiar theory of distribution of loss must be very much higher, while the source from which such premiums must be paid is very much more limited. Thus remaining upon the strict basis of actuarial (or insurance business) principles, the premium necessary to protect all these emergencies is so high that the working class as a whole are either unable or unwilling to meet it. A point is arrived at where the certainty of the economic cost of insurance overbalances the fear of the danger of possible loss, and insurance is not effected.

But why necessarily insurance? . . . It is often argued that, inasmuch as all these emergencies are quite common and frequent, each individual family must take the necessary steps to be prepared for them through the instrumentality of savings.

No student of economics would deny the educational, character-building value of thrift, meaning elimination of waste and respect for the proper value of property, which in the last analysis means respect for the results of human effort. But the assertion that, in the case of the wage-earning class, individual saving may solve the problem of poverty, necessarily presupposes the existence of a surplus in the budget of the average wage-earner's family. There was a time when that assertion could be glibly made for lack of accurate scientific material to contradict it. That time is fortunately gone. A series of able and painstaking investigations both of the actual and normal standards of living, has conclusively shown that, even in the United States, a very large proportion of the wage earners have an income which is insufficient for the maintenance of a normal standard, and surely have no surplus. . . .

Here, then, is the social problem underlying the need of insurance of the wage-earning millions. Their economic condition is precarious; the economic dangers threatening them many; and the degree of risk in each case is very high. Individual provision is insufficient, social provision through distribution of loss is necessary but costly, often much too costly.

If we have grasped the substance of these principles, we are prepared to draw the line between commercial and social insurance, and we understand the main purpose and functions of social insurance. Both forms of insurance are social institutions. But there is also a vast difference, easily explained by the differences in the economic status, and, therefore, in the psychological attitude towards the insurance of the two social groups concerned. . . .

But there is the very much larger class of wage-earners or persons in similar economic conditions, whose need of insurance is very much greater, because the hazards are many and grave, but who nevertheless are unable to meet the true cost of insurance conducted as a business. To provide them with such insurance or some equivalent form of protection has become the concern of the modern progressive state, and this is properly the field of social insurance. There are many different ways, or perhaps more accurately, different degrees of assistance, which society or the state can furnish, and they may be all considered as efforts to reduce the amount of premium or cost of insurance and to extend its application. Thus the state may begin by simply providing a safe insurance organization, devoid of the elements of profit. This alone reduces the premium, for profits are a necessary element of the premium of commercial insurance. It may take the next step and assume part or the entire cost of administration of the insurance institutions, and thus further reduce the cost, for this cost is a very important fact in "loading" or increasing the premium. It may take still one more step and directly subsidize insurance, thus assuming a part of the true cost, or it may impose such assumption of cost upon other elements of society, such as the employing class, or it may further assume or shift the entire cost of the premium, thus virtually granting an insurance without payment of premium by the insured, as is the case with the insurance against accidents in most countries and with old-age pensions in some. And it may finally counteract the unwillingness of the working class to pay even a small subsidized premium by making insurance compulsory. All this the modern state may and does do to develop social insurance, to furnish protection to those who need and are unable to purchase it in the open market. . . .

In this brief exposition of the general aims of the movement known as "social insurance," the needs of the working class were primarily emphasized. Undoubtedly it is the wage-working class which has mostly felt the new economic dangers of the social system based upon purchase of labor, the insecurity of means of existence, and the pressure of the cost of living upon the earnings. But poverty is not altogether limited to this class. The lower middle class has felt the same conditions quite acutely, both because there is a constant influx from the middle class to the wage-working class, and because its own means of existence are often insecure. Thus the very large and rapidly growing group of salaried employees, and even the groups of small independent artisans, small property-owners, a very large proportion of the farmers, and even the small employers of labor are not at all free from the dangers of discontinuance of income and consequent poverty or even pauperism. Thus modern social insurance has gradually taken in many of these economic groups. And in so far the term social insurance is rather more extensive than the more modest and limited term "workmen's insurance." . . .

Source: I. M. Rubinow, *Social Insurance: With Special Reference to American Conditions* (New York: Henry Holt, 1913), 3–12.

Document 1.6
The Townsend Plan, 1934

Francis E. Townsend, a doctor living in Long Beach, California, devised a plan known as the Old Age Revolving Pension Plan—or the Townsend Plan, for short—to solve the problem of economic security for the aged. The basic idea of the plan was that the government would provide a pension of $200 per month to all citizens age sixty and older—on conditions that they fully retire and that they spend the entire amount each month. The pensions would be funded by a national sales tax. Townsend published his plan in a local Long Beach newspaper in early 1933 and within two years there were approximately 7,000 Townsend Clubs around the country with more than 2.2 million members actively working to make the Townsend Plan the nation's old-age pension system.

The Townsend Plan had some serious support in Congress, as well. Because Social Security benefits remained less generous than old-age assistance pensions until after the amendments in 1950, the Townsend organization stayed in business and continued to lobby for its views well after the original Social Security Act was passed in 1935. Indeed, there is some evidence that Roosevelt was prodded to introduce his Social Security proposal to counter the growing influence of the Townsend Plan.

*Reprinted below are two documents regarding the Townsend Plan—one that was published in the millions in 1934–1935 and one that has never been published before. The first (Document 1.6) is an excerpt from the Townsend Plan itself—*Old Age Revolving Pensions: A Proposed National Plan—*"Youth for Work, Age for Leisure"; the second (Document 1.7) is an unpublished Committee on Economic Security analysis of the Townsend Plan.*

Foreword by the Editor

The author of the plan for combining liberal retirement compensation for the aged with national financial recovery and permanent prosperity as described in the subsequent pages is a physician who has been employed by the city of Long Beach, California, for the past two years, through its health department, in caring for the indigent sick. A large percentage of his patients were old folks whose life savings have been swept away by the financial collapse of institutions in which their savings were invested.

With a suddenness that bewildered them these folks found themselves not only helpless but a burden to their financially embarrassed relatives. That was the last straw. To feel that they were not only helpless and useless but also in the way caused a rapid decline in their health and spirits and an actual, ardent wish for death as their only hope of relief.

This pathetic collapse of their morale with the hopeless apathy it produced in them made their care a double burden upon their anxious relatives who were impelled to stretch their already meager finances in an effort to provide little luxuries and means of amusement for their beloved elders. Many of the old folks went into a rapid decline and died, the sorrow for their loss and the added obligations of the funeral expenses but adding to the desperate situation faced by their sons and daughters.

Daily association with affliction, grim want and hopeless sorrow obsessed this physician with a consuming desire to provide a cure for the national folly of permitting blighting, destructive want in a land of superabundance.

He believes that he has found the cure. He believes with President Roosevelt that poverty and its useless horrors can be abolished. He believes that our nation with its vast creative power needs but one important principle to be established through legislation to banish poverty and its attendant evils forever. . . .

Analysis of the Plan

Retirement at Age of Sixty

Insurance statistics show that only 8% of people reaching that age have achieved financial success to such a degree that they may live comfortably thereafter without depending upon further earnings. Eighty-five percent of the 92% of all people sixty years of age and over are still employed or are endeavoring in some manner to earn all or a part of their livelihood and the remainder are dependent upon public or private charity for their keep. Those of the 85% who are still earning are capable of producing only enough to partially pay for their living. A very small percentage actually earn enough for their total needs and but very few earn any surplus for their declining years.

Approximately 8,000,000 people will be eligible to apply for the pension. Economists estimate that each person spending $200.00 per month creates a job for one additional worker. The retirement of all citizens of 60 years and over from all productive industry and gainful occupation, will thereby create jobs for 8,000,000 workers which will solve our national labor problem.

Retirement on a Monthly Pension of $200

The spending of $200 per month is for a constructive purpose. First, to place an adequate amount of buying power in the hands of these citizens which will permit them to satisfy their wants that have been so restricted for the past four years. Second, to create such a demand for new goods of all description that all manufacturing plants in the country will be called upon to start their wheels of production at full speed and provide jobs for all workers.

This money made suddenly available to the channels of trade will immediately start a tremendous flood of buying, since the country has been on short commodity rations for the past four years, and since all sections of the country will be affected alike (the old are everywhere) and the poorest sections will at once become important buying centers.

All factories and avenues of production may be expected to start producing at full capacity and all workers called into activity at high wages, since there will be infinitely more jobs available and many less workers to fill the jobs, the old folks having retired from competition for places as producers. . . .

Pensioners to Retire without Further Gain from Labor or Profession

This is an important feature of the plan since the idea is to create jobs for the young and able, eliminating competition for such jobs and positions on the part of elderly people.

Consumption of the products of farm and factory is the vital problem now facing our nation. The success of this plan is based entirely on the creation of jobs of production and by retiring all those pensioned, with adequate spending power, that they may consume for all their need in comforts, necessities and pleasure. . . .

Saving for Old Age

We have been taught in the past that saving was essential in planning for security in old age. But recent experience has taught us that no one has yet been able to devise a sure method of saving. Statistical records show that ninety-two percent of all people reaching the age of sixty-five have, in spite of their best efforts, been unable to save enough to guard them from the humiliation of accepting charity in some form, either from relatives or from the state. Experience proves that no form of investment is infallible that human mind can devise which is based upon the small group or individual financing. The Townsend plan proposes that all who serve society to the best of their ability in whatever capacity shall not be denied that security in their declining years to which their services in active years have entitled them.

Costs of Maintaining the Huge Revolving Fund

The unthinking see a great increase in the cost of living due to the necessity for the retailer to raise his prices to meet the government tax for maintaining the pension roll. He fails to take into consideration the fact that the elimination of poor houses, organized state and county relief agencies, public and private pension systems, community chests, etc., are now costing the country the many millions of dollars per month that the Townsend plan would eliminate. And, too, would not the cost of crime and insane asylums be greatly reduced after the public became assured of the permanency of our prosperity? Further, the tremendous increase in the volume of retail business which this huge revolving fund would insure makes certain that bigger profits would be possible to the retailer through his old rates than ever before and make unnecessary the advance in prices on any articles except those classed as luxuries. Estimated from the sources available a tax of 10% will be ample to raise this fund and the tax can be materially lowered as the volume of trade increases. . . .

No one will object to paying the slight advance in price for commodities for the purpose of re-establishing prosperity and, in so doing, making it possible for the elderly people to retire and live comfortably the remainder of their days, since everyone in making his purchases will be providing for his own security when he reaches the age of sixty.

Sales Tax to Be Used Exclusively for the Pensions

It is the intent of the plan to apply the sales tax solely to the one purpose of maintaining the pensions roll until such time as the public becomes fully assured of the beneficent and fair system of taxation involved in a universal retail tax. Here is the only fair system of taxation for all that can be devised. . . .

No Change in Form of Government

This plan of Old Age Revolving Pensions interferes in no way with our present form of government, profit system of business or change of specie in our economic setup. It is a simple American plan dedicated to the cause of prosperity and the abolition of poverty. . . .

The Meaning of Security to Humanity

Here lies the true value in the Townsend Plan. Humanity will be forever relieved from the fear of destitution and want. The seeming need for sharp practices and greedy accumulation will disappear. Benevolence and kindly consideration for others will displace suspicion and avarice, brotherly love and tolerance will blossom into full flower and the genial sun of human happiness will dissipate the dark clouds of distrust and gloom and despair. . . .

Source: Social Security Administration History Archives, Revolving Files, Folder: "Townsend, Francis."

Document 1.7
Edwin E. Witte on "Why the Townsend Old Age Revolving Pension Plan Is Impossible" January 1935

As part of the work of President Roosevelt's Committee on Economic Security, the executive director of the group, Edwin Witte, drafted an internal report on the Townsend Plan. Witte, who was an economist from the University of Wisconsin, dismissed the Townsend Plan as a wildly impractical scheme.

Costs

The Townsend plan proposes that pensions of $200 per month shall be granted to all citizens of the United States who are 60 years of age or over, other than habitual criminals, and who will forego all gainful occupation and agree to spend the pensions during the month in which they are received. No income or property limitations whatsoever are prescribed; even millionaires would be entitled to the Townsend pensions.

There were 10,385,000 persons over 60 years of age in the United States in 1930, as shown by the Census of that year. At this time the number is considerably greater, being estimated at 11,582,000. The number of habitual criminals among the aged is very small and the number who are not citizens only about 600,000. While 4,155,495 persons over 60 years of age were in 1930 still "gainfully occupied," the great majority of these persons would gladly forego gainful occupation and agree to spend their pensions each month as received, if they were assured a pension of $200 per month. Even if one fourth of all now gainfully occupied would refuse the pensions, the total number of the pensioners under the Townsend plan would still approximate 10,000,000. This is the figure for the number of pensioners most commonly given in the Townsend literature, although sometimes 8,000,000 is stated as the number to be pensioned.

If there are 10,000,000 pensioners, the cost is 2 billion dollars per month or 24 billions per year; if there will be only 8,000,000 pensioners, these figures would be reduced to $1,600,000,000 per month or $19,200,000,000 per year. Either figure is considerably more than double the present combined federal, state, and local taxes, which in 1932 totalled only $8,212,000,000. . . .

These figures would represent the costs only in the first year. Persons who reach age 60 still have more than 15 years of life ahead of them on the average. Under the Townsend plan the average pensioner would be entitled to $200 per month for more than 15 years. Actuaries employed by the Committee on Economic Security have computed that merely to pay pensions to these now 60 or over, represents a cost to the Government of a present value of 245 billion dollars—which is to be compared with a total estimated public and private debt of 126 billion dollars at the peak of the boom period in 1929. . . . This total almost equals the entire estimated taxable wealth of the United States, which . . . a sub-committee of the Committee on Ways and Means . . . places at less than 260 billion dollars, and is 50% greater than the actual assessed value of all property, found by this sub-committee to be 163 billion dollars.

As the plan contemplates that not only shall pensions of $200 per month be paid to those now 60 and over but also to all persons as they become 60, the actual liability assured by the Government is much greater than this staggering total of 245 billion dollars. For many years to come, the number of pensioners will increase each year, and the annual cost and total liability will mount rapidly.

Taxes

To finance the Townsend pensions, the McGroarty bill (H.R. 3977), which is the official Townsend plan bill, provides that a 2% tax (which may be reduced by the President to 1% or increased to 3%) shall be levied "on the gross value of each business, commercial, and/or financial transaction," to be paid by the seller.

In the Townsend literature the claim is made that the total money value of all transactions in 1933 was 1200 billion dollars and the *55th Statistical Abstract of the United States* . . . indicates that no figure for the total money value of all transactions appears anywhere in the volume. The nearest approach to such a figure is the total of all bank debits (representing the total of all business transactions in which bank checks, drafts, etc., are used) in the 141 principal cities of the country, which in 1933 was . . . 442 billion dollars, while, roughly representing the total of all "business, commercial, and/or financial transactions" not all of this amount will be taxable under the Townsend Plan, as it specifically exempts "salaries for personal services." Allowing for this exemption, approximately 400 billion dollars of transactions would have been taxable in 1933. At the 2% rate in the McGroarty bill, this tax would have yielded 8 billion dollars, or about one-third the amount needed for the Townsend pensions. A rate not of 2% or 3%, as provided in the McGroarty bill, but of 6% is indicated as necessary for payment of the Townsend pensions on the basis of 1933 money value of all transactions.

Even a 2% rate on the money value of all business, commercial and financial transactions (to say nothing of a 6% rate) is so heavy that it would stop all business and could not possibly be collected. It would mean a tax of 2% of the face value of every check written in the course of ordinary business transactions. It would apply to manufacturer's sales, wholesalers' sales, and retail sales, and for nearly all commodities would represent a duplication of taxes, which inevitably, would have to be added to the price paid by the consumers. In glassware for instance, 11 transactions are customary between the producer of the raw materials and the consumer. On all of these transactions there would be a 2% (or 3%) tax and at each stage something more than the tax (to allow for investment and handling charges) would be added to the price.

Such increases in prices would have a pronounced tendency to restrict purchases. Many other types of transactions would be rendered entirely impossible, while in the Townsend literature the claim is repeated time and again that a very large part of the entire cost of pensions would come from the sale of stocks and bonds, the probable effect of a tax of 2% (or 3%) on the money value of all sales of securities would be to close all stock exchanges, since the margin at which business is done on these exchanges is much less than 2%. A tax of 2% on the money value of all transactions would dry up the sources of revenue and would probably produce much less than the $2,000,000,000 per year indicated as the probable yield on the basis of the 1933 business of the country. In fact, it is doubtful whether such a heavy tax could be collected at all.

Administrative Problems

Aside from the difficulties of collecting three times the amount of the federal, state, and local taxes combined (which, as noted, would require a tax rate, not of 2%, but of 6% on the money value of all business, commercial an financial transactions), the Townsend plan involves other great administrative difficulties. It provides that all sellers shall be licensed by the Secretary of the Treasury. The Bureau of the Census in 1933 had a record of 2,359,497 establishments engaged in manufacturing, wholesale and retail trade, hotel, service industries, and places of amusement, and this is by no means the entire number of sellers who would have to be licensed and from whom taxes would have to be collected monthly. Provisions would also have to be made for up to the minute lists of pensioners and their identification, to prevent frauds. Under the McGroarty bill, further local pension boards would have to be set up in each of the 3,071 counties and, approximately, 3,500 wards in cities of the country.

Most difficult of all would be the necessary checking to see that the 10,000,000 pensioners all spent their $200 within the month in which received. This would require going into the private affairs of the pensioners to an extent never before attempted and would necessitate a vast army of additional Government employees.

Final Appraisal of Plan

The Townsend advocates base practically their entire argument on the "revolving" feature of their plan. If there does not result from the plan a very great increase in incomes and in the money value of transactions, the promised pensions cannot possible be paid for any length of time without wholesale inflation. The total income of all of the people of the United States in 1933 was only 46 billion dollars. The people who are over 60 years of age are less than 9% of the entire population of the country. The Townsend proposal, consequently, might be described as a plan under which more than half the national income is to be given to the less than 9% of the people who are over 60 years of age. Unless there is a very great increase in the national income, this could be done only through reducing the incomes of the people under 60 years of age by approximately one-half.

The Townsend advocates claim that such a result will not be produced because business will be enormously stimulated through placing such a large amount of money in the hands of the old people to spend within the month in which received. They say nothing about the fact that the people under 60 will have approximately the same amount less to spend, and they will have to pay in taxes the amount which the people over 60 will get in pensions.

The Townsend literature states that the United States Government would have to pay only the 2 billion dollars required for the first month's pensions and that the plan would thereafter be self-sustaining because it would create enough new business to return to the

Government the entire pension costs, without burdening the taxpayers. As the rate of tax proposed is only 2%, it is manifest that the 2 billion dollars paid out in the first month would have to increase to 100 billion during that month, to justify the expectations of the Townsend advocates. The Townsend plan contemplates that pensioners shall spend their money within the month—but in order to produce sufficient revenue to pay the pensions of the second month, without burdening the people under 60, there must be fifty turnovers of the pension within the first month.

Even the Townsend advocates acknowledge that this is impossible, but they are reduced to the dilemma, either of burdening the people under 60 with heavy taxes which will greatly reduce their incomes or of having the Government pay the pension costs for a much longer period than the first month. Since it is inconceivable that the people under 60 would submit to have their incomes reduced by one-half, the latter course is the only possibility. This will mean a rapid increase in the national debt and in effect pronounced inflation.

Through inflation it may be possible to keep up the pension payments for some time. The final result, however, cannot be in doubt. The inflation and duplicate taxation involved in the Townsend plan will cause prices to soar and soon, even with $200 per month, the pensioners will not be better off than they were before, while those below 60 will be immeasurably worse off. The Townsend plan is one which involves not only revolving pensions but revolving taxes. It is a plan which arouses great hopes but actually will give the old people little, or nothing.

Source: Social Security Administration History Archives, Lateral File 3, Drawer 2.

Document 1.8
President Roosevelt's Message to Congress, June 8, 1934

On June 8, 1934, President Roosevelt sent a message to Congress announcing his legislative agenda and indicating his intention to propose social insurance legislation. This was the beginning initiative in what would become a prominent aspect of the New Deal's political and policy legacy.

To the Congress:

You are completing a work begun in March 1933, which will be regarded for a long time as a splendid justification of the vitality of representative government. . . .

You and I, as the responsible directors of these policies and actions, may, with good reason, look to the future with confidence, just as we may look to the past fifteen months with reasonable satisfaction.

On the side of relief we have extended material aid to millions of our fellow citizens.

On the side of recovery we have helped to lift agriculture and industry from a condition of utter prostration.

But, in addition to these immediate tasks of relief and of recovery we have properly, necessarily and with overwhelming approval determined to safeguard these tasks by rebuilding many of the structures of our economic life and reorganizing it in order to prevent a recurrence of collapse. . . .

Our task of reconstruction does not require the creation of new and strange values. It is rather the finding of the way once more to known, but to some degree forgotten, ideals and values. If the means and details are in some instances new, the objectives are as permanent as human nature.

Among our objectives I place the security of the men, women and children of the Nation first.

This security for the individual and for the family concerns itself primarily with three factors. People want decent homes to live in; they want to locate them where they can engage in productive work; and they want some safeguard against misfortunes which cannot be wholly eliminated in this man-made world of ours. . . .

. . . [S]ecurity was attained in the earlier days through the interdependence of members of families upon each other and of the families within a small community upon each other. The complexities of great communities and of organized industry make less real these simple means of security. Therefore, we are compelled to employ the active interest of the Nation as a whole through government in order to encourage a greater security for each individual who composes it. . . .

The third factor relates to security against the hazards and vicissitudes of life. Fear and worry based on unknown danger contribute to social unrest and economic demoralization. If, as our Constitution tells us, our Federal Government was established among other things, "to promote the general welfare," it is our plain duty to provide for that security upon which welfare depends.

Next winter we may well undertake the great task of furthering the security of the citizen and his family through social insurance.

This is not an untried experiment. Lessons of experience are available from States, from industries and from many Nations of the civilized world. The various types of social insurance are interrelated; and I think it is difficult to attempt to solve them piecemeal. Hence, I am looking for a sound means which I can recommend to provide at once security against several of the great disturbing factors in life—especially those which relate to unemployment and old age. I believe there should be a maximum of cooperation between States and the Federal Government. I believe that the funds necessary to provide this insurance should be raised by contribution rather than by an increase in general taxation. Above all, I am convinced that social insurance should be national in scope, although the several States should meet at least a large portion of the cost of management, leaving to the Federal Government the responsibility of investing, maintaining and safeguarding the funds constituting the necessary insurance reserves.

I have commenced to make, with the greatest of care, the necessary actuarial and other studies for the formulation of plans for the consideration of the 74th Congress.

These three great objectives—the security of the home, the security of livelihood, and the security of social insurance—are, it seems to me, a minimum of the promise that we can offer to the American people. They constitute a right which belongs to every individual and every family willing to work. They are the essential fulfillment of measures already taken toward relief, recovery and reconstruction.

This seeking for a greater measure of welfare and happiness does not indicate a change in values. It is rather a return to values lost in the course of our economic development and expansion. . . .

We must dedicate ourselves anew to a recovery of the old and sacred possessive rights for which mankind has constantly struggled—homes, livelihood, and individual security. The road to these values is the way of progress. Neither you nor I will rest content until we have done our utmost to move further on that road.

Source: The Public Papers and Addresses of Franklin D. Roosevelt, 1934 (New York: Random House, 1938), 287–293.

Document 1.9
President Roosevelt Establishes the Committee on Economic Security, June 29, 1934

To give form to his message to Congress, President Roosevelt created—by executive order—a cabinet-level Committee on Economic Security to research, study, and design a viable social insurance system for America.

Executive Order No. 6757—June 29, 1934

By virtue of and pursuant to the authority vested in me by the National Industrial Recovery Act (ch. 90, 48 Stat. 195), I hereby establish (1) the Committee on Economic Security (hereinafter referred to as the Committee) consisting of the Secretary of Labor, Chairman, the Secretary of the Treasury, the Attorney General, the Secretary of Agriculture, and the Federal Emergency Relief Administrator, and (2) the Advisory Council on Economic Security (hereinafter referred to as the Advisory Council), the original members of which shall be appointed by the President and additional members of which may be appointed from time to time by the Committee.

The Committee shall study problems relating to the economic security of individuals and shall report to the President not later than December 1, 1934, its recommendations concerning proposals which in its judgment will promote greater economic security.

The Advisory Council shall assist the Committee in the consideration of all matters coming within the scope of its investigations.

The Committee shall appoint (1) a Technical Board on Economic Security consisting of qualified representatives selected from various departments and agencies of the Federal Government, and (2) an executive director who shall have immediate charge of studies and investigations to be carried out under the general direction of the Technical Board, and who shall, with the approval of the Technical Board, appoint such additional staff as may be necessity to carry out the provisions of this order.

Source: The Public Papers and Addresses of Franklin D. Roosevelt, 1934 (New York: Random House, 1938), 321–322.

Document 1.10

Report of the Committee on Economic Security, January 15, 1935

The President's Committee on Economic Security was formed in June 1934 and it issued its final report in January 1935. Not everything contemplated by the CES at the outset made it into their final proposal. Health insurance was deferred for later study. A proposal for voluntary old-age annuities as supplements to the basic contributory social insurance system did not survive congressional review. But the CES's final report provided the basic blueprint for what would come to be the Social Security Act.

*In this report the CES advocated a financing plan that would have left the program in a deficit condition by 1965, at which point it was suggested that general revenues be used to make up the shortfall. This aspect of their proposal was deleted at the insistence of President Roosevelt and thus was not part of the administration's final proposals (**Document 1.12**).*

Need for Security

The need of the people of this country for "some safeguard against misfortunes which cannot be wholly eliminated in this man-made world of ours" is tragically apparent at this time, when 18,000,000 people, including children and aged are dependent upon emergency relief for their subsistence and approximately 10,000,000 workers have no employment other than relief work. Many millions more have lost their entire savings, and there has occurred a very great decrease in earnings. The ravages of probably the worst depression of all time have been accentuated by greater urbanization, with the consequent total dependence of a majority of our people on their earnings in industry. . . .

. . . At least one-third of all our people, upon reaching old age, are dependent upon others for support. Less than 10 percent leave an estate upon death of sufficient size to be probated.

There is insecurity in every stage of life. . . .

For those now old, insecurity is doubly tragic, because they are beyond the productive period. Old age comes to everyone who does not die prematurely and is a misfortune only if there is insufficient income to provide for the remaining years of life. With a rapidly increasing number and percentage of the aged, and the impairment and loss of savings, this country faces, in the next decades, an even greater old-age security problem than that with which it is already confronted. . . .

The one almost all-embracing measure of security is an assured income. A program of economic security, as we vision it, must have as its primary aim the assurance of an adequate income to each human being in childhood, youth, middle age, or old age—in sickness or in health. It must provide safeguards against all of the hazards leading to destitution and dependency.

A piecemeal approach is dictated by practical considerations, but the broad objectives should never be forgotten. Whatever measures are deemed immediately expedient should be so designed that they can be embodied in the complete program which we must have ere long.

To delay until it is opportune to set up a complete program will probably mean holding up action until it is too late to act. A substantial beginning should be made now in the development of the safeguards which are so manifestly needed for individual security. . . .

Old-Age Security

The Old-Age Problem

In 1930 there were 6,500,000 people over 65 years of age in this country, representing 5.4 percent of the entire population. This percentage has been increasing quite rapidly since the turn of the century and is expected to continue to increase for several decades. . . .

No even reasonably complete data are available regarding the means of support of aged persons, and the number in receipt of some form of public charity is not definitely known. The last almshouse survey was made more than 10 years ago, and the number of people in institutions of this kind can only be approximated. There are about 700,000 people over 65 years of age on F.E.R.A. [Federal Emergency Relief Administration] relief lists, and the present cost of the relief extended to these people has been roughly estimated at $45,000,000 per year. In addition there are a not definitely known but large number of old people in receipt of relief who are not on F.E.R.A. relief lists. All told, the number of old people now in receipt of public charity is probably in excess of 1,000,000.

The number in receipt of some form of pension is much smaller. Approximately 180,000 old people, most of them over 70 years of age, are receiving pensions under the State old-age assistance laws, the average pension last year being $19.74 per month.

A somewhat smaller number of the aged are receiving public retirement or veterans' pensions, for which the expenditures exceed those under the general old-age assistance laws. Approximately 150,000 aged people are in receipt of industrial and trade-union pensions, the cost of which exceeds $100,000,000 per year.

The number of the aged without means of self-support is much larger than the number receiving pensions or public assistance in any form. Upon this point the available data are confined to surveys made in a few States, most of them quite a few years ago. . . . At this time a conservative estimate is that at least one-half of the approximately 7,500,000 people over 65 years now living are dependent.

Children, friends, and relatives have borne and still carry the major cost of supporting the aged. Several of the State surveys have disclosed that from 30 percent to 50 percent of the people over 65 years of age were being supported in this way. During the present depression, this burden has become unbearable for many of the children, with the result that the number of old people dependent upon public or private charity has greatly increased. . . .

General Outline of Recommendations

An adequate old-age security program involves a combination of noncontributory pensions and contributory annuities. Only noncontributory pensions can serve to meet the problem of millions of persons who are already superannuated or shortly will be so and are without sufficient income for a decent subsistence. A contributory annuity system, while of little or no value to people now in these older age groups, will enable younger workers, with the aid of their employers, to build up gradually their rights to annuities in their old age. Without such a contributory system the cost of pensions would, in the future, be overwhelming. Contributory annuities are unquestionably preferable to noncontributory pensions. They come to the workers as a right, whereas the noncontributory pensions must be conditioned upon a "means" test. Annuities, moreover, can be ample for a comfortable existence, bearing some relation to customary wage standards, while gratuitous pensions can provide only a decent subsistence. . . .

. . . Difficult administrative problems must be solved before people who are not wage earners and salaried employees can be brought under the compulsory system, and it is to be expected that some people from higher income groups will come to financial grief and dependence in old age. Until literally all people are brought under the contributory system, noncontributory pensions will have a definite place even in long-time old-age-security planning.

There also is need for a voluntary system of annuities to supplement the compulsory system we advocate, intended primarily for persons of low and moderate income who are not included in the compulsory system. While the latter is not as important as the noncontributory pensions and the compulsory system of contributory annuities, we recommend the establishment of a related, but distinct, voluntary system of Government old-age annuities, for restricted groups in the population who do not customarily purchase annuities from commercial insurance companies. . . .

Contributory Annuities (Compulsory System)

It is only through a compulsory, contributory system of old-age annuities that the burden upon future generations of the support of the aged can be lightened. With an increasing number and even more rapidly increasing percentage of the aged, the cost of supporting old persons will be a heavy load on future generations regardless of any legislation that may be enacted. . . . In order to reduce the pension costs and also to more adequately provide for the needs of those not yet old but who will become old in time, we recommend a contributory annuity system on a compulsory basis, to be conducted by the Federal Government. . . . [W]e deem it desirable that the taxes to finance this system should not become effective until January 1, 1937, but believe that the necessary legislation should be enacted at an early date, to enable the Board to make the necessary studies and other preparations for putting this plan into operation.

Outline of plan.—We recommend that the contributory annuity system include, on a compulsory basis, all manual workers and non-manual workers earning less than $250 per month, except those of governmental units and those covered by the United States Railroad Retirement Act. . . .

The compulsory contributions are to be collected through a tax on pay rolls and wages, to be divided equally between the employers and employees. To keep the reserves within manageable limits, we suggest that the combined rate of employers and employees be 1 percent in the first 5 years the system is in effect; 2 percent in the second 5 years; 3 percent in the third 5 years; 4 percent in the fourth 5 years and 5 percent thereafter. If it is deemed desirable to reduce the burden of the system upon future generations, the initial rate may well be doubled and the taking effect of each higher rate advanced by 5 years. . . .

We suggest that the Federal Government make no contribution from general tax revenues to the fund during the years in which income exceeds payment from the funds, but that it guarantee to make contributions, when the level of payment exceeds income from contributions and interest, sufficient to maintain the reserve at the level of the last year in which income exceeded payments. According to our actuarial estimates the reserve on this basis would be maintained at about $15,250,000,000.

No benefits are to be paid until after the system has been in operation for 5 years, nor to any person who has not made at least 200 weekly contributions, nor before the member has reached the age of 65 and retired from gainful employment. Persons retiring after having passed the age of 65 will receive only the same pension as if they had retired at that age. The benefits are normally to take the form of annuities payable during the remainder of the life of the annuitant. Should a member die before the age of 65 or before the amount of his own contributions has been paid to him as an annuity, the difference between his contributions and the amount which he may have received as an annuity, with interest at 3 percent, is to be paid as a death benefit to his dependents. Members who have made contributions for a short time but who, on reaching the age of 65 are not entitled to an annuity (because they have not made 200 contributions) are to be refunded their own contributions with 3-percent interest. . . .

Explanation.—The plan outlined above contemplates that workers who enter the system after the maximum contribution rate has become effective will receive annuities which have been paid for entirely by their own contributions and the matching contributions of their employers. Workers now middle aged or older will receive annuities which are substantially larger than could be purchased by their own and the matching contributions, although considerably less than the annuities which will be paid to workers who contribute for longer periods. Larger annuities than on a strictly earned basis would seem desirable because annuities build up only very slowly. . . .

The allowance of larger annuities than are warranted by their contributions and the matching contributions of their employers to the workers who are brought into the system at the outset, will involve a cost to the Federal Government which if payments are begun immediately will total approximately $500,000,000 per year. Under the plan suggested, however, no payments will actually be made by the Federal Government until 1965, and will, of course, be greater than they would be if paid as incurred, by the amount of the compound interest on the above sum. This plan thus involves the creation of a debt upon which future generations will have to pay large amounts annually, the Federal contributions representing the interest at 3 percent on the debt thus incurred to pay (partially) unearned annuities in the early years of the system.

While the creation of this debt will impose a burden on future generations which we do not wish to minimize, we, nevertheless, deem it advisable that the Federal Government should not pay its share of the cost of old-age annuities (the unearned part of annuities to persons brought into the system at the outset) currently. To do so would create a reserve which would reach a total of about $75,000,000,000. Further, to pay this cost now would unfairly burden the younger part of the present generation, which would not only pay for the cost of its own annuities but would also pay a large part of the annuities to the people now middle-aged or over. Expressed differently, the plan we advocate amounts to having each generation pay for the support of the people then living who are old. However, we favor showing the debts to the fund currently incurred by the Government, which debts should be evidenced by formal Government obligations issued to the fund. We accordingly recommend that an actuarial audit of the annuity fund be made and published annually which shall set forth clearly the present status of the fund taking into account future payments and future income and will show the present worth of the obligations being incurred by the Federal Government.

This plan also contemplates only small contributions by employers and employees during the early years of the system. Somewhat larger payments in the early years may be advisable, to reduce the necessary Government contributions later on. . . .

Costs.—Actuarial estimates based on the plan we have described indicate that the income of the compulsory annuity fund will in the first 5 years that the system is in operation amount to a little more than $300,000,000. With increases in rates and interest earnings on the reserve this income will increase quite rapidly until by 1980 it will amount to $2,200,000,000 per year. Benefit payments will be light in the early years, but will increase steadily until by 1965 they will exceed the annual receipts. It is at this stage, that the Federal Government would begin to make contributions to the annuity system, which, under the figures submitted by the actuaries reach a maximum of above $1,400,000,000 per year by 1980. (These contributions by the Federal Government, as has been stated, represent the unearned part of the pensions paid to people now approaching old age, with interest on these amounts calculated at 3 percent.)

We realize that there may be valid objection to this plan, in that it involves too great a cost upon future generations. This cost can be reduced by putting the rate of 5 percent into effect at an earlier date; it can be entirely eliminated only through not paying any annuities that have not been fully earned. If the Congress deems it advisable to make either or both of these changes, we are prepared to suggest detailed plans for doing so. . . .

In considering the costs of the contributory system, it should not be overlooked that old-age annuities are designed to prevent destitution and dependency. Destitution and dependency are enormously expensive, not only in the initial cost of necessary assistance but in the disastrous psychological effect of relief upon the recipients, which in turn, breeds more dependency.

The contributions required from employers and employees have an equally good justification. Contributions by the employees represent a self-respecting method through which workers make their own provision for old age. In addition many workers themselves on the verge of dependency will benefit through being relieved of the necessity of supporting dependent parents on reduced incomes, and at the expense of the health and well-being of their own families. To the employers, contributions toward old-age annuities are very similar to the revenues which they regularly set aside for depreciation on capital equipment. There can be no escape from the costs of old age; and since these costs must be met, an orderly system under which employers, employees, and the Government will all contribute appears to be the dignified and intelligent solution of the problem. . . .

Source: Social Security Administration History Archives, Revolving Files, Folder: "Social Security Beginnings and History, 3."

Document 1.11
President Roosevelt's Message to Congress, Transmitting the Report of the CES, January 17, 1935

In this message President Franklin D. Roosevelt highlights the principles that will become the foundation of the Social Security Act of 1935. Particularly noteworthy is the president's expla-nation that the old-age insurance plan "should be self-sustaining in the sense that funds for the payment of insurance benefits should not come from the proceeds of general taxation." Also, it is instructive to note that the administration viewed state old-age assistance pensions as even-tually being replaced by the federal social insurance scheme.

(In the parlance of the era, old-age "annuities" were what are now called Social Security benefits and old-age "pensions" meant welfare-type programs run by the states.)

To the Congress of the United States:

In addressing you on June 8, 1934, I summarized the main objectives of our American program. Among these was, and is, the security of the men, women, and children of the Nation against certain hazards and vicissitudes of life. This purpose is an essential part of our task. In my annual message to you I promised to submit a definite program of action. This I do in the form of a report to me by a Committee on Economic Security, appointed by me for the purpose of surveying the field and of recommending the basis of legislation.

I am gratified with the work of this Committee and of those who have helped it; the Tech-nical Board on Economic Security drawn from various departments of the Government, the Advisory Council on Economic Security, consisting of informed and public spirited private citizens and a number of other advisory groups, including a committee of actuarial consult-ants, a medical advisory board, a dental advisory committee, a hospital advisory committee, a public health advisory committee, a child welfare committee and an advisory committee on employment relief. All of those who participated in this notable task of planning this major legislative proposal are ready and willing, at any time, to consult with and assist in any way the appropriate Congressional committees and members, with respect to detailed aspects.

It is my best judgment that this legislation should be brought forward with a minimum of delay. . . .

The detailed report of the Committee sets forth a series of proposals that will appeal to the sound sense of the American people. It has not attempted the impossible, nor has it failed to exercise sound caution and consideration of all of the factors concerned; the national credit, the rights and responsibilities of States, the capacity of industry to assume financial responsibilities and the fundamental necessity of proceeding in a manner that will merit the enthusiastic support of citizens of all sorts.

It is overwhelmingly important to avoid any danger of permanently discrediting the sound and necessary policy of Federal legislation for economic security by attempting to apply it on too ambitious a scale before actual experience has provided guidance for the permanently safe direction of such efforts. The place of such a fundamental in our future civilization is too precious to be jeopardized now by extravagant action. It is a sound idea—a sound ideal. Most of the other advanced countries of the world have already adopted it and their experience affords the knowledge that social insurance can be made a sound and workable project.

Three principles should be observed in legislation on this subject. First, the system adopted, except for the money necessary to initiate it, should be self-sustaining in the sense that funds for the payment of insurance benefits should not come from the proceeds of general taxation. Second, excepting in old-age insurance, actual management should be left to the States subject to standards established by the Federal Government. Third, sound financial management of the funds and the reserves, and protection of the credit structure of the Nation should be assured by retaining Federal control over all funds through trustees in the Treasury of the United States.

At this time, I recommend the following types of legislation looking to economic security:

1. Unemployment compensation.
2. Old-age benefits, including compulsory and voluntary annuities.
3. Federal aid to dependent children through grants to States for the support of existing mother's pension systems and for services for the protection and care of homeless, neglected, dependent, and crippled children.
4. Additional Federal aid to State and local public-health agencies and the strengthening of the Federal Public Health Service. I am not at this time recommending the adoption of so called "health insurance," although groups representing the medical profession are cooperating with the Federal Government in the further study of the subject and definite progress is being made. . . .

In the important field of security for our old people, it seems necessary to adopt three principles: First, noncontributory old-age pensions for those who are now too old to build up their own insurance. It is, of course, clear that for perhaps thirty years to come funds will have to be provided by the States and the Federal Government to meet these pensions. Second, compulsory contributory annuities which in time will establish a self-supporting system for those now young and for future generations. Third, voluntary contributory annuities by which individual initiative can increase the annual amounts received in old age. It is proposed that the Federal Government assume one-half of the cost of the old-age pension plan, which ought ultimately to be supplanted by self-supporting annuity plans.

The amount necessary at this time for the initiation of unemployment compensation, old-age security, children's aid, and the promotion of public health, as outlined in the report of the Committee on Economic Security, is approximately $100,000,000.

The establishment of sound means toward a greater future economic security of the American people is dictated by a prudent consideration of the hazards involved in our national life. No one can guarantee this country against the dangers of future depressions but we can reduce these dangers. We can eliminate many of the factors that cause economic depressions, and we can provide the means of mitigating their results. This plan for economic security is at once a measure of prevention and a method of alleviation.

We pay now for the dreadful consequence of economic insecurity—and dearly. This plan presents a more equitable and infinitely less expensive means of meeting these costs. We cannot afford to neglect the plain duty before us. I strongly recommend action to attain the objectives sought in this report.

Source: The Public Papers and Addresses of Franklin D. Roosevelt, 1935 (New York: Random House, 1938), 43–46.

Document 1.12
Testimony of Treasury Secretary Morgenthau on Tax Rates, February 5, 1935

The most significant change in the proposed bill during the hearings came when Treasury Secretary Henry Morgenthau Jr., speaking for the administration, asked the House Committee on Ways and Means to revise the tax schedule in the initial proposal. Morgenthau was recommending an increase in the initial tax rates to build up the program's reserves, as a strategy to avoid larger tax increases in the future or the use of general revenues.

Old-Age Provisions

1. By inaugurating a national contributory old-age annuity system, the Federal Government is undertaking very heavy responsibilities extending from year to year into the indefinite future. Under the modification that we shall suggest, as well as under the plan now incorporated in the economic security bill, the sums to be paid out each year in benefit payments will rise to more than $4,000,000,000. It is obvious that we must make sure now that the provisions incorporated in the bill will enable the Federal Government continuously to meet the heavy and recurring liabilities that will be imposed upon it.

2. Under the provisions now embodied in the economic security bill, the Federal Government is called upon to defray, out of its general revenues . . . the cost of substantial unearned gratuities that are provided under the contributory system for persons who will retire during the next 40 years. The benefits provided for such persons will be substantially in excess of the contributions, plus interest, made in their behalf. Such excess benefit payments would be borrowed from current contributions to the fund and repaid with compound interest in subsequent years. In consequence, under the present bill, by 1980 and forever after, the cost of the contributory system on the Federal Government is estimated at $1,500,000,000 a year. This burden is in addition to a Federal cost estimated at $504,000,000 a year in 1980 and thereafter for the noncontributory system.

3. The alteration that we recommend will make it possible, without the imposition of onerous burdens upon the future, to provide annuities ranging from $22.50 to $82.50 per month. . . . The aggregate benefit payments under the plan that we propose are substantially identical with those now incorporated in the bill. . . .

4. Any actuarial computations extending indefinitely into the future, such as are necessary for the establishment of a national contributory old-age annuity system, inevitably rest upon assumptions and forecasts that are subject to a very considerable margin of error. Subject to this acknowledged limitation, it is our opinion that the national contributory system can be launched and maintained on a sound financial basis by establishing the combined rate of pay roll and earnings taxes at 2 percent for the first 3 years, 3 percent for the next 3 years, 4 percent for the third 3-year period 5 percent for the fourth 3-year period, and 6 percent thereafter; in substitution for the rates now incorporated in the bill. . . .

5. A combined contributory tax rate of 5 percent is the minimum that will permit the payment of adequate annuities and at the same time maintain the financial integrity of the system under both the present economic security provisions and under our proposed alteration. But a 5 percent rate can do this only if it is imposed from the start. Under the pres-

ent provisions of the economic security bill, a 5-percent rate does not go into effect for 20 years. Hence, under the bill a heavy deficit is accumulated in the early years, and the small sums paid on behalf of individuals now middle-aged or over are kept so low as to be far out of keeping with the benefit payments scheduled for them upon retirement. . . .

6. Under our proposal, the Federal Government would guarantee an investment return of 3 percent on all receipts from the pay-roll and earnings taxes that were not currently disbursed in benefit payments. Such sums would be used progressively to replace the outstanding public debt with the new liability incurred by the Federal Government for old-age annuities. To the extent that the receipts from the old-age annuity taxes are used to buy out present and future holders of Government obligations, that part of the tax revenues that is now paid out to private bond holders will be available for old-age annuity benefits; thereby minimizing the net additional burdens upon the future. . . .

7. It should be emphasized that the Federal Government, by inaugurating a national contributory old-age annuity system, is undertaking responsibilities of the first magnitude. Not only is it committed to paying a 3-percent return upon all collections in excess of current benefit payments involved, but it is also diverting for the purpose of old-age security a very large fraction of its possible tax revenues. But we recommend this deliberately, in view of the outstanding importance of the objective. We know, moreover, that, even in the absence of the well-considered legislation, we cannot avoid important financial outlays for the care of the aged. Students of our population trends tell us that the proportion of the aged and of the dependent aged in our population gives promise of increasing very materially in the course of the next few generations.

8. There are some who believe that we can meet this problem as we go by borrowing from the future to pay the costs. They are willing to incur the large and growing new liability for old-age annuities without effecting any compensating reductions in the outstanding public debt, reductions that could be represented by a reserve account in the Treasury. They would place all confidence in the taxing power of the future to meet the needs as they arose.

We do not share this view. We have already cited the fact that the aggregate benefit payments under our proposal, as under that of the economic security bill, will eventually exceed $4,000,000,000 a year. We cannot safely expect future generations to continue to divert such large sums to the support of the aged unless we lighten the burdens upon the future in other directions. If we fail to do this, the $4,000,000,000 a year will be a net additional burden. Such a burden might well jeopardize the continued operation of the system. If, on the other hand, we are able to reduce the necessary outlays of future generations in other directions, as by retiring a large part of the public debt, and by the provision of useful public works, we can look forward with far more assurance to the continued support of the system. This, then, is the purpose of our proposal. We desire to establish this system on such sound foundations that it can be continued indefinitely in the future; and, at the same time, to meet the highly desirable social objective of providing an adequate annuity without a means test to all eligible workers upon retirement.

9. We recognize that the incidence of the pay-roll and earnings taxes appears to be largely upon the mass of our population. But it should be emphasized that the effect of these taxes is to provide a substitute form of savings from which our workers will receive far greater and more assured benefits than from many other forms of savings now in existence. These taxes,

in other words, will not be a net deduction from workers' incomes. They will release funds, as well as relieve anxiety, hitherto directed toward the universal problem of providing against one's old age.

10. Further, it is entirely possible that improvements in our revenue system may permit us in the course of time to reduce various taxes on consumption goods; and thereby to return to the mass of our population in this form what is taken from it in the form of payroll and earnings taxes. . . .

Source: Economic Security Act, Hearings before the Committee on Ways and Means, House of Representatives, on H.R. 4120 (Washington, D.C.: U.S. Government Printing Office, 1935), 897–900.

Document 1.13
Testimony of Treasury Secretary Morgenthau on Coverage Exclusions, February 5, 1935

Near the end of his testimony before the House Ways and Means Committee, Secretary Morgenthau diverted from his expected testimony regarding tax rates and the reserve and brought up the issue of coverage of workers under the program. The CES staff developing the old-age insurance proposal had recommended four exclusions from participation in the new program: high-paid white collar workers, government employees, railroad employees, and agricultural and domestic workers (this last group on the grounds that there were various administrative difficulties involved in their coverage). The executive body of the CES overruled the staff and recommended coverage of the agricultural and domestic workers but left the other three exclusions in the final proposal. As the administration's bill was before the Ways and Means Committee, CES executive member Morgenthau requested that the committee reinstate the exclusion of agricultural and domestic workers, again on the grounds of administrative difficulties.

. . . Before taking up the next paragraph, which is entitled "Administrative Simplification," I would like to say that from here on I am presenting the Treasury's own attitude toward the collection of this tax; that is, this is the attitude of the Bureau of Internal Revenue on whom the burden of collecting these taxes will fall. As I say, this is purely the Treasury's statement. Up to this point, those of us who have worked on this bill are in complete accord. But I wish to point out that from here on the matter discussed is one which has been brought to my attention by the Bureau of Internal Revenue. I feel it is my duty to point that out to the committee, and I want to emphasize once again that this is purely the Treasury's attitude. . . .

Mr. COOPER. By that, Mr. Secretary, we are to understand that the Economic Security Committee is in agreement and submits jointly all of the statement which you have read up to this point?

Secretary MORGENTHAU. Up to this point, yes.

Secretary PERKINS. Yes, sir. . . .

Mr. TREADWAY. From the point where you are now about to read, your Department is not in agreement with the bill as submitted to us? Is that what you mean, Mr. Secretary?

Secretary MORGENTHAU. I would not put it that way. I simply feel that this is a matter the responsibility for the carrying out of which will fall on the Bureau of Internal Revenue. They

Secretary of Labor Frances Perkins was chair of the Committee on Economic Security and one of the principal political architects of the Social Security Act of 1935. Perkins is seen here, at far right, in April 1938 speaking to a national broadcast audience on the occasion of the issuance of the 26 millionth Social Security card. Also shown, left to right: Arthur J. Altmeyer, chairman of the Social Security Board, and Martha Carlson, recipient of the card.
Source: SSA History Archives.

raised the point as to whether they can enforce this, and I, as Secretary of the Treasury, feel that I should bring it to the attention of this committee.

Mr. TREADWAY. I assume that you concur with the Bureau of Internal Revenue on this point?

Secretary MORGENTHAU. Oh, yes.

Mr. TREADWAY. You approve what they are recommending to you for you to submit to the committee?

Secretary MORGENTHAU. Yes. Otherwise, I would not read it.

Mr. TREADWAY. That is what I assumed.

Secretary MORGENTHAU. I would not read it unless I believed in it.

Mr. TREADWAY. I wanted it to be perfectly clear in the record.

Secretary MORGENTHAU. I want to make it clear that Miss Perkins and I are in complete accord, but this particular matter is purely one of administration.

The CHAIRMAN. Please proceed.

Secretary MORGENTHAU.

Administrative Simplification

This committee is well acquainted with the Treasury's attitude on law enforcement. If there is a law on the statute books to be enforced by the Treasury, we insist on enforcing it to the utmost of our powers. But in one respect the bill in its present form imposes a burden upon the Treasury that it cannot guarantee adequately to meet.

The national contributory old-age annuity system, as now proposed, includes every employee in the United States, other than those of governmental agencies or railways, who earns less than $251 a month. This means that every transient or casual laborer is included, that every domestic servant is covered, and that the large and shifting class of agricultural workers is covered. Now, even without the inclusion of these three classes of workers, the task of the Treasury in administering the contributory tax collections would be extremely formidable. If these three classes of workers are to be included, however, the task may well prove insuperable—certainly, at the outset.

I want to point out here that personally I hope these three classes can be included. I am simply pointing out the administrative difficulty of collecting the tax from those classes.

Mr. Reed. Mr. Secretary, your views with regard to the difficulty of collecting this tax coincide with the experience of Great Britain insofar as the domestic-service class is concerned over there.

Secretary Morgenthau. I am sorry, Mr. Congressman, that I am not familiar with the experiences of Great Britain. I am simply pointing out what I feel is a difficulty. Perhaps we can work out some way of overcoming that difficulty.

Mr. Reed. The British Government had that difficulty, exactly along the lines you mention, and those people were eliminated from the provisions of their security act.

Secretary Morgenthau. I do not happen to be familiar with the British experience or practice in that respect.

The Chairman. In other words, you are presenting a very serious difficulty which you have thus far not been able to find a way of overcoming?

Secretary Morgenthau. Up to now. But I am asking the Bureau of Internal Revenue to try their best to find some way whereby this tax can be collected. As soon as they find a way, I shall ask them to bring it to this committee's attention.

Under the income-tax law, the Bureau of Internal Revenue last year handled something less than 5 million returns; with the present nearly universal coverage of the bill's provisions with respect to contributory old-age annuities, we estimate that some 20 million returns would be received. In addition, there would be required the sale of stamps to be used in connection with hundreds of thousands of odd payments for casual work, often for only a few hours' duration. We recognize, without question, the need of these classes of workers for the same protection that is offered other employed workers under the bill. But we should like to ask the committee to consider the question whether it is wise to jeopardize the entire contributory system, as well as, possibly, to impair tax-collecting efforts in other fields, by the inclusion under the system of the necessity for far-flung, minutely detailed, and very expensive, enforcement efforts.

In view of the great importance of our objective, we should greatly regret the imposition of administrative burdens in the bill that would threaten the continued operation of the entire system. After the system has been in operation for some years, more inclusive coverage may prove to be entirely practicable; but we should like to see the system launched in such fashion that its administrative as well as its financial provisions contribute directly to the assurance of its success. . . .

Mr. Knutson. Mr. Secretary, you are making some recommendations of changes in the bill that we have before us?

Secretary Morgenthau. Yes, sir.

Mr. Knutson. It was my understanding that the bill we have before us, H.R. 4120, was the product of the Economic Security Committee appointed by the President.

Secretary Morgenthau. That is right.

Mr. Knutson. When were these changes agreed upon, Mr. Secretary?

Secretary Morgenthau. Mr. Knutson, the fact that the changes have been made as late as this is purely my own fault. Unfortunately, I had so many administrative duties to perform. I worked for 3 months on the $4,800,000,000 bill that was recently before the Congress. I took part in the preparation of the Budget. So it is my fault that I did not get to this earlier. I simply felt that I had better be late and be right.

Mr. KNUTSON. We have put in 2 weeks of hearings on H.R. 4120. I am just wondering whether the changes that you have proposed this morning would necessitate continued hearings, perhaps for as long a time as we have been in session on this bill.

Secretary MORGENTHAU. Of course, that is up to the committee, as to whether they want to have further hearings on the bill.

Mr. VINSON. May I suggest to the gentleman from Minnesota that several of these suggestions that have been made this morning were mentioned during the course of the hearings. For instance, the exclusion of the agricultural workers, domestics, and the casual workers from the compulsory contributory plan was discussed freely, as I recall it.

Dr. Witte made the statement that the exclusion of those from the contributory system could be had without any added burden to the fund or to the system.

Mr. KNUTSON. That is true.

The CHAIRMAN. If Mr. Knutson will yield.

Mr. KNUTSON. Of course.

The CHAIRMAN. The Chair would like to suggest that unless someone should request to be heard in opposition to the proposed changes, further hearings will not be necessary on those proposed changes. Should anyone request that they be heard in opposition to those changes that might change the situation.

Mr. MCCORMACK. Mr. Secretary, referring to the casuals, and the domestics, and I assume those engaged in agricultural pursuits, they are the ones you have in mind in connection with your expression of doubt conveyed to the committee of the feasibility of practical administration of the provisions of the bill as applied to them, is that right?

Secretary MORGENTHAU. Yes, sir. . . .

Mr. MCCORMACK. Why should they be excluded from the benefits of old-age assistance? . . .

Secretary MORGENTHAU. I tried to make clear, and I am glad to have the opportunity again, that I do not suggest that anybody be excluded. I simply point out that the Bureau of Internal Revenue feels that a plan has not yet been devised which will make it practical to collect this tax.

We just came out of one of the most difficult eras of selling liquor. I have been struggling with that for about 13 months. We are beginning to see daylight now, and getting the public to realize that it is a question of buying tax-paid or non-tax-paid liquor. The American public got itself into a frame of mind where they just did not think they had to obey the Federal laws.

What I am afraid of is that if we make it so difficult to collect this tax that we may again build up a large population or group who will get themselves into that same sort of frame of mind. I feel that it is up to us to find a way to collect that tax, and the Internal Revenue Bureau should do that. But we have not been smart enough yet to do it. I want to make it very clear that we are not recommending that any group should be excluded.

Mr. VINSON. May I suggest that the testimony before the committee, Mr. Secretary, has shown that the moneys that would be paid in by this group in taxes, under the contributory plan, would buy very small annuities. You would take the benefits that would accrue, and, of course, there is no suggestion here that this group would be excluded from the noncontributory features, or what we generally call the old-age pension plan.

Mr. McCORMACK. I recognize the force of the argument that there are administrative difficulties, but that is taking an attitude of defeatism, it seems to me. If we do not get them in the bill, then you are going to have a lot of difficulty in the future getting them into the bill. If we are going to do anything, we might as well embrace them now, and if necessary suspend payments from them for a year or two until you have devised a method of obtaining those payments in a practical way. That would be my thought on the matter.

Secretary MORGENTHAU. I would say that that would be ideal.

The CHAIRMAN. If there are no further questions, we thank you for your appearance and the testimony you have given the committee, Mr. Secretary.

Source: Economic Security Act, Hearings before the Committee on Ways and Means, House of Representatives, on H.R. 4120 (Washington, D.C.: U.S. Government Printing Office, 1935), 901–902, 910–911.

Document 1.14
House Ways and Means Committee Report—Republican Views, April 5, 1935

In the 74th Congress the House Ways and Means Committee had an 18–7 Democratic majority. Thus the committee reported out a bill that in its essentials incorporated the goals of the administration's proposals. The Republicans on the committee were deeply antagonistic to major aspects of the proposed legislation, a fact they made clear in separate dissents to the formal committee report on the bill.

Minority Views

We, the undersigned members of the minority, submit the following statement showing in brief our attitude toward this proposed legislation. . . .

Old-Age Pensions

We favor such legislation as will encourage States already paying old-age pensions to provide for more adequate benefits, and will encourage all other States to adopt old-age pension systems.

However, we believe the amount provided in the bill to be inadequate, and favor a substantial increase in the Federal contribution. . . .

Compulsory Old-Age Annuities

Title II provides for compulsory old-age annuities, and title VIII provides the method by which the money is to be raised to meet the expense thereof.

These two titles are interdependent, and neither is of any consequence without the other. Neither of them has relation to any other substantive title of the bill. Neither is constitutional. Therein lies one of the reasons for our opposition to them.

The Federal Government has no power to impose this system upon private industry.

The best legal talent that the Attorney General's office and the Brain Trust could marshal has for weeks applied itself to the task of trying to bring these titles within constitutional limitations. Their best effort is only a plain circumvention. They have separated the proposition into two titles. This separation is a separation in words only. There is no separation in spirit or intent. These two titles must stand or fall together.

The learned brief submitted by the Attorney General's Office contains in its summation the following weak, apologetic language:

> There may also be taken into consideration the strong presumption which exists in favor of the constitutionality of an act of the Congress, in the light of which and of the foregoing discussion it is reasonably safe to assume that the social security bill, if enacted into law, will probably be upheld as constitutional.

We also oppose these two titles because they would not in any way contribute to the relief of present economic conditions, and might in fact retard economic recovery.

The original bill contained a title providing for voluntary annuities. This was another attempt to place the Government in competition with private business. Under fire, this title has been omitted. It was closely akin to title II. In fact, it had one virtue that title II does not possess in that it was voluntary while title II is compulsory.

These titles impose a crushing burden upon industry and upon labor.

They establish a bureaucracy in the field of insurance in competition with private business.

They destroy old-age retirement systems set up by private industries, which in most instances provide more liberal benefits than are contemplated under title II. . . .

Conclusion

The minority membership of the Ways and Means Committee have at no time offered any political or partisan opposition to the progress of this measure, but on the contrary have labored faithfully in an effort to produce a measure that would be constitutional and that would inure to the general welfare of all the people. . . .

Supplemental Views of Mr. Knutson

While I concur in a general way with the conclusions of my colleagues of the minority, there are certain provisions of the bill so obnoxious to me that I cannot support it. My reasons for voting against the measure are as follows:

1. It is obvious from the provisions of this bill that it cannot be made effective for several years, hence it will be a bitter disappointment to those who have looked hopefully to this administration for immediate relief.
2. The measure is wholly inadequate and therefore will not give the result sought to be obtained.
3. The age limit of 65 is too high to give the needed relief. The limit should be fixed at 60, which would help the unemployment situation materially and at the same time care for a large number now out of work and who by reason of age are unemployable.

4. The old-age pension to be granted under H.R. 7260 would be wholly inadequate in the relief of distress. The amount paid would be so small that its effect upon business would be negligible.

5. The administering of this law will result in discrimination. People living in States that are bankrupt, or nearly so, will receive absolutely no benefits from this legislation. These people must be taken care of by the National Government.

6. The two pay-roll taxes which the bill imposes will greatly retard business recovery by driving many industries, now operating at a loss, into bankruptcy, or by forcing them to close down entirely, thereby further increasing unemployment, which would greatly retard recovery.

7. Many small concerns having 12 or 15 employees would discharge enough employees to exempt them from the payment of the pay-roll taxes which would yet further aggravate the unemployment situation.

8. The proposal to establish a new bureau to administer this law is indefensible and a needless expense to the taxpayers. . . .

Source: The Social Security Bill, House Report to accompany H.R. 7260, April 5, 1935, Report No. 615, 42–45.

Document 1.15
Congressional Floor Debates—House, April 1935
This document features excerpts from debates in the House of Representatives on three issues:
    Townsend Plan. *Probably the single most discussed topic in the House was the Townsend Plan (and a related plan from Rep. Ernest Lundeen of the Farmer Laborite Party) as an alternative to both Title I and Title II of the bill. The brief excerpt here raises this issue, in the form of a challenge issued by a rank-and-file member, Rep. James Mott (R-Ore.), and remarks in indirect answer by Ways and Means Committee Chairman Robert Doughton (D-N.C.).*
    General Opposition. *Some in the House—particularly Republicans on the Ways and Means Committee—were opposed on principle to the Social Security program. This was not a view widely shared, even within the Republican caucus, but it was vigorously expressed by several Republicans members and is represented here in an excerpt from Rep. Allen Treadway (R-Mass.), who was the ranking member on the committee.*
    Coverage Exclusion of Agricultural and Domestic Workers. *While this was not a major issue at the time and, in fact, was remarked upon only briefly during the House debates, excerpts of those remarks have been included because some contemporary scholars have considered this a matter of some importance. (The issue was not raised at all in the Senate.)*

[Townsend Plan]

Mr. MOTT. . . . Now, let me say frankly at the outset that the only part of the President's economic-security bill that I am very greatly interested in for the moment, or that many Members are very greatly interested in, is section 1 of that bill, which contains the old-age pensions provisions. I dare say not 2 percent of the people of the United States either know or care a great deal about any part of this administration bill, except the old-age pension part of it. But, on the other hand, I venture to say that 90 percent of the people of the United States do know and do care about the old-age pension features of it and that they are very much interested in knowing whether or not we intend at this session of Congress to give to them an adequate old-age pension bill.

. . . I desire to say in this connection that the old-age pension provided in the administration bill is not an adequate old-age pension and that most of the membership of the House freely admit that it is not adequate. . . .

Mr. Speaker, there are millions of people in this country who in good faith have petitioned the Congress to consider and discuss and to decide upon the merits of certain old-age pension plans which they believe to be solutions to the old-age-pension problem. It is said that 20,000,000 people have signed petitions asking Congress to consider the so-called "Townsend plan," which is now before the Congress in the shape of a new bill known as the revised McGroarty bill. It is reported also that more than a million people have by the similar orderly method of petition prayed Congress to consider the Lundeen bill, which has been favorably reported to the House by the Committee on Labor. Is this body, the duly constituted representatives of the people and the law-making authority of the people, going to deny completely these petitions of the people? . . .

I am not contending that you must grant those petitions by enacting their proposals into law. . . . But I do say to you that you have no right to refuse to allow the legislation prayed for in those petitions to be considered on the floor of this House. I do say that you have no right, figuratively speaking, to throw those petitions in the waste basket. And finally I say that although you may have the legal right you have no moral right to adopt any rule today which will render it impossible for the House to consider and act upon either the revised McGroarty bill, the Lundeen bill, or any other old-age-pension bill now before Congress which proposes a different old-age-pension plan than that proposed in the President's bill. . . .

Mr. DOUGHTON. . . . The social-security bill is one of the most important measures ever placed before Congress for its consideration. While it is designed to enhance very greatly the security of the American worker and to provide a larger measure of social justice, it does so within the scope of our existing economic order. In no way does it resemble the many panaceas and nostrums which propose that we legislate ourselves into prosperity by lifting ourselves by our bootstraps and which would upset our established economic and political institutions. The fact that several of these proposals have attracted a wide-spread following implies a threat to our existing institutions which should not be regarded lightly. . . .

The social-security program of the administration is an attempt to mitigate and to prevent the distress and suffering which so frequently arise from our industrial economy. . . .

. . . We must certainly deplore the extent to which large masses of our people are weighed down by privation and suffering, and we cannot overlook the grave social danger implied in the deterioration and pauperization of a large section of our population. We cannot afford to delay further the legislation which is necessary to protect our American workers against the many hazards of our industrial order which lead to huge relief rolls and threaten the foundations of our society.

The social-security program of the administration grew out of a determination to find a better way of dealing with the causes which have brought about the present acute situation. It should not be regarded as a substitute for relief, for there will always be the necessity for some public charity. It will not benefit immediately all of those now on relief, but other protection is provided for them. What the bill will do is this: Relieve much of the present distress and greatly lessen the incidence of destitution and dependency in future years.

[General Opposition]

Mr. TREADWAY. . . . If legislation of this character is to be passed by Congress there should have been 4 separate bills instead of 1, divided into 2 categories: First, those which, according to the view of the minority of the committee, "spring from the desire of the Federal Government to provide economic assistance to those who need and deserve it"; and, second, those which are based upon the principles of compulsory insurance. . . .

In the first class are titles I, IV, V, and VI, granting aid to the States for old-age pensions, for the care of dependent children, for maternal and child welfare, and for public health. . . .

The other group consists of titles II and VIII relating to compulsory contributory annuities, and titles III and IX relating to unemployment insurance. I am opposed to these four titles of the bill. They are not in any sense emergency measures. They would not become effective in time to help present economic conditions, but, on the contrary, would be a definite drag on recovery. . . .

I am strongly opposed to the provisions of titles II and VIII which impose upon private industry a compulsory Federal retirement system for superannuated employees and exact a contribution from such employees and their employers, in the guise of a pay-roll tax, to set up reserves out of which to pay retirement benefits. . . .

The Federal Government has no express or inherent power under the Constitution to set up such a scheme as is proposed. No one knows this any better than the administration and the Democratic majority of the committee. They have been working for months trying to give titles II and VIII some color of constitutionality. . . .

The reason that these two titles are separated in the bill is that if they were combined, as they should be, they would on their face be unconstitutional, since the Federal Government cannot lay a tax for any other purpose than the raising of revenue for public uses. The tax imposed under title VIII is not a tax at all, but an enforced insurance premium for old-age annuities. The money raised by the tax is not intended for the support of the Government, but to pay the benefits provided under title II to the same employees who are taxed under title VIII. . . . Personally, I think this attempt to delude the Supreme Court is rather childish. Either the Federal Government has the power to set up this compulsory-insurance system or it has not. The Constitution should either be respected or abolished. What is the sense of having it if we are going to spend most of our time trying to devise ways and means to circumvent it? . . .

Considering the pay-roll taxes under titles VIII and IX together, industry and business are faced with an additional tax burden of $228,000,000 in 1936 . . . and gradually increasing amounts in future years, reaching $1,800,000,000 in 1950. . . .

In my opinion, the proposed imposition of the pay-roll taxes imposed under titles VIII and IX constitutes the greatest single threat to recovery of all the administration's ill-advised policies. . . .

There is one feature of the compulsory annuity provisions to which I wish to call attention that is generally overlooked. I refer to the matter of reserves.

According to the report of the committee, the reserve for the payment of retirement benefits will reach a maximum of about $32,000,000,000. That is more than the present national debt. . . .

What would be the consequence of having $32,000,000,000 of credit standing in the name of the National Government? Would it not be an invitation for all sorts of pork-barrel schemes and wild-spending sprees? We would have such an orgy of extravagance that even the unprecedented expenditures of the Roosevelt administration would seem small in comparison. . . .

[Coverage Exclusion of Agricultural and Domestic Workers]

Mr. VINSON of Kentucky. . . . Now, I want to deal with the exemption features in title VIII. We have been actually criticized because agriculture, casuals, and domestics, and certain other people have been exempted from title VIII. I would like to know, and I am willing to yield in my time for reply, what Member of this House is willing to stand on this floor and say that agriculture, domestics, and casuals should be taxed for old-age benefits.

Mr. LUNDEEN. Will the gentleman yield?

Mr. VINSON of Kentucky. I yield.

Mr. LUNDEEN. I would like to say that the millionaires and billionaires and the men who have fortunes and incomes over $5,000 ought to be taxed.

Mr. VINSON of Kentucky. Oh, yes; and the gentleman would talk loudest and longest if the farmers of his section had to pay a tax under title VIII. Am I right or wrong?

Mr. LUNDEEN. If there is a farmer who has an income of over $5,000, I would tax him.

Mr. VINSON of Kentucky. Oh, no. I am not talking of incomes over $5,000. Do not dodge it, my friend. The amount of income is not involved in title VIII. If farmers were subject to the tax under title VIII, he would pay $1 for each $100 he earned; if it were $10 he would pay 10 cents. Does the gentleman from Minnesota assert that the farmer of his district should pay that tax? [After a pause.] The gentleman is eloquent as usual, but it is the eloquence of silence. I say to you there were real reasons why those exemptions were made. . . .

Mr. VINSON of Kentucky. The farmer, the casual, the domestic were not taxed in this bill, because we knew that the House and Senate would not keep it in the bill. Nobody would want a farmer to pay a dollar a year for 45 years, with all of the nuisance features attached thereto, with all of the cost of administration. Suppose a man plowed for a farmer for a day, and he paid him a dollar a day, the employer would have to take out a penny and give him 99 cents for his day's work.

Then at the end of the road he would not have accumulated enough money to have paid for any substantial old-age benefits.

This bill exempts the farmer, exempts casuals, and exempts domestics, because the amount of the tax would be inconsiderable and its collection would be such a nuisance and cause such a clamor that the very ideal of the structure—the ideal to which the President refers—would be endangered. It would be too ambitious; no comparable benefits would come from it. No Member on the floor of this House, seriously understanding the bill, is going to complain about not taxing the farmer, the domestic, the casual and the others exempted under the bill.

Mr. LEWIS of Maryland. Mr. Chairman, will the gentleman yield for a suggestion?

Mr. VINSON of Kentucky. I yield.

Mr. LEWIS of Maryland. Did not the administrative authorities, in fact, the present Secretary of the Treasury, appeal to us not to extend it into those fields at this time because he felt that its administration would break down?

Mr. VINSON of Kentucky. Yes, sir. He said that in his opinion it would be very difficult if not impossible of administration. In other words, I repeat, if you had put that in there, it would have been analogous to the situation that obtains in regard to the ambitions of certain folks under the N. R. A. legislation. You would have such confusion and such clamor that the good in the legislation well might be destroyed. . . .

Mr. REED of New York. . . . Now, my colleagues, you know that what you are attempting to do is unconstitutional, and you know that for that reason title II and title VIII ought to be eliminated from the bill. They are not relief provisions, and they are not going to bring any relief to the destitute or needy now, nor for years to come. It is more of your compulsory, arbitrary program. You are saying to a specified class of wage earners, not all for, as I have I said, you are not giving these benefits to the needy at all but you are saying to the wage earner, "We are going to force you to pay a tax to buy an annuity from the Government." You propose to whip and lash the wage earner into paying this tax, but you are not treating everybody alike. Millions who labor are exempted from benefits. People who work on farms grow old; people who work as domestic servants grow old; they have the problems of old age, but they can starve in their old age so far as getting aid from this bill. Gentlemen, why talk about the difficulty of administering the act as an excuse for omitting them? You found no difficulty in providing for the administration of title I of the act, which reaches every person who is in need; but when it comes to certain classes, then you discriminate. This title ought to be removed from the bill. . . .

Mr. MCCORMACK. Mr. Chairman, I hardly think that the closing argument of my distinguished friend the gentleman from New York, with reference to the fact that farmers and domestic servants are not included in title II, and there is less administrative difficulty, or no more at least than there is with reference to title I where they are included, presents a fair picture as to the reasons why farm laborers or the domestic servants are included in title I and are excluded from title II.

Title I is a noncontributory law. Title II is a contributory law. Title I, being noncontributory, every person in need who meets the requirements imposed by a State and is over the age limit and meets the requirements imposed by this particular bill in the State plan, without regard their previous employment, should receive the amount set out, provided and intended by this bill.

When we come to the contributory provision, there is entirely different situation. The administrative cost enters into the picture. Furthermore, whether or not farm laborers and domestic servants receive a salary so that when they reach the age of retirement they will receive an earned annuity above $10 a month is also a matter of consideration. We have also excluded those employed in educational and religious activities and in all kinds of charitable activities. The committee has tried to draft a contributory annuity provision which will not only meet the purposes desired but do so in a manner that can be administered without any great difficulty.

Mr. WADSWORTH. Will the gentleman yield?

Mr. MCCORMACK. I am glad to yield to the gentleman from New York.

Mr. WADSWORTH. I am seeking information. Is it a fact that it is hoped title II will grow and expand if soundly managed to such a point at which title I will cease to be an important obligation to the Government?

Mr. MCCORMACK. That is the purpose as I understand it.

Mr. WADSWORTH. All right. Will the gentleman tell the House, if that is the case, why domestic servants are exempt from carrying their part of that burden, which is eventually to relieve the Federal Government of a major part of the straight-out old-age pensions?

Mr. VINSON of Kentucky. Will the gentleman yield to me to answer that question?

Mr. MCCORMACK. I yield to the gentleman from Kentucky.

Mr. VINSON of Kentucky. The tax levy in title VIII is upon wages. Taking as a basis the total wage of the domestic servants, then 1 percent of that, and 1½, finally a maximum of 3, then if you multiplied it by 40 you would not have money in the account sufficient to purchase a substantial annuity. You would have a nuisance feature, such as a person being paid $1 wage and taking out 1 penny and having at the end of the road a small sum that would purchase a very small annuity. The same thing applies to agriculture, and the same thing applies to other occupations.

Mr. WADSWORTH. On the ground that the wages are low?

Mr. VINSON of Kentucky. On the ground the total wages over a period of years taxed would be inconsiderable.

Mr. WADSWORTH. That is not true in the field of domestic servants.

[Here the gavel fell.]

Source: Congressional Record, House, April 11, 1935, 5468, 5528–5535; April 17, 1935, 5902–5903; April 18, 1935, 5991–5992.

Document 1.16
Congressional Floor Debates—Senate, June 1935

This document features excerpts from the Senate floor debates on three issues:

Generational Equity. *In an excerpt from the June 14th Senate floor debate the issue of subsidies for early program participants is raised by Sen. Daniel Hastings (R-Del.), and he is answered by Finance Committee Chairman Byron "Pat" Harrison (D-Miss.) and Sen. Robert M. La Follette (R-Wis.).*

Clark Amendment. *The Clark Amendment was a proposal introduced by Sen. Bennett Champ Clark (D-Mo.) to exempt from participation in the Social Security system any company that had an existing company system.*

Senator Clark introduced his amendment on the Senate floor on June 17th. The amendment was adopted by a vote of 51–35. As there was no such provision in the House-passed version of the bill, the matter went to conference, where the two bodies could not reach an agreement—stalling passage of the entire bill. The issue of Clark amendment was finally bypassed by a promise from the Democrats to allow the amendment to be considered as a stand-alone bill in the next Congress. (This bill never materialized.)

Voluntary Treasury Annuities. *The Roosevelt Administration's legislative proposal contained a third program to address economic security in old age. Under this provision, the Treasury Department would sell special Treasury securities in the open market to anyone wishing to purchase them. These securities could then be redeemed upon retirement for a government-provided retirement annuity. This was the only major provision of the Roosevelt proposal that Congress rejected.*

The bill as received from the House contained no provision for voluntary annuities. The voluntary annuity provision was included in the Finance Committee's bill. During the final day of Senate debate on the bill, Sen. Augustine Lonergan (D-Conn.) introduced an amendment to delete the voluntary annuities from the bill. Following a brief debate, the Senate voted by voice vote to delete the provision from its bill.

[Generational Equity]

Mr. HASTINGS. Mr. President, I do not know whether or not the Senator covered the point I am about to make, as I did not hear the very first part of his discussion; but I wish to give an illustration and see whether the Senator can explain how this situation is to be met:

For instance, if a man 50 years of age going into this plan on January 1, 1937, is earning $100 a month and pays in until he is 65 and lives out his expectancy of 12 years, he will be entitled under this plan to $17.50 a month, or $210 a year. In 12 years that will amount to something like $2,500. There will have been paid in by him and for him during that time $24 for the first, second, and third years, and $36 for the next 2 years, making $144. If that $144 were invested in an annuity, as is the plan here, it would earn him only $1.17 a month, something like $14 a year, or a total of $168 during the 12 years as against twenty-five hundred and some odd dollars he would get under the plan proposed by the bill. It costs for that particular individual something over $2,300.

In view of the fact that this plan contemplates that the taxes collected shall pay all the expenses. . . . I should like to have the chairman of the committee explain to the Senate how this difference of $2,300 in that particular class is made up.

Mr. HARRISON. I may say here to the Senator from Delaware that, without question, under the plan favored treatment is accorded to those who are now of advanced years. . . .

Mr. HASTINGS. I have based all the figures I am using upon the figures which it is contemplated the Government uses under the plan. The theory of the Government under this plan is that the amounts paid in plus 3-percent interest will take care of the whole plan. The point I make is that in order for that to be true . . . we must discriminate between the young man of today and the old man of today and give the older man a great advantage. My theory is that in the later years the young man who participates in this plan, when he, too, grows to be old, will call upon the Congress to make up to him in 1980 that which has been taken from him in order to take care of some older man who lived in the year 1940. . . .

Mr. HARRISON. . . . It is quite true that when the bill shall go into effect as a law, those persons of advanced age will be favored. However, as suggested by the Senator from Illinois, this is not an investment plan. It is a plan which is worked out for security in the years to come. We are trying to be of help to people in their old age. I cannot believe that those of the younger generation, who are to realize in later years under the plan, will begrudge the possible advantage to those men who now have reached 55 or 60 years of age. . . .

Mr. LAFOLLETTE. I think the Senator has completely answered the suggestion of the Senator from Delaware, but I did want to add one or two suggestions if he will permit.

In the first place, the shedding of tears about the burdens placed upon the youth under this plan would be viewed with less sympathy if we should stop to think that without this plan . . . the youth of the Nation would be, as usually they now are, called upon to meet, without any assistance, the burden of the aged dependent.

In the second place, the Senator from Delaware lumps in the contributions made by the employer in arriving at this apparent differentiation between the treatment of the younger group and those who are in the older groups at the time the system shall go into operation. I see no reason in the world, if the plan is to be agreed to at all, why we should not require the employer to help take care of the aged in his employ for whom he has made in the past no provision whatsoever.

In that connection I desire to point out that, as a matter of fact, if we separate the contributions of the employee and the employer, we find in every instance, whether they the younger group, that when they become eligible for annuities under the proposed plan they will receive more than they themselves will have contributed. . . .

[Clark Amendment]

Mr. CLARK. . . . The purpose may be very briefly stated. The purpose of the amendment is to permit companies which have or may establish private pension plans, which are at least equally favorable or more favorable to the employee than the plan set up under the provisions of the bill as a Government plan, to be exempted from the provisions of the bill and to continue the operation of the private plan provided it meets the requirements of the amendment and is approved by the board set up by the bill itself. . . .

Mr. BARKLEY. Let me ask the Senator another question. Would not the employer be permitted or induced to discriminate as between younger employees and older employees, so that the older ones might be shunted off on the Government, while the younger ones were taken care of by the private plan?

Mr. CLARK. . . . For the purpose of meeting such an objection as that . . . a provision was inserted in this amendment . . . which provides that the employer must in every case pay into the private pension fund, and to the reserve set up under the private pension fund, an amount not less than the amount of the tax, so that it is impossible for him to profit in any way by going under a private pension system. . . .

Mr. HARRISON. Mr. President, before a vote is taken on the amendment I desire to say to the Membership of the Senate that there was no question presented to the committee related to the pending legislation to which we gave more consideration than to the question before us. . . .

When the question was first presented to the committee, the amendment appealed to me, as one member of the committee, and I am sure it appealed to others. I thought that those institutions which had built up private pension systems of their own should be commended; that they had taken a great forward and progressive step and that they should be encouraged because they were forward looking; and personally I did not want to see anything done by legislation which might hamper their progressive march.

When we begin to analyze the proposition, however, from every angle and to stop, look, and listen, we find there is more to it than might appear at first glance, and I changed from the first opinion that I held about the matter. . . .

It was pointed out by the distinguished Senator from Delaware [Mr. HASTINGS] the other day that there is favored treatment accorded to those in the old, ripe years over those of younger years. We admit that. It is just so. It cannot be otherwise. They have worked many years in comparison with the short period they will be under the proposed annuity system, and consequently we give them proportionately more for the time they are in the system than we do younger men.

. . . If these private institutions are permitted to carry on their private pension plan, there is nothing in the amendment of the Senator from Missouri [Mr. CLARK] which prevents them from doing what they please in the matter of discharging men when they reach a certain age, because of the heavy obligations which are imposed upon the private industrial institutions, and take on in their places younger men, because the younger the men are the less heavy are the obligations. . . .

However, aside from all the analysis which we might go on with here, which I was hopeful we might avoid, the simple question, Members of the Senate, is this: We did not adopt this amendment which was offered in the committee because, first, we thought it might be an encouragement to private institutions to stay out of the system, weakening the Federal plan and giving a leverage to private institutions to discharge their employees when they had reached a certain age, and to take on younger men, or that same institution would go out and take Federal insurance under this plan to the number of its older men. . . .

Mr. SHIPSTEAD. It seems to me there is a question of policy involved here. I have had, in recent years, complaints from people who supposed they were the beneficiaries of private retirement systems but who found that the reserve funds invested to carry on the retirement plan had been so badly invested that when the time came for them to receive the benefits which were anticipated, and which they expected to receive annually, the condition of the fund was such that the amount received by them, in many cases, was very little. Others have complained that they have been discharged from the service a year before the date for their retirement without, at least so they claim, any just cause. I wonder if the committee has considered the injustices and the disappointments which in many cases have come to those who are supposed to be beneficiaries of private pension systems.

Mr. HARRISON. That, as I have stated, was among the reasons that caused some of us to oppose the adoption of such an amendment as is now pending. There is nothing in this proposed legislation that will prevent private institutions from carrying on their pension systems just as they have carried them on in the past. . . .

Mr. CLARK. If any private plan were loosely run, it would be directly chargeable to the holy social security board set up by the Senator himself in this measure, because they are specifically charged with the responsibility of seeing that these plans are not loosely run; and since we are giving them practically powers of life and death over the population of the

United States anyway, it does not seem to me too much to require that they should see that these private plans are not loosely run.

Mr. WAGNER. . . . The Senator happened to mention one company which has had an excellent system; but there are many bad ones. In addition, this bill does not abolish any system. If any employer desires to give to his employees an advantage in addition to that which is given under this bill, he is at liberty to do so. He can supplement our efforts. . . .

Mr. LAFOLLETTE. . . . If this amendment should be agreed to and the employer should sit down to compare the Federal system, as provided in title II, with the system being urged upon him by some insurance broker, one of two things would inevitably result. Either he would decide that it was better for him to employ only those in the younger age groups and to provide a system embracing all his employees under a private plan, or he would employ a fair share of the older men but do all in his power to encourage the older employees in his employment to elect to come under the Government plan, so that under either course he would be able to provide as liberal benefits as the Federal system without paying as much for them, because the Federal system would have too carry the older workers. . . .

Mr. GEORGE. . . . I know that the Senator is not making an argument against the bill; but it does seem to me that an argument against the amendment is an argument against the whole philosophy of the bill. I do not share the view that American industries as a whole will undertake to take advantage of this amendment, and will employ only young men, because their obligation would be the same as it is under the plan set out in the bill. But if the Senator is correct, it seems to me that we might as well accept as an established fact in the beginning that the same selfish motives will induce the American employer to hire and employ the young man who can produce more per hour than the old man. Remember, the employer's tax is measured by his pay roll, and that will also induce him to use every bit of labor-saving machinery he can put into his establishment. If selfishness is the driving motive of all American business, it seems to me the Senator's argument is against the whole bill as much as it is against the amendment.

Mr. BARKLEY. . . . I believe the effect of the Clark amendment . . . will be to disorganize and disarrange the reserve fund set up in the Treasury under the Federal plan, and that it will gradually and effectually undermine the Federal system which we are trying to set up. . . .

As the Senator from Wisconsin [Mr. LAFOLLETTE] said yesterday, the employers of the United States have not asked for this amendment. Only one employer of labor came before our committee and suggested it. . . . The only other man who came before the committee to suggest the amendment was a man who represents an annuity company which desires to write policies for employers throughout the United States. . . .

My contention is . . . that we cannot safely take away from this uniform, universal system which we are trying to establish here the universality and the uniformity of its application by holding out an invitation or an encouragement to private individuals to impinge upon the system set up by the Federal Government, and utterly to destroy its reserve fund, and thereby break down its application, because the Federal Government will be compelled to bear the burden of it on the seamy side, while private employers may so manipulate their employment as to age as to have a large majority of younger men who would not be an immediate burden upon them, while shifting to the Federal Government all of the older employees whom they do not desire to carry on their rolls because of the greater burden that might be attached to payment of annuities to them over a term of years. . . .

[Voluntary Treasury Annuities]

Mr. LONERGAN. Mr. President, title XI relates to annuity bonds.

The proposal was submitted before the House Ways and Means Committee, and was rejected. It was not incorporated in the bill which came to the Finance Committee of the Senate. At a meeting of our committee, when this proposal was considered, 12 members out of 21 were present. Seven voted in favor of the proposal and five voted against it. Three of the four Senators who voted for the proposal, according to their statements in the committee, were under the belief that insurance companies do not sell annuity bonds, especially for small sums. . . .

Mr. President, I think these reports point out conclusively that private insurance companies have developed and are developing a much more stable field of annuities than the Senate has perhaps heretofore realized. Here we have a bill including a section which would put the Government into that business in such a way that it would intrude upon private business enterprise, and no doubt discourage the widespread development of annuities which is being undertaken. . . .

The Government already offers, through the Treasury and the Post Office Departments, numerous opportunities for investments of small savings in the tax-exempt field. An extension of this program to include annuity insurance bonds would definitely compete with an important business, and, moreover, would tend to invite individuals to lean upon the Government instead of private business and the various State and municipal governments which are expected to participate in this social security program. . . .

Now, Mr. President, is the Senate of the United States going to enact into law a provision in this bill which will injure these companies? Is the Senate going to place the Government into a definitely private business? . . .

Mr. HARRISON. Mr. President, I merely desire to make a brief statement. The provision giving an opportunity to people to buy annuity bonds, with the limitation which is in the bill, that in no instance may they receive an annuity of more than $100 a month. It was placed there to take care of a group that did not come within the other provisions of the measure. I think it is one of the minor features of the bill; in other words, I think the annuities provided in title II of the bill, and the old-age pensions and the unemployment features under other titles are much more important than is this; but, for the reasons I have just stated, we placed this provision in the bill on the recommendation of the President's committee which investigated the matter. . . .

Mr. COSTIGAN. It is my understanding that the annuity bond feature of the bill is designed to offer many million people an opportunity to purchase cheap annuity insurance, free from premiums to agents, and that the persons who, under the committee amendment, are offered this security are employers or employees who do not come under other provisions of the bill.

Mr. HARRISON. The Senator has stated the facts correctly. . . .

Mr. COSTIGAN. Mr. President, may I say that it was on my motion that these provisions were included in the bill in the Finance Committee. The motion was made following . . .

a very able presentation of the reasons for the amendment by Representative DAVID J. LEWIS of Maryland who has been a lifelong student of this and allied questions. Representative LEWIS pointed out . . . that there are about 22,000,000 persons in the United States at this time who do not come under the protective clauses of the pending bill. Among those are the self-employed and the members of professions, who are estimated at this time to be about 11,125,000, and approximately 10,000,000 workers. The purpose of the provisions, of course, is to permit the purchase from the Government, on reasonable terms, of annuity bonds which will guarantee the purchasers incomes running from a minimum of $60 a year to $1,200 a year per person.

When Representative LEWIS presented this matter to the Senate Finance Committee he persuasively enumerated reasons which make these amendments particularly appealing to Members of the Senate, to professional men of all sorts, and to employers who are unable, for one reason or another, to guard against the likelihood that old age will find them reduced to need. . . .

Mr. LONERGAN. Does the Senator know whether or not the United States Government can issue insurance at a cheaper rate than can insurance companies of long experience?

Mr. COSTIGAN. It is my understanding that under these amendments the Government of the United States would sell annuity bonds to investors—

Mr. LONERGAN. That is correct.

Mr. COSTIGAN. And that there would be an absence of the premiums which ordinarily go to insurance representatives. . . .

I suggest, therefore, that this amendment should be seriously considered by the Senate. It should at least go to conference. In my judgment, there is no serious opposition to it on the part of the leading insurance companies of the country. The only objection comes from those who, like the Senator from Connecticut [Mr. LONERGAN], are reluctant to see any form of Government activity which may be regarded, even theoretically, as competitive with private business. . . .

Mr. MCKELLAR. Does not this title put the Government into the insurance business?

Mr. COSTIGAN. It does in a minor way, in a very limited field. . . .

Mr. MCKELLAR. During the war we went into the insurance business for our soldiers, but since the war we have found it to be very impracticable for the Government to continue that activity, and we are getting out of it as rapidly as possible. With that experience in mind, it seems to me to be most unwise for us now to go into the insurance business even in a limited way. . . .

Mr. ADAMS. I wish to ask a question which is very unwelcome these days. In what clause of the Federal Constitution does the Senator find justification for the issuance of a Federal insurance policy? . . .

Mr. BARKLEY. . . . Undoubtedly we have the power to issue bonds, and we have the power to use the credit of the United States. If I have $2,000 to invest in such a bond, the terms of which are that I will be paid back in monthly or annual installments the money I put in, there is certainly nothing unconstitutional about that. It is merely a different way by which the United States would repay its debts or the money that it borrowed from the people, just as in the case of Liberty bonds. The Government could pay them back all at once, or, if it desired to do so, it could authorize repayment in installments. That is all this provision undertakes to do. When we come down to brass tacks, that is all it amounts to. I place a certain amount of money in a Government bond, and we provide for paying it back in annual installments, which is simply a method by which the Government repays its debt. . . .

Source: Congressional Record, Senate, June 14, 1935, 9272–9273; June 18, 1935, 9511–9513, 9520–9521, 9523, 9525; June 19, 1935, 9626, 9532–9533, 9634–9639.

Document 1.17
Original Actuarial Estimates for Social Security, 1935

For Franklin Roosevelt it was critical that Social Security be financed by payroll contributions, not by general tax revenues. The initial proposal presented to the president by the Committee on Economic Security contained plans for some general revenue financing in the out-years. The CES staff had devised a proposal using general revenue subsidies because they were trying to solve the start-up problem faced by any new pension system: how to make benefits adequate for early participants. Generally, this is done by subsidizing the benefits of early participants, which requires increased revenues in the early years of the program. The CES was proposing paying the subsidies, in part, by using general revenues.

The plan developed by the CES thus assumed there would be both a general revenue component to program financing and a significant subsidy to early program participants. But when tasked with providing some alternative actuarial calculations, the CES produced three alternatives: their original proposal, their original proposal without general revenues (but with subsidies), and a plan with no general revenues or subsidies to early program participants. These three plans were submitted to the Senate Finance Committee by Edwin Witte in a letter dated February 4, 1935, and were made part of the record of the committee's hearings on the bill. Ultimately, Congress opted for a financing scheme without the use of general revenues but with subsidies to early program participants.

Following final action on the legislation, CES actuary Robert J. Myers produced an actuarial table to reflect the provisions of the final bill. This table was not published, but its bottom-line—a $47 billion surplus by 1980—became a famous figure used in estimating the future costs of the program.

Original CES Proposal (with general revenues and program subsidies)

Table II. Old-Age Insurance Plan of Bill: Part A—Progress of Reserve
(all estimates in millions of dollars)

Year	Net Contributions	Interest on Reserve	Federal Subsidy	Benefit Payments	Reserve End of Year
1937	306.0	0.0	0.0	0.7	305.3
1938	308.9	9.2	0.0	2.0	621.5
1939	312.0	18.7	0.0	3.3	948.8
1940	314.9	28.4	0.0	4.8	1,287.3
1945	672.3	106.0	0.0	190.1	4,123.5
1950	1,073.3	211.9	0.0	577.1	7,770.7
1955	1,520.0	329.6	0.0	1,149.6	11,687.2
1960	1,979.2	431.9	0.0	1,924.8	14,880.1
1965	2,058.3	470.0	0.0	2,532.8	15,660.4
1970	2,137.5	468.0	507.3	3,112.8	15,600.0
1975	2,216.7	468.0	926.5	3,611.2	15,600.0
1980	2,216.7	468.0	1,387.9	4,072.5	15,600.0

Assumed tax rates (total, employer and employee rates combined):

    1937–1941 1%
    1942–1946 2%
    1947–1951 3%
    1952–1956 4%
    1957–1980 5%

Authors' note: This plan shows an annual general revenue contribution of $507 million in 1970, increasing thereafter, and a final 1980 Trust Fund reserve of $15.6 billion. The 5% tax rate was to remain in place after 1980.

Revised CES Proposal (no general revenues or subsidies)

Table III. Plan M2—No Unearned Annuities, Rates as in Bill: Part A—Progress of Reserve
(all estimates in millions of dollars)

Year	Net Contributions	Interest on Reserve	Federal Subsidy	Benefit Payments	Reserve End of Year
1937	306.0	0.0	0.0	0.7	305.3
1938	308.9	9.2	0.0	2.0	621.5
1939	312.0	18.7	0.0	3.3	948.8
1940	314.9	28.4	0.0	4.8	1,287.3
1945	672.3	113.5	0.0	26.8	4,541.5
1950	1,073.3	266. 5	0.0	91.5	10,134.7
1955	1,520.0	497.2	0.0	227.6	18,364.7
1960	1,979.2	807.5	0.0	488.7	29,214.1
1965	2,058.3	1,155.7	0.0	863.9	40,874.3
1970	2,137.5	1,505.2	0.0	1,372.7	52,444.3
1975	2,216.7	1,830.4	0.0	2,087.3	62,974.5
1980	2,216.7	2,086.7	0.0	3,038.1	70,822.5

Assumed tax rates same as under the original proposal, Table II.

Authors' note: This plan projects the largest reserve—$70.8 billion by 1980. This result is due to a combination of three factors: loss of the general revenues, a dramatic decline in the cost of benefit payments due to the lack of subsidies, and an increased interest income to the program due to the larger year-to-year reserve produced by the reduction in initial benefits.

Revised CES Proposal (no general revenues, but with program subsidies)

Table IV. Plan M11—2 to 6 Percent Contribution Rate with Partially Unearned Annuities to Persons Now Half Old: Part A—Progress of Reserve (all estimates in millions of dollars)

Year	Net Contributions	Interest on Reserve	Federal Subsidy	Benefit Payments	Reserve End of Year
1938	629. 5	18.7	0.0	4.0	1,266.1
1939	635.6	38.0	0.0	6.7	1,933.0
1940	980.0	58.0	0.0	10.8	2,960.2
1945	1,393.3	237.5	0.0	207.6	9,338.8
1950	2,185.1	498.7	0.0	623.6	18,682.8
1955	2,280.0	796.8	0.0	1,223.5	28,413.5
1960	2,375.1	1,046.5	0.0	2,023.2	36,281.7
1965	2,470.0	1,231.5	0.0	2,628.4	42,122.5
1970	2,565.1	1,370.0	0.0	3,191.2	46,408.9
1975	2,660.0	1,462.3	0.0	3, 692.3	49,173.3
1980	2,660.0	1,502.3	0.0	4,146.3	50,093.7

Assumed tax rates (total, employer and employee rates combined):

    1937–1939 2%
    1940–1942 3%
    1943–1945 4%
    1946–1948 5%
    1949 and thereafter 6%

Authors' note: The tax rates under this plan would be higher than those under the original CES plan, due to the loss of the general revenue funding and due to the need to build up the reserve more rapidly in other to take advantage of greater interest incomes (to offset the loss of the general revenues).

Unpublished Myers Calculations Based on Final Congressional Action

Table IIIa. Plan M2—No Unearned Annuities, Rates as in Bill: Part A—Progress of Reserve (all estimates in millions of dollars)

Calendar Year	Appropriation for Reserve	Benefit Payments (82.5% Col. 10)	Interest on Reserve	Balance in Reserve
1937	511.0	3.7	0.0	507.3
1938	515.9	10.7	15.2	1027.7
1939	520.9	18.2	30.8	1561.3
1940	803.3	25.7	46.8	2385.8
1941	811.0	33.7	71.6	3234.7
1942	818.6	71.9	97.1	4078.5
1943	1121.4	116.5	122.4	5205.7
1944	1131.8	169.2	156.2	6324.5
1945	1142.2	213.2	189.7	7443.3
1946	1440.6	285.2	223.4	8822.0
1947	1453.6	343.7	264.4	10196.3
1948	1466.6	411.1	305.9	11557.7
1949	1775.5	473.0	346.7	13207.0
1950	1791.1	537.9	396.2	14856.3
1951	1806.6	622.3	445.7	16486.5
1952	1822.2	690.6	494.6	18112.8

Table IIIa (*continued*)

Calendar Year	Appropriation for Reserve	Benefit Payments (82.5% Col. 10)	Interest on Reserve	Balance in Reserve
1953	1837.8	762.9	543.4	19731.1
1954	1853.4	854.7	591.9	21321.7
1955	1869.0	920.8	639.7	22909.6
1956	1884.5	1032.4	687.3	24449.0
1957	1900.1	1117.6	733.5	25965.0
1958	1915.7	1231.4	779.0	27428.2
1959	1931.3	1329.6	822.8	28852.8
1960	1946.8	1430.2	865.6	30235.0
1961	1962.5	1551.2	907.0	31553.2
1962	1978.0	1652.2	946.6	32825.6
1963	1993.5	1728.3	984.8	34075.6
1964	2009.1	1813.2	1022.3	35293.8
1965	2024.7	1874.7	1059.4	36503.2
1966	2040.3	1982.0	1095.1	37656.5
1967	2055.8	2065.3	1129.7	38776.7
1968	2071.5	2162.3	1163.3	39849.2
1969	2087.0	2252.0	1195.4	40879.7
1970	2102.6	2355.0	1226.4	41853.7
1971	2118.1	2462.0	1255.6	42765.4
1972	2133.8	2570.6	1282.9	43611.5
1973	2149.3	2686.5	1308.3	44382.6
1974	2164.9	2810.0	1331.5	45069.1
1975	2180.5	2934.1	1352.0	45667.5
1976	2180.5	3058.3	1370.0	46159.8
1977	2180.5	3184.3	1384.8	46540.8
1978	2180.5	3318.8	1396.2	46798.7
1979	2180.5	3446.8	1403.9	46936.3
1980	2180.5	3575.8	1408.1	46949.1

Tax rate schedule same as in Table IV.

Authors' note: This table represents the final actuarial estimates for the original Social Security program of 1935, even though the table was not published at the time. The tax rate schedule is as proposed by the CES in their revised M11 Plan (Table 1.3). The detailed figures in the table are not identical to those in Table 1.3 because Congress made other changes in the benefit provisions of the final law.

Sources: Tables II, III, and IV from Economic Security Act, Hearings before the Committee on Finance, United States Senate, on S. 1130, Jan. 22–Feb. 20, 1935 (Washington, D.C.: Government Printing Office, 1935), 251–253. Table IIIa showing the Myers actuarial projections is from a copy of Myers's original worksheets retained in the Social Security Administration history archives.

Document 1.18
President Roosevelt's Remarks on Signing the Social Security Act, August 14, 1935

According to Frances Perkins, Franklin Roosevelt's secretary of labor, the Social Security Act of 1935 was FDR's proudest domestic achievement of his presidency.

Today a hope of many years' standing is in large part fulfilled. The civilization of the past hundred years, with its startling industrial changes, has tended more and more to make life insecure. Young people have come to wonder what would be their lot when they came to old age. The man with a job has wondered how long the job would last.

This social security measure gives at least some protection to thirty millions of our citizens who will reap direct benefits through unemployment compensation, through old-age pensions and through increased services for the protection of children and the prevention of ill health.

We can never insure one hundred percent of the population against one hundred percent of the hazards and vicissitudes of life, but we have tried to frame a law which will give some measure of protection to the average citizen and to his family against the loss of a job and against poverty-ridden old age.

This law, too, represents a cornerstone in a structure which is being built but is by no means complete. It is a structure intended to lessen the force of possible future depressions. It will act as a protection to future Administrations against the necessity of going deeply into debt to furnish relief to the needy. The law will flatten out the peaks and valleys of deflation and of inflation. It is, in short, a law that will take care of human needs and at the same time provide the United States an economic structure of vastly greater soundness.

I congratulate all of you ladies and gentlemen, all of you in the Congress, in the executive departments and all of you who come from private life, and I thank you for your splendid efforts in behalf of this sound, needed, and patriotic legislation.

If the Senate and the House of Representatives in this long and arduous session had done nothing more than pass this Bill, the session would be regarded as historic for all time.

Source: The Public Papers and Addresses of Franklin D. Roosevelt, vol. 4: The Court Disapproves, 1935 (New York: Random House, 1938), 324–325.

Document 1.19
Text of the Social Security Act, August 14, 1935

The 1935 Social Security Act was an omnibus bill, which combined provisions of separate but related items into one piece of legislation. In this case, the act created seven distinct programs from its eleven titles. In addition to the Social Security program, this law also created programs for state old-age assistance, national unemployment insurance, and aid to dependent children, among others. (Only those sections of the act relevant to the Social Security program are included here.)

Social Security was split into two separate titles in the bill: Title II, which authorized the payment of benefits, and Title VIII, which raised the taxes to fund the benefits. This was a legal strategy undertaken by the act's designers in an effort to suggest that the two aspects of the program were not connected to each other, so that if one or the other was eventually ruled to be unconstitutional the other title might survive.

The Social Security Act (Act of August 14, 1935) [H.R. 7260]

An act to provide for the general welfare by establishing a system of Federal old-age benefits, and by enabling the several States to make more adequate provision for aged persons, blind persons, dependent and crippled children, maternal and child welfare, public health, and the administration of their unemployment compensation laws; to establish a Social Security Board; to raise revenue; and for other purposes.

Be it enacted by the Senate and House of Representatives of the United States of America in Congress assembled. . . .

[Title I: Grants to States for Old-Age Assistance omitted.]

Title II: Federal Old-Age Benefits Old-Age Reserve Account

Section 201. (a) There is hereby created an account in the Treasury of the United States to be known as the Old-Age Reserve Account hereinafter in this title called the Account. There is hereby authorized to be appropriated to the Account for each fiscal year, beginning with the fiscal year ending June 30, 1937, an amount sufficient as an annual premium to provide for the payments required under this title, such amount to be determined on a reserve basis in accordance with accepted actuarial principles, and based upon such tables of mortality as the Secretary of the Treasury shall from time to time adopt, and upon an interest rate of 3 per centum per annum compounded annually. The Secretary of the Treasury shall submit annually to the Bureau of the Budget an estimate of the appropriations to be made to the Account.

(b) It shall be the duty of the Secretary of the Treasury to invest such portion of the amounts credited to the Account as is not, in his judgment, required to meet current withdrawals. Such investment may be made only in interest-bearing obligations of the United States or in obligations guaranteed as to both principal and interest by the United States. For such purpose such obligations may be acquired

(1) on original issue at par, or
(2) by purchase of outstanding obligations at the market price. The purposes for which obligations of the United States may be issued under the Second Liberty Bond Act, as amended, are hereby extended to authorize the issuance at par of special obligations exclusively to the Account. Such special obligations shall bear interest at the rate of 3 per centum per annum. Obligations other than such special obligations may be acquired for the Account only on such terms as to provide an investment yield of not less than 3 per centum per annum.

(c) Any obligations acquired by the Account (except special obligations issued exclusively to the Account) may be sold at the market price, and such special obligations may be redeemed at par plus accrued interest.

(d) The interest on, and the proceeds from the sale or redemption of, any obligations held in the Account shall be credited to and form a part of the Account.

(e) All amounts credited to the Account shall be available for making payments required under this title.

(f) The Secretary of the Treasury shall include in his annual report the actuarial status of the Account.

Old-Age Benefit Payments
SEC. 202. (a) Every qualified individual (as defined in section 210) shall be entitled to receive, with respect to the period beginning on the date he attains the age of sixty-five, or on January 1, 1942, whichever is the later, and ending on the date of his death, an old-age benefit (payable as nearly as practicable in equal monthly installments) as follows:

(1) If the total wages (as defined in section 210) determined by the Board to have been paid to him, with respect to employment (as defined in section 210) after December 31, 1936, and before he attained the age of sixty-five, were not more than $3,000, the old-age benefit shall be at a monthly rate of one-half of 1 per centum of such total wages;

(2) If such total wages were more than $3,000, the old-age benefit shall be at a monthly rate equal to the sum of the following:

(A) One-half of 1 per centum of $3,000; plus
(B) One-twelfth of 1 per centum of the amount by which such total wages exceeded $3,000 and did not exceed $45,000; plus
(C) One-twenty-fourth of 1 per centum of the amount by which such total wages exceeded $45,000.

(b) In no case shall the monthly rate computed under subsection (a) exceed $85. . . .

(c) If the Board finds . . . more or less than the correct amount has therefore been paid to any individual . . . proper adjustments shall be made. . . .

(d) Whenever the Board finds that any qualified individual has received wages with respect to regular employment after he attained the age of sixty-five, the old-age benefit payable to such individual shall be reduced, for each calendar month in any part of which such regular employment occurred, by an amount equal to one month's benefit. Such reduction shall be made, under regulations prescribed by the Board, by deductions from one or more payments of old-age benefit to such individual.

Payments upon Death

SEC. 203. (a) If any individual dies before attaining the age of sixty-five, there shall be paid to his estate an amount equal to 3½ per centum of the total wages determined by the Board to have been paid to him, with respect to employment after December 31, 1936.

(b) If the Board finds that the correct amount of the old-age benefit payable to a qualified individual during his life under section 202 was less than 3½ per centum of the total wages by which such old-age benefit was measurable, then there shall be paid to his estate a sum equal to the amount, if any, by which such 3½ per centum exceeds the amount (whether more or less than the correct amount) paid to him during his life as old-age benefit.

(c) If the Board finds that the total amount paid to a qualified individual under an old-age benefit during his life was less than the correct amount to which he was entitled under section 202, and that the correct amount of such old-age benefit was 3½ per centum or more of the total wages by which such old-age benefit was measurable, then there shall be paid to his estate a sum equal to the amount, if any, by which the correct amount of the old-age benefit exceeds the amount which was so paid to him during his life.

Payments to Aged Individuals Not Qualified for Benefits

SEC. 204. (a) There shall be paid in a lump sum to any individual who, upon attaining the age of sixty-five, is not a qualified individual, an amount equal to 3½ per centum of the total wages determined by the Board to have been paid to him, with respect to employment after December 31, 1936, and before he attained the age of sixty-five.

(b) After any individual becomes entitled to any payment under subsection (a), no other payment shall be made under this title in any manner measured by wages paid to him, except that any part of any payment under subsection (a) which is not paid to him before his death shall be paid to his estate. . . .

Definitions

SEC. 210. When used in this title—(a) The term wages means all remuneration for employment, including the cash value of all remuneration paid in any medium other than cash; except that such term shall not include that part of the remuneration which, after remuneration equal to $3,000 has been paid to an individual by an employer with respect to employment during any calendar year, is paid to such individual by such employer with respect to employment during such calendar year.

(b) The term employment means any service, of whatever nature, performed within the United States by an employee for his employer, except—

(1) Agricultural labor;
(2) Domestic service in a private home;
(3) Casual labor not in the course of the employer's trade or business;
(4) Service performed as an officer or member of the crew of a vessel documented under the laws of the United States or of any foreign country;
(5) Service performed in the employ of the United States Government or of an instrumentality of the United States;
(6) Service performed in the employ of a State, a political subdivision thereof, or an instrumentality of one or more States or political subdivisions;
(7) Service performed in the employ of a corporation, community chest, fund, or foundation, organized and operated exclusively for religious, charitable, scientific, literary, or educational purposes, or for the prevention of cruelty to children or animals, no part of the net earnings of which inures to the benefit of any private shareholder or individual.

(c) The term qualified individual means any individual with respect to whom it appears to the satisfaction of the Board that—

(1) He is at least sixty-five years of age; and

(2) The total amount of wages paid to him, with respect to employment after December 31, 1936, and before he attained the age of sixty-five, was not less than $2,000; and

(3) Wages were paid to him, with respect to employment on some five days after December 31, 1936, and before he attained the age of sixty-five, each day being in a different calendar year. . . .

[Titles III: Grants to States for Unemployment Compensation Administration, IV: Grants to States for Aid to Dependent Children, V: Grants to States for Maternal and Child Welfare, and VI: Public Health Work omitted.]

Title VII: Social Security Board

Establishment
SECTION 701. There is hereby established a Social Security Board . . . to be composed of three members to be appointed by the President, by and with the advice and consent of the Senate. During his term of membership on the Board, no member shall engage in any other business, vocation, or employment. Not more than two of the members of the Board shall be members of the same political party. Each member shall receive a salary at the rate of $10,000 a year and shall hold office for a term of six years, except that

(1) any member appointed to fill a vacancy occurring prior to the expiration of the term for which his predecessor was appointed, shall be appointed for the remainder of such term; and

(2) the terms of office of the members first taking office after the date of the enactment of this Act shall expire, as designated by the President at the time of appointment, one at the end of two years, one at the end of four years, and one at the end of six years, after the date of the enactment of this Act. The President shall designate one of the members as the chairman of the Board.

Duties of the Social Security Board
SEC. 702. The Board shall perform the duties imposed upon it by this Act and shall also have the duty of studying and making recommendations as to the most effective methods of providing economic security through social insurance, and as to legislation and matters of administrative policy concerning old-age pensions, unemployment compensation, accident compensation, and related subjects. . . .

Title VIII: Taxes with Respect to Employment

Income Tax on Employees
SECTION 801. In addition to other taxes, there shall be levied, collected, and paid upon the income of every individual a tax equal to the following percentages of the wages (as defined in section 811) received by him after December 31, 1936, with respect to employment (as defined in section 811) after such date:

(1) With respect to employment during the calendar years 1937, 1938, and 1939, the rate shall be 1 per centum.

(2) With respect to employment during the calendar years 1940, 1941, and 1942, the rate shall 1½ per centum.

(3) With respect to employment during the calendar years 1943, 1944, and 1945, the rate shall be 2 per centum.

(4) With respect to employment during the calendar years 1946, 1947, and 1948, the rate shall be 2½ per centum.

(5) With respect to employment after December 31, 1948, the rate shall be 3 per centum.

Deduction of Tax from Wages

SEC. 802. (a) The tax imposed by section 801 shall be collected by the employer of the tax-payer by deducting the amount of the tax from the wages as and when paid. Every employer required so to deduct the tax is hereby made liable for the payment of such tax, and is hereby indemnified against the claims and demands of any person for the amount of any such payment made by such employer. . . .

Deductibility from Income Tax

SEC. 803. For the purposes of the income tax imposed by Title I of the Revenue Act of 1934 or by any Act of Congress in substitution therefore, the tax imposed by section 801 shall not be allowed as a deduction to the taxpayer in computing his net income for the year in which such tax is deducted from his wages.

Excise Tax on Employers

SEC. 804. In addition to other taxes, every employer shall pay an excise tax, with respect to having individuals in his employ, equal to the following percentages of the wages (as defined in section 811) paid by him after December 31, 1936, with respect to employment (as defined in section 811) after such date:

(1) With respect to employment during the calendar years 1937, 1938, and 1939, the rate shall be 1 per centum.

(2) With respect to employment during the calendar years 1940, 1941, and 1942, the rate shall be 1½ per centum.

(3) With respect to employment during the calendar years 1943, 1944, and 1945, the rate shall be 2 per centum.

(4) With respect to employment during the calendar years 1946, 1947, and 1948, the rate shall be 2½ per centum.

(5) With respect to employment after December 31, 1948, the rate shall be 3 per centum. . . .

Definitions

SEC. 811. When used in this title—(a) The term wages means all remuneration for employment, including the cash value of all remuneration paid in any medium other than cash; except that such term shall not include that part of the remuneration which, after remuneration equal to $3,000 has been paid to an individual by an employer with respect to employment during any calendar year, is paid to such individual by such employer with respect to employment during such calendar year.

(b) The term employment means any service, of whatever nature, performed within the United States by an employee for his employer, except—

(1) Agricultural labor;
(2) Domestic service in a private home;
(3) Casual labor not in the course of the employers trade or business;
(4) Service performed by an individual who has attained the age of sixty-five;
(5) Service performed as an officer or member of the crew of a vessel documented under the laws of the United States or of any foreign country;
(6) Service performed in the employ of the United States Government or of an instrumentality of the United States;
(7) Service performed in the employ of a State, a political subdivision thereof, or an instrumentality of one or more States or political subdivisions;
(8) Service performed in the employ of a corporation, community chest, fund, or foundation, organized and operated exclusively for religious, charitable, scientific, literary, or educational purposes, or for the prevention of cruelty to children or animals, no part of the net earnings of which inures to the benefit of any private shareholder or individual. . . .

[Titles IX: Tax on Employers of Eight or More and X: Grants to States for Aid to the Blind omitted.]

Title XI: General Provisions
Definitions Section 1101. . . .

Separability
SEC. 1103. If any provision of this Act, or the application thereof to any person or circumstance is held invalid, the remainder of the Act, and the application of such provision to other persons or circumstances shall not be affected thereby.

Reservation of Power
SEC. 1104. The right to alter, amend, or repeal any provision of this Act is hereby reserved to the Congress.

Short Title
SEC. 1105. This Act may be cited as the Social Security Act.

Source: Full text of the act available online on the Social Security Administration website at: www.ssa.gov/history/35actinx.html (accessed September 19, 2006).

Document 1.20
First Government Pamphlet on Social Security, 1936
Headlined with "Security in Your Old Age," this is the text of the official government pamphlet that was issued to the nation's workers to explain the new Social Security program.

To Employees of Industrial and Business Establishments

Factories • Shops • Mines • Mills • Stores • Offices and Other Places of Business

Beginning November 24, 1936, the United States Government will set up a Social Security account for you, if you are eligible. To understand your obligations, rights, and benefits you should read the following general explanation.

THERE is now a law in this country which will give about 26 million working people something to live on when they are old and have stopped working. This law, which gives other benefits, too, was passed last year by Congress and is called the Social Security Act.

Under this law the United States Government will send checks every month to retired workers, both men and women, after they have passed their 65th birthday and have met a few simple requirements of the law.

What This Means to You

THIS means that if you work in some factory, shop, mine, mill, store, office, or almost any other kind of business or industry, you will be earning benefits that will come to you later on. From the time you are 65 years old, or more, and stop working, you will get a Government check every month of your life, if you have worked some time (one day or more) in each of any 5 years after 1936, and have earned during that time a total of $2,000 or more.

The checks will come to you as a right. You will get them regardless of the amount of property or income you may have. They are what the law calls "Old-Age Benefits" under the Social Security Act. If you prefer to keep on working after you age 65, the monthly checks from the Government will begin coming to you whenever you decide to retire.

The Amount of Your Checks

How much you will get when you are 65 years old will depend entirely on how much you earn in wages from your industrial or business employment between January 1, 1937, and your 65th birthday. A man or woman who gets good wages and has a steady job most of his or her life can get as much as $85 a month for life after age 65. The least you can get in monthly benefits, if you come under the law at all, is $10 a month.

If You Are Now Young. Suppose you are making $25 a week and are young enough now to go on working for 40 years. If you make an average of $25 a week for 52 weeks in each year, your check when you are 65 years old will be $53 a month for the rest of your life. If you make $50 a week, you will get $74.50 a month for the rest of your life after age 65.

If You Are Now Middle-Aged. But suppose you are about 55 years old now and have 10 years to work before you are 65. Suppose you make only $15 a week on the average. When you stop work at age 65 you will get a check for $19 each month for the rest of your life. If you make $25 a week for 10 years, you will get a little over $23 a month from the Government as long as you live after your 65th birthday.

If You Should Die before Age 65. If you should die before you begin to get your monthly checks, your family will get a payment in cash, amounting to 3.5 cents on every dollar of wages you have earned after 1936. If, for example, you should die at age 64, and if you had earned $25 a week for 10 years before that time, your family would receive $455. On the other hand, if you have not worked enough to get the regular monthly checks by the time you are 65, you will get a lump sum, or if you should die your family or estate would get a lump sum. The amount of this, too, will be 3.5 cents on every dollar of wages you earn after 1936.

Taxes

The same law that provides these old-age benefits for you and other workers, sets up certain new taxes to be paid to the United States Government. These taxes are collected by the Bureau of Internal Revenue of the U.S. Treasury Department, and inquiries concerning them should be addressed to that bureau. The law also creates an "Old-Age Reserve Account" in the United States Treasury, and Congress is authorized to put into this reserve account each year enough money to provide for the monthly payments you and other workers are to receive when you are 65.

Your Part of the Tax

The taxes called for in this law will be paid both by your employer and by you. For the next 3 years you will pay maybe 15 cents a week, maybe 25 cents a week, maybe 30 cents or more, according to what you earn. That is to say, during the next 3 years, beginning January 1, 1937, you will pay 1 cent for every dollar you earn, and at the same time your employer will pay 1 cent for every dollar you earn, up to $3,000 a year. Twenty-six million other workers and their employers will be paying at the same time.

After the first 3 years—that is to say, beginning in 1940—you will pay, and your employer will pay, 1.5 cents for each dollar you earn, up to $3,000 a year. This will be the tax for 3 years, and then, beginning in 1943, you will pay 2 cents, and so will your employer, for every dollar you earn for the next 3 years. After that, you and your employer will each pay half a cent more for 3 years, and finally, beginning in 1949, twelve years from now, you and your employer will each pay 3 cents on each dollar you earn, up to $3,000 a year. That is the most you will ever pay.

Your Employer's Part of the Tax

The Government will collect both of these taxes from your employer. Your part of the tax will be taken out of your pay. The Government will collect from your employer an equal amount out of his own funds.

This will go on just the same if you go to work for another employer, so long as you work in a factory, shop, mine, mill, office, store, or other such place of business. (Wages earned in employment as farm workers, domestic workers in private homes, Government workers, and on a few other kinds of jobs are not subject to this tax.)

Old-Age Reserve Account

Meanwhile, the Old-Age Reserve fund in the United States Treasury is drawing interest, and the Government guarantees it will never earn less than 3 percent. This means that 3 cents will be added to every dollar in the fund each year.

Maybe your employer has an old-age pension plan for his employees. If so, the Government's old-age benefit plan will not have to interfere with that. The employer can fit his plan into the Government plan.

What you get from the Government plan will always be more than you have paid in taxes and usually more than you can get for yourself by putting away the same amount of money each week in some other way.

Note.—*"Wages" and "employment" wherever used in the foregoing mean wages and employment as defined in the Social Security Act.*

Source: Social Security Administration History Archives, Lateral Files 1, Drawer 5, Folder: "Pamphlets and Informational Materials—1930s."

CHAPTER 2

The First Controversy over Financing and the Creation of Family Benefits, 1935–1939

The period between the enactment of the Social Security Act in 1935 and the 1939 amendments began with a fundamental challenge to Social Security, in the context of the presidential election campaign of 1936. The first three documents in this chapter recount some of the political discussion sparked by the economic security issue in the buildup to the election.

The 1939 amendments grew out of the work of an advisory council, jointly chartered by the Social Security Board and the Senate Finance Committee. Committee member Arthur Vandenberg (R-Mich.) was the principal advocate of a new advisory council, and he hoped to use it to challenge the reserve financing scheme of the original law. The Social Security Board wanted to use the council to further its objective of program expansion. So these two matters—financing and potential program expansion—were at the center of the council's deliberations.

The 1939 amendments made a fundamental change in the Social Security program by adding two new categories of benefits: payments to the spouse and minor children of a retired worker (so-called dependents benefits) and sur-

MORE SECURITY FOR THE AMERICAN FAMILY

WHEN AN INSURED WORKER DIES, LEAVING DEPENDENT CHILDREN AND A WIDOW, BOTH MOTHER AND CHILDREN RECEIVE MONTHLY BENEFITS UNTIL THE LATTER REACH 18.

FOR INFORMATION WRITE OR CALL AT THE NEAREST FIELD OFFICE OF THE
SOCIAL SECURITY BOARD

This government poster, issued following the enactment of the 1939 amendments, announces the major change of this period—the transformation of the Social Security program from an individual retirement program to a family-based social insurance benefit. Source: SSA History Archives.

vivors' benefits paid to the family in the event of the premature death of a covered worker. The 1939 amendments also increased benefit amounts and accelerated the start of monthly benefit payments to 1940. On the financing issues, the size of the reserve was reduced and a formal trust fund mechanism was created to embody the reserve.

Document 2.1
Excerpts from Governor Landon's Speech on Social Security, September 27, 1936

During the 1936 presidential campaign the Republican challenger to President Franklin D. Roosevelt, Gov. Alf Landon of Kansas, made repeal of the newly enacted Social Security program a major plank in his campaign. On September 26, during a Sunday night speech in Milwaukee, Wisconsin, Landon denounced Social Security in strong terms, suggesting that if he were elected the program would be replaced with a noncontributory, needs-based, scheme.

I am going to talk tonight about economic security—economic security for the men and women obliged to earn their daily bread through their own daily labor.

There is no question that is of deeper concern to us all. Even in good times there is ever present in the minds of workers the fear of unemployment. In periods of deep depression there is the fear of protracted idleness. And always, in prosperity and in depression, there is the ever-present dread of penniless old age.

From the standpoint of the individual, I know of no more intensely human problem than that of economic security. From the standpoint of the government there is no problem calling more for a sympathetic understanding and the best efforts of heart and mind.

But to solve the problem we must have more than a warm heart and a generous impulse. We must have the capacity and the determination to translate our feelings into a practical, workable program. Daydreams do not pay pensions.

Now in broad terms there are two ways to approach the development of a program of economic security. One is to assume that human beings are improvident—that it is necessary to have the stern management of a paternal government to force them to provide for themselves—that it is proper for the government to force them to save for their old age.

The other approach is to recognize that in an industrial nation some people are unable to provide for their old age—that it is a responsibility of society to take care of them.

The act passed by the present administration is based upon the first of these approaches. It assumes that Americans are irresponsible. It assumes that old-age pensions are necessary because Americans lack the foresight to provide for their old age. I refuse to accept any such judgment of my fellow-citizens.

I believe that, as a nation, we can afford old-age pensions—that in a highly industrialized country they are necessary. I believe in them as a matter of social justice.

Because of my firm belief in the justice, necessity and feasibility of old-age pensions, I am going to discuss the present act with the utmost frankness. It is a glaring example of the bungling and waste that have characterized this administration's attempts to fulfill its benevolent purposes. It endangers the whole cause of social security in this country.

In my own judgment—and I have examined it most carefully—this law is unjust, unworkable, stupidly drafted and wastefully financed.

Broadly speaking, the act is divided into three main sections. One deals with compulsory old-age insurance. It applies to about one-half of our working population. It excludes, among others, farmers and farm laborers and domestic servants.

Another part of the act attempts to force States to adopt unemployment insurance systems.

The third part of the act provides old-age pensions for those in need who do not come under the compulsory plan.

Now let us look at the so-called old-age insurance plan in more detail, and on a dollars and cents basis. In other words, let us see just how much the old people of this country are going to get, when they are going to get it and who is going to pay for it.

Here we are dealing not with opinions but with hard facts, with the provisions of the law.

Under the compulsory insurance plan of the present law, none of our old people will get any pension at all until 1942. If you happen to be one of those insured—and remember about half of our workers are not—you have to earn, on the average, $125 a month every single month for the next twenty years to get a monthly pension of $37.50. And you have to earn $125 a month for the next forty-five years to get a pension of $59.38 a month. Besides, these sums have to support both the worker and his wife.

But meanwhile, beginning Jan. 1 of next year, 26,000,000 working people begin paying taxes to provide these pensions. Beginning next January employers must start deducting these taxes from the pay envelopes of their employees and turn them over to the government.

Beginning next January employers must, in addition, begin paying taxes on the payrolls out of which your wages are to come. This is the largest tax bill in history. And to call it "social security" is a fraud on the working-man.

These taxes start at the rate of $2 in taxes for every $100 in wages. They increase until it is $6 in taxes for every $100 in wages.

We are told that this $6 will be equally divided between the employer and the employee. But this is not so, and for a very simple reason. The actual fact will be, in almost every case, that the whole tax will be borne either by the employee or by the consumer through higher prices. That is the history of all such taxes. This is because the tax is imposed in such a way that, if the employer is to stay in business, he must shift the tax to someone else.

Do not forget this: Such an excessive tax on payrolls is beyond question a tax on employment. In prosperous times it slows down the advance of wages and holds back re-employment. In bad times it increases unemployment, and unemployment breaks wage scales. The Republican party rejects any feature of any plan that hinders re-employment.

Yet it is solely by such tax that the plan of this administration is financed. Its entire cost is to be raised by a 3 per cent tax on wages and a 3 per cent on payrolls. I do not see how any one can believe that the average man making $100 a month should be compelled to save 3 per cent of his wages. Certainly he is not in a position to save 6 per cent of his wages.

One more sample of the injustice of this law is this: Some workers who come under this new Federal insurance plan are taxed more and get less than workers who come under State laws already in force.

For instance, under the new law many workers now 50 years old must pay burdensome taxes for the next fifteen years in order to receive a pension when they are 65; whereas those of the same age who come under some State laws pay no taxes and yet actually get a larger pension when they reach the age of 65.

These are a few reasons why I called this law unjust and stupidly drafted.

There is a further important point in connection with the compulsory saving provided by the plan of the present administration. According to this plan, our workers are forced to save for a lifetime. What happens to their savings? The administration's theory is that they go into a reserve fund, that they will be invested at interest and that in due time this interest will help pay pensions. The people who drew this law understand nothing of government finance.

Let us trace the process step by step.

The worker's cash comes into the treasury. What is done with it? The law requires the treasury to buy government bonds. What happens when the treasury buys government bonds? Well, at present when there is a deficit, the treasury gives some nice new bonds in exchange for the cash which the treasury gives the treasury. Now what happens to the cash which the treasury gives the treasury? The answer is painfully simple. We have good spenders in Washington, and they spend the cash that the treasury gives the treasury.

Now I know all this sounds silly, but it happens to be an accurate recital of what this administration has been foolish enough to enact into law.

Let me explain it in another way—in simple terms of the family budget.

The father of the family is a kindly man, so kindly that he borrows all he can to add to the family's pleasure. At the same time he impresses upon his sons and daughters the necessity of saving for their old age.

Every month they bring 6 per cent of their wages to him so that he may act as trustee and invest their savings for their old age. The father decides that the best investments are his own IOU. So every month he puts aside in a box his IOU carefully executed, and, moreover, bearing interest at 3 per cent.

And every month he spends the money that his children bring him, partly in meeting his regular expenses, and the rest in various experiments that fascinate him.

Years pass, the children grow old, the day comes when they have to open their father's box. What do they find? Roll after roll of neatly executed IOUs.

I am not exaggerating the folly of this legislation. The saving it forces on our workers is a cruel hoax.

There is every probability that the cash they pay in will be used for current deficits and new extravagances. We are going to have trouble enough to carry out an economy program without having the Treasury flush with money drawn from the workers.

Personally, I do not want the Treasury flush with trust funds—funds which the trustee can mingle with its own general funds. I want the Treasury to be a position where it must consider every penny it spends. I want the Secretary of the Treasury to be obliged to say to committees of Congress every time a new appropriation is proposed, "Gentlemen, you will have to provide some new taxes if you do this."

With this social security money alone running into billions of dollars, all restraint on Congress will be off. Maybe some people want that, but I don't.

And even if the budget is balanced, the fact that there is a billion dollars and more of extra cash on hand each year that can be made instantly available for any purpose by issuing special bonds to the trust fund is too great a temptation.

This temptation is further increased by another provision of the law—that provision relating to how much of the cash collected will be paid out in pensions. During the next ten years only 10 cents out of every dollar collected from the workers will be paid out as benefits. And from now until 1950 only 16 cents out of every dollar collected will be paid out as benefits.

The workers asked for a pension and all they have received is just another tax.

There is one more point I want to mention about the compulsory old age pension system. This is the question of keeping records.

The administration is preparing a plan, the exact nature of which we shall not know until after the election, for keeping the life records of 26,000,000 of our working people. These records are necessary because the amount of the pension anyone is to receive depends upon how much he has earned after the act goes into effect.

The record must show every job a man has, and every dollar he earns so long as he is working at something that brings him under the plan. If he is working in a factory and changes to another factory, a government agent must keep track of him.

Imagine the vast army of clerks which will be necessary to keep these records. Another army of field investigators will be necessary to check up on the people whose records are not clear, or regarding whom current information is not coming in. And so bureaucracy will grow and grow, and Federal snooping flourish.

To get a workable old-age pension plan we must repeal the present compulsory insurance plan. The Republican Party is pledged to do this. The Republican Party will have nothing to do with any plan that involves prying into the personal working records of 26,000,000 people. . . .

This brings us to the third main feature of the present act—the section dealing with pensions for the needy aged not covered by the compulsory insurance plan. This part of the present law can be made to serve as the foundation of a real old age pension plan. This, the Republican Party proposes to do. It proposes to overhaul this section and make of it a workable, common-sense plan—a plan to be administered by the States.

We propose through amendments to this section to provide for every American citizen over 65 the supplementary payment necessary to give a minimum income sufficient to protect him or her from want.

Frankly, I am not in a position to state with finality the total cost of this plan. . . . [T]he plan which we propose will be much less expensive than the plan of the present administration because we will not create a needless reserve fund of $47,000,000,000.

Our plan will be on a pay-as-you-go basis, with the result that we will know year by year just what our pensions are costing us. That is sound, common-sense financing. . . . The precise method of taxation used will depend upon the decision of Congress working in cooperation with the Treasury. But there are three essential principles which should be complied with: The necessary funds should be raised by means of a special tax earmarked for this purpose so that the already difficult problem of budget-balancing may not be further complicated. The tax should be direct and visible. And the tax should be widely distributed. . . .

Let me repeat! I am a profound believer in the justice and necessity of old age pensions. My criticism of the present act is not that its purpose is bad. It is that this act will involve a cruel disappointment for those of our people least able to bear the shock of disappointment.

To these—our old people, our workers struggling for better conditions, our infirm—I will not promise the moon. I promise only what I know can be performed: economy, a living pension and such security as can be provided by a generous people.

Source: "Text of Gov. Landon's Milwaukee Address on Economic Security," *New York Times,* September 27, 1936, 6. Copyright © 1936 by The New York Times Co. Reprinted with permission.

Document 2.2
Governor Winant's Letter of Resignation, September 28, 1936

The Republican head of the Social Security Board, former New Hampshire governor John Winant, temporarily resigned his position so that he could publicly speak out against Landon's stance on Social Security and in defense of the program. In his letter of resignation, Winant expressed his view that the Social Security program ought not be a subject of partisan dispute.

My dear Mr. President:

On August 14, 1935 the Social Security Act became law. The administration of its major provisions was entrusted to a Board of three members. Under the law not more than two members of the Board could be "members of the same political party." You named me to the Board and as a Republican and as the minority member my appointment was confirmed by the Senate on August 23, 1935, together with the other two members, without objection.

It was clearly the intention of Congress to create a nonpartisan Board, with personnel protected under Civil Service, and to insure non-partisan administration of the Act. It has been so administered.

The Act itself was viewed as a non-partisan, humanitarian measure. Three times as many Republicans in Congress voted for the Social Security Act as voted against it.

Having seen the tragedy of war, I have been consistently interested in the ways of peace. Having seen some of the cruelties of the depression, I have wanted to help with others in lessening the hardships, the suffering, and the humiliations forced upon American citizens because of our previous failure as a nation to provide effective social machinery for meeting the problems of dependency and unemployment. The Social Security Act is America's answer to this great human need.

The references to the problems of social security in the platform of the Republican Party were disappointing. It was my hope that the position of the Republican presidential nominee might be less so.

Today we know that both the Republican platform and the Republican candidate have definitely rejected the constructive provisions of the Social Security Act, only to fall back upon the dependency dole—a dole with a means test, which in my state includes the pauper's oath and disenfranchisement.

The statements that provisions of this Act are "a fraud on the working man" and "a cruel hoax" I believe are untrue. They are charges with regard to a measure which had the support of 372 members of the House of Representatives, as against 33 opposed—which met with the approval of 77 members of the United States Senate with only six against—which was upheld by the votes of Senator Hiram Johnson, Senator LaFollette, Senator Costigan, Senator Wagner and Representative David J. Lewis—a measure which was advocated by such advisers to the Committee on Economic Security as President Green of the American Federation of Labor, President Frank P. Graham of the University of North Carolina, Miss Grace Abbott, former Chief of the Children's Bureau, and Monsigneur John A. Ryan of the National Catholic Welfare Conference.

I have never assumed that the Social Security Act was without fault. I had assumed and even hoped that time and experience might dictate many and important changes. As you stated when you signed the Act on August 14, 1935: "This law represents a cornerstone in

John G. Winant was the first chair of the new Social Security Board and an ardent defender of the ideal of the Social Security program as nonpartisan and nonparticipatory in party politics.
Source: SSA History Archives.

a structure which is being built, but is by no means complete." But Governor Landon's address at Milwaukee on the Social Security Act was not a plea for the improvement of the Act; it was a plea to scrap the Act.

I am interested in the social security program not from a partisan viewpoint. I am interested in it as a humanitarian measure. Governor Landon has made the problem of social security a major issue in this campaign and I cannot support him. I do not feel that members of independent Commissions or Boards, such as the Social Security Board, should take an active part in politics and moreover I was appointed and confirmed as the minority member. While I retain this position I am not free to defend the Act. Therefore, I am tending you my resignation as a member of the Social Security Board.

No work I have ever undertaken seemed more worthwhile to me than my brief service on the Social Security Board. May I thank you for the opportunity of this service and join you in defending it.

Sincerely,

John G. Winant

Source: Copy of letter in Social Security Administration History Archives, Revolving Files, Folder: Winant, John G.

Document 2.3
President Roosevelt's Reply to Winant's Letter of Resignation, September 30, 1936

President Roosevelt appointed Winant to head the Social Security Board in order to convey a message that the program ought to be above partisan considerations. So he viewed the issue here in the same way as Winant and was in agreement with Winant's arguments and reasons for resigning. Roosevelt was also probably genuinely reluctant to see Winant leave, as they had a long-standing political friendship dating from their days as fellow governors. Winant, for his part, was dedicated to Franklin Roosevelt, and upon Roosevelt's death in 1945 Winant abruptly ended his own career in public life.

Dear Governor Winant:

Your letter tendering your resignation as a member of the Social Security Board greatly distresses me. You are, of course, right in regarding the Social Security Act as "America's Answer" to the "great human need" of "effective social machinery for meeting the problems of dependency and unemployment."

Like you, also, "I have never assumed that the Social Security Act was without fault. I had assumed and even hoped that time and experience might dictate many and important changes."

The Act was conceived and passed by the Congress as a humanitarian measure. Its passage transcended party lines. The opposition in both houses was, practically speaking, negligible. I share your regret that the evanescent passions of a political campaign have fanned the flames of partisan hostility to this non-partisan legislation.

Equally right are you in recognizing the "intention of Congress to create a non-partisan board, with personnel protected under civil service, and to insure non-partisan administration of the Act." Your appointment was intended to insure that it would be so administered. And, as you state, "it has been so administered."

Under such conditions I should have thought that you might have felt free to correct any misconception of the purpose of the legislation or any misinterpretation of its details. Appropriate education of the public mind regarding public measures is one of the inherent duties of an administrator.

For that reason I have hesitated to accept your resignation. I did not wish to lose the benefit of your devoted and disinterested service in the administration of the social security program. Yet, upon reflection and after talking with you, I have come to appreciate your position and the sense of public duty which impelled your resignation and your wish to be free as a citizen, not simply to clear up misconceptions and misinterpretations of the Act, but actively to defend the "constructive provisions" of the Act and to oppose spurious substitutes.

It is, therefore, with the deepest regret that I yield to your wish and accept your resignation. My regret is tempered by the knowledge that you have resigned only in order the better to defend the great work which you have so well begun.

Very sincerely yours,

Franklin D. Roosevelt

Source: Copy of letter in Social Security Administration History Archives, Revolving Files, Folder: Winant, John G.

Document 2.4
The Supreme Court Ruling on the Social Security Act, May 24, 1937

Four Social Security Act cases made their way to the Supreme Court during its October 1936 term (two were joined in a single ruling, resulting in only three rulings from the Court). One case challenged the old-age insurance program, and three challenged the unemployment compensation program of the Social Security Act.

On May 24, 1937, the Supreme Court handed down its decision in the three cases. Justice Benjamin Cardozo wrote the majority opinion in the first two cases. The first, Steward Machine Co. v. Davis, *upheld the unemployment provisions of the act and was cited several times in the second case,* Helvering v. Davis, *which established that the Social Security program passed constitutional muster. In* Helvering, *the Court ruled 7–2 in support of the old-age insurance program, and even though two justices disagreed with the decision, no separate dissents were written.* (Authors' note: *Footnotes and most legal references have been deleted in this excerpt.*)

Helvering v. Davis, 301 U.S. 619

Mr. Justice CARDOZO delivered the opinion of the Court.

. . . In this case Titles VIII and II are the subject of attack. Title VIII lays another excise upon employers in addition to the one imposed by Title IX (though with different exemptions). It lays a special income tax upon employees to be deducted from their wages and paid by the employers. Title II provides for the payment of Old Age Benefits, and supplies the motive and occasion, in the view of the assailants of the statute, for the levy of the taxes imposed by Title VIII. . . .

First: Questions as to the remedy invoked by the complainant confront us at the outset. . . .

Second: The scheme of benefits created by the provisions of Title II is not in contravention of the limitations of the Tenth Amendment.

Congress may spend money in aid of the "general welfare.". . . There have been great statesmen in our history who have stood for other views. We will not resurrect the contest. It is now settled by decision. *United States v. Butler, supra.* The conception of the spending power advocated by Hamilton and strongly reinforced by Story has prevailed over that of Madison, which has not been lacking in adherents. Yet difficulties are left when the power is conceded. The line must still be drawn between one welfare and another, between particular and general. Where this shall be placed cannot be known through a formula in advance of the event. There is a middle ground or certainly a penumbra in which discretion is at large. The discretion, however, is not confided to the courts. The discretion belongs to Congress, unless the choice is clearly wrong, a display of arbitrary power is not an exercise of judgment. This is now familiar law. . . . Nor is the concept of the general welfare static. Needs that were narrow or parochial a century ago may be interwoven in our day with the well-being of the nation. What is critical or urgent changes with the times.

The purge of nation-wide calamity that began in 1929 has taught us many lessons. Not the least is the solidarity of interests that may once have seemed to be divided. Unemployment spreads from state to state, the hinterland now settled that in pioneer days gave an avenue of escape. . . . Spreading from state to state, unemployment is an ill not particular but general, which may be checked, if Congress so determines, by the resources of the nation. If this can have been doubtful until now, our ruling today in the case of the *Steward Machine Co., supra,* has set the doubt at rest. But the ill is all one or at least not greatly different whether men are thrown out of work because there is no longer work to do or because the disabilities of age make them incapable of doing it. Rescue becomes necessary irrespective of the cause. The hope behind this statute is to save men and women from the rigors of the poor house as well as from the haunting fear that such a lot awaits them when journey's end is near.

Congress did not improvise a judgment when it found that the award of old age benefits would be conducive to the general welfare The President's Committee on Economic Security made an investigation and report, aided by a research staff of Government officers and employees, and by an Advisory Council and seven other advisory groups. Extensive hearings followed before the House Committee on Ways and Means and the Senate Committee on Finance. A great mass of evidence was brought together supporting the policy which finds expression in the act. Among the relevant facts are these: The number of persons in the United States 65 years of age or over is increasing proportionately as well as absolutely. What is even more important the number of such persons unable to take care of themselves is growing at a threatening pace. More and more our population is becoming urban and industrial instead of rural and agricultural. The evidence is impressive that among industrial workers the younger men and women are preferred over the older. In time of retrenchment the older are commonly the first to go, and even if retained, their wages are likely to be lowered. The plight of men and women at so low an age as 40 is hard, almost hopeless, when they are driven to seek for reemployment. Statistics are in the brief. . . .

The problem is plainly national in area and dimensions. Moreover laws of the separate states cannot deal with it effectively. Congress, at least, had a basis for that belief. . . .

Whether wisdom or unwisdom resides in the scheme of benefits set forth in Title II, it is not for us to say. The answer to such inquiries must come from Congress, not the courts. Our concern here as often is with power, not with wisdom. Counsel for respondent has recalled to us the virtues of self-reliance and frugality. There is a possibility, he says, that aid from a paternal government may sap those sturdy virtues and breed a race of weaklings. If Massachusetts so believes and shapes her laws in that conviction must her breed of sons be changed, he asks, because some other philosophy of government finds favor in the halls of Congress? But the answer is not doubtful. One might ask with equal reason whether the system of protective tariffs is to be set aside at will in one state or another whenever local policy prefers the rule of *laissez faire.* The issue is a closed one. It was fought out long ago. When money is spent to promote the general welfare, the concept of welfare or the opposite is shaped by Congress, not the states. So the concept be not arbitrary, the locality must yield. . . .

Third: Title II being valid, there is no occasion to inquire whether Title VIII would have to fall if Title II were set at naught.

The argument for the respondent is that the provisions of the two titles dovetail in such a way as to justify the conclusion that Congress would have been unwilling to pass one without the other. The argument for petitioners is that the tax moneys are not earmarked, and that Congress is at liberty to spend them as it will. The usual separability clause is embodied in the act.

We find it unnecessary to make a choice between the arguments and so leave the question open.

Fourth: The tax upon employers is a valid excise or duty upon the relation of employment.

As to this we need not add to our opinion in *Steward Machine v. Davis, supra,* where we considered a like question in respect of Title IX.

Fifth: The tax is not invalid as a result of its exemptions.

Here again the opinion in *Steward Machine Co. v. Davis, supra,* says all that need be said.

Sixth: The decree of the Court of Appeals should be reversed and that of the District Court affirmed.

Ordered accordingly.

Mr. Justice MCREYNOLDS and Mr. Justice BUTLER are of opinion that the provisions of the Act here challenged are repugnant to the Tenth Amendment, and that the decree of the Circuit Court of Appeals should be affirmed.

Source: Supreme Court of the United States, No. 910, *Guy T. Helvering et al. vs. George P. Davis, Respondent,* 301 U.S. 619, May 24, 1937.

Document 2.5
Press Release Announcing Advisory Council, May 10, 1937

As part of their continuing opposition to the financing structure created in the 1935 Social Security Act, and in particular to the buildup of a large trust fund reserve, Sen. Arthur Vandenberg (R-Mich.), Sen. John G. Townsend (R-Del.), Rep. Daniel Reed (R-N.Y.), and Rep. Thomas Jenkins (R-Ohio), introduced Concurrent Resolution No. 4 in Congress in January 1937. This resolution called on the Social Security Board to report to Congress by May 1, 1937, on its "recommendations" concerning the "abandonment" of the full reserve system of Social Security financing.

The Senate Finance Committee held a hearing on the resolution on February 22, 1937, at which Senator Vandenberg tried to persuade Arthur Altmeyer, the Social Security Board chairman, to commit to abandoning full reserve financing. Altmeyer was determined to resist any such suggestion. The compromise solution that emerged called for the creation of an external advisory council to study this issue, as well as potential program expansion. Thus Vandenberg was able to put the issue of interest to him—the trust fund reserve—on the policy agenda, while Altmeyer got his issue of interest—program expansion—on the agenda as well.

Following the agreement between Vandenberg and Altmeyer, the chairman of the Senate Finance Committee, Pat Harrison (D-Miss.), and Altmeyer issued a joint press release—through the Press Service of the Social Security Board—announcing their sponsorship of the 1937–1938 Advisory Council on Social Security. The board went to great lengths to emphasize that it did not expect major changes to be recommended by this council. This would, however, prove to be a faulty expectation as the council report proved to be a major milestone on the path to the 1939 Social Security Amendments.

The bipartisan Social Security Board administered the Social Security program until a 1946 government reorganization. Shown here are board members at the time of the enactment of the 1939 Amendments. Left to right: Chairman Arthur J. Altmeyer, Ellen S. Woodward, and George E. Bigge. Source: SSA History Archives.

Social Security Advisory Council Is Appointed

Senator Pat Harrison, Chairman of the Committee on Finance of the United States Senate, and Arthur J. Altmeyer, Chairman of the Social Security Board, issued the following announcement concerning the creation of an Advisory Council on Social Security:

"At a hearing before the Committee on Finance of the United States Senate on February 22, 1937, it was agreed that the Chairman of the Committee on Finance would appoint a special committee to cooperate with the Social Security Board to study the advisability of amending Titles II and VIII of the Social Security Act. The Chairman of the Committee on Finance has appointed such a special committee consisting of Senator Pat Harrison, Senator Harry Flood Byrd, and Senator Arthur H. Vandenberg. It was agreed that this special committee in cooperation with the Social Security Board would appoint an Advisory Council on Social Security to assist in studying the advisability of amending Titles II and VIII of the Social Security Act.

"It is desired that the Advisory Council on Social Security cooperate with the Special Committee of the Committee on Finance of the United States Senate and with the Social Security Board in considering the following matters:

"(1) The advisability of commencing payment of monthly benefits under Title II sooner than January I, 1942;

"(2) The advisability of increasing the monthly benefits payable under Title II for those retiring in the early years;

"(3) The advisability of extending the benefits in Title II to persons who become incapacitated prior to age 65;

"(4) The advisability of extending the benefits of Title II to survivors of individuals entitled to such benefits;

"(5) The advisability of increasing the taxes less rapidly under Title VIII;

"(6) The advisability of extending the benefits under Title II to include groups now excluded;

"(7) The size, character and disposition of reserves;

"(8) Any other questions concerning the Social Security Act about which either the Special Senate Committee or the Social Security Board may desire the advice of the Advisory Council.

"It is understood that the Social Security Board will make all necessary studies and furnish all necessary technical assistance in connection with the consideration of the foregoing subjects. It is further understood that these subjects will be considered jointly by the Advisory Council, the Special Senate Committee, and the Social Security Board. . . ."

"The Advisory Council will be called together within the next thirty days for a preliminary discussion of the subjects concerning which advice is sought. At that time a program will be developed for future meetings. It is not expected that any fundamental changes in the Act will be recommended at this session of Congress."

The Social Security Board announced that it would not recommend any fundamental changes in the Social Security Act to this Congress, but would only make recommendations as regards matters of immediate concern regarding which there appears to be rather general agreement. The Board stated that most of the proposed amendments are designed to improve the administrative features of the Act as it is now written.

Source: Social Security Board press release, May 10, 1937. Copy in Social Security Administration History Archives, Revolving Files, Folder: Advisory Council 1938.

Document 2.6
Eleanor Lansing Dulles: "An Examination of the Reserve Problem," November 5, 1937

Eleanor Dulles, sister of Secretary of State John Foster Dulles, worked in Social Security Board's research and statistics component from early 1936 until 1942. In this capacity, she was part of the staff to the 1937–1938 Social Security advisory council. This report, presented as a briefing paper to the council, touches on the whole range of issues involving the role of the Social Security Trust Fund reserves, which was a topic of major interest for the council.

A. The Importance of the Reserve Question

The problem of the reserve method of financing old-age insurance is without doubt extremely important. Even though *some* critics have misinterpreted certain aspects of the question, it still raises major issues and calls for careful consideration.

One cause for misunderstanding is that many have failed to recognize, in considering the various aspects of the reserve question, that it should never be considered an end in itself. It is a means to an end; it is a carefully considered attempt to adjust federal financial planning to future obligations, to avoid double burdens in years to come, and to educate the public with regard to the cost and benefits of any old-age retirement system. If it falls to accomplish those purposes, it is indeed subject to serious criticism, but the objects are reasonable, constructive, and important to public welfare. . . .

Various measures have been suggested in Congress and elsewhere which affect both the theory and practice of financing old-age insurance. Some would so alter the present plan as to leave a very narrow margin at all times between receipts under Title VIII and expenditures under Title II. Various changes in the benefit formulas particularly those that increase the payments in the early years would, if allowed to have a direct influence on the reserve, reduce the accumulations and necessitate later Government subsidies. Other suggestions which delay or eliminate the higher tax rates under the present schedule would tend, if they are to be linked with appropriations and reserve, to prevent any substantial funds being transferred to the reserve. . . .

. . . There are three main lines of criticism of the reserve method of financing old-age insurance, first, contentions that it is unjust; second, assertions that it is based on unsound economic ideas; and third, that it is politically dangerous. . . .

B. Problems of Equity

. . . Many critics have charged that the younger workers could do better under private insurance, some have contended that the older workers benefit in an unfair way, while others believe that it is inequitable to secure the main financial support from the low income groups who will be taxed under the plan. These criticisms raise questions both with regard to fact and equity.

Those who argue that the younger workers could do better if they bought annuities from private companies are, of course, assuming that the employers' tax will in effect be paid by the workers themselves. This point can neither be proved or disproved at this time. For the sake of argument this assumption will be taken as substantially correct. It is, then, obvious from a study of the tables that some individuals . . . might . . . buy annuities from private companies which will be slightly to their advantage as compared with the Federal plan.

The assumptions which have to be made to establish the possibility of cases of this type are so exacting as to limit very greatly the number of persons to whom they might be applied. Workers have not in fact financed annuities of this sort on their own initiative and out of their own resources to any significant extent. . . . It is also evident that the entire tax is not apt to be passed on by the employer at all times and in all cases. . . .

Another suggested unfairness in giving older workers more benefits than they have bought by their contributions is a criticism not properly applicable to a *social* insurance system. . . . If it is good social policy to permit the older workers to qualify for benefits a little sooner, and at higher rates than would otherwise be the case, a method of financing these additional sums which diffuses the cost broadly over many groups and over a considerable period of time seems both fair and wise. . . .

The reasons for establishing a reserve method of financing for old-age insurance are connected in a number of ways with the desire to have a contributory system, but are even more definitely the outgrowth of the desire to equalize burdens ever time. . . .

Once the general characteristics of a contributory system have been accepted, it is practically impossible to justify any financial methods which do not set up a plan which is independent and self-sustaining for a considerable span of years. How far the budgeting for future benefits should be projected ahead is perhaps a matter of dispute, but clearly reasonable provision for later expenditures must be made. . . .

Efforts have been made to see that no individual suffers any real injustice. The attempt has been made to protect him as to both the capital value of the amounts paid in and the investment yield of these amounts. In certain instances, however, the plan has been modified so as to subordinate these individual rights and claims to the general aims of the social security program. . . .

Various new modifications of the contributory idea have been discussed by different groups. Some of these can quite easily be grafted on the present old age insurance system. Each of them, if adopted, would make reasonable some modification in the present reserve idea. . . .

In the first place if *coverage* were extended, either directly through taking in new groups or indirectly through adding survivors, dependents, or special types of benefits, the recourse to Federal revenue could be justified in theory because the individual benefiting would have paid taxes as a citizen to general revenues even though no special contributions had been made.

In the second place, if the benefit amounts could be made to approach the "normal levels" sooner, something closer to a pay-as-you-go system would inevitably result, but tax rates might have to approach more rapidly the maximum rate now anticipated. . . .

. . . if the minimum benefits were raised, subsidies to meet the cost of the lower scale annuities would be almost inevitable. It would be unreasonable to ask a special group of wage earners, such as those covered by the Act, to pay this additional expense. Similarly the reduction of the higher benefits would so modify the insurance idea as to lead to measures calling for a wider diffusion of the cost. . . .

. . . It is probable that most of the advocates of such a system would be less eager to see it adopted if they put their emphasis on the possible 9 or 10 percent deductions from pay rolls which it might necessitate at a later date. On no sound basis can anyone, who has studied the trend of future payments and calculated the probable effects of various formulae, advocate the substitution of this method of financing for the present method without indicating the necessity of these higher pay-roll taxes at a later date, or else suggesting now types of revenue which might be used when pay-roll levies already indicated fail to meet the bill.

Those who suggest that the present plan is inequitable do not usually consider the danger that any other plan might deceive present contributors and bring such more injustice to the worker and the citizen than any of those characteristics now alleged as flaws in the system. The greatest possible injustice would be the failure to make good at a later date. . . .

C. Economic Criticisms

A number of arguments have been advanced to show that the reserve method of financing old-age insurance in economically unsound. These arguments are partly theoretical and partly practical. Some of these relate to the pay-roll tax, as it now stands in the Act, and some to the accumulation of funds derived from the annual appropriation to meet a future obligation. . . .

It is obvious that those who wish to see a general rise in the standard of living wish to keep taxes from pay rolls and other sources as low as possible in view of the many other obligations of the Government. They may advocate a one, two, or three percent tax rate in the abstract, but they can hardly insist that such rates are wise or sound without showing what portion of the social security program such taxes will pay and without supplementing their arguments with calculations of funds which might perhaps be secured with other sources of revenue.

Few of the present advocates of lower taxes, or "pay-as-you-go" financing, are likely to prefer to postpone increases in schedules for very long if they think that in the end they will have to pay more in taxes than would otherwise have been the case. . . . It is probable that some of those who attempt to do away with the reserve by cutting pay-roll taxes think that these higher rates of taxes can be avoided. It is natural for the individual to think that he can escape. It is less justifiable for a Nation to assume that it can escape the cost merely by keeping the rates temporarily below figures which have been agreed to by all competent authorities as necessary to pay for the program. . . .

The attack on the reserve system which takes the form of urging a lower pay-roll tax now seems in the light of these various factors to be an attempt to avoid the issue. At no time is the rate of the pay-roll tax above what is estimated to be necessary to finance the system. If it should be cut to a lower figure, it can only be on the assumption of Federal subsidies. In other words, any cut in the pay-roll tax implies an increase in other forms of taxation. . . .

Similarly, it is not reasonable to think that this year's reserve can worry any one. It is unlikely that a Reserve Account of two or three billion dollars could be seriously attacked by any economist. The argument has been projected into a dimly seen distant future and the discussion focused on the figure of 47 billion dollars, which we might know to be remote from realities if we could see into the future. . . .

One of the offsetting factors that should be noted is the fact that funds collected under the social security taxes may affect Treasury financing in such a way as to release funds otherwise absorbed by government borrowing and increase the industrial demand for consumer and producer goods. Another offsetting factor would be the use of pay-roll tax collections as a substitute for other forms of saving. If, for instance, the wage earner knowing that he would receive a retirement income ceased to buy other types of insurance, the result might be that he would spend exactly the same amount on his current budget but would save through the old-age insurance rather than through private companies. Clearly such a result would prevent pay-roll taxes from having a deflationary influence. . . .

The economic criticisms which bear on the investment of the fund have been alluded to above in connection with the possibility of national saving. . . . Almost certainly a large part of the debt held by the public would be retired under the reserve system. . . .

D. Political Questions

Certain doubts and fears have been brought forward which are largely political in nature. They relate to future Congressional appropriations and the expenditure of public funds as affected by social security finance. Many commentators have indicated that they consider future Congressional action highly uncertain and unpredictable. They allege for this reason that the plan gives a fictitious illusion of security unwarranted by the legal guarantees and requirements of the Act. They point to the lack of direct connection between Titles II and VIII, and say that since they are not directly linked together, Congress may fail to appropriate funds according to schedule.

Some go further than this and say that, although Congress may follow the schedule of payments set before them by the Secretary of Treasury on advice of actuaries, the fund will be merely a "paper" reserve, and that Congress at a certain stage may consider the Reserve Account an easy source of money. This criticism overlooks the fact, in the first place, that the reserve is not an appropriable sum of money but consists of government obligations which a Congress or Administration could not spend. The possible extravagance which might result, in case regular appropriations to the reserve are made, would take the form of devoting the funds currently received from the Reserve Account, when the Treasury borrows from the Account, to wasteful and unnecessary purposes. The appropriate use as indicated in the Act would be the retirement of the outstanding debt. If there were extravagance of this sort, the debt both to the Old-Age Reserve Account and to the public would rise. This course of action would indeed be an exploitation of public confidence if it should be followed.

These objections call for little comment here. No law can be so drawn as to tie future Congresses against their own interests and their own ideas of the public welfare. If some later session of Congress wishes to pursue a shortsighted policy and to squander public funds, there are dozens of ways in which these ends can be accomplished. There are various ways of borrowing or inflating the currency and exploiting the tax capacity of the nation which cannot be excluded by any clause in this or in any other Act against the unwillingness or inability of Congress to follow the program laid down. There are bulwarks stronger than legislative devices. These bulwarks are supported by a tremendous political pressure of 30 or 40 million holders of Social Security Account Numbers, and almost as many persons who have claims for future benefits.

This group of objections does not seem sufficiently strong to justify any modification in the plan for financing social security if that plan proves on other grounds to be desirable and sound.

Another group of questions which bear on the advisability of the reserve method of financing is raised by those who are concerned with the influence it will have on the Federal debt. . . . Some say that the debt now standing at a little over 36 billion dollars is less than the estimated reserve by approximately 30 percent. They go on to say that even if the present debt were big enough to equal the probable reserve or, to put the matter in another way, if the reserve should rise to approximately 36 billion dollars, some of the new obligations would prove to be a net increase in the total government debt. This being true, the debt service or annual interest charge would increase.

One reason why these arguments are difficult to handle in a conclusive manner is that it is impossible to estimate what the debt is likely to be come 30 or 40 years hence if there were no reserve fund. The future size of the present debt will be the result of a number of different economic and political considerations, and will be expressed in government policy quite independent, for the most part, of social security financing. The total debt will increase only if it is the deliberate intent of Congress to permit such a situation to result from the tax and spending programs. It is quite possible to use a major part of the social security reserves to reduce the present publicly-held debt. To put this more concretely, funds coming in as a result of social security taxes can, if equaled by appropriations to the reserve, furnish resources for the retirement, either at maturity or by purchases in the open market, of the existing publicly-held debt. . . .

As at present set forth in the Act, the reserve holds government obligations, but the Treasury is free to use the funds resulting from this borrowing process in a variety of ways. It can spend the cash for current expenditures, avoiding other types of borrowing. It can retire certain parts of its debt as indicated above. It can also invest in new enterprises which will yield a return currently in new income in much the same way as private business. The fourth possibility is that the funds will be sterilized or hoarded which is extremely unlikely, although it might occur for short times in respect to small portions of the funds. . . .

It may, of course, prove advisable after further exploration of the subject to provide for special types of investments for designated portions of the reserve fund, but such a course of action is not necessary to give security or meaning to the reserve fund. The present provisions safeguard the interests of the beneficiary without disturbing the natural course of Treasury activities.

A further set of objections to the reserve have been brought forward in connection with the interest payable to the Reserve Account. Some have said that these payments constitute Federal subsidies and are a disguised form of assistance to the fund. They urge that an outright subsidy would be more honest and call for less complicated bookkeeping. There is no valid support for this argument. Other trust funds have been set up in the government on a similar basis and have stood the test of time. The fact that these trust funds are smaller does not alter the nature of the relations involved in accumulating securities and investing these funds. Also, the Treasury would have to borrow elsewhere and, in that case, would have to pay both interest and subsidy.

One might well ask whether, if the funds in the reserve fund are to be used by the Treasury, they should be free of all interest charges, when the government, borrowing from outside investors, pays a regular return? If such a policy were pursued, it would, of course, mean that the beneficiaries were subsidizing the general taxpayer. . . .

If the interest fixed in the Act is not "too high," there is no element of subsidy. It is possible that a different procedure might be developed, allowing some fluctuation in the rate of interest payable on the fund. If this rate were tied to the rates on other outstanding government obligations, it would not fluctuate very much from the present level prescribed. It is obvious why this alternative policy was not developed in the first instance. It would complicate considerably the attempt to estimate future reserve accumulations. Moreover, there would be little gain except for the moral and psychological effect of keeping more closely in touch with current money market conditions. Each of these aspects of the situation becomes important only when a very *large* reserve has been accumulated. If and when such funds are held in the Reserve Account, further consideration of these matters might be called for. . . .

[Section E—How the System Works—omitted.]

F. Types of Change Suggested

. . . The main types of modification so far suggested are two. One would be the stepping up of the rates more gradually, the other to the elimination from the present Act of the higher rates and stopping the schedule at a total of 4 or 5 percent.

The first of these suggestions has been urgently brought forward by those who wish to shift the balance somewhat between generations, and also those who wish to pare down the amounts going to reserve. It would be the less drastic of the two suggestions and for that reason would give less satisfaction to the critics. The main principles are not sacrificed and in the main the contributory idea is safeguarded. The arguments against such a move are that it gives no great relief to the taxpayer while it does lessen the self-sufficiency of the scheme. Moreover, it might well happen that the years of step-up were unfavorable years. Many unpredictable factors would determine whether or not it was easier on the economic system. It is clearly a compromise plan and one which does not elicit a very eager response for that reason.

The second suggestion has been more actively put forward. It would actually face more squarely the possibility of a Federal subsidy. . . .

G. General Conclusions

A few remarks in summary may indicate some of the reasons for holding to the general principles of a financial program such as that already outlined. . . .

. . . [I]t is clear that if there is a contributory system and if the coverage is limited, it is almost necessary to have a reserve system. If opinion and policy should swing to the other extreme and greatly extend coverage, modifications in the contributory plan would have to be made and these would in turn indicate the reasonableness of subsidies out of general taxation. This other policy would, however, call for a large increase in total benefits because of new and non-contributing groups of beneficiaries, and the question of how much tax paying capacity the country has for this purpose would be squarely before Congress.

The general purposes of the reserve have been indicated at the outset. It is the purpose of this type of system to set the financial house in order so that later commitments will be met. Its object is also to see that those who are to benefit later shall face honestly the extent of the costs. Someone must pay for these benefits and the man who is to receive the annuity must participate on a sound basis. Since the Treasury sets up the machinery which makes possible the payment of monthly annuities, its task must be lightened by reasonable provisions for coming expenditures. Its debt and tax positions must be adjusted gradually to a growing load.

Changes must be made from time to time, but it would be unfortunate to go backward just as forward progress is becoming more evident.

Source: Social Security Administration History Archives, Revolving Files, Folder: Dulles, Eleanor Lansing.

Document 2.7
Senator Vandenberg's Letter on the Reserve, April 25, 1938
While the debate over the reserve was taking place within the Advisory Council, Senator Vandenberg attempted to lobby for his viewpoint by sending a letter to the Social Security Board asking the board to agree in advance that payroll taxes needed to be cut. (Authors' note: *The emphases are in the original document.*)

My dear Mr. Altmeyer,

If the pay roll taxes—now 2% divided equally on 30,000,000 employees and their employers—could be reduced at the present time, it would clearly be a great and essential relief not only to Business but also to labor. These pay roll taxes now constitute a major load on commerce. If the load may be *safely* lightened, without impairing the integrity of the pension system, the stimulation to suffering Business will be profound. I do not need to reiterate my own view, which I have been urging for more than a year, that the load *can* be safely lightened, still leaving the pension system on a sound actuarial basis, *if we frankly abandon the needless full reserve system and proceed on a pay-as-you-go basis with a contingent reserve only.* I do not need to reiterate that I have produced the Presidents of seventy of the leading life insurance companies to sustain the propriety and wisdom of this change.

One year ago your Board, in cooperation with Congress, created an able, expert, non-partisan Advisory Council to study this and other related problems connected with the Social Security Act. Six months ago the Council proceeded to its task. It has not yet reported. I fully realize the size and perplexity of its assignment; and the importance of *sound* findings. I have declined, thus far, to join in any efforts to change the pay roll taxes ahead of a report from this Council—because I believe the "full reserve" system must change *before* the taxes can change. The taxes, in my view, *must* depend upon the *system*.

Under these circumstances, and in the presence of the present economic emergency, I inquire whether we may not now hopefully ask for a preliminary report from the Advisory Council within the next few weeks as a basis for Congressional action on pay roll taxes before the present session adjourns. If it be authentically determined that the present pay roll taxes *can* be safely reduced *now*—through a change in the "reserve system"—I believe Congress would greatly welcome a recommendation for the alternative system on a sound actuarial basis—and I am certain nothing would be more helpful as a powerful factor in the anti-depression campaign in which we are all now engaged.

I shall appreciate a report indicating the status of the work of the Advisory Council and answering the request for an immediate report.

Cordially and faithfully,

(signed) A. H. Vandenberg

Source: National Archives II, RG-47, Records of the Social Security Board, Records of the Office of the Commissioner, Chairman's File, 1935–1942, Box 99, Folder 705 (Old-Age Reserves Correspondence).

Document 2.8
President Roosevelt's Letter to the Social Security Board, April 28, 1938

As the advisory council was nearing the final stages of its work, Arthur Altmeyer arranged for President Roosevelt to send a letter, drafted by Altmeyer, to the Social Security Board expressing FDR's broad support for significant program expansion.

My dear Mr. Chairman:

I am very anxious that in the press of administrative duties the Social Security Board will not lose sight of the necessity of studying ways and means of improving and extending the provisions of the Social Security Act.

The enactment of the Social Security Act marked a great advance in affording more equitable and effective protection to the people of this country against widespread and growing economic hazards. The successful operation of the Act is the best proof that it was soundly conceived. However, it would be unfortunate if we assumed that it was complete and final. Rather, we should be constantly seeking to perfect and strengthen it in the light of our accumulating experience and growing appreciation of social needs.

I am particularly anxious that the Board give attention to the development of a sound plan for liberalizing the old-age insurance system. In the development of such a plan I should like to have the Board give consideration to the feasibility of extending its coverage, commencing the payment of old-age insurance annuities at an earlier date than January 1, 1942, paying larger benefits than now provided in the Act for those retiring during the earlier years of the system, providing benefits for aged wives and widows, and providing benefits for young children of insured persons dying before reaching retirement age. It is my hope that the Board will be prepared to submit its recommendations before Congress reconvenes in January.

Very truly yours,

[President Roosevelt]

Source: The Public Papers and Addresses of Franklin D. Roosevelt, 1938 Volume (New York: Macmillan, 1941), 300–301.

Document 2.9
Edwin Witte on the Reserve, June 17, 1938

Edwin Witte and Albert Linton were members of the 1937–1938 Advisory Council on Social Security. Witte—the former executive director of President Roosevelt's Committee on Economic Security—and Linton—an insurance company executive—were at opposite ends of the debate about the reserve fund. Witte viewed it as essential to the sound operation of the Social Security program; Linton supported the Republican critique of the reserve as unnecessary and problematic. They debated this matter at length within the council. In this speech, Witte emphasizes the importance of the trust fund reserve.

. . . Of the present social security program, old-age insurance remains the part that is most criticized. The criticisms come from both the Left and the Right, and, strangely, both the Left and the Right are making essentially the same arguments. The criticisms of both center around the alleged large reserve in the old age insurance system. Both the radicals and conservatives are saying that if the attempt to build up any reserve is abandoned and a "pay-as-you-go" system of financing is submitted, it will be possible at one and the same time to increase benefits and to reduce taxes.

The term "pay-as-you-go" has great popular appeal and thus far the public has not grasped the idea that the so-called pay-as-you-go method of financing old-age insurance is a complete misnomer. As used by both its radical and conservative advocates, it means raising enough money only to meet current cash outlays, without paying any attention to accruing liabilities. In old-age insurance, the accruing liabilities are necessarily the major part of the costs in the early years of the system. The benefits provided in the Social Security Act were estimated by the actuaries to cost forty-three times as much in 1980 as in 1942. Under the so-called pay-as-you method of financing, however, no provision would be made to meet the rapidly accruing liabilities. It is even proposed by some that no record be kept of these accruing liabilities, so were this plan adopted, the United States government would have a vast hidden debt, in addition to the acknowledged federal debt.

University of Wisconsin professor of economics Edwin E. Witte was the executive director of the Committee on Economic Security and one of the nation's foremost experts on the new program. Source: SSA History Archives.

Conservative groups, by hammering away at the reserves in the old-age insurance system, hope to get a reduction in social security taxes. Were the old-age insurance system financed as are commercial annuities sold by private insurance companies, taxes equal to 5.5 per cent of payrolls would be necessary from the beginning. Actually, the present combined rates on employers and employees total only 2 per cent and 5.5 per cent will not be collected until 1949, beginning in which year, however, 6 per cent will be collected to make up for the insufficient collections in the early years. But while the present taxes are less than those which would have to be charged were the old-age insurance system financed on private insurance company principles, the advocates of pay-as-you-go financing urge that these taxes be lowered, because even the present inadequate rates yield more money than is necessary to meet the cash disbursements of the old-age insurance system.

Radicals of all stripes want the benefits increased. Concern is expressed by them over the inadequate benefits which will be paid to the wage-earners who will reach retirement age in 1942 or soon thereafter. While the people retired in 1942 will, on the average, receive sixty times as much in benefits as they paid in taxes, it is nevertheless urged that their benefits be further increased, so they can live in comfort on their retirement annuities without income from any other source. There are also proposals for supplementing old-age insurance with invalidity insurance and with widows' and orphans' pensions which alone would cost fully as much as do the old-age insurance benefits now provided. At the extreme are the advocates of the General Welfare Bill, the 1938 version of the Townsend Plan. While the $200 per month has been dropped out of the formal statement of the plan, the poor old people who are contributing to the many organizations that support this measure still hope for $200 per month for everybody over sixty.

As I see the situation, either the conservatives or the radicals are bound to be disappointed should they be able to continue to work together until the Social Security Act is amended.

While, for a few years, it is possible to keep taxes down and increase benefits if no account is taken of accruing liabilities, this possibility will not long endure. The present taxes will prove to be inadequate to fully finance the old-age benefits now contemplated, without subsidies, in distant future years, from the general treasury. Any increase in these benefits will necessitate additional taxes.

It is my conviction that the conservative groups who have assailed the old-age insurance system are playing with fire and are likely to produce a blaze that will cause tremendous losses to American businesses ere long. If the people who are attacking the reserves succeed in convincing the American public that it is not necessary to pay any attention to accruing liabilities, we will have such a large increase in benefits that they cannot possibly be financed without a very great increase in taxes.

As I see it, the underlying principles of the federal old-age insurance system are fundamentally sound. This country faces a very serious old-age problem in the years lying ahead. That problem can be most wisely met through a contributory insurance system, in which the principles are observed that accruing liabilities shall, as far as practicable, be met currently and that the prospective beneficiaries must pay one-half of the costs. Abandon the contributory principle, or substitute for the principle of meeting all accruing costs currently an assessment system of financing, of which is given the misleading designation of a "pay-as-you-go" plan and you will find it impossible to keep the old-age security costs within reasonable limits. . . .

Source: Edwin Witte, "Social Security: A Wild Dream or a Practical Plan," address to the Wisconsin Alumni Institute, June 17, 1938." *Edwin E. Witte Papers,* Wisconsin Historical Society.

Document 2.10
Report of the Advisory Council on Social Security, December 10, 1938

The advisory council's report contained recommendations on program expansions and on financing. Those for program expansion covered two broad areas: benefits *(which types of benefits are to be paid and under what conditions) and* coverage *(who participates in the system). On benefits, the council recommended adding wives (but not husbands) to the retirement benefit, and widows (but not widowers) and for mothers with young children (but not similarly situated fathers) to survivors' benefits. On coverage, the council set an ambitious agenda for encompassing more occupational groups under the program. In the financing area, the council supported a "reasonable contingency reserve" rather than the full reserve enacted under the 1935 law. The council also recommended the provision of general revenues as part of the system's funding.*

One small, technical change in the way benefits are computed—from using cumulative wages to using average wages—had a significant effect in that it produced higher benefits for early beneficiaries, which was the reason it was being suggested.

The cost of adding dependents' and survivors' benefits to the Social Security program, and paying higher benefits to earlier cohorts, was to be met through a reduction in benefits to future single beneficiaries.

Recommendations and Conclusions

A. Recommendations on Benefits

I. The average old age benefits payable in the early years under Title II should be increased.

Since it is the purpose of old-age insurance to prevent dependency in old age, the benefits payable under the program should, as soon as possible, be sufficient in amount to afford the aged recipient at least a minimum subsistence income. . . . After study . . . the Council believes that in a considerable proportion of cases, the schedule of old-age benefits established in Title II will not provide reasonable benefits in the early years of the program. . . .

The policy of paying higher benefits to persons retiring in the earlier years of the system than are the equivalent of the individual contributions is already established in the present Act. Such a policy is not only sound social insurance practice but has long been recognized as necessary in private pension programs. Only through the payment of reasonable benefits can older workers be retired. It is believed that the reasoning which led to the application of the principle in the law in 1935 inevitably leads to a further application of the principle in the light of experience now available. . . .

II. The eventual annual cost of the insurance benefits now recommended, in relation to covered payroll and from whatever source financed, should not be increased beyond the eventual annual disbursements under the 1935 Act. [Several members of the Council believe, in view of the other types of benefits which later may be added to the plan, that in adopting revised old-age and survivors' benefits their eventual cost should be kept within 10 per cent of payrolls, the original estimate of the probable eventual cost of the present old age benefits when the Act was adopted.]

. . . So far as possible . . . the Council has sought to level out the progressive increases in the annual costs of the system to avoid a great upward acceleration of future disbursements, at the expense of inadequate protection in the early years, and at the risk of exceeding proper eventual limits. While old-age insurance disbursements will increase in years to come, a closer approximation of disbursements to available tax proceeds is in itself desirable in financing a continuing social insurance program. . . .

III. The enhancement of the early old-age benefits under the system should be partly attained by the method of paying in the case of a married annuitant a supplementary allowance on behalf of an aged wife equivalent to fifty per cent of the husband's own benefit. . . .

The inadequacy of the benefits payable during the early years of the old-age insurance program is more marked where the benefits must support not only the annuitant himself but also his wife. In 1930, 63.8 per cent of men aged 65 and over were married. Payment of supplementary allowances to annuitants who have wives over 65 will increase the average benefit in such a manner as to meet the greatest social need with the minimum increase in cost. The Council believes that an additional 50 per cent of the basic annuity would constitute a reasonable provision for the support of the annuitant's wife. . . .

In addition, the Council believes that careful study should be given to the substitution of an average wage formula for the accumulated wage formula incorporated in the present

Act. An average wage formula would more readily permit an increase in the early benefit payments and enable eventual costs to be kept within the limits prescribed under Recommendation II. . . .

. . . [T]he Council recommends that the cost of the program of wives' allowances here proposed be financed in part through some reduction in the eventual rates of benefits payable to individuals as single annuitants. Not only does such a readjustment of the benefit structure seem socially desirable but such an adjustment can and should be made without doing violence to the principle of individual equity in the case of widowers, bachelors, and women workers, since such persons should receive in all cases insurance protection at least equal in value to their individual direct contributions invested at interest. . . .

V. The widow of an insured worker, following her attainment of age 65, should receive an annuity bearing a reasonable relationship to the worker's annuity. . . .

A haunting fear in the minds of many older men is the possibility, and frequently, the probability, that their widow will be in need after their death. The day of large families and of the farm economy, when aged parents were thereby assured comfort in their declining years, has passed for a large proportion of our population. This change has had particularly devastating effect on the sense of security of the aged women of our country.

Women as a rule live longer than men. Wives are often younger than their husbands. Consequently, the probabilities are that a woman will outlive her husband. Old age insurance benefits for the husband, supplemented during his life by an allowance payable on behalf of his wife, fall considerably short, therefore, of providing adequate old-age security.

Lump-sum death benefits, such as payable under the present Act, are a very unsatisfactory and ineffective form of protection. The amount in the individual case is quite unlikely to bear any reasonable relationship to the needs of the surviving widow. Payable immediately in one sum, such settlements are likely to be used for many other purposes long before her old age.

The Council believes, therefore, that the old-age insurance program should include provision for old-age annuities for the widows of all covered workers. Where the worker had been an annuitant at time of death, it appears reasonable that his widow, if 65 or over, should receive an annuity equal to approximately three-fourths of the husband's annuity which would be equal to one-half of their combined annuity. Similar protection should be afforded if death occurred before the husband had reached old age. . . .

The cost of financing the program of widows' protection here recommended can be met, in the judgment of the Council, from the savings to the system in the revision of the present provisions for death benefits (as proposed in Recommendation IX), and in the reduction of the eventual rates of old-age benefits payable to single annuitants (as proposed in Recommendation VIII). . . .

VI. A dependent child of a currently insured individual upon the latter's death prior to age 65 should receive an orphan's benefit, and a widow of a currently insured individual, provided she has in her care one or more dependent children of the deceased husband, should receive a widow's benefit.

The Council believes that a program of survivors' insurance, intended primarily for the protection of the dependent orphans of deceased wage earners, is of as much importance to the community as an old-age insurance program. . . . The method of survivors' insurance not only sustains the concept that a child is supported through the efforts of the parent, but affords a vital sense of security to the family unit. . . .

The Council recommends that, in addition to benefits for such children, benefits be payable to widows who have in their care one or more of their children of the deceased wage earner. Such payments are intended as supplements to the orphans' benefits with the purpose of enabling the widow to remain at home and care for the children. . . .

VII. The provision of benefits to an insured person who becomes permanently and totally disabled and to his dependents is socially desirable. On this point the Council is in unanimous agreement. There is difference of opinion, however, as to the timing of the introduction of these benefits. Some members of the Council favor the immediate inauguration of such benefits. Other members believe that on account of additional costs and administrative difficulties, the problem should receive further study. . . .

While recognizing the desirability of providing protection against total and permanent disability and the advantages of contributory insurance as a method of attacking this problem, other members believe it is undesirable to recommend the initiation of a program of disability insurance at this time. The probable costs of such a program are extremely difficult to determine. . . . Until the probable costs of the old-age and survivors' insurance, recommended in this report, can be more accurately projected, it is unwise to recommend the assuming of the burden of a distinctly new type of protection, the cost of which is indeterminate and heavy.

Further, these members believe that disability insurance would introduce many administrative problems of great difficulty, and of a character apart from those involved in the program here recommended. . . .

VIII. In order to compensate in part for the additional cost of the additional benefits herein recommended, the benefits payable to individuals as single annuitants after the plan has been in operation a number of years should be reduced below those now incorporated in Title II. . . .

In order to provide more adequate basic protection to the wage earners of the country and at the same time fit the pattern of benefits to the financial cloth, it is believed that the formula used in the computation of old-age benefits should be revised in such a manner as to reduce the eventual rates of benefit payable to individuals as single annuitants. The Council is convinced of the necessity of broadening the scope of insurance protection to include allowances for aged wives and benefits for aged widows and surviving dependent children. It is of the conclusion that the use of a part of the funds otherwise allocated to the payment of relatively high benefits to single individuals in future years to permit the immediate broadening of the protection afforded by the system is both socially justifiable and financially necessary. . . .

IX. The death benefit payable on account of coverage under the system should be strictly limited in amount and payable on the death of any eligible individual.

With the introduction of a systematic and adequate plan of survivors' protection under the old-age insurance program, all justification of the large lump-sum death benefits now possible under the existing provisions of Title II disappears. . . . The Council, therefore, recommends the substitution of a strictly limited death benefit such as three months' average wages but not in excess of $200 and payable in all cases where the insured individual is eligible. . . .

X. The payment of old-age benefits should be begun on January 1, 1940.

Since it is convinced of the importance of enhancing the effectiveness and adequacy of the contributory system of old age protection in this country, the Council recommends that benefits under the broadened program be begun on January 1, 1940. . . .

B. Recommendations on Coverage

. . . The Council wishes to repeat the . . . proposals developed by the Social Security Board for the amendment of Titles II and VIII in the following particulars:

1. An amendment which would permit an individual to qualify for monthly benefits and to secure a larger monthly benefit because of employment after age 65. . . .

In addition, the Council makes the following recommendations at this time:

I. The employees of private non-profit religious, charitable, and educational institutions now excluded from coverage under Titles II and VIII should immediately be brought into coverage under the same provisions of these Titles as affect other covered groups. . . .

II. The coverage of farm employees and domestic employees under Titles II and VIII is socially desirable and should take effect, if administratively possible, by January 1, 1940.

Farm and domestic employees are, in general, among those wage earners most in need of protection against dependent old age and premature death. Low wages and intermittent employment frequently combine to make individual savings difficult. Their exclusion from the existing legislation was based to a considerable extent on grounds of administrative difficulties foreseen with respect to wage reporting and tax collections. Recent studies indicate that the additional cost of extending the coverage of the system to these classes of workers will be considerably less than originally estimated. . . . These groups could probably be covered by means of some form of stamp-book system applied to a limited number of broad wage classifications.

III. The old-age insurance program should be extended as soon as feasible to include additional groups not included in the previous recommendations of the Council and studies should be made of the administrative, legal, and financial problems involved in the coverage of self-employed persons and governmental employees.

Consistent with its acceptance of the contributory insurance method as socially necessary and desirable, the Council recommends the extension of the coverage of this method to the largest possible proportion of our gainfully employed population. An important group outside the existing program are those persons working on their own account such as business and professional men, farmers, and mechanics. Not only would the inclusion of this group be socially desirable, but it would also be a marked advantage in planning the financial program of the system. . . .

Despite the reasons in its favor, extension of coverage to the self-employed cannot be recommended at this time. The Council finds that the administrative problems of obtaining reports of earnings and of collecting contributions from persons without an employer, together with the problems of financing the benefits to be paid such persons are extremely difficult. The Council believes that attempts to find a solution should be made, and urges that studies directed toward this end be continued.

C. Recommendations on Finance

. . . Much of the present controversy in regard to the financing of the old-age insurance program has been concerned with long-run future policy. . . . After thorough canvassing of this aspect of the insurance program, the Council makes the following recommendations.

I. Since the nation as a whole, independent of the beneficiaries of the system, will derive a benefit from the old-age security program, it is appropriate that there be Federal financial participation in the old-age insurance system by mean of revenues derived from sources other than payroll taxes.

. . . The Council has indicated its conviction of the importance of an adequate contributory insurance program in the prevention of the growth of dependency in a democratic society. Since the nation as a whole will materially and socially benefit by such a program, it is highly appropriate that the Federal government should participate in the financing of the system. With the broadening of the scope of the protection afforded, governmental participation in meeting the costs of the program is all the more justified since the existing costs of relief and old-age assistance will be materially affected.

Governmental participation in financing of a social insurance program has long been accepted as sound public policy in other countries. Definite limits exist in the proper use of payroll taxes. An analysis of the incidence of such taxes leads to the conviction that they should be supplemented by the general tax program. The prevention of dependency is a community gain in more than social terms.

II. The principle of distributing the eventual cost of the old-age insurance system by means of approximately equal contributions by employers, employees, and the government is sound and should be definitely set forth in the law when tax provisions are amended.

The Council believes that this recommendation is a logical implementation of the principle of governmental financial participation.

III. The introduction of a definite program of Federal financial participation in the system will affect the consideration of the future rates of taxes on employers and employees and their relation to future benefit payments.

Future taxes under the program must be determined in relation to the future volume of benefits as knowledge becomes more definite. The introduction of Federal financial participation will permit redetermination of tax rates and intervals between adjustments of tax rates in relation to benefit costs, as then estimated, if such redetermination is deemed appropriate. Such adjustments may, under these conditions, be so determined as to affect the amount remaining on balance in the old-age insurance fund without the creation of serious financial problems as the system matures. The Council believes that with Federal financial participation, problems of financial policy can be far more readily resolved.

IV. The financial program of the system should embody provision for a reasonable contingency fund to insure the ready payment of benefits at all times and to avoid abrupt changes in tax and contribution rates.

The Council is of the conclusion that, in the financing of the insurance program, it is desirable to make provision for a contingency fund to insure ready payment of benefits at all stages of the business cycle and under varying conditions resulting from fluctuations in such factors as the average age of retirement, the total coverage under the program, and average wage rates. It is desirable that the payment of benefits should not be dependent upon quick Congressional action in levying emergency taxes to meet deficits or in sudden raising of contribution rates when disbursements exceed current tax collections or normal appropriations to the system.

With the changes in the benefit structure here recommended and with the introduction of a definite program of governmental contributions to the system, the Council believes that the size of the old-age insurance fund will be kept within much lower limits than are involved in the present act. Under social insurance programs it is not necessary to maintain a full invested reserve such as is required in private insurance, *provided* definite provision is made for governmental support of the system. The only invested fund then necessary would be a reasonable contingency fund as outlined above. The financial program inherent in the present Act offers one means of meeting the future costs of an old-age insurance program. If the method of accumulating a relatively large reserve is eliminated, there must be, instead, the definite assurance that the program will be financed not by payroll taxes alone but, in addition, by governmental contributions from other sources. Without interest returns on a relatively large fund, payroll taxes alone would prove insufficient to meet the current disbursements necessary as the system matures. For this reason, the Council insists that the principle of adequate governmental contributions should be definitely established in the law when tax provisions are revised, if the reserve policy under the old-age insurance program is changed.

V. The planning of the old-age insurance program must take full account of the fact that, while disbursements for benefits are relatively small in the early years of the program, far larger total disbursements are inevitable in the future. No benefits should be promised or implied which cannot be safely financed not only in the early years of the program but when workers now young will be old.

VI. Sound presentation of the government's financial position require full recognition of the obligations implied in the entire old age security program and treasury reports should annually estimate the load of future benefits and the probable product of the associated tax program.

The Council wishes to reiterate the necessity of taking full account of the greatly increasing costs of the old age insurance program in future years. The Council has kept this fact constantly in mind in its study of recommended revisions. It is of the belief that we should not commit future generations to a burden larger than we would want to bear ourselves. It is therefore important that Congress be kept fully informed of the obligations implied in the entire old age security program in the years to come under both the assistance and the contributory insurance provisions of the Social Security Act.

VII. The receipts of the taxes levied in Title VIII of the law, less the costs of collection, should through permanent appropriation be credited automatically to an old-age insurance fund and not to the general fund for later appropriation to the account, in whole or in part, as Congress may see fit. It is believed that such an arrangement will be constitutional.

VIII. The old-age insurance fund should specifically be made a trust fund, with designated trustees acting on the behalf of the prospective beneficiaries of the program. The trust fund should be dedicated exclusively to the payment of the benefits provided under the program and, in limited part, to the costs necessary to the administration of the program.

At the time the Social Security Act was drafted it was deemed necessary for constitutional reasons to separate legally the taxation and benefit features of the program. It is believed that in the light of subsequent court decisions such legal separation is no longer necessary. Since the taxes levied are essentially contributions intended to finance the benefit program, it is not only logical but expedient to provide for automatic crediting of tax proceeds to the old age insurance fund. It is believed by the Council that such a procedure would enhance public understanding of the contributory insurance system. Since the tax proceeds thus credited are intended for payment of benefits, it is recommended that they be deposited in a trust fund under the control of designated trustees in accordance with appropriate legal provisions. The trust fund should be dedicated to the payment of benefits and, to a restricted amount, to the costs necessary to the administration of the program. It is recommended that these funds should continue to be invested in securities of the Federal government as at present. . . .

IX. The consideration of change in the tax schedule under Title VIII of the law should be postponed until after the rates of 1.5 per cent each on employer and employee are in effect. . . .

With these and many other variable elements now present in any estimate of the future costs of a revised program under Title II, the majority of the Council is not ready to recommend any change in the tax schedule under Title VIII of the Act at this time. It does not feel that it could determine intelligently or with proper caution any precise adjustment of rates. Nor is immediate change considered necessary since in any case the amount accumulated in the old-age insurance fund for some years will not exceed that deemed appropriate for the contingency fund previously recommended. In view of the probable increase in the immediate cash outlay to begin in 1940 which the Council's recommendations of benefits will entail, it is conservative policy to continue the taxes now provided in the present Act. It seems the part of wisdom to make changes, as warranted, on the basis of more certain knowledge. [Several members of the Council feel that the increase of 50 per cent in the tax rate from 2 per cent to 3 per cent now provided by the law to be made in 1940 should be reconsidered. Unless the cost of the benefits payable in 1940 and 1941 shall exceed current income from the present 2 per cent payroll tax, and in view of the probable size of the contingency fund on January 1, 1940, they feel that the increase in the tax rate should not take place before the study herein recommended to be made in 1941 shall have been completed. They believe that under the present conditions it would be better policy to allow the sum involved in the increase in the tax rate to remain in the hands of employees and employers than to use it to increase the contingency fund.]

. . . After thorough canvassing of the problem, the Council is of the conclusion that by the close of 1941, sufficiently comprehensive knowledge will be available for definitive recommendations on changes in the tax program, if then deemed appropriate, and for definitive recommendations as to the timing of governmental contributions toward the financing of the insurance system. By that time approximately five years of experience in tax collection under varying conditions will be available. Even more important, approximately two years of benefit experience under a revised program will have developed, if suggested revisions are made. Further change in the tax rates under the existing schedules will not take place until January 1, 1943.

At that time, the determination of the long-run philosophy as to the financing of the program will come to have significance in terms of tax rates. Discussion of such philosophy, while of great concern to all far-sighted students of fiscal policy, does not warrant departure from the recommendations on financial policy here presented. . . .

Appendix

On April 29, 1938, the Council unanimously approved the following statement concerning the financing of the old-age insurance system:

"The Advisory Council on Social Security has been giving much attention to the problem of financing the old age insurance system. The Council recognizes that there are other ways of financing the old-age insurance system which upon further study may prove to have greater advantages than the present system. The entire subject, however, is so complex that the Council is not yet prepared to express a final judgment as to the method of financing which would be most desirable from a social and economic standpoint.

"Upon one aspect of the general problem the Advisory Council deems it advisable to make a public statement at this time to allay unwarranted fears. This relates to the method of handling the funds collected for old-age insurance purposes.

"In accordance with the statutes, the taxes collected from employers and employees under Title VIII of the Social Security Act are paid into the general fund of the Treasury. While not expressly provided by law, it was understood at the time of the enactment of the Social Security Act that amounts equivalent to the entire proceeds of these taxes, less costs of administration, shall be appropriated annually by Congress to the old age reserve account. Congress has not only done so, but to date has appropriated somewhat more to the old-age reserve account than has been collected from the taxes levied in Title VIII of the Social Security Act. Thus, up to the end of March, 1938, $636,100,000 had been invested to the credit of the old-age reserve account, and $577,447,532 had been collected from the taxes for old-age insurance purposes.

"A proportionate part of the moneys appropriated by Congress to the old-age reserve account has been turned over periodically to this account and has been immediately invested in special securities of the United States Government bearing 3 per cent interest.

"The special securities issued to the old-age reserve account are general obligations of the United States Government, which differ from other securities of the Government only in the higher rate of interest they bear and in the fact that they are not sold in the open market. The issuance of such special securities is not only expressly authorized by law, but is required by the provision of the Social Security Act that the old-age reserve funds are to be invested so as to yield an interest return of 3 per cent.

"The United States Treasury uses the moneys realized from the issuance of these special securities by the old-age reserve account in the same manner as it does moneys realized from the sale of other Government securities. As long as the budget is not balanced, the net result is to reduce the amounts which the Government has to borrow from banks, insurance companies and other private parties. When the budget is balanced, these moneys will be available for the reduction of the national debt held by the public. The members of the Advisory Council are in agreement that the fulfillment of the promises made to the wage earners included in the old age insurance system depends upon, more than anything else, the financial integrity of the Government. The members of the Council, regardless of differing views on other aspects of the financing of old-age insurance, are of the opinion that the present provisions regarding the investment of the moneys in the old-age reserve account do not involve any misuse of these moneys or endanger the safety of these funds."

Source: Full text of the council report is available on the Social Security Administration Web site: www.ssa.gov/history/reports/38advise.html (accessed September 28, 2006).

Document 2.11
President Roosevelt's Remarks on the Third Anniversary of Social Security, August 15, 1938

On the day following the third anniversary of the Social Security Act, President Roosevelt went on national radio to broadcast his report of the act's progress to date, entitled "A Social Security Program Must Include All Those Who Need Its Protection." He also took the opportunity to signal his intentions about future program expansion.

The Social Security Act is three years old today. This is a good vantage point from which to take a long look backward to its beginnings, to cast an appraising eye over what it has accomplished so far, and to survey its possibilities of future growth.

Five years ago the term "social security" was new to American ears. Today it has significance for more than forty million men and women workers whose applications for old-age insurance accounts have been received; this system is designed to assure them an income for life after old age retires them from their jobs. . . .

These accomplishments of three years are impressive, yet we should not be unduly proud of them. Our Government in fulfilling an obvious obligation to the citizens of the country has been doing so only because the citizens require action from their Representatives. If the people, during these years, had chosen a reactionary Administration or a "do nothing" Congress, Social Security would still be in the conversational stage—a beautiful dream which might come true in the dim distant future.

But the underlying desire for personal and family security was nothing new. In the early days of colonization and through the long years following, the worker, the farmer, the merchant, the man of property, the preacher and the idealist came here to build, each for himself, a stronghold for the things he loved. The stronghold was his home; the things he loved and wished to protect were his family, his material and spiritual possessions.

His security, then as now, was bound to that of his friends and his neighbors.

But as the Nation has developed, as invention, industry and commerce have grown more complex, the hazards of life have become more complex. Among an increasing host of fellow citizens, among the often intangible forces of giant industry, man has discovered that his individual strength and wits were no longer enough. This was true not only of the worker at shop bench or ledger; it was true also of the merchant or manufacturer who employed him. Where heretofore men had turned to neighbors for help and advice, they now turned to Government.

Now this is interesting to consider. The first to turn to Government, the first to receive protection from Government, were not the poor and the lowly—those who had no resources other than their daily earnings—but the rich and the strong. Beginning in the nineteenth century, the United States passed protective laws designed, in the main, to give security to property owners, to industrialists, to merchants and to bankers. True, the little man often profited by this type of legislation; but that was a by-product rather than a motive.

Taking a generous view of the situation, I think it was not that Government deliberately ignored the working man but that the working man was not sufficiently articulate to make his needs and his problems known. The powerful in industry and commerce had powerful voices, both individually and as a group. And whenever they saw their possessions threatened, they raised their voices in appeals for government protection.

It was not until workers became more articulate through organization that protective labor legislation was passed. While such laws raised the standards of life, they still gave no assurance of economic security. Strength or skill of arm or brain did not guarantee a man a job; it did not guarantee him a roof; it did not guarantee him the ability to provide for those dependent upon him or to take care of himself when he was too old to work.

Long before the economic blight of the depression descended on the Nation, millions of our people were living in wastelands of want and fear. Men and women too old and infirm to work either depended on those who had but little to share, or spent their remaining years within the walls of a poorhouse. . . .

Because it has become increasingly difficult for individuals to build their own security single-handed, Government must now step in and help them lay the foundation stones, just as Government in the past has helped lay the foundation of business and industry. We must face the fact that in this country we have a rich man's security and a poor man's security and that the Government owes equal obligations to both. National security is not a half and half manner: it is all or none.

The Social Security Act offers to all our citizens a workable and working method of meeting urgent present needs and of forestalling future need. It utilizes the familiar machinery of our Federal-State government to promote the common welfare and the economic stability of the Nation.

The Act does not offer anyone, either individually or collectively, an easy life—nor was it ever intended so to do. None of the sums of money paid out to individuals in assistance or in insurance will spell anything approaching abundance. But they will furnish that minimum necessity to keep a foothold; and that is the kind of protection Americans want.

What we are doing is good. But it is not good enough. To be truly national, a social security program must include all those who need its protection. Today many of our citizens are still excluded from old-age insurance and unemployment compensation because of the nature of their employment. This must be set aright; and it will be.

Some time ago I directed the Social Security Board to give attention to the development of a plan for liberalizing and extending the old-age insurance system to provide benefits for wives, widows and orphans. . . .

I am hopeful that on the basis of studies and investigations now under way, the Congress will improve and extend the law. I am also confident that each year will bring further development in Federal and State social security legislation—and that is as it should be. One word of warning, however. In our efforts to provide security for all of the American people, let us not allow ourselves to be misled by those who advocate short cuts to Utopia of fantastic financial schemes.

We have come a long way. But we still have a long way to go. There is still today a frontier that remains unconquered—an America unclaimed. This is the great, the nationwide frontier of insecurity, of human want and fear. This is the frontier—the America—we have set ourselves to reclaim. . . .

Source: The Public Papers and Addresses of Franklin D. Roosevelt, 1938 Volume (New York: Macmillan, 1941), 477–481.

Document 2.12
Treasury Secretary Morgenthau's Testimony to the House Committee on Ways and Means, March 24, 1939

In his appearance before the House Ways and Means Committee in 1939 Treasury Secretary Henry Morgenthau Jr. reversed his views on the necessity of building a large trust fund reserve. Instead, he suggested that the program needed only to retain a "contingency reserve." This allowed a fundamental shift in the financing of the program by increasing benefits in the near term and freezing tax rates, thereby reducing the projected trust fund buildup to contingency reserve levels.

. . . In 1935, when the act was before this committee, I urged adoption of a self-supporting contributory old-age insurance system in which the future tax beneficiaries on the beneficiaries would be lightened by interest earned on a reserve fund accumulated by an excess of taxes over benefits during the early years of the system. I believe now as I believed then that a sound old-age insurance system must be on a contributory basis. Our experience in these

4 years leads me, however, to recommend to you an important alteration in the role which a reserve fund should play in this contributory insurance system.

Four years ago when the old-age insurance program was being planned we expected that the act as passed would provide old-age security for a fairly limited group in the community. We realized, of course, that many workers who might not be insured under the act at any one time would later obtain protection by shifting into the insured occupations. It was generally supposed, however, that the group so shifting would be small compared with the great mass of workers, who throughout their working life would remain continuously either in the insured category or in the uninsured category.

Because the limited group of employments for which insurance was provided had been selected primarily upon the basis of administrative feasibility, it did not seem fair that uninsured persons should be taxed in order to provide old-age benefits as of right for the insured group. I therefore recommended to your committee in 1935 that the old-age insurance system be made self-supporting from pay-roll taxes on uninsured employees and their employers.

Operation of the act has provided significant information bearing on this question. This information shows that the extent of migration, temporary or permanent, from uninsured to insured employment is far greater than was assumed by the President's Committee on Economic Security in 1935. In my last annual report I pointed out that the consequences of this migration was that the scheduled tax rates were insufficient to maintain the system on the actuarial reserve basis provided by the law.

There is, however, another and more cheerful result of this migration. As a consequence of the migration, a much larger proportion of the total population of the United States is qualifying under the contributory system to receive old-age benefits than had been expected. My latest annual report presented the estimate that, without extension of the coverage under the present law, 80 percent of the population of the United States ultimately will have qualified during their working life for at least the minimum annuity under Title II of the act.

This experience throws new light on our original belief that the act ought to be self-supporting. Four years of experience have show that the benefits of the act will be so widely diffused that supplemental funds from general tax revenues may be substituted—without substantial inequity—for a considerable portion of interest earnings from the large reserve contemplated by the present law. Therefore, it becomes apparent that the argument for a large reserve does not have the validity which 4 years ago it seemed to possess.

There is no need at the present time and, I believe, there will be no need in the near future, for supplementing pay roll taxes from general revenue. For all classes of beneficiaries, the values of the benefits which the act provides are, and for a long time will be, substantially in excess of the contributions under the schedule provided in the law.

There is another reason for questioning the schedule of tax rates and the resultant reserve set-up in 1935. We adopted a gradual step-up in the tax rate in 1935 in order to give industry an opportunity to accustom itself to the new taxes and so to avoid any undue restrictive effects. The trend of business conditions in specific future years could not, of course, then be accurately foreseen. In periods of incomplete business recovery like the present, the contributory old-age insurance system should be financed as to have the least possible deterring effect on business. It is, therefore, a pertinent question whether a substantial increase in the tax rate should be allowed to occur at the present stage of business recovery.

The depressing effect of the present disturbed state of world affairs upon the American economy makes it especially urgent that at this time we do not place any avoidable burdens on American productive enterprise. . . .

With these factors in mind, I recommend the following changes in the act:

1. We should not accumulate a reserve fund any larger than is necessary to protect the system against unforeseen declines in revenues and increases in the volume of benefit payments. Specifically, I would suggest to Congress that it plan the financing of the old-age insurance system with a view to maintaining for use in contingencies an eventual reserve amounting to not more than three times the highest prospective annual benefits for the ensuing 5 years. . . .

Source: Social Security Hearings Relative to the Social Security Amendments of 1939 before the Committee on Ways and Means, House of Representatives, Seventy-Sixth Congress, vol. 3 (Washington, D.C.: Government Printing Office, 1939), 2111–2113.

Document 2.13
Excerpts from Congressional Debates, June 6–8, 1939

Congress approved the work of the advisory council and the Ways and Means Committee in floor debate that took place in the summer of 1939. Questions related to the reserve fund, tax rates, and old-age assistance as provided by grants-in-aid to the states dominated the debate. Family benefits and other innovations in Social Security received almost no mention.

Mr. Taylor of Tennessee. . . . The bill, consisting of over 100 pages, is so complex and complicated that it would take the sapience of the proverbial Philadelphia lawyer and a great deal of actuarial knowledge to interpret its provisions. . . .

Mr. Doughton. Mr. Chairman, H.R. 6635, now before the Committee for discussion and consideration is the result of the work of the Committee on Ways and Means, which began the 1st of February last. The committee conducted hearings for about 50 days, during which approximately 2,500 pages of testimony were taken. The committee was then in executive session for something like 6 weeks, giving diligent and painstaking thought and consideration to the very important matter it had before consideration.

The report on the bill contains about 120 pages and is a full and detailed explanation of the bill. Much of the bill, I may say, is technical and somewhat complicated and difficult to understand. . . .

The bill has the unanimous support, I believe, of the Committee on Ways and Means. . . .

The bill changes the old-age reserve account to a trust fund, with the Secretary of the Treasury, the Secretary of Labor, and the Chairman of the Social Security Board, all ex officio, acting as a board of trustees. . . . Instead of the mythical $47,000,000,000 reserve of which we have heard so much, it will probably never exceed eight to ten million dollars, and will conform to the recommendation of the Secretary of the Treasury of not more than three times the highest prospective annual benefits in the ensuing 5 years. . . .

Mr. Treadway. We are continually urging reemployment, but at the same time we are putting increased burdens on employers for giving employment. If we keep on adding burdens to business, the time is not far distant when the Government will have to take over all business, industry, and commerce if it is to be carried on at all. Then the Government will indeed become the Great White Father. So I repeat, let us proceed slowly in liberalizing the Social Security Act, lest in pursuing security we lose it altogether, and with it the liberties of the people.

Mr. Burdick. . . . Experience with the present social security law has established some facts which should guide us in our present deliberations.

First. That the amount paid to the aged has been so inadequate that there has, in fact, been no pension at all, but merely a dole.

Second. The law has not been operated as a decent dole; for a dole is a gift and no gifts were made to the aged under this law if they possessed any tangible piece of property. If an old couple, an old man, or an old lady possessed what they called their home—some instances the actual value was not over $200, no benefits could be received under this law until the property was deeded over to the State administration. . . .

Third. We have failed to offer any direct Government assistance to any old person. We have offered aid if and when the State is willing to match funds.

Mr. Gearhart. . . . because Title II of the Social Security Act is an abomination, a monstrosity, one that should be eliminated from the whole scheme of Social Security.

In the first place, although it is named "insurance," it is not insurance. In the second place, it draws a line of demarcation between American people—those who shall have benefits and those who shall be denied benefits. It is therefore inequitable, unjust, unfair, and un-American. It provided that only those who are fortunate enough as to have jobs shall have security. Those who are not so fortunate as to have jobs are denied security. Now, I ask you, my colleagues, who is the more in need of security, those who go through life having jobs or those, the more unfortunate, who, though desiring work, can find nothing to do. . . .

Mr. McCormack. . . . Congress provides a certain rate of interest. In order to meet that rate of interest under special circumstances special obligations would be issued. Precedent has been established for this. These obligations occupy the same status as a bond. They are in the same category as a bond. . . .

The characterization of these obligations as I O U's, of course, has no greater strength than if the same characterization were directed against a bond issued by the Government. Insofar as this committee is humanly able, we have provided in the pending bill a separate fund and provided for its administration by trustees and insofar as we are humanly able we have directed those trustees to go into the open market when it is not inconsistent with the best interest of our Government and purchase bonds. In doing this, I submit to the gentleman from Wisconsin and my colleagues on both sides of the aisles, we are doing everything we can possibly do. . . .

Mr. Gearhart. Mr. Chairman, even at the risk of being accused again of cheap politics, I rise to make a little more plain, I hope, just what a legalistic fiction all of this is. The gentleman from Massachusetts has carefully explained to you the elaborate method they have of handling those so-called pay-roll taxes. They levy a pay-roll tax and they get the money, and then the slippery bookkeeping begins. They make out IOU's, they appropriate the money from one fund to another, and they say it is invested when it is gone. And where is it? As soon as the Government got this payroll tax from the poorest people in the country—those least able to pay it—they immediately spent the money building battleships, paying benefits to people, and spending it on the P.W.A. and the W.P.A and upon every other routine activity of the Government. But not a bit of it on Social Security. When spent, the money is gone, and it is gone forever as soon as it is spent, because there is no necessity for the Government ever to pay it back for the simple reason that the interest on those I O U's furnishes the money which must be raised to care for the maturing demands against the social-security system set up in title II. Since none of the moneys collected as pay-roll taxes will be needed to pay the workers under title II, where will the Government get the money to pay the old-age pensions?

It will get it just the way it gets all the other money it must have, it will borrow it or levy an additional tax. It will levy a tax on the people, all the people, and not a part of the people. . . . And when they levy that tax on all the people, they catch again the man who had already paid the pay-roll tax. In other words, this ridiculous, unfair, and unjust system is a double system of taxation upon the poorest, and the humblest, the man least able to pay. . . .

Source: Congressional Record, House, June 6, 1939, 6682, 6689, 6692, and 6697; *Congressional Record,* House, June 8, 1939, 6849, 6853, 6855, and 6856.

Document 2.14
Social Security Bulletin Announcement, September 1939
In addition to summarizing President Roosevelt's signing statement, this announcement reported on the initial administrative actions being undertaken to implement the new legislation.

Social Security in Review

Following his approval of the Social Security Act Amendments of 1939, President Roosevelt on August 11 made a public statement in which he declared the amendments to be "another tremendous step forward in providing greater security for the people of this country." The President commented specifically on the changes in the old-age insurance system, expressing his gratification that in liberalizing the provisions a reasonable relationship had been retained between wage loss sustained and benefits received. "This," he declared, "is a most important distinguishing characteristic of social insurance as contrasted with any system of flat pensions." With regard to changes in coverage of the system, the President remarked: "I am glad that the insurance benefits have been extended to cover workers in some occupations that have previously not been covered. However, workers in other occupations have been excluded. In my opinion, it is imperative that these insurance benefits be extended to workers in all occupations.". . .

The President concluded his statement by calling attention to the work of the Committee on Economic Security. "In 1934," he declared, "I appointed a committee called the Committee on Economic Security made up of Government officials to study the whole problem of economic and social security and to develop a legislative program for the same. The present law is the result of its deliberations. That Committee is still in existence and has considered and recommended the present amendments. In order to give reality and coordination to the study of any further developments that appear necessary I am asking the Committee to continue its life and to make active study of various proposals which may be made for amendments or developments to the Social Security Act. . . .

Immediately on adoption of the Social Security Act Amendments of 1939, the Social Security Board discontinued acceptance of claims for lump-sum payments under the old-age insurance program from workers reaching age 65. This type of payment is terminated by the amendments, and workers who might have been eligible to receive such payments are given opportunity to qualify instead for monthly benefits. . . .

In connection with the announcement of discontinuance of lump-sum payments to workers reaching age 65, it was indicated that, on the basis of preliminary estimates, approximately 485,000 persons past the age of 65 will be entitled to monthly benefits in 1940 and that the benefits payable during that year will exceed $110 million. Under the provisions of the original Social Security Act, it was indicated, lump-sum benefits probably would not have amounted to more than $30 million in 1940, including both payments to workers reaching age 65 and death payments. From January 1, 1937, when the program went into effect, through July 31, 1939, approximately 397,400 claims for lump-sum payments amounting to more than $21.5 million were certified by the Social Security Board to the Secretary of the Treasury. . . .

Source: *Social Security Bulletin,* vol. 2, no. 9 (Washington, D.C.: U.S. Government Printing Office, 1939): 1–2.

Document 2.15
Summary of the 1939 Amendments, December 1939

This summary of the major changes introduced in the 1939 amendments was prepared by the Social Security Board staff and published in their in-house research publication. This document provides an introduction to the concepts and program policies involved in Social Security benefits when there are dependents' benefits involved. It details how the program was changed by the 1939 amendments, as many concepts of the modern program have their origin in these changes. The growth of the program during its postwar expansionary period would often take the form of liberalizations of these basic program principles.

Federal Old-Age and Survivors Insurance: A Summary of the 1939 Amendments

The Amendments to the Social Security Act . . . revised provisions for the Federal old-age insurance system in four major respects:

1. Advance in the date of first payment of monthly benefits to January 1, 1940, to make the benefits immediately effective.

2. Increase in the average amounts of benefits payable in the early years.
3. Extension of scope to provide protection for certain dependents of beneficiaries and survivors of insured workers.
4. Liberalization of eligibility requirements to provide protection for more persons now aged or approaching retirement age.

The effect of these amendments is to shift the emphasis of the system from protection of the individual worker and principles of individual equity to protection of the family and a recognition of the broader goal of meeting social needs. In addition, certain changes in the financial framework of the system and in taxing provisions were made by this legislation. . . .

. . . The types of benefits payable under the old-age and survivors insurance plan are:

1. Primary insurance benefits, which are old-age insurance benefits for wage earners who have attained the age of 65 and who are "fully insured" under the program (as explained later).
2. Wife's insurance benefits for wives aged 65 and over of wage earners entitled to primary insurance benefits.
3. Child's insurance benefits, for children under the age of 16, or under 18 if attending school, of wage earners entitled to primary insurance benefits and of deceased insured wage earners.
4. Widow's insurance benefits for widows aged 65 and over of wage earners who died fully insured.
5. Widow's current insurance benefits for widows of any age caring for the dependent children of wage earners who died either fully or "currently insured.". . .
6. Parent's insurance benefits for parents over age 65 of wage earners who died fully insured leaving no widow or unmarried surviving child under the age of 18.
7. Lump-sum death payments under certain circumstances. . . .

I. Covered Employment and Wages

As in the original act, taxes and benefits depend on wages received in covered employment. . . .

Under the original act, wages with respect to services performed after age 65 were not taxable and did not count toward benefits. The age limitation now contained in the definition of employment applies only to services after age 65 performed prior to 1939. Services performed in 1939 and thereafter are thus considered to be employment regardless of the employee's age, and wages received for such employment are taxable and are counted toward benefits. . . .

II. Insured Status

For the purposes of determining who may qualify for the various types of benefits, the terms "fully insured individual" and "currently insured individual" are used. In the definition of the first of these terms, the term "quarter of coverage" appears.

a. A *quarter of coverage* is a calendar quarter in which an individual has been paid not less than $50 in wages. . . .

b. *Fully Insured Individual.*—For the primary and supplementary benefits, and for certain of the survivors benefits, the wage earner must be "fully insured." To be fully insured an individual must satisfy either one of the following two requirements: (1) He must have had at least half as many quarters of coverage as the number of calendar quarters elapsing after 1936 or after the quarter in which he attained age 21 . . . and prior to the quarter in which he attained the age of 65 or died . . . and in no case less than six quarters of coverage; or (2) he must have had at least 40 quarters of coverage.

The requirements for fully insured status can best be understood if the term "elapsed quarters" . . . is explained.

Elapsed quarters include all quarters in the normal working lifetime of an individual, except, of course, any quarters occurring before 1937 when the program first went into effect. . . .

The general rule is that to be fully insured an individual must have had at least half as many quarters of coverage as the number of elapsed quarters. However, a minimum of six quarters of coverage is required if the number required by the general rule is less than six. Furthermore, if a person has 40 quarters of coverage he is fully insured, regardless of the requirement of the general rule. . . .

c. *Currently Insured Individual.*—In order that protection for orphans and widows caring for orphans may become available even when a wage earner has not had a considerable period in covered employment before his death, benefits are payable not only to such survivors of fully insured individuals but also to such survivors of "currently insured individuals." Certain lump-sum death payments may also be paid with respect to either type of individual.

A currently insured individual is an individual who has been paid wages of not less than $50 for each of six or more quarters out of the 12 calendar quarters immediately preceding the quarter in which he died. . . .

d. Thus, an individual may be currently insured without being fully insured. All the monthly benefits are payable with respect to fully insured individuals; but if a wage earner was only currently insured, only his surviving orphans and widow caring for them can receive monthly benefits. . . .

III. Average Monthly Wage

The amounts of all benefits are directly or indirectly dependent on the average wage of the individual with respect to whose wages the benefits are payable. This fact represents a further recognition of the fundamental purpose of social insurance, i.e., to replace the wages lost which formerly provided support for the beneficiaries. As a general rule, the average monthly wage is determined by dividing the total wages paid to the individual by the total number of months in which he could have earned wages. . . .

This method of determining the average monthly wage gives an average of the employee's monthly wages in covered employment over that part of his working lifetime subsequent to the original date on which the old-age insurance provisions became operative, regardless of whether he was actually engaged in covered employment during the entire period. This has the result of reducing the average wage of and consequent benefits to any person who is not a full-time participant in the system. Such a course is necessary in order to safeguard the system against disproportionate payments to those who are in covered employment and are contributors for only part of the time they might have been covered. . . .

IV. Primary Insurance Benefits

a. After December 31, 1939, every individual who (1) has attained the age of 65, (2) is a fully insured individual, and (3) has filed application for monthly benefits, known as "primary insurance benefits," is to be entitled to such insurance benefits. . . .

b. The amount of the primary insurance benefit is computed in two parts: (1) a basic amount equal to 40 percent of the first $50 of average monthly wage plus 10 percent of the next $200 of average monthly wage; (2) an increase of 1 percent of the basic amount for each year in which the individual was paid at least $200 of wages in covered employment. . . .

c. If the primary insurance benefit thus computed is less than $10, it is raised to $10 in all cases. . . .

V. Wife's Insurance Benefits

a. A wife of an individual entitled to primary insurance benefits is entitled to monthly benefits based on her husband's wage record if all the following four requirements are satisfied: (1) She has attained the age of 65; (2) she has filed an application for wife's insurance benefits; (3) she was living with her husband at the time such application was filed; and (4) she is not entitled to a primary insurance benefit in her own right equal to or greater than one-half the primary insurance benefit of her husband. . . .

d. The wife's insurance benefit is equal to one-half of the primary insurance benefit of her husband unless she is entitled to a primary insurance benefit in her own right. If she is entitled to a primary insurance benefit in her own right which is smaller than half of her husband's primary insurance benefit, her benefit will be the difference between the two plus her primary benefit. . . . if she is entitled to a primary insurance benefit of her own equal to or greater than half of her husband's primary insurance benefit, she will receive her own primary insurance benefit instead of a wife's insurance benefit. . . .

e. Since every primary insurance benefit must be at least $10, a wife's benefit will be computed at not less than $5; in other words, the combined benefits of husband and aged wife cannot be less than $15. . . .

f. The combined primary insurance and wife's insurance benefits payable with respect to the husband's wages are subject to a maximum of $85, or 80 percent of his average monthly wage, whichever is smaller. If there are any child's insurance benefits payable, the combined benefits are subject to an additional maximum. . . .

VI. Child's Insurance Benefits

(Payable in conjunction with primary insurance benefits.)

a. Every child of an individual entitled to primary insurance benefits becomes entitled to monthly benefits if all of the following three requirements are met: (1) The child is unmarried and under the age of 18; (2) the child is dependent upon such individual at the time of filing application; and (3) the child has filed application for child's insurance benefits. . . .

b. The definition of "child" includes a step-child of an individual by a marriage contracted prior to the date upon which the individual attained the age of 60 and a child legally adopted by an individual prior to the date upon which the individual attained age 60. . . .

c. A child is deemed dependent upon a father or adopting father if, at the time the child's application for benefits was filed, either of the following requirements is met: (1) Such individual was living with or contributing to the support of such child; or (2) the child is either the legitimate or adopted child of such individual and has not been adopted by some other individual. A child shall be deemed dependent upon the mother, adopt mother, stepmother, or stepfather, unless such, child is receiving contributions toward his support from his father or adopting father or he is living with his father or adopting father. . . .

d. The child's insurance benefit is equal to one-half of the primary insurance benefit of the person with respect to whose wages the child is entitled to receive such benefit. When a child is entitled to benefits with respect to more than one parent . . . the child's insurance benefit shall be equal to one-half of whichever primary insurance benefit is greater. . . .

e. Since every primary benefit must be at least $10, a child's benefit as computed will not be less than $5. . . .

f. The maximums placed upon benefits . . . apply also to the total of all monthly benefits payable with respect to an individual's wages. Besides these maximums, the total of all monthly benefits payable with respect to one individual's wages is also limited to twice the primary insurance benefit of such individual. The maximum of twice the primary insurance benefits has the effect of limiting to two the number of dependents (of a primary insurance beneficiary) who can draw full benefits. In other words, unless limited by the other maximums a primary insurance beneficiary with a wife over age 65 and one child can draw full benefits, or, if there is no wife over age 65, a primary insurance beneficiary and two children can draw full benefits. If there is a larger number of eligible dependents or if the other maximums serve to reduce the total benefits which would otherwise be payable, a pro rata reduction is made in all benefits payable with respect to one individual's wages except the primary insurance benefit. . . .

VII. Widow's Insurance Benefits

a. Widows of individuals who die after December 31, 1939, are entitled to monthly benefits if all of the following requirements are met: (1) The widow has attained the age of 65; (2) the husband was a fully insured individual at the time of his death; (3) the widow has not remarried; (4) she was living with her husband at the time of his death; (5) she has filed an application for widow's insurance benefits; (6) she is not entitled to a primary insurance benefit, based on her own wages, equal to or greater than three-fourths of the primary insurance benefit based on her husband's wage record. . . .

e. The widow's insurance benefit is equal in amount to three-fourths of the primary insurance benefit computed on her deceased husband's wage record, provided she is not entitled to a primary insurance benefit on the basis of a wage record of her own. If she is entitled to a primary insurance benefit which is less than three-fourths of the primary insurance benefit based on the wage record of her deceased husband, her benefit will be the difference between the two plus her own primary benefit. . . . [I]f she is entitled to receive a primary insurance benefit equal to or greater than three-fourths of the primary insurance benefit based on the wage record of her deceased husband, she will receive her own primary insurance benefit instead of the widow's insurance benefit. . . .

f. Since every primary insurance benefit is at least $10, every widow's insurance benefit, as computed, will be at least $7.50. Furthermore, if the widow is the only survivor entitled to benefits, her benefit will be raised to the minimum of $10 payable with respect to one individual's wages. . . .

g. If she is the only survivor, the maximum provisions do not affect a widow's insurance benefits, since the latter could not reach any of the maximums set. In the rare event that an aged widow is entitled to benefits and there are also orphans entitled to benefits, the maximum provisions . . . apply here also. . . .

VIII. Widow's Current Insurance Benefits

a. A widow, regardless of age, of an individual who dies after December 31, 1939, is entitled to monthly benefits based upon the deceased husband's wage record if all the following requirements are met: (1) The widow, at the time of filing her application, has in her care one or more children of such deceased individual entitled to receive child's benefits; (2) the husband was either a fully or currently insured individual at the time of his death; (3) the widow has not remarried; (4) she was living, with her husband . . . at the time of his death; (5) she has filed an application for these benefits; (6) she is not entitled to a widow's insurance benefit; and (7) she is not entitled to a primary insurance benefit equal to or greater than three-fourths of the primary insurance benefit of her husband. . . .

b. The widow's current insurance benefit is equal in amount to three-fourths of the primary insurance benefit computed on her deceased husband's wage record provided that she is not entitled to a primary insurance benefit on the basis of a wage record of her own. If she is entitled to a primary insurance benefit which is less than three-fourths of the primary insurance benefit based on her husband's wage record, her benefit will be the difference between the two plus her primary benefit. . . . if she is entitled to a primary insurance benefit in her own right which is equal to or larger than three-fourths of her husband's primary insurance benefit, she will receive her own primary benefit instead of the widow's current insurance benefit. . . .

c. For the purpose of computing the widow's current insurance benefit, the primary insurance benefit upon which it is based is subject to a minimum of $10. Therefore the widow's current benefit as computed cannot be less than $7.50. Since a widow's current benefit is payable only if there is at least one child eligible to draw child's benefits, the combined benefits cannot be less than $12.50. . . .

d. The maximum . . . of twice the primary insurance benefit, while equally applicable to the widow's current insurance benefits, does not affect these benefits if she has only one or two children of the deceased individual in her care. However, if there are three or more orphans in the care of the widow, the combined benefits will be reduced because they must not exceed twice the primary benefits of the deceased individual. . . .

e. The widow's current insurance benefits begin with the month in which all the requirements outlined in paragraph (a) are satisfied. . . . The benefits end with the month immediately preceding the first month in which she remarries, dies, or there ceases to be a child of the deceased individual entitled to receive child's insurance benefits. . . .

IX. Orphan's Benefits

(Child's Insurance Benefits payable in the event of the death of the worker.)

a. Every child of an individual who dies after December 31, 1939, is entitled to monthly benefits based on such deceased individual's wage record if all the following requirements are met: (1) The child is unmarried and under the age of 18; (2) the individual with respect to whose wages the child's benefit is payable was either a fully or a currently insured individual at the time of his death; (3) the child was dependent upon such individual at the time of such individual's death or at the time of original application for child's insurance benefits if such individual had been a primary beneficiary; and (4) the child has filed an application for these benefits. . . .

d. The orphan's benefit is equal in amount to one-half of the primary insurance benefit computed on the wage record of the individual with respect to whose wages the child is entitled to receive such benefit. If there is more than one such individual the child's insurance benefit is equal to one-half of whichever primary insurance benefit is the greatest. . . .

e. Since every primary insurance benefit must be at least $10, the benefit computed for each child would be at least $5. However, if a single orphan is the only survivor eligible for benefits, his benefit will be at least $10 because of the $10 minimum applying to the total of the benefits payable with respect to one individual's wages. . . .

f. The total of benefits payable for a month with respect to an individual's wages is subject to the same maximum provisions. . . . The maximum of twice the primary insurance benefit has the effect of reducing the orphans' benefits otherwise payable if there are more than two orphans and a widow, all eligible for benefits with respect to the same deceased individual's wage record. Likewise, this maximum will serve to reduce the orphans' benefits (in the event that there is no widow eligible for benefits) when there are more than four orphans eligible for benefits with respect to one individual's wages. Whenever any of the maximums serves to reduce the total benefits which would otherwise be payable, a pro rata reduction is made in all benefits. . . .

X. Parent's Insurance Benefits

a. Each parent of an individual who dies after December 31, 1939, leaving no widow or unmarried surviving child under the age of 18, is entitled to receive monthly benefits if all the following requirements are met: (1) The individual was fully insured at the time of his death; (2) the parent has attained the age of 65; (3) the parent was wholly dependent upon and supported by such individual at the time of such individual's death and filed proof of such dependency and support within 2 years of such death; (4) the parent has not married since such individual's death; (5) the parent is not entitled to any other insurance benefits under the benefit provisions of the amended act, the total of which is greater than one-half of the primary insurance benefit of such deceased individual; and (6) the parent must have filed an application for parent's insurance benefits. . . .

c. The term "parent" includes the stepparent of an individual by a marriage contracted before such individual attained the age of 16; it also includes an adopting parent by whom an individual was adopted before he attained the age of 16.

d. The amount of the parent's insurance benefit is equal to one-half of the primary insurance benefit computed on the basis of the wage record of the deceased individual, provided the parent is not entitled to receive any other insurance benefits. If the parent is entitled to receive other insurance benefits of which the total is less than one-half of the primary insurance benefit of the deceased individual, the parent's insurance benefit will be reduced by the amount of such other benefits. If the parent is entitled to receive any other such insurance benefits of which the total is equal to or greater than one-half the primary insurance benefit of the deceased individual, no parent's insurance benefit is payable. . . .

e. When there is more than one individual with respect to whose wages the parent is entitled to receive a parent's insurance benefit, the parent's benefit is equal to one-half of whichever such primary insurance benefit is greatest. . . .

f. Since every primary insurance benefit must be at least $10, each parent's insurance benefit payable must be at least $5. Furthermore, the total of benefits payable with respect to any one individual's wages is subject to a minimum of $10. Therefore, if there is only one eligible parent, he or she will receive a benefit of at least $10. The maximum provisions cannot affect the parents' insurance benefits except in the unlikely event of there being more than two "parents" entitled to benefits. . . .

XI. Lump-Sum Death Payments

a. A lump-sum payment is made upon the death of an individual after December 31, 1939, if (1) such individual was either fully or currently insured at the time of his death, and (2) there was no surviving widow, child, or parent who would, on filing an application in the month in which such individual died, be entitled to a survivor's benefit for such month. . . .

b. The amount of such lump-sum death payment is equal to six times the primary insurance benefit computed upon such individual's wage record. . . .

c. The lump-sum death payment is payable to the following person (or, if more than one, will be distributed among them) . . . (1) to the widow or widower of the deceased; (2) if no widow or widower is then living, to any child or children of the deceased and to any other persons who are entitled to share as distributees with such children under the intestacy law of the State where the deceased was domiciled; (3) if none of the aforementioned are living, then to the parents of the deceased in equal shares; (4) if none of the aforementioned are living, such amounts shall be payable to any person or persons equitably entitled thereto to the extent that he or they shall have paid the burial expenses of the deceased. . . .

e. Lump-sum payments under section 203 of the original Social Security Act are to be discontinued in cases of death on and after January 1, 1940. . . .

XII. Lump-Sum Payments at Age 65

a. Lump-sum payments upon attainment of age 65 under section 204 of the original Social Security Act were discontinued immediately upon the enactment of these amendments. . . .

XIII. Special Deductions from Benefits

a. Deductions will be made from benefits for any month in which either the person entitled to benefits or (in the case of wife's or child's benefits) the individual on the basis of whose wage record the benefit is payable rendered services for wages of $15 or more (in covered employment). . . .

XVI. Taxing Provisions

a. The tax rate continues to be 1 percent each on employers and employees for the years 1940, 1941, and 1942, as well as for the remainder of 1939. After 1942, the schedule in the original act is resumed so that the rate is 2 percent on employers and 2 percent on employees in 1943, 1944, and 1945, 2½ percent on each in 1946, 1947, and 1948, and 3 percent on each thereafter. . . .

e. The taxing provisions formerly in title VIII of the Social Security Act are included under the Internal Revenue Code in subchapter A of chapter 9, which can be cited as the "Federal Insurance Contributions Act.". . .

XVII. Reserves

a. The old-age reserve account of the original act is replaced as of January 1, 1940, by a trust fund to be termed the "Federal old-age and survivors insurance trust fund." Securities and amounts held by or credited to the old-age reserve account are transferred to the trust fund. This fund is administered by a board of trustees composed of the Secretary of the Treasury, who is to be the Managing Trustee, the Secretary of Labor, and the Chairman of the Social Security Board. There is to be credited to the trust fund through permanent appropriation amounts equivalent to the full amount of taxes received annually under the Federal Insurance Contributions Act. The amounts credited to the trust fund shall be available for making the payments required under title II and for the administrative expense of the Treasury Department and Social Security Board in connection with the old-age and survivors insurance provisions of the act. This method of administering the old-age insurance reserve fund will tend to avoid misunderstanding of the use of the funds and will increase confidence in their proper investment. . . .

b. That portion of the fund not needed to meet current claims or administrative expenses is to be invested in obligations of or guaranteed by the United States, purchased by the trust fund at the market price. If the Managing Trustee determines that the purchase of securities on the open market is not in the public interest, special obligations may be acquired at par. Interest on special certificates will be at the current average rate of interest borne by all outstanding interest-bearing obligations composing the public debt. . . .

c. It will be the duty of the Board of Trustees to (1) hold the trust fund, (2) report annually to the Congress on the operation and status of the trust fund and its expected operation during the ensuing 5 fiscal years, and (3) report to the Congress immediately whenever they are of the opinion that during the ensuing 5 fiscal years the trust fund will exceed three times the highest annual expenditures anticipated during that 5-year period and whenever they are of the opinion that the amount of the trust fund is unduly small. . . .

Source: "Federal Old-Age and Survivors Insurance: A Summary of the 1939 Amendments," *Social Security Bulletin,* vol. 2, no. 12 (Washington, D.C.: Social Security Board, 1939): 3–16.

CHAPTER 3

Political Struggles over Social Security in the 1940s and Program Expansion in 1950

Bookended by the watershed 1939 amendments and the very significant 1950 amendments, the 1940s saw relatively little action in Social Security, but there were two significant developments.

The first was a long sequence of rate freezes whereby the tax rate schedules from the 1935 and 1939 laws were not allowed to take effect. This sequence of decisions was implicitly engaging policymakers in issues about the trust fund reserve and the interplay of current versus future taxation as a source of program funding.

President Harry Truman campaigned for national health insurance and for expansion of the coverage of the Social Security program. He signed the 1950 Amendments into law. Source: Library of Congress.

In the Social Security Act of 1935 the trust fund was an implicit financing structure, and the program was on a full-reserve basis. Following the 1939 amendments, the financing was shifted to be virtually a pay-as-you-go system, with the trust funds formalized in the law. During World War II, the debate about the reserves took place in the context of proposals to "freeze" increases in the tax rates that were written into existing law. This happened for the first time in the 1939 amendments and then seven more times between 1942 and 1949.

The economy in the war years produced a financial windfall for the Social Security system. At the same time that demand for benefits declined by more than 50 percent, tax revenues doubled. The unexpected high balance in the trust funds prompted lawmakers to propose ways to prevent additional buildups, primarily by freezing tax rates. In general, a shift to a more "pay-as-you-go" approach would mean lower taxes in the early years and higher taxes in the distant future. The alternative to higher future payroll taxes would be general revenue subsidies to the Social Security program—and this option was continually suggested by some throughout the freeze debates.

The Social Security Board was uncomfortable with the idea of using general revenues to cover future income shortfalls. Board officials believed that when it came time to raise future tax rates, Congress and taxpayers would balk, resorting to benefit cuts to make up the shortfall. Board officials thus argued against the freezes in the tax rates (after the 1939 changes, which the administration supported), and President Franklin D. Roosevelt tried unsuccessfully to veto some of them.

No provision of law permitted general revenue contributions to Social Security until 1943, when as an amendment to this effect was introduced on the Senate floor (at the request of the Social Security Board) by Sen. James Murray (D-Mont.). Board officials believed that if long-range program finances were to depend in part on general revenues, then this needed to be in the law. The Murray amendment was enacted into law in 1943 and repealed in the 1950 amendments without ever having been used.

This chapter also documents the passage of the Social Security Act Amendments of 1950. These amendments dramatically increased the value of Social Security benefits and started the program on its glide path to the nearly universal coverage it has today.

Prior to the 1950 amendments, there were more elderly in America receiving welfare-based old-age pensions than Social Security, and the average old-age pension benefit was higher than the average Social Security retirement benefit. After the 1950 amendments, Social Security would bypass welfare on both scores.

The 1950 amendments were to a considerable degree the product of the 1948–1949 advisory council. The report of this council, and President Harry Truman's adoption of their recommendations, started the legislative process and shaped the legislation that followed.

The 1950 law rerationalized the financing of the system, dramatically increased the value of benefits, and extended coverage. Overall, the amendments brought 8 million new workers into mandatory coverage under the system—more than half of whom were in various forms of self-employment. In addition, another 2.5 million workers (mostly state and local government employees) were offered optional coverage at their election. The law increased the value of benefits by an average of 77 percent, which was slightly more than the increase in prices since 1937 but only about two-thirds of the increase in average wage levels since then.

One seemingly minor technical change eliminated the "increment" in the benefit formula. Under this provision, the benefit calculation increased the benefit amount by 1 percent for each year the person participated in the program—as a way of rewarding longevity in the labor force. The effect on benefits was that initial benefits (and program costs) would be higher and future benefits (and program costs) would be lower. Eliminating the increment thus allowed policymakers to raise benefits in the short run for early beneficiaries without having to pay higher benefits in the long-run to later beneficiaries.

Document 3.1
Unpublished First Report on the Social Security Trust Funds, January 3, 1941

The trustees of the Social Security trust funds began the practice of issuing an annual report in 1941. The first report was transmitted to the Speaker of the House and the president of the Senate as a letter from the trustees, but it was never subsequently published either by Congress or the Social Security Board. This earliest formal statement of the operations of the Social Security trust funds points to the special role in Social Security policymaking played by the actuaries and their annual estimates of program financing.

Introductory Statement

The Federal old-age and survivors insurance trust fund was created pursuant to section 201 of the Social Security Act Amendments of 1939, approved August 10, 1939. This trust fund became effective on January 1, 1940, and superseded the old-age reserve account established under the Social Security Act of 1935. . . .

Resources made available to the trust fund included the securities held by the Secretary of the Treasury for the old-age reserve account, accounts standing to the credit of the old-age reserve account on the books of the Treasury as of January 1, 1940, and interest on the investments. . . .

The trust fund was in operation for only 6 months of the fiscal year 1940. The transition from the old-age reserve account to the new fund was accomplished in such a manner that the financial operations of the program may be considered as continuous from the active beginning of the old-age insurance program in January 1937 to the end of the fiscal year 1940.

The Social Security Act Amendments of 1939, creating the old-age and survivors insurance trust fund and establishing the Board of Trustees, made other significant changes affecting the financing of the old-age and survivors insurance program. . . . The expected effect of these modifications was to increase disbursements from the trust fund in the next two or three decades and to reduce contributions during the fiscal years 1940 through 1943. . . .

. . . At the end of June 1940 approximately 50 million persons already held social security account numbers and about 42 million workers had made contributions toward benefits under the system. In the future, millions of additional workers will come under the program as they obtain jobs in covered employments. Most of the rights now being accumulated toward benefits by these contributors and insured workers will not mature for many years. Consequently, benefits under the program are expected to increase markedly over a long period. This results from the fact that larger numbers of workers will be eligible and will qualify for benefits and from the expectation that the proportion of the population in ages 65 and over, estimated at 7 percent in 1940, may eventually rise to perhaps 14 to 16 percent. Hence the essential assurance of future financial soundness of the system, with its rising rate of disbursement, rests on a graduated increase in contribution rates or provision of income from other sources, or both. . . .

Actuarial Status of the Trust Fund

. . . Illustrations of future cost possibilities must recognize an upward trend in benefit outgo for long periods ahead. The amendments of 1939 greatly improved the protection afforded covered groups in the population by bringing monthly benefits to widows and children of deceased covered workers. These new protections, while of major significance to the security of insured workers and their families, represent only about one-fourth of the costs of the program; the remaining portion of the disbursements is for old-age protection. This is significant since, with a larger number and percentage of the population at ages above 65 definitely anticipated for the future, the number of qualified beneficiaries may be expected to increase more or less steadily for perhaps a century.

The actuarial status of the trust fund may be measured by a variety of methods. One method is to estimate the income and disbursements of the fund during specified future periods . . . according to which annual tax collections would be expected to rise from an average of almost $1 billion for the first 5 years of operation under the amended set to an average of $1.7 billion during the second 5 years of operation and to approximately $2.5 billion 35 or 40 years hence.

Annual benefit payments may be expected to increase from an average of about $0.3 billion for the first 5 years to almost $1 billion for the second 5 years. After a 40-year period, average annual benefit payments may have risen to a magnitude of about $3.5 billion and, after a 50-year period to over $4 billion. A further rise after that period may be expected because of the anticipated increase in the number of persons qualifying for benefits and in the average benefit payments. . . .

. . . [T]hroughout the initial period taxes exceed benefits. This would result in a fund accumulation which provides interest earnings to meet a portion of the current benefit payments. . . . Because of the cumulative growth of the disbursements, any long-term deficiency in the finances of the program would be apparent well in advance, and, therefore, could be met without serious shock or disturbance, by moderate changes in the financial provisions.

Expected Relations between Size of the Trust Fund and Disbursements

. . . The primary consideration with respect to the size of the trust fund is its role in relation to the financial integrity of the social insurance program. In addition, the Board of Trustees must have regard for the relationship of the fund to the fiscal position of the Government and the economic position of the Nation.

The present low level of current disbursements may be increased sharply with a change in employment conditions within the next few years; nor is this level representative of what is likely to be the long-term experience. The probable future level of benefit payments is high and the trend of such payments will be steeply ascending over the next generation and longer. The actuarial analysis . . . indicates that a generation hence disbursements will be at least three to four times greater than the maximum disbursements which may be expected in the next five fiscal years. Prudent management, therefore, requires emphasis on the long-range consideration of income and disbursements.

Having regard for these long-range as well as for short-range commitments and for fiscal and economic relationships, the Board believes that the trust fund is not excessive in size.

Summary and Conclusion

In presenting this report to Congress . . . the Board of Trustees reports that the purposes to be served by the amendments of 1939 have been safeguarded in every respect.

The essential functions performed by the old-age reserve account have been taken over by the new trust fund. These functions are strengthened and the interests of the beneficiaries emphasized by the modification of procedure under which appropriations to the fund are now related directly to the tax collections.

During the six months of operation of the old-age and survivors insurance trust fund (January 1 to June 30, 1940), receipts of the fund, including the investments held by and amounts credited to the old-age reserve account, the transfers from the 1940 appropriation balance, and interests on investments, totaled $1,766.9 million. Disbursements from the fund for benefit payments and reimbursements for administrative expenses were $22.2 million. On June 30, 1940, assets of the trust fund amounted to $1,744.7 million of which $1,738.1 million represented investments.

The trust fund augmented by the anticipated income of the next five fiscal years is ample to assure the payment of benefits and administrative expenses for this period. However, the next five-year period is but the introduction to several generations during which the trend in benefits, while predictable in degree, will be pronouncedly upward.

The future benefits to which we are now committed will require large scale outlays many times greater than the level of payments in the first five years. Expected income will also be increasing, but whether or not additional income will be needed in the long-distant future cannot be determined at this time. In view of the short period during which the amended act has been in force and the magnitude of the long-range commitments of the program, the Board makes no recommendation at this time for changing the tax rates under sections 1400 and 1410 of the Federal Insurance Contributions Act.

Source: Trust Fund Reports, "Letter of Transmittal," January 3, 1941. Manuscript copy in the Social Security Administration History Archives and full report available on the Social Security Administration Web site: www.ssa.gov/history/reports/trust/tf1941.html (accessed March 18, 2007).

Document 3.2
Arthur Altmeyer on the "Desirability of Expanding the Social Insurance Program Now," November 1942

In this article from the Social Security Bulletin *(the in-house research publication of the Social Security Board), chairman Arthur Altmeyer is urging that the nation should dramatically expand the scope and role of Social Security by providing a comprehensive social insurance system. He makes this argument during a time of full national mobilization for war and uses the war effort, and the unique effect it has on the Social Security system's finances, to argue that this is the optimum time to expand the program.*

Arthur J. Altmeyer was the principal administrator of the Social Security program for most of its first twenty years and the single greatest influence on Social Security policymaking during that period.
Source: SSA History Archives.

. . . While greatly furthering individual and family security, the present system still fails to provide protection against several major economic hazards confronting every individual, notably income loss resulting from temporary and permanent disablement and heavy costs incurred for hospitalization and medical care. It also omits from the scope of even its present protections a substantial proportion of the Nation's workers. Moreover, benefits payable under existing programs are admittedly inadequate at various points.

Timeliness of Expanding Social Insurance

Because of the economic dislocations which may characterize the aftermath of the war, it is important to provide greater security against economic risks to workers and their families by remedying these deficiencies and strengthening our social insurance system before that time. Unless action is taken now, there is grave danger that the postwar period will arrive before a well-rounded system has been put in operation. It may then be impossible to install the necessary measures sufficiently rapidly to care for the urgencies of the moment, and we might have to face emergency problems with hastily improvised devices.

The obvious question which will occur to many—who may agree with the inherent desirability of having a comprehensive social insurance system available at the end of the war—is whether the present is a practical and appropriate time for such action. The enormous outlays and the vast administrative undertakings now necessary for the prosecution of the war may appear to suggest that action be deferred, regardless of other consequences.

The answer to this question—entirely apart from the social gains involved—is that expansion of the social insurances would be more appropriate now from the standpoint of the Nation's economic and fiscal circumstances than at any time since 1935 or for some time to come.

Two of the major economic problems of the war effort are to control inflation and to obtain revenues through taxation or borrowing or both. Because of the accumulation of reserves which characterizes the early stages of social insurance systems, new or expanded, and the operation of such systems in a period of high employment such as now prevails, immediate expansion of our social insurance system would contribute substantially toward meeting these economic problems. The enlarged excess of contributions over disbursements which would accompany the early phase of social insurance expansion would reduce current purchasing power and serve as a potent force in the fight against inflation. Investment of the excess in Government obligations would make corresponding sums available to the Treasury. These investments would aid in financing the war just as do the war savings bonds purchased by individuals.

Thus, a measure can be taken now which will provide the basis for a better society after the war and at the same time will serve the general economic and fiscal needs of the moment.

Contents of an Expanded Program

Before examining the possible contribution of social insurance expansion to these problems, it is desirable to outline briefly the general nature of the changes which should be made in the present system. In the first place, new types of protection should be added: (1) benefits for permanently disabled workers and for their dependents, irrespective of the worker's age and generally similar in amount to old-age benefits; (2) benefits for workers temporarily disabled through illness or injury and for their dependents, payable for a limited number of months and more or less similar in amount to unemployment benefits; and (3) payments with respect to hospitalization costs incurred by insured workers or their dependents.

A second part of the expansion should be the extension of social insurance coverage to occupations now excluded from even the present programs. Among the major occupations not now covered at all or only partially covered under the existing system are agricultural labor, domestic service, employment in certain nonprofit organizations, governmental service, maritime employment, employment in small firms, and self-employment. . . . It would be desirable, so far as it is administratively and otherwise feasible, to extend both the present and the proposed new protections to these groups. . . .

Post-War Considerations

Because of the manner in which benefit and eligibility rights are accumulated in advance of the receipt of benefits under social insurance, the contributory nature of its financing, and the automatic processes inherent in its operation, it is inevitably destined for an important role in the postwar period. The only basic question is whether a comprehensive system should be set up now, so that benefits will be immediately available at the end of the war to assist in alleviating the hardships of that period, or whether changes should be delayed until these hardships are actually occurring for millions of families.

Provided expansion is undertaken now, social insurance can play a dual role in the economic readjustment and reconstruction that will be necessary when the war ends. On the one hand, it can provide protection to individuals and families against the loss of income which they may suffer for one reason or another after the war, when a decline from the high levels of wartime production would increase greatly the incidence of risks leading to such losses. On the other hand, from the standpoint of the economic system as a whole, social insurance can aid in maintaining consumer purchasing power if national income exhibits a tendency to shrink and thus can assist in maintaining employment at higher levels.

Under an expanded program, more nearly adequate benefits would be available to support the unemployed and their dependents until they can get new employment in peacetime production. More nearly adequate annuities would be paid to aged workers who, though they normally might have retired, remained at work until the end of the war. Permanently disabled persons, too young to be eligible for old-age benefits, would for the first time be able to obtain similar benefits. Workers who are temporarily disabled would be eligible for weekly benefits until they are able to return to work. When sickness entails hospitalization, payments would be available to ease the heavy burden of the cost. Finally, the widows, orphans, and other survivors of workers who die would continue to receive benefits which would, in large measure, replace their loss of support. . . .

The economic effect of an expanded program upon the economy as a whole during the post-War period will depend largely upon the relation of disbursements to contributions. Social insurance benefits represent active purchasing power used immediately for consumption goods. Social insurance contributions in the main come out of income otherwise used for consumption. Thus, the extent to which the social insurance programs as a whole will give a stimulus to the economy after the war will depend on the extent, if any, to which disbursements exceed receipts in that period. The net balance between receipts and disbursements will vary widely according to the levels of post-war production and employment. If employment declines sharply after the war, the need for a strong social insurance system will be critically urgent. Even if our economy stays geared for the long run to high levels of employment, many millions of workers and soldiers may be temporarily unemployed while we are changing over from a war to a peacetime economy. It is precisely in such circumstances that disbursements under an expanded program will be most likely to exceed receipts and will be most useful in sustaining general purchasing power.

Contribution Rates

The question now arises as to the over-all rate of contribution which, from the standpoint of sound principles of social insurance financing, should be imposed at the outset of an expanded program. . . .

. . . [A] total basic contribution rate of 10 percent of pay roll for employments covered under all protections is indicated for the first years of the program outlined above. For employments omitted from the coverage of some of the protections, an appropriate downward adjustment in the basic rate would be necessary. A 10-percent rate would be double the total basic rate levied in 1942 for old-age and survivors insurance and unemployment compensation combined.

Receipts and Expenditures

The suggested contribution rates would produce receipts substantially in excess of disbursements in the first years of the expanded program. . . .

While adhering firmly to accepted principles of social insurance financing, immediate expansion of the social insurance program along lines strongly dictated by social needs would thus lead to a substantial increase in reserves. Investment of these additional reserves in Federal obligations would make funds in corresponding amount available to the Treasury. These obligations would be credits available to the social insurance program, to be drawn upon later as required to meet benefit disbursements.

War-Revenue Requirements

A revised estimate of $85 billion for expenditures by the Federal Government in the fiscal year 1942–43 was issued on October 7 by the Bureau of the Budget. After taking into account net budget and trust-account receipts and borrowing from Government trust accounts under existing legislation, it is estimated that during the fiscal year 1942–43 the Treasury will have to obtain approximately $60 billion over and above expected income to finance expenditures.

The deficit amount will have to be obtained either through additional taxation or by borrowing from individuals and banks. It is generally recognized that financing the war through potentially inflationary measures, such as borrowing from commercial banks, should be kept to the lowest possible level. If excessive reliance on bank borrowing is to be avoided, additional funds beyond those now provided must be transferred from the hands of the public into the Treasury.

The first question in considering methods of attaining the Treasury's necessary goal is whether or not the imposition of further levies should be accompanied by some type of post-war return. To the extent that additional funds are obtained through outright taxation, no such return is provided. Expansion of the social insurance system or the introduction of a compulsory lending plan would, however, involve additional levies which would provide a return to the lender after the war. . . .

The increased revenue accompanying an expansion of the social insurance program differs from other types of taxation in that a post-war credit is provided to contributors. It resembles compulsory lending plans to that extent, but it differs from such lending plans in that the post-war return is in the form of insurance protection rather than lump-sum amounts. . . .

To advance as an argument in support of an expansion of social insurance—a desirable and timely step on its own merits—that the increase in net receipts in the early years would aid the Treasury in financing the war should not be understood as advocating diversion of social security taxes to general revenue purposes. The increased collections, as in the past, would still flow into trust funds, rather than into the general fund of the Treasury; their investment in interest-bearing Government obligations would still be manifested by a corresponding rise in the public debt; and—most important of all—contributors would receive benefit rights, and such benefit rights would be a full "money's worth" per dollar contributed.

In view of these considerations, immediate expansion of the social insurance program would seem to be well adapted as a part of a well-rounded program for financing the war. . . .

In summary, expansion of social insurance is urgently required now to provide security against the uncertainties arising out of the war. Changes in our economic life caused by the war increase the potential economic risks facing individuals and their families, and emphasize the need for an adequate system of insurance to allay fear of the future and provide the security essential for an all-out effort. Taking this socially desirable action now would not interfere with the war effort but would assist in alleviating the pressing economic problems of raising more funds for the war and of checking inflation.

Source: Social Security Bulletin, vol. 5, no. 11 (November 1942): 5–9.

Document 3.3
Arthur Altmeyer's Statement before the Ways and Means Committee, November 27, 1944

The Roosevelt administration had supported the first of the tax rate freezes (in the 1939 amendments) but opposed the subsequent freezes, starting in 1942. By 1944 the administration and the Congress were at loggerheads over the issue of the continual freezing of the tax rates. In this 1944 testimony before the House Ways and Means Committee, Arthur Altmeyer was trying to head off another freeze of the contribution rates. He refers to the "level annual cost" of the program, and he mentions figures of an implied deficit to date based on the current tax rate. This level annual cost is the tax rate that would have to be charged throughout a period in order for the system to be fully funded. At a given point in time, if the tax rate has been running below the level annual cost, then an implicit deficit-to-date has accrued; this is the deficit-to-date to which Altmeyer is referring in his testimony.

The question which I understand the Committee wishes to discuss today is whether Congress should act to prevent the automatic increase in the present 1-percent contribution rate payable by employers and employees respectively under the Federal old-age and survivors insurance system. As you know, if Congress does not act this rate will increase automatically to 2 percent each on January 1, 1945, in accordance with the schedule provided in the Social Security Act of 1935 and retained in the 1939 amendments to that Act. If Congress acts to retain the rate at 1 percent it will be the fourth time Congress has delayed the automatic increase provided in the law.

As you know from my previous appearances before this Committee, the Social Security Board believed that it was necessary from the standpoint of sound financing of a contributory social insurance system that the automatic increases be permitted to go into effect. The Social Security Board believes that the longer these necessary increases in the contribution rate are deferred the greater is the impairment of the financial soundness of this contributory social insurance system and the greater the impairment of the whole idea of contributory social insurance.

. . . A sound contributory social insurance system has four main characteristics. First, it provides for benefits on a specific and predetermined basis. Second, it provides these benefits as a matter of right without a means or a needs test. Third, it finances these benefits largely out of contributions made by or on behalf of the beneficiaries. Fourth, it provides a long-range systematic method of financing rather than a year-to-year unsystematic method.

There is no question that the benefits promised under the present Federal old-age and survivors insurance system will cost far more than the 2 percent of payrolls now being collected. As I pointed out in my testimony of last year, none of the actuarial estimates which have been made on the basis of present economic conditions and other factors now clearly discernible result in a level annual cost of this insurance system of less than 4 percent of payroll. Indeed, under certain assumptions the level annual cost has been estimated to be as much as 7 percent of payrolls. On the basis of a 4-percent level annual cost it may be said that the reserve fund of this system already has a deficit of $6,600 million. On the basis of 7-percent level annual cost it may be said that the reserve fund already has a deficit of about $16,500 million.

Another indication of the magnitude of the liability which the Federal Government has assumed can be obtained from the fact that the present value of the benefits payable to those now eligible amounts to approximately four and one-half billion dollars. Let me emphasize that this figure represents only the liabilities which the Federal Government has assumed for those persons already eligible for benefits. Since the reserve fund as of January 1, 1945, will be only six billion dollars, this leaves only a billion and a half dollars in the reserve fund to meet the liabilities which the Federal Government has assumed for the payment of benefits to the 69 million persons who have accumulated wage credits but have not yet died or reached the retirement age of 65.

I hope that the foregoing figures will help to clear up the misunderstanding that some people have that because we are collecting as much in contributions at the present rate of 1 percent each on employers and employees as it was estimated in 1939 we would collect at 2 percent each it is not necessary to permit the automatic increase in the rate to go into effect. I wish to emphasize that for every dollar of contributions which is collected the Federal Government assumes a liability for the payment of benefits. It is true that we are collecting at the present rate of 1 percent as much as we estimated in 1939 we would collect at 2 percent. However, this is because more people have become insured and larger wage credits, upon which benefits are based, have been accumulated by the workers insured under this system. Therefore, it is quite fallacious to assume that because we are collecting as much at the present 1-percent rate as we estimated in 1939 we would collect at the 2-percent rate it is not necessary to permit the increased rate to go into effect. A private insurance company that wrote twice as much business and, therefore, had twice as much premium income as it had previously estimated does not cut its premium rates in half, because it realizes that it has also assumed an increased liability. In my judgment, it is likewise unsound for the Federal Government to do so.

I do not wish to take the time of this Committee by repeating all of the facts and arguments I have presented on previous occasions. However, it may be helpful to the Committee if I list the following points upon which I believe all experts are in agreement:

(1) In the early years of the operation of the old-age and survivors insurance system, the actuarial value of the benefits paid are many times the actuarial value of the individual worker's contributions. . . .

(2) Even a contribution rate of 2 percent each by employers and employees is probably inadequate to finance the cost of benefits promised.

(3) It is a mathematical certainty that the longer the present pay-roll tax rate remains in effect, the higher the future pay-roll tax must be if the insurance system continues to be financed wholly by payroll taxes. Therefore, the indefinite continuation of the present contribution rate . . . will eventually necessitate raising the . . . contribution rate later. . . .

(4) Retaining the present rate creates a moral obligation on the part of Congress to provide a Government subsidy later on to the extent necessary to avoid levying inequitably high pay-roll tax rates in the future. . . .

(5) The Government obligations held by the Old-Age and Survivors Insurance Trust Fund would otherwise be in the hands of banks, insurance companies, and other private investors. . . .

I think it is concerning the implications of this last point that there has not been a complete meeting of minds. Thus, the following statement is contained in a report of the Senate Finance Committee concerning the tax freeze last year: "It makes no difference to the taxpayer whether this $1,500,000,000 is appropriated to pay the interest on $50,000,000,000 of Government bonds in a reserve fund or whether it is a direct appropriation to the support of the old-age and survivors system."

However, I feel that that statement fails to recognize that with no reserve funds the taxpayers would be required to pay a $1.5 billion *subsidy* to the insurance system *and also be required to pay $1.5 billion interest to private investors on securities held by them instead of by the insurance trust fund.* With a $50 billion reserve fund, the taxpayers would pay *only* $1.5 billion into the insurance trust fund in the form of interest on the securities held by it. Therefore, without a reserve fund the taxpayers' burden would be exactly double.

If my analysis is correct, I believe that this Committee is confronted with a question of public policy rather than a technical question upon which experts might differ. This question of policy may be summarized as follows:

(1) The Social Security Board believes that there is greater assurance that the benefits promised will be paid if the future annual excess of benefit payments over pay-roll tax receipts is met by a Congressional appropriation to pay the interest on the insurance trust fund rather than in the form of an outright subsidy out of general revenues.

(2) Those who disagree believe that the larger the accumulated trust fund, the greater is the temptation to extravagance on the part of Congress, if not for general Government purposes, at least for the payment of higher benefits than they would consider warranted. The Board believes that this argument is unsound for two reasons: First, because while this fund represents an *asset* of the insurance system it represents a *liability* of the Government just as truly as any other outstanding Government obligations. Second, because the Board believes that the present contribution rate, so far below the value of the protection provided, creates a temptation to increase the benefits without giving proper consideration to the true costs involved. Parenthetically, I should also like to point out that the continuation of the present 1-percent rate not only tends to depreciate the true costs involved, but also depreciates in the minds of employees, employers and the public generally the great value of the protection afforded.

In my testimony before this Committee last January, I made the following statement: "In the history of social insurance throughout the world the major difficulty of social insurance systems has been the lack of adequate financing of old-age retirement benefits. It is always easiest to delay levying the necessary insurance contributions, thus perpetuating and strengthening the belief that the insurance benefits are meager and the costs of the insurance system are low. Inevitably, when the time comes to increase the taxes, many reasons can always be advanced as to why the imposition of the additional taxes is unwise or impossible. In this country we are still in a position to avoid these mistakes by getting clearly established now that if our people want social insurance they must be willing to pay for it. The time to obtain the necessary contributions is when people are able to pay for the insurance and are willing to pay for it because they can be shown that they are getting their money's worth. If we should let a situation develop whereby it eventually becomes necessary to charge future beneficiaries rates in excess of the actuarial cost of the protection afforded them, we would be guilty of gross inequity and gross financial mismanagement, bound to imperil our social insurance system."....

Source: Arthur J. Altmeyer, "A Statement on the Automatic Increase in the Tax Rate under the Federal Old-Age and Survivors Insurance System," testimony before the House Ways and Means Committee, November 27, 1944; available on the Social Security Administration Web site: www.ssa.gov/ history/aja1144a.html (accessed November 10, 2006).

Document 3.4
House Ways and Means Committee Report and Dissent, December 1, 1944

Following the hearing in November 1944, the House Ways and Means Committee issued a report to the House favoring the proposal to freeze the payroll tax rates at the existing level. The Republican members of the committee unanimously supported the bill and were joined by several Democratic members—producing a 17–7 vote in favor of reporting the bill to the House. The seven dissenting Democrats joined in a formal dissent to the committee's report. Their four-page dissent was twice the length of the report itself.

Report

This bill provides for "freezing" the rate of tax on pay rolls and wages for old-age and survivors benefits on employees and employers at the rate of 1 percent for the year 1945, thus postponing an increase to 2 percent on employers and employees as would otherwise result under existing law. Your committee is convinced that it is not necessary to double existing rates for 1945 in order to protect the solvency of the old-age and survivors insurance fund.

When the social security law was amended in 1939, your committee and the Congress were both definitely of the opinion that the reserve contemplated in the original act, and variously estimated under the original schedule of tax rates to reach from 47 billion to 49 billion dollars, was not necessary for the solvency of the fund.

The estimate furnished to the committee and the Congress in 1939 indicated that the reserve would amount to $3,122,000,000 in 1944 with a graduated schedule of tax rates. However, the reserve has now reached the sum of approximately $6,000,000,000 with a tax rate of 1 percent on employee and employer, and will approximate $7,250,000,000 by the end of 1945. Thus the reserve fund will be more than 2 times the amount that was contemplated under the estimates used when the social security system was revised in 1939, and was placed on what was then considered to be a sound actuarial basis. In the hearings of 1939, the Secretary of the Treasury, Mr. Morgenthau, testified as follows:

"Specifically, I would suggest to Congress that it plan the financing of the old-age insurance system with a view to maintaining for use in contingencies an eventual reserve amounting to not more than 3 times the highest prospective annual benefits in the ensuing 5 years."

Congress has upon three occasions applied this rule and as a result has three times postponed the statutory increase in pay-roll taxes. Your committee finds that the old-age reserve as of June 30, 1944, was $5,450,000,000, and approximately $6,000,000,000 as of the end

*This World War II-era poster presents a
perennial Social Security issue—the importance
of the Social Security card—in terms of a patriotic appeal in support of the war effort.*
Source: SSA History Archives.

of this year and that according to the most recent estimates of the Social Security Board the highest annual expenditure will be between $450,000,000 and $700,000,000 in the next 5 years. Therefore, the existing reserve is from 8 to 12 times the highest annual expenditure instead of 3 times, as recommended by the Secretary of the Treasury.

It should also be pointed out that the tax collections at 1 percent on employee and 1 percent on employer now exceed the amount originally anticipated from the higher tax rate provided in the Social Security Act as amended in 1939. Tax collections, even with the tax rate retained at 1 percent on employee and employer respectively, have substantially exceeded the estimates furnished in 1939 and the benefits paid have fallen far below the estimates furnished to the Congress in 1939. Therefore, since the automatic increase in tax to 2 percent on employer and employee, respectively, effective next January is unnecessary for benefit payments (for many years to come), or for the maintenance of a contingent reserve 3 times the highest anticipated expenditure in the next 5 years, we submit that these taxes should not be doubled at this time.

The committee does not feel that any unnecessary increase in the existing high tax burden should be made now in view of the problems of reconversion from war to peace that soon will confront us and which must be solved. It should be clearly understood that this legislation has no connection with the question of expansion of social security benefits or coverage, but refers solely to the problem of financing existing benefits and coverage. It does not involve in any way, benefit payments under the old-age assistance or so-called old-age pension systems which are paid out of annual appropriations.

As has been stated, actual experience in the operation of the system has demonstrated the inaccuracy of the estimates made only 5 years ago to say nothing of those made in 1935. . . .

Dissenting Views

The undersigned members of the Ways and Means Committee respectfully submit their dissenting views relative to H. R. 5564, which has been favorably reported by the majority of the committee.

We deeply regret that our considered opinion with respect to this bill is at variance with a majority of our colleagues and that we cannot concur in the recommendation that the bill should be reported favorably.

The bill reported by a majority of the committee will prevent the rate of contributions under the Federal old-age and survivors insurance system from increasing on January 1, 1945, in accordance with the schedule contained in the present law. We believe this action to be unwise and detrimental to the basic principles underlying a contributory social-insurance system. Our reasons are summarized as follows:

Summary of Objections to the Bill

1. The success of a contributory system of social insurance is at stake.

We believe that the very success of this contributory social-insurance system which Congress established in 1935 is at stake and not merely the fixing of a tax rate in the usual sense of the term. The Congress of the United States in 1935 took a long step forward in undertaking to substitute for a hit-and-miss method of relieving destitution through a Government dole a systematic long-range method known as contributory social insurance. Under a system of contributory social insurance, benefits are paid as a matter of right without a means or a needs test and are related in an equitable manner to the length of time a person has been insured and the amount of his past earnings. An essential characteristic of any contributory social-insurance system is that the benefits are financed wholly or in large part from contributions made by or on behalf of the beneficiaries. It is just as true of a social-insurance system as of any insurance system that its security depends upon the certainty and soundness of the methods used to finance it. In financing a contributory social-insurance system it is necessary to make certain that the promises made today to pay benefits in the future can be and will be fulfilled. Under a social-insurance system providing old-age annuities based upon the length of time insured initial costs are low and ultimate costs are high. In the case of this social-insurance system it has been estimated that the eventual annual cost will be 15 to 20 times what they are today.

2. The cost of benefits promised is far in excess of the contributions being collected.

None of the witnesses appearing before the committee placed the average annual cost of this insurance system at less than 4 percent of pay roll. Some of the estimates placed the average annual cost as high as 7 percent and the eventual annual cost as high as 11 percent. Therefore, it is obvious that the actuarial soundness of this insurance system will continue to deteriorate so long as the current rate of contributions is kept at the present low level. Even if we accept the lowest estimate of 4 percent average annual cost, it may be said that the reserve fund of this system already has a deficit of $6,600,000,000. If we take the higher estimate of 7 percent average annual cost, it may be said that the reserve fund already has a deficit of about $16,500,000,000. The fact that we are collecting as much at the present 1-percent rate as it was estimated in 1939 we would collect at the 2-percent rate does not affect these estimates of cost and the size of the deficit, since the liabilities assumed by the insurance system have likewise increased.

One of the arguments advanced for not permitting the automatic increase in rate to take effect is that there should be a study made of the financing of this system and of social security generally. Another argument advanced is that Congress will soon consider the extension and broadening of the social security law. These arguments lack validity, since the minimum cost estimate set forth above has not being disputed by any witness appearing before the committee and it is obvious that any extension and broadening of the social-security law will certainly not result in a reduction in cost. Therefore, there appears to be no good reason why present costs, which are not disputed, should not be properly financed.

3. The continuance of the present pay-roll tax rate will require an eventual Government subsidy.

If the rate of contributions is continued at less than the average annual cost of this insurance system, it is a mathematical certainty that there will be one of the following three results: (1) The future pay-roll tax rates will have to be much higher if the insurance system continues to be financed wholly by pay-roll taxes, or (2) the benefits promised will have to be reduced, or (3) the Federal Government will be obliged to provide a subsidy out of general tax revenues.

There is of course a limit to the amount of pay-roll taxes that can be levied in justice to employers and workers. In the case of the workers the actuarial figures indicate that if the eventual rate is placed higher than 3 percent large numbers will be required to pay more for their benefits under this insurance system than if they obtained similar protection from a private insurance company. Since such a result would be clearly inequitable and since the repudiation by the Government of benefits promised is unthinkable, the only real alternative is an outright Government subsidy.

In making these statements, it should not be concluded that we are opposed to some eventual contribution by the Government to the social insurance system out of general revenues, provided it is not caused solely by the fact that an unjustifiably low rate is levied in the early years of operation and provided there is complete coverage of the workers in this country. However, at the present time, there are some 20,000,000 individuals engaged in occupations which are excluded from the insurance system. We believe, therefore, that before any such contribution is made to the social insurance system out of general revenues consideration should be given to broadening the coverage of the insurance program.

4. Freezing costs taxpayers more later on.

A major argument that has been made by persons in favor of the tax freeze is that it does not make any difference to the taxpayers of the future whether they are required to pay taxes to cover the interest on Government bonds held by the reserve fund or are required to pay taxes for an outright Government subsidy to this insurance system. This argument was completely disproved in the course of the hearings, since not only the Chairman of the Social

Security Board but M. A. Linton, president of the Provident Mutual Life Insurance Co., who advocates the freeze, both agreed that the amount of taxes to be raised in the future if there is no reserve fund will be twice as much as if there is a reserve fund. Both of these witnesses agreed that the interest payable on Government obligations held by the reserve fund would otherwise have to be paid to private investors who would be holding these obligations and in addition a subsidy of an equal amount would still have to be made to the insurance system.

5. Delay in automatic step-up will create future hardship for employers and workers.

It has been suggested that now is a difficult time for employers and workers to meet the additional 1-percent tax on pay rolls. We sympathize with the difficulties of meeting the present tax burden made necessary by the war. However, we are of the opinion that it will be far more difficult for employers and workers to absorb an increase in the rate a year from now or at any date in the near future. The profits of most employers are at a high level today. In fact, the majority of employers will be required to pay excess-profits taxes. Therefore, in most cases the increased pay-roll tax payable by employers will be partially offset by the reduction in the excess-profits taxes they will be required to pay. So far as the workers are concerned, the committee was informed that both the American Federation of Labor and the Congress of Industrial Organizations are in favor of permitting the automatic increase to take effect. As members of the Committee on Ways and Means, the committee which has the difficult task of raising taxes, we are impressed by the willingness of the workers of this country to pay their equitable share of the cost of these benefits. We wish to commend these labor organizations for their statesmanlike action which indicates that they truly understand and appreciate the value of this contributory social-insurance system, and therefore desire to maintain its financial integrity.

6. Low contributions imply low benefits.

The real reason why many people advocate keeping the contribution rate at a level below the true cost of the benefits provided is that they fear the accumulation of a reserve fund will create a demand for an increase in the size of the benefits. However, in our opinion the continuation of the present unjustifiably low contribution rate has the effect of making people believe that the cost of the benefits provided is low and that the value of the benefits provided is inconsequential. As already pointed out the real cost and value is far in excess of the rate of contribution now being collected. The survivors benefits alone have a face value between $3,000 and $10,000 for most families and as high as $15,000 for some families. The total amount of survivors benefits provided have a face value of $50,000,000,000.

Most people estimate the value of what they buy by the price which they pay. Therefore, we believe that an increase in the contribution rate will result in less extravagant rather than more extravagant demands being made upon the Congress for an increase in the benefits provided.

7. Freezing not consistent with general congressional policy.

The policy embodied in the majority's recommendations to freeze the rate of contributions under the old-age and survivors' insurance system is defended on the ground that only sufficient contributions should be collected to cover the cost of benefits currently being paid out. However, this policy is diametrically opposed to the policy which the Congress follows in the national service life insurance system for veterans of World War II, the Government life insurance system for veterans of World War I, the civil-service retirement fund, the Foreign Service life insurance fund, and several other of the retirement funds set up by the Congress. In completely departing from this principle for the Federal old-age and survivors insurance fund, we believe that the Congress is making a grave mistake.

Conclusion

For the reasons outlined above, we oppose the freezing of social security contributions at the present time. We believe that the action of the majority of the committee is unwise and unsound.

We believe that it is important to strengthen the social-insurance provisions of the Social Security Act. We cannot do so unless we assure the continuation of the social-insurance provisions on a sound financial basis that will guarantee to every American citizen that he will get his social-insurance benefits as a matter of right and not as a dole.

We do not believe that the present provisions of the Social Security Act are perfect. We believe that many of the provisions in the existing law should be strengthened and expanded. We believe that the Committee on Ways and Means should give consideration to a comprehensive review of all of the provisions of the Social Security Act. Only in this way can the contributions and the benefit provisions be seen in proper perspective. However, we do not believe it is wise, pending such consideration, to emasculate the proper financing of the admitted true cost of the benefits now provided. We are opposed, therefore, to the piecemeal consideration of one aspect of social security legislation and favor a comprehensive study of the entire social-security program with a view toward broadening, expanding, and strengthening its provisions so that it will make its full contribution to the preservation of our democracy and our system of free enterprise in the difficult reconversion and post-war periods.

Source: House Committee on Ways and Means, Report and Dissent, *Fix Rate of Tax under Federal Insurance Contributions Act on Employer and Employee for Calendar Year 1945,* Report no. 2010, December 1, 1944 (Washington, D.C.: U.S. Government Printing Office), 1–7.

Document 3.5
Congressional Floor Debate on 1945 Rate Freeze, December 5, 1944

The politics of the 1945 freeze featured the Democratic leadership, and pretty much the entire Republican caucus, united against a minority of Democrats. Of the seventy-three members of the House who voted against final passage of this bill, only five were Republicans.

In general, there were three main reasons to support the freeze: to keep short-term tax rates down, to reduce the size of the reserve, and to avoid long-term planning. All three are on display in these excerpts from congressional debate. The excerpts provide a sample of the arguments made in support of the freeze.

Mr. Jenkins. . . . If we increase this rate to 2 percent from the employee and also from the employer it does not give the employee any more money in case of death or accident. He does not get any more benefits; the benefits stay just as they are.

Mr. Speaker, it is absolutely unfair to compel those who labor to pay these exorbitant surpluses if there is no additional benefit to them. If we are going to increase these rates we should by all means increase the benefits.

From a standpoint of economy some say that we should not raise the benefits now in these prosperous times. The time they will need greater benefits is in less prosperous times. I say this just to show how confusing these arguments can be. I still say, however, that the benefits must be raised if the payments are raised and the big surpluses are maintained. . . .

Mr. Gifford. . . . Blessed be the man who expects nothing because he will not be disappointed; but the man who expects something and does not get it might well be disappointed.

Are we entering into a system of swindling posterity on a huge scale? Are we really collecting this money and spending it for the general purposes of government and not treating it as a trust fund? Can the Government spend trust funds for general expenses without challenge? I have here a letter that came to my desk this morning from a chamber of commerce, calling this method a swindle because we are spending these funds for the general expenses of the Government. . . . I am frankly worried as to whether or not the Government is so different from individuals as the custodian of such contributions. If you as an individual hold my trust funds, do not buy an automobile for yourself. I am worried about the many comments of wise men who are critical of the road we are traveling. It is stated that the foremost superstition in the United States today is that we think that we can get social security by voting for it. . . .

Mr. Eberharter. I just want to call the gentleman's attention to the fact that the majority report of the committee, which all of his Republican colleagues signed, states that there definitely is a trust fund amounting to over five and one-half billion dollars. That is a trust fund upon which the membership who voted to pass out this bill depend.

Mr. Gifford. It is indeed a trust fund. Should it be spent for general purposes? This has been questioned. Maybe you will be able to reassure these critics. Here is a Government faced as it is with many billions of dollars to be paid out for subsidies and pensions in various forms after this war. Our Government is traveling fast in those directions. . . .

Mr. Doughton. . . . The issue we have placed squarely before the House is whether the reserve in the trust fund is adequate at the present time and that it can be maintained within the reasonable limit of safety by retaining the tax at 1 percent during the year 1945.

In 1939 the law was revised and the basis of the trust fund was changed, after long and deliberate study, from a so-called full reserve to a contingent reserve to meet unusual conditions or emergencies. At that time the Social Security Board, with the help of experts and actuaries, estimated that the trust fund would be $3,000,000,000 at the end of 1944. They estimated that it would be only that amount if the tax increases as written into the law should become effective. However, without the increases, instead of only $3,000,000,000 we have, or will have at the end of 1944, approximately $6,000,000,000 in the trust fund—or 100 percent more than was estimated. In other words we will have double the amount it was estimated we would have and we have built this reserve at a lower rate of tax than the social-security experts and actuaries used in their calculations for securing only $3,000,000,000. Today, mark you, we are collecting more in taxes at 1 percent than it was anticipated we would collect at 2 percent, which amount we were told would be adequate to fully protect the system.

The opponents of this bill will contend that this is all due to the war, which we deny. Some of it is probably due to the war, but the estimates of receipts before the war were far from accurate. We have always collected more, both before and since the war, in taxes and paid out considerably less in benefits than was estimated. . . .

The opponents of this bill also contend that the claims or liabilities against the fund have increased greatly. In the report they use the figures $50,000,000,000, which as far as I can determine is the most extreme possibility that the human mind could imagine and not within the realm of any reasonable probability. . . .

The estimates on receipts and disbursements and the growth of the trust fund made by Dr. Altmeyer and his experts have fallen so wide of the mark up to the present that it is difficult for anyone to view with any reliance whatever estimates they make as to many, many years hence, which must necessarily be based upon economic conditions and human factors that can only be guessed at—and so far they have been the wildest guessers with whom I have ever attempted to work. I know that I cannot personally look into the future and tell what economic conditions and human factors will be 20, 30, or 40 years from now. So how can we, on the basis of such estimates and when the fund is adequate at present or within the reasonably near future, justifiably increase the already high tax burden on workers and employers. Even opponents of the bill admit that a tax of 1 percent will be adequate for 10 years, and I have no doubt it might be sufficient for 20 years.

The Secretary of the Treasury . . . testified before our committee in 1939, as follows:

> "Specifically, I would suggest to Congress that it plan the financing of the old-age insurance system with a view to maintaining for use in contingencies an eventual reserve amounting to not more than three times the highest prospective annual benefits in the ensuing 5 years."

. . . [A]s a matter of fact, the amount in the trust fund is now from 8 to 12 times the highest prospective annual expenditure in the next 5 years—8 to 12 times, instead of 3 times as recommended by Secretary Morgenthau, who must surely know, or should know, whereof he speaks.

If the Morgenthau rule is sound . . . we then have a wide margin of safety. Under these circumstances and in view of the extremely high tax burden the people necessarily are carrying, how can we justify doubling the tax at this time? . . .

Mr. ROBSION. . . . All the taxes that have been paid in and that will in the future be paid in are intended to create and maintain a reserve or trust fund to be paid out to the beneficiaries as their claims to part of this trust fund accrue. All of the taxes that have been paid by the workers and the employers into this trust fund up to this time and including the $6,000,000,000 of reserve have been from day to day transferred to the general fund in the Treasury and in the place of the tax money there is placed the IOU of the Federal Government, and the money paid out of these funds has not been limited to the beneficiaries, but it is expended by the administration for almost every and any activities of the Federal Government. This social-security tax money may be spent, and part of it, no doubt, has been expended for a lot of the boondoggling projects of the Government, and other parts of it have been squandered and wasted. It is handled the same as other tax money paid into the Treasury.

It is no secret that the administration desires through these taxes to build up a so-called reserve or trust fund amounting to approximately $50,000,000,000 and, of course, the administration will, in the future as in the past, in my opinion, place this money in the general fund and spend the money as it comes in, and there will be nothing in its place except the IOU and bonds of the Federal Government. This is where the Government takes the tax money of the workers and the employers and turns over to itself and gives IOUs and bonds. When we realize the great desire of this administration to tax, squander, and spend, it is easy to understand why they complain, because this so-called trust fund is only $6,000,000,000. These taxes roll in day by day, and it affords the administration an easy way to get billions of dollars without going out and publicly borrowing the money and selling the bonds.

This surplus reserve fund is already 8 to 12 times as much as the estimated outlay for benefits to the workers for any 1 year for the next 5 years, when Secretary Morgenthau stated that this reserve should not amount to more than 3 times the highest prospective annual benefits in any one of the ensuing years. . . .

. . . Some persons talk as if today is the last day that this or any Congress will ever meet. The people have already elected the Seventy-ninth Congress and will elect other Congresses. We have amended the Social Security Act heretofore and as the years come and go it will likely be amended in other respects that will be necessary and helpful. I have no doubt but what the Congress will watch this reserve or trust fund carefully so that so far as it is practicable under the present administration the rights of the beneficiaries under this legislation will be fully protected. I have no doubt but what it is protected today so far as the amount of money that has been paid in and no harm can come to this reserve fund during this investigation in 1945. If this reserve fund is weakened, it will be due to the improvident spending and wasting of the present administration. . . .

Mr. SIMPSON. . . . I think that anyone who thinks about social security and the question of the reserve must recognize that we are worrying about a situation which may arise some 40 or 50 years from now, in 1990 or the year 2000. It is probable that it will approach that date before, on the basis of the present tax payment . . . there will be occasion to worry about the reserve. We forget, however, that between this year and that distant year many Congresses will change this law, year after year, increasing the benefits and coverage, for as pointed out but a moment ago, it is undoubted that the payments being received by many today are far less than necessary to properly maintain one's livelihood. So, I think as we are in the war, and as we face the reconversion period in this country, we can, with entire safety, consider the facts as we find them today and determine on the situation today—whether we cannot with safety delay this increase next year. It is unquestioned but that there are ample funds in current collections at 1 percent to meet all liabilities which will arise during the coming 9 years. . . .

So I think that inasmuch as the reserve fund is today ample to take care of any possible contingency which may arise within the coming 10 years, without any increase in tax, we would be foolish, in this day, to impose a further burden upon the small businessman, the employer of today. . . .

Source: House floor debate, *Congressional Record,* House, December 5, 1944, 8836–8857.

This 1948 poster expresses the government's long-standing philosophy of program administration—that it is the government's duty to make certain that members of the public are informed of the benefits to which they may be entitled. Source: SSA History Archives.

Document 3.6
Report of the 1948–1949 Advisory Council, December 31, 1948
The Social Security Act Amendments of 1950 grew out of the work of an advisory council appointed in 1948. The advisory council of 1948–1949 actually issued its report in two parts. The first dealt with desired changes in the old-age and survivors part of the program and was mostly enacted into law. The second reported on the desirability of adding disability benefits to the program; this part was not adopted by Congress.

Part I: Old-Age and Survivors Insurance

Introduction and Summary

Opportunity for the individual to secure protection for himself and his family against the economic hazards of old age and death is essential to the sustained welfare, freedom, and dignity of the American citizen. For some, such protection can be gained through individual savings and other private arrangements. For others, such arrangements are inadequate or too uncertain. Since the interest of the whole Nation is involved, the people, using the Government as the agency for their cooperation, should make sure that all members of the community have at least a basic measure of protection against the major hazards of old age and death. . . .

The Council has studied the existing system of old-age and survivors insurance and unanimously approves its basic principles. The Council, however, finds three major deficiencies in the program:

1. Inadequate coverage—only about three out of every five jobs are covered by the program.
2. Unduly restrictive eligibility requirements for older workers—largely because of these restrictions, only about 20 percent of those aged 65 or over are either insured or receiving benefits under the program.
3. Inadequate benefits—retirement benefits at the end of 1947 averaged $25 a month for a single person.

The Council's recommendations are designed to remedy these major defects.

The Council has agreed unanimously on 20 of its 22 specific recommendations. . . .

Summary of Recommendations

1. *Self-employment.*—Self-employed persons such as business and professional people, farmers, and others who work on their own account should be brought under coverage of the old-age and survivors insurance system. . . .

2. *Farm workers.*—Coverage of the old-age and survivors insurance system should be extended to farm employees.

3. *Household workers.*—Coverage of the old-age and survivors insurance system should be extended to household workers.

4. *Employees of nonprofit institutions.*—Employment for nonprofit institutions now excluded from coverage under the old-age and survivors insurance program should be brought under the program, except that clergymen and members of religious orders should continue to be excluded.

5. *Federal civilian employees.*—Old-age and survivors insurance coverage should he extended immediately to the employees of the Federal Government and its instrumentalities who are now excluded from the civil-service retirement system. . . .

6. *Railroad employees.*—The Congress should direct the Social Security Administration [SSA] and the Railroad Retirement Board to undertake a study to determine the most practicable and equitable method of making the railroad retirement system supplementary to the basic old-age and survivors insurance program. . . .

7. *Members of the armed forces.*—Old-age and survivors insurance coverage should be extended to members of the armed forces, including those stationed outside the United States.

8. *Employees of State and local governments.*—The Federal Government should enter into voluntary agreements with the States for the extension of old-age and survivors insurance to the employees of State and local governments. . . .

11. *Insured status.*—To permit a larger proportion of older workers, particularly those newly covered, to qualify for benefits, the requirements for fully insured status should be [reduced]. . . .

12. *Maximum base for contributions and benefits.*—To take into account increased wage levels and costs of living, the upper limit on earnings subject to contributions and credited for benefits should be raised from $3,000 to $4,200. . . .

14. *Benefit Formula.*—To provide adequate benefits immediately . . . the primary insurance benefit should be [increased] . . . Present beneficiaries, as well as those who become entitled in the future, should receive benefits computed according to this new formula. . . .

15. *Increased survivor protection.*—To increase the protection for a worker's dependents, survivor benefits for a family should be at the rate of three-fourths of the primary insurance benefit. . . .

17. *Maximum benefits.*—To increase the family benefits, the maximum benefit amount payable on the wage record of an insured individual should be three times the primary insurance benefit amount. . . .

18. *Minimum benefit.*—The minimum primary insurance benefit payable should be raised to $20.

19. *Retirement test.*—No retirement test (work clause) should be imposed on persons aged 70 or over. . . .

20. *Qualifying age for women.*—The minimum age at which women may qualify for old-age benefits (primary, wife's, widow's, parents') should be reduced to 60 years.

21. *Lump-sum benefits.*—To help meet the special expenses of illness and death, a lump-sum benefit should be payable at the death of every insured worker even though monthly survivor benefits are payable. . . .

22. *Contribution schedule and Government participation.*—The contribution rate should be increased to 1.5 percent for employers and 1.5 percent for employees at the same time that benefits are liberalized and coverage is extended. The next step-up in the contribution rate, to 2 percent on employer and 2 percent on employee, should be postponed until the 1.5 percent rate plus interest on the investments of the trust fund is insufficient to meet current benefit outlays and administrative costs. There are compelling reasons for an eventual Government contribution to the system, but the Council feels that it is unrealistic to decide now on the exact timing or proportion of that contribution. When the rate of 2 percent on employers and 2 percent on employees plus interest on the investments of the trust fund is insufficient to meet current outlays, the advisability of an immediate Government contribution should be considered. . . .

Goal of Universal Coverage
The basic protection afforded by the contributory social insurance system under the Social Security Act should be available to all who are dependent on income from work. The character of one's occupation should not force one to rely for basic protection on public assistance rather than insurance.

Earlier decisions to exclude the self-employed, workers in agriculture, and workers in domestic service from coverage of the insurance system were based on the expectation that there would be administrative difficulties in collecting contributions and obtaining wage reports for these groups. Other groups such as railroad workers, government employees, and employees of religious, charitable, and educational institutions were excluded for various reasons—because some of the workers were protected under existing retirement plans, because of the constitutional barrier to the levy of a Federal tax on State and local governments, or because of objections to taxing traditionally tax-exempt nonprofit organizations.

The Council believes that none of the reasons for the original exclusions justifies continued denial of basic social insurance protection to these groups. The administrative difficulties which may arise from including the self-employed and workers in agriculture and domestic service seem far less formidable today than they did 10 years ago when the social insurance system was new and in the early stages of developing its administrative organization. . . .

An incidental but important result of extension of coverage will be a reduction in the percentage of pay rolls required to meet the costs of old-age and survivors insurance. Extension of coverage would increase the revenue of the program more than it increases benefit payments. The net saving would be roughly one-half percent to 1 percent of pay roll under the present provisions. Under a program of liberalized benefits such as we recommend, costs would, of course, be increased, but under such a program the net saving as a result of the extension of coverage would also be increased—possibly to as much as 2 percent of pay roll. . . .

Purchasing Power of Benefits

For millions of persons the social security system represents a guaranty of future security. If that guaranty is to be valid and meaningful, the purchasing power of benefits must not be destroyed by large increases in price levels. A special obligation rests on the Government and all groups in the community with an interest in the social-insurance system and in the security it offers to make sure that monetary policies, price policies, and wage policies contribute to the objective of preventing such a large rise in the price level. If the people of the United States are unable to prevent steep increases in price levels, benefits will have to be readjusted to preserve their purchasing power for unless the purchasing power of the benefits is preserved, the security guaranteed by the social-insurance plan will be illusory. . . .

Source: Recommendations for Social Security Legislation, "The Reports of The Advisory Council on Social Security to the Senate Committee on Finance" (Washington, D.C.: Government Printing Office, 1949), 1–14.

Document 3.7
President Truman's Annual Budget Message to Congress, January 10, 1949

In his budget to Congress—given shortly after he received the first part of the advisory council's report—President Harry Truman seconded its recommendations, in broad terms, and even expanded upon them to include a renewed call for national health insurance—something the advisory council did not consider.

Social Welfare, Health, and Security

In the last 15 years the Federal Government has established a basic pattern of activities in the field of social welfare, health, and security. The national system of old-age and survivors insurance, the system of regular grants to States for public assistance payments to the needy aged and blind and to dependent children, the Federal-State system of unemployment insurance, and several grant programs for the promotion of public health and of children's welfare were established by the Social Security Act of 1935. . . .

Under the Social Security Act, the national policy contemplated that old-age and survivors insurance would be the primary Government measure affording economic protection to the needy aged and dependent children. . . . Other types of social insurance were to be added later to provide more adequate protection against major economic hazards of our society. Public assistance was designed as a backstop, a second line of defense, eventually to be replaced in large measure by social insurance benefits. We have not made progress toward this objective in the last decade. Individual benefit payments under public assistance now are substantially higher than under old-age and survivors insurance. . . .

Three principal steps should be taken now to strengthen and complete the system of social insurance, and thereby to make our governmental programs consistent with the basic national policy in this field.

First, old-age and survivors insurance should be extended to nearly all the 25 million gainfully employed persons not now covered; the scale of benefits should be sharply raised; benefits should be provided for women at an earlier age; and higher part-time earnings should be permitted. . . .

Second, disability insurance should be provided to protect against loss of earnings during illness or other temporary disability, and to assure continuing annuities to workers who become permanently disabled and therefore unable to earn a livelihood.

Third, a comprehensive national health program should be established, centering in a national system of medical care insurance, accompanied by improved services and facilities for public health and medical care.

These recommendations have had extended public discussion. Action is long overdue. I am confident that the Congress will enact promptly the legislation needed to achieve an integrated, comprehensive system of social insurance. . . .

The needed legislation includes not only measures to establish administrative procedures and authorize benefit payments, but also provisions for financing them. . . . My recommendations contemplate raising the tax rate on presently covered employment on July 1, 1949, the date when increased benefits should be made available. In addition, I propose that we raise the ceiling on taxable earnings, as well as extend the pay-roll tax to workers and employers not now covered. The addition of insurance coverage for medical care and disability benefits will also require some additions to the pay-roll tax rates in order that the whole social insurance system will continue to be substantially self-supporting.

The financial impact of these recommendations is mainly in the trust accounts. For the fiscal year 1950, benefit payments and administrative expenses from the major trust accounts in the field of social welfare (other than unemployment insurance) are estimated at 1.3 billion dollars under existing laws. Under the legislation which I recommend, these payments would be doubled. . . .

Source: Public Papers of the Presidents of the United States: Harry S. Truman, 1949 (Washington, D.C.: Government Printing Office, 1964), 66–67.

Document 3.8
Ways and Means Committee Report, August 22, 1949

In February 1949 the Truman administration submitted two bills to Congress: one covered the public assistance titles, and the other covered the social insurance program. Ultimately, the Ways and Means Committee would combine them in a single bill—H.R. 6000. In most other respects, the bill followed the administration's proposals, including many of the extensions of coverage, the increase in the value of benefits, and the disability plan.

Since the 1950 changes made the program much more generous, the question of financing was discussed at length in the Ways and Means report, and a sample of this debate is included. The committee felt the need to make an express defense of the trust funds and the idea of the trust funds as a repository of program assets, as this basic principle of the program continued then (as now) to be subject to broad criticisms.

All ten Republican members of Ways and Means signed a separate dissent in opposition to key provisions of the bill and expressed their antipathy to central policies and practices of the social insurance model. Notwithstanding their opposition, the bill was voted out of committee on a 23–2 vote, and when it was considered on the House floor, under a closed rule, the bill eventually passed on a vote of 333–14.

Introduction

I. Purpose and Scope of the Bill

. . . Ten years have elapsed since the last major revision of the Social Security Act established the scale of monthly benefits under the old-age and survivors insurance system in effect today. . . .

The Congress is faced with a vital decision which cannot long be postponed. Inadequacies in the old-age and survivors insurance program have resulted in trends which seriously threaten our economic well-being. The assistance program, instead of being reduced to a secondary position as was anticipated, still cares for a much larger number of people than the insurance program. Furthermore, the average payments under assistance have more than doubled in amount since 1939 while benefits under insurance have scarcely risen at all. There are indications that if the insurance program is not strengthened and expanded, the old-age assistance program may develop into a very costly and ill-advised system of noncontributory pensions. . . . Without an adequate and universally applicable basic social insurance system, the demands for security by segments of the population threaten to result in unbalanced, overlapping, and competing programs. . . . There is a pressing need to strengthen the basic system at once before it is undermined by these forces. . . .

The time has come to reaffirm the basic principle that a contributory system of social insurance in which workers share directly in meeting the cost of the protection afforded is the most satisfactory way of preventing dependency. . . .

III. Summary of Principal Provisions of the Bill

A. Old-age and survivors insurance

1. *Extension of coverage.*—Old-age and survivors insurance coverage would be extended to add approximately 11,000,000 new persons to the 35,000,000 persons now covered during an average week. . . .

2. *Liberalization of benefits.*—(a) About 2.6 million persons currently receiving old-age and survivors insurance benefits would have their monthly benefit increased on the average by about 70 percent. Increases would range from 50 percent for highest benefit groups to as much as 100 percent for lowest benefit groups. The average primary benefit is now approximately $26 per month for a retired insured worker, and under the bill it would be approximately $44. . . .

B. Permanent and total disability insurance

1. *Coverage.*—All persons covered by the old-age and survivors insurance program would have protection against the hazard of enforced retirement and loss of earnings caused by permanent and total disability.

2. *Benefits.*—Permanently and totally disabled workers would have their benefits and average wage computed on the same basis as for old-age benefits, but no payments would be available for dependents of disabled workers. . . .

IX. Permanent and Total Disability Insurance

A. Need for disability insurance

The old-age and survivors insurance system does not now meet the needs of those who become disabled before they reach the normal age of retirement. At least 2,000,000 persons in the United States are chronic invalids. . . . Chronic invalidism spares no age group, but it is more common to the older worker, the one who has been in covered employment for a number of years and has made substantial contributions to the social-insurance system. The system today actually penalizes the disabled worker by reducing, or extinguishing his right to, eventual benefits, depending on his insured status and the length of his absence from the labor market. The addition of permanent and total disability benefits will inject more realism into the retirement concept, and will effectively counteract pressures for a reduction in the age of normal retirement. . . .

Consideration has been given to the proposal that benefits for permanent and total disability be confined solely to a separate category of public assistance. Your committee believes, however, that public assistance can meet only part of the problem. Notwithstanding the present size of its rolls, public assistance is essentially a supplementary measure which should taper off as the insurance program matures. In permanent and total disability we are dealing fundamentally with the problem of involuntary, premature retirement. The worker who has paid social insurance contributions for a number of years—perhaps over much of his working lifetime—has a real stake in the system which deserves to be recognized. He should not be required to show need to become entitled to benefits. . . .

Accordingly, the bill provides for permanent and total disability benefits under old-age and survivors insurance, as well as under public assistance. The assistance payments will be available only to those needy disabled who either cannot qualify for insurance payments or who need supplementary aid.

The committee recommends a conservative disability insurance program to fill the present gap in the social insurance system. The program would apply only to those wage earners and self-employed persons who have been regular and recent members of the labor force and who can no longer continue gainful work. Disability benefits for the worker will be computed in the same manner as old-age benefits (the amount of the benefit is computed as though the individual had attained age 65 on the date he became disabled). Mindful of the added costs, your committee does not recommend payment of benefits to dependents of disabled beneficiaries. . . .

X. Actuarial Cost Estimates and Financing of Old-Age, Survivors, and Disability Insurance

. . . Your committee recognizes and, in fact, wishes to stress the difficulties involved in estimating the long-range costs of the system. Because of numerous factors such as the aging of the total population of the country and the inherent slow but steady growth of the benefit roll in any retirement program, benefit payments may be expected to increase continuously for at least the next 50 years. . . .

Your committee has very carefully considered the problems of cost in determining the benefit provisions recommended. Also your committee is firmly of the belief that the old-age, survivors, and disability insurance program should be on a completely self-supporting basis. Accordingly, the bill eliminates the provision added in 1943 authorizing appropriations to the program from general revenues. At the same time, your committee has recommended a tax schedule which it believes will make the system self-supporting (or in other words, actuarially sound) as nearly as can be foreseen under present circumstances. Future experience may differ from the estimates so that this tax schedule, at least in the distant future, may have to be modified slightly either upward or downward. This may readily be determined by future Congresses after the revised program has been in operation for a decade or two. . . .

XI. Investments of the Old-Age and Survivors Insurance Trust Fund

The trust fund has been invested in United States Government securities, which represent the proper form of investment. Your committee does not agree with those who criticize this form of investment on the ground that the Government spends for general purposes the money received from the sale of securities to the fund. Actually such investment is as reasonable and proper as is the investment by life insurance companies of their own reserve funds in Government securities. The fact that the Government uses the proceeds received from the sales of securities to pay the costs of the war and its other expenses is entirely legitimate. It no more implies mishandling of moneys received from the sale of securities to the trust fund than is the case for money received from the sale of United States securities to life insurance companies, banks, and individuals.

The investment of the excess income of the trust fund in Government securities does not mean that people have been or will be taxed twice for the same benefits, as has been charged. The following example illustrates this point: Suppose some year in the future the outgo under the old-age and survivors insurance system should exceed pay roll tax receipts by $100,000,000. If there were then $5,000,000,000 of United States 2-percent bonds in the trust fund, they would produce interest amounting to $100,000,000 a year. This interest would, of course, have to be raised by taxation. But suppose there were no bonds in the trust fund. In that event, the $100,000,000 to cover the deficit in the old-age and survivors insurance system would have to be raised by taxation. In addition, another $100,000,000 would have to be raised by taxation to pay interest on $5,000,000,000 of Government bonds owned by someone else; if the Government had not been able to borrow from the trust fund, it would have had to borrow the same amount from other sources. In other words, the ownership of the $5,000,000,000 in bonds by the old-age and survivors insurance system would prevent the $100,000,000 from having to be raised twice—quite the opposite from the "double taxation" criticism that has been raised. . . .

Views of the Minority on H. R. 6000

Part I: The Compulsory Social Insurance System

. . . We recommend that coverage of the social-insurance system be broadened and that the amount of benefit payments be increased.

We are unable, however, to support all the provisions of this proposed legislation. . . .

The provisions we oppose will increase the cost of this system at its maturity by approximately $3,500,000,000 a year and this amount when added to the huge and pyramiding cost of the other features of the program may well mean the difference, between the success or break-down of the system.

Our opposition to certain features of the bill is based, in addition to the cost factor, on our strong conviction that they are inconsonant with the fundamental purpose of compulsory social insurance.

In our opinion, the purpose of compulsory social insurance is to provide a basic floor of economic protection for the individual and his family and in so doing to encourage and stimulate voluntary savings through personal initiative and ambition. It should not invade the field historically belonging to the individual.

We believe that such a form of compulsory social insurance which unnecessarily takes from the individual funds which he would invest or otherwise use for building his own security is incompatible with our free-enterprise system. Accordingly, we do not conceive it to be a proper function or responsibility of the Federal Government either to compensate individuals for all types of losses in earning capacity or to provide a scale of benefits which pay substantially higher amounts to those with higher income.

We believe further that if this vast program is to fulfill its social objectives, the most important factor is to restrict the burden of its pyramiding cost within an amount which the economy can bear. This is so because in the final analysis the basis of all security is a productive economy, and the burden in any one year of the mounting cost of this program will have, in the main, to be paid for out of the production of the goods and services which the system seeks to distribute. In 20 years the pay-roll tax provided for in this bill will be 6.5 percent or a dollar cost based on present wage levels of over $8,000,000,000 a year for this one program alone. If this burden becomes too great, the system may well be repudiated by future generations, and if benefit payments are carried to extreme, the inevitable result of the companion tax burden will be a stifling of the incentive and ambition to produce.

Summary of Our Recommendations

1. *Continuation of the present $3,000 wage base.*—Increasing the wage base to $3,600 as proposed in H. R. 6000 results in higher benefits to those better able to provide their own protection and does nothing to increase the benefits for those with average wages below $3,000 for whom the system should be primarily concerned. . . .

5. *Realistic coverage for household workers.*—The bill purports to extend coverage to household workers but in reality does so for only a small group—1,300,000 of these workers are excluded under the bill. Coverage should be real, not theoretical.

6. *Teachers, firemen, and policemen with their own pension systems should be excluded.* . . .

8. *Continuation of existing law with respect to lump-sum death payments.*—More than 78,000,000 persons have already paid for the same private life-insurance protection which this provision in the bill would duplicate or replace. Encroachment by the Federal Government into this field is accordingly unjustified.

9. *Confine total and permanent disability payments to the public assistance program.* . . .

Effect of Our Recommendations

If the above changes are made in this proposed legislation, the compulsory social-insurance system will be kept within its fundamental purpose and its cost and the necessary taxes required for its support will be substantially reduced. According to actuarial advice, the average annual saving until the maturity of the program, some 50 years hence, will be in the neighborhood of $1,250,000,000. This saving is real and not illusory and the result would be wholly compatible with the aims of the social-security program. More than that, an adoption of our recommendations will aid in preserving the proper relationship between security achieved through social insurance and that which is to be had through individual self-reliance. The approximately $60,000,000,000 so saved over this period would be available to the American people for their individual use in providing for their own additional financial security in the manner most appropriate and fitting to their own circumstances. . . .

Source: Social Security Amendments of 1949, House Report no. 1300 (Washington, D.C.: Government Printing Office, August 22, 1949), 2–8, 27–31, 36–37, 157–159.

Document 3.9
Senate Finance Committee Report, May 17, 1950

The Senate Finance Committee held two months of hearings on H.R. 6000, starting in January 1950—resulting in a 2,400 page hearing report. The Senate debated the bill for a week in June, passing it on a vote of 81–2.

The major differences between the House and Senate bills were that the Senate dropped the "increment" in the benefit formula and did not adopt a disability program. Other relatively minor differences were adjudicated in conference in August, producing the first major Social Security legislation since 1939.

In this excerpt from the committee report, the Finance Committee explains its views on the increment and disability issues and on Social Security more broadly. The committee again expresses the ideal that a central goal of the contributory social insurance system is to lessen the role of welfare provision in the nation's system of economic security.

I. Purpose and Scope of the Bill

More than a decade has passed since the Congress amended the Social Security Act and established the present benefit provisions under old-age and survivors insurance. In the interim, tremendous changes have taken place in our economy. The onrush of broad social and economic developments has completely unbalanced the Nation's social security system. Congressional action is, therefore, urgently needed to reestablish the proper relationship among the basic programs in this system.

Your committee is greatly disturbed by the increasing burden on the general revenues caused by dependency in the United States. Currently Federal expenditures are running at a rate of $1.1 billion a year for public assistance as contrasted to expenditures of less than $800 million under the old-age and survivors insurance program.

Total expenditures for the three State-Federal public assistance programs in calendar year 1949 were $2.0 billion. The cost to the Federal Treasury for assistance to needy persons was $1.0 billion in 1949. This was $235 million more than in 1948 and $350 million more than in 1947. More than three-fourths of the costs of public assistance grants from the Federal Treasury are for dependent old people. In 1949 the Federal Government spent

$795 million for payments to needy old people alone, and the combined amounts spent by Federal, State, and local governments for old-age assistance was $1.4 billion. The magnitude of expenditures for old-age dependency gives us special concern because of the growing number of aged in the population. The number of persons age 65 and over has increased from 7 million in 1935 when the Social Security Act was passed to 11 million today. By 1960 we may expect 14 to 15 million aged persons and 25 years from now 17 to 20 million.

Your committee's impelling concern in recommending passage of H. R. 6000, as revised, has been to take immediate, effective steps to cut down the need for further expansion of public assistance, particularly old-age assistance. Unless the insurance system is expanded and improved so that it in fact offers a basic security to retired persons and to survivors, there will be continual and nearly irresistible pressure for putting more and more Federal funds into the less-constructive assistance programs. . . . We believe that improvement of the American social-security system should be in the direction of preventing dependency before it occurs, and of providing more effective income protection, free from the humiliation of a test of need. Accordingly your committee recommends action designed to immediately bolster and extend the system of old-age and survivors insurance by extension of coverage, increasing benefit amounts, liberalizing eligibility requirements, and otherwise improving this basic system for dealing with income losses. . . .

To keep assistance at a minimum in the future will also require even further extension of coverage than is provided in this bill. We recommend particularly that further extension of coverage to farm groups be given attention. In the absence of clear-cut expressions on the part of farm operators that they want this protection the provisions of the committee-approved bill seem to us to be as far as it is desirable to go without fuller consultation with the farm groups. This should be a matter for further study. . . .

Your committee has not included permanent and total disability insurance or assistance provisions in the bill. We recognize that the problem of disabled workers is one which requires careful attention, especially because of the increasing proportion of older workers and the rising rate of chronic invalidity in the population. Moreover, the problem is not limited to the feasibility of providing income or pensions merely to maintain disabled workers. At least of equal significance is the need for assuring fullest use of rehabilitation facilities so that disabled persons may be returned to gainful work, whenever this is possible. Your committee believes that the Federal Government should increase the grants-in-aid to the States for vocational rehabilitation and that further study should be made of the problem of income maintenance for permanently and totally disabled persons.

Your committee believes that further study should also be given to the problems involved in the long-range financing of an old-age and survivors insurance system, particularly the issue of reserve financing versus pay-as-you-go.

Although your committee recognizes that the bill does not solve all the problems, we believe that its passage would constitute a very significant step forward in the establishment of a sound social-security program. . . .

VI. Old-Age and Survivors Insurance Benefits Liberalized

General

A major change provided by the committee-approved bill is to establish a level of old-age and survivors insurance benefits which would be roughly double the amounts provided in the present Social Security Act and somewhat higher, for some time to come, than the amounts provided in H. R. 6000 as passed by the House of Representatives. . . .

. . . Several factors contribute to this increase. The new benefit formula itself gives a much higher proportion of the average monthly wage than the present formula; another factor of significance is the increase in the minimum benefit from $10 to $20. An increase in benefits would also result from the provision for basing benefits solely on wages earned after 1950 if such wages result in a higher benefit than that derived from all wages earned under the program. . . .

B. Computation of benefits

. . . There are compelling social and economic reasons for liberalizing benefits for those now on the rolls. Present beneficiaries, no less than persons who become beneficiaries in the future, need benefits which are revised to take into account that the 1939 benefit formula proved to be inadequate soon after its enactment and that prices have risen since then. This type of adjustment is common practice in private pension plans and in retirement plans of State and local governments. . . .

The increase in benefit amounts for persons now on the rolls would be accomplished by the use of a conversion table . . . This would avoid the necessity of recomputing benefit amounts individually, a procedure which would be extremely time consuming and expensive. . . .

The conversion table will apply not only to present beneficiaries but to all future beneficiaries . . . those who qualify for the "new start" will have the alternative available to them of applying the benefit formula in the present law (except no increment would be given for years after 1950) to an average monthly wage starting with 1937 and then using the conversion table. In the great majority of cases, however, the "new start" would be more advantageous. . . .

We believe that benefits should be related to the continuity of the worker's coverage and contributions to the system, as well as to the amount of his earnings. . . . Thus, in figuring the average monthly wage, a worker's total wage credits are—and would continue to be—divided by the total number of months that he might have been contributing to the system after 1950 or after 1936. His average wage, and consequently his primary benefit, will therefore be the smaller for each month lacking in his record of covered employment. In our opinion, this method of adjusting benefits permits sufficient differentiation between workers who are steadily employed in covered jobs and those whose covered employment is only brief or intermittent. An increment, the 1-percent increase for each year of coverage, is not needed for this purpose.

There is no need for the increment moreover to provide equitable treatment as between persons now of the same age. A young worker who contributes to the system for his entire working lifetime will under the committee-approved bill receive a larger benefit than a worker of the same age who was in covered employment for only part of the time, but at the same wage level while employed; the latter will, as explained previously, have a lower average monthly wage for benefit purposes and, correspondingly, a lower benefit. Thus the increment is not needed to distinguish between members of the same generation who have different covered-employment continuity histories.

With coverage broadly extended, the increment would serve largely to reward younger workers for their greater contributions by paying them higher retirement benefits than those paid to persons who were old when the system started. To us, such an advantage seems undesirable. The older worker should not be penalized for the fact that he could not contribute throughout his life. We propose, in effect, that, as in many private pension plans, the older worker receive credit for his past service and acquire rights to the full rate of benefits now.

The benefit formula of the present program, with its automatic increase of 1 percent for each year of coverage, in effect postpones payment of the full rate of benefits for more than 40 years from the time the system began to operate. Under such provisions, if the benefit amount of a retired worker after he has had a lifetime of coverage represents a reasonable proportion of his average wage, that for older workers who have been in the system for only a few years and for the survivors of younger workers will almost of necessity be inadequate. Thus, the survivors of a man who began working at age 20 and dies at age 30 will have rights to benefits only about three-fourths as large as those which the same average monthly wage would have provided if he had lived to age 65. Yet the worker who dies at an early age has had less opportunity than have older workers to accumulate savings and other resources to supplement the benefits payable to his survivors. Your committee believes that adequate benefits should be paid immediately to retired beneficiaries and survivors of insured workers, but considers it unwise to commit the system to automatic increases in the benefit for each year of covered employment. . . .

Source: Social Security Amendments of 1950, Senate Report no. 1669 (Washington, D.C.: Government Printing Office, May 17, 1950), 1–24.

Document 3.10
SSA Director's Bulletin, July 27, 1950

Following the conclusion of the conference in which the differences between the House and Senate bills were resolved, the director of the SSA's Bureau of Old-Age and Survivors Insurance sent a global memorandum to agency employees explaining the provisions in the final version of the new law and expressing the views of the program's administrators on the legislation.

In addition to the issues noted in previous documents, this memorandum is a good illustration of the complexities involved in the issue of coverage. Expanding program coverage was one of the defining features of the 1950 amendments, but the actual rules on coverage were quite complicated—as this excerpt makes clear.

The last of the Conference Committee decisions on H.R. 6000 are now public knowledge and the Committee staff is engaged in drafting the final version of the bill. Thus more than 18 months of intensive congressional action on improvements in the Social Security Act now approach their culmination. I am sure that you have followed with deep interest (and, at times, anxiety) the events beginning with the introduction of H.R. 2893 on February 21, 1949, through the long months of hearings which resulted in the passage of H.R. 6000 by the House last October and by the Senate a few weeks ago. The enactment of H.R. 6000 will be a tremendous advance in the long journey toward a universal, sound, and adequate means of providing security for all Americans through a method consistent with our system of individual incentives and free enterprise. This legislation does not bring that journey to its end, but the goal is much nearer than at any time in the past.

In some instances, the new legislation does not go as far as we think it should, or in the direction we think it should take, but this is inevitable in any subject in which so many different interests are involved. In other instances, the provisions provide greater security than would have resulted had H.R. 6000 been enacted last fall and not revised this year.

Disability insurance, probably the most controversial issue in the bill, was defeated only after prolonged Committee consideration which revealed a good deal of strength in its favor. The decision of the conferees to drop efforts to find an acceptable compromise on permanent total disability insurance and to restore disability assistance was adopted to prevent a delay which might have held up the entire bill. . . .

I. Coverage

The amendments will extend coverage on a compulsory basis to about 7.7 million persons and on a voluntary basis to about 2 million. . . . About 45 million workers will be covered by the expanded OASI program. . . .

The major groups who will still not have systematic retirement protection under a public program even after the amendments, are self-employed farmers and self-employed professional persons and those agricultural and domestic workers who are not "regularly" employed. These groups represent only about 10 percent of the Nation's 60 million paid workers.

Employees of Nonprofit Institutions

The amendments afford opportunity for coverage—subject to certain conditions—to 600,000 employees of nonprofit institutions. . . .

Clergymen and members of religious orders are manditorily excluded from coverage. The amendments continue the exclusion of certain services performed by students, student nurses, and interns. The existing exclusion of services performed in the employ of certain income-tax exempt organizations is modified to exclude such services if the remuneration is less than $50 a quarter.

These compromise provisions for covering employees of nonprofit institutions leave much to be desired from an administrative and program viewpoint. . . .

Employees of State and Local Governments

The legislation makes coverage available to 1.4 million employees of States and their political subdivisions and instrumentalities by means of voluntary agreements to be negotiated between the States and the Federal Security Administrator. Excluded from coverage are about 2.4 million employees of State and local governments in positions covered by retirement systems. . . .

. . . The otherwise complete exclusion of retirement system members is a disappointing result, but one which is understandable in view of the pressure exerted on Congress by public school teachers, policemen, and firemen who objected to the mere possibility of coverage under old-age and survivors insurance.

Federal Employment

The great majority of Federal employees are covered under the civil service retirement system, the armed forces retirement systems, or under some other system established by a law of the United States. Under the amendments these Federal employees (including all members of the armed forces) are excluded. . . .

Self-Employed Persons

The amendments will extend coverage to some 4.6 million self-employed persons. In general, those covered are persons other than farm operators and certain specified professional people. . . . The excluded professional groups are: lawyers, physicians, dentists, osteopaths, chiropractors, naturopaths, Christian Science practitioners, optometrists, veterinarians, professional engineers, architects, funeral directors, and certified . . . public accountants.

The covered group included proprietors (sole owners and partners) of retail stores, service establishments, wholesale and jobbing businesses, manufacturing plants, and transportation, communication, insurance, real estate, publishing, and financial enterprises. In addition, it includes about 225,000 borderline workers, such as part-time life insurance salesmen, house-to-house salesmen, operators of leased taxicabs, and "newsboys" over 18, who are excepted from coverage as employees but will be treated as self-employed persons. . . .

Although this extension of coverage is an extremely important one, there are still significant groups of the self-employed for whom coverage has not been provided. There are, in an average week, some 2,800,000 farm operators and about 480,000 persons in the named professional groups. . . . The farm operators were excluded principally because Congress has insufficient evidence that farmers desired coverage. The National Grange and the Farmers' Union favored immediate coverage but the American Farm Bureau Federation counseled delay. With respect to the professional groups, Congress felt that a large proportion of members of the groups did not wish to come under the program. As a result the House Committee first excluded such major groups as doctors, lawyers, and dentists. As the bill proceeded through the legislative process, the exclusion of some other groups was requested by various professional associations which feared that coverage under the program would cast doubt on their members' professional standing.

Domestic Service

Approximately 1 million of the estimated 1.8 million persons who work in domestic service will be covered under the amendments. The newly covered domestic workers are those who are regularly employed in non-farm private homes, and non-students working in college clubs and local chapters of fraternities and sororities. Domestic workers in private homes on farms operated for-profit constitute a special category and are covered on the same basis as agricultural labor. Students working in college clubs are excluded. . . .

Agricultural Labor

The amendments extend coverage to about 850,000 workers excluded as "agricultural labor" under present law. . . .

The amendments will result in the first large-scale application in this country of a social insurance program to agriculture. Through this coverage, farm people will be afforded their first opportunity to become directly acquainted with old-age and survivors insurance.

World War II Military Service

The amendments give World War II veterans wage credits of $160 for each month of military service performed during the war period. . . .

The wage credits will be taken into account in computing monthly benefits payable for months beginning with September 1950 and in determining lump-sum death payments in cases where the veteran dies after August 1950. . . .

II. Insured Status

For newly covered workers and for older workers who had only small amounts of covered employment before the effective date, the provision approved by the Conference Committee liberalizes insured status requirements to a greater extent than was recommended by the Administration. . . .

The immediate effect of the revised eligibility requirements will be to make eligible for benefits a large number of aged individuals who now have 6 or more quarters of coverage, but not enough to give them an insured status under the present law.

This provision, recommended by the Advisory Council and adopted by the Senate, was approved largely because of its effect on future public assistance loads and because it would hasten the time when the old-age and survivors insurance program would provide more effective security for the aged. . . .

III. Benefit Amounts

The amendment provides for substantial increases in benefit amounts, both for beneficiaries now on the rolls and for individuals who will become entitled to benefits in future. The benefits of individuals now on the rolls will be increased through the medium of a "conversion table" . . . set forth in the law. . . . The average increase in present benefits that would result from the use of the table would be about 77 percent. This will raise the average husband and wife benefit for aged couples now on the rolls from $41 to about $75. The minimum benefit for those now on the rolls would be $20. . . .

. . . This basic formula will produce higher benefits in the near future . . . but it will not reach as high a level in the long run because of the omission of increments for years of coverage. The act as approved by the Conference Committee follows the recommendations of the Advisory Council in this respect. The Council had recommended that the increment be dropped, on the ground that it would result in inadequate benefits in the early years, if the formula is adjusted to adequate benefits some 30 or 40 years in the future. Conversely, if benefits are made adequate now, the Council felt an increment would commit the system at this time to costs which might prove to be excessive. The Administration recommended retention of the increment as a means of differentiating the benefits of long-term workers, who have made very substantial amounts of contribution over a long period, from those of workers who qualified on a shorter period of employment. . . .

The increase in the wage base to $3,600 is a definite improvement, though it falls short of the $4,800 base recommended by the Administration. Strong feelings were expressed during hearings for retaining the present $3,000 wage base, and it was only on the closing day of debate in the Senate that the higher amount was voted, thus taking the wage base out of the area of consideration by the Conference Committee. The importance of the change is greater than the $600 might indicate. It establishes the principle that when wage rates rise generally, the benefit formula should be adjusted so that benefits will reflect actual wage loss for the great majority of covered workers. This is of basic importance in preserving the American social insurance plan of benefits geared to wages.

The method of computing the average monthly wage remains essentially the same as in present law. The only substantial difference is the establishment of a "new start," effective after 1950, for those individuals whose benefits are to be computed under the new benefit formula. This "new start" will be especially important for workers newly covered under the amendments, since otherwise their average monthly wage would be greatly reduced by the inclusion, in the elapsed period, of all the time back to the beginning of 1937. . . . Without a "new start," the average monthly wage of these covered workers would be pulled down by their previous low wages. . . .

VI. Cost and Financing

The tax schedule agreed to by the conferees is as follows:

Calendar Year	Employee Percent	Employer Percent	Self-employed Percent
1951–53	1½	1½	2¼
1954–59	2	2	3
1960–64	2½	2½	3¾
1965–69	3	3	4½
1970 and after	3¼	3¼	4⅞

The level premium cost of the expanded program (that is, the rate which would be required to carry the full cost of the program from the present time indefinitely into the future) is about 6%. Thus, the cost of benefits as a percent of payroll will be about the same under the expanded program as was contemplated under either the original 1935 Act or the 1939 Amendments.

The development of the Nation's economic system in the past has been accompanied by a rising level of income and earnings. If past trends continue, earnings in the future will be substantially higher than they are now. The cost estimates, and hence the contribution rate schedule, are based on the assumption that benefits in the long-range future will be raised so as to bear about the same relationship to future average earnings that benefits under the conference bill bear to present average earnings. To the extent that benefit changes fail to keep pace with rising earnings levels, the cost of the program as a percent of payroll will be lower than the estimates indicate. This is due to the weighted nature of the benefit formula; as average earnings approach the $300 maximum a larger portion of such earnings becomes subject to the 15% factor rather than the 50% factor in the benefit formula and, therefore, benefits based on high average earnings are smaller in relation to such earnings.

The cost of the protection under the new program for a generation of workers covered during their full working lifetime is estimated to be approximately 4% of payroll. Thus, under the schedule in the bill the combined rate in 1954 would approximate the value of the benefits for the group of young workers who enter covered employment at that time. The excess of the 6% level premium cost over the 4% rate results from the fact that persons retiring during the next 30 or 40 years will receive full benefits even though they have not contributed over a full working lifetime.

Although the Administration and the Senate Advisory Council recommended a Government contribution, the rates in the bill were established with the intent that the system would be self-supporting. The 1943 Amendment authorizing appropriations to the Trust Fund out of general revenues has been deleted.

Source: "Director's Bulletin No. 169 from O.C. Pogge, Director of the Bureau of Old-Age and Survivors Insurance, to All Bureau Employees," July 27, 1950. SSA History Archives, Downey Books, 1950 Amendments, vol. 4.

Document 3.11
President Truman's Statement on Signing the 1950 Amendments, August 28, 1950

In this signing statement President Truman makes reference to "insurance rights" that were "taken away" by the 80th Congress. This refers to the fact that during the 1940s Congress removed from coverage—over Truman's veto—about 500,000 newspaper and magazine vendors. The 1950 amendments brought part of this occupational group back under coverage.

I have today approved H.R. 6000, the Social Security Act Amendments of 1950. These amendments greatly strengthen the old-age and survivors insurance system and the public assistance programs originally established by the Social Security Act of 1935.

The passage of this legislation is an outstanding achievement. In this act the 81st Congress has doubled insurance benefits and brought 10 million more persons under old-age and survivors insurance—including those whose insurance rights were taken away by the 80th Congress. Millions of others will benefit from the new public assistance provisions giving help to the disabled and to dependent children. For the first time American citizens in Puerto Rico and the Virgin Islands will be covered under both the insurance and assistance programs. In addition, veterans of World War II will now receive wage credits for military service in computing their insurance benefits.

This act will help a great many people right away. Three million aged persons, widows, and orphans will receive increased insurance benefits beginning with the month of September. A million more will begin to receive increased payments within the next few months. Nearly 3 million needy persons will benefit from increased Federal aid to the States for public assistance purposes.

By making it possible for most families to obtain protection through the contributory insurance system, and by increasing insurance benefits, the act will ultimately reduce dependence on public charity. This measure demonstrates our determination to achieve real economic security for the American family. This kind of progressive, forward-looking legislation is the best possible way to prove that our democratic institutions can provide both freedom and security for all our citizens.

We still have much to do before our social security programs are fully adequate. While the new act greatly increases coverage, many more people still need to be brought into the old-age and survivors insurance system. Expanded coverage and increased benefits in old-age insurance should now be matched by steps to strengthen our unemployment insurance system. At the same time, we urgently need a system of insurance against loss of wages through temporary or permanent disability. These and other vital improvements in our social security laws are needed in addition to the act which I have signed today. I shall continue to urge action on this unfinished business and I know that the committees of Congress are now preparing to give these matters serious consideration. . . .

Both the House Committee on Ways and Means and the Senate Committee on Finance have already announced that they intend to study proposals for further improvement in our social security programs. Members of these committees have worked long and faithfully on the act which I have signed today. I am confident that their future efforts will be equally productive in advancing social security in this country.

Source: Public Papers of the Presidents of the United States: Harry S. Truman, 1950 (Washington, D.C.: Government Printing Office, 1965), 600–601.

CHAPTER 4

Extending Coverage and Benefits, 1951–1965

A major expansion of Social Security and, more generally, of the federal social insurance system took place in the 1951–1965 period. The Social Security legislation adopted during this period focused on four themes: expansion of the program's coverage, the inclusion of disability benefits, liberalizations in benefits, and financing matters—both increasing the value of benefits and adjusting the tax rates and the wage base to strengthen the program's financial condition.

First, with the 1952 amendments, Congress extended coverage to some occupational categories that had been excluded since enactment in 1935.

The biggest change to the nation's social insurance system during this period was the creation of the Medicare program, which is promoted through this 1968 government poster. Source: SSA History Archives.

These amendments also increased Social Security benefits by 12.5 percent. Amendments in 1954 and 1956 also significantly expanded the coverage of the program, the 1954 law alone adding more than 10 million new workers to the system. Amendments in 1958, 1960, and 1961 focused mainly on various types of benefit liberalization, while the 1965 legislation addressed both benefit liberalization and program financing. But, with the exception of Medicare, which falls outside the scope of this volume, by far the most important development during this period involved the addition of disability benefits to the Social Security program.

After the election of Dwight D. Eisenhower to the presidency, Social Security entered a brief period of uncertainty. The new administration eventually gave its support to the program, but it remained opposed to the advent of disability insurance. Despite this opposition, Congress adopted disability insurance in two steps: a "disability freeze" in 1954 and cash benefits in 1956. The "disability freeze" provision meant that a worker's periods of disability would not held against him or her when calculating retirement benefits, and it was a helpful prelude to the introduction of cash benefits two years later.

Following enactment of the disability freeze, proponents of expanding Social Security to include disability insurance once again pushed to obtain cash benefits for the disabled.

Supporters stressed that such benefits would address basic economic security needs. But a disability program posed significant problems, including costs, potential disincentives to rehabilitation, and the difficulty of making disability determinations. Policymakers had wrestled with these from the earliest days of consideration by the Committee on Economic Security until Congress and President Eisenhower made the final decision to add disability to the Social Security package of protection. Both sets of concerns were well articulated in the debates leading up to passage of the 1956 Amendments. The inclusion of disability represented a major expansion of the federal social insurance system.

Document 4.1
SSA Director's Bulletin on the 1952 Amendments, July 18, 1952

The aim of the 1952 amendments was to increase benefits, liberalize the retirement test, and provide gratuitous wage credits for military service. The House Ways and Means Committee also wanted to provide for a "disability freeze." The Senate Finance Committee supported the first three of these proposals but opposed the disability freeze. Ultimately, the conference on the two versions of the bill yielded a somewhat unusual provision whereby the freeze became law for a limited period with the proviso that no claims could be taken under the provision until after it had expired! That is, the effective date of the legislation was after the program was scheduled to terminate. It was, one might say, a provision in principle only.

This document is a memorandum from the director of the Bureau of Old-Age and Survivors Insurance at the Social Security Administration (SSA), explaining the provisions in the new law and their rationales to SSA employees.

The Social Security Act Amendments of 1952 became law today with signature by the President. The fact that there is new social security legislation within two years of the comprehensive changes made in 1950 is highly significant. The increased benefits indicate a realization by the Congress that the old-age and survivors insurance program must and can be kept in line with the level of the economy. Even more important, it indicates recognition of the fact that rising wage levels permit some liberalizations in the program without the need for increasing tax rates or changing the self-supporting basis of the system.

We in the Bureau were, of course, disappointed that some of the provisions originally in H.R. 7800 were dropped or drastically changed. The bill as originally passed by the House of Representatives on June 17 contained a provision for "freezing" the insured status and average monthly wage of individuals who become permanently and totally disabled before reaching retirement age. This provision . . . would have corrected a serious anomaly in the present law which affects the benefit rights of a very large number of persons covered under the program. From 75,000 to 100,000 persons now on the rolls would have had their benefits increased immediately by recomputation to take account of past disability. In all, perhaps as many as 500,000 persons disabled in the past would have gained some advantage for themselves or their survivors in present or future benefits from this provision. This is not to speak of the approximately 150,000 persons a year who are currently becoming disabled in 1953, 1954, 1955, and in later years. . . .

Following is a summary of the amendments.

I. Increase in Benefits

Benefits are increased for both present and future beneficiaries, whether their benefit amounts are computed under the conversion table or the formula. . . .

. . . The increases thus range from $5 to $8.60. The average increase to old-age insurance beneficiaries on the rolls will be $6. . . .

. . . *Maximum Provisions*—The amendments raise, beginning with September, the $150 maximum to $168.75, and the amount below which the 80 percent maximum does not apply from $40 to $45. Both of these amounts are 12½ percent larger than the corresponding amounts in the 1950 provisions. . . .

II. Work Clause

When H.R. 7800 came under consideration, there appeared to be wide agreement as to the need for an increase in the work-clause amount. The extent of the increase to be provided was, however, in dispute. As passed by the House, H.R. 7800 provided for a $70 work clause although there were many who favored raising the amount to $100. The Senate did raise the figure to $100. The conferees agreed upon $75. The new amount will be effective for wage earners beginning with September 1952, and for the self-employed beginning with the first taxable year which ends after August 1952. . . .

III. Wage Credits for Military Service

The legislation provides old-age and survivors insurance wage credits of $160 for each month of service in the active military or naval service of the United States after July 24, 1947, and before January 1, 1954. Thus all such service performed at any time from September 1940 through December 1953 is now creditable for old-age and survivors insurance purposes.

The new wage-credit provisions are similar in virtually all respects to those enacted in 1950 to provide wage credits for World War II service. The new credits may be used regardless of whether death occurred in or out of service, or whether Veterans Administration benefits are payable. . . .

. . . Beneficiaries now on the rolls may, on application, have their benefit amounts recomputed to reflect the new credits. . . . There is no change in the financing of the wage credits; their cost will continue to be borne by the trust fund. As in the case of World War II provisions enacted in 1950, the Conference Committee rejected the provision favored by the Social Security Administration and included in the House version of the bill which would have authorized appropriations from the General Treasury to meet the additional costs of the wage credits. . . .

IV. Disability "Freeze"

As finally enacted into legislation, this provision has no effect on benefit rights. As indicated earlier, the provision is included in the law as a basis for further study and is completely inoperative.

The disability "freeze" provision was, as is known to most of you, hotly contested. The purpose of such a provision is to prevent persons insured under our program and forced into premature retirement on account of permanent and total disability from losing their insured status or suffering a reduction in the amount of their old-age insurance benefit and the benefits of their dependents and survivors. Aged beneficiaries now on the rolls, as well as individuals who will qualify in the future as permanently and totally disabled persons, would have their primary insurance amounts computed so as to exclude periods prior to age 65 during which permanent and total disability prevented them from working.

When first introduced on the floor of the House, the disability provision of the bill met the unexpected opposition of the American Medical Association which charged that it was "socialized medicine." Nevertheless, the bill containing this provision later passed the House by a vote of 331 to 22.

The House version of the bill would have authorized the Federal Security Administrator to set up the necessary administrative processes in our Bureau for determining permanent and total disability. The provision, now included in the law for study purposes, would transfer the responsibility of determining whether an applicant is permanently and totally disabled from the Federal Security Administrator to appropriate State agencies . . . as may be designated in agreements entered into with the States by the Administrator. The Federal Security Administrator would retain the right to veto a State determination holding an individual disabled if, after reasonable notice and opportunity for a hearing, he found such individual not disabled. The administrative costs incurred by the States in making determinations of disability would be borne by the trust fund. . . .

The statement of the House conferees explains that the provisions which postpone the effective date and cause the authority to expire without becoming effective are intended to permit "the working out of tentative agreements with the States for possible administration of these provisions. It is the intent of the conferees that hearings will be held on this entire matter early in 1953 and at that time the congressional committees will go into the administrative and other provisions. It is intended to obtain the views at that time of interested groups on the methods of obtaining evidence of disability, under what circumstances and by whom such determinations should be made, and whether or not these provisions or any modification thereof should be enacted into permanent law."

Before January 1953, the Bureau must not only explore the possibilities for administering the "freeze" program through use of State agency services, but must also develop any modifications of the present provision that we may wish to present to Congress. We believe there are a number of objections to the plan as now written in the law. The Bureau is hopeful that any legislation providing permanent machinery for the determination of disability will take account of recommendations that we will want to make in the interest of economy, efficiency, and the safeguarding of the substantive rights of contributors. . . .

VI. Cost of the Program under 1952 Amendments

The schedule of contributions now in the law was based on an intermediate cost estimate showing that the level-premium cost of the program as amended in 1950 would be 6.05 percent of pay roll. These estimates were based on the wage levels of 1947. Based on 1951 wage levels, which are some 20 to 25 percent higher, and on interest rates currently yielded by investments of the trust fund (2.25 percent), the level-premium cost of the program under the 1952 amendments according to the intermediate cost estimates is slightly lower (5.85) than the cost of the program as estimated in 1950. . . .

Source: O. C. Pogge, SSA Director, to Administrative, Supervisory and Technical Employees, "Social Security Amendments of 1952 (H.R. 7800)," Director's Bulletin no. 188, SSA History Archives, Bookcase 4, Downey Books, 1951–1952, vol. 1.

Document 4.2
President Truman's Remarks on the Disability Freeze, July 18, 1952

In his remarks at the signing of the 1952 legislation, President Harry S. Truman departed markedly from the usual form in which a president celebrates the achievements of the bill. Truman made a few fleeting remarks about the content of the law, then expended the bulk of his remarks on an extended critique of the disability freeze provision and Congress's actions in enacting it.

. . . In this new law, otherwise so generally desirable, there is one drawback which I feel requires comment at this time. I deeply regret that the Congress failed to take proper action to preserve the old-age and survivors insurance rights of persons who become permanently and totally disabled. There is a provision in the Act which purports, beginning July 1, 1953, to preserve an individual's rights in the event of disability—but, unfortunately, the Act also includes a sentence, saying that this provision shall cease to be in effect on June 30, 1953. The net effect of this is that the provision will expire on the day before it can go into effect. Thus, in the Act I have just signed, the Congress takes away with one hand what it appears to give with the other.

The provision thus nullified by this extraordinary effective date arrangement, is analogous to the waiver of premiums in private insurance policies. This provision would permit aged persons whose disability has forced them into early retirement to have their benefits recomputed so that lost time due to their disability would not count against them.

No fair-minded individual denies the justice of such a provision. No procedures would be involved that are not already a part of the daily routine of scores of private life insurance companies. No administrative methods would be required that are not already used by any one of several Government disability programs for veterans, railroad employees, and Government workers, including Members of the Congress themselves.

The way in which this provision was, in effect, defeated is such a revealing example of how the Republicans dance when a well-heeled lobbyist pipes a tune that I think it warrants being brought to the particular attention of the American people in this election year.

The disability provision was recommended to the House of Representatives by its Committee on Ways and Means. On May 19th, the bill was taken up on the House floor under a motion to suspend the rules, a procedure which permits quick action but requires a two-thirds favorable vote to pass, a bill. This procedure was agreed to because no one foresaw any opposition to this sensible and reasonable piece of legislation.

At that point, the Washington lobbyist for the American Medical Association got the notion that here was a chance for him to attack what he chose to call a "socialistic" proposal.

So he sent a letter or telegram to every Member of. the House. There had been no other opposition to H.R. 7800.

There was, as Chairman Doughton stated on the floor of the House, "no more social-ized medicine in . . . [this provision] . . . than there is frost in the sun." Yet, when the House voted on the measure, nearly 70 percent of the Republicans were against the bill. A great majority of the Democrats, to their credit, stood firm and voted for the bill, but with the solid Republican opposition, they were unable to muster the necessary two-thirds vote.

After that defeat, the bill was sent back to the Ways and Means Committee. Then the story began to get around as to what had really happened. A great number of Republicans apparently decided they couldn't take the heat when they got caught, for when the bill was again reported and again brought to the floor, only 12 percent of the Republicans persisted in their opposition.

On this second try, the bill passed the House, on June 17th. But the American Medical Association lobby had accomplished what it wanted just the same. For the month's delay in the House had created such a situation that the Senate could act before adjournment only by dispensing with hearings. It was then the strategy of the American Medical Association to put up a great demand to be heard on the disability provision. Faced with the Associa-tion's insistence, the Senate committee decided to drop this provision rather than schedule hearings which might consume the time before adjournment and thus lose the chance for Senate action on the bill.

The net result of the medical lobby's maneuvering was the impairment of insurance pro-tection for millions of disabled Americans. What the lobby could not engineer outright, it won by delay. And be it noted that this victory for the lobby, at the people's expense, was accomplished by a great majority of the Republicans in the House. They were perfectly will-ing to deny to millions of Americans the benefits provided by this bill in order to satisfy the groundless whim of a special interest lobby—a lobby that purports to speak for, but surely fails to represent, the great medical profession in the United States.

I earnestly hope that the Congress next year will override the foolish objections of the medical lobby and put a proper disability provision in the law. . . .

In addition, I hope the Congress at that time will also consider the entire question of fur-ther extending and liberalizing the Social Security Act as a whole.

Source: Public Papers of the Presidents of the United States: Harry S. Truman, 1952–53 (Washington, D.C.: Government Printing Office, 1966), 486–488.

Document 4.3
Report of the "Hobby Lobby," June 24, 1953

At the beginning of the Eisenhower administration the newly appointed secretary of Health, Education, and Welfare (HEW), Oveta Culp Hobby, convened a small panel of experts to advise her on Social Security policy. This group—formerly known as the Consultants on Social Security, but more commonly called the "Hobby Lobby"—initially appeared to be formulating conserva-tive alternatives to Social Security, but ultimately it ended up recommending significant expan-sions in coverage of the retirement and survivors program. The scope of the Social Security pro-

gram would be significantly increased during the Eisenhower administration through amendments it supported in 1954, 1956, 1958, and 1960. This report was the foundation for the administration's Social Security policy during this period.

Dear Mrs. Secretary [Hobby]:

When you asked us to serve as consultants on social security, you referred to the President's recommendation in his State of the Union Message on February 2 that the "old-age and survivors insurance law should promptly be extended to cover millions of citizens who have been left out of the social-security system.". . .

As requested by you, we have given consideration in our study of social security to various alternatives for extending old-age and survivors insurance to additional groups of current workers, both employed and self-employed. . . .

There is transmitted herewith a report which includes the proposals which we have developed for your consideration in carrying out the President's recommendation for extending old-age and survivors insurance. . . .

Introduction and Summary

As requested by Secretary Hobby, we have given consideration to various alternatives for extending old-age and survivors insurance to additional groups, of current workers, both employed and self-employed. . . .

In evaluating the possibility of including each additional group of current workers not now included, we have considered first of all the question of technical feasibility. . . .

We have, however, been forced to recognize that the distinction between what is technically feasible and what is fair, socially desirable, and in the public interest is useful mainly as a device for breaking down the broad subject of social security into divisions that lend themselves to separate study. In actual practice, the various phases and aspects of social insurance such as coverage, benefits, and financing are not separable. In complying with the request that we make recommendations regarding extension of coverage, it has not been possible for us to make a study of certain other features of the old-age and survivors insurance program, the existence of which means that the present plan falls short in certain respects of providing all the various advantages which a contributory old-age and survivors insurance system can have for the country. The objectives of this program as we understand it are:

(*a*) Inclusion of all workers, employed and self-employed;
(*b*) Payment of benefits related to prior earnings and as a matter of right without a needs test; and
(*c*) Financing on a contributory basis.

We have operated on the premise that participation in the old-age and survivors insurance program will prove of real benefit to the members of most groups of current workers and that broader participation therein will be in the public interest. We have, therefore, tried to take into account the question of fairness, justice, and consistent treatment for each group considered, no matter how small the group or what initial difficulties would have to be overcome in administering the program for that group. . . .

Under the coverage provisions of the Social Security Act as originally enacted, about six out of ten paid civilian jobs were included. Subsequent amendments to the Social Security Act, including the major revisions made in 1950, extended coverage so that now about eight out of ten paid civilian jobs are included. Although there has been at least one cogent reason why each group of excluded workers has been left out in the past, we believe that it is feasible at this time to extend coverage to most of the jobs now excluded.

Several of the groups for whom we recommend coverage do not raise any particular administrative or technical difficulty not already encountered under present coverage. Coverage for State and local government employees under retirement systems, self-employed professional persons, fishermen, and home workers is almost entirely a matter of policy rather than administrative or technical feasibility. Coverage of some of the other groups does present certain difficulties but we believe these can be overcome in the ways which we suggest in the report. The groups which present some special, but not insuperable, problems include self-employed farm operators, hired farm workers, and domestic workers.

On the other hand, our recommendations for extension of coverage at this time do not include the blanketing-in of persons already age 65 or over who because they have not become eligible through prior work in covered employment are not receiving insurance benefits. We have excluded this group from consideration in this report because their inclusion would involve very substantial modifications of the present program which would require careful and prolonged study.

Since special studies were initiated last year by Congress in regard to the relationship of the old-age and survivors insurance program to the Railroad Retirement Act and to Federal employee retirement systems, we have not included in this report any recommendations with respect to railroad workers or to employees of the Federal Government and its instrumentalities who are currently excluded. . . .

Our proposal is designed to meet the problem of the newly covered groups, who under existing legislation would in many instances have substantially lower benefits than those already covered because they do not have wage credits in 1951, 1952, and 1953. Our proposal solves this problem of the newly covered groups as part of an overall improvement in the program. It represents a recognition that for the long run the present average monthly wage provision results in reductions in the benefit amount for every year a worker is out of the system. Unemployment or disability for even part of a year can now cause benefit reductions. . . .

By making possible the payment of full-rate benefits where earnings were reduced or nonexistent in as many as three years, the proposal does away with the need for any special provision for the newly covered groups. At the same time it gives to those already covered the advantage of some future protection against the lowering of the average monthly wage because of periods of unemployment, disability, or low earnings. . . .

Our proposal solves the immediate problem arising from extension of coverage. We recognize, however, that it may be desirable for the long run to allow individuals who have been under the program for a considerable period of time to disregard more than three years in computing the average monthly wage. This is particularly important because the groups brought under coverage after 1953 will in general be unable to utilize the three-year provision to offset future periods of low earnings or absence from the system. We are not intending by our present recommendation to prejudge later consideration of broader proposals designed to solve the long-range problem of the adverse effect of periods of low earnings or absence from the system on monthly benefits.

It will be noted that we have not recommended a new start for newly covered groups similar to what was done in 1950. While we think such an arrangement would probably be practical if coverage were extended to substantially all workers now excluded we believe that our proposal is superior to the alternative of a series of new starts.

We have not included in this report any recommendations relative to the retirement test. We recognize that extension of coverage will increase the number of anomalous situations which are created by the existing retirement test and, to this extent, intensify the need to find a more satisfactory retirement provision. However, this problem, like the question of benefit levels and methods of financing, raises broad questions relating to the system as a whole, whatever its coverage, and lies beyond the specific subjects we were asked to consider. . . .

. . . On the basis of the intermediate cost estimates shown in the appendix, universal coverage without other changes in the system would result in a reduction of about 0.4 in the percentage of payrolls required over the years to meet the costs of old-age and survivors insurance. Comparative figures for the extension of coverage that we propose . . . show a reduction of 0.25 percent of payroll over the years.

The saving occurs first of all because under limited coverage, those who move in and out of covered employment have low average monthly wages in covered employment and receive the advantage of a formula weighted in favor of those with low average wages. . . . Under extended coverage, their wages in covered employment will be greater. This means a corresponding increase in contribution income from those persons and their employers, with some but proportionately smaller increase in benefit outgo. This, in turn, means that over time the contribution income will increase more than benefit outgo. Second, extension of coverage means that there will be fewer cases in which earnings from uncovered employment are disregarded in applying the retirement test.

Our proposal for a change in the method of computing the average monthly wage will, on the basis of the intermediate cost estimate, increase long-range costs by about 0.1 percent of payroll. Thus since our proposals for extension of coverage will save about 0.25 percent it is estimated that on balance our proposals taken together will have no significant effect on the percentage of payroll required to meet the costs of the old-age and survivors insurance program.

Summary

In accordance with the President's policy to extend old-age-and survivors insurance coverage, we recommend the following:

1. Allow coverage under Federal-State agreements of members of State and local government retirement systems under provisions requiring that all members of a coverage group be brought in if any are covered.
2. Cover self-employed professional persons on the same basis as other self-employed now covered and cover interns by deleting the present exclusion of services of interns in the definition of employment.

3. Cover farm operators on a basis consistent with that on which other self-employed are now covered.

4. Cover cash wages earned in hired farm work regardless of the number of days the individual works for a single employer, and remove the exclusion of workers employed in cotton ginning and the production of gum naval stores.

5. Cover cash wages of domestic workers regardless of the number of days the individual works for a single employer.

6. Allow coverage for ministers and members of religious orders (other than those who take a vow of poverty) on a basis similar to that on which other employees of nonprofit organizations may now be covered.

7. Cover employees engaged in fishing and similar activities who are now excluded.

8. Cover home workers in States without licensing laws on the same basis as those in States with licensing laws.

9. Cover American citizens employed on vessels of foreign registry by American employers on the same basis as other American citizens working outside the United States for American employers.

10. Extend for a limited period the present provision giving "free" wage credits of $160 a month for service in the armed forces.

11. Revise the method for computing the average monthly wage to provide that the three years in which earnings credits were the lowest (or nonexistent) would ordinarily be disregarded, but in no case shall the period over which the average monthly wage is computed be less than the period of time required for the worker to obtain fully insured status.

Source: Consultants on Social Security, "A Report to the Secretary of Health, Education, and Welfare on Extension of Old-Age and Survivors Insurance to Additional Groups of Current Workers," 1953, SSA History Archives, Revolving Files, Folder: "Hobby, Oveta Culp."

Document 4.4
Ways and Means Committee Report on Disability Freeze Legislation, May 28, 1954

The purpose of the disability freeze was to preserve the eligibility for and the amount of any eventual retirement or survivors benefits a disabled worker would be entitled to receive. When a worker became disabled prior to age sixty-five, the worker's years of nonearning due to the disability could reduce the retirement benefit amount or even cause a loss of retirement benefits altogether due to the inability to accrue sufficient credits for work under the system. The concept of the freeze was devised to address this side effect of becoming disabled, the idea being that any period in which the worker is disabled would not be considered in assessing eligibility for Social Security retirement and survivors benefits.

The enactment of the freeze was important since it meant that the SSA had to set up the entire apparatus for making disability determinations and had to address the key policy issues involved in disability, such as making determinations of whether a person was truly disabled. Hence, passage of a disability freeze in 1954 became an important incremental step toward passage of disability insurance in 1956.

This 1954 photograph shows a Social Security employee inform-ing the public about the benefits available under the law in the wake of the 1954 amendments. Such information campaigns usually followed significant changes in the law.
Source: SSA History Archives.

Preservation of Benefit Rights for Disabled

A. Need for Disability Freeze

Under present law old-age and survivors insurance rights are impaired or may be lost entirely when workers have periods of total disability before reaching retirement age. Unless the worker is already permanently insured when he becomes disabled, he may have lost his fully insured status when he reaches retirement age because the entire period of his disability is included in the elapsed time which is the basis for determining his insured status. When ben-efit amounts are computed under present law, whether for retirement benefits or survivors benefits, his total earnings after a specified starting date and up to age 65 or death are divided by the total elapsed time, including any periods of total disability, in determining his aver-age monthly wage, on which monthly benefits are based. A freeze of old-age and survivors insurance status during extended total disability would remove this disadvantage by pre-venting such periods of disability from reducing or denying retirement and survivors bene-fits. In addition there is available to the disabled individual the 4- or 5-year dropout period provided by this bill for all persons.

Such a freeze provision is analogous to the "waiver of premium" commonly used in life insurance and endowment annuity policies to maintain the protection of these policies for the duration of the policyholder's disability. About 200 life-insurance companies (many of the largest) operating in the United States offer a "waiver of premium" clause to individu-als purchasing ordinary life insurance. It has been estimated that about half of the standard ordinary life insurance issued currently is protected through "waiver of premium" in the event of the disability of the insured.

B. Emphasis on Rehabilitation

Your committee recognizes the great advances in rehabilitation techniques made in recent years and appreciates the importance of rehabilitation efforts on behalf of disabled persons. It is a well-recognized truth that prompt referral of disabled persons for appropriate voca-tional rehabilitation services increases the effectiveness of such services and enhances the probability of success. The bill is framed to carry out your committee's objective that disabled individuals applying for disability determinations be promptly referred to State vocational rehabilitation agencies, to the end that as many disabled individuals as possible may be restored to gainful work.

C. Earnings Requirements

The earnings requirements which must be met to qualify for the freeze are intended to limit the application of this provision to individuals who have had a reasonably long, as well as recent, record of covered earnings. They operate to screen out those who have not established a reasonably substantial attachment to the labor force and those who had voluntarily retired from gainful activity, and had not been compelled to leave the labor force by reason of their disability.

D. Definition of Disability

Only those individuals who are totally disabled by illness, injury, or other physical or mental impairment which can be expected to be of long-continued and indefinite duration may qualify for the freeze. The impairment must be medically determinable and preclude the individual from performing any substantially gainful work. An individual would also be disabled, by definition, if he is blind within the meaning of that term as used in the bill. A person who does not meet the statutory definition, but who nevertheless has a severe visual impairment would be in the same position as all other disabled persons, that is, he may qualify for a period of disability under the general definition of disability if he is unable to engage in any substantially gainful activity by reason of his impairment.

There are two aspects to disability evaluation: (1) There must be a medically determinable impairment of serious proportions which is expected to be of long-continued and indefinite duration or to result in death, and (2) there must be a present inability to engage in substantially gainful work by reason of such impairment (recognizing, of course, that efforts toward rehabilitation will not be considered to interrupt a period of disability until the restoration of the individual to gainful activity is an accomplished fact). The physical or mental impairment must be of a nature and degree of severity sufficient to justify its consideration as the cause of failure to obtain any substantially gainful work. Standards for evaluating the severity of disabling conditions will be worked out in consultation with the State agencies. They will reflect the requirement that the individual be disabled not only for his usual work but also for any type of substantially gainful activity.

Disability must have lasted for 6 months before it may be considered. This provision is intended to exclude from consideration temporary conditions which terminate within 6 months.

In prescribing that the freeze apply only in the case of impairments "which can be expected to be of long-continued and indefinite duration" your committee seeks to assure that only long-lasting impairments are covered. This provision is not inconsistent with efforts toward rehabilitation since it refers only to the duration of the impairment and does not require a prediction of continued inability to work. An individual would not meet the definition of disability if he can, by reasonable effort and with safety to himself, achieve recovery or substantial reduction of the symptoms of his condition.

E. Determinations of Disability

By and large, determinations of disability will be made by State agencies, administering plans approved under the Vocational Rehabilitation Act. This would serve the dual purpose of encouraging rehabilitation contacts by disabled persons and would offer the advantages of the medical and vocational case development undertaken routinely by the rehabilitation agencies. These agencies have well-established relationships with the medical profession and would remove the major load of case development from the Department.

By agreement, the State agencies will apply the standards developed for evaluating severity of impairments for purposes of the freeze. This will promote equal treatment of all disabled individuals under the old-age and survivors' insurance system in all States. The cost to these agencies for their services in making disability determinations will be met out of the trust fund.

In the relatively few cases where there may be no agreement with a State or there is delay in obtaining agreement, disability determinations will be made by the Department of Health, Education, and Welfare. Such determinations will also be made in certain types or classes of cases, which, because of their characteristics or their volume (e. g., the backlog), are excluded from the agreement at the State's request.

F. Effective dates

January 1, 1955, has been specified as the earliest date a disability freeze application can be accepted in order to give the Department of Health, Education, and Welfare time to prepare its forms and procedures and negotiate necessary agreements with State agencies. An individual who files a freeze application before July 1, 1955, must, however, be alive on July 1, 1955, in order to get a period of disability.

Until July 1, 1957, a disability "freeze" application could establish a period of disability beginning on the earliest date the individual was disabled and met the covered work requirements described above. This means that an individual who was disabled as early as the fourth quarter of 1941 could have had sufficient qualifying earnings and could establish a period of disability provided he was continuously disabled and filed a disability freeze application before July 1, 1957. Despite the administrative difficulties created, your committee believes that the large number of persons who have been totally disabled for the years before the enactment of this provision should be included in the group receiving the advantages of the freeze provision, but only for periods of disability continuing to the date of application.

Benefit increases for disabled individuals already on the benefit rolls would be payable beginning July 1955. Newly entitled persons would be able to have their benefits computed with the exclusion of a period of disability, beginning with the month of July 1955. Survivors of workers who died after having qualified for a period of disability would receive increased benefits. . . .

Source: Social Security Amendments of 1954, House Report no. 1698 (Washington, D.C.: Government Printing Office, 1954), 22–24.

President Eisenhower signed the precursor to cash disability benefits (the disability freeze bill) into law while on vacation in Byers Peak, Colorado, on September 1, 1954.
Source: SSA History Archives.

Document 4.5
President Eisenhower's Statement on Signing the Social Security Amendments of 1954, September 1, 1954

In this signing statement, President Eisenhower explains the main provisions of the 1954 amendments—which he explicitly endorsed. This shows that the Eisenhower administration had embraced the incremental expansion of the increasingly popular Social Security program.

I am very happy to sign the Social Security Amendments of 1954. By enabling some 10,000,000 more Americans to participate in the Old-Age and Survivors Insurance Program, it gives them an opportunity to establish a solid foundation of economic security for themselves and their families.

Beyond broadening the coverage of this program, this new law contains four other important provisions:

First, it raises payments to all retired workers by at least five dollars a month. It also raises—by $13.50 a month for retired workers and by $31.25 a month for families—the ceiling on payments to people now receiving monthly checks. People becoming eligible in the future will also receive higher payments, including increases that result from raising from $3,600 to $4,200 the maximum wage base from which the amount of their benefit checks is determined.

Second, the law eliminates the four or five lowest years of earnings from the computation of the OASI checks of workers who retire in the future. This provision is of great importance to many people whose years of unusually low earnings—for reasons of unemployment, illness, or otherwise—would sharply reduce their benefits.

Third, all retired workers under the program are permitted to earn more without forfeiting OASI checks. The amount of exempt earnings is increased to $1,200 a year, and this annual exemption is applied equally to wage earners and self-employed workers.

Fourth, the Act preserves the benefits rights, under Old-Age and Survivors Insurance, of those workers regularly covered under the program who become totally disabled for long and indefinite periods.

This new law is an important part of the broad program of the Administration and the 83d Congress to improve the well-being of our people. In the past month I have signed into law a number of other Acts directly affecting the human problems of each family in the land. These include:

1. More hospitals and nursing homes for persons who are chronically ill, special medical facilities for people not requiring hospitalization, and rehabilitation facilities for disabled people.
2. A start toward increasing from 60,000 to 200,000 by 1959, the number of disabled people rehabilitated each year.
3. Three Acts helping the States and local communities meet the nation's educational problems.
4. Help to provide and improved housing, to prevent and eliminate slums, and to conserve and develop urban communities.
5. Extension of the unemployment insurance program to almost 4,000,000 more workers.

These Acts and the Social Security amendments I have approved today will bolster the health and economic Security of the American people. They represent one of the cornerstones of our program to build a better and stronger America.

Source: Public Papers of the Presidents of the United States: Dwight D. Eisenhower, 1954 (Washington, D.C.: Government Printing Office, 1960), 801–802.

Document 4.6
Secretary Hobby's Letter of Opposition to Cash Disability Benefits, June 21, 1955

While the House of Representatives was considering the disability legislation, the Eisenhower administration expressed its opposition to any cash disability program. It did so primarily through a letter from HEW secretary Oveta Culp Hobby directed to the Ways and Means Committee. Committee chairman Rep. Jere Copper (D-Tenn.) had asked for HEW's position on the legislation, and Hobby's letter was the reply.

The disability program would be enacted without administration support, although President Eisenhower would sign the bill into law.

Dear Mr. Chairman:

Thank you very much for your letter of June 17, 1955, enclosing copies of a confidential draft of a bill you are submitting to the full Committee on Ways and Means. Our staff has made such review as is possible in the time available. . . .

You have asked, also, that our staff be ready to present to the committee the position of the Department on these proposed amendments. I would like to take this opportunity to set forth our views. . . .

. . . [T]he 1954 amendments, which were adopted by an overwhelming bipartisan vote in both Houses of Congress, reflect in a way even more eloquent than a statement of principles the deep concern of this administration for improving the welfare of our people by strengthening and improving the OASI system.

We come now to consider how the administration policy for strengthening the OASI system applies in the situation presented by your . . . letter. . . .

. . . We believe that this committee could best serve the American people in this particular instance by setting up the mechanism for an intensive study . . . A study commission or advisory council, particularly if given a mandate to consider certain specified problem areas, could assure that no important consideration is overlooked and the views of all are taken into account. . . .

While it is true that testimony on related proposals was received by this committee in 1949, we are convinced that a full inquiry is needed with respect to the proposals contained in the confidential draft for the following reasons:

1. The social-security system is a system of the people. It represents the source of security for many millions of Americans, and it has a tremendous significance for our economy. It has reached practically universality in coverage of employment. Legislation dealing with a structure of such universal impact and significance should be considered widely by employers, employees, the self-employed, and other interested groups and discussed fully and openly.

2. Though the confidential draft is similar in many respects to parts of a bill considered by your committee in 1949, there are important differences. Just for example the provisions of the 1949 bill dealing with cash disability benefits provided that a disability benefit could be terminated if the disabled person refused without good cause to accept available rehabilitation services.

3. There are many alternative approaches to even the proposals in the draft bill. For example, as to cash disability benefits, the terms of eligibility, the administrative provisions and the appropriate review of administrative determinations are all matters of key importance with respect to which we do not purport to be able to give the Congress our best counsel at this time.

4. The OASI system has changed significantly since 1949 from a system under which about 6 out of 10 jobs were covered to one under which 9 out of 10 jobs are covered. Millions of self-employed persons have now been brought within the system—paying social security taxes at a rate 150 percent of the rate paid by employees. Self-employed farmers will commence paying taxes for the first time on January 1, 1956. The benefit structure of the system has been completely revised since 1949. The overall costs of the system have increased substantially, and a substantially higher ultimate tax rate is projected than was the case in 1949.

5. Because the OASI system is becoming a more costly one (with an 8 percent combined employer-employee tax already projected at the end of 20 years), every additional item of cost must be considered with the greatest care. The system could lose its attractiveness, particularly for many self-employed persons, if additional cost items are added without the most careful evaluation of the benefits they confer.

6. There are many praiseworthy objectives which have taken the form of numerous proposals for amendment of the OASI system other than the 2 or 3 proposals included in the confidential draft. There should be full opportunity carefully to consider which of the many proposals have the highest priority.

7. Since 1949 there have been many developments outside the OASI system which call for a thorough consideration. For example, there has been a tremendous growth in private insurance, private pension plans, and voluntary health insurance. These developments have an important bearing on the proposals contained in the confidential draft.

Within the Administration, we have not had an opportunity to make a real study of the proposals contained in the confidential draft bill, and have particularly not had an opportunity to solicit the views of groups and individuals outside of Government.

Furthermore, there has not been an opportunity to assess and evaluate the results of the 1954 amendments, nor will there be for some time yet. The first few State determinations of disability under the disability "freeze" provision enacted last year have just been received. We are convinced that best interests of the OASI system and the American people would be served by obtaining more experience under the "freeze" and having that experience evaluated carefully before coming to far-reaching decisions which have important implications for the OASI trust fund. Similarly, there has been no real opportunity to evaluate the effect of the Vocational Rehabilitation Act of 1954, expanding the Federal-State program of rehabilitation for the disabled, or the effect of the referral to State rehabilitation agencies under the disability "freeze" provision mentioned above. We regard all of these as matters of crucial significance in the development of sound legislation. . . .

There are many issues which a commission of inquiry might fruitfully consider. For example, the following major questions are raised by the proposals in the confidential draft bill:

Cash Disability Benefits

1. Recognizing that self-sufficiency and independence through rehabilitation are more important goals for the individual than dependence on cash payments: What are the implications of cash disability benefits with respect to rehabilitation efforts?

(*a*) Has experience under veterans' programs, workmen's compensation, or other programs indicated any lessening of incentive toward rehabilitation as a result of payments of cash benefits?
(*b*) Do we yet know the full potential of the expanding Federal-State vocational rehabilitation program?
(*c*) Could greater social gain be achieved by backing rehabilitation efforts with additional funds—whether from the OASI trust fund or other sources—rather than paying the same funds in cash benefits on the condition of continued disability?
(*d*) Could the desired objectives be better achieved by making more liberal maintenance payments during rehabilitation?

2. What are the actuarial problems involved in cash disability benefits? What is the recent experience of insurance companies, labor union funds, and the like? What experience is there with respect to disabilities of women in middle and upper age brackets?

3. Do we need a broad "health census" to better ascertain the incidence and scope of "permanent and total disability" in this country? . . .

4. Would a cash disability program be utilized by employers as a means for retiring disabled persons from the labor market, especially persons in upper age groups?

5. Is there in fact a changing concept of disability, as a result of developments which have broadened the extent to which handicapped persons may be restored to activity and gainful employment? Is it true, as stated in the 1952 report of the Task Force on the Handicapped (Office of Defense Mobilization) that "The idea of disability itself is outmoded," and that the significance of medical and rehabilitation advances of the last 10 years have not yet been fully comprehended? How should long-range policy in our social insurance system toward disability be developed in the light of these factors, if they are found to be true?

6. What guidance to the administrative problems involved in determining disability can be derived from experience under the disability "freeze" which has just gone into effect?

7. What would be the relationship of a Federal cash disability program to—

(*a*) The program of aid to the permanently and totally disabled, enacted in 1950;
(*b*) "Permanent and total disability" benefits provided under workmen's compensation;
(*c*) Unemployment compensation;
(*d*) Temporary disability programs in the States; and
(*e*) Private disability programs and voluntary health insurance plans?

8. Could benefits for "permanent and total disability" be handled more effectively under any of the foregoing programs at the State level rather than at the Federal level?

9. Should cash disability benefits, if adopted, be paid at any age, or only at age 55 or 60? . . .

The foregoing questions, many of which involve issues of broad economic and social policy, are stated not to discourage action in further amending the OASI law, but rather to lend sincere encouragement to the soundest possible approach to strengthening our social insurance system. It is because of these questions, Mr. Chairman, that we are anxious that your committee should exercise its traditional prerogatives with respect to the social security system and conduct a full inquiry into these and the many other questions which might be raised.

In addition to stating these views as Secretary of Health, Education, and Welfare, I wish to express the same opinions in my capacity as a trustee of the old-age and survivors insurance trust fund. The integrity of the fund cannot, in my opinion, be protected if we are to commence now to deviate from the pattern of deliberate, full, and careful consideration which has marked all prior major amendments of the OASI system. The actuarial status of the fund is too vital to the welfare of our people—the employed, the self-employed, and their families—to permit of even the possibility of hasty action without full understanding by all members of this committee, the Congress, and the American people of the implications of that action.

At the very minimum as a trustee of the fund, I feel compelled to call attention to the financial impact which the proposals in the confidential draft might have as a result of their average annual cost to excess of $2 billion—and to stress the importance of full and forthright financing of any additional costs imposed. . . .

Sincerely yours,

OVETA CULP HOBBY, *Secretary.*

Source: Social Security Amendments of 1955, House Report no. 1189, July 14, 1955 (Washington, D.C.: Government Printing Office, 1955), 58–62.

Document 4.7
House Committee Report on H.R. 7225, July 14, 1955

The 1956 amendments brought two notable changes: one large and important, and one seemingly small that would become important in the future. The big change was the inclusion of cash disability benefits. The small change was the offering of an early retirement option at age sixty-two—but only for women. This early retirement option had little immediate impact because relatively few women were among Social Security's retiring workers. But it opened the door for the early retirement option for men, which would eventually become one of the major cost factors in the program. (Although early retirement benefits are reduced to a level that in principle produces no net long-term cost to the trust funds, in practice the introduction of early retirement increased costs significantly in the short term and fueled a trend toward more and more workers taking the early retirement option.) Also, this provision benefiting only women continued the disparate gender treatment of women (to their advantage) that had first been introduced in 1939 and that would not be fully eliminated until 1983.

Also included in this Ways and Means Committee report was a separate "supplemental views" statement authored by seven of the Republican members of the committee, at least four of whom voted with the majority to report the bill. However, the minority members opposed the disability provisions of the bill, for reasons similar to those announced by Secretary Hobby, and they opposed the change in the retirement age as well.

Report

[To accompany H. R. 7225]. . . .

B. Disability Insurance Benefits

. . . *Need for disability benefits.*—The old-age and survivors insurance system now pays benefits to retired people who are age 65 or over. These benefits are designed primarily to protect workers against the loss of earning power due to age.

Your committee believes that retirement protection for the 70 million workers under old-age and survivors insurance is incomplete because it does not now provide a lower retirement age for those who are demonstrably retired by reason of a permanent and total disability. We recommend the closing of this serious gap in the old-age and survivors insurance system by providing for the payment of retirement benefits at age 50 to those regular workers who are forced into premature retirement because of disability.

The provision of social insurance protection against the risk of permanent and total disability has been considered for many years. After considerable study of the subject, the Advisory Council to the Senate Committee on Finance recommended such a program in 1948. After extensive hearings and careful consideration in executive sessions, your committee in 1949 recommended the passage of a permanent and total disability insurance program, and the House of Representatives passed the bill, H. R. 6000, providing for such protection. The Senate-approved version of the bill did not provide for this protection and, although a Federal-State program of disability assistance for the needy was established in the bill as finally passed in 1950, no provision was made for disability insurance benefits.

We have now had 4½ years of experience with the special category of aid to the permanently and totally disabled and longer experience with other measures for meeting the income maintenance needs of disabled people through the means-test assistance programs, supported by general revenues. Forty States and three Territories have established programs under the special category of aid to the permanently and totally disabled.

In fiscal year 1955 the Federal Government and the States spent about $145 million on this category of assistance. Approximately $70 million has been spent on aid to the needy blind and an estimated $145 million on aid to dependent children who are in need because of the disability of the father. Furthermore, much of the $225 million approximate cost to the States and local governments of general assistance (which excludes vendor payments for medical care) also arises because of disability. It is true that a part of this $585 million in total assistance costs results from the needs of people with congenital disabilities and of women who have never worked, and that perhaps half of the assistance costs arising from disabilities may be attributable to disability among persons who are not yet 50 years of age. Nevertheless, the program we recommend will, over the years, make the burden of public assistance, and therefore on general revenues, very substantially less than it would be in the absence of such a program.

The adoption, in 1950, of the assistance program to provide for the income maintenance needs of the disabled clearly expressed the intention of the Congress that the disabled should not be allowed to go without the necessities of life. It also indicated the judgment of the Congress that it was administratively feasible to determine who is disabled. Therefore, the question before your committee was one of method of providing for the disabled. Your committee concluded that the disabled should be provided for by contributory social insurance rather than to continue to be solely provided for through needs-test assistance financed out of general revenues. These disability insurance benefits would afford additional protection to the 70 million workers now protected by the social security system and would relieve the general taxpayers to a considerable extent from the burden of providing funds for such benefits.

Your committee has consistently been of the belief that the foundation of the social security system should be the method of contributory social insurance with benefits related to prior earnings and awarded without a needs test. As stated in the committee's report on the Social Security Act Amendments of 1949:

> the contributory system of old-age and survivors insurance, with benefits related to earnings and paid as a matter of right, should continue to be the basic method for preventing dependency. Insurance against wage loss due to permanent and total disability will round out the protection of the insurance system. The assistance program, with payments related to need, should continue to serve the function of filling the gaps left by the social insurance program.

Your committee believes that the covered worker forced into retirement after age 50 and prior to age 65 should not be required to become virtually destitute before he is eligible for benefits as he must under the assistance program. Certainly there is as great a need to protect the resources, the self-reliance, the dignity and the self-respect of disabled workers as of any other group. As the Advisory Council to the Senate Committee on Finance pointed out:

> The protection of the material and spiritual resources of the disabled worker is an important part of preserving his will to work and plays a positive role in his rehabilitation.

We believe that everything possible should be done to support and strengthen vocational rehabilitation. Rehabilitation, where it is possible, is the most economical method of providing for disabled persons and is the most satisfactory for the individual.

Under your committee's bill the determination of disability will be made by the State agencies which make the determinations under the disability "freeze" provisions enacted last year. The Department of Health, Education, and Welfare now has agreements with 36 States, the District of Columbia, and Puerto Rico to make such determinations. In all but 5 of these 38 jurisdictions, there are agreements with State vocational rehabilitation agencies. Eleven additional States and two Territories have designated vocational rehabilitation agencies to enter into agreements for this purpose and it is expected that these agreements will be completed in the near future. In the few States where the State agency designated is the public welfare agency rather than the rehabilitation agency, working relationships have been developed for the proper referral of individuals for rehabilitation purposes.

In order to avoid setting up barriers to vocational rehabilitation the bill specifically provides that a person who performs work while under a State rehabilitation program will not, solely by reason of this work, lose his benefits during the first 12 months while he is testing out a new earning capacity. On the other hand, the legislation also contains as a special safeguard a provision that stops the benefits of anyone who, without good cause, refuses rehabilitation available to him.

Important as rehabilitation is, it cannot be a substitute for disability benefits. Many disabled persons cannot be vocationally rehabilitated and even those who can will need benefits during rehabilitation. The major proportion of the disabled people who can be successfully rehabilitated are those who are only partially disabled or who are under age 50.

Your committee has designed a conservative program of disability insurance benefits. Under the bill eligibility for these benefits will be limited to persons who, through a record of work over a considerable period of time, have demonstrated a capacity and a will to work and who at the time of their disablement have had recent work. Moreover, the definition of the term "disability" requires inability to engage in any substantial gainful activity by reason of any medically determinable physical or mental impairment which can be expected to result in death or to be of long-continued and indefinite duration. Thus, an individual who is able to engage in any substantial gainful activity will not be entitled to disability insurance benefits even though he is in fact severely disabled. Also, a waiting period of 6 consecutive months of disability is required. The requirement that the disability can be expected to result in death or to be of long-continued and indefinite duration is more exacting than the disability provisions of commercial insurance policies now being issued, which permit a total disability that has persisted for 6 months to be compensated on the presumption that it is "permanent" until shown to be otherwise. The 6-month waiting period is long enough to permit most temporary conditions to be corrected or to show definite signs of probable recovery. The fact that the worker will frequently be without income during that period would make it unprofitable for a person who could work not to do so.

Under your committee's bill if another Federal disability benefit or a State workmen's compensation benefit is also payable to the disabled individual, the disability insurance benefit would be suspended if it is smaller than the other disability benefit; or, if larger, it would be reduced by the amount of the other benefit.

Basically the present framework for carrying out the disability "freeze" provision established by the 1954 amendments would be used for the payment of monthly disability benefits. As under the disability "freeze" provision the use of State agencies in making disability determinations will mean the utilization of well-established relationships with the medical profession. The near-universality of the coverage of old-age and survivors insurance program means that through its earnings reports and records the Bureau of Old-Age and Survivors Insurance will have an automatic check on earnings of the disabled.

Although present law provides for the preservation of the insurance rights of disabled workers, so as to insure that when they attain age 65 they will get full retirement benefits, many will not survive to age 65. The time they need their retirement protection is when they are in fact permanently retired whether it results from age or disability.

Covered workers have no protection under old-age age survivors insurance against income loss by reason of disability and for most such workers there is no protection under any other program, public or private. Employees disabled on the job may benefit from State workmen's compensation laws—but only about 5 percent of all permanent and total disability cases are work connected. The coverage provided by private insurance is very limited in this area. For the average worker, such insurance protection against income loss due to disability is not, as a practical matter, available.

Your committee believes that protection under the old-age and survivors insurance program should be provided in this area.

C. Payment of Monthly Benefits to Women at Age 62

Summary of Provision.—The qualifying age for receipt of monthly insurance benefits under present law is 65 for all aged beneficiaries. Your committee's bill would lower the qualifying age to 62 for all women beneficiaries. Altogether about 1,200,000 women would derive immediate protection from this provision of the bill. Of the 1,200,000 about 800,000 could draw monthly benefits beginning in January 1956. The remaining 400,000, who are working or the wives of workingmen, could receive benefits when they or their husbands retire. The reduction in the qualifying age for widows means the addition of about $15 billion in face value of the survivor protection of insured workers under the program.

Need for Provision.—Your committee has given careful attention to the special problems resulting from the requirement that women must be 65 before qualifying for old-age and survivors insurance benefits. In the hearings before the committee on the Social Security Amendments of 1950 the great majority of witnesses testifying on the retirement age for women favored lowering the age at which they could qualify for benefits. Although the eligibility age for women was not actively considered at the time of the 1954 amendments, representatives of many different groups again recommended that the qualifying age for women be lowered. In recommending a reduction in eligibility age for women your committee took cognizance of the personal hardship encountered by older women who have to wait until age 65 to receive monthly benefits under the old-age and survivors insurance program.

Your committee is concerned about the situation of elderly couples after the husband retires. The principle underlying wife's benefits under old-age and survivors insurance is that a married couple should not have to get along on the same amount that is sufficient for a single person. Wives are generally a few years younger than their husbands. Thus, when the husband has to retire many couples have only the husband's benefit until the wife also reaches age 65. With the age of eligibility for wife's benefits reduced to 62, about 400,000 wives would become immediately eligible for monthly benefits. Of this number 275,000 could draw benefits beginning January 1956, the effective date of the provision.

Your committee also is keenly aware of the plight of women widowed when they are not many years below age 65. Many of these widows have never worked or have not had recent work experience. As a result, when the death of the family earner makes a search for employment necessary many widows find it impossible to secure jobs. Some 175,000 widows and dependent mothers of insured workers would become immediately eligible for benefits with the age reduced to 62; virtually all of them could draw benefits beginning in January 1956. With the present qualifying age of 65, insured workers now have the equivalent of some $70 billion in face value of survivors insurance protection under the old-age and survivors insurance program for their wives in the event of the worker's death. As mentioned above, reduction in the qualifying age for widows from 65 to 62 means the immediate addition of about $15 billion in survivor protection under the program for these insured workers.

Your committee believes that the age of eligibility should be reduced to 62 for women workers, also. A recent study by the United States Employment Service in the Department of Labor showed that age limits are applied more frequently to job openings for women than for men and that the age limits applied are lower. Under your committee's bill some 650,000 women workers now between 62 and 65 years of age would be immediately eligible for benefits; about half of them could draw benefits beginning in January 1956. . . .

Supplemental Views

A majority of the undersigned voted to report this bill favorably. . . . Nevertheless, we are impelled to express our concern over certain aspects of this vital legislation.

The social security system is fast reaching maturity. Under Republican leadership, practically universal coverage was finally achieved last year. The system is no longer an experimental innovation but has become an integral part of our economy. . . . The Committee on Ways and Means is charged by law with responsibility for initiating all legislation affecting the social security system, and, in a very real sense, therefore, the members of our committee are trustees of the public interest in this program. This trusteeship imposes upon us an obligation not only to current social security beneficiaries but also to succeeding generations of beneficiaries. We must state with regret that we do not believe that the committee has properly discharged its trust in this instance.

The proposals contained in this bill will involve increased benefit payments from the trust fund of $2 billion a year, on the average. . . .

. . . The ultimate social and economic implications of these proposals are tremendous. . . .

Basic Problems

1. *Cost.*—In order to finance the multi-billion-dollar increase in benefits contained in this bill, a higher tax schedule is provided. . . . As a result, the ultimate tax rate projected under the bill, effective in 1975, is 9 percent shared equally by employees and their employers. . . .

It is estimated that in 1975 the total social security tax collections will approximate $20 billion annually, a colossal sum. Moreover, this estimate assumes continuation of existing wage levels and makes no allowance for the increase in those levels which past experience indicates will occur. The $20 billion estimate, is therefore, extremely conservative.

We point out these facts concerning future social-security tax rates and tax collections in order to show both the ultimate individual tax burdens and the total burden on the economy which are projected under this program. We believe that realism requires us to face the cold fact that these projected tax burdens are so high as to effectively preclude any significant social-security liberalizations in the future. . . .

We are concerned over this fact, moreover, because by their very nature, the liberalizations contained in this bill will create demands for additional changes involving further costs. For example, the bill provides benefits for the disabled children of a deceased worker. This liberalization is, in itself, highly desirable and involves very little cost. Once enacted, however, how long can the Congress deny equivalent benefits to a widow who is likewise permanently and totally disabled? The bill provides for the payment of cash disability payments to workers once they have reached the age of 50. How long can Congress deny equal treatment to permanently and totally disabled workers who are 49, 45, or younger? The bill provides retirement benefits to women on attaining age 62 even though the statistics show that women retire only slightly earlier than men. How long can Congress refuse to lower the retirement age for men?

We do not cite these problems as criticisms of the provisions of the bill. One cannot deny the serious need of many disabled people or elderly women. On the other hand, we have pointed out that the costs projected under the provisions of the bill are so great as to preclude serious additions to those costs in the future. At the same time we have created the basis for further liberalization which it will be almost impossible to refuse. That is the dilemma which we are creating for ourselves.

We are further concerned over these ultimate costs because of the danger that they may eventually weaken or even destroy public acceptance of the social security system. A social insurance program cannot be expected to provide against all insurable risks. It must be designed to provide a basic protection at a cost within the reach of all, especially those in the lower income brackets who are most in need of that protection. Despite this fact, we are creating a scale of benefits which must be supported by a social security tax which, in the not too distant future, will be equal to and in many cases higher than the Federal income tax. . . .

Finally, insofar as the cost of this program is concerned, we should take sober warning that, in our zeal to provide ever greater benefits . . . and to provide against an ever wider area of need, we do not destroy the very system which we have created. We have succeeded in avoiding the full impact of the cost by shifting most of the burden to the future. At that time, the high tax rates may make it very difficult to retain the contributory principle which we believe so essential to the program. However, we would be deluding ourselves should we believe that the general revenue could be depended upon to support the system. We have already pointed out that, under the present schedule, social security tax collections in 1975 will amount to about $20 billion. If such a vast sum were financed through the individual income tax, for example, it would necessitate approximately a 50 percent across-the-board increase in that already burdensome tax. These figures show clearly the magnitude of the problem we are so casually creating.

Cash Disability Benefits

There are several aspects of the disability benefit provisions which received little or no serious study by our committee and which we believe deserve the most careful consideration. These are, among others—

First, what should the relationship be between a cash disability payment program and rehabilitation programs, including State plans? To what extent may disability payments interfere with the objective of rehabilitation?

Second, have we had sufficient experience under the disability "freeze" program to provide a sound basis for intelligent legislation in this area?

Third, what are the implications of charging the States with responsibility for administering Federal benefit payments?

Fourth, the cost of the disability program has not been fully analyzed by the committee.

A very serious question raised by the payment of cash disability benefits involves its relation to rehabilitation. . . . We believe that a primary goal of any disability program should be to encourage disabled individuals to regain their position as useful, self-supporting members of society. . . . However, many sincere students of the problem feel that cash disability payments may discourage individual incentives for rehabilitation.

We do not believe that a cash disability program need necessarily operate to the disadvantage of rehabilitation. On the other hand, we do believe that our committee has failed completely to face up to the problem. . . .

As was done with respect to the disability freeze, this bill provides that the determination of total and permanent disability shall be made by the States. However, there are substantial differences between the two programs. For purposes of the "freeze," the State determination simply protects benefit rights to which individuals may become entitled at some time in the future. Under the disability benefit program, however, the State determination will provide the basis for the payment of immediate cash benefits out of the OASI trust fund. In many cases, such a determination will make it possible for the State to reduce or eliminate its own benefit payments, entirely at the expense of the Federal program. This fact raises a serious question of whether the administration of this program may not be subject to abuse. . . .

The cost of the disability program is at best conjectural. The actuary of the Social Security Administration, in whom our committee has always had great confidence, admitted that his actuarial estimate of the cost could be subject to wide variation. Insurance actuaries have generally testified to their conviction that the cost would be substantially in excess of that estimated by the committee for this portion of the bill. . . .

Eligibility Age for Women

The bill lowers the age of eligibility for all women beneficiaries (widows, wives, and women workers) from 65 to 62. There has been widespread demand over the years for lowering the eligibility age both for retirement and survivors' benefits, and the major interest in this question has been with respect to women beneficiaries. Such a proposal was rejected by this committee in 1949 as being too costly.

A number of the undersigned favor the principle of creating more liberal eligibility requirements for women. Here again, however, there are a number of questions which our committee either failed to explore completely or did so only in a cursory and inconclusive manner. We do not raise these questions as objections to the merits of the proposal contained in this bill. We do believe, however, that these matters should have been studied carefully in order to prevent the creation of new discriminations, in order to determine the areas of greatest need, and in order to avoid any possible detriment to other objectives of great social importance.

The longevity of the American people is increasing at a significant rate. The proportion of people over 65 is very large and becoming larger all the time. As a result of this situation, one of the most encouraging trends in the country has been the effort toward creating a favorable climate for the employment of older workers. . . . Certainly, those who wish to work beyond 65, or any other age for that matter, should be afforded an opportunity to do so and should not be forced arbitrarily out of employment.

There is a serious question in the minds of many as to whether the reduction of the statutory social-security eligibility age, for women, desirable as such action is in many individual cases, may not run counter to this major social and economic objective of wider employment opportunity. Private industrial pension plans are generally geared to the social-security system. This fact has led most such plans to adopt age 65 as the compulsory retirement age for both men and women. If age 62 is established for social-security purposes, it must be expected that the same pattern will be adopted by private industry. Our committee made no effort to appraise the implications of its action in this regard.

Lowering the retirement age for women workers is supported on the ground that they typically retire at an earlier age than men. However, the statistics indicate that this is true only to a slight extent. In 1953, the average age was 68.0 for men and 67.6 years for women. We do believe that a serious hardship, however, exists under present law with respect to women who are widowed before age 65. We question whether making benefits available to this group at age 62 will make any significant improvement in the situation. . . .

Source: Social Security Amendments of 1955, House Report no. 1189, July 14, 1955 (Washington, D.C.: Government Printing Office, 1955), 3–7, 57–67.

Document 4.8
Senate Committee Report on H.R. 7225, June 5, 1956

The Senate Finance Committee rejected out-of-hand any provision for the introduction of disability benefits into the program. Even though the committee was controlled by the Democrats, the majority argued a position very similar to that taken by the Eisenhower administration and by the Republicans on the Ways and Means Committee. So the committee refused to recommend disability benefits in its report.

In this report, it was liberal Democrats who wrote a separate set of "minority views" on the legislation. These minority views contained the most sustained argument in favor of including cash disability benefits in the law. On the early retirement issue, the committee favored limiting benefits at age sixty-two to widows; the dissenting Democrats supported the more generous House position.

. . . The committee does not believe that the following proposals, which were included in the House-approved bill but are not in the committee bill, are necessary or desirable:

1. *Provision for lowering minimum eligibility age for wives and women workers.*—Lowering the eligibility age for women workers would have the undesirable effect of encouraging employers to lower their maximum hiring ages and compulsory retirement ages for women. Lowering the eligibility age for wives would be costly and there is not as great a need as in the case of widows, since the family has income from the husband's benefit.

2. *Provision of cash disability benefits for permanently and totally disabled persons at age 50.*—Your committee recognizes that prolonged and severe disability is a serious problem to the worker, his family, and the community. As the testimony before the committee has shown, however, there are important differences of opinion as to how the problem can best be met. Your committee has concluded, on the basis of the preponderance of the evidence submitted at the public hearings, that the adoption of a provision for paying cash disability benefits to insured workers under the old-age and survivors insurance program would not be desirable. Under the system now, cash payments are made only upon death or retirement. These conditions are easy to determine. Under the disability proposal, however, the primary condition for payment would be, in the terms of the bill, inability—

> to engage in any substantial gainful activity by reason of any medically determinable physical or mental impairment which can be expected to result in death or to be of long continued and indefinite duration.

These conditions for payment are much more difficult to determine. Monthly disability benefits have a completely different nature as compared with the present provisions for old-age benefits and survivor benefits. Lack of objectivity in determination of disability makes it both easier for the claimant to maintain, and harder for the administration to deny, the presence of qualifying disability. In many instances, physical disability does not necessarily produce economic disability, although this would in many cases be the tendency if monthly benefits were available.

In reaching this conclusion your committee has taken into account the significant progress that has already been made in meeting the needs of disabled workers. In 1950, when the question of disability benefits came before this committee, the committee rejected the proposal for paying cash disability benefits under the old-age and survivors insurance system. This position was sustained by the Senate. In conference with the House, a fourth category of assistance grants to States was approved—aid to the permanently and totally disabled.

Since 1950, 42 States have begun operations under this program some of them only recently. About 244,000 needy disabled persons are now receiving monthly assistance payments, which total about $165 million annually. . . . In most of the States, therefore, provisions already have been made to meet the basic needs of those who cannot support themselves because of extended and serious disability.

Significant strides have been made, too, in the Federal-State program of vocational rehabilitation under the impetus of the 1954 amendments, which greatly expanded the program. Many witnesses who appeared before your committee expressed the belief that payment of cash disability benefits would in some cases discourage rehabilitation.

The 1954 amendments to the Social Security Act included in the law the so-called disability "freeze," which protects the old-age and survivors insurance rights of workers during periods of total disability. The freeze provisions will be helpful to many disabled persons in protecting rights to old-age and survivors insurance benefits, in providing higher retirement and survivor benefits, and in bringing more individuals promptly to the attention of State rehabilitation agencies.

More time is needed to develop more fully all of the existing programs for the disabled and to evaluate their results. In particular it would be desirable to have more experience with the disability freeze.

Your committee has been impressed by the testimony of the many medical experts who have testified that many problems would be encountered in evaluating physical and mental impairments for purposes of determining eligibility for disability benefits.

Difficulties in determining eligibility, and other factors, lead to uncertainty as to the future costs of a cash disability program. Cost estimates in the field of disability benefits, as pointed out by the Chief Actuary of the Social Security Administration, are subject to a wider range of variation than are estimates for other types of benefits. The basic cost estimates which have been presented to the committee were based on high employment conditions; under low employment conditions, the cost would be significantly higher. The old-age and survivors insurance system is on a sound financial basis; your committee strongly believes that it must be kept so and should not be altered by adding a benefit feature that could involve substantially higher costs than can be estimated.

In view of all these considerations your committee has decided against including provisions for cash benefits to disabled workers. . . .

Minority Views on H. R. 7225

The Senate Committee on Finance had almost a full year during which the House-passed bill was before it. While the bill has been improved in several respects, the actions of the Senate Committee on Finance resulted in striking out some of the most beneficial provisions of the bill passed by the House. Specifically, we feel that the committee should never have eliminated those provisions which provided disability benefits for workers who become disabled after age 50 and those provisions which lowered the retirement age for working women, wives of retired workers and dependent mothers. . . .

Disability Benefits

The old-age and survivors insurance system now pays benefits to retired people who are 65 or over. To a considerable extent these benefits rest on a general presumption of the likelihood of serious disabilities in later life. Yet there is no magic in the selection of age 65 as the point at which workers no longer young are forced out of the labor market because of disabilities. There are around a million persons between ages 50 and 65, for example, who would be working but for serious long-term disability. At present they have little recourse but the charity of friends and relatives and the Federal-State programs of assistance to the needy.

We believe that retirement protection for the 70 million workers under old-age and survivors insurance is woefully incomplete because it does not now provide a lower retirement age for those who are demonstrably retired by reason of a permanent and total disability. We recommend the narrowing of this serious gap in the old-age and survivors insurance system by providing for the payment of retirement benefits at age 50 to those regular workers who are forced into premature retirement because of disability.

The majority report states that through the assistance programs in most of the States—

provisions have already been made to meet the basic needs of those who cannot support themselves because of extended and serious disability.

Such State welfare plans no more meet the needs of insurance to care for disability than do the welfare plans for the needy aged eliminate the need of old-age insurance. . . .

Prior Consideration of Disability Insurance

For almost 20 years it has been maintained that disability benefits should be paid under our social security program but that such benefits should be delayed for further study. Additional delay is completely unjustified.

In 1937 the Senate Special Committee on Social Security appointed a 25-member Advisory Council on Social Security composed of individuals representing employers, employees, and the public to study the social-security system. . . . The council reported unanimous agreement on the social desirability of paying benefits to insured persons who became totally and permanently disabled, and disagreed only as to whether such benefits should be inaugurated immediately, or after further detailed study.

In 1947 the Senate Finance Committee appointed an Advisory Council on Social Security composed of 17 members from representative areas of American life to consider, among other questions, the advisability of initiating disability payments as a part of the social-insurance system. In 1948 the chairman, the late Edward R. Stettinius, Jr., reported back to the committee that, after careful study of all aspects of the question, 15 of the 17 members felt that the time had come to extend social-insurance protection to the risk of loss of income from disability. . . .

Of the need for such a program, the council felt no doubt:

Income loss from permanent and total disability is a major economic hazard to which, like old age and death, all gainful workers are exposed. . . . The economic hardship resulting from permanent and total disability is frequently even greater than that created by old age or death.

In 1950, following extensive hearings, the House Ways and Means Committee favorably reported a social-security bill containing provisions for permanent and total disability insurance. The committee pointed out that the proposed public assistance program for the disabled could meet only part of the problem and that the worker who had paid social insurance contributions over a number of years had a real stake in the system which deserved to be recognized.

The Senate Finance Committee, however, disapproved the disability insurance provisions, stating in its report that

. . . further study should be made of the problem of income maintenance for permanently and totally disabled persons.

The 1950 bill, as finally passed, did not include the provisions for disability insurance, although the disability problem was recognized to a degree by the establishment of a separate public assistance program for the disabled.

In 1954 recognition was again given to the equity involved in the case of an insured worker who became disabled. The "disability freeze" allowed the disabled worker to leave out the years of disability in computing his average wages for the purpose of determining benefits payable at 65. The experience thus far under this legislation has been highly useful in demonstrating that disability can be determined administratively within the framework of our social-security system without unusual difficulty.

Over the years the experience of foreign governments in providing disability insurance has not been without value to those concerned with the problem in the United States. By 1954, 37 foreign countries had put into effect programs of disability insurance on a contributory basis, as compared to only 4 countries which had disability benefits restricted to a needs test. . . .

Despite the plea by the Secretary of Health, Education, and Welfare for more time, we know that the Department of Health, Education, and Welfare has made exhaustive studies over the years, and we are convinced that it is prepared to conduct a sound disability benefits program. . . .

In the light of the experience now available from so many sources, and in view of the consideration given the question of disability insurance for almost 20 years, it seems to us that the continued objections regarding the uncertainties of such a program and the continued call for further study constitute a tactical maneuver on the part of those who basically are opposed to the idea. . . .

Cost of Disability Benefits

Much has been said about the cost aspects of the proposed disability benefits program. Seldom is this cost explained in terms of additional insurance the worker is buying. American people are perfectly willing to pay a nominal increase in taxes to obtain this vital protection against expensive and unpredictable risk of a crippling illness or injury. . . .

. . . In our judgment the Chief Actuary of the Social Security Administration has made as good an estimate of the probable cost of these proposed new benefits, and of the benefits already provided under the old-age and survivors' insurance system, as is humanly possible. But it is important to remember that, according to past experience, the estimates usually have been higher, rather than lower, than actual costs. They are based upon the assumption that there will be no future increase in the general level of earnings. . . .

We doubt that the cost would approach the high-cost estimates, but even if, as some people have predicted, costs would greatly exceed the intermediate estimate used in our proposal, we believe that the families of this country would want the added protection.

Administration of Disability Benefits

Under our proposal the determination of disability will be made by the State agencies which make the determinations under the disability "freeze" provision enacted in 1954. The Department of Health, Education, and Welfare now has agreements with 36 States, the District of Columbia, and Puerto Rico to make such determinations. . . .

The use of these State agencies in making disability determinations for a program of disability benefits will avoid duplicating use of existing medical facilities and records and will utilize well-established relationships with the medical profession. The near-universality of the coverage of old-age and survivors insurance means that through its earnings reports and records the Bureau of Old Age and Survivors Insurance will have an automatic check on the earnings of the disabled. . . .

The majority report stresses the difficulty of determining disability in a public program providing such benefits. But we know that disability determinations are being made successfully every day, not only in connection with the "disability freeze" provision of the old-age and survivors insurance system, but also in numerous public programs which pay benefits. As a matter of fact, some 420,000 people are now receiving disability benefits under . . . federally administered programs. . . .

We submit that the experience with these well-established programs has demonstrated that the extent of disability can be determined with sufficient precision to make such a program administratively feasible and financially sound. We also wish to point out that the rehabilitation features of the program we propose make an important contribution in this respect because they bring into play other factors—such as attitude and work record—to supplement the medical diagnosis as to the extent of disability.

Effect on Rehabilitation

The majority report takes the position that the payment of disability benefits might discourage rehabilitation. Belief that rehabilitation would be hindered or malingering encouraged seems to us to be unjustified in view of the stringent eligibility requirements, limited benefits, and positive stress on rehabilitation contained in the proposal to which we subscribe.

The eligibility requirements would require a substantial and recent attachment to the labor force, determined by a work history. . . .

The definition of disability contained in the proposal is a conservative one, limited to medically determinable physical or mental impairment which prevents the individual from engaging in any substantial gainful activity. Furthermore, a waiting period of 6 consecutive months of disability prior to eligibility for benefits is required.

Since benefits under our proposal would not be paid to the dependents of a disabled worker, the income available to a worker's family from disability insurance would not be sufficient to encourage persons on the borderline of total disablement to seek benefits if employment alternatives were open to them. . . .

The disability provisions which we support incorporate the rehabilitation process with the disability benefit plan. Refusal, without good cause, to accept rehabilitation would result in termination of the individual's benefits. . . .

A great deal of emphasis must rightly be placed on rehabilitation. However, the fact must be recognized that a great many older disabled workers cannot be rehabilitated successfully. Our best information indicates that it has not been possible to rehabilitate more than 25 percent of disabled persons who are age 50 or over. Furthermore, rehabilitation cannot be a substitute for income for the disabled worker.

Lowering the Eligibility Age for Women

We wholeheartedly agree with the provision of the Senate bill which lowers from 65 to 62 the age at which surviving widows may first become eligible for their benefits, but we believe this provision should also apply to working women, wives, and dependent mothers. . . .

We believe that the policy adopted by the committee of excluding two groups of women—wives and women workers—from the same privilege which they extend to other women is a serious departure from a well-established principle of the old-age and survivors insurance system. Under such a provision, a widow who normally works and supports herself would be able to receive benefits if she lost her job at age 62, and was unable to find work, while a woman worker in the same circumstances would be forced to wait until her 65th birthday for benefits. This would be true even though she may have contributed throughout her working life to the old-age and survivors insurance system.

Any woman who loses her job between the ages of 62 and 65 cannot easily get other employment. . . .

Men almost universally retire because they become disabled, because they reach the retirement age in the industry in which they work, or because the employer terminates the employment for other reasons. Although lowering the eligibility age to 62 does not solve the problem for all elderly couples, we cannot overlook the fact that it would provide immediate benefits to over 20 percent more wives than at present and a shorter waiting period for the remainder. . . .

It is not realistic to assume that an elderly wife will be able to go out and get a job when the family income is reduced because of the retirement of the husband. They experience the same problem of obtaining employment as do other older women. Over 90 percent of all wives between the ages of 62 and 65 are not in the labor force. . . .

The level premium cost of adding benefits for working women, wives, and dependent mothers, would be only 0.36 percent of payroll. These relatively small added costs are more than justified so that all women will have the right to retire at age 62, which committee bill grants only to widows. . . .

Source: Social Security Amendments of 1956, Senate Report no. 2133, June 5, 1956 (Washington, D.C.: Government Printing Office, 1956), 3–5, 127–135.

Document 4.9
Senate Floor Debate on the 1956 Amendments, July 17, 1956

The House version of the 1956 legislation (including the disability program) passed easily in July 1955 with little controversy and with a vote of 372–29. The Senate version was passed one year later, in July 1956.

The bill as introduced in the Senate did not include the disability provision and had only a limited reduction in the age sixty-five requirement. However, the three Democratic members of the Finance Committee who authored the minority dissent to the committee's report (along with several cosponsors) introduced the disability provision as a floor amendment; it was known as the George Amendment, after Sen. Walter George (D-Ga). Sen. Robert Kerr (D-Okla.) introduced a separate amendment to expand the early retirement option to additional categories of women, to parallel the House version, but with a variation requiring reduced benefit amounts under early retirement.

The George Amendment was vigorously resisted by the chairman of the Finance Committee, Sen. Harry Flood Byrd (D-Va.), but ultimately the amendment passed by a close vote of 47–45.

Senator Kerr's amendment was again opposed by Chairman Byrd but was argued against on the floor by a handful of Republican senators, most notably by Sen. Thomas Martin of Iowa and Sen. Carl Curtis of Nebraska. Martin's argument was that granting women this special treatment was a form of discrimination against them. The Kerr amendment passed overwhelmingly on a vote of 86–7. After these two contentious matters were settled, the legislation went on to be passed in the Senate by a vote of 90–0.

Mr. BYRD: . . . I shall discuss two provisions relating to old-age and survivors insurance that were included in the House bill but deleted by the Committee on Finance. They are disability benefits to disabled workers and payment of benefits to all insured women at age 62.

. . . I wish to make it clear that the committee decided against recommending this disability program, because of doubt that such a system of benefits would accomplish the objective of those who advocate the proposal. . . .

Pronounced differences of opinion were found among experts. Many of them believe that a system of cash disability benefits would operate to discourage efforts toward rehabilitation. . . .

The question of adding a cash disability payment to the list of benefits now provided under the old-age and survivors insurance system is complicated also by difficulty in estimating costs. Experience under the so-called disability freeze provision . . . is too brief to provide a firm basis for estimating the cost of cash disability payments.

The Chief Actuary of the Social Security Administration, in presenting his estimates to the committee, acknowledged that they were subject to a broader variation than are estimates for other types of benefits—types for which eligibility can be determined from fact. The estimates are based on high-employment assumptions. Decrease in employment would mean still higher costs, but by even the low-cost figures a system of cash disability benefits would result in a significant acceleration of expenditures from the trust fund.

In summary, the Committee on Finance concluded from extensive hearings and study that the apparent disadvantages and uncertainties of the proposed system of cash disability payments are far too great to warrant its recommendation to the Senate and to the people, who would bear its costs.

The other provision to which I referred a moment ago related to lowering the eligibility age for all women from age 65 to age 62. The bill reported by the Committee on Finance would make that change for widows only. Women whose lifelong occupation has been that of homemaker and who are widowed rather late in life commonly have a very reduced chance of employment, both because of age and because of lack of outside work experience. The same is only slightly less true of older widows who worked outside the home when younger but have been out of the labor market for many years.

For these reasons, the bill now before the Senate would make benefits available to widows at age 62, despite the fact that the Finance Committee regards the general question of reduction in the retirement eligibility age with misgivings for reasons in addition to the heavy cost that would be involved. . . .

Mr. GEORGE: Mr. President, I ask Senators to give me their attention, because I want to speak very earnestly against the committee amendment. . . .

Mr. President, I feel strongly that we have arrived at the time when we should improve our social-security program by providing for the payment of insurance benefits to the men and women of our country who are unfortunate enough to become permanently and totally disabled. . . .

The hearings which the Finance Committee conducted in 1950, 1954, and this year have amply demonstrated that it is imperative to liberalize the social-security program to help disabled persons. The burden of disability is a crushing load on many families. Not only does the disabled person have the worry, the discouragement, and the frustration due to the loss of his health, but he has the heavy weight of increased medical and hospital bills, nursing services and drugs, the loss of his regular income, and the continued financial responsibility for the support of his wife and the education and care of his children.

Every Senator knows individual cases where prolonged sickness and disability have reduced a proud and self-supporting person to a helpless, dependent individual who must look to his wife, or to his children or relatives, or to private or public charity to support him. . . .

Every time we cut short the education of a promising young boy or girl we are not only making it difficult for him or for her to have a successful career, but we are losing for our Nation productive or inventive skills which may have been developed through proper schooling. Every time we force a mother into the labor market against her will we are disrupting family life and sowing the seeds of further hardship, even delinquency, and sometimes despair.

Today in the United States, more than 400,000 permanently and totally disabled persons are receiving public relief. Think of that. I ask Senators to stop and reflect for a moment what it would mean if someone they knew, some one they held dear to them, some friend of theirs, had to apply for public relief because he or she was permanently and totally disabled. . . .

I find it singularly distressing and very strange in the year 1956 to hear the arguments of those who say we can rely upon public assistance to meet the needs of those who are disabled. We have not followed this principle with respect to the aged, widowed mothers, and dependent children, or the unemployed; and we have not followed it as to ourselves as Members of Congress. As a progressive and enlightened Nation we have adopted the policy that assistance is a second line of defense, and that we want to rely on the tried and tested method of contributory social insurance to meet the major economic hazards of our industrial society. I believe we should, we can, and we must now apply the contributory social insurance principle to the risk of permanent total disability. . . .

Mr. President, another feature of our proposal is that the funds for disability payments are earmarked in a wholly separate fund. . . . It is necessary to provide another social security system and a collection system, through the Commissioner of Internal Revenue, to bring that about, but that is done. The moneys for disabled persons will not be commingled in any way with the funds for old-age insurance or for widows and orphans. The contribution income and the disbursements for disability payments will be kept completely distinct and separate. In this way the cost of disability benefits always will be definitely known and the costs always will be shown separately. . . .

Thus, the argument which was made against the original proposal as considered by the Finance Committee, namely, that the cost of the proposal could not be determined, has been met by our amendments. The cost may not be easily ascertained, because we cannot determine how many permanently disabled cases exist at the moment, but assuredly, with one-third or more of them being under 50 years of age, no burden will be imposed which the one quarter of 1 percent payroll tax cannot bear. . . .

Mr. Byrd: Mr. President, we must recognize that cash disability payments to those covered by social security would establish an entirely new concept, never contemplated when the program was inaugurated. It may well involve the question of the physical fitness of 70 million persons who are currently under social security, and this number will increase as the years go on. The pending amendment for cash payments to the totally disabled of 50 years of age and over is merely the entering wedge.

The distinguished Senator from Georgia, himself, has indicated the probability of rapid expansion of this program. He has said there should be no age limitation, and he has offered this amendment to the pending bill after the Finance Committee failed to adopt his previous proposal to pay disability benefits without regard to age.

Various representatives of trade unions testified before the committee that they regarded the pending amendment as only the instrument for establishment of the principle of disability payments under social security. If this amendment is adopted, it is certain that in the immediate future the effort will be made to enlarge the scope. It is not difficult to anticipate the contention that younger persons with their young children are more entitled to disability payments than are the older group.

I emphasize that, once this principle of disability payments under social security is established, it is likely, and I think probable, that the program will be broadened to partial disability. Broadening the scope would be according to the pattern already established in other social-insurance and pension programs.

I am thoroughly sympathetic with those who are totally disabled, but I submit that relating the program proposed in this amendment to the system in which 70 million citizens are investing against their old age is an improper approach.

The private insurance companies have had unfavorable experience with total disability insurance, resulting in millions of dollars of loss. A public disability insurance program, such as this, is likely to have the same experience in the event of a recession. Under such circumstances, the tax proposed under this amendment may have to be increased substantially at a time when individual taxpayers would be least able to pay additional taxes.

It has been impossible to date to safeguard a Federal system of disability benefits against abuse. This is primarily because of the difficulty in defining total disability. A person may be disabled physically, but at the same time capable of making economic and social contributions. He may be disabled in a manner preventing one type of work, but not another. He may be disabled as a farmer, but not disabled as a watchman. He may be a malingerer exploiting the program, purely and simply. What would be the status of a married woman who is able to establish disability for outside employment, but who is perfectly capable of housework at home?

There is competent testimony and historical experience to demonstrate that disability rises and falls with prosperity and recession. Determination of disability is difficult enough in times of high employment conditions. . .

Mr. Kerr: Mr. President, the amendment allows full benefits for widows at age 62, as does the bill reported by the Committee on Finance, but in addition it also provides full benefits at 62 for the dependent mothers of workers who have died. It also extends to working women and wives the privilege of electing early retirement at or after age 62 with proportionately reduced benefits—a principle used in the Civil Service Retirement System, the

Railroad Retirement System, and in many private pension plans to add flexibility to their retirement programs without excessively increasing the cost to the contributor.

Thus the proposal would extend the right of retirement to 600,000 women workers and wives, and dependent mothers, in addition to the 200,000 widows who would become eligible for benefits under the bill as reported by the committee.

I believe that our amendment provides a logical compromise between the bill as reported by the Committee on Finance and the bill as passed by the House.

An important consideration, in connection with our amendment, is the fact that the choice of the date of retirement is voluntary in our social security system. No woman will, of course, be required to retire at age 62. The choice will be hers. If she does not elect to take a slightly lower benefit to qualify before age 65, and instead decides to wait until she is 65 years of age to apply, she will still be entitled to her full benefit. . . .

Mr. President, in view of these considerations, I believe that the Members of the Senate will agree that the liberalization proposed by means of the amendment can be made in line with sound financing principles, to preserve the integrity of the old-age and survivors insurance trust fund, while at the same time making social-security benefits available to hundreds of thousands of women who would choose to receive them at an earlier retirement age. . . .

Mr. MARTIN: Mr. President, today we are considering proposed legislation which may have more complex effects upon the future of the United States than we now contemplate. . . . This amendment would write into law an unwarranted discrimination against women, and would adversely affect the 19 million women in the labor force in this country.

We men often speak of the inconsistency of women, but at times we may find women who show a shining example of consistency. I refer to the action taken at their recent national convention, in Miami Beach, Fla., by the National Federation of Business and Professional Women's Clubs.

More than 3,000 delegates, representing a membership of over 170,000 business and professional women, and coming from all 48 States, the District of Columbia, Hawaii, and Alaska, voted to support uniform retirement age under the Social Security Act. This organization is also one of the strongest advocates of the equal rights amendment, Senate Joint Resolution 39, which 32 of my distinguished colleagues have joined me in cosponsoring.

The National Federation of Business and Professional Women's Clubs recognizes that one cannot speak for equal rights out of one side of his mouth, and for lowering the retirement age for women only out of the other. In their statement to the Senate Finance Committee, in opposition to the proposed provision for lower retirement age for women, the business and professional women say this:

A difference in the age of eligibility for retirement for men and women negates the principle of equality for women, both in law and in custom. Such a difference would hold women back perhaps for years, until the legislation establishing it was revoked, from obtaining either equal rights or equal pay. It would wipe out many of the gains which employed women have been able to win, through the years, in recognition of the common justice of having their abilities and their performances in their jobs or their careers judged on their merits. . . .

Why do women work? One might as well ask why men work; for the answer is basically the same. Women work, as men do, because of economic necessity. They work to support themselves; to support others (their dependents, either of an older or younger generation); to maintain homes; to maintain standards of living; to provide for their old age. These, to a large extent, are the major economic reasons which place women in jobs. . . .

We see no advantage which employed women can gain from any retirement-age difference based on sex, but only great and accumulative disadvantage. We are opposed to a difference in the retirement age for men and women.

As we are well aware, this is an election year. No doubt some of us have felt that this proposed amendment might have considerable appeal for the voters of both parties. We sometimes, however, fail to credit our constituents with the astute evaluation of the actions of this great deliberative body which they actually merit. . . .

Remember, there are more than 2 million more women voters than men. Are these women, denied their constitutional equality, likely to be fooled by a sop of lowered retirement age, which in the end would further discriminate against their employment opportunities? . . .

I submit that every known fact—economic, sociological, biological, psychological and simple justice—argues against lowering the retirement age for women. To review very briefly—a lowered retirement age for women would have an adverse effect:

Economically—because it would make employment harder to secure for older women. . . .

Sociologically—it would set back women's fight to secure equality under the law and set a precedent for other discriminatory legislation. . . . Biologically—it is a proven fact that women have a longer life expectancy than men and therefore need the financial security of longer years of productivity and employment. Psychologically—when women's years as homemakers and mothers have passed they need the additional interest of belonging in the world of business activity and of contributing as economic producers; a discrimination against women under the Social Security Act would place upon them the stigma of being second-class citizens whose skills and experience were considered of less value than those of men.

Simple justice—should we take upon ourselves the role of deciding that at a certain age one group of citizens should be treated differently than another; women are citizens and taxpayers—let us consider whether we have the right to relegate them, as a class, into earlier retirement than men, and, at that, at a reduced rate of benefit.

Mr. President, I urge that the proposed amendment to H. R. 7225 be defeated because the amendment would adversely affect the economy of the Nation and establish a precedent for discrimination against women. . . .

Mr. CURTIS: Mr. President, there are two reasons why the retirement age should not be lowered for any individuals.

In the first place, the life span is lengthening. Individuals are not only living longer, but their health is better because of the great advance made in medicine and in medical research. An individual's active and productive years have been greatly lengthened and that will be the trend in the future. To enact a law to hasten the day when individuals are labeled as retired runs contrary not only to the lengthening of the life span and the productive years, but it may invite undesirable employment trends.

In the second place, the reduction of the retirement age will add greatly to the costs of the program. The immediate cost is important, but it is far less than the long range and ultimate cost.

At the turn of the century, we only had a little over 3 million people in this country who were over 65 years of age. . . . In the year 2000, the estimate of the number of people that we will have that are over 65 will be 26.5 million.

In considering the future social security costs, we must keep in mind that the program was designed to run in perpetuity. We cannot avoid the consideration of the long-range costs. We not only will have more people over 65, but those people will be drawing benefits over a longer period of time. At the present time, the life expectancy of a man aged 65 is about 13.1 years and for women it is about 15.7.

If we lower the retirement age for any group by 3 years, we very materially add to the future costs of the program.

By and large, the benefits that are paid under OASI are paid by the young and middle-aged producers. At the present time, and for many years to come, the beneficiaries pay only a small part of their own retirement. . . .

If we consider the present OASI trust fund and the obligations that are accruing against it, we can get a picture of the very heavy burden of the future costs of social security, even though benefits are never again raised. At the end of 1955, the trust fund amounted to 21.7 billion. It is estimated that the cost of paying out the benefits to the 7.9 million beneficiaries now on the roll amounts to $48 billion. However, during the period that this trust fund would be paid out, we would have an interest accrual of almost $4 billion.

In other words, if we were to close the books on January 1, last, and apply the existing trust fund and its accruing interest to the payment of the future benefits to those beneficiaries already on the roll, we would be short $23 billion. With such an application of the trust fund, there is no money in it to pay the benefits to individuals eligible to retire but have not done so, nor any money in it to pay the individuals who might become 65 today or tomorrow or next month and, of course, there is nothing saved up in the trust fund to pay the benefits of the current workers.

Mr. President, about 5 million of our aged are not now drawing OASI benefits. The time will soon come when practically all of our aged will draw benefits. The total number of aged people during the lifetime of our children will double. These future costs will be heavy. We should not add to it by lowering the retirement age for any group.

Source: Congressional Record, Senate, July 17, 1956, S13037–S13068.

Document 4.10
President Eisenhower's Statement on Signing the 1956 Amendments, August 1, 1956

Even though the Eisenhower administration initially opposed the disability program, the president decided to sign the bill into law. In his signing statement, the president chose to focus attention on the other aspects of the bill. To the extent that he talked about the disability provisions, he made sure to place them in the context of state rehabilitation programs and to express his determination to control costs—two traditional conservative viewpoints regarding disability. Although the president claimed that changes to the bill improved the disability provisions (explaining the administration's about-face on the issue), his remarks also suggest that the administration had continuing reservations about the disability program. The vote in Congress was perhaps also an indication that this type of program expansion had become too politically popular to oppose.

*This 1968 poster promotes the
addition of disability benefits to
the cash benefits program.*
Source: SSA History Archives.

I have today signed H.R. 7225, the Social Security Amendments of 1956. The new law embraces a wide range of changes in old-age and survivors insurance, the public assistance programs, and child welfare services.

This Administration's strong support of the social security program was demonstrated by the broad expansion and improvements enacted in 1954 at my recommendation. The 1954 Amendments, which extended coverage of the program to millions of additional persons and included higher benefits for all who were then or who would become beneficiaries, have had a major impact in bringing greater security to our people.

The new law also contains certain major provisions which were recommended by the Administration. It extends social security coverage to about 600,000 additional farm owners or operators and about 225,000 self-employed lawyers, dentists, and others.

It provides for increased Federal funds to encourage better medical care for the needy aged, blind, disabled, and dependent children. This will help meet a critical problem for these groups.

Another Administration proposal placed increased emphasis, in public assistance programs, on services to help more needy people build toward independence. The law initiates new programs of grants to train more skilled social workers and to support research in ways of helping people overcome dependency. Another Administration proposal will increase funds for child welfare services.

The law also includes provisions about which the Administration had serious reservations in their initial form; these provisions were modified and improved before their final enactment and now meet, in part, some of the Administration's objections.

The original proposal to lower the retirement age for all women was changed to provide that employed women and wives may accept reduced benefits at an earlier age or obtain full benefits at age 65. I am hopeful that this provision will now have no adverse effect on employment opportunities for older women. The law allows full benefits at age 62 for widows because of their special needs.

Congress also modified somewhat the original proposal to provide disability benefits at age 50 or above. A separate trust fund was established for the disability program in an effort to minimize the effects of the special problems in this field on the other parts of the pro-gram—retirement and survivors' protection. We will, of course, endeavor to administer the disability provisions efficiently and effectively, in cooperation with the States. I also pledge increasing emphasis on efforts to help rehabilitate the disabled so that they may return to useful employment.

The original proposal would have imposed a 25 percent increase in social security taxes on everyone covered by the system. I am pleased that the tax increase has now been cut in half. Our actuaries report that while they cannot estimate costs of the disability program with certainly, the tax increase should be adequate to finance the benefits, assuming effective administration.

Although there were differences of opinion over separate provisions, the final legislation was approved overwhelmingly by Congress. In signing this legislation, I am hopeful that this new law, on the whole, will advance the economic security of the American people.

Source: Public Papers of the Presidents of the United States: Dwight D. Eisenhower, 1956 (Washington, D.C.: Government Printing Office, 1958), 638–639.

Document 4.11
House Ways and Means Committee Report on the 1958 Amendments, July 28, 1958

The amendments of 1958 once again raised benefit amounts, liberalized disability benefits and the retirement test, raised tax rates, and increased the benefit base. The bill passed the House on a vote of 374–2 (with 54 not voting) and a virtually identical bill passed the Senate by a vote of 79–0 (with 17 not voting).

This excerpt from the House committee report not only reviews the proposed changes, but also includes an extended discussion of the financing principles underlying the program, as they were understood in that period.

I. Purpose and Scope of Old-Age, Survivors, and Disability Insurance Provisions

The old-age and survivors insurance benefit structure and the contribution schedule by which the benefits are financed have not been revised by the Congress since 1954. Since that date there have been significant increases in wages and prices; also, new cost estimates have shown an increase in the actuarial deficit of the program. In the light of these developments, it is imperative that the Congress take prompt action to assure that the program be kept both effective and actuarially sound.

Twelve million now rely on monthly checks from the social-security system as the foun-dation of their economic security. For the overwhelming majority of these aged and disabled persons, widows and orphans, these benefits are the major source of their support. As prices have risen in recent years the purchasing power of social security benefits has been cut.

Your committee is equally concerned about the 75 million people who are currently con-tributing under the social-security program toward the benefits that they and their families will need when they in their turn become too old or too disabled to work or when they die. These 75 million persons, together with their dependents, represent practically all Americans not already in the retired group. The benefit protection toward which these workers are contributing has been deteriorating in relation to the wages they are now earning. For although wages have gone up, the system has not been adjusted to take this fact into account. In a dynamic economy such as ours it is necessary that the social-security system be periodically amended to keep up to date the maximum earnings base which governs how much of each worker's annual earnings is subject to contributions and counted toward his social-security protection, in order to keep benefit amounts generally in line with changing prices, wages, and levels of living.

Your committee has not been able to recommend benefits at as high a level as, in our opinion, would be justified if one considered solely the need for this protection. The increase of approximately 7 percent provided by the bill is actually somewhat short of the rise in the cost of living that has taken place since 1954. We believe, however, that it is essential that a significant part of the additional contributions to the system that we are recommending be used to strengthen the financing of the system rather than to improve benefit protection.

The latest long-range cost estimates prepared by the Chief Actuary of the Social Security Administration show that the old-age and survivors insurance part of the program (as distinct from the disability part) is further out of actuarial balance than your committee considers it prudent for the program to be. When the last major changes were made in 1956 the estimates prepared at that time showed an expected long-range actuarial deficit for old-age and survivors insurance of two-tenths of 1 percent of payroll on an intermediate cost basis. More recent estimates show that the old-age and survivors insurance part of the program is now expected to be out of balance by fifty-seven one-hundredths of 1 percent of payroll. Your committee believes that a deficit of the size indicated by present cost estimates should not be permitted to continue.

The disability insurance part of the program, on the other hand, shows a definite actuarial surplus. This is not unexpected; your committee, when it recommended the adoption of disability insurance benefits in 1956, decided that it would be best to go into the program on a conservative basis. Not only are the contributions imposed for the purpose of financing the disability side of the program fully adequate to meet outgo, so far as can be determined at this time, but there is some room for improvements in the protection afforded to disabled workers and their families. . . .

A. Strengthening the Financial Basis of the System

In addition to the need for action to reduce the insufficiency in the financing of old-age and survivors insurance over the long range, there is need for action to improve the condition of the system over the next few years. This year, for the first time in the 18 years since benefits were first paid, the income to the old-age and survivors insurance trust fund is slightly less than the expenditures from the fund. If no changes are made, outgo will continue to exceed income in each year until 1965. Your committee believes that a situation where outgo exceeds income for 7 or 8 years is one that should not be permitted to continue. We believe that public confidence in the system—so necessary if it is to provide real security for the people—may be impaired if the trust fund continues to decline.

Your committee also thinks it important that the present generation of contributors bear a greater proportion of the true cost of the benefits provided by the program than they will under the present schedule of contribution rates. The level-premium cost of the present program on an intermediate basis is estimated at about 8¼ percent of payroll—somewhat over 4 percent each if split equally between employers and employees. Under the present tax schedule the contributors will not pay taxes as high as their share of the level-premium cost until 1975. While your committee believes that the taxes required to support the program should be imposed on the economy gradually, under the present schedule the reflection of the true cost of the program in the contribution rate is being too long postponed.

All of these considerations have led the committee to recommend that a new schedule of contribution rates be put into effect immediately. . . .

B. Increase in Benefit Amounts

Your committee believes that adjustments in old-age, survivors, and disability insurance benefit amounts are necessary at this time. Since the last benefit increase was put into effect in 1954, wages have increased by about 12 percent and prices by 8 percent. The generally higher level of the economy means that a benefit increase is required now if the program is to continue to be effective and if the serious hardships beneficiaries are facing are to be relieved.

. . . [S]ince their benefits are such all important part of their income, the beneficiaries will be in real need if benefit amounts are not adjusted in the light of rising prices, wages, and levels of living.

C. Increase in the Maximum Earnings Base

Provision is made in your committee's bill for increasing from $4,200 to $4,800 the maximum on the annual amount of earnings on which workers pay social-security taxes and which count in the computation of their benefits. Your committee believes the rise in earnings levels makes such an increase appropriate. If the earnings base is not increased as wages rise, the wage-related character of the system will be weakened and eventually lost. In 1950 about 64 percent of regularly employed men would have had all their wages credited toward benefits under the $3,600 base that was adopted in that year. The $4,200 earnings base adopted in 1954 would have covered all the wages of about 56 percent of such workers. In 1957 only 43 percent had all their wages credited; about 56 percent would have received full credit under a $4,800 base. An increase to $4,800 would restore the situation which prevailed in 1954 and thus, in our opinion, would be a conservative adjustment to the rise in wages that has taken place.

D. Improvements in Disability Protection

In 1955 your committee recommended that the insurance protection of the social security programs be extended to provide monthly benefits for insured workers who are no longer able to work because of an extended total disability. This much-needed improvement in the protection provided under the national social security system was accomplished by the Social Security Amendments of 1956. The disability provisions that were decided upon at that time were purposely conservative in order to reduce to a minimum the problems that are inevitable in a new program of this kind. It was expected that, as experience under these provisions was gained, and as the soundness of the program was confirmed by this experience, necessary improvements would follow. Your committee believes that it is now time to take steps in the direction of improving the disability insurance program. In recognition of the favorable experience that has developed not only under the cash benefit provisions but also under the so-called disability freeze provisions that have been in effect since 1955, your committee is recommending a broadening of the protection now provided against the risk of extended, total disability. It is also recommending removal of certain provisions that have proved unnecessarily strict and, in some situations, have caused inequities.

All of the recommended improvements in the disability provisions of the program can be adequately financed from the contributions already earmarked for the Federal disability insurance trust fund.

(1) Benefits for Dependents of Disability Insurance Beneficiaries

Your committee believes that additional protection can and should be provided for the families of disabled workers. Present law provides monthly benefits for disabled workers who have attained age 50, but no provisions are made for the dependents of these people. This is a serious gap in the protection provided under the program and your committee believes it should be closed. Accordingly, we are recommending the provision of monthly benefits for the dependents of disability insurance beneficiaries. These benefits would parallel those now provided for the dependents of retired workers.

(2) Elimination of the Disability Benefits Offset Provision

Your committee is recommending also that the disability benefits offset provision of present law be eliminated. This provision requires that the monthly social security benefits payable to disabled workers . . . be reduced by the amount of any periodic benefit payable on account of disability under other Federal programs. . . .

Your committee believes that disability benefits payable under the national social security system should be looked upon as providing the basic protection against loss of income due to disabling illness and we have concluded that it is undesirable, and incompatible with the purposes of the program, to reduce these benefits on account of disability benefits that are payable under other programs.

(3) Retroactivity for Applications for Disability Benefits and the Disability Freeze

Your committee is also recommending two changes in the disability provisions of the program that are designed to protect the benefit rights of disabled workers. To avoid penalizing disabled workers who do not file timely applications for disability benefits, the bill includes a provision under which these benefits, like old-age insurance benefits, may be payable retroactively for as many as 12 months before the month in which the worker applies for them. . . .

(4) Modifications in the Work Requirements for Eligibility for Disability Protection

Under present law a disabled worker may fail to qualify for disability insurance benefits or a disability freeze only because he did not work in covered employment during the last year or two before his impairment developed into a total disability. A disabled worker in this unfortunate position is likely to be one who, because he has a progressive illness, is unemployed for quite a few months before his impairment meets the law's requirement of disability for all substantial gainful employment. Your committee would alleviate this problem by relaxing the present recency-of-work test. The work requirements for eligibility for disability benefits and for the disability freeze would be made identical—the worker would have to be fully insured and have about 5 years of covered work out of the last 10 years before his disability began. . . .

J. Actuarial Cost Estimates for the Old-Age, Survivors, and Disability Insurance System

(1) Financing Policy

The Congress has always carefully considered the cost aspects of the old-age, survivors, and disability insurance system when amendments to the program have been made. In connection with the 1950 amendments, the Congress was of the belief that the program should be completely self-supporting from contributions of covered individuals and employers. Accordingly, in that legislation, the provision permitting appropriations to the system from general revenues of the Treasury was repealed. This policy has been continued in subsequent amendments. Thus, the Congress has always very strongly believed that the tax schedule in the law should make the system self-supporting as nearly as can be foreseen and therefore actuarially sound.

The concept of actuarial soundness as it applies to the old-age, survivors, and disability insurance system differs considerably from this concept as applicable to private insurance although there are certain points of similarity—especially as concerns private pension plans. Thus, the concept of "unfunded accrued liability" does not by any means have the same significance for a social insurance system as it does for a plan established under private insurance principles. In a private insurance program, the insurance company or other administering institution must have sufficient funds on hand so that if operations are terminated, the plan will be in a position to pay off all the accrued liabilities. This, however, is not a necessary basis for a national compulsory social insurance system. It can reasonably be presumed that under Government auspices such a system will continue indefinitely into the future. The test of financial soundness then is not a question of sufficient funds on hand to pay off all accrued liabilities. Rather the test is whether the expected future income from tax contributions and from interest on invested assets will be sufficient to meet anticipated expenditures for benefits and administrative costs. Thus, it is quite proper to count both on receiving contributions from new entrants to the system in the future and on paying benefits to this group. These additional assets and liabilities must be considered to determine whether the system is estimated to be in actuarial balance.

Accordingly, it may be said that the old-age, survivors, and disability insurance program is actuarially sound if it is in actuarial balance by reason of the fact that future income from contributions and from interest earnings on the accumulated trust funds will over the long run support the disbursements for benefits and administrative expenses. Obviously, future experience may be expected to vary from the actuarial cost estimates made now. Nonetheless, the intent that the system be self-supporting (or actuarially sound) can be expressed in law by utilizing a contribution schedule that, according to the intermediate-cost estimate, results in the system being in balance or substantially close thereto.

The actuarial balance under the 1952 act was estimated, at the time of enactment, to be virtually the same as in the estimates made at the time the 1950 act was enacted. . . . This was the case because of the rise in earnings levels in the 3 years preceding the enactment of the 1952 act being taken into consideration in the estimates for that act and this virtually offset the increased cost due to the benefit liberalizations made. New cost estimates made 2 years after the enactment of the 1952 act indicated that the level-premium cost (i.e., the average long-range cost, based on discounting at interest, relative to payroll) of the benefit disbursements and administrative expenses were somewhat more than 0.5 percent of payroll higher than the level-premium equivalent of the scheduled taxes (including allowance for interest on the existing trust fund).

The 1954 amendments as passed by the House of Representatives contained an adjusted contribution schedule that met not only the increased cost of the benefit charges in the bill, but also reduced the aforementioned lack of actuarial balance to the point where, for all practical purposes, it was sufficiently provided for. The bill as it passed the Senate, however, contained several additional liberalized benefit provisions without any offsetting increase in contribution income. . . . The benefit costs for the 1954 amendments as finally enacted fell between those of the House and Senate-approved bills. . . .

The estimates for the 1954 act were revised in 1956 to take into account the rise in the earnings level that had occurred since 1951–52, which period had been used as the basis for the estimates made in 1954. Taking this factor into account reduced the lack of actuarial balance under the 1954 act to the point where, for all practical purposes, it was nonexistent; accordingly, the system was in approximate actuarial balance. The benefit changes made by the 1956 amendments were fully financed by the increased contribution income provided so that the actuarial balance of the system was unaffected. . . .

New cost estimates have been made for the old-age, survivors, and disability insurance program taking into account recent experience and modified assumptions as to anticipated future trends. In the past 2 years, there has been a very considerable number of retirements from among the groups newly covered by the 1954 and 1956 amendments so that benefit expenditures have run appreciably higher than had been previously estimated. Moreover, the analyzed experience for the recent years of operation indicate that retirement rates have risen or in other words, that the average retirement age has dropped significantly. This may be due in large part to the liberalizations of the retirement test made in recent years, under which aged persons are better able to effectuate a smoother transition from full employment to full retirement. These new cost estimates indicate that the program as it is under the provisions of the 1956 act is out of actuarial balance by over 0.4 percent of payroll.

Your committee believes that not only should any liberalizations in benefit provisions be fully financed by appropriate changes in the tax schedule or through other methods, but also that the actuarial status of the system should be improved in similar manner so that the actuarial insufficiency is reduced to the point where it is virtually eliminated, namely below one fourth of 1 percent of payroll, as has been the case generally in the previous legislation. . . .

Source: Social Security Amendments of 1958, House Report no. 2288, July 28, 1958 (Washington, D.C.: Government Printing Office), 1–6, 26–28.

Social Security Commissioner Robert M. Ball (center) presents new Medicare cards to the principal House and Senate sponsors of the legislation, Rep. Cecil B. King (D-Calif.), left, and Sen. Clinton P. Anderson (D-N.M.).
Source: SSA History Archives.

Document 4.12
Summary of the 1958 Amendments, August 29, 1958

This memorandum from Robert M. Ball, the acting director of the Bureau of Old-Age and Survivors Insurance, to the SSA employees describes the final provisions of the 1958 law.

Benefit Increase

Benefit amounts for all beneficiaries—those now on the rolls and those who will come on after the effective date of the legislation—are increased by about 7 percent, with an increase of at least $3 in the amount payable to a retired worker (except that women workers and wives receiving benefits before age 65 get actuarially reduced amounts). The dollar ceiling on total family benefits is increased from $200 to $254. . . .

The benefit increase provided by the amendments would bring benefits approximately into line with price changes between September 1954 (when the last benefit increase became effective) and June 1958 (when hearings began before the Committee on Ways and Means of the House of Representatives). In that interval, the Consumer Price index had risen 7.7 percent. The Committee on Ways and Means, in its report on the bill, recognized that the benefit increase did not quite offset the full rise in prices, but pointed to the need for using the additional tax income that the bill provides to strengthen the financial basis of the system, as well as to increase benefit amounts. . . .

Increase in Earnings Base

The maximum amount of annual earnings taxable and creditable toward benefits is increased from $4,200 to $4,800, beginning with 1959. This change recognizes the rise in earnings levels since the $4,200 base was established in 1954.

Unless the maximum is increased as earnings levels rise, fewer workers will receive benefits based on all of their earnings. Also, as more and more workers have earnings in excess of the maximum there tends to be a concentration of workers receiving benefits at or near the maximum and benefits tend to reflect differences in individual earnings to a lesser extent.

The $4,800 maximum restores the relationship between workers' creditable earnings and total earnings that existed in 1954, when the $4,200 earnings base was adopted. The $4,200 base would have covered all the earnings of about 56 percent of the regularly employed male workers in 1954. In 1957 only 43 percent of such workers had all their earnings credited; about 56 percent would have had all their earnings credited under a $4,800 base.

Financing

The amendments provide the following new schedule of contribution rates:

Year	Percent		
	Employers	Employees	Self-employed
1959	2½	2½	3¾
1960–62	3	3	4½
1963–65	3½	3½	5¼
1966–68	4	4	6
1969 and thereafter	4½	4½	6¾

Congress has always carefully considered the cost of the program when amending the law. In 1950 the belief that the program should be completely supported from contributions by covered individuals and employers was so strong that a provision authorizing appropriations from general revenues was removed from the law. The tax schedules under major amendments since 1950 have been designed to make the system self-supporting.

The new schedule of contributions provided in the amendments will yield income more than sufficient to pay for the additional benefits. It will decrease the estimated actuarial insufficiency of the old-age and survivors insurance trust fund from 0.57 percent of payroll to 0.25 percent of payroll. The Chief Actuary has stated that with a deficiency of this size the systems can be considered in actuarial balance, and in fact the Board of Trustees had considered the fund to be in actuarial balance when a similar imbalance was estimated under the law as amended in 1956. Under the 1958 amendments, the disability insurance trust fund will have a favorable actuarial balance of 0.01 percent of payroll.

Congress was also concerned with improving the relation between income and outgo over the next few years. The expected excess of outgo over income in 1959 will be greatly reduced, and in 1960–64 contribution and interest income will again exceed benefit payments and administrative expenses.

Dependents of Disabled Workers

The legislation provides monthly benefits for dependents of disability insurance beneficiaries like those provided for the dependents of old-age insurance beneficiaries. These dependents benefits will be payable for the first time for the month of September 1958.

In providing these new benefits, the Congress recognized that the needs of the family of a disability insurance beneficiary are as great as, or greater than, the needs of the family of an old-age insurance beneficiary. . . .

The categories of dependents eligible for the new benefits parallel those eligible for benefits as dependents of old-age insurance beneficiaries. . . .

Other Changes in Disability Provisions

1. The amendments repeal the disability benefits offset provision. . . .

2. The work requirements for both cash disability benefits and the disability freeze are modified so as to make it easier for people whose disabilities have a gradual onset to qualify. . . .

3. The amendments provide retroactive payment of disability insurance benefits for as many as 12 months before the month in which application is filed for these benefits. Applications for disability insurance benefits are thus accorded the same retroactive effect as applications for all other types of monthly benefits under the program. . . .

Retirement Test

Three changes have been made in the retirement test provision:

1. The most important change provides that excess earnings will not be allocated to months in which a beneficiary earns wages of $100 or less (rather than $80 as previously provided). Hereafter, as a result, regardless of a beneficiary's total earnings during his taxable year, he will not lose a benefit for any month in which he earns wages of $100 or less (and does not render substantial services in self-employment). . . .

Dependents' Benefits

A number of changes are made in provisions relating to dependents' benefits. . . .

1. Where a child who has been disabled since before age 18 is over age 18 when his parent dies or becomes entitled to an old-age insurance benefit, the new law provides for the payment of benefits to the child without requiring proof (required under former law) that he has been dependent upon his parent for one-half of his support. The change makes the dependency requirements for the disabled child the same as for the child under age 18. . . .

2. The amendments provide benefits for the dependent parent of a deceased worker even though a widow, dependent widower, or dependent child of the worker also survived. . . .

The bar to the payment of parents benefits has been in the law since 1939, when parents' benefits were first provided. With this bar, it was possible for the existence of a child or widow who would never receive benefits to preclude a dependent parent from receiving benefits. . . .

It is not uncommon for a worker with a family to have also assumed responsibility for the support of one or both of his parents, and there is no reason why, within the limit on payment of benefits to a family, benefits should not be paid to a parent where he was dependent on the worker for more than one-half of his support.

3. The amendments provide for the payment of a lump-sum to the widow of a deceased worker only if she was living in the same household with him or had paid his burial expenses.

Before 1957, for a widow to receive; either monthly benefits or the lump-sun, death payment based on the earnings record of her deceased husband, the law required that she have been living in the same household with the worker or receiving contributions from him or that the worker have been under a court order to contribute to her support. In 1957 Congress removed the "living-with" provision as a requirement for entitlement to monthly benefits.

Since the purpose of the lump-sum death payment is to help with the expenses incident to the death of a worker, it is appropriate to pay the lump-sum death payment to the spouse only where it can be presumed that she will take responsibility for those expenses. This presumption can most reasonably be made where the spouse was actually living in the same household with the worker.

4. The amendments remove the 3-year waiting period before an adopted child can qualify for benefits on the earnings record of a retired or disabled worker. . . .

5. The new law makes eligible for child's insurance benefits a child adopted by the widow of a worker within 2 years after the worker died (or 2 years after the date of enactment) if the child had been living in the worker's household and if the child had not been supported by anyone else. . . .

6. The new law makes a person eligible for widow's, widower's, or mother's insurance benefits if he or she is the parent of a child adopted by the deceased spouse. . . .

The provision eliminates the anomalous situation where a child can qualify for benefits but his mother who is caring for him cannot qualify for mother's benefits even though the child's stepfather, on whose earnings record the child qualified for benefits, had been married to her and had adopted the child.

7. The new law makes a wife, husband, widow, or widower eligible for benefits if in the month before marriage the person was eligible for dependents' or survivors' benefits. . . .

Under former law, a woman who was receiving widow's benefits and who married an old-age insurance beneficiary had her widow's benefits terminated and had to wait for 3 years before she could qualify for wife's benefits based on her new husband's earnings record.

Inasmuch as the former duration-of-marriage requirements were intended to prevent exploitation of the trust fund by claims for benefits from persons who married beneficiaries solely to get wife's benefits, it does not seem unreasonable to delete those requirements for persons who have already established their entitlement to dependents' benefits. . . .

8. The new law eliminates marriage as a terminating event in cases where a person entitled to widow's, widower's, mother's, parent's, or childhood disability benefits marries another person receiving any such benefits and where a childhood disability or mother beneficiary marries an old-age insurance beneficiary or a disability insurance beneficiary. . . .

9. The new law provides for the reinstatement of mother's and widow's benefits terminated by remarriage when the second husband dies within a year and benefits are not payable on his earnings. . . .

Coverage

Nonprofit Employment

1. The legislation provides for a limited period of retroactive coverage for employees of nonprofit organizations which elect coverage. . . .

2. . . . Coverage would . . . be made possible for employees of certain nonprofit organizations which under prior law could not secure the necessary concurrence of two-thirds of their employees because some of their employees were covered by a public retirement system and did not desire social security coverage. . . .

Wage Credits for Military Service with Our World War II Allies

14. The amendments broaden the provisions of prior law for gratuitous wage credits of $160 for each month of active military service for the United States to provide such credits for certain American citizens who served in the armed forces of our allies during World War II. . . .

Source: Robert M. Ball, acting director of the Bureau of Old-Age and Survivors Insurance, to the SSA administrative and technical employees, "Enactment of Social Security Amendments of 1958 and Minor Social Security Bills," August 29, 1958, SSA History Archives, *Director's Bulletins nos. 195–299,* Bookcase 8, Shelf 2.

Document 4.13
President Eisenhower's Statement on Signing the 1958 Amendments, August 28, 1958

In contrast to his remarks upon signing the 1956 amendments, this brief speech shows President Eisenhower giving full support to the new legislation—which he describes as a "significant forward step"—and to the incremental expansion of the program.

I have today approved H.R. 13549, "To increase benefits under the Federal Old Age, Survivors, and Disability Insurance System, to improve the actuarial status of the Trust Funds of such System, and otherwise improve such System; to amend the public assistance and maternal and child health and welfare provisions of the Social Security Act; and for other purposes."

This act is a significant forward step in the old-age, survivors, and disability insurance program of the social security system. The increases in benefits and in the tax base are desirable in the light of changes in the economy since these provisions were last amended in 1954. The increase in social security contribution rates and the accelerated tax schedule in the bill will further strengthen the financial condition of this system in the years immediately ahead and over the long-term future. It is, of course, essential that the old-age, survivors, and disability insurance program, which is so vital to the economic security of the American people, remain financially sound and self-supporting. . . .

Source: Public Papers of the Presidents of the United States: Dwight D. Eisenhower, 1958 (Washington, D.C.: Government Printing Office, 1959), 661–662.

Document 4.14
Secretary Flemming's Testimony before the Ways and Means Committee,
March 23, 1960

The 1960 amendments removed the age-fifty limitation for disability benefits and loosened
requirements involving the trial work period and the insured status rules governing disability
benefits. President Eisenhower signed the bill into law on September 13, 1960. Somewhat unusu-
ally, the president did not issue a signing statement or make any public remarks on the occasion.
During the House Ways and Means Committee hearings on the legislation, Arthur Flemming,
secretary of Health, Education, and Welfare, appeared before the committee to state the admin-
istration's position on the bill.

First of all this morning, I would like to discuss with your Committee some changes in the
Old Age, Survivors and Disability Insurance provisions of the Social Security Act that the
administration desires to recommend.

We recommend removing the age-50 limitation on the payment of disability insurance
benefits.

About 250,000 people—125,000 disabled workers and 125,000 dependents of these
workers—would be made immediately eligible for benefits by this provision. This would
mean additional benefits of about $200 million in 1961, increasing in the future to an aver-
age of over $600 million a year.

We also recommend changes in the disability program discussed with your Committee
last week. These are: (1) a proposal for eliminating the second six-month waiting period
for applicants with a previous period of disability; (2) a proposal for extending a six-month
trial work period to those who are not under State rehabilitation programs; (3) a proposal
for authorizing the Secretary of Health, Education, and Welfare to reverse unfavorable disability determinations by the States, provided applicants request reconsideration of such decisions. The last provision is necessary in this nationwide program in order to provide full
assurance of a reasonable degree of uniformity in the determination of rights to benefits in
the various States. It would also speed up the processing of some cases and avoid needless
and time-consuming appeals.

We recommend also that the benefit for each child of a deceased worker be increased to
three-fourths of the worker's benefit amount. . . .

About 900,000 children would get benefit increases immediately as a result of this proposal. This would mean additional benefits of about $60 million in 1961, increasing later to
an average of about $65 million a year.

Another change that we recommend at this time is to provide benefits for the survivors
of people who died fully insured before 1940.

In recent years amendments to the law have usually made eligible not only those who in
the future meet certain conditions but also those who met comparable conditions in the
past. This was not done, however, in the case of survivors of persons who died prior to 1940.

We believe it would be desirable to apply to this group left out in the 1939 amendments
the principle of retroactivity which has been generally applied in the more recent amendments. There are about 25,000 widows 75 years of age and over who would be made eligible for benefits by this proposal. This would mean additional benefits of about $10 million
in 1961 for this group.

Another proposal we recommend that would enable more people to qualify for benefits is one that would remedy the situation in present law under which a widow and her children are denied benefits because of a defect in a marriage that she entered into in good faith and believed to be valid.

We also recommend five extensions of coverage under the Old Age, Survivors, and Disability Insurance program. We propose:

1. That coverage be extended to include services (other than domestic services) performed by a parent for a son or daughter.
2. That coverage be made available to policemen and firemen under State or local retirement systems in all States.
3. That coverage be extended to self-employed physicians on the same basis as that applicable to self-employed people now covered.
4. That the protection of the program be extended to employees and self-employed people in Guam.
5. That nonprofit organizations be permitted to extend coverage to employees who want to be covered without requiring that two-thirds of the employees of the organization consent to be covered. All new employees would be covered compulsorily as under present law.

These changes which I have proposed would constitute a significant advance in the Old Age, Survivors and Disability Insurance program. . . .

Source: Social Security Amendments of 1960, SSA History Archives, Downey Books, vol. 2.

Document 4.15
Report of the House Ways and Means Committee on the 1960 Amendments, June 13, 1960
The majority report of the Ways and Means Committee adopted most of the recommendations of the Eisenhower administration, some with variations. The report contained an extended discussion of the financing of the program, which is touched upon in several sections and is challenged in a dissent written by three of the Republican members of the committee. The dissent might be viewed as somewhat unrepresentative of congressional sentiment, since the legislation had the support of the administration and it passed the House on a vote of 381–23.

[Sections I through III(d) omitted.]

E. Investment of the Trust Funds

The bill would provide for putting into effect certain recommendations made by the Advisory Council on Social Security Financing. . . .

Under present law, the interest on special obligations issued for purchase by the trust funds is related to the average coupon rates on outstanding marketable obligations of the

United States that are neither due nor callable until after the expiration of 5 years from the date of original issue. Thus the interest rate on new special obligations is related to the coupon rate that prevailed at some time in the past rather than to the market yield prevailing at the time the special obligation is issued. As a result of the formula in the law, the average interest rate on special obligations issued to the trust funds is now about 2⅝ percent, while the average yield on outstanding marketable obligations is above 4 percent.

The Advisory Council thought that the rate of return on trust fund investments in special issues should be more nearly equivalent to what the Treasury has to pay for the long-term money it borrows from other investors. This, the Council believed, would avoid both special advantages and special disadvantages to the trust funds. . . .

Your committee recognizes the need to give the-investments of the old-age, survivors, and disability insurance program more equitable treatment by relating the interest earnings of the funds to the average yield on outstanding long-term obligations. . . . Accordingly, the bill would relate the interest received on future obligations issued exclusively to the trust funds to the average market yield of all marketable obligations of the United States that are not due or callable for 4 or more years from the time at which the special obligations are issued. Current actuarial cost estimates indicate that this change would, over the long range, provide additional income to the trust funds equivalent to 0.02 percent of payroll on a level-premium basis. . . .

(2) Actuarial Balance of Program in Past Years

. . . The cost estimates made in early 1958 indicated that the program was out of actuarial balance by somewhat more than 0.4 percent of payroll.

The 1958 amendments recognized this situation and provided additional financing for the program—both to reduce the lack of actuarial balance and also to finance certain benefit liberalizations made. In fact, one of the stated purposes of the legislation was "to improve the actuarial status of the trust funds." This was accomplished by introducing an immediate increase (in 1959) in the combined employer-employee contribution rate, amounting to 0.5 percent, and by advancing the subsequently scheduled increases so that they would occur at 3-year intervals (beginning in 1960) instead of at 5-year intervals.

The revised cost estimates made in 1958 for the disability insurance program contained certain modified assumptions that recognized the emerging experience under the new program. As a result, the moderate actuarial surplus originally estimated was increased somewhat, and most of this was used in the 1958 amendments to finance certain benefit liberalizations, such as inclusion of supplementary benefits for certain dependents and modification of the insured status requirements.

At the beginning of 1960, the cost estimates for the old-age, survivors, and disability insurance system were reexamined and were modified in certain respects. The earnings assumption had previously been based on the 1956 level, and this was changed to reflect the 1959 level. Also, data first became available on the detailed operations of the disability provisions for 1956, which was the first full year of operation that did not involve picking up "backlog" cases. It was found that the number of persons who meet the insured-status conditions to be eligible for these benefits had been significantly overestimated. It was also found that the disability experience in respect to eligible women was considerably lower than had been originally estimated, although the experience for men was very close to the interme-diate estimate. Accordingly, revised assumptions were made in regard to the disability insur-ance portion of the program.

Your committee believes that it is a matter for concern if either portion of the old-age, survivors, and disability insurance system shows any significant actuarial insufficiency. Tra-ditionally, the view has been held that for the old-age and survivors insurance portion of the program, if such actuarial insufficiency has been no greater than 0.25 percent of payroll, it is at the point where it is within the limits of permissible variation. The corresponding point for the disability insurance portion of the system is about 0.05 percent of payroll (because of the relatively smaller financial magnitude of this program). Furthermore, traditionally when there has been an actuarial insufficiency exceeding the limits indicated, any subsequent liberalizations in benefit provisions were fully financed by appropriate changes in the tax schedule or through other methods, and at the same time the actuarial status of the program was improved. The changes provided in the bill are in conformity with these principles.

(3) Basic Assumptions for Cost Estimates

. . . An important measure of long-range cost is the level-premium contribution rate required to support the system into perpetuity, based on discounting at interest. It is assumed that benefit payments and taxable payrolls remain level after the year 2050. If such a level rate were adopted, relatively large accumulations in the old-age and survivors insurance trust fund would result, and in consequence there would be sizable eventual income from inter-est. Even though such a method of financing is not followed, this concept may neverthe-less be used as a convenient measure of long-range costs. This is a valuable cost concept, especially in comparing various possible alternative plans and provisions, since it takes into account the heavy deferred benefit costs.

The estimates are based on level-earnings assumptions. This, however, does not mean that covered payrolls are assumed to be the same each year; rather, they are assumed to rise steadily as the population at the working ages is estimated to increase. If in the future the earnings level should be considerably above that which now prevails, and if the benefits are adjusted upward so that the annual costs relative to payroll will remain the same as now esti-mated for the present system, then the increased dollar outgo resulting will offset the increased dollar income. This is an important reason for considering costs relative to payroll rather than in dollars.

The cost estimates have not taken into account the possibility of a rise in earnings levels, although such a rise has characterized the past history of this country. If such an assumption were used in the cost estimates, along with the unlikely assumption that the benefits, nev-ertheless, would not be changed, the cost relative to payroll would, of course, be lower. If benefits are adjusted to keep pace with rising earnings trends, the year-by-year costs as a per-centage of payroll would be unaffected. In such case, however, this would not be true as to the level-premium cost—which would be higher, since, under such circumstances, the rel-ative importance of the interest receipts of the trust funds would gradually diminish with the passage of time. If earnings do consistently rise, thorough consideration will need to be given to the financing basis of the system because then the interest receipts of the trust funds will not meet as large a proportion of the benefit costs as would be anticipated if the earnings level had not risen. . . .

(4) Results of Intermediate-Cost Estimates

. . . The Congress, in enacting the 1950 act and subsequent legislation, was of the belief that the old-age, survivors, and disability insurance program should be on a completely self-supporting basis or, in other words, actuarially sound. Therefore, a single estimate is necessary in the development of a tax schedule intended to make the system self-supporting. Any specific schedule will necessarily be somewhat different from what will actually be required to obtain exact balance between contributions and benefits. This procedure, however, does make the intention specific, even though in actual practice future changes in the tax schedule might be necessary. Likewise, exact self-support cannot be obtained from a specific set of integral or rounded fractional tax rates increasing in orderly intervals, but rather this principle of self-support should be aimed at as closely as possible. . . .

(6) Summary of Actuarial Cost Estimates

The old-age, survivors, and disability insurance system, as modified by the bill, has an estimated benefit cost that is very closely in balance with contribution income. This also was the case for the 1950 act and subsequent amendments at the time they were enacted.

The old-age and survivors insurance system as modified by the bill is about as close to actuarial balance, according to the intermediate cost estimate, as is the present law. The system as modified by the bill, and the system as it was modified by the previous amendments, has been shown to be not quite self-supporting under the intermediate cost estimate. Nevertheless, there is close to an exact balance, especially considering that a range of variation is necessarily present in the long-range actuarial cost estimates and that rounded tax rates are used in actual practice. Accordingly, the old-age and survivors insurance program, as it would be amended by this bill, is actuarially sound. The cost of the liberalized benefits is, for all practical purposes, met by the financing provided.

The separate disability insurance trust fund established under the 1956 act shows a small lack of actuarial balance because the contribution rate allocated to this fund is slightly less than the cost for the disability benefits, based on the intermediate-cost estimate. Considering the variability of cost estimates for disability benefits and certain elements of conservatism believed to be present in these estimates, this small actuarial deficit is not significant. . . .

XV. Further Separate Views of Messrs. Mason, Utt, and Alger

We are opposed to the enactment of the bill, H. R. 12580, which purports to strengthen and improve the social security program but which in fact merely makes the program broader in coverage and benefit eligibility and thereby compounds the weakness and actuarial unsoundness of the existing program. . . .

Our purpose in filing these further separate views is to state concern over the lack of actual soundness of the old-age, survivors, and disability insurance program and to call that concern to the attention of the membership of the House.

It is our belief that the Congress has a moral obligation to those who are now benefit recipients and to those who will look to the program for retirement and survivorship income in the future to safeguard against the insolvency of the Old-age and Survivors Insurance Trust Fund and the Disability Insurance Trust Fund.

There are several built-in factors in the social security program which may cause its destruction.

The actuarial soundness of the social security trust funds is based on two uncertain assumptions: (1) continued high employment and income and (2) constantly increasing population.

Even with the present high rates of employment and income and a high level of new entrants to the working force, expenditures from the OASI trust fund exceeded fund income in 1958 and 1959. For a time it was thought income would exceed expenditures in 1960; now it is a distinct likelihood that expenditures again will be higher. It is now maintained that because of the increase in the tax rate from 2½ to 3 percent which took effect on January 1, 1960, that the fund should resume building up reserves in 1961. This estimate is based on present allowances and expectations—it may not allow realistically for increased benefit amounts or increased benefit recipients.

Should we run into any period of curtailed employment which would reduce tax payments into the fund, there would be a further drain on the fund. Should there be a drop in population growth figures, again we would place the funds in further imbalance. . . .

What will happen if the program in this way destroys itself and these people, who are planning to live out their old age on anticipated benefits, find there are no balances in the trust funds to pay those benefits? . . .

The undersigned have expressed these views because of our conviction that we owe an obligation to our older citizens who plan on these retirement benefits, and to our young citizens just entering the Nation's working force, who will face ever-increasing taxes to support a program from which they may never draw benefits. In good conscience we feel an obligation to warn against the insecurity of a program based on assumptions which, to say the least, are open to question. . . .

Future generations will presumably have the same problems that beset us today of paying for the cost of Government first, and then with what is left, of providing for their necessities and the education of their children. It is of doubtful responsibility that we should now further obligate the income of future generations by an unsound program that has become political insurance instead of individual insurance. . . .

Source: Report of the Committee on Ways and Means, Social Security Amendments of 1960, House Report no. 1799, June 13, 1960 (Washington, D.C.: Government Printing Office), 6–9, 326–336.

Document 4.16
Supreme Court Ruling in *Flemming v. Nestor,* June 20, 1960

Apart from the main flow of policy development during this period, another significant event appeared, on a separate track from the legislative process. A 1960 Supreme Court ruling established the principle that the Social Security program—like any piece of federal legislation—is subject to amendment and modification by subsequent acts of Congress. The case pitted a former beneficiary (Ephram Nestor) against the administration in the person of Arthur Flemming, the secretary of health, education and welfare. The issue here is fairly simple.

The fact that workers contribute to the Social Security program's funding through a dedicated payroll tax establishes a somewhat unique connection between those tax payments and future benefits. This is often expressed in the idea that Social Security benefits are "an earned right." But like all federal laws, Congress can change the rules regarding benefits, and it has done so many times over the years. There was, however, an argument that Federal Insurance Contributions Act (FICA) payroll taxes entitle persons to a benefit in a contractual sense. Flemming v. Nestor *settled this issue.*

In this 1960 Supreme Court decision Nestor's denial of benefits was upheld even though he had contributed to the program for nineteen years and was already receiving benefits. Under a 1954 law, Social Security benefits were denied to persons deported for, among other things, having been a member of the Communist Party. Accordingly, Nestor's benefits were terminated when the Justice Department deported him for having been a communist. He appealed the termination arguing, among other claims, that promised Social Security benefits were a contract and that Congress could not renege on that contract. In its ruling, the Supreme Court rejected this argument and established the principle that entitlement to Social Security benefits is not a contractual right.

Flemming v. Nestor

Mr. Justice HARLAN delivered the opinion of the Court.

From a decision of the District Court for the District of Columbia holding 202 (n) of the Social Security Act unconstitutional, the Secretary of Health, Education, and Welfare takes this direct appeal. The challenged section . . . provides for the termination of old-age, survivor, and disability insurance benefits payable to . . . an alien individual who . . . is deported under Sec. 241 (a) of the Immigration and Nationality Act . . . on any one of certain grounds specified in 202 (n).

Appellee, an alien, immigrated to this country from Bulgaria in 1913, and became eligible for old-age benefits in November 1955. In July 1956 he was deported pursuant to . . . the Immigration and Nationality Act for having been a member of the Communist Party from 1933 to 1939. This being one of the benefit-termination deportation grounds specified in 202 (n), appellee's benefits were terminated soon thereafter, and notice of the termination was given to his wife, who had remained in this country. . . . [T]he District Court ruled for appellee, holding Sec. 202 (n) unconstitutional under the Due Process Clause of the Fifth Amendment in that it deprived appellee of an accrued property right. The Secretary prosecuted an appeal to this Court. . . .

I.

We think that the District Court erred in holding that 202 (n) deprived appellee of an "accrued property right.". . . Appellee's right to Social Security benefits cannot properly be considered to have been of that order.

The general purposes underlying the Social Security Act were expounded by Mr. Justice Cardozo in *Helvering v. Davis.* . . . The issue here, however, requires some inquiry into the statutory scheme by which those purposes are sought to be achieved. Payments under the Act are based upon the wage earner's record of earnings in employment or self-employment covered by the Act, and take the form of old-age insurance and disability insurance benefits. . . . Broadly speaking, eligibility for benefits depends on satisfying statutory conditions as to (1) employment in covered employment or self-employment (2) the requisite number

of "quarters of coverage" . . . and (3) attainment of the retirement age. . . . Of special importance in this case is the fact that eligibility for benefits, and the amount of such benefits, do
not in any true sense depend on contribution to the program through the payment of taxes,
but rather on the earnings record of the primary beneficiary.

The program is financed through a payroll tax levied on employees in covered employment, and on their employers. . . .

The Social Security system may be accurately described as a form of social insurance,
enacted pursuant to Congress' power to "spend money in aid of the 'general welfare,'"
whereby persons gainfully employed, and those who employ them, are taxed to permit the
payment of benefits to the retired and disabled, and their dependents. Plainly the expectation is that many members of the present productive work force will in turn become beneficiaries rather than supporters of the program. But each worker's benefits, though flowing
from the contributions he made to the national economy while actively employed, are not
dependent on the degree to which he was called upon to support the system by taxation. It
is apparent that the noncontractual interest of an employee covered by the Act cannot be
soundly analogized to that of the holder of an annuity, whose right to benefits is bottomed
on his contractual premium payments.

It is hardly profitable to engage in conceptualizations regarding "earned rights" and
"gratuities." The "right" to Social Security benefits is in one sense "earned," for the entire
scheme rests on the legislative judgment that those who in their productive years were functioning members of the economy may justly call upon that economy, in their later years,
for protection from "the rigors of the poor house as well as from the haunting fear that such
a lot awaits them when journey's end is near." But the practical effectuation of that judgment has of necessity called forth a highly complex and interrelated statutory structure. Integrated treatment of the manifold specific problems presented by the Social Security program
demands more than a generalization. That program was designed to function into the indefinite future, and its specific provisions rest on predictions as to expected economic conditions which must inevitably prove less than wholly accurate, and on judgments and prefer-
ences as to the proper allocation of the Nation's resources which evolving economic and
social conditions will of necessity in some degree modify.

To engraft upon the Social Security system a concept of "accrued property rights" would
deprive it of the flexibility and boldness in adjustment to ever-changing conditions which it
demands. It was doubtless out of an awareness of the need for such flexibility that Congress included in the original Act, and has since retained, a clause expressly reserving to it
"[t]he right to alter, amend, or repeal any provision" of the Act. That provision makes
express what is implicit in the institutional needs of the program. . . .

We must conclude that a person covered by the Act has not such a right in benefit payments as would make every defeasance of "accrued" interests violative of the Due Process
Clause of the Fifth Amendment.

II.

This is not to say, however, that Congress may exercise its power to modify the statutory
scheme free of all constitutional restraint. The interest of a covered employee under the Act
is of sufficient substance to fall within the protection from arbitrary governmental action

afforded by the Due Process Clause. In judging the permissibility of the cut-off provisions of 202 (n) from this standpoint, it is not within our authority to determine whether the Congressional judgment expressed in that section is sound or equitable, or whether it comports well or ill with the purposes of the Act. "Whether wisdom or unwisdom resides in the scheme of benefits set forth in Title II, it is not for us to say. The answer to such inquiries must come from Congress, not the courts. Our concern here, as often, is with power, not with wisdom.". . . Particularly when we deal with a withholding of a noncontractual benefit under a social welfare program such as this, we must recognize that the Due Process Clause can be thought to interpose a bar only if the statute manifests a patently arbitrary classification, utterly lacking in rational justification.

Such is not the case here. The fact of a beneficiary's residence abroad—in the case of a deportee, a presumably permanent residence—can be of obvious relevance to the question of eligibility. One benefit which may be thought to accrue to the economy from the Social Security system is the increased over-all national purchasing power resulting from taxation of productive elements of the economy to provide payments to the retired and disabled, who might otherwise be destitute or nearly so, and who would generally spend a comparatively large percentage of their benefit payments. This advantage would be lost as to payments made to one residing abroad. For these purposes, it is, of course, constitutionally irrelevant whether this reasoning in fact underlay the legislative decision, as it is irrelevant that the section does not extend to all to whom the postulated rationale might in logic apply. . . . Nor, apart from this, can it be deemed irrational for Congress to have concluded that the public purse should not be utilized to contribute to the support of those deported on the grounds specified in the statute. We need go no further to find support for our conclusion that this provision of the Act cannot be condemned as so lacking in rational justification as to offend due process. . . .

Reversed.

Source: U.S. Supreme Court, *Flemming v. Nestor,* 363 U.S. 603 (1960). Full text available on the Social Security Administration Web site: www.ssa.gov/history/nestor.html (accessed March 18, 2007).

Document 4.17
Finance Committee Report on the 1960 Amendments, August 19, 1960

The Senate Finance Committee—starting from the House bill—adopted much of the House package. One proposal that failed was the matter of allowing men the option of early retirement at age sixty-two. This was in the Finance Committee report (excerpted here) and was passed in the Senate. However, since the provision was not in the House bill, it had to go to conference and it was deleted upon insistence of the House conferees.

The overall bill passed the Senate on an initial vote of 91–2, and after the conference the final version of bill was accepted on a 74–11 vote, after two days of debate.

Reduction of Retirement Age for Men to 62

Under present law, male workers cannot receive retirement benefits before age 65, but female workers may do so as early as age 62 by accepting permanently reduced benefits (by

20 percent for retirement at age 62; proportionately less for later ages at retirement). Similarly, men who are (or have been) dependents of female workers—such as husbands and widowers and fathers of a deceased worker—cannot now receive benefits before age 65, but women who are (or have been) dependents of male workers can receive benefits as early as age 62 (or even before that if they have an eligible child in their care). The benefit payable to a widow or to a mother of a deceased worker is not reduced if it is claimed at ages 62 to 64, but a wife's benefit is permanently reduced by 25 percent if taken at age 62 (proportionately less for later ages at claim).

The principle underlying the reduction in women's benefits on account of early retirement is that the additional amount payable before age 65 will be exactly counterbalanced by the reduced benefits payable after attainment of age 65 (i.e., the actuarial-reduction principle). . . .

The earlier minimum retirement age for women under present law is also beneficial to women because it is this age that determines the "closing date" for determining fully insured status and average monthly wage. Thus, for example, a man born in January 1900 must have 28 quarters of coverage to be fully insured for retirement benefits, whereas a woman born in the same month need have only 22 quarters of coverage. Also, if a man has no earnings in the year he becomes age 62 and thereafter, his average wage is decreased by reason of the 3 "zero" years (at ages 62 to 64), whereas this would not be the case for a woman worker, who can base the calculation on the period before age 62 (even if she chooses to wait until age 65 and then receive the full benefit).

The Committee on Finance added an amendment which would reduce the minimum retirement age for men to 62 so that they can qualify for benefits in the same way that women can under existing law. Men workers and dependent husbands, under the amendment, could elect to receive an actuarially reduced benefit if they chose this early-retirement feature, in the same way that women workers and wives can now qualify. Similarly, dependent widowers and dependent fathers (of deceased workers) could qualify for full benefits at age 62, as widows and dependent mothers do under existing law. Full benefits (at the rate of 50 percent of the primary insurance amount, but subject to the maximum family benefit provisions) would be paid in respect to eligible children (under age 18 or permanently and totally disabled since before age 18) of a man who retires before age 65, and in such cases also to the wife regardless of her age. If both the husband and wife are aged 62 to 64 when he retires (and no eligible children are present), the wife can claim an actuarially reduced benefit based on her husband's reduced benefit. . . . Approximately 1.8 million men would be eligible to retire immediately under this amendment, which would be effective for the month of November 1960.

The committee recognizes, however, that not all men will wish to elect this early reduction since it represents a permanent reduction in the amount of the benefit they will receive for the rest of their lives, as well as a reduction in the benefits payable to their wives. We recognize as well that there is some question as to whether it is desirable policy for the Government to encourage early retirement at a time when medical science is lengthening the lifespan, but we recognize as well that many men in their early sixties are unable to find work or unable to work, even though they may not be so seriously disabled as to meet the strict conditions for disability benefits under the program. . . .

The same actuarial reduction factors are used for men as for women. This is appropriate—despite the longer life expectancy of women because what is of relevance is the relationship of the male expectation of life at age 65 to the male expectation at age 72 and the corresponding relationship for women. These two relationships are substantially the same, according to standard actuarial tables of mortality.

The bill would provide for men—just as present law does for women—equitable adjustment and correlation provisions where there is eligibility for benefits both on his own work record and as a spouse, adjustment of reduced benefits at age 65 when benefits have been withheld for 3 or more months before age 65, and more advantageous results in the determination of fully insured status and average monthly wage for benefit computation purposes. . . .

Source: Report of the Committee on Finance, Social Security Amendments of 1960, Senate Report no. 1856, August 19, 1960 (Washington, D.C.: Government Printing Office), 18–21.

Document 4.18
Summary of the 1960 Amendments, November 1960

This summary of the final provisions of the 1960 amendments was written by Social Security Commissioner William L. Mitchell. Its list of relatively minor changes illustrates quite well the incremental manner in which changes in Social Security policy have been made over the years. Big legislative changes—like the addition of disability benefits in 1956—have been relatively rare. More common are the types of changes seen in this review.

Old-Age, Survivors, and Disability Insurance

Improvements in Disability Provisions

Benefits for disabled workers under age 50.—Under the amendments, a disabled worker under age 50 and his dependents can qualify for monthly benefits, if they meet the other requirements. Previously, such benefits were payable only to disabled workers aged 50–64 and their dependents. . . .

This amendment considerably strengthens the disability protection provided under old-age, survivors, and disability insurance. An estimated 125,000 disabled workers under age 50 and at least that many dependents can qualify immediately.

The age limitation of the old law was included as part of the conservative approach of the 1956 disability benefit provisions, which took into account the difficulty of predicting costs under the new program. The need of younger workers for protection in the event of disability was not seriously questioned. In 1959, the Department of Health, Education, and Welfare concluded from its experience in operating the disability insurance provisions that it would be feasible to extend the benefits to younger workers, and subsequently it recommended to Congress the elimination of the age requirement.

Trial-work period.—The amendments broaden the provision under which persons who return to work pursuant to a State-approved vocational rehabilitation plan could continue to draw benefits for as many as 12 months even though they engaged in substantial gainful activity. Under the new law, disability beneficiaries who work under any kind of rehabilitation plan or are rehabilitating themselves may perform services in each of 12 months, as long as they do not medically recover from their disability, before their benefits are terminated as a result of such services.

After 9 months of the trial period, however, the services a person has performed during the period or performs afterward will be considered in determining if he has demonstrated an ability to engage in substantial gainful activity. If he demonstrates such ability, 3 months later his benefits will be terminated. . . .

The Department recommended the trial-work provision as a means of relieving disabled people of anxiety concerning loss of benefits while they test their possible ability to work. . . .

Modification of the waiting-period requirement.—For persons who again become disabled within 60 months of the termination of disability insurance benefits or an earlier period of disability, the amendments eliminate the requirement that the worker must be under a disability during a 6-month waiting period before qualifying for benefits.

This change had also been recommended by the Department as a means of removing a disincentive to the rehabilitation of disabled beneficiaries in doubt about their ability to work and therefore unwilling to risk termination of their disability benefits when there was the threat that they would be without benefits for 6 months after they once again became unable to work. . . .

Changes in the Retirement Test

The amendments establish a new retirement test. . . The former requirement that a month's benefit be withheld for each $80 of earnings above $1,200 is eliminated. Under the new test, if a beneficiary under age 72 earns more than $1,200 in a year, $1 in benefits will be withheld for each $2 of earnings from $1,200 to $1,500 and for each $1 of earnings above $1,500. . . .

Liberalization of the Requirements for Fully Insured Status

The amendments liberalize requirements for fully insured status. . . .

The number of additional persons—workers, dependents, and survivors—who will, as a result of the change, become eligible for monthly benefits beginning October 1960 is estimated to be about 400,000. By January 1, 1966, an estimated 1 million persons who could not qualify under the earlier provision will be eligible for monthly benefits.

Changes in Benefit Amounts

Increase in the benefits of children of deceased workers.—The amendments provide that the benefit payable to each child of a deceased worker shall be three-fourths of the worker's primary insurance amount (subject, of course, to the maximum limitation on the amount of family benefits payable on the worker's earnings record). . . . Beginning with benefits for the month of December 1960, about 400,000 children will get some increase in benefits as a result of the change. . . .

Changes in Eligibility Provisions

Benefits for survivors of certain people who died before 1951.—The amendments provide for payment of child's, widow's, mother's, and parent's insurance benefits to survivors of workers who had 6 quarters of coverage and died before 1940. Under the old law, monthly benefits were provided only for the survivors of workers who died after 1939. . . .

Benefits in certain situations when a marriage is legally invalid.—Under the amendments, benefits are now payable to a person as the wife, husband, widow, or widower of a worker if (1) the person had gone through a marriage ceremony with the worker in good faith in the belief that it was valid, (2) the marriage would have been valid had there been no impediment, and (3) the couple had been living together at the time of the worker's death or at the time an application for benefits was filed. For the purposes of this provision, an impediment is defined as an impediment resulting from a previous marriage—its dissolution or lack of dissolution—or resulting from a defect in the procedure followed in connection with the marriage.

Benefits are also payable to a child of a person who had gone through a marriage ceremony with a worker even though an impediment prevented the ceremony from resulting in a valid marriage.

Reduction in the length of time needed to acquire the status of child, wife, or husband.—The amendments simplify the duration-of-relationship requirement by making the conditions that apply when the worker has died also applicable when the worker is alive. Wives, husbands, or stepchildren can qualify for benefits payable on a retired or disabled person's earnings if the relationship had existed for 1 year, rather than 3 years as previously required.

Benefits for a child based on his father's earnings record.—Under the amendments, benefits will be payable to a child on his father's earnings record even though the child is living with and being supported by his stepfather. Under the previous law a child was not deemed dependent upon his father, and therefore was not eligible for benefits on the father's earnings record, if the child was living with and being supported by his stepfather. . . .

Benefits for a child who is born to, becomes a stepchild of, or is adopted by a disabled worker.—Because of a defect in the 1958 amendments to the Social Security Act, benefits have not been payable to a child who is born to, becomes the stepchild of, or is adopted by a worker after the worker becomes disabled. The amendments provide for benefits to be paid to a child who is born or who becomes a worker's stepchild after the worker becomes entitled to disability insurance benefits. . . .

Changes in Coverage Provisions

Family employment.—Under the old law any services performed by a parent for his child have been excluded from coverage. This exclusion is changed to provide coverage for services performed after 1960 by parents in the employ of their adult children, if the services are those that are performed by the parent for his child in the course of a trade or business. Domestic services in or about the employer's home or other work not in the course of his trade or business continue to be excluded.

State and local government employees.—A number of new amendments are designed, in general, to facilitate coverage under the Social Security Act for employees of State and local governments. . . .

Employees of foreign governments, instrumentalities of foreign governments, and international organizations.—Services performed within the United States by citizens of the United States in the employ of foreign governments or of international organizations . . . are covered on a compulsory basis under the self-employment provisions.

Guam and American Samoa.—Coverage is extended to about 8,000 employees and self-employed persons in Guam and about 2,000 in American Samoa. . . .

Employees of nonprofit organizations.—An amendment, which the Department recommended, eliminates the requirement that two-thirds of the employees of a nonprofit organization must consent to coverage before the organization can obtain coverage for concurring present employees and all future employees. . . .

Financing

Investment of the trust funds.—The amendments provide for putting into effect certain recommendations made by the Advisory Council on Social Security Financing. Under these provisions the interest on future obligations issued exclusively to the trust funds is related to the average market yield of all marketable obligations of the United States that are not due or callable for 4 or more years from the time at which the special obligations are issued. Current actuarial cost estimates indicate that this change will, over the long range, provide additional income to the trust funds equivalent to 0.02 percent of payroll on a level-premium basis. . . .

Advisory councils on social security financing.—The amendments provide that advisory councils on social security financing will be appointed in 1963, 1966, and every fifth year thereafter. . . .

The amendments also expand the function of the council to be appointed in 1963 so that, in addition to reviewing the status of the trust funds, it will review and report on the overall status of the old-age, survivors, and disability insurance program, including coverage, adequacy of benefits, and all other aspects. . . .

Source: William L. Mitchell, "Social Security Legislation in the Eighty-Sixth Congress," *Social Security Bulletin,* vol. 23, no. 11 (November 1960): 2–28.

Document 4.19
President Kennedy's Budget Proposals, February 2, 1961

In a special message to Congress, President John F. Kennedy outlined five proposals for Social Security legislation that would become the core of the 1961 amendments. President Kennedy initially proposed the changes in the context of his economic recovery package, as it was thought they would have the effect of increasing program spending in the immediate term (without much long-term impact) and thus would have a potentially stimulative effect on the economy.

His proposal to loosen the disability requirement of "indefinite duration" would fail to become law in 1961 but would do so (in a modified form) in the 1965 amendments. The main provision of the 1961 law created an early retirement option at age sixty-two for men. The legislation passed in the House by a vote of 400–14 and in the Senate by a vote of 90–0.

Improvements in the Old-Age, Survivors, and Disability Insurance Program.

The current softness of the economy underscores the inadequacy of social security benefits in relation to the needs of many present beneficiaries. The average retired worker's benefit is only $74 a month. A majority of these beneficiaries have no other significant income. The basic principle of our social insurance system is undermined when a substantial number of retired individuals must seek public assistance or else subsist below minimum standards of health and comfort. We must not permit the benefits of retired workers and their families to lag behind rises in living costs; we cannot decently exclude our older population from the general advances in standards of living enjoyed by employed workers.

I recommend that Congress enact five improvements in benefits, to become effective April 1. All are clearly justified in equity and decency. They will increase benefit payments for between four and five million people in the next twelve months. Besides meeting pressing social needs, the additional flow of purchasing power will be a desirable economic stimulus at the present time. Early enactment will serve this end.

The Old-Age, Survivors, and Disability Insurance program is financed on a sound actuarial basis, with insurance contributions adjusted to scheduled benefit payments. The benefit improvements I am proposing can be covered by additions of ¼ of 1 percent each to the employer's and employees contributions, beginning at the next scheduled increase in contributions on January 1, 1963.

The five proposals are:

(1) Raise the minimum monthly benefit for the retired worker from $33 per month to $43 per month, increasing benefits for more than 2,200,000 people in the first 12 months. . . .

(2) Improve retirement protection by paying actuarially reduced benefits to men beginning at age 62. Present law does not permit a man to become eligible for optional retirement benefits before age 65 although such benefits are available to women at age 62 on an actuarially reduced basis. Provision for paying reduced benefits to men beginning at age 62 would make benefits available to older unemployed workers at comparatively little additional program cost. . . . Provision for actuarially reduced benefits at age 62 to men as well as women will provide income for 600,000 people, some of whom would otherwise have to turn to public assistance for support.

(3) Provide Benefits for 170,000 Additional People by Liberalizing the Insured Status Requirement. . . .

(4) Increase the Aged Widow's Benefit from 75% to 85% of her Husband's Benefit Amount, raising benefits for 1,550,000 widows. . . .

(5) Broaden disability insurance protection. The social security program should provide disability insurance benefits for insured workers and their families after the workers have been totally disabled for 6 months. Under present law, disability benefits are available only if the disabled worker's condition is expected to result in death or to last for a long and indefinite period. The proposed change provides benefits in the first 12 months for 85,000 people (totally disabled workers and their dependents) many of whom otherwise have to resort to public assistance. Since it would no longer be necessary to determine that the disabled person is unlikely to recover, the change removes an important barrier to rehabilitation. It also speeds up determinations of disability. While the change has these desirable effects, it would in no sense be an innovation. Similar provisions are contained in many private insurance contracts and other disability programs. . . .

Source: Public Papers of the Presidents of the United States: John F. Kennedy, 1961 (Washington, D.C.: Government Printing Office, 1962), 47–49.

Document 4.20
Secretary Ribicoff's Hearing Testimony, March 9, 1961

During the Ways and Means Committee hearings on the Social Security Amendments of 1961, the secretary of health, education, and welfare, Abraham Ribicoff, appeared as a witness to argue the case for the administration's legislative proposals.

. . . [T]he administration recommends five improvements in the social security program. We believe these are necessary to meet pressing social needs. The changes will provide new or increased benefits for almost 5 million people in the next 12 months amounting to over a billion dollars in desperately needed purchasing power for these people. Because generally they are needy people and will spend the additional income promptly to meet their current needs, enactment of the proposals will get money into the economy quickly and, thereby, help to combat the current recession. While the proposals were selected for enactment at this time because they will contribute to overcoming the current recession, they are significant permanent improvements, adding to the flexibility and effectiveness of our social security program for the long run.

Increase in the Minimum Benefit

We propose that the present minimum monthly benefits of $33 be raised to $43. This change will provide additional income under the Social security program to an estimated 2,455,000 people during the first 12 months of operation. The total additional benefits that will be paid out during this period will be $255 million. . . .

The level-premium cost of an increase to $43 is estimated at 0.11 percent of payroll.

Reduction in the Age of Eligibility for Benefits for Men

We recommend also that the age of eligibility for benefits for men be reduced from 65 to 62, with the benefits payable to those who claim them before age 65 reduced to take account of the longer period over which benefits will be paid. . . .

Under the proposal, an estimated 600,000 people including dependents will get benefits during the first 12 months of operation. The additional benefits that will be paid out during the first 12 months are estimated at $515 million. . . .

The proposal will increase the level-premium cost of the program by 0.10 percent of payroll. The reason why the proposal increases cost is that in lowering the age of first eligibility to age 62 it would for all men reduce the insured-status requirement slightly (since the period over which insured status is measured would end at 62 instead of 65) and would also shorten the period over which the average monthly wage, on which benefits are based, must be computed. (Similar changes were made for women when the age of eligibility was reduced for them.) These collateral changes that go along with the reduction in the age of eligibility will mean that a somewhat larger number of men will be insured than otherwise would be and that benefit amounts will in most cases be slightly higher.

Change in the Insured-Status Requirement

We recommend that the requirement for insured status be changed so that a worker will be fully insured if he has 1 quarter of coverage for every 4 calendar quarters elapsing after 1950 and up to the year of death or attainment of retirement age, instead of 1 for every 3. Under the proposal, about 170,000 people who are not now insured would become eligible for benefits in the first 12 months of operation. . . . [T]he total amount that would be payable to these people in the first 12 months would be $65 million. . . .

The proposal would help many people who are uninsured, not because they worked irregularly over their lifetimes, but because the work they did in the prime of life was not covered. By the time their regular occupations were covered they were already so old that they could not work regularly enough to meet the insured status requirements in the law.

The level-premium cost of the proposal would be 0.02 percent of payroll.

Increase in Widow's Benefits

We recommend that the aged widow's benefit be increased to 85 percent of her husband's retirement benefit. Under present law an aged widow gets 75 percent of her husband's retirement benefit. As a result aged widows as a group have very much lower benefits than older people who get benefits based on their own earnings. It is estimated that some 1,465,000 people would have their benefits increased during the first 12 months of operation by the change in the widow's benefit amount; the additional benefits that would be paid out during the first 12 months would amount to about $140 million. . . .

The increase for widows is one of the most urgently needed changes in the social security program. Aged widows are among the neediest groups in our population. The average benefit for an aged widow in June 1960 was $57.20 a month. Widows not only get lower benefits than do retired workers, they also have less in other income. Almost none of them, for example, are getting private pensions. . . . The proposed change would provide desperately needed additional funds for these older women.

The level-premium cost of increasing the widow's benefits . . . is estimated at 0.22 percent of payroll.

Improvement in Disability Protection

Under existing law, disability benefits can be paid only if the worker's total disability is expected to result in death or to last for a long continued and indefinite period.

We recommend that disability insurance benefits be provided for insured workers and their families after the worker has been totally disabled for 6 months without requiring a prognosis of how long it will last. . . .

About 85,000 people—disabled workers and their families—would be paid benefits in the first year of operation of the proposed amendment. Benefit payments in the first year would amount to about $35 million.

From the standpoint of rehabilitation, also, the proposal has merit. In some cases a psychological barrier to rehabilitation results from the finding that a person's total disability is likely to result in death or continue for a long and indefinite period. It is quite understandable that some totally disabled people have their morale and attitudes, and therefore their chances of rehabilitation, impaired if they know that they have been classified as "unlikely to recover." Since under the proposed definition it would no longer be necessary to classify totally disabled people in this way, the proposal would be in harmony with the rehabilitation objectives of the disability insurance provisions. It should also simplify administration and help to make possible more rapid payment of the first benefit check in cases where a prognosis of the duration of disability is difficult to make. . . .

The level-premium cost of the proposal is estimated at 0.03 percent of payroll.

Financing the Proposed Changes

In order to finance the proposed changes we recommend that beginning in 1963 there be an increase of one-quarter of 1 percent each in the contribution rates for employees and employers and three-eighths of 1 percent in the contribution rate for the self-employed.

The increase in the level-premium cost of the program resulting from the proposals is estimated to be 0.48 percent of payroll, and the level-premium equivalent of the additional income to the trust funds is estimated to be 0.48 percent of payroll. . . .

Source: Social Security Amendments of 1961, SSA History Archives, Downey Books, Bookcase 4, Shelf 2.

Document 4.21
Wilbur Mills's Comments on the House Floor, April 20, 1961

The Ways and Means Committee adopted four of President Kennedy's five proposals and the House passed the bill by a vote of 400–14. The proposal for a change in the definition of disability was dropped. In this excerpt, Ways and Means Chairman Wilbur Mills (D-Ark.) explains the provisions the committee adopted and how they differ from the president's proposals. The House version of the bill went on to be adopted in the Senate, where a few very minor technical amendments were added.

Mr. MILLS: . . . Mr. Chairman, some weeks ago the President transmitted to the Congress a message setting forth five changes in the old-age, survivors, and disability insurance program under the Social Security Act that the administration desired the Congress to make during this session. . . .

The bill which is before the committee today is along the lines suggested by the President but is not in all respects similar to the recommendations made by the President relative to changes in the social security law. The President suggested that we increase the minimum benefit. The committee bill, the one presently before us, does increase the minimum benefit.

The President requested that we increase the percentage of the widow's benefit, that is, as a percent of the worker's benefit. The bill before us does provide for an increase in the widow's benefit.

The President suggested that we make a change with respect to the insured status provision, as one of the eligibility requirements for social security benefits. The bill contains a provision changing the insured status provision.

The President asked for a provision that men 62 years of age have the option of retiring, with a reduced benefit, without having to wait until 65 to be eligible for social security benefits. The bill before us does contain such a provision.

The President, in addition, recommended that with respect to the disability program we change the requirements for eligibility from what they are in the law today, namely, total and so-called permanent disability, to one of total disability without the requirement that it must be determined by medical science that the disability is permanent. There is nothing in the committee bill that bears on that recommendation of the President.

As compared to the President's recommendations, there are differences in degree or amount with respect to three or four recommendations that are contained in the bill. For example, under the committee bill, in the case of the minimum benefit, the committee bill raises the minimum benefit from $33 to $40, but not to the amount originally recommended by the President, which was $43. The bill does raise the percentage of the husband's primary benefit that a widow may draw to 82½ percent over 75 percent which is the provision of existing law, but not to the 85 percent recommended by the President in his message.

The bill does include the provision for the retirement of men at age 62, but the benefit to be derived at age 62 by one retiring is computed by a method which differs from that which would have been used under the recommendation that came to us from the President.

The sum of all these changes makes it possible for us to report this legislation to the House with an accompanying tax increase of not one-half of 1 percent on both employer and employee, but with a combined tax of one-quarter of 1 percent on both the employer and the employee.

Thus, the actual cost of the committee bill on the basis of a percent of payroll is approximately one-half of the cost of the program submitted to us by the President. . . .

On the whole, Mr. Chairman, there are about 4,420,000 people who will derive some new or increased benefit under this program. . . .

In the case of the minimum benefit, approximately 2,175,000 people will be benefited during the first 12 months of operation. . . . That will cost, in the first 12 months of operation, approximately $170 million.

There are about 560,000 people that we estimate will take optional retirement at age 62 if the provisions of this bill become effective. If that is the case, in the first 12 months of the operation of that provision there will be expended $440 million.

The change in the insured status requirement from 1 out of 3 . . . to 1 out of 4 elapsed quarters . . . will make 160,000 more people eligible for benefits than are presently eligible and will cost in the first 12 months of the operation of the provision around $65 million.

The increase in the benefits for widows, widowers, and parents . . . would apply to 1,525,000 people and will cost in the first 12 months of the operation of the provision around $105 million.

Altogether, therefore, there will be expended under this bill, over the provisions of existing law, from the social security trust fund during the next 12 months approximately $780 million, benefiting, as I have said, some 4,420,000 people, There would have been spent under the administration program submitted to us around $1 billion in the first 12 months, and that would have gone to approximately 4,775,000 people. The primary difference in the number is due to the deletion by the committee of the change with respect to eligibility for disability benefits under the program which was enacted several years ago. The dollar amount is largely the difference in the percentage of change voted by the committee under that recommended by the President for the minimum payment and for widows' benefits. . . .

Source: Congressional Record, House, April 20, 1961, H6088–H6089.

Document 4.22
Secretary Celebrezze's Testimony before the Ways and Means Committee, January 27, 1965

The major change introduced by the 1965 amendments was the enactment of the Medicare and Medicaid programs. On the cash benefits side, the changes involved increases in benefit levels and in the wage base, along with half a dozen small changes in the eligibility rules. In this excerpt, Anthony J. Celebrezze, secretary of health, education, and welfare, addressed the Committee on Ways and Means on H.R. 1, which was the pending Social Security legislation.

H. R. 1, introduced by the distinguished gentleman from California, Mr. King, incorporates the recommendations of the Administration for changes in the Social Security Act.

The bill would establish a program of social insurance for hospital and related care for the aged; it would provide a 7 percent increase in cash benefits and otherwise improve the benefit and coverage provisions and the financing structure of the Federal Old-Age, Survivors, and Disability Insurance system. . . .

Proposed Changes in the Old-Age, Survivors, and Disability Insurance Provisions

I would like to discuss now the principal changes that would be made by the bill in the old-age, survivors, and disability insurance provisions. . . .

7-Percent Across-the-Board Increase in Benefit Payments

The bill would provide a 7-percent increase in cash benefits to take account of increases in the cost of living. . . .

The effect of a 7-percent benefit increase on present and future social security beneficiaries can be seen by comparing the percentage of covered average monthly earnings that is replaced by benefits under present law with the percentage that would be replaced if benefits were increased by 7 percent.

At and below the $110 average monthly earnings level, retirement benefits payable at age 65 now replace approximately 59 percent of average earnings and would, under the bill, replace about 63 percent. At the $200 average monthly earnings level (the equivalent of full-time earnings at the Federal minimum wage), the replacement is now 42 percent and, under the bill, would be 45 percent. At the $400 average monthly earnings level, the maximum possible under present law, the percentage replacement is 31 percent under present law and would be 34 percent under the bill.. Since the bill would increase the contribution and benefit base from $4800 to $5600, a new maximum average monthly earnings of $466 would become possible at that level the percentage replacement would be 32 percent. . . .

Increase in the Contribution and Benefit Base

An increase in the contribution and benefit base to $5600. . . .

As the Advisory Council on Social Security stated in its recent report, the contribution and benefit base must be increased from time to time as earnings levels rise in order to maintain the wage-related character of the benefits, to restore a broad financial base for the program, and to distribute the cost of the system among low-paid and higher-paid workers in the most desirable way. A $5600 earnings base will make it possible to provide, for workers at and above average earnings levels, benefits that are more reasonably related to their actual earnings, and, by taxing a larger proportion of the Nation's growing payrolls, will improve the financial base of the program.

If benefits were raised without increasing the base, the increases in the contribution rates would have to be higher than they would have to be if the base were raised, and lower-paid workers as well as those earning at or above the maximum would have to pay these higher rates. . . .

About 90 percent of the additional income from the increase in the contribution and benefit base will go to the cash benefit program and about 10 percent of the additional income from the base increase will go to the new hospital insurance program. . . .

Source: Social Security Amendments of 1965, SSA History Archives, Downey Books, vol. 5.

*Left to right: Arthur J. Altmeyer,
Robert M. Ball (at rear),
and Wilbur J. Cohen, the three
most influential bureaucratic
Social Security policymakers
of the twentieth century, at a
White House event in 1965.*
Source: SSA History Archives.

Document 4.23
Summary of the 1965 Amendments, July 21, 1965

*When it came to the cash benefit programs in the 1965 Social Security amendments, Congress
pretty much followed the proposals introduced by Secretary Celebrezze in his March testimony.
Congressional debate focused on the health care proposals in the bill, leaving the changes in the
cash benefit provisions essentially uncontested—although both the House and Senate made slight
changes to the administration's initial proposals. At the conclusion of the House-Senate conference on the 1965 bill, H.R. 6675, the commissioner of Social Security, Robert Ball, circulated a
"commissioner's bulletin" to agency personnel summarizing the provisions of the final legislation.*

II. Old-Age, Survivors, and Disability Insurance Amendments

A. Benefits

1. Increase in Monthly Cash Benefits

The bill provides a 7-percent across-the-board benefit increase, effective retroactively
beginning with January 1965, with a minimum increase of $4 for retired workers age
65 and older. Benefits will be increased for the 20 million social security beneficiaries on the
rolls at the time of enactment and for all future beneficiaries.

The minimum monthly benefit for workers retiring at or after age 65 is $44; the maximum
. . . is $135.90. In the future, higher creditable earnings under the increase in the contribu-
tion and benefit base to $6600 a year will make possible a maximum benefit of $168. . . .

The bill also provides for the benefits of people on the rolls to be recomputed automatically each year to take account of any covered earnings that the worker might have had in
the previous year and that can increase his benefit amount. . . .

2. *Change in the Retirement Test*

The bill provides that a beneficiary may have annual earnings of $1500 and still get all of his benefits for the year; if his earnings exceed $1500, $1 in benefits will be withheld for each $2 of annual earnings up to $2700 and for each $1 of earnings thereafter. The bill also provides that a beneficiary will get benefits, regardless of the amount of his annual earnings, for any month in which he earns $125 or less in wages and does not render substantial services in self-employment. . . .

3. *Payment of child's insurance benefits to children attending school or college after attainment of age 18 and up to age 22.* . . .

4. *Changes in the Disability Program*

a. Definition of disability.—The bill eliminates the requirement that a worker's disability must be expected to be of long-continued and indefinite duration and provides that an insured worker is eligible for disability benefits if he has been under a disability which can be expected to result in death or which has lasted or can be expected to last for a continuous period of not less than 12 calendar months. . . .

5. *Benefits for widows at age 60*

Widows can elect to receive benefits at age 60; the benefits payable to those who claim them before age 62 will be actuarially reduced to take account of the longer period over which they will be paid. . . .

7. *Dependents' Benefits*

. . . The bill provides that benefits will be payable to widows (and widowers) even though they have remarried if the remarriage was after age 60 (age 62 for widowers). The amount of the remarried widow's or widower's benefit will be equal to 50 percent of the primary insurance amount of the deceased spouse rather than 82½ percent of that amount, which is payable to widows and widowers who are not married. . . .

. . . The bill authorizes payment of wife's or widow's benefits to the divorced wife of a retired, deceased, or disabled worker if she had been married to the worker for at least 20 years before the date of the divorce and if her divorced husband was making . . . a substantial contribution to her support when he became entitled to benefits, became disabled, or died. The bill also provides that a wife's benefits will not terminate when the woman and her husband are divorced if the marriage has been in effect for 20 years. . . .

D. Number of People Immediately Affected and Amount of Additional Cash Benefit Payments in First Full Year, 1966

Provision	Amount of payments in first full year, 1966	Number of people immediately affected
7-percent benefit increase ($4 minimum in primary benefits)	$1,470,000,000	20,000,000
Reduced benefits for widows at age 60	165,000,000[1]	185,000
Benefits for people aged 72 and over with limited periods in covered work	140,000,000	355,000
Improvements in benefits for children:		
Benefits for children to age 22 if in school	195,000,000	295,000
Broadened definition of "child"	10,000,000	20,000
Modifications in disability provisions:		
Change in definition	40,000,000	60,000
Liberalized requirements for benefits for the blind	5,000,000	7,000
Modification of earnings test	295,000,000	750,000[2]
Total additional benefit payments	$ 2,320,000,000	

[1] No long-range cost to the system because the benefits are actuarially reduced.
[2] Number affected in 1996; modification does not become effective until then.

E. Financing of Old-Age, Survivors, and Disability Insurance Amendments

The old-age, survivors, and disability insurance provisions of the bill are financed by (1) an increase in the earnings base from $4,800 to $6,600, effective January 1, 1966, and (2) a revised tax rate schedule.

The revised tax rate schedule provided by the bill for the old-age, survivors, and disability insurance program follows:

Year	Employer-employee rate (each)	Self-employed rate
1966	3.85%	5.8%
1967–68	3.9	5.9
1969–72	4.4	6.6
1973 and after	4.85	7.0

Source: Social Security Amendments of 1965, "SSA Commissioner's Bulletin," July 21, 1965, SSA History Archives, Downey Books, vol. 5.

CHAPTER 5

Enlarging the Program and Indexing Benefits to the Rate of Inflation, 1966–1972

This chapter covers a period of expansion that began with the 1967 Social Security amendments and reached its peak at the end of the first administration of President Richard Nixon, who signed two major pieces of legislation in 1972.

The 1967 amendments had their roots in studies done during 1966, in legislative proposals that President Lyndon Johnson suggested that year and in the favorable financing news reported in 1966.

In the summer of 1966 the actuaries announced that the Social

Robert M. Ball served as the commissioner of Social Security under Presidents Kennedy, Johnson, and Nixon. Seen here in Social Security's computer center in suburban Baltimore, Maryland, Ball was both the main administrator and a major influence on Social Security policy during this era. SSA History Archives.

Security program was somewhat overfinanced—by about three-quarters of one percent of payroll. This overfinancing occurred naturally due to wage growth in the economy and its impact on the actuarial estimates, which were based on static wage assumptions. That is, the actuarial estimates assumed no growth in average wage levels over time; thus, when such growth occurred, revenues to the system were higher than had been predicated, resulting in a surplus in the Social Security accounts. In this manner the program would from time to time during these years appear to be overfinanced as the economy grew, and this condition permitted raising benefits without raising taxes. The actuaries reported in 1966 that the program could support a general 8 percent increase in benefits.

This combination of factors led to the president making a set of formal legislative proposals and to action in the House and Senate in 1967.

During the period 1966–1972 a main form of program expansion involved increasing benefit levels, and, in 1972, the introduction of automatic annual benefit increases, known as cost-of-living adjustments (COLAs). President Nixon came to support indexation as a conservative device that could prevent larger ad hoc benefit increases by Congress. Democratic congressional leaders like Wilbur Mills resisted automatic indexation in order to preserve the power of Congress to enact popular benefit increases. In the late 1960s and early 1970s, Congress enacted such increases before adopting automatic indexation in 1972. The combined effect of large benefit increases and automatic indexation considerably raised the amount of a person's pre-retirement earnings that Social Security replaced.

Document 5.1
President Johnson's Message to Congress, January 23, 1967

Following his State of the Union address on January 10, 1967, in which he called for increases in Social Security benefits, President Lyndon Johnson followed with a detailed message to Congress on aid to the aged. In this message he outlined the changes he asked Congress to make in the Social Security program.

To the Congress of the United States:

America is a young nation. But each year a larger proportion of our population joins the ranks of the senior citizens. Today, over 19 million Americans are 65 or older—a number equal to the combined populations of 20 States. One out of every 10 citizens is in this age group—more than twice as many as a half century ago.

These figures represent a national triumph. The American born in 1900 could expect to reach his 47th birthday. The American born today has a life expectancy of 70 years. . . .

These figures also represent a national challenge. . . .

The historic Social Security Act of 1935, sponsored by that great President, Franklin D. Roosevelt, first proclaimed a Federal role in the task of creating a life of dignity for the older American. By 1951, the number of our senior citizens who had earned and received social security benefits exceeded the number on public welfare. Today, more than 15 million Americans over 65 draw social security, while only 2 million remain on the welfare rolls. . . .

When he signed the 1935 Social Security Act, President Franklin Roosevelt said, "This law . . . represents a cornerstone in a structure which is being built but is by no means complete." President Truman in 1950 and President Kennedy in 1961 proposed and the Congress passed legislation to improve the social security system. . . .

Toward an Adequate Income

Social security benefits today are grossly inadequate.

Almost 2½ million individuals receive benefits based on the minimum of $44 a month. The average monthly benefit is only $84.

Although social security benefits keep 5½ million aged persons above the poverty line, more than 5 million still live in poverty.

A great nation cannot tolerate these conditions. I propose social security legislation which will bring the greatest improvement in living standards for the elderly since the act was passed in 1935.

I recommend effective July 1, 1967:

1. *A 20-percent overall increase in social security payments.*
2. *An increase of 59 percent for the 2.5 million people now receiving minimum benefits—to $70 for an individual and $105 for a married couple.*
3. *An increase of at least 15 percent for the remaining 20.5 million beneficiaries.*
4. *An increase to $150 in the monthly minimum benefit for a retired couple with 25 years of coverage—to $100 a month for an individual.*

5. *An increase in the special benefits paid to more than 900,000 persons 72 or over, who have made little or no social security contribution—from $35 to $50 monthly for an individual; from $52.60 to $75 for a couple.*
6. *Special benefits for an additional 200,000 persons 72 or over, who have never received benefits before.*

During the first year, additional payments would total $4.1 billion, almost five times greater than the major increase enacted in 1950, almost six times greater than the increase of 1961. These proposals will take 1.4 million Americans out of poverty this year—a major step toward our goal that every elderly citizen have an adequate income and a meaningful retirement.

The time has also come to make other improvements in the act.

The present social security system leaves 70,000 severely disabled widows under age 62 without protection.

The limits on the income that retired workers can earn and still receive benefits are so low that they discourage those who are able and willing to work from seeking jobs.

Some farmworkers qualify for only minimum social security benefits. Others fail to qualify at all. As a result, many farmworkers must go on the welfare rolls in their old age.

Federal employees in the civil service and Foreign Service retirement systems are now excluded from social security coverage. Those having less than 5 years service receive no benefits if they die, become disabled, or leave Federal employment. Those who leave after longer service lose survivor and disability protection.

I propose legislation to eliminate these inequities and close these loopholes.

I recommend that

Social security benefits be extended to severely disabled widows under 62.

The earnings exemption be increased by 12 percent, from $125 to $140 a month, from $1,500 to $1,680 a year.

The amount above $1,680 a year up to which a beneficiary can retain $1 in payments for each $2 in earnings be increased from $2,700 to $2,880.

One-half million additional farmworkers be given social security coverage.

Federal service be applied as social security credit for those employees who are not eligible for civil service benefits when they retire, become disabled, or die.

Social security financing must continue on an actuarially sound basis. This will require future adjustments both in the amount of annual earnings credited toward benefits and in the contribution rate of employers and employees.

I recommend

A three-step increase in the amount of annual earnings credited toward benefits—to $7,800 in 1968; to $9,000 in 1971; and to $10,800 in 1974.

That the scheduled rate increase to 4.4 percent in 1969 be revised to 4.5 percent; and that the increase to 4.85 percent in 1973 be revised to 5 percent. . . .

Source: "Special Message to the Congress Proposing Programs for Older Americans," *Public Papers of the Presidents of the United States: Lyndon B. Johnson, 1967,* vol. 1 (Washington, D.C.: Government Printing Office, 1968), 32–34.

Document 5.2
Ways and Means Committee Report, August 7, 1967

The bill reported to the House by the Ways and Means Committee (H.R. 12080) was cospon-sored by the chairman, Rep. Wilbur Mills (D-Ark.), and the ranking member, Rep. John Byrnes (R-Wis.). It was debated for two days in mid-August 1967, under a closed rule, and passed by a vote of 415–3.

The House bill scaled backed many of the administration's proposals, accepting most of them in principle but making them less generous. For example, the committee bill proposed a 12.5 per-cent benefit increase instead of the 15 percent the president requested.

1. Increase in OASDI Benefits

Your committee believes that if the social security program is to continue to fulfill its vital role in the Nation's economy, it should be realistically reappraised by the Congress from time to time in the light of the changes which occur within the economy. Periodic review has been a basic characteristic of the program from its inception.

Your committee is recommending a 12½-percent across-the-board benefit increase for those now on the rolls.

In developing this recommendation, your committee has carefully studied the matter of wage-replacement, upon retirement, disability or death of the wage-earner and has sought to establish a reasonable relationship between former wages and benefits. Thus, the bill embodies the principle that the retirement benefit for a man age 65 and his wife should rep-resent at least 50 percent of his average wages under the social security system.

Your committee's decision with respect to the recommended benefit increase takes into account the fact that wage levels have risen by about 10 percent and the consumer price index has risen by about 7 percent since the level of benefits was last adjusted in 1965.

In considering the level of benefits under the social security program a number of facts are pertinent. Today, universal social security coverage has been nearly reached. More than 90 percent of the people who are employed are earning future social security retirement pro-tection. Ninety-two percent of the people currently reaching age 65 are eligible for cash ben-efits; 87 percent of the people aged 25–64 have protection in the event of long-term dis-ability; and 95 percent of all children under age 18 and their mothers have survivorship protection.

According to Social Security Administration studies, social security benefits are virtually the sole reliance of about half the beneficiaries and the major reliance for most beneficiar-ies. Thus, the level at which social security benefits are set determines in large measure the basic economic well-being of the majority of the Nation's older people.

The determination at any given time of the appropriate level of social security benefits is a difficult task. Your committee is constrained to take into account not only the immediate effect on the economic well-being of the aged, disabled people, widows, and orphans which will result from an increase in social security benefits, but also the immediate effect on the economic situation of workers, of employers, and of the Nation as a whole. Of equal impor-tance is the recognition which must be given to the fact that the social security program is a long-range program which taxes today's workers on current earnings, and provides for benefits in the future. Within this matrix, it is necessary to provide as nearly adequate benefits as possible for those who are now receiving them as well as to make advance provision for as nearly adequate benefits as can be foreseen for today's workers who, together with their employers, are the current payers of social security taxes. . . .

In the future, the higher creditable earnings resulting from the increase in the earnings base (to $7,600) would make possible benefits that are more reasonably related to the actual earnings of workers at the higher earnings levels. If the base were to remain unchanged, more and more workers would have earnings above the creditable amount and these workers would have benefit protection related to a smaller and smaller part of their full earnings. Such a static situation might eventually mean that the program would provide a flat benefit unrelated to total earnings because almost everyone would be earning at the maximum creditable amount. In 1968, the present $6,600 base would mean that only a little over one-half of regularly employed men would get social security credit for their full earnings; under the proposed $7,600 base, it is estimated that about two-thirds of all regularly employed men would have their full earnings counted toward benefits. . . .

Unfortunately, your committee could discover no definitive guide for determining what the level of the minimum benefits should be. At this time, a $50 minimum appears appropriate to the continuation of a wage-related system. . . .

11. Actuarial Cost Estimates for the Old-Age, Survivors, and Disability Insurance System

(a) Summary of actuarial cost estimates
The old-age, survivors, and disability insurance system, as modified by your committee's bill, has an estimated cost for benefit payments and administrative expenses that is very closely in balance with contribution income. This also was the case for the 1950 and subsequent amendments at the time they were enacted.

The old-age and survivors insurance system as modified by your committee's bill shows a favorable actuarial balance of 0.04 percent of taxable payroll under the intermediate-cost estimate. This is, of course, very close to an exact balance, especially considering that a range of variation is necessarily present in the long-range actuarial cost estimates and, further, that rounded tax rates are used in actual practice. Accordingly, the old-age, and survivors insurance program, as it would be changed by your committee's bill, is actuarially sound.

The separate disability insurance trust fund, established under the 1956 act, shows exact actuarial balance under the provisions that would be in effect after enactment of your committee's bill, because the contribution rate allocated to this fund is exactly the same as the cost of the disability benefits, based on the intermediate-cost estimate. Accordingly, the disability insurance program, as it would be modified by your committee's bill, is actuarially sound.

(b) Financing policy
(1) Contribution rate schedule for old-age, survivors, and disability insurance in bill
    The contribution schedule for old-age, survivors, and disability insurance contained in your committee's bill, as to the combined employer-employee rate, is the same as that under

present law in 1968, is lower by 0.4 percent in 1969–70, is higher by 0.4 percent in 1971–72, and is higher by 0.3 percent in 1973 and thereafter. The maximum earnings base to which these tax rates are applied is $7,600 per year for 1968 and after under your committee's bill as compared with $6,600 under present law. . . .

(2) Self-supporting nature of system

The Congress has always carefully considered the cost aspects of the old-age, survivors, and disability insurance system when amendments to the program have been made. In connection with the 1950 amendments, the Congress stated the belief that the program should be completely self-supporting from the contributions of covered individuals and employers. Accordingly, in that legislation the provision permitting appropriations to the system from general revenues of the Treasury was repealed. This policy has been continued in subsequent amendments. The Congress has very strongly believed that the tax schedule in the law should make the system self-supporting as nearly as can be foreseen and thus actuarially sound.

(3) Actuarial soundness of system

The concept of actuarial soundness as it applies to the old-age, survivors, and disability insurance system differs considerably from this concept as it applies to private insurance and private pension plans, although there are certain points of similarity with the latter. In connection with individual insurance, the insurance company or other administering institution must have sufficient funds on hand so that if operations are terminated, it will be in a position to pay off all the accrued liabilities. This, however, is not a necessary basis for a national compulsory social insurance system and, moreover, is frequently not the case for well-administered private pension plans, which may not, as of the present time, have funded all the liability for prior service benefits.

It can reasonably be presumed that, under Government auspices, such a social insurance system will continue indefinitely into the future. The test of financial soundness, then, is not a question of whether there are sufficient funds on hand to pay off all accrued liabilities. Rather, the test is whether the expected future income from tax contributions and from interest on invested assets will be sufficient to meet anticipated expenditures for benefits and administrative costs over the long-range period considered in the actuarial valuation. Thus, the concept of "unfunded accrued liability" does not by any means have the same significance for a social insurance system as it does for a plan established under private insurance principles, and it is quite proper to count both on receiving contributions from new entrants to the system in the future and on paying benefits to this group during the period considered in the valuation. These additional assets and liabilities must be considered in order to determine whether the system is in actuarial balance.

Accordingly, it may be said that the old-age, survivors, and disability insurance program is actuarially sound if it is in actuarial balance. This will be the case if the estimated future income from contributions and from interest earnings on the accumulated trust fund investments will, over the long-range period considered in the valuation, support the disbursements for benefits and administrative expenses. . . . [T]he intent that the system be self-supporting (and actuarially sound) can be expressed in law by utilizing a contribution schedule that, according to the intermediate-cost estimate, results in the system being in balance or substantially close thereto.

Your committee believes that it is a matter for concern if the old-age, survivors, and disability insurance system shows any significant actuarial insufficiency. Traditionally, the view has been held that for the old-age and survivors insurance portion of the program, if such actuarial insufficiency has been no greater than 0.25 percent of payroll, when measured over perpetuity, it is at the point where it is within the limits of permissible variation. The corresponding point for the disability insurance portion of the system is about 0.05 percent of payroll (lower because of the relatively smaller financial magnitude of this program). Based on the recommendation of the 1963–64 Advisory Council on Social Security Financing . . . the cost estimates are now being made on a 75-year basis, rather than on a perpetuity basis. On this approach, the margin of variation from exact balance should be smaller—no more than 0.10 percent of taxable payroll for the combined old-age, survivors, and disability insurance program.

Furthermore, traditionally when there has been an actuarial insufficiency exceeding the limits indicated, any subsequent liberalizations in benefit provisions were fully financed by appropriate changes in the tax schedule or through raising the earnings base, and at the same time the actuarial status of the program was improved.

The changes provided in your committee's bill are in conformity with these financing principles. . . .

Source: House Ways and Means Committee, Social Security Amendments of 1967, Report no. 544, August 7, 1967 (Washington, D.C.: Government Printing Office), 21–24, 76–79.

Document 5.3
Finance Committee Report, November 14, 1967

The Senate Finance Committee adopted without change twenty provisions of H.R. 12080 and added or modified twenty-five more. The Senate version of the bill reinstated the administration's position on most of the issues. The committee report shows that the Finance Committee was financing its more generous benefit increase by changes in the tax base and the tax rates. The committee bill also put on the table a striking proposal to allow early retirement at age sixty, but this ultimately failed to become law. The Republican members of the committee appended a set of dissenting views to the report, complaining in a general way about the potential future tax burdens implicitly imposed by the bill.

In the Senate, the bill was debated for a week, during which time nine additional amendments were added. The bill passed on November 22 by a vote of 78–6. The changes made in conference moved the bill back closer to the House version of the legislation, and the conference report was quickly adopted in the House by a final vote of 388–3. The Senate debated the conference report for two days, ultimately adopting it on a 62–14 vote. (Welfare, rather than Social Security, was the sticking point of the bill.)

The committee has carefully considered the need for increased social security benefits and has concluded that the present level of benefits is so low that a greater increase than the 12½-percent increase provided in the House-passed bill is required. In its deliberations the committee considered the fact that the cash-benefit increase as well as the hospital and health insurance benefits enacted in 1965 did much to improve the economic situation of social security beneficiaries. However, cash benefits are still insufficient for the vast number of people who must rely on social security benefits for a very significant part of their support. Therefore, the committee's bill would provide a guaranteed increase in cash benefits of 15 percent for all beneficiaries now on the social security rolls. This increase is needed not just to bring the benefits for the aged, the disabled, the widowed, and the orphaned up to date in terms of increases in the level of living since the last benefit increase, but also to provide some improvement in the adequacy of benefits. The earnings levels of all wage earners covered under the social security program have risen by about 14 percent and the Consumer Price Index has risen by about 8 percent since the level of benefits was last adjusted in 1965.

In keeping with the decision to increase benefits above the level of the House bill and to improve the income of the beneficiaries in the lower part of the benefit scale, the committee recommends that the minimum worker's benefit for retirement at or after age 65 be increased to $70, rather than to $50 as in the House bill. . . .

12. Actuarial cost estimates for the old-age, survivors, and disability insurance system

(a) Summary of actuarial cost estimates
The old-age, survivors, and disability insurance system, as modified by the committee-approved bill, has an estimated cost for benefit payments and administrative expenses that is very closely in balance with contribution income. . . .

The old-age and survivors insurance system as modified by the committee-approved bill shows an actual balance of –0.05 percent of taxable payroll under the intermediate-cost estimate. Accordingly, the old-age and survivors insurance program, as it would be changed by the committee-approved bill, is in close actuarial balance, and thus remains actuarially sound.

The separate disability insurance trust fund, established under the 1956 act, shows an actuarial balance of - 0.05 percent of taxable payroll under the provisions that would be in effect after enactment of the committee-approved bill, according to the intermediate-cost estimate. Accordingly, the disability insurance program as it would be modified by the committee bill, is in close actuarial balance. . . .

The contribution schedule for old-age, survivors, and disability insurance contained in the committee-approved bill, as to the combined employer-employee rate, is lower than under present law by 0.2 percent in 1968, and 0.4 percent in 1969–70, and higher by 0.4 percent in 1971–72, 0.3 percent in 1973–75, and 0.4 percent in 1976 and after. The maximum earnings base to which these tax rates are applied is $8,000 in 1968, $8,800 per year for 1969 through 1971, and $10,800 for 1972 and after under the committee-approved bill as compared with $8,600 under present law and $7,600 in 1968 and after under the House-approved bill. . . .

Source: Senate Finance Committee, Social Security Amendments of 1967, Report no. 744, November 14, 1967 (Washington, D.C.: Government Printing Office), 40–42, 124–127.

Document 5.4
Robert Ball's Remarks at SSA Conference of Top Staff, December 18, 1967

In this speech to SSA staff, commissioner of Social Security Robert M. Ball offers a description of the 1967 amendments to the Social Security Act, which President Johnson would sign two weeks later. This speech—in addition to providing a summary of the provisions of the 1967 amendments and their effects—is also an expression of the program philosophy and the policy goals of the program's administrators. It also reflects the antipoverty rhetoric of the era.

My friends and fellow workers throughout social security, the amendments of 1967 constitute an extremely important improvement in the social security program. They will result, for example, under the cash program, in paying $3.6 billion more in the first full year of operation—16 percent more in benefits than would have been the case in the absence of the benefit improvement. This is the largest total increase in cash benefits in a single year since the program began. The largest percentage increase occurred in 1950, when benefits were increased about 77 percent. (I have to add that it was 77 percent of a pretty low figure in those days—we were paying average benefits of about $22 a month.)

These major increases in the '67 amendments are extraordinary when we consider that they are being made just 2½ years after the sweeping amendments of 1965, which established a whole new program of Medicare and provided a 7½ percent increase in benefits.

The social security program has indeed come a very long way in these 2½ years. In June of 1965, just before the 1965 amendments, we were making payments at the annual rate of somewhat less than $17 billion a year, a very large figure, but, after the conversion in February, Social Security expenditures, including both cash payments and Medicare, will increase to an annual rate of about $30 billion—an increase of about 75 percent in 2½ years. About three-fourths of this increase is the result of legislative change and the rest, of course, is the result of the expected growth of the program. Nearly 24 million people every month—that is, more than one out of every nine Americans—will be receiving higher benefits in March.

The recent improvements, of course, will affect not only those now receiving benefits but will be of equal or greater importance to the 86 million workers who are presently contributing to the program and to the families of those 86 million contributors.

Social Security today affects just about every American family. It is an insurance program providing protection against contingencies that may occur in the future. Its value is in the protection provided, as well as in the benefits being currently paid. Now, this is a difficult point to get across, and yet one of absolutely critical importance.

Many newspapers have been writing about Social Security during this period of legislative consideration as if it were something enjoyed by those getting benefits currently, but as if it were solely a burden to current workers. In some quarters, a deliberate attempt has been made to foster conflict between the beneficiary group and the contributing group.

We have a big job to do in our interpretation of the program, in making sure that the 86 million contributors see the program improvements as additional current value to them as well as to immediate beneficiaries. Part of the problem is that the program is frequently presented as if it were largely retirement insurance. Age 65 or 62 seems a long way off to young workers. The fact is, however, that nearly 30 percent of social security contributions go to pay for benefits to survivors and benefits to the disabled and their families. These are current risks of immediate importance to workers of all ages.

The amendments of 1967 increased the face value of survivorship protection under the program by something over $200 billion. The face value of survivorship protection alone—not disability, not retirement, and not Medicare—just the survivorship protection alone, will increase from about $720 billion under the old law to a new total of $940 billion. This $940 billion is almost equal to the total amount of the face value of all private life insurance now in force in the United States. This big increase is a result not only of the overall benefit improvement but also of greatly improved protection for the survivors of women workers. This change makes it easier for the survivors of women workers to draw benefits, and about 175,000 children will become immediately eligible.

Survivorship protection has also been improved in the 1967 amendments by the addition of a whole new category of beneficiaries, disabled widows and widowers. Under the old law, widows under the age of 60 could receive cash benefits only if they had children under the age of 18 in their care. But now, disabled widows and widowers will receive benefits on a reduced basis at age 50. About 65,000 new beneficiaries will be made immediately eligible under this provision. Of course this change is part of that big increase in the value of survivorship protection.

Now, the other risk of particular importance to current contributors is the risk of total disability. No matter how young he may be, a worker can see survivorship and disability protection as something that may be needed by his family or himself tomorrow, not 30, 35, or 40 years from now. The provision for total disability was significantly improved by these amendments, particularly for the young worker. Until now, in order to be eligible for disability benefits, a worker must have worked 5 years out of the 10 years preceding the time he became disabled. Under these amendments, especially helpful for the young worker, there are special insured status requirements which range from a year and a half of coverage up to 5 years, depending upon the worker's age. . . . Young workers who have become totally disabled in the past, without having had the opportunity to work long enough in covered employment, will now be protected by this new provision. We will pick up a backlog of about 100,000 disabled workers and their dependents, who will become immediately eligible because of this provision.

One of the President's proposals that would have increased the protection to disabled people was not adopted—hospitalization for the disabled. However, Congress did authorize the establishment of an advisory council to examine the question of the extension of Medicare to the disabled. . . .

The across-the-board benefit increase was 13 percent, with an increase in the minimum from $44 to $55, as compared with the President's recommendation of a 15 percent increase and a minimum of $70. . . . [W]e got about 80 percent of what was recommended, which is a pretty good result in a legislative process.

Although most people know about the 13 percent increase, few realize that the increase in the maximum earnings base from $6,600 to $7,800 will mean considerably greater protection for current workers who earn above $6,600 or who will earn above $6,600 in the future. These are the people who are going to pay significantly more in contributions as a result of the amendments. They are also the ones who are going to get benefit protection that is significantly higher than 13 percent.

I think this is an extremely critical point for us to get across in our interpretation of the program, and again a very difficult one to get across. The fact is that workers who earn less than $6,600 a year under the new program will pay only slightly higher contributions than they are scheduled to pay under the present law. . . . For those earning over $6,600, the ultimate increase in contributions can be as high as $7.55 a month, but, since higher earnings will count in benefit computations, these workers will get significantly more in benefit protection than the 13 percent increase, the publicized figure. . . .

The earnings base is often discussed as if it were primarily an issue of finance, as if its sole purpose is to get more money for the system. This is partly true, but it's also true that only by increasing the earnings base can the program be kept up to date and continue to perform adequately for the average worker. If the base is not kept up to date, then people earning average and slightly above-average earnings will get benefits that represent a continually smaller part of what they were living on while working. A $3,000 increase in the earnings base in a 2½ year period has not been hailed as the major accomplishment in the program, but I think it's important to realize that in many respects it is the most important accomplishment.

Of course, Social Security's goal is not only to do a good job for the average or above-average worker. The program is by far the largest anti-poverty program that we've ever had in the United States. Prior to the 1967 amendments, about 5.7 million people were kept out of poverty, as defined by the Social Security Administration, by their Social Security benefits. If they didn't have those benefits they would have dropped below this minimum standard. The rest of their income was not sufficient to bring them up to it. The '67 amendments alone added nearly a million people to this group. Nearly a million more people are lifted above that level of poverty by these amendments.

So when we put these two things together—the weighted benefit formula which gives a special break to the low-income worker and the higher earnings base—the conclusion is that Social Security is a great anti-poverty program and also a universal insurance system offering protection to nearly all. It's the base upon which all workers—the poor, the near poor, the average earner, and the above-average earner—build their own security. Of course, there is more to be done before the program does as good a job throughout the whole range of earnings as we would like it to do and as it could do. But certainly the '65 and '67 amendments have brought us a long way toward our goals in the cash benefit area.

I'm sure you're aware of the fact that the liberalization in the retirement test increases the value of the protection of the program. Individuals will now be able to earn up to $1,680, instead of $1,500, without loss of any Social Security benefits in the year, and there are other comparable changes in the retirement test. More than three-quarters of a million Social Security beneficiaries will get some additional benefits as a result of this change.

The new legislation also provides that the 3 million people in the Armed Forces will get additional protection under Social Security without having to pay more for it; $100 a month additional wage credits will be given for each month of service, in recognition of the fact that the credits under the old law did not take into account anything except the cash wage for a serviceman. The additional $100 is a recognition of room and board and other prerequisites of members of the Armed Forces. It would be very difficult to assess an additional contribution based upon the $100 which no one ever sees as money. So general revenues will pay that additional credit. . . .

Source: Social Security Administration Web site: www.ssa.gov/history/67amend.html (accessed September 25, 2006).

Document 5.5
President Johnson's Statement on Signing the 1967 Amendments,
January 2, 1968

In his speech upon signing the 1967 amendments to the Social Security Act, President Johnson depicted them as one of the greatest steps forward in Social Security since the original 1935 law. Although this was perhaps a bit of hyperbole, the combination of the recently passed 1965 amendments and these amendments in 1967 represented a significant expansion of the Social Security system.

Social Security Amendments

This coming year will mark one-third of a century since social security became the law of the land.

Because of social security, tens of millions of Americans have been able to stand straighter and taller—unafraid of their future.

Social security has become so important to our lives, it is hard to remember that when it was first proposed it was bitterly attacked—much as Medicare was attacked and condemned before it came into being 2 years ago.

Today, for the second time in 30 months, I am signing into law a measure that will further strengthen and broaden the social security system. Measured in dollars of insurance benefits, the bill enacted into law today is the greatest stride forward since social security was launched in 1935.

In March, 24 million Americans will receive increased benefits of at least 13 percent. In the years to come, as the 75 million American earners now covered by social security become eligible, they will gain even greater benefits.

- For a retired couple, maximum benefits will rise from $207 to $234 and ultimately to $323 per month.
- Minimum benefits for an individual will be increased from $44 to $55 a month.
- Outside earnings can total $140 a month with no reduction in benefits.
- 65,000 disabled widows and 175,000 children will receive benefits for the first time. . . .

Combined, the Social Security Amendments of 1965 and 1967 bring an average dollar increase of 23 percent. Medicare protection amounts on the average to an additional 12 percent. This makes total increases of 35 percent in the past 30 months.

When the benefit checks go out next March, 1 million more people will be lifted above the poverty line. This means that 9 million people will have risen above the poverty line since the beginning of 1964.

Social security benefits are not limited to the poor. They go to widows, orphans, and the disabled who without them would be reduced to poverty. They relieve an awful burden from the young who would otherwise have to divert income from the education of their children to take care of their parents.

Franklin Roosevelt's vision of social insurance has stood the test of the changing times. . . .

Source: "Statement by the President upon Signing the Social Security Amendments and upon Appointing a Commission to Study the Nation's Welfare Programs," *Public Papers of the Presidents of the United States: Lyndon B. Johnson, 1968–69*, vol. 1 (Washington, D.C.: Government Printing Office, 1970), 14–15.

Document 5.6
President Nixon's Special Message to Congress on Social Security, September 25, 1969

Two significant pieces of Social Security legislation were enacted into law in 1972. The first— which became law in July—provided for an across-the-board benefit increase of 20 percent, along with a major policy shift under which there would be automatic benefit increases—COLAs— and an automatic increase in the wage base every year, beginning in 1975. The 20 percent benefit increase followed a 10 percent increase enacted in 1971. The shift to the "automatics" (as they were sometimes called) is a major feature of the modern program, and the value of benefits are greatly influenced by the various automatic provisions now in the law.

The second piece of legislation marked the conclusion of a long debate over the Family Assistance Plan, which culminated in October 1972 in the passage of a comprehensive Social Security and welfare bill. Among other things, this bill created a new welfare program, Supplemental Security Income, which became the responsibility of the Social Security Administration, alongside its responsibilities for the Social Security program.

In this 1969 speech, President Nixon attempts to convince the Democratic leadership in Congress to enact an automatic indexation system that would implicitly make ad hoc benefit increases harder to enact. To compensate for the effects of inflation since the adoption of the 1967 amendments, the president also recommends a 10 percent across-the-board increase in Social Security benefits. During the two following years, Congress would increase benefits well above the 10 percent mark while postponing the enactment of automatic indexation.

To the Congress of the United States:

This nation must not break faith with those Americans who have a right to expect that Social Security payments will protect them and their families.

The impact of an inflation now in its fourth year has undermined the value of every Social Security check and requires that we once again increase the benefits to help those among the most severely victimized by the rising cost of living.

I request that the Congress remedy the real losses to those who now receive Social Security benefits by increasing payments by 10 per cent.

Beyond that step to set right today's inequity, I propose that the Congress make certain once and for all that the retired, the disabled and the dependent never again bear the brunt of inflation. *The way to prevent future unfairness is to attach the benefit schedule to the cost of living.*

This will instill new security in Social Security. This will provide peace of mind to those concerned with their retirement years, and to their dependents.

By acting to raise benefits now to meet the rise in the cost of living, we keep faith with today's recipients. By acting to make future benefit raises automatic with rises in the cost of living, we remove questions about future years; we do much to remove this system from biennial politics; and we make fair treatment of beneficiaries a matter of certainty rather than a matter of hope. . . .

There are certain changes in the Social Security program . . . for which the need is so clear that they should be made without awaiting the findings of the Advisory Council. The purpose of this message is to recommend such changes.

I propose an across-the-board increase of 10% in Social Security benefits, effective with checks mailed in April 1970, to make up for increases in the cost of living.

I propose that future benefits in the Social Security system be automatically adjusted to account for increases in the cost of living.

I propose an increase from $1680 to $1800 in the amount beneficiaries can earn annually without reduction of their benefits, effective January 1, 1971.

I propose to eliminate the one-dollar-for-one-dollar reduction in benefits for income earned in excess of $2880 a year and replace it by a one dollar reduction in benefits for every two dollars earned, which now applies at earnings levels between $1680 and $2880, also effective January 1, 1971.

I propose to increase the contribution and benefit base from $7800 to $9000, beginning in 1972, to strengthen the system, to help keep future benefits to the individual related to the growth of his wages, and to meet part of the cost of the improved program. From then on, the base will automatically be adjusted to reflect wage increases.

I propose a series of additional reforms, to ensure more equitable treatment for widows, recipients above age 72, veterans, for persons disabled in childhood and for the dependent parents of disabled and retired workers.

I emphasize that the suggested changes are only first steps, and that further recommendations will come from our review process. . . .

The Benefit Increase

With the increase of 10%, the average family benefit for an aged couple, both receiving benefits, would rise from $170 to $188 a month. . . .

The proposed benefit increases will raise the income of more than 25 million persons who will be on the Social Security rolls in April, 1970. Total budget outlays for the first full calendar year in which the increase is effective will be approximately $3 billion.

Automatic Adjustments

Benefits will be adjusted automatically to reflect increases in the cost of living. The uncertainty of adjustment under present laws and the delay often encountered when the needs are already apparent is unnecessarily harsh to those who must depend on Social Security benefits to live.

Benefits that automatically increase with rising living costs can be funded without increasing Social Security tax rates so long as the amount of earnings subject to tax reflects the rising level of wages. Therefore, I propose that the wage base be automatically adjusted so that it corresponds to increases in earnings levels.

These automatic adjustments are interrelated and should be enacted as a package. Taken together they will depoliticize, to a certain extent, the Social Security system and give a greater stability to what has become a cornerstone of our society's social insurance system.

Reforming the System

I propose a series of reforms in present Social Security law to achieve new standards of fairness. These would provide:

1. *An increase in benefits to a widow who begins receiving her benefit at age 65 or later.* The benefit would increase the current 82½% of her husband's benefit to a full 100%. This increased benefit to widows would fulfill a pledge I made a year ago. It would provide *an average increase of $17 a month to almost three million widows.*
2. *Non-contributory earnings credits of about $100 a month for military service* from January, 1957 to December, 1967. During that period, individuals in military service were covered under Social Security but credit was not then given for "wages in kind"—room and board, etc. A law passed in 1967 corrected this for the future, but the men who served from 1957 (when coverage began for servicemen) to 1967 should not be overlooked.
3. *Benefits for the aged parents of retired and disabled workers.* Under present law, benefits are payable only to the dependent parents of a worker who has died; we would extend this to parents of workers who are disabled or who retire.
4. *Child's insurance benefits for life* if a child becomes permanently disabled before age 22. Under present law, a person must have become disabled before age 18 to qualify for these benefits. The proposal would be consistent with the payment of child's benefit to age 22 so long as the child is in school.
5. *Benefits in full paid to persons over 72,* regardless of the amount of his earnings in the year he attains that age. Under present law, he is bound by often confusing tests which may limit his exemption.
6. *A fairer means of determining benefits payable on a man's earnings record.* At present, men who retire at age 62 must compute their average earnings through three years of no earnings up to age 65, thus lowering the retirement benefit excessively. Under this proposal, only the years up to age 62 would be counted, just as is now done for women, and three higher-earning years could be substituted for low-earning years.

Changes in the Retirement Test

A feature of the present Social Security law that has drawn much criticism is the so-called "retirement test," a provision which limits the amount that a beneficiary can earn and still receive full benefits. I have been much concerned about this provision, particularly about its effects on incentives to work. The present retirement test actually penalizes Social Security beneficiaries for doing additional work or taking a job at higher pay. This is wrong.

In my view, many older people should be encouraged to work. Not only are they provided with added income, but the country retains the benefit of their skills and wisdom; they, in turn, have the feeling of usefulness and participation which employment can provide.

This is why I am recommending changes in the retirement test. Raising the amount of money a person can earn in a year without affecting his Social Security payments—from the present $1680 to $1800—is an important first step. But under the approach used in the present retirement test, people who earned more than the exempt amount of $1680, plus $1200, would continue to have $1 in Social Security benefits withheld for every $1 they received in earnings. A necessary second step is to eliminate from present law the requirement that when earnings reach $1200 above the exempt amount, Social Security benefits will be reduced by a full dollar for every dollar of added earnings until all his benefits are withheld; in effect, we impose a tax of more than 100% on these earnings.

To avoid this, I would eliminate this $1 reduction for each $1 earned and replace it with the same $1 reduction for each $2 earned above $3000. . . .

These alterations in the retirement test would result in added benefit payments of some $300 million in the first full calendar year. Approximately one million people would receive this money—some who are now receiving no benefits at all and some who now receive benefits but who would get more under this new arrangement. . . .

Contribution and Benefit Base

The contribution and benefit base—the annual earnings on which Social Security contributions are paid and that can be counted toward Social Security benefits—has been increased several times since the Social Security program began. The further increase I am recommending—from its present level of $7800 to $9000 beginning January 1, 1970—will produce approximately the same relationship between the base and general earnings levels as that of the early 1950s. This is important since the goal of Social Security is the replacement, in part, of lost earnings; if the base on which contributions and benefits are figured does not rise with earnings increases, then the benefits deteriorate. The future benefit increases that will result from the higher base I am recommending today would help to prevent such deterioration. These increases would, of course, be in addition to those which result from the 10% across-the-board increase in benefits that is intended to bring them into line with the cost of living.

Financing

. . . I also propose to decelerate the rate schedule of the old-age, survivors and disability insurance trust funds in current law. These funds taken together have a long-range surplus of income over outgo, which will meet much of the cost. The combined rate . . . already scheduled by statute, will be decreased from 1971 through 1976. Thus, in 1971 the currently scheduled rate of 5.2% to be paid by employees would become 5.1%, and in 1973 the currently scheduled rate of 5.65% would become 5.5%. The actuarial integrity of the two funds will be maintained, and the ultimate tax rates will not be changed in the rate schedules which will be proposed. . . .

In the coming months, this Administration will give careful study to ways in which we can further improve the Social Security program. The program is an established and important American institution, a foundation on which millions are able to build a more comfortable life than would otherwise be possible—after their retirement or in the event of disability or death of the family earner.

The recommendations I propose today, which I urge the Congress to adopt, will move the cause of Social Security forward on a broad front. We will bring benefit payments up to date. We will make sure that benefit payments stay up to date, automatically tied to the cost of living. We will begin making basic reforms in the system to remove inequities and bring a new standard of fairness in the treatment of all Americans in the system. And we will lay the groundwork for further study and improvement of a system that has served the country well and must serve future generations more fairly and more responsively.

Source: Public Papers of the Presidents of the United States: Richard Nixon, 1969 (Washington, D.C.: Government Printing Office, 1971), 740–745.

Document 5.7
President Nixon's Statement on Signing the Debt Ceiling Increase, March 17, 1971

In December 1969, President Nixon signed the Tax Reform Act of 1969, which included a 15 percent increase in Social Security benefits. Then, in early 1970, the House passed an omnibus Social Security bill raising benefits another 5 percent and providing for automatic COLAs, as President Nixon had been urging. However, when the bill got before the Senate, additional measures were added relating to welfare reform and even import quotas. House Ways and Means Committee Chairman Wilbur Mills, opposed to the COLA provision, declined to go to conference with the Senate, effectively killing the bill. Following this series of events, Senate Finance Committee Chairman Russell Long (D-La.) attached a rider to the 1971 debt ceiling bill, raising Social Security benefits another 10 percent and providing some of the benefit changes the president had sought. Putting aside his discontent over failing to get automatic cost-of-living adjustments, President Nixon signed the debt ceiling extension into law on March 17, 1971.

I have signed H.R. 4690, which in addition to raising the ceiling on the national debt, also increases social security benefits by 10 percent. This measure provides some of the relief which the 26 million social security recipients have urgently needed for a long time. I have felt keenly that it is intolerable that millions of these men and women, who did so much to build the Nation's productivity and to provide our youth with the abundance and the many opportunities they enjoy, are not sharing equitably in that abundance. . . . This measure will help. . . .

Unfortunately, however, the measure does not include the vital cost-of-living escalator. I have repeatedly asked the Congress to provide for automatic increases in social security benefits as the cost of living increased. Only if such a provision is included can we overcome the rigidity of the social security benefit system, and the long delay that ensues before senior citizens receive the real benefits of a system that most have supported by their contributions throughout their adult lives.

The measure has other serious deficiencies in it. In this bill the Congress has departed from the cardinal principle which should govern the social security system: The Congress

President Richard Nixon was an advocate of automatic cost-of-living adjustments (COLAs)—a major innovation in Social Security program policies. Here he relaxes at the "western White House" in San Clemente, California, in July 1972. During this vacation Nixon signed the law establishing procedures for yearly automatic COLAs.
Source: National Archives.

has not provided for sufficient revenues in the current year to cover fully the added costs of the new benefits. It has deferred the effective date of increased contributions required to pay for these new and much deserved benefits. . . .

If these urgently needed social security increases are enacted but the means to pay for them currently are defaulted, we are faced with the very real prospect of increased inflation. For that reason, I urge the Congress to act promptly on a social security revenue measure so that the current cost of these increased benefits will be financed. . . .

Increasing social security benefits is essential, as I have said many times. Increasing social security benefits in a way that carries with it the seeds of a resumption of the inflation it has taken us more than 2 years to control would benefit no one. We owe to the elderly people in this country something more than a social security increase which is only an illusion. . . .

Source: Public Papers of the Presidents of the United States: Richard Nixon, 1971 (Washington, D.C.: Government Printing Office, 1972), 438–439.

Document 5.8
The Church Amendment, June 29, 1972

While the debate over the administration's welfare reform proposals continued, with particular opposition from the Senate Finance Committee, the federal government came up against the existing statutory debt limit and needed to enact another increase in that limit, just as it had done the previous year. In June 1972 the debt limit extension came before the Senate. Frank Church (D-Idaho) used the same maneuver as Russell Long had the year before to attach a rider to the bill proposing a 20 percent increase in benefits and to add automatic annual COLAs and automatic annual increases to the Social Security program. The bill passed the Senate on a vote of 78–3 and was easily accepted by the House in conference. The president signed it into law in July 1972.

Thus, a two-year, 30 percent increase in benefits, and the addition of automatic COLAs, became law as riders on debt limit extension bills. These two bills—along with the Tax Reform

Act of 1969—increased Social Security benefits 45 percent in three years and put benefits on automatic annual increases after that point (starting in 1975).

This excerpt from the Congressional Record *documents Senator Church's successful effort to add the COLAs and the automatic increase in the wage base to the Social Security program.*

The Church proposal was not universally supported, as can be seen in the comments from Sen. Carl Curtis (R-Neb.), but it easily passed in the Senate. Curtis was skeptical that these generous provisions (a 20 percent benefit increase and automatic COLAs) could be added to the program without raising taxes. Church was arguing that there would be no need for an increase in payroll tax rates if Congress embraced pay-as-you-go financing along with automatic annual increases in the wage base. To an extent, they were talking past each other, as the increase in the wage base would result in higher taxes for high-income workers even though rates might remain unchanged or even be lowered.

Mr. CHURCH: . . . a few days ago I announced my intention to amend the debt ceiling bill by adding a 20-percent across-the-board increase in social security benefits.

Today, I would like to confirm that intention and to offer additional arguments for my amendment.

That amendment, I should add, will include a mechanism for automatic cost-of-living adjustments which will keep social security inflation-proof, now and in the future.

This two-pronged approach, it seems to me, can and should be adopted by the Congress in the few remaining days before we recess for the Democratic National Convention.

How else, during a session which will later be interrupted by the Republican Convention and all the subsequent activities related to a presidential campaign, can our elderly be sure of receiving a desperately needed increase in retirement income?

How else are we to avoid the trap into which we have fallen in the past—the trap which opens up and closes shut when social security reforms are tied to welfare measures?

Such a prospect is before us again. H.R. 1—the welfare reform bill—is a cumbersome, controversial legislative package. And entrapped in this massive and complex bill is an urgently needed social security increase. . . .

In addition to providing an immediate increase in benefits, my amendment also would provide a mechanism for keeping benefits up to date with increases in prices.

Our elderly citizens are the least able to suffer losses in the purchasing power of their limited incomes. Social security benefits are the only regular income for half of our retired workers. Benefit increases have too often lagged behind increases in the cost of living. We have an obligation to guarantee, in the law, that social security benefits will not deteriorate because of inflation.

Equally important, all this can be achieved without impairing the actuarial soundness of the social security trust funds and without any increase in the contribution rates for the cash benefits part of the social security program for several decades. In fact, the cash benefit improvements in my amendment can be financed until well into the next century with contribution rates that are lower than the rates under present law. . . .

. . . [T]he contribution rates are based on the assumptions that benefits will rise in the future to take account of increases in prices—as my amendment would provide—and that the maximum amount of earnings counted for social security purposes will increase as earnings levels rise—also as my amendment would provide. The Advisory Council recommended the adoption of contribution rates based on rising benefits and earnings assumptions in lieu of the past practice of basing rates on the assumption that earnings levels would not rise. . . .

After 1974, the maximum amount of a worker's annual earnings that can be counted for social security benefit and contribution purposes would be adjusted to reflect future increases in average earnings in employment covered under social security. . . .

Further, this provision is of considerable significance in the financing of the automatic benefit increases provided under my amendment. With the realistic assumption that earnings levels will rise and will rise significantly faster than price levels, as has been the case over the last several decades, the additional financing needed to meet the cost of the automatic benefit increases will come from the contributions paid by workers at increasing earnings levels. About two-thirds of the cost of each successive automatic benefit increase under the provisions of this amendment would be financed by the additional contribution income generated directly by rising earnings levels. The remaining one-third of the cost of each successive benefit increase would be financed by the additional income to the system that would result from the application of the scheduled contribution rate to those with earnings in the upper brackets. Thus, all workers will share in the cost of the automatic adjustment in social security benefits, and the automatic adjustment in the base merely assures that workers at upper earnings levels will share proportionately in this cost with workers at lower earnings levels. . . .

Let me just say, Mr. President, that I am not here attempting to play the role of Merlin the Magician. I am not saying we are not going to spend more money when we increase social security benefits by 20 percent. . . .

What I am saying is that, based upon actuarial assumptions—assumptions approved by the Finance Committee, the 1971 Social Security Advisory Council, and the Nixon administration, the actual tax rate can be decreased for the great majority—three-quarters of the workers—under the program—and a 20 percent benefit increase authorized by not providing funds in excess of the needs of the program. . . .

Under present law those reserves would build up, between calendar year 1972 and calendar year 1977, to about $120 billion. It is not true that the social security system needs reserves that even begin to amount to such a fantastic sum. . . .

. . . [U]nder this amendment, in 1973 the total tax rate would be 5.5 percent, compared to 5.65 percent under present law. This is not the result of any act of magic; it is simply the result of a prudent decision . . . that it is unnecessary to base these rates on old assumptions of how to build up a tremendous reserve. We can operate social security soundly on a pay-as-you-go basis and maintain a reasonable reserve for contingencies. This is all that this kind of program requires. . . .

Mr. CURTIS: . . . [T]he projection as to what the reserves will be in 1977 is purely speculative. The Congress is going to meet every year between now and then, and we will have several elections in the meantime, and there will be no such accumulation.

The trend of the reserves has been to go down in relation to the outgo. There was a time, not many years ago, when we had about a 3-year reserve. We are now down to a year's reserve. Under this proposal it will go to a 9-month reserve.

Again I repeat that the statement that the taxes are going to go down is inaccurate. What is going to go down is somebody's speculation about what is going to happen in the future, without regard to the grim fact that Congress has never let those reserves accumulate in that way. But the fact remains that everyone is going to have a tax increase, in every bracket, and there will be no person who will pay lesser social security taxes than he pays now. . . .

Mr. CHURCH: . . . I shall place in the *Record* tables that fully substantiate everything I have said with respect to the tax rates in the coming years under this amendment as compared with tax rates in the coming years under present law. They will show that this amendment not only finances itself, but finances itself in the coming years at a rate which is less than the rate that would otherwise obtain under present law, and at the same time accomplishes a 20-percent increase in benefits. . . .

If in the future the Congress adds the benefits, then I think they would not be self-financing; we would have to add more financing. We will face that when we get to it. But for the purpose of pointing up this amendment, it not only finances an increased benefit of 20 percent, but in future years it means a lesser rate of taxes and automatic cost-of-living benefit increases. . . .

Source: Congressional Record, Senate, June 29, 1972, S10781–S10784.

Document 5.9
President Nixon's Statement on Extending the Temporary Ceiling on National Debt and Increasing Social Security Benefits, July 1, 1972

In early July 1972, President Nixon finally signed legislation creating an automatic indexation system for Social Security. This legislation also included a 20 percent benefit increase, which had been financed by reducing the surplus in the trust fund reserve rather than by additional taxes or benefit cuts. This meant that the overall federal budget would thereby suffer an increase in its deficit, which caused problems for the administration's "full employment budget" initiatives. So, while President Nixon signed the bill, he expressed some key complaints about its Social Security provisions.

I have today signed H.R. 15390, which extends the temporary ceiling on the national debt, and which, among other measures, provides for an across-the-board increase of 20 percent in social security benefits.

One important feature of this legislation which I greet with special favor is the automatic increase provision which will allow social security benefits to keep pace with the cost of living. This provision is one which I have long urged, and I am pleased that the Congress has at last fulfilled a request which I have been making since the first months of my Administration. This action constitutes a major break-through for older Americans, for it says at last that inflation-proof social security benefits are theirs as a matter of right, and not as something which must be temporarily won over and over again from each succeeding Congress. . . .

As I have indicated on other occasions, however, H.R. 15390 includes some serious shortcomings.

It fails the test of fiscal responsibility by failing fully to finance its increase in social security benefits. As a result of this failure, it would add an additional $3.7 billion to the more than $3 billion by which earlier actions and inactions by the Congress have already thrown the full employment budget for fiscal year 1973 into deficit—thus threatening dangerously to escalate the rate of inflation at a time when this Administration's economic policies are succeeding in turning it back.

I am determined that we shall win the battle against inflation—and that fiscally irresponsible policies shall not again penalize all Americans, and especially the older citizens whom these benefit increases are designed to help, by taking away in higher prices what they have gained in higher wages and higher benefits.

Therefore, it will be necessary for the Congress and the Administration to offset the additional $3.7 billion deficit created by this measure through cuts in other Federal programs.

An additional fault with H.R. 15390 is that it jeopardizes the integrity of the Social Security Trust Fund by substantially reducing the necessary coverage of trust fund reserves to ensure annual benefit payments. I shall request the next Congress to restore this full 100-percent protection. . . .

Beyond the shortcomings I have noted in this measure, it should be noted that the added benefits will not come without cost. Even though it is not fully funded, the measure still imposes considerable additional tax burdens on all wage earners. However, the overriding and finally determining factor in my decision to give my approval to this act is my deep concern for the well-being of our older Americans. They both need and deserve a significant increase in social security benefits.

With the signing of H.R. 15390, social security benefits since this Administration took office will have increased by a compound total of 51 percent. It is now our responsibility to see that these needed increases in income for our senior citizens are not eaten up by increases in the cost of living. The Congress has a solemn responsibility to join me in fighting inflation, adopting an unbreakable rule—that there shall be no future increases in spending above my budget without providing for tax increases to pay for such spending increases. Our older Americans deserve full and fair consideration at the hands of their Government, and I have made every effort to see that they receive it. It is in consideration of their just requirements, and in spite of the fiscal irresponsibility that the Congress has demonstrated in its deficit funding of this legislation, that I have signed H.R. 15390.

Source: Public Papers of the Presidents of the United States: Richard Nixon, 1972 (Washington, D.C.: Government Printing Office, 1974), 723–724.

Document 5.10
Robert Ball on the Legislative History of the 1972 Amendments, March 1973

This document offers a brief summary by Robert M. Ball, the commissioner of Social Security, of the various changes introduced in the two sets of amendments enacted in 1972.

President Nixon's signature on H.R. 1, the Social Security Amendments of 1972, brought to a close 3 years of consideration of and deliberations on proposals to improve the social security program. What the President called "landmark legislation" became Public Law 92–603 on October 30, 1972. Among its most significant and far-reaching provisions are:

- Higher benefits for most people eligible for benefits as aged widows and widowers;
- For men reaching age 62 in the future, repeal of the provisions under which a man the same age and with the same earnings as a woman generally got a lower benefit than the woman worker and under which men needed more social security credits to qualify for retirement benefits than women did (the change will be accomplished over a 3-year period beginning with 1973);
- Changes in the retirement test to assure that the more a beneficiary works and earns, the more spendable income (social security benefits plus earnings after taxes) he will have, and to raise from $1,680 to $2,100 the annual exempt amount of earnings with future automatic adjustment to keep pace with increases in earnings levels;
- A special minimum benefit for those who have worked in covered employment for many years, but at low earnings;
- Higher benefits for workers who do not get social security retirement benefits before age 65 but continue to work past that age;
- Improvements in disability insurance protection (including a reduction in the waiting period for benefits and extension of childhood disability benefits to persons disabled between ages 18 and 22) as well as improved protection for a worker's dependents and survivors;
- Extension of Medicare protection to disability insurance beneficiaries who have been on the social security disability benefit rolls for at least 2 years. . . .

Other major social security legislation was enacted in July 1972. Those amendments (1) provided a 20-percent across-the-board increase in social security benefits effective for September 1972; (2) included provisions for keeping social security benefit amounts up to date automatically in the future as the cost of living rises; and (3) increased from $9,000 in 1972 to $10,800 in 1973 and to $12,000 in 1974 the maximum amount of a worker's annual earnings that may be counted in figuring his and his family's social security benefits (and on which he pays social security contributions) and provided in addition for keeping the amount up to date automatically in the future as average wages rise. . . .

Source: Robert M. Ball, "Social Security Amendments of 1972: Summary and Legislative History," *Social Security Bulletin,* vol. 36, no. 3, March 1973 (Washington, D.C.: Government Printing Office): 3.

Document 5.11
Oral History Interview with Robert Ball, May 1, 2001

SSA commissioner Robert Ball was both an eyewitness and a key participant in the decisions made around the issue of the having automatic COLAs as a specific provision of the law. This excerpt is from an interview conducted by Larry DeWitt in May 2001, in which Commissioner Ball recounts the development of the COLA provision, including some interesting behind-the-scenes reports on how this key provision of the Social Security program became law.

BALL: . . . The history of the automatics has some depth to it. It didn't just happen in 1972. Among the first people who were actually for the automatic provision was Mel Laird, a Wisconsin Congressman, later Secretary of Defense. He was the Ranking Republican on the Appropriation Subcommittee that dealt with Social Security. Dan Flood was the Chair, and Mel Laird was the Ranking Republican. They worked very well together. Mel was very supportive of Social Security. We got to the point where he considered himself a good friend of mine. When he left the Defense Department, as he was leaving, he was going to tour the military posts all across the country to say, "Goodbye," to the troops and the officers. He wanted me to go with him. He called me up and asked me to fly around with him. (*Laughs.*) That was just not something I was likely to do. At that time, he was in extremely bad repute with Democrats, particularly liberals.

INTERVIEWER: Over Vietnam?

BALL: Over Vietnam, and I wasn't about to fly around with the Secretary of Defense. But, that's just an illustration of how much he had come to regard me as a friend, out of the role that he had back as a Congressman, when he was the Ranking Republican on the Appropriations Sub-Committee.

So, I don't know where it actually came from, but he was the first person I knew to actually introduce a bill on this. Of course the Appropriations Committee doesn't have substantive jurisdiction. This was just something he wanted to be associated with, because he was interested in Social Security and he thought it was a good idea. He used it in his campaigns—that sort of thing.

But the first time that it was supported in the substantive committee, Ways and Means, was by John Byrnes, who also was from Wisconsin, and he was the Ranking Republican on the Ways and Means Committee—where his views would make a lot of difference. I think this idea, to an extent, came from Bob Myers. Bob originally was very intrigued with the concept of automatics, and still is. In fact, he would like to make almost everything automatic. Maybe it makes it easier to make estimates if you know everything is going to keep up with everything else. So I think probably, he was a source of Byrnes' interest in this.

It became quite an important public issue before 1972, in terms of pushing the idea.

Now, the line up, pros and cons, was pretty interesting in the light of later developments. On the one hand there was Labor and Wilbur Cohen, who were always allies. Wilbur almost never let any kind of daylight between him and the labor movement, in terms of policy in Social Security. Usually I was with them too. But they took the opposite view of the Republicans. I guess the way to say this in an orderly way is to ask, "The people who were for the COLA, the Republicans, what was in their minds? Why were they proposing this?" They made it very clear; there was no secret about it, they were for it because the program dropping behind, so that the benefits were less in purchasing power because of inflation, had been the excuse that was used time after time to amend the Social Security Act. Whenever benefits slipped behind, that started a major drive by Labor and the Democrats, generally, to fix that. And, almost always, when attention was paid to the program, more was done than just keeping up with the cost of living. It wasn't just the COLA. The Democrats would add other things to it. So the whole strategy by the Republicans in supporting automatic cost of living increases, was to keep the program from being amended—which almost always expanded the program. Their idea was to slow it down; and the way they thought to do that was through the cost of living proposal.

INTERVIEWER: That's ironic.

BALL: Yes. Now the Labor Movement and Wilbur, as I started to say, fell in with that analysis and took the opposite view for the same reason. They were afraid that once you had an automatic provision for the cost of living, they wouldn't be able to get the attention of the Congress for other improvements in the program.

Well, I disagreed with that strategy. I had been concerned about the degree of lag that there was between the time the cost of living increased and when benefits were adjusted. Although the program did keep up to date, not just with the cost of living, but with wages. Over a period of time the benefits would fall behind, and then they would be increased, and they would fall behind, and then be increased. But in the mean time, people were dying by the thousands. I mean, old people have high mortality rates. And if you take three or four years, or even two, to catch up with the cost of living, a lot of people had the experience of not being able to buy what they had previously been able to buy. So, I thought the automatic cost of living was really a very desirable and good addition to the program.

I had an occasion, as Commissioner, to have a part in getting a cost of living adjustment for federal employees. John Macy, who was the Chairman of the Civil Service Commission at the time I'm speaking of, proposed an automatic cost of living adjustment for retired civil servants in the Civil Service Retirement System. And he had to deal with the Bureau of the Budget in trying to get support for making it an Administration program.

Maybe not everybody who reads this oral history will know that the President's program is made up of recommendations from the major agencies. But they don't become part of his program until he gives approval to that particular legislative initiative. And the arm of the government that he uses to staff out proposals is what's now the Office of Management and Budget, OMB, and was the Bureau of the Budget. There was a legislative section in the old Bureau of the Budget, and there probably still is, that reviews all new proposals for the President, and clears reports on pending bills introduced by others. Congressmen were always introducing bills on subjects in the jurisdiction of some department. And the Congressional Committees would ask the agencies to tell the Committee what they think of those bills. Well, they would write a report. But, before it's released, it goes to a section of the Bureau of the Budget (or OMB). When I was there, it was headed by a really competent guy named "Sam" Hughes. They provide clearance to a report by saying it's in concord with the program of the President. And, if it isn't, you are not supposed to send the report. You have to let your views be known, if you want them known, some other way, but not through an official review.

So, to get back to the main line of this story on civil service COLAs, when it came to a question of getting support for automatic provisions in the civil service retirement system, the Bureau of the Budget and Macy wanted my views as head of the Social Security system, since it was a retirement program and similar to Social Security, and so on. I attended meetings at the Bureau of the Budget with Macy on this. I was very enthusiastic about it, not because I was particularly focused on civil servants, but because I wanted it as a precedent for the Social Security system, because having it there would be very important in the argument to have it be part of the President's program when came Social Security's turn.

So I was well on board in favor of automatic provisions to keep up with the cost of living, as a matter of principle within the program, and did not take this tactical view of the situation that Labor and Wilbur Cohen did. That was also reflected in the difference between

Wilbur Mills and John Byrnes. Mills took the view—not so much that you wouldn't get the attention of the Congress for expansion, because he was very conservative and he wasn't interested in expanding it all that much. On that theory, he might have been on the side of Byrnes.

INTERVIEWER: Yes, that's what I would've thought.

BALL: But, what he was interested in was the Congress getting credit with beneficiaries for voting for it. If it's automatic, the politicians get nothing out of it, except the first time they vote. He was willing to have it come up every couple of years, and vote for it every couple of years. He liked that a lot.

So, Mills opposed it on those grounds. The Democrats had been in charge of the Congress for so long (there was just one exception for a couple of years there) and he expected to stay in control of the Congress, and he wanted all of his Democratic colleagues to help him stay there. So every few years, when they're up for re-election, they could put out what they characterized as a benefit increase, even though it was just keeping up to date with purchasing power. So, that was his view. And, as I say, he had liberal support on the basic idea, for other reasons.

So, Democrats and liberals, for slightly different reasons, were opposed to the automatic cost of living adjustments, whereas the Republicans—or at least John Byrnes as a leader of the Republicans, he didn't have all the Republicans—was for it as a brake on the expansion of the program.

INTERVIEWER: Now, what about Nixon? Nixon supported the automatics.

BALL: Yes, now we come to. . . .

INTERVIEWER: He proposed it himself several times.

BALL: Yes. Although, I don't know if it was several times.

INTERVIEWER: What was his motivation?

BALL: When he came into office in 1968, one of his major proposals was an automatic Social Security cost of living—he just picked it up from Byrnes and the Republicans in the Congress and made it part of his program. I was still Commissioner in the first Nixon term and that was very compatible with what I thought, so that was fine. Nixon didn't have enthusiastic support of all his own immediate staff—Arthur Burns, who was his Chief Economic Advisor—was very much opposed to the automatic cost of living on the ground that it removed one of the brakes on inflation. Burns' main focus—and economists generally, but particularly conservative economists—main focus had been for a long, long time to prevent inflation. He thought if older people getting Social Security had their benefits protected against inflation, they wouldn't care whether there was inflation or non-inflation and therefore one of the powerful voting blocks would be neutralized, in terms of a fight against inflation. So he fought within the Administration to prevent going ahead with an automatic provision and really pretty much argued it right up to the end. He and I held a joint press conference when it finally passed. I had to carry most of it because he didn't. . . .

INTERVIEWER: He didn't want to do it?

BALL (*laughing*): He still didn't like the idea.

INTERVIEWER: Was Nixon's motivation the same as Byrnes' motivation? Do you think he wanted it to be a legislative brake?

BALL: I would think so. He may not have thought it through to the same extent. He recognized it to be a Republican position that he could promote as being pro-Social Security, so it's not entirely unmixed. Nixon was less of a domestic conservative than people now paint him. He was for quite a few ideas that would be considered liberal today, most notably the Family Assistance Program.

Source: Social Security Administration Web site: www.ssa.gov/history/orals/ball4.html (accessed September 25, 2006).

Document 5.12
President Nixon's Statement on Signing the Social Security Amendments of 1972, October 30, 1972

The 1972 amendments made additional modest changes in the Social Security program. The major Social Security provision in what remained of H.R. 1 was a provision to allow Social Security disability beneficiaries to participate in Medicare.

The main change in the amendments was the federalizing of various state welfare programs under the new federal Supplemental Security Income program. This new program was all that remained of the Nixon administration's ambitious welfare reform initiatives—much to the president's disappointment.

It gives me very great pleasure to sign H.R. 1, landmark legislation that will end many old inequities and will provide a new uniform system of well-earned benefits for older Americans, the blind, and the disabled. This bill contains many improvements and expansions of the social security, Medicare, and Medicaid programs which this Administration recommended and is proud to bring into reality today.

But this legislation aims at goals which are larger than the sum of all of its various program improvements:

- It represents another step in my effort to end the gap that separates far too many older Americans from the mainstream of American life.
- It furthers my concept that, rather than being viewed as a problem, older Americans should be recognized and utilized as a priceless American resource whose energy, ideals, and commitment the Nation needs. But first they have to be protected against both the realities and the fears of income and health problems—and this bill will do much to advance such protections. . . .

H.R. 1's cost has always been a part of my budget estimates for fiscal year 1973. Due to its late enactment, the bill will actually provide a $900 million surplus over the additional outlays in fiscal year 1973.

Therefore, I am able to sign this bill without violating my promise to hold down Federal spending in order to avoid a general tax increase.

The social security taxes imposed by this bill, to pay for these benefits, also were included in my fiscal year 1973 budget estimates.

H.R. 1, as enacted, does not contain my proposals for reforming the welfare system for families with dependent children. This is a deep disappointment to all—including the taxpayers—who are the victims of the existing welfare mess. . . .

Despite this major omission, H.R. 1 does give life to many of my recommendations to improve the quality of life for older Americans, the blind, and the disabled.

Social Security—It provides increased benefits for 3.8 million widows and widowers; it liberalizes the retirement earnings test by increasing from $1,680 to $2,100 the amount a beneficiary can earn without having benefits reduced, a provision that will aid 1.6 million persons; it establishes a special minimum benefit of $170 per month for 150,000 persons who have worked for long years at low wages; and it improves benefits for men retiring at age 62 and for those who work beyond 65.

Medicare/Medicaid—It extends Medicare to cover 1.5 million social security disability beneficiaries. . . .

Source: Public Papers of the Presidents of the United States: Richard Nixon, 1972 (Washington, D.C.: Government Printing Office, 1974), 1069–1071.

Document 5.13
President Nixon's Radio Address on Older Americans, October 30, 1972

After his signing statement on the 1972 amendments, President Nixon also made a radio address in which he provided more detail about the bill he had just signed into law.

Good afternoon:

A President signs many bills, but one that I signed today gave me special satisfaction because of the enormous impact it can have on the lives of millions of individual Americans.

I refer to the legislation known as H.R. 1—and especially to its provisions for helping, older Americans. Many of these provisions grew out of recommendations which I have been urging the Congress to act on for several years.

Let's look at some of the things H.R. 1 will do:

First, nearly 4 million widows and widowers will get larger social security benefits—the full 100 percent of what was payable to the individual's late husband or wife. This will mean more than $1 billion in additional income for these deserving people in the next fiscal year.

Second, over a million and a half older Americans who are now working can earn more income without having their benefits reduced.

Until today, if you were receiving social security, every dollar you earned above $1,680 cost you 50 cents in benefits—and every dollar you earned above $2,880 cost you a full dollar. But under the new provision—which I have advocated for years—you can earn up to $2,100 without losing a cent of social security, and every dollar you earn above that $2,100—no matter how many—will cost you only 50 cents in benefits. This will encourage more older Americans to work—helping them and helping the country. . . .

In addition, H.R. 1 will pay a special minimum benefit of $170 per month to 150,000 older persons who worked for long years at low wages. Men who retire at 62 will also be helped. . . .

Altogether, H.R. 1 will improve the income position of millions of older Americans. That, in my judgment, is the best way to help older people—by providing them with more money so they can do more things for themselves.

H.R. 1 is only the latest in a series of steps we have taken to improve the incomes of older people. In the last 4 years, for example, social security benefits have gone up 51 percent. That is the largest and most rapid increase in history. But the important thing is not just that benefits have been brought up to date. The important thing is that they now can be kept up to date. That is a result of the automatic increase provisions which I have been pushing for many years and which finally became law this summer.

Social security, in short, is now "inflation proof." Payments that keep pace with the cost of living are no longer something the elderly have to battle for in the Congress year after year. They have at last become a guaranteed right for older Americans. . . .

I believe that millions of older Americans can make great contributions to our Nation's progress if only they have the chance. This really is the point of our Government programs and policies—to help older Americans play a full, continuing role in the great adventures of America.

Thank you and good afternoon.

Source: Public Papers of the Presidents of the United States: Richard Nixon, 1972 (Washington, D.C.: Government Printing Office, 1974), 1075–1079.

CHAPTER 6

The Second Controversy over Financing and the 1977 Social Security Amendments, 1973–1977

This chapter contains documents relating to three distinct issues: (1) the growing financial problems the system began experiencing in the 1970s, which resulted in the passage of the 1977 amendments; (2) the closely related but distinct issue known as "decoupling" of benefit adjustments; and (3) the conceptually distinct but chronically related issue of gender biases in Social Security law. Each of these issues requires some background by way of introduction to the documents.

THE FINANCING PROBLEMS

Between fiscal years 1970 and 1975, the trust fund reserves fell from 125 percent to 75 percent of annual payout. This indicated a short-term financing problem for the system. By 1976 the disability insurance (DI) trust fund was projected to be exhausted as early as 1979 and the Old Age and Survivors Insurance (OASI) trust fund by 1984.

The Social Security legislation signed by President Nixon in 1972 marked the end of a major period of policy expansion. Nixon's immediate successors—Gerald Ford and Jimmy Carter—both had to struggle with the need to restrain the costs of the program. Source: Jimmy Carter Presidential Library.

Not all the problems facing program planners were of short duration. There were continuing financing shortfalls projected over the entire seventy-five-year valuation period. In the 1976 estimates the deficit (expressed as a percentage of payroll) ranged from 2 percent in the early years to more than 15 percent by the end of the valuation period (and the average deficit over the seventy-five years was about 8 percent of payroll).

These financing problems are documented in a set of excerpts from the annual reports of the Social Security trustees.

THE ANNUAL SOCIAL SECURITY TRUSTEES REPORTS, 1973–1977

The Social Security trust funds are administered by a board of trustees, who report annually to Congress on the financial status of the program. The trustees reports contain actuarial estimates, with explanatory material. The reports are written by the actuaries at the Social Security Administration (SSA) and released to the public under the signatures of the trustees. The reports provide estimates for both the short-range (the next five to ten years) and the long-range estimating period (currently seventy-five years). Thus, they attempt to assess the summary question: Is the Social Security program solvent (i.e., in actuarial balance) in the short run and over the long term? Often, the reports contain multiple cost projections, based on differing sets of assumptions. Traditionally, when more than one set of estimates is provided, the so-called intermediate set is the one preferred for most purposes.

The first annual trustees report was issued in 1941. That report and each subsequent one until 1973 generally projected that the Social Security trust funds were in long-range actuarial balance (see Appendix C). In the 1973 report, the trustees for the first time raised concern about the system's long-range financing. This concern was repeated throughout the subsequent reports as the financial picture worsened. The 1977 amendments ultimately reduced the shortfall from 8.2 percent of payroll to only 1.2 percent, but it did not fully restore long-range solvency.

THE "DECOUPLING" PROBLEM

One particular policy change central to the financing issues in the 1977 amendments was the "decoupling" of Social Security benefits. Understanding this issue requires some significant background.

Without periodic adjustments for price inflation, the purchasing power of a Social Security benefit would continuously decline. Likewise, because of the general rise in wage levels over the years, an initial benefit computed based on wages earned years before would tend to lower benefits to levels beneath prevailing standards of living. So there needs to be some type of adjustment for wage inflation.

To handle these problems, Congress has traditionally raised the general level of all Social Security benefits through occasional legislation. Not only has that increased the benefits of people already receiving Social Security, but it has also raised the benefits of people who will receive Social Security in the future. So there was both a "price adjustment" and a "wage adjustment" in the prior benefit increases, and they were "coupled" together—that is, both existing and future benefits were inflated by the same percentage. Historically, coupling had kept initial benefits in step with wage growth and ongoing benefits in step with price inflation.

In the period prior to 1972, wages had tended to increase about 2 percent faster than prices. If this relationship remained stable, the coupled technique for increasing benefits would continue to function as designed. But the automatic annual cost-of-living adjustment (COLA) made the system more sensitive to instabilities in the relationship between prices and wages. Hence, the combination of the automatic increases and the adverse economics of the 1970s together created a problem in program financing. The coupled mechanism began producing dramatically higher benefits for future beneficiaries and dramatically increased costs to the program. Policymakers tried to address these problems by "decoupling" the two types of increases.

Although proposals for decoupling the price adjustment from the initial benefit adjustment had been under study even before the 1972 amendments, the worsening financial position of the program after 1972 made some form of decoupling a necessity. Essentially, what was done in 1977 was to separate the two adjustments. COLAs for current beneficiaries are applied only to their benefits and are not used to inflate the wages of future beneficiaries. The initial benefit amount for a new beneficiary is calculated separately and is indexed to the growth in average wages during their working career. This two-part, separated, procedure thus took the place of the old "coupled" mechanism. (This sequence of policymaking is documented by excerpts from internal government memoranda and published legislation.)

The 1977 Amendments

Social Security's financing problems (both the general problems documented by the trustees and the specific issue of the decoupling) led to the passage of the 1977 amendments, which represented the first major contraction of program policy in the entire post-1935 history of Social Security in America. The 1972 amendments and a few minor acts in 1973 and 1974 marked the end of the expansionary period in Social Security policy; the 1977 amendments began the contractionary period that persists to the present day.

The 1977 legislation produced a partial fix of the long-range financing problem and a lessening of some of the pressure on short-range financing. But both problems were incompletely addressed by the 1977 amendments, thus a second round of major financing legislation would follow in 1983 (see Chapter 7).

Supreme Court Rulings on Gender Discrimination, 1975–1979

On a separate policy track during this period was the issue of gender bias in the Social Security program—an issue documented here in the form of excerpts from several Supreme Court rulings and congressional reports.

Beginning with the 1939 changes in the law, the Social Security program contained a number of gender discriminations in its policies. Generally, these discriminations were designed to advantage women and disadvantage men—by, for example, requiring men to meet eligibility requirements not imposed on women or granting women types of benefits unavailable to males (such as widow's benefits under the 1939 law). Generally, these policies were adopted due to a paternalistic view of the dependent status of women vis-à-vis men. Nevertheless, the result was overt policy discrimination against male beneficiaries. By the mid-1970s this gender bias in the program had come under assault, and starting in 1975 a series of Supreme Court decisions overturned certain of these gendered policies. This triggered a policy shift in which all remaining residual gender distinctions were eliminated in the amendments of 1983.

Document 6.1
1973 Trustees Report, July 16, 1973

The 1973 trustees report was the first to project a long-range deficit in the Social Security program's financing. This report—the first issued after the "automatic" provisions of the 1972 law were enacted—attributed the cause of the financing shortfall to rising rates of disability and not to the poor economic climate of the era.

Long-Range Cost Estimates

Long-range cost estimates for the old-age, survivors, and disability insurance system presented in this report are computed under dynamic assumptions with respect to the future levels of the benefits and the taxable base. These assumptions are based on the automatic adjustment provisions enacted in 1972. . . .

The 1971 Advisory Council on Social Security recommended that the level-benefit level-earnings assumption used in the past be replaced by dynamic assumptions as to benefit table increases and as to the rate of increase in taxable earnings. These recommendations have now been adopted. The two sets of amendments to the Social Security Act enacted in 1972 were based on financing schedules that incorporate the dynamic assumptions. Estimates based on such dynamic assumptions basically assume (1) that the provisions automatically adjusting the benefit table in accordance with the Consumer Price Index [CPI], and automatically adjusting the taxable earnings base in accordance with the increase in covered earnings per worker, will continue to be a part of the structure of the system, and (2) if Congress were to grant larger benefit table increases, to liberalize the benefits in any other sense, or to hold down the taxable earnings base, it would simultaneously provide additional financing. Tax schedules based on such dynamic methodology provide the financing needed to increase the benefit table in step with the Consumer Price Index, but do not provide financing for benefit table increases in excess of the increase in prices. . . .

. . . [T]he old-age, survivors, and disability insurance system is shown to be underfinanced over the long-range, with a negative actuarial balance of –0.32 percent of taxable payroll. This underfinancing is largely due to the disability insurance program, which is shown to have an actuarial deficit of –0.23 percent of taxable payroll, while the old-age and survivors insurance program is shown as having a negative actuarial balance of –0.09 percent of taxable payroll.

As compared with the long-range cost estimates prepared at the time that the 1972 Social Security Amendments were under consideration, the present estimates show a higher cost. The higher cost is attributed mostly to the disability insurance portion of the system. In the last two years the disability rates—that is, the number of allowed claims as a percentage of the insured population—has shown an increase over previous experience. If the higher rates continue, there will be an increase in costs in later years sufficient to require additional financing. Although it is not yet possible to have a firm judgment on whether or not the increases will be permanent, the actuaries are of the opinion that a significant portion of the increase in the rates may not be temporary and that the possibility of higher costs in the long run should now be recognized in the long-range planning of the program. The Trustees agree and have, therefore, shown the cash benefit program to be out of balance for the long run. However, since much more needs to be known about the change in disability rates before a solid opinion can be made concerning the certainty of higher costs for the later years, the Trustees are not, at this time, recommending an actual change in the contribution rates. . . .

Conclusion

The long-range actuarial cost estimates for the old-age, survivors, and disability insurance program . . . currently show an actuarial imbalance of –0.32 percent of taxable payroll, a deficit of about 3 percent of the long-range cost of the program. The deficit, which did not appear in the actuarial estimates prepared for use by the Congress in connection with its consideration of the Social Security Amendments of 1972, arises from two sources.

A small part arises from the sensitivity of the methodology to short-term changes in consumer prices and average covered wages. The rate at which consumer prices have increased since the last benefit increase was granted (for September 1972) makes it now appear that the benefit increase called for as of January 1, 1975, may be over 7 percent, whereas the earlier projections were based on the assumption of a benefit increase amounting to just over 5 percent. The estimates as to the rate of increase in average covered earnings have also been increased, further increasing the estimates of future benefits (since increases in taxable earnings are reflected later in the benefit payments), but increasing the estimates of future trust fund income as well. . . .

The larger part of the deficit arises from the projection of disability rates that are significantly higher than those used in previous estimates. A higher rate of disability was used because the 1972 data now available indicate that the rather sharp increase in the rate of disability awards first noted in 1971 was apparently not due to temporary causes. The reasons for the increase in the rate of disability awards are not entirely clear, and an intensive study of disability experience has already been begun to ascertain these reasons, and to determine whether additional financing may eventually be required. The actuarial deficit shown in this Report serves as a notification that an increase in the contribution rate for the disability program is likely to be needed sometime in the future.

The combined old-age and survivors and disability insurance trust funds at the beginning of 1973 ($42.8 billion) are 80 percent of the estimated combined trust fund expenditures for calendar year 1973 ($53.7 billion). The 1973 ratio is below that for 1972 due to the substantial benefit increase enacted in 1972. The ratio is projected to decrease slowly, but to remain in the 76–78 percent range for the 1974–77 period. However, in absolute dollar amounts, the trust funds are projected to increase from $42.8 billion at the end of 1972 to $58.3 billion at the end of 1977.

The Board of Trustees, in viewing the system beyond the next 5-year period, recognizes the possibility that there may need to be some increase in the rate of contribution to cover higher rates of disability. The need for any extra financing is rather long delayed, however, and can be considered after the studies of disability experience now being undertaken have been completed. The Trustees do not, at this time, propose any changes in financing.

Source: 1973 Annual Report of the Board of Trustees of the Federal Old-Age and Survivors Insurance and Disability Insurance Trust Funds (Washington, D.C.: Government Printing Office, 1973), 29–33.

Document 6.2
1974 Trustees Report, June 8, 1974

This second negative trust fund report contained some important findings: (1) the magnitude of the financing shortfall had increased ten times over what had been shown in the 1973 report, (2) demographic and economic factors were now being cited as causes of the shortfall, (3) a short-run deficit was now being reported along with the long-run deficit, and (4) the actuaries were clearly indicating that financing modifications were needed, although they deferred any recommendations to the upcoming 1974–1975 advisory council.

One point of interest is the fact that the trustees suggested borrowing from the Medicare trust fund to shore-up the Social Security trust funds—a policy intervention briefly adopted in the 1983 amendments. Following the 1965 creation of the Medicare program, a separate trust fund (called the hospital insurance—HI—trust fund) was established for Medicare and a portion of the Social Security payroll tax was allocated to go to this fund. Thus there are three separate trust funds: OASI, DI, and HI, and the Social Security actuaries are here suggesting allowing inter-fund borrowing as a way to shore up the OASDI parts of the trio. (Technically, there is a fourth "trust fund" for the medical services portion of Medicare, called the supplemental medical insurance, or SMI, trust fund. But SMI is not a real trust fund—it holds no assets—and its only purpose is to summarize the amount of the federal taxpayer subsidy to this part of Medicare, that is, the amount not covered by the Part B Medicare premiums.)

Note also that the actuaries stated their expectation that inflation would soon abate, and that if it did not, the estimates would worsen—which is what happened.

Actuarial Status of the Trust Funds

. . . [T]he OASDI System is shown to be underfinanced over the long-range, with a negative actuarial balance of about 3 percent of taxable payroll. . . . Both OASI and DI have a long-range actuarial deficit equivalent to about 21 percent of their costs.

Table 20 Estimated Actuarial Balance of Old-Age, Survivors, and Disability Insurance Systems as Percent of Taxable Payroll . . . (in percent)

Item	OASI	DI	Total
Average-cost of system	11.97	1.92	13.89
Average rate in present tax schedule	9.39	1.52	10.91
Actuarial balance	−2.58	−.40	−2.98

. . . As compared with the long-range cost estimates prepared last fall when the Social Security Amendments (P.L. 93–233) were under consideration, the present estimates show substantially higher costs. These higher costs are attributed mostly to a change in the population projections that are used to project the costs of the social security programs. . . .

Although most of the increase in cost is expected to occur after the turn of the century (when the effects of the changes in the population projections are fully felt), part of it will already occur within the next few years, thereby producing a marked decline in the near future in the ratio of assets to expenditures in the absence of an immediate increase in income to both the OASI and DI Trust Funds. In the very short run (for the next 5-10 years) a real-location of the current contributions could cover this problem. The overall OASHDI contribution rate in present law would be enough, if reallocated, to adequately support all three trust funds (OASI, DI and HI) during this period. However, after the next 5-10 years, a tax increase or constraints in the growth of benefits will nonetheless be needed for each of the three programs. . . .

Conclusion

The long-range actuarial cost estimates for the old-age, survivors, and disability insurance program prepared in accordance with dynamic assumptions as to both benefits and taxable earnings show an actuarial balance of –2.98 percent of taxable payroll over the valuation period of 75 years, which substantially exceeds the acceptable limit of variation of 5 percent of the cost of the program (0.69 percent of taxable payroll).

The principal reason for the increase in the actuarial imbalance, as compared to that reflected by the cost estimates used last fall by the Congress, is a change in the long-range population projections underlying the cost estimates, which are now based on the results of the 1970 Census and on lower future fertility assumptions than were previously used for such projections.

Although the new population and fertility projections will have a major impact after the turn of the century on the long-range cost estimates, they will not have a significant effect in the short run. According to present short-range cost estimates, action to increase the combined income of the OASDI and hospital insurance systems for the next 5-10 years is not necessary right now. Although, when considered separately, the Disability Insurance Trust Fund and, to some extent, the Old-Age and Survivors Insurance Trust Fund decline in terms of both absolute dollar amounts and as a percent of outgo, the Hospital Insurance Trust Fund is increasing more rapidly than previously projected, with the result that it is developing an excess of funds. The Board noted that one of the possible ways that the projected short-range excess of outgo over income in the cash benefit funds can be avoided is a reallocation of the total program income among the three funds (OASI, DI, and HI) by revising the contribution rates scheduled in present law without increasing the total rate. However, in order to maintain the HI Trust Fund in actuarial balance, any reduction in the HI tax rates in the early years would have to be offset by compensatory increases in later years.

The present assumptions as to the rate of increase in the CPI, in both the short-range and the long-range estimates, assume some deceleration from recent rates of increase. If this deceleration does not occur, or occurs more slowly than assumed, the reallocation noted above may not be sufficient over the next 5–10 years to prevent a decline in the funds. And, of course, if such deceleration does not occur and if, as is assumed, recent fertility trends should continue, the additional financing needed over the long-range will be increased.

Although there is of necessity a considerable degree of uncertainty inherent in the long-range demographic and economic assumptions and consequently in the projections that flow from those assumptions, it is certain that additional income to the cash benefits program or some adjustment in the benefit structure will be needed eventually. However, in view of this inherent uncertainty and the fact that the newly appointed Advisory Council on Social Security is studying the long-range financial status of the social security system, the Board is not recommending a specific increase in the combined OASDHI contribution rates scheduled in present law. The Board believes that there is ample time to await the Council's findings and recommendations before making specific proposals.

Source: 1974 Annual Report of the Board of Trustees of the Federal Old-Age and Survivors Insurance and Disability Insurance Trust Funds (Washington, D.C.: Government Printing Office, June 3, 1974), 35–38.

Document 6.3
1975 Trustees Report, May 6, 1975

In the 1975 report the long-range financial situation has again gotten markedly worse. There appears the first discussion of the effects of the inflation adjustments on long-range financing (the "decoupling" problem discussed in the next section of this chapter), and the warnings of financial trouble have gotten more dire.

Long-Range Actuarial Status of the Trust Funds

Significance of Long-Range Cost Estimates

Long-range cost estimates are essential to the evaluation and planning of the OASDI program over the long-range future. . . .

Long-Range Cost Estimates

. . . According to this projection the cost of the old-age and survivors insurance program will increase slowly during the remainder of this century. After the turn of the century, the cost will be subject to accelerated increases until leveling at about 18½ percent of taxable payroll around the year 2030. For the disability insurance program the projection shows a steady increase in cost to around the year 2020, after which the cost will level at about 3¾ percent of taxable payroll.

The combined cost of the total old-age, survivors, and disability insurance system, using the central set of economic assumptions, is projected to increase to about 12 percent of taxable payroll by the end of the century; thereafter the costs will increase rapidly to about 22 percent of taxable payroll by the year 2030 and will remain essentially level during the remainder of the valuation period. These future costs would be substantially ameliorated, however, if the provisions of law were modified to avoid the phenomenon that causes future projected benefits under the automatic adjustment provisions to increase out of proportion to the levels of wage replacement established by benefits currently paid under the program. . . .

. . . According to these calculations the old-age, survivors, and disability insurance system is estimated to be underfinanced over the customary long-range 75-year period by an average annual amount equivalent to 5.32 percent of taxable payroll. . . .

One significant element of the sensitivity of the projected costs to economic assumptions is the fact that most of the effect of changes in the CPI occurs after the turn of the century. . . . it can be concluded that over the remainder of this century the old-age, survivors, and disability insurance system will need additional financing equivalent to about 1.3 percent of taxable payroll under reasonable sets of economic assumptions.

After the turn of the century, the amount of required additional financing would be significantly higher. . . . However, to a large extent, the higher cost that is projected to occur after the turn of the century is due to what may be considered unintended and undesirable results of the automatic benefit adjustment provisions in present law.

These present provisions in the law automatically increase the benefits of retired workers as increases occur in the CPI. These CPI increases are also given (indirectly through increases in the benefit table) to workers who have not yet retired and who therefore have an opportunity to improve their future benefits as a result of increases in their future taxable earnings. Thus, in a large proportion of cases the future benefits of those who are still working increase at annual rates that are in excess of increases in either CPI or average wages under economic conditions which may be considered likely to prevail. The duality of benefit increases that is possible under present law can result in future benefits being substantially higher than the highest gross earnings on which the worker was taxed. . . .

Conclusion

The short-range actuarial cost estimates indicate that the assets of both the old-age, and survivors insurance trust fund and the disability insurance trust fund will decline during the 5-year period 1975–79. Without legislation to provide additional financing, the assets of both trust funds will be exhausted soon after 1979.

The Board recommends that prompt action be taken to strengthen the financing of the old-age, survivors, and disability insurance system over the near term. The required additional income to the trust funds should be obtained through increases in the tax rate, in the taxable earnings base, or in both rate and base. The Board opposes the use of additional general revenue financing for the old-age, survivors, and disability insurance program. The Board noted that the amount of additional income required for the program would be reduced if the Congress adopted the President's proposal to limit to 5 percent the automatic benefit increase scheduled for June, 1975. *[Authors' note: The COLA increase adopted in 1975 would in fact be 8 percent.]*

The long-range actuarial cost estimates indicate that for every year in the future the estimated expenditures will exceed the estimated income from taxes. This excess increases with time and is estimated to average about 1.3 percent of taxable payroll over the next 25-year period. . . .

The long-range cost of the OASDI program projected to occur after the turn of the century will substantially exceed the taxes scheduled in present law. . . .

To some extent the high cost of the old-age, survivors, and disability insurance program projected to occur after the turn of the century is due to unintended results in the automatic benefit adjustment provisions enacted in 1972, which cause future projected benefits to increase out of proportion to levels of wage replacement established by benefits currently paid under the program. The Board fully concurs with the intent of the recommendation by the 1975 Advisory Council on Social Security that the benefit structure be revised to maintain the levels of benefits in relation to pre-retirement earnings levels that now prevail.

The Board recommends that development of specific plans for strengthening of the long-range financing of the old-age, survivors, and disability insurance program be pursued immediately with special priorities given to ways of modifying the automatic benefit adjustment provisions in present law. . . .

Source: 1975 Annual Report of the Board of Trustees of the Federal Old-Age and Survivors Insurance and Disability Insurance Trust Funds (Washington, D.C.: Government Printing Office, May 6, 1975), 34–45.

Document 6.4
1976 Trustees Report, May 25, 1976

*This report explores for the first time two sets of proposals for addressing long-range costs: a small set of changes recommended by the Gerald Ford administration (**Document 6.11**) and the impact of "decoupling" the inflation-adjustment mechanism.*

In an attempt to separate the impact of the inflation-adjustment problem from the deficit caused by demographic and other factors, the actuaries developed a concept they called the "modified theoretical system," and they concluded that about half the program deficit was caused by the inflation-adjustment problem.

Long-Range Actuarial Status of the Trust Funds

Significance of Long-Range Cost Estimates

. . . Throughout its history the old-age, survivors, and disability insurance program has been self-supporting and since the 1950's has been operated on what may be termed a current-cost financing basis. It is self-supporting in that the only source of funds to pay benefits and administrative expenses is the social security taxes collected from workers and their employers covered under the program (and the interest earned on the invested balances of the trust funds). Under the current-cost method of financing, the amount of taxes collected each year is intended to be approximately equal to the benefits and administrative expenses paid during the year plus a small additional amount to maintain the trust funds at an appropriate contingency reserve level. The purpose of the trust fund under current-cost financing is to reflect all financial transactions and to absorb temporary differences between income and expenditures. Thus, whatever normal ratio of trust fund assets to expenditures is established, it can be expected that the funds will vary somewhat from that level from time to time as they absorb those fluctuations.

Since the inception of the old-age, survivors, and disability insurance program, past payroll taxes together with interest on the trust funds have been adequate to provide all past benefits and administrative expenses. Specifically, with respect to the old-age, survivors, and disability insurance program from 1937 through calendar year 1975, cumulative income to the trust funds amounted to $586 billion and cumulative disbursements were $542 billion. The balance of $44 billion was still in the trust funds at the end of calendar year 1975. Based upon projections made under the intermediate assumptions (alternative II), it is estimated that, during the calendar years 1976–1981, income to the trust funds will total $581 billion and disbursements will be $616 billion. . . . This is a projected decrease in the trust funds of $35 billion during the period 1976–1981. . . .

When estimated future disbursements and estimated future income over the 75-year valuation period are not in balance, an "actuarial deficit" or an "actuarial surplus" exists—depending upon whether disbursements are greater than income, or vice versa. The old-age, survivors, and disability insurance program has been in close actuarial balance throughout most of the program's existence. When there was an imbalance, i.e., an actuarial deficit or actuarial surplus, the Congress has acted in due course to revise either taxes, benefits, or both so as to bring the program into close actuarial balance over the 75-year valuation period. Therefore, it is essential to the sound financial operation of the old-age, survivors, and disability insurance program that periodic estimates be made of the estimated future income and outgo to ensure that they are still in balance, and, if not, to provide information to enable appropriate action to be taken to restore the balance. . . .

Long-Range Cost Estimates

. . . Under the intermediate set of assumptions the cost of the old-age and survivors insurance program is projected to increase slowly during the remainder of this century. After the turn of the century two effects combine to cause the expenditures to increase very rapidly. One is that the replacement ratio continues to increase. The second is that workers born during the period of very high birth rates, from post-World-War-II years through the late 1950's and into the 1960's, reach retirement age and begin to receive benefits.

During the last years of the projection period the expenditures continue to increase but at a much slower rate, thereby reflecting both the decelerated increases in the replacement ratios and the low birth rates of the 1970's.

. . . According to these calculations the old-age, survivors, and disability insurance system is estimated to be underfinanced over the customary long-range 75-year period by an average annual amount equivalent to 7.96 percent of taxable payroll. . . .

Long-Range Cost Estimates under a Modified Theoretical System

As stated previously, it is unlikely that the expenditures projected under present law and current economic assumptions will be allowed to materialize, since they result from the unreasonably high awarded benefits that are produced by the complex relationship between such benefits and future changes in wages and the Consumer Price Index. Consequently, based on the assumption that it would be useful for long-range financial planning to illustrate the general trends in the expenditures for a system under which the previously mentioned relationship is more stable, cost projections have been prepared on the basis of a "modified theoretical" old-age, survivors, and disability insurance system which would maintain through time the relationship between average awarded benefits and average earnings existing at the beginning of calendar year 1978. . . .

. . . It can also be noted . . . that the overall level of estimated expenditures is reduced as a result of eliminating the "excess" benefits which stem from rising replacement rates. . . .

. . . [T]he actuarial imbalance over the customary 75-year period would be reduced to a range of about 2.64 to 5.66 percent of taxable payroll. . . .

Estimated Operations and Status of the Trust Funds under the System as Modified by the President's Financing Proposals

The President has proposed increases in the contribution rates payable under the old-age, survivors, and disability insurance program, in order to strengthen the financing of the program over the near term. Under the President's proposals, contribution rates would be increased, effective January 1, 1977 . . .

Enactment of the President's financing proposals would reduce the long-range average annual deficit of the old-age, survivors, and disability insurance system over the next 75 years by 0.69 percent of taxable payroll—0.59 percent due to the increase in the contribution rate for employees and employers and 0.10 percent due to the increase in the contribution rate for self-employed persons. As a result, under the intermediate assumptions, the 75-year average annual deficit would be 7.27 percent of taxable payroll based on the benefit structure in present law, and 3.59 percent based on the modified theoretical system described in an earlier section.

Conclusion

The short-range actuarial cost estimates indicate that the assets of the old-age and survivors insurance and disability insurance trust funds will decline during the period 1976–1981. . . . Without legislation to provide additional financing, the assets of the disability insurance trust fund will be exhausted in 1979. . . . Similarly, the assets of the old-age and survivors insurance trust fund will be exhausted in . . . 1984 under the intermediate set . . . of assumptions.

The Board recommends that prompt action be taken to strengthen the financing of the old-age, survivors, and disability insurance system over the near term by means of appropriate increases in the tax rates. The Board opposes the use of additional general revenue financing for the old-age, survivors, and disability insurance program. The Board recommends against an increase in the taxable earnings base, other than increases which will occur automatically as average wages in covered employment increase, as a means of producing additional income because of the effect this would have on increased benefits and expenditures in future years.

The long-range actuarial cost estimates indicate that for every year in the future, under present law, the estimated expenditures will exceed the estimated income from taxes. . . .

The Board recognized in the 1975 annual report, as it does in this report, that the high cost of the old-age, survivors, and disability insurance program projected to occur after the turn of the century is partially due to unintended results in the automatic benefit adjustment provisions enacted in 1972. . . . The Board is in full concurrence with the intent of the 1975 Advisory Council on Social Security that the benefit structure be revised in a responsible manner. The Board recommends the adoption of a specific plan as soon as possible in order to improve the predictability of future benefit levels and to reduce the long-range cost of the system. . . .

Source: 1976 Annual Report of the Board of Trustees of the Federal Old-Age and Survivors Insurance and Disability Insurance Trust Funds (Washington, D.C.: Government Printing Office, May 25, 1975), 40–59.

Document 6.5
1977 Trustees Report, May 10, 1977

The 1977 report shifted focus to the medium-range period (the next twenty-five years), as well as expressing continuing concerns about the long-range period. The projected long-range deficit had increased yet again, although not as dramatically as in some of the prior reports. At this stage—on the eve of the 1977 legislation—the actuaries were telling policymakers that the system had an 8.2 percent long-range actuarial deficit.

Actuarial Status of the Trust Funds

Significance of Long-Range Cost Estimates

. . . [U]nder present law, because of the particular method by which future benefits are related to future changes in wages and the Consumer Price Index, the benefits projected to materialize under certain assumptions regarding such changes reach extremely high levels for persons who first become entitled to benefits in the next century. It is clearly imperative that legislative changes be made too prevent such benefit levels from materializing. . . .

. . . [F]rom 1937 through calendar year 1976, cumulative income to the trust funds amounted to $661 billion ($30 billion of which is from interest earned on the trust funds) and cumulative disbursements were $620 billion. The balance of $41 billion was held in the trust funds at the end of calendar year 1976.

Based upon projections made under the intermediate assumptions . . . it is estimated that during the calendar years 1977–81, income to the trust funds will total $499 billion ($7 billion of which is from interest earned on the trust funds) and disbursements will be $540 billion. . . . This is a projected decrease in the trust funds of $41 billion during the period 1977–81, which would reduce the trust funds to less than $½ billion by the end of calendar year 1981. . . .

Medium-Range Cost Estimates: 1977–2001

. . . [T]he 25-year average cost of 12.24 percent of taxable payroll under present law is 0.28 percent of taxable payroll higher than the 25-year average cost of 11.96 percent of taxable payroll under the modified theoretical system. This illustrates the reduction in cost over the next 25 years that can be obtained by stabilizing replacement ratios at their 1979 levels. . . .

A comparison of the average expenditures . . . for the next 25 years with the corresponding average tax rate of 9.9 percent in present law shows that the old-age, survivors, and disability insurance system is estimated to be underfinanced by 2.34 percent of taxable payroll under present law and by 2.06 percent of taxable payroll if the replacement ratios are stabilized as under the modified theoretical system. Thus, although the medium-range financial problem of the old-age, survivors, and disability insurance system can be alleviated by stabilizing the replacement ratios, it cannot be solved by that action alone. . . .

Long-Range Cost Estimates: 1977–2051

(*Excerpt from*) Table 31 Total Seventy-Five Year Period (1977–2051)			
	OASI	DI	Total
Expenditures as percent of payroll	15.51	3.68	19.19
Tax Rate in Law	9.45	1.54	10.99
Difference	–6.06	–2.14	–8.20

Conclusion

The actuarial cost estimates presented in this report indicate that the declines in the assets of the old-age and survivors insurance and disability insurance trust funds which began in 1975 will continue. Without legislation to improve the financial status of the program, the assets of the disability insurance trust fund will be exhausted in 1979 under all three of the alternative sets of economic assumptions for which estimates have been presented in this report. Similarly, the assets of the old-age and survivors insurance trust fund will be exhausted in 1982 under the most pessimistic set of assumptions, in 1983 under the intermediate set, and in 1984 under the most optimistic set of assumptions.

The Board recommends that action be taken to strengthen the actuarial status of the old-age, survivors, and disability insurance system over the near term beginning in calendar year 1978, if feasible, and certainly no later than calendar year 1979. . . .

The Board recommends that high priority be given to the development of plans to strengthen the actuarial status of the old-age, survivors, and disability insurance program over the next 25 years.

The long-range cost of the present program projected to occur after the turn of the century will substantially exceed the taxes scheduled in present law. . . .

Source: 1977 Annual Report of the Board of Trustees of the Federal Old-Age and Survivors Insurance and Disability Insurance Trust Funds (Washington, D.C.: Government Printing Office, May 10, 1977), 42–60.

Document 6.6
Recommendations on Decoupling from the 1974–1975 Advisory Council, March 6, 1975

The report of the 1974–1975 advisory council set the stage for the changes introduced in the 1977 amendments, and this council made a particular point of studying the decoupling problem and making a recommendation for solving it.

As a first step, the council commissioned the services of an outside panel of five experts (two economists and three actuaries) to examine the financing issues in general and the decoupling issue in particular and to make recommendations to the council. Following receipt of the consultants' report, a special council subcommittee made their report to the full council on the financing issues, including decoupling. The council then made its final decisions and recommendations.

The first excerpt is from the consultants' report to the council, followed by an excerpt from the final council report on the issue of the decoupling.

Decoupling of OASDI System

Your consultants suggest to the Subcommittee, and hence to the entire Advisory Council, that the Council recommend the gradual phasing out of the "coupled" OASDI system now established by law, and the phasing in of a "decoupled" system. . . .

Rationale

We recognize that the rationale behind this suggestion is not immediately apparent. We do not claim that a decoupled system is per se superior to a coupled one. . . .

The goal of the decoupling suggestion is to improve the stability of the OASDI system under conditions of price and wage inflation. . . .

The difficulty that decoupling is intended to cure is that potential benefits do not increase directly with average wages (as one would expect in a wage-related system), but instead increase in a complicated way, mixing consumer price increases with a portion (something less than-half) of wage increases. This mixed rate will be always greater than the CPI Increase, but it may be *either* greater or less than the average wage increase. The important replacement ratio . . . is therefore unstable. It rises when the gain in real wages is small, falls when it is large. This instability not only thwarts good pension design, but it makes future cost estimates depend heavily upon price and wage increase rates, over which the system can exercise no effective control.

A decoupled system can be designed to correct this instability, without negative effect on other aspects of the system. Potential benefits for those still working would fully reflect increase in average wages, but would be made independent of CPI changes. Replacement ratios, wherever they may be set initially, are therefore preserved, since potential benefits and wages increase together.

Cost Effects

If the gain in real wages happens to follow the 2% assumption chosen by the Social Security Administration for long range cost estimate purposes, then replacement ratios will tend to rise. . . . Increasing replacement ratios are responsible for a part of the deficit shown in the most recent Trustees report. The adoption of a decoupling proposal would therefore be helpful in reducing the deficit.

It is important to realize, however, that a decoupling proposal is *not necessarily* a cost-reducing one. If gains in real wages were to average 3% annually, replacement ratios under the coupled system would slowly fall. Under these circumstances a decoupled system would prevent replacement ratio deterioration, and hence be more costly than the present coupled system.

Your consultants recommend the decoupled system because of its improved stability under forces of inflation, not because it appears to reduce the actuarial deficit. The fact that decoupling would improve the actuarial balance (under assumptions which the consultants find reasonable) also commends it to us—but we would recommend it even if we thought that the effect would be in the opposite direction.

The Average Indexed Monthly Wage

As a first step toward achieving our objectives, we suggest that benefits be based on an "average indexed monthly wage."

We propose no change in the averaging periods, in the rules about dropout years, or any other feature of the AMW [average monthly wage] calculation, except that an indexing system will be applied to change the AMW to an AIMW (average indexed monthly wage).

The wage record of any past year is indexed by multiplying it by the ratio that average wages of the most recent calendar year bear to the average wages of the year being indexed. . . .

Section 1. Summary

The Council recommends that until retirement all earnings should be "indexed." That is, the actual money earnings of a worker before retirement should be adjusted in accordance with an index of changes in the average earnings of all workers. Average monthly indexed earnings (AMIE) would be used as the basis for determining benefits instead of actual average monthly earnings (AME) as now. After retirement, benefits should be adjusted according to an index of changes in the cost of living, as they now are under the 1972 amendments. Replacement rates (the proportion of earnings replaced by benefits) that are currently produced by present law should be continued. . . .

. . . With the steady inflation in the post-war period, the benefits of retired individuals soon failed to keep pace with increases in prices. Congress, in recognition of this erosion of benefits, raised benefits from time to time on an ad hoc basis to maintain the real purchasing power of social security benefits. . . Congress generally has raised benefits more than in proportion to increases in consumer prices. . . .

The automatic cost-of-living adjustments are made only in the level of payments to beneficiaries (present and future). There is, however, an important effect of inflation while the worker is still earning. Since wages as well as prices increase during inflation, wages earned just before retirement tend to reflect the level of prices and productivity at the time of retirement, and to that extent move the worker to a higher level of benefits. Wages earned many years before retirement, however, do not reflect the effects of inflation between the time they were earned and the time of retirement, so at retirement when an average is taken of monthly earnings (AME) it is lower than it would be if each month's work had been done at the wage levels prevailing at the date of retirement.

The effects of inflation while a worker is still earning should be allowed for explicitly, and by a different method from that used to allow for the effects of inflation after a worker begins to draw benefits.

The Council therefore recommends that a worker's earnings should be "indexed"—that is, adjusted to reflect increases in average earnings over his working lifetime—up to retirement, and after retirement his benefits should be adjusted according to changes in the cost of living. . . .

2.2 Stability of Replacement Ratios

. . . Benefits have been carefully controlled by Congress in the past. But the method used for automatic cost-of-living adjustments in benefits has the side-effect of making replacement ratios . . . subject to unpredictable variations caused by changes in wage and price levels, an effect that presumably was not intended. The result is that replacement rates, instead of being controlled by conscious and deliberate policy set by the Congress, can fluctuate up or down with the tides of inflation.

This loss of control and stability comes about in large part because of a compounding in the inflation adjustment. For those who have retired, the adjustment takes place only in the benefit schedule, and works well. Those who have not retired, however, will get a partial adjustment for inflation through higher earnings before retirement. . . .

The extent to which this compounding will change replacement ratios, and even whether it will raise them or lower them, cannot be foreseen. . . . [S]ustained inflation at a high rate—especially if prices rise as fast as wages—would lead to replacement ratios substantially greater than 100 percent. Under the present provisions for financing the system, such replacement ratios would impose an excessive burden on those still working, so they could ultimately jeopardize the whole system, or at least necessitate substantial reductions of benefits from the levels that people had been led to expect.

Indexing earnings before retirement to changes in average earnings and indexing benefits after retirement to changes in prices will make it possible to eliminate the compounding of adjustments to inflation, to restore stability and predictability of replacement ratios and put them firmly under congressional control, and to strengthen the long-run financial integrity of the system. . . .

2.3 Some Considerations of Equity

. . . Our recommendation is that actual earnings for each year be multiplied by the ratio of average earnings of all workers in the year of retirement to average earnings of all workers in each past year used in computing the benefit. If a worker retires in 1975, for example, and if all earnings averaged 4 times as high in 1975 as in 1951, 4 times the worker's actual earnings in 1951 would be the indexed earnings used in computing the AMIE. Thus, everyone retiring in 1975 would have all his actual earnings, regardless of when they were earned, restated to an equivalent 1975 figure. . . .

Source: Reports of the Advisory Council on Social Security 1974–75 (Washington, D.C.: U.S. Advisory Council on Social Security, 1975), 163–168; 19–25. Bound manuscript copy available in the SSA History Archives.

Document 6.7
Secretary Simon's Memo to the Economic Policy Board, October 2, 1975

The Ford administration was actively at work on the decoupling problem and produced many internal memoranda on the subject.

In the first memorandum, Secretary of the Treasury William E. Simon is writing to the executive committee of the Economic Policy Board, which was a Ford administration economic policy planning unit. In the memo, Simon is crafting the issue of the decoupling in the context of a broader policy reform of the program. This memo shows that the Ford administration was thinking of how to use the decoupling question as part of a broader effort to control the costs of the Social Security system.

During the past several years, the financial condition of the Old Age, Survivors' and Disability Insurance (OASDI) system has rapidly worsened. . . . Outlays have grown from $30.3 billion in FY 1970 to a currently projected $73.7 billion for FY 1976—an average 16% annual growth rate. OASI is already the largest of all Federal programs, and it grows automatically with the cost of living.

Once beyond controversy, Social Security has come under persistent attack in the news media for its inequities, its financial uncertainties and its complexity. And economists have called attention to its negative effects on private capital formation, employment, and economic activity generally. The common cause of these various problems lies largely in the benefit and contribution formulas prescribed by present law, and in the weakness of the link between contributions and benefits.

The most obvious defect of the present system is the fact that benefits being "earned" by current workers are tied to both wage rates and the consumer price index. There is widespread agreement that the system must be "decoupled" to eliminate automatic increases in future benefits that outpace the CPI, and work is underway within the Domestic Council framework to design an explicit "decoupling" proposal. This effort deserves a high priority.

Decoupling is expected to remove about half of the long-term financial deficiency. Unfortunately, the half which remains is likely to be far less tractable. This is where the real problem lies—the source of the need for reform.

Reasons Why Social Security Reform Should Not Be Delayed
- Reform of Social Security would logically be an integral part of the President's ongoing strategy for rationalizing Federal welfare programs. The system is based on benefit formulas which have been explicitly designed to redistribute income from high to low-wage workers, and it contains many other features which, accidentally or otherwise, have major redistributive effects.
- The OASDI trust funds are expected to be extinguished by 1981, unless additional funding is obtained. This crisis, together with the decoupling of the system, provides an opportunity for more basic reform.
- The net liability to be overcome will continue to grow rapidly as the "baby boom" generation gets closer to retirement.
- Public confidence in the system could evaporate, with serious political consequences, as its financial problems mount.

An ideal Social Security system would be economically sound in at least the following respects:

1. Economic activity and growth not to be discouraged,
2. Tax rates to be moderate, predictable and stable,
3. No threat of sharp tax increases in the future,
4. No intergenerational or other obvious inequities.

In addition, the program needs simplification. Participants should be able to understand it, and policymakers should be able to predict its future development.

Recommendations

I recommend that a small task force be established by the Economic Policy Board in cooperation with the Department of Health, Education, and Welfare to study options for Social Security reform beyond decoupling. Working along the lines of the goals suggested in this memorandum, the task force would be expected to provide an outline of a reformed system, together with related cost, revenue, and outlay estimates. The Board should be able to present its recommendations to the President in time for the State of the Union Massage in January 1976.

William E. Simon

Source: Copy in SSA History Archives, Mary Ross Papers, Box 34, Binder: "Decoupling Memoranda."

Document 6.8
Secretary Simon's Memo to James Cannon, November 11, 1975

In this memorandum from Secretary Simon to James Cannon, assistant to the president for domestic affairs, Simon is moving the argument along to another center of power in the Ford administration. Notice that at one point Simon is suggesting that wage inflation adjustments be abandoned altogether.

. . . The Social Security system is in great need of decoupling, but more than decoupling is required to reduce its negative effects on employment, capital formation and economic activity generally. We must not lose this chance to plan a basic financial reform. I believe that the timetable suggested in your memo is too short to make possible more than some ad hoc adjustments in the system. With a little more time, we can put together a package which simultaneously accomplishes the following objectives:

- Reduction through decoupling of the long-run growth rate of benefits, to a point where these benefits can be financed without sharp increases in payroll taxes
- Trimming away some overly generous features of the system, such as the minimum benefit which federal workers can collect on the basis of minimal outside work experience
- A much closer correspondence between each individual's lifetime contributions paid and expected benefits earned. This reform is basic to restoring undistorted economic incentives for output and capital formation.

Specific Comments

1. Different decoupling schemes would have widely divergent financial impacts. These are not adequately explored in your memo. For example, Option No. 3 could more than meet the entire long range deficit and even allow payroll taxes to decline slowly in the future. This is the option which keeps the purchasing power of initial benefits constant for successive retiring generations, instead of increasing it to keep pace with earnings.

   It is an option which restores inter-generational equity to some degree, and should be studied seriously. . . .

3. Your short term financing alternatives do not include options to reduce benefits in the short term. Some of the options in section C should be considered in the context of reducing the short range deficit.

4. If taxes must be raised, the tax rate, and not the wage base, should be adjusted. An increase in the wage base would raise not only current receipts, but also future benefits, and actually worsen the long range financing problem. . . .

Source: Copy in SSA History Archives, Mary Ross Papers, Box 34, Binder: "Decoupling Memoranda."

Document 6.9
Draft HEW Memo to the President, December 1975

There was some significant internal dissension within the Ford administration over the issue of decoupling. While Secretary Simon was moving the issue to the president for a decision, officials in the Social Security Administration and the Department of Health, Education, and Welfare (HEW) were concerned that Treasury had larger agendas beyond simply fixing the problem in the Social Security benefit formula. As the Treasury package was moving through the bureaucracy, a draft memorandum from HEW secretary David Mathews to President Ford was prepared, attempting to block the broader use of the decoupling issue. The HEW position was that this was a narrow technical issue that ought to be addressed as a specific problem, without trying to use it as an opportunity for broader policy objectives. (It is unclear whether the draft memo was sent to the president, but it does reflect the views of the SSA and HEW on this issue within the administration.)

The purpose of this memorandum is to comment on two important social security issues that need to be decided as a part of your 1976/77 budget and legislative program: what to do about the short-term deficit and about "decoupling."

Both of these issues are the subject of a comprehensive memorandum that has either been sent to you or is on its way to you from the Director of the Domestic Council. HEW and others at interest have had a full and fair opportunity to participate in the preparation of this memorandum. However, as the Cabinet officer responsible for managing the social security program and as a principal Administration spokesman about the program, I thought it important to express my separate views about these two issues, as follows:

Short-Term Financing

The memorandum lays out several options for dealing with the short-term financing problem. Without debating the merits of any of them, it seems to me that given the overall budget strategy that you have already adopted, the only consistent choice would be to assume that the short-term deficit will be met through the budgetary device constraining social security benefit payments during the 1976–77 fiscal years. The 60 percent cap, plus other constraints that are being included in the budget, would be sufficient to keep trust fund reserves at an adequate level through at least 1981. We should emphasize, of course, that these devices will not avoid the long-term deficit that is clearly facing the system.

"Decoupling"

I would start out by saying that I am a strong believer in decoupling the system as soon as possible. I would like to see the Administration take the initiative on decoupling as a part of its 1976 legislative program. It is my belief that if we do not do so, the Congress will and, in the process, label us as being either indecisive about or unconcerned with this obvious fault in the system.

I would recommend that you go forward with a social security legislative strategy that incorporates the budgetary policy discussed above with decoupling in the name of "fiscal responsibility."

We would be saying, "We are not going to make the same mistake with this pension system that New York made with its system. The present coupled system results in unpredictable future costs and requires unnecessarily high taxes. We are taking steps to correct it now rather than later."

I am aware that Secretary Simon (and perhaps others within the Administration) would prefer to use decoupling as a device for fundamental change in the overall social security system—change that goes well beyond decoupling per se. The options contained in the Domestic Council memorandum that call for declining future social security "replacement rates" are, in my opinion, options that represent fundamental change. They would employ decoupling as a vehicle for reducing the role of social security relative to the private pension system in providing retirement income.

Because these options have the practical effect of reducing the scope and coverage of social security—reducing benefit levels relative to preretirement earnings—they are certain to be controversial and are certain to attract a great deal of opposition from the labor movement and others interested in promoting the cause of social security.

While I cannot argue against examination of the system in terms of its impact on capital formation, the private pension system and tax and income maintenance policy, I do argue that we lack the time to make such an examination in sufficient depth and be able to present a well-rounded proposal to the next session of Congress—something that I think we would be well-advised to do. As I have already indicated, if we are not on the side of early action, just about everybody else will be, and we will appear to be less than concerned about the system's financial stability.

In short, I recommend that the Administration adopt a decoupling plan that is as neutral as possible on the matter of future fundamental changes in the system and that the plan be included in the Administration's 1976 legislative program.

Source: Copy in SSA History Archives, Mary Ross Papers, Box 34, Binder : "Decoupling Memoranda."

Document 6.10
James Cannon's Memo to President Ford, December 17, 1975

At this stage in the process, the issue has finally percolated up to the president for a decision. The following document is a memo to the president that spells out the main policy options seen at the time. After a discussion of the policy and political implications of the issue, the memo continued for fifteen pages, listing nine different policy options. But at this point in 1975 President Ford declined to adopt any of the suggested approaches to decoupling. At the end of the memo there is a handwritten notation: "Pres made no choice here."

Purpose

The purpose of this memorandum is to present for your decision options for dealing with the serious short and long term financing problems facing the Social Security System. The timing of any legislative proposal is clearly a key element in your decision. Therefore, options must be examined in terms of the impact on the trust fund, the budget, and broad policy considerations. . . .

Problems

The OASDI trust funds are underfinanced in the short and long-term. Benefit outlays are expected to exceed payroll tax receipts in 1975 and every year thereafter. If no changes are made in current law, the projected deficit over the next 25 years (1975–1999) will average 1.3% (.65% each for employees and employers) of taxable earnings. In the following 25-year period (2000–2024) the deficit will rise to 4.1% (2.05% each for employees and employers) of taxable earnings.

Unless some action is taken, OASDI trust funds will fall from the current 66% of yearly outgo to 43% in 1977, 33% in 1978, 11% in 1981, 3% in 1982, and the trust funds will be exhausted by 1983.

The projected rapid decline in trust fund assets over the next few years can be attributed to:

- Increased benefits resulting from wage growth and inflation.
- Legislation since the late 1960's which raised benefits.
- Absence of equivalent increases in payroll tax revenues. (In fact, payroll tax receipts have lagged due to high rates of unemployment and slowed wage growth).

The projected long-term deficit beyond 2000 can be attributed to:

- Population trends which include a substantially increasing ratio of retired persons to the working population after the beginning of the 21st Century.

- A flaw in the current system which *over adjusts* the benefits of *future* retirees to inflation. The current formula which determines future benefits for workers increases the weighting of earnings by the rate of inflation. Since wages normally grow with inflation, the result is an overcompensation—commonly referred to as a "coupled" system. There is a general consensus in the Congress and among outside experts that the inflation adjustment in the formula should be eliminated, thus "decoupling" the system. Such a change would not affect the automatic CPI increases in benefits *after* retirement. It should be emphasized here that "decoupling" will have virtually *no* effect on the short-term deficit.

Political Context

A review of the political environment surrounding the Social Security System is useful as we sort out these very important issues. Social Security decisions have traditionally followed a pattern which has insulated the system from sudden and far reaching changes. Structural modifications take place usually after extensive public debate including exhaustive studies and visible commissions. Protection of the system is fostered by one of the strongest and largest constituencies in the public policy arena, including the elderly, organized labor and all of the wage earners who are contributing to the system and expect to benefit from it in the future.

Members of Congress and especially of the Finance and Ways and Means Committees have institutionalized this process of incremental reform. The Committees have jointly established an advisory group (the Hsiao Panel) to examine the long-term financing— "decoupling" problem and to recommend policy changes to the Committees in the spring of 1976.

Although some hearings have been held on the short-term financing problem, no proposals have come out of the Committees. Secretary Weinberger testified before Ways and Means last May and took the position that the Administration would be pleased to cooperate in developing a proposal to alleviate the short-term deficit. You decided then not to propose any tax or wage base increase noting that the Congress had failed to act on the 5% cap on benefit increases proposed in the FY 1976 budget. The stand-off has continued since that time as the trust fund continues to decline.

Because of the financing problems, the public has begun to question the stability of Social Security. Although the subtleties and complexities are not widely understood, there exists general pressure to move toward stabilizing the trust fund with a minimum of change for those in the system.

Decisions

The discussion of alternatives for your decision are presented in three categories:

I. Options to deal with the short-term decline in trust fund assets.
II. "Decoupling" options which alleviate part or all of the long-term deficit.
III. Mechanism for analyzing the structure and role of Social Security.

Source: Copy in SSA History Archives, Mary Ross Papers, Box 34, Binder: "Decoupling Memoranda."

Document 6.11
President Ford's Special Message to Congress, February 9, 1976

Despite his hesitation in December 1975 to commit to a specific set of Social Security reforms, in February 1976 President Ford sent a special message to Congress outlining a set of policy proposals on Social Security financing, which included both limiting benefits to specific "replacement rates" and increasing the payroll tax by 0.6 percent. Fixing benefits to specific replacement rates would result in a benefit reduction for many future beneficiaries. This dual proposal was Ford's effort to address problems both in the short-term (with the tax hike) and the long-term (with the fixed replacement rates).

The change Ford proposed to deal with decoupling was to force the computation formula to yield certain results, which, on average, would produce a benefit that was a fixed percentage of the retiree's pre-retirement income. Ford's idea was to place limits in the computation formula such that the inflation adjustments could not exceed certain general limits. The Ford plan would have resulted in benefit replacement rates that were approximately the same as those in place in 1969, prior to the 1972 changes. On average, this would have meant a replacement rate of about 27 percent for high-wage workers, 41 percent for average-wage workers, and 55 percent for low-wage workers.

The Ford administration proposals were not enacted by Congress, leaving the decoupling problem for the next president, Jimmy Carter.

To the Congress of the United States:

. . . The single greatest threat to the quality of life of older Americans is inflation. Our first priority continues to be the fight against inflation. We have been able to reduce by nearly half the double digit inflation experienced in 1974. But the retired, living on fixed incomes, have been particularly hard hit and the progress we have made in reducing inflation has not benefited them enough. We will continue our efforts to reduce federal spending, balance the budget, and reduce taxes. The particular vulnerability of the aged to the burdens of inflation, however, requires that specific improvements be made in two major Federal programs, Social Security and Medicare.

We must begin by insuring that the Social Security system is beyond challenge. Maintaining the integrity of the system is a vital obligation each generation has to those who have worked hard and contributed to it all their lives. I strongly reaffirm my commitment to a stable and financially sound Social Security system. My 1977 budget and legislative program include several elements which I believe are essential to protect the solvency and integrity of the system.

First, to help protect our retired and disabled citizens against the hardships of inflation, my budget request to the Congress includes a full cost of living increase in Social Security benefits, to be effective with checks received in July 1976. This will help maintain the purchasing power of 32 million Americans.

Second, to insure the financial integrity of the Social Security trust funds, I am proposing legislation to increase payroll taxes by three-tenths of one percent each for employees and employers. This increase will cost no worker more than $1 a week, and most will pay less. These additional revenues are needed to stabilize the trust funds so that current income will be certain to either equal or exceed current outgo.

Third, to avoid serious future financing problems I will submit later this year a change in the Social Security laws to correct a serious flaw in the current system. The current formula which determines benefits for workers who retire in the future does not properly reflect wage and price fluctuations. This is an inadvertent error which could lead to unnecessarily inflated benefits.

The change I am proposing will not affect cost of living increases in benefits after retirement, and will in no way alter the benefit levels of current recipients. On the other hand, it will protect future generations against unnecessary costs and excessive tax increases.

I believe that the prompt enactment of all of these proposals is necessary to maintain a sound Social Security system and to preserve its financial integrity. . . .

Source: Public Papers of the Presidents of the United States: Gerald Ford, 1976–77, vol. 1 (Washington, D.C.: Government Printing Office, 1979), 235–239.

Document 6.12
President Carter's Message to Congress, May 9, 1977

This message to Congress just months after taking over the presidency marked the initial effort of the Carter administration to address the Social Security financing issues.

The Carter plan contained some departures from existing policy. The proposal to introduce partial general revenue financing was a return to the pre-1950 debates over this issue. The Carter administration also favored truncating the standard seventy-five-year period involved in assessing long-range solvency by advocating proposals that would only restore solvency to the "end of the century." Similarly, favoring a removal of the wage-base cap for employers but not for workers was also a drastic change from past practice. None of these more dramatic policy proposals survived congressional consideration, although the heart of the Carter administration proposals—their decoupling scheme—was adopted.

To the Congress of the United States:

The Social Security system affects the lives of more Americans than almost any other function of government. . . .

Today, the Board of Trustees of the Social Security Trust Funds is submitting its 1977 report to the Congress. The report tells us that the system critically needs financial support in the short term. The high unemployment of recent years has curtailed Social Security's revenues, while benefits have risen with inflation. Since 1975 expenditures have exceeded income; and existing reserves will soon be exhausted.

Unless we act now, the Disability Insurance Trust (DI) Fund will be exhausted in 1979 and the Old Age and Survivors Insurance (OASI) Trust Fund will run out in 1983.

The Trustees' Report indicates that there are serious longer term problems as well. Under current law the Social Security system will have an estimated deficit of 8.2 percent of taxable payroll over the next seventy-five years. About half of this deficit is due to changes in the projected composition of our population over those years. Higher life expectancy and lower birthrates will make the nation older as a whole. About half is due to a technical flaw in the automatic cost of living formula adopted in 1972.

While campaigning for President, I stressed my commitment to restore the financial integrity of the Social Security system. I pledged I would do my best to avoid increases above those already scheduled in tax rates, which fall most heavily on moderate and lower-income workers. I also promised to correct the technical flaw in the system which exaggerates the adjustment for inflation, and to do so without reducing the relative value of retirement benefits as compared with pre-retirement earnings.

I am announcing today a set of proposals which meet those commitments and which solve both the short-term and long-term problems in the Social Security system through the end of the twentieth century. . . .

I will ask the Congress to take the following specific actions:

1. Compensate the Social Security trust funds from general revenues for a share of revenues lost during severe recessions. General revenues would be used in a counter-cyclical fashion to replace the payroll tax receipts lost as a result of that portion of unemployment in excess of six percent. General revenues would be used only in these carefully limited situations. Because this is an innovative measure, the legislation we submit will provide this feature only through 1982. The next Social Security Advisory Council will be asked to review this counter-cyclical mechanism to determine whether it should be made permanent.

2. Remove the wage-base ceiling for employers. Under present law employers and employees pay a tax only on the first $16,500 in wages. Under this proposal the employer ceiling would be raised over a three-year period, so that by 1981 the ceiling would be removed. This action will provide a significant source of revenue without increasing long-term benefit liabilities.

3. Increase the wage base subject to the employee tax by $600 in 1979, 1981, 1983, and 1985, beyond the automatic increases in current law. This will provide a progressive source of financing.

4. Shift revenues from the Hospital Insurance Trust Fund to the Old Age, Survivors, and Disability Trust Funds. In part, this shift will be made possible because of substantial savings to the Medicare system from the hospital cost containment legislation that I have proposed.

5. Increase the tax rate on the self-employed from 7 percent to 7.5 percent. This will restore the historical relationship between the OASI and the DI rates paid by the self-employed to one and one-half times that paid by employees.

6. Correct certain technical provisions of the Social Security Act which differentiate on the basis of sex. This will include a new eligibility test for dependent benefits. Recent Supreme Court decisions would result in unfinanced increases in the cost of the system and some inequities without this change.

These six steps, along with measures already contained in existing law, will eliminate the short-term financing problem and improve the overall equity of the Social Security system.

In order to guarantee the financial integrity of the system into the next century, two additional steps must be taken. I will be asking the Congress to:

1. Modify the Social Security benefit formula to eliminate the inflation over-adjustment now in law. This modification, known as "decoupling," should be done in a way that maintains the current ratio of retirement benefits to pre-retirement wages.

2. Adjust the timing of a tax rate increase already contained in current law. The one percent tax rate increase presently scheduled for the year 2011 would be moved forward so that .25 percent would occur in 1985 and the remainder in 1990.

Taken together, the actions I am recommending today will eliminate the Social Security deficit for the remainder of this century. They will reduce the estimated 75-year deficit from the Trustee Report forecast of 8.2 percent of payroll to a manageable 1.9 percent.

Prompt enactment of the measure I have recommended will provide the Social Security system with financial stability. This is an overriding immediate objective. . . .

I call upon the Congress to act favorably on these major reform initiatives.

Source: Public Papers of the Presidents of the United States: Jimmy Carter, 1977, vol. 1 (Washington, D.C.: Government Printing Office, 1977), 836–838.

Document 6.13
Secretary Califano's Memo on Proposed Legislation, July 11, 1977

The Carter administration legislative proposal for Social Security had three parts: (1) a fix for the short-term financing problem, (2) proposals for the long-term (decoupling), and (3) a set of changes to make the program gender-neutral. The decoupling proposal—by far the largest piece in terms of revenue impacts—was identical to the Ford administration's proposal.

The administration presented its draft bill as three separable pieces of legislation, with individual titles. This may have made it easier for Congress to drop whole sections of the draft bill (which was the ultimate the fate of the gender-neutrality proposals).

This memorandum—from HEW secretary Joseph Califano Jr. to Walter Mondale, in his capacity as the president of the Senate—was the cover letter sent with the administration's draft bill.

Dear Mr. President:

Enclosed for the consideration of the Congress is a draft bill, "To amend the Social Security Act and the Internal Revenue Code of 1954 to strengthen the financing of the social security system, to reduce the effect of wage and price fluctuation on the system's benefit structure, and to eliminate gender-based distinctions from the social security provisions of the Act." The bill would be cited as the Social Security Financing, Benefit indexing, and Equal Rights Amendments of 1977.

The draft bill embodies the recommendations contained in the Message from the President to the Congress of May 9, 1977, transmitting proposals for restoring the financial integrity of the social security system.

Title I of the bill, to be cited as the Social Security Financing Amendments of 1977, would prevent the predicted default of the trust funds by increasing the level at which the system is currently financed.

Title II of the bill, to be cited as the Social Security Benefit Indexing Amendments of 1977, is designed to protect the system's integrity over the next 75 years by stabilizing the rates at which social security benefits replace income lost at retirement.

Title III of the bill, to be cited as the Social Security Equal Rights Amendments of 1977, would eliminate gender-based distinctions from title II of the Social Security Act. . . .

We urge the Congress to give the draft bill its prompt and favorable consideration. We are advised by the Office of Management and Budget that its enactment would be in accord with the program of the President.

Sincerely,

Joseph A. Califano, Jr.

Source: Copy of memo in the SSA History Archives, Mary Ross Papers, Box MR 13.

Document 6.14
Senate Hearing Report on the Social Security Financing Proposals, June–July, 1977

The Subcommittee on Social Security in the Senate held five days of hearings during the June 13 through July 15 period on the administration's Social Security financing prosals. HEW secretary Joseph Califano and James Bruce Cardwell, Social Security commissioner, testified before the subcommittee.

Senator NELSON [D-Wis.]: . . . Dealing with these deficits is no easy task. Ultimately it means reducing current benefits, increasing taxes, or combining these two approaches. But no matter what financing mechanism is used to compensate for the social security deficits, any proposal or set of proposals which impose new taxes or decrease benefits will inevitably be extremely controversial.

Nevertheless, the social security trust funds cannot be allowed to go bankrupt. At stake is the stability of one of this country's most important and enduring institutions. The economic and social well being of the American people hangs in the balance. . . .

Of the various proposals made by the Carter administration, two of them are of particular significance: using general revenues to help finance the social security trust funds during periods of excessive unemployment and removing the ceiling on the amount of an individual's wage or salary on which the employer pays social security taxes. These two proposals, more so than any of the others, would establish landmarks in the social security law if adopted by Congress.

Until this time, general revenues have not generally been used to finance the social security cash benefits programs, nor the hospital insurance program. And the wage base upon which employers pay social security payroll taxes thus far has been equal to the wage base upon which workers contribute their share of the payroll tax. The administration's financing proposals would modify the traditional method of financing the social security benefits programs. . . .

One thing is very certain. Before any new taxes are imposed to pay for fiscal shortfalls or to maintain current benefits, it is vitally important for Congress and this subcommittee to consider every viable option and to ascertain the economic and social benefits and costs of these new financing mechanisms. . . .

Senator LAXALT [R-Nev.]: . . . In virtually every advanced industrial country mounting social security deficits are posing profound social, political, and economic problems.

Although the United States was one of the last industrial countries to establish a social insurance structure, I would like to see our country become the first in the world to solve its financing problems. Hopefully, these hearings will assist us in formulating financing solutions which will not only restore our own system to a firmer footing but also provide a model for other countries facing similar difficulties. . . .

. . . [T]he Carter package is likely to constitute a bench mark, or perhaps more accurately, a lightning rod during these proceedings and I would like to venture several observations of my own at this time.

(1) Decoupling is essential. There are few things in social security on which there is anything approaching universal agreement. One of these is the over indexing technical error made by the 1972 Social Security Act Amendments. . . .

Certainly our retirees need to be protected from the ravages of inflation and the intent of the 1972 amendments was to do precisely that. However, we must separate the indexation of the benefit schedule from the positive [sic] at which future retirees will enter that schedule. . . .

(2) General revenue financing is wrong. The social security trust funds are just moving into deficit. The Treasury has been there for a long time. Although my good friend, Congressman Bill Archer, described the proposal for general revenue financing in the Ways and Means Committee as the blind leading the blind, I think general revenue financing for social security is more a case of adding fuel to the fire—the fire of ever greater Federal deficits.

Also, although social security is not in a strictly technical sense an insurance program, social security recipients and their employers have contributed substantial sums toward their retirement. They are entitled to the benefits they receive irrespective of their overall financial condition. To use general revenue funding is to ignore this contribution aspect. With taxpayers' moneys being expended, it is logical to assume that they should be allocated on the basis of need. Once this happens, social security becomes indistinguishable from AFDC or any other welfare program. Personally, I cannot accept any diminution of the earned right principle.

(3) The wage base for employers should not be removed. We need to encourage the creation of high wage, productive jobs rather than discourage it. And the last thing we need is to stimulate another round of inflation. Yet, the proposal to remove the wage base on employers succeeds in both discouraging job creation and sparking inflation. The Secretary may really believe that employers will absorb the additional $30 billion out of profits and furthermore that businesses will not be deterred from creating high wage jobs by the additional costs involved. But I don't. I see the removal of the employers' wage base as costly for consumers and workers alike.

(4) The reserve level should not be lowered. The present 50 percent level is already inadequate to assuage public concern about the financial integrity of the system. Although the administration argues that with the Treasury backing inherent in general revenue financing, the reserve level can safely be reduced to 33 percent, I see this as merely adding to the public perception of social security as a financial house of cards. I am even more concerned that in the event general revenue financing is denied, the administration will still seek to reduce the reserve level.

. . . Quite obviously I am unhappy with a good portion of the Carter package. I certainly commend the President for confronting a difficult problem. But I believe we need to do better. Perhaps Chairman Ullman is right and we need a whole new approach to social security. . . .

Secretary CALIFANO: . . . It is our proposal, essentially, to let the active duty workers' future benefits reflect wage increases due to inflation and productivity but not adjust again for inflation. If we do not change this, we will have workers in this country who will be receiving more than 100 percent of their active duty pay.

We have benefit levels that are reasonably high now. The proposal, I should note, would also keep benefits at about the relative levels they are today, a commitment the President made during the Presidential campaign.

Senator NELSON: May I ask a question? As I recall from your testimony, that was one of the two major causes of the deficit.

Secretary CALIFANO: That is correct, Mr. Chairman. Almost half the deficit in the long term.

Senator NELSON: I am interested in a little bit of history so that we might avoid this kind of thing in the future.

Where did this proposal, this consequence come from? The Social Security Advisory Council, the Congress, or where?

Secretary CALIFANO: It was a proposal that many people in Congress suggested, a proposal also recommended by the Nixon administration. The manner in which it was done, I honestly believe, from everyone whom I have talked to, was inadvertent. People did not fully appreciate what would happen.

Senator NELSON: I suspect that is so, since nobody seemed to know it at the time of its passage into law.

My question is, what were the methodologies, the procedures, for getting this result? We ought to know so we can avoid such a blunder in the future.

Secretary CALIFANO: I think the recommendation was made by the Nixon administration. Congress enacted it. I do not know exactly—I do not know if there is anyone to blame for the mistake here. . . .

Mr. CARDWELL: Mr. Chairman, the previous Advisory Council recommended that the system be indexed and that is what this formula was intended to do when it was adopted in 1972.

They did not prescribe the formula. This particular approach to indexing tends . . . to follow the traditional behavior of the Congress in the way in which they authorized benefit increases for social security.

They would tend to authorize the higher benefit rate for both current workers and current retirees. That is what the present formula does.

Senator CURTIS: It has always done that, has it not?

Mr. CARDWELL: Yes, sir. . . .

Senator NELSON: . . . I cannot understand how, even with the old math, some 8th grade graduate could not have made a computation to tell us we would get this disastrous result. What bothers me, in dealing with this matter of tremendous consequence, is that everybody in the United States, the executive branch, the Congress, the Social Security administration, all the actuaries could have let this blunder happen. . . .

Senator LONG [D-La.]: . . . When you talk about financing social security out of general revenues. I think that is very misleading. We do not have any general revenues to finance it with.

The income tax is not paying for the full cost of general government. The Federal Government is running a $60 billion deficit. The only way you are going to find the general revenues is just by stepping up the printing press and running off a lot of printing press dollars to pay for social security, which is the way the deficit in the Federal fund is being covered now. . . .

That is the burden on us: to find people to vote for the taxes to pay for benefits that they want to fund. . . .

If we offer them the easy way out, to say if we will just finance this thing by running off more printing press money, that is how I read this general fund. There is no general fund except that printing press down at Federal Reserve. How are we going to fund this thing and find the folks to pay for all of this without funding first the general fund, the so-called Federal fund, then the trust funds, out of printing press money? . . .

Secretary CALIFANO: . . . There is no need for you and your colleagues to pass any law raising an additional $14 billion in taxes over a 5-year period. . . . This is, in effect, an insurance policy.

We would hope that the time would never come when we would be in the kind of recessionary situation where you would have to have that money. If the situation were that bad, if the economy of this country were so bad that we had to dip into the general funds in order to pay these benefits, it would make probably a lot of sense to have those benefits paid and to have a deficit like that. It is not that much money. That is the best I can answer. . . .

Senator LONG: Over the past years, Mr. Secretary, I have had to fight on the floor against amendments to provide benefits that would be paid out of the deficit. I dislike the idea of getting this on the basis of where Senators and Members of the House can come up with these politically appealing proposed benefits, and take the view that they can be financed without any tax.

The last big increase was financed by changing the assumptions on which the program was based. We cannot do that anymore, can we? *[Authors' note: Here Senator Long is referring to the "windfalls" made possible by static actuarial assumptions prior to the introduction of the automatic adjustments introduced in the 1972 Act.]*

Financing it just by changing it will not work. We are going to have to find money somewhere for it.

Secretary CALIFANO: That is right . . . We feel that we have found enough money here. As you know, we are asking for a decoupling plan of stabilizing the benefit rate level. We are asking for an additional $30 billion in taxes on employers. We are increasing the wage base on employees by $600 in 1979, $600 in 1981 which will effectively increase the amount of money that will pay for this system. . . .

Senator HATHAWAY [D-Maine]: With regard to the decoupling program, actually it saves 12 percent, but you get 8 percent put in by increasing benefits by the results of the decoupling. Is that correct? . . .

Mr. CARDWELL: It would reduce the long term 75-year deficit that is estimated at 8.2 percent of payroll. It would reduce that by half, so the deficit would be about 4 percent. . . .

[The following was subsequently supplied for the record:]

. . . [T]he device of showing a saving from decoupling of 12 percent of payroll and then a 7.9 percent cost for maintaining current replacement rates for future retirees tends to be confusing, since, as is recognized elsewhere in the Committee print, "simple decoupling" without some mechanism for adjusting initial benefits which produces the 12 percent saving is not a viable option, because of the resulting very sharp decline in initial benefits. Since viable decoupling options also address the question of future benefits of current workers, the cost of such provisions is generally included in calculating the net saving from decoupling proposals. Thus it is generally said that the Administration plan results in reducing costs by 4.1 percent of payroll, rather than by 12 percent with a cost increase of 7.9 percent.

Senator HATHAWAY: My point is, part of that 4 percent savings is a net figure. Your proposal increases benefits by 8 percent. If instead we increase the retirees' benefits by 4 percent, then with decoupling you would take care of the long term deficit because you would be serving a net of 8 percent. . . .

Secretary CALIFANO. What you have to do, is to reduce benefits below the rates they are at presently. If you do that, you will save even more money by decoupling, if you decouple in that way. We propose to leave benefit levels where they are. We think it is about right, the present benefit rate. . . .

Source: Social Security Financing Proposals, Hearings before the Subcommittee on Social Security of the Committee on Finance, 95th Congress, 1st sess. (Washington, D.C.: Government Printing Office, 1977), 3–36.

Document 6.15
House Committee Report on the Social Security Financing Amendments of 1977, October 12, 1977

The House Ways and Means Committee report on the proposed 1977 amendments contained a discussion of the decoupling issue and the changes in law the House bill was proposing to address this problem. The solution described here is essentially the one that was enacted into law in the 1977 amendments.

Notice at the end of the excerpt the brief mention of the issue of transition rules, which expressed the committee's concern that the new financing policies be gradually phased in over a number of years. These transition rules would inadvertently create a new policy problem that would come to be known as the "notch."

B. Revised Benefit Structure

A major factor contributing to the long-range deficit is the projected rise in social security benefit replacement rates. . . . Current projections show that benefit levels will rise by about 50 percent more than wages over the next 75 years, with most of this increase occurring after the 1990's. Replacement rates can fluctuate widely in the future, either up or down, depending on future changes in wages and prices. When the automatic provisions were enacted in 1972, it was expected, on the basis of the economic assumptions made then, that future replacement rates would remain fairly constant. . . .

Under your committee's bill, the benefit structure would be "decoupled," that is, current workers' future benefits would be separated from those of beneficiaries currently on the rolls; the automatic cost-of-living increases would apply only to beneficiaries on the rolls when such benefit increases becomes effective. The decoupling proposal provides a new benefit formula for future beneficiaries that would produce replacement rates and costs that are much more predictable than under present law. The benefit amounts payable to workers who retire in the future would generally reflect the increase in the standard of living that occurs during their working years.

A major feature of the plan is that the worker's earnings would be indexed to reflect the change in general wage levels that has occurred during his working lifetime. These indexed earnings would be averaged and a three-step, weighted benefit formula would be applied to his average indexed monthly earnings (AIME) to produce the worker's benefit amount. [*Note:* The formula for 1979 follows: 90 percent of the first $180 of AIME, plus 32 percent of AIME over $180 through AIME of $1,085, plus 15 percent of AIME above $1,085.]

For those becoming entitled to benefits in the future, the benefit factors (percentage amounts) would not be indexed, but the bend points (dollar amounts) in the formula would be adjusted automatically as average wages increase.

By providing for the indexing of earnings and the benefit formula to the increase in general wage levels, benefits would be based on the worker's relative earnings position averaged over his working lifetime. As a result, all workers with the same relative earnings positions would be treated the same regardless of when they become entitled to benefits. Thus, while the dollar amounts of benefits of, say, workers with average earnings retiring 20 or 30 years apart would be substantially different, their replacement rates would be virtually the same.

In addition, your committee recommends that replacement rates be stabilized at a level 5 percent lower than the levels that will prevail in January 1979, when the revised benefit structure will be implemented. This recommendation would result in replacement rates more nearly in line with those that could have been anticipated under the 1972 legislation than those that have in fact occurred. Your committee believes that the gradual increase in replacement rates (and costs) that has occurred was unintended and that replacement rates that existed in recent years should be reestablished and maintained at relatively constant levels in the long-range future.

Your committee's bill would assure that social security benefit protection will generally keep pace with rising wages during the worker's lifetime and with the cost of living after the worker and his family start to receive benefits. This was the underlying premise of the 1972 automatic adjustment provisions and, in fact, the way the system generally operated before the automatic provisions were enacted. . . .

The plan included in your committee's bill necessarily involves many substantial changes in provisions of present law, transitional provisions for the period during which the new system is implemented, and a number of "conforming" amendments to minimize possible disruptions that such a basic change in the benefit structure might otherwise produce. . . .

A worker's earnings would be indexed by multiplying the actual earnings by the ratio of average wages. . . . For example, if a worker earned $3,000 in 1956, and retired at age 62 in 1979, the $3,000 would be multiplied by the ratio of average annual wages in 1977 ($10,002) to average annual wages in 1956 ($3,514), as follows:

$$\$3,000 \times \frac{\$10,002}{\$3,514} = \$8,539$$

Thus, while the worker's actual earnings for 1956 were $3,000, his relative or indexed earnings would be $8,539. The worker's earnings each year would be adjusted in this manner.

The result would be that the worker's benefits would be based on earnings levels that prevail just prior to age 62, and benefits would be based on the worker's relative earnings (that is, relative to average wages) averaged over the time the worker could reasonably be expected to have worked in covered employment. . . .

In addition, indexing wages as proposed by your committee assures that benefit amounts would generally be related to the standard of living that prevails when the worker retires, becomes disabled, or dies; that is, workers would share in the general rise in the standard of living that occurs during their working lifetimes. . . .

Your committee's bill would provide a transitional provision to protect the benefit rights of people who are now approaching retirement and whose retirement plans have taken social security benefits into account.

Under your committee's bill, the transitional provision would "guarantee" that a worker (and his dependents or survivors) who first becomes eligible for retirement benefits within 10 years after the effective date would get an initial benefit that would be the higher of:

1. The benefit derived under the new, wage-indexing formula;

or

2. The benefit based on the present law benefit as it is in the law on the effective date of the revised system. . . .

Source: Social Security Financing Amendments of 1977, House Report no. 702, to Accompany H.R. 9346 (Washington, D.C.: U.S. Government Printing Office, 1977), 22–28.

Document 6.16
President Carter's Remarks on Signing the 1977 Amendments, December 20, 1977

The signing ceremony for the 1977 amendments took place in the ornate Indian Treaty Room of the Old Executive Office Building. President Carter released a written statement and made some oral remarks.

[President's Written Statement]

Before I became President, the concern expressed to me most often was the fear that the social security system was in danger of bankruptcy. This fear was backed up by facts:

- A flaw had been introduced into the benefit formula which overcompensated for inflation and threw the system out of actuarial balance.
- Declines in birth rates meant that there would be fewer workers to support the system in the future—down from over 100 to 1 when the system started, to 14 to 1 in 1950, to 3 to 1 today, and to 2 to 1 in the next century.
- The worst recession since the Great Depression and the worst inflation since the Civil War had depleted the reserves in the trust funds to the point that the Disability Trust Fund would be depleted by 1979 and the Old Age and Survivors Trust Fund would run out by 1983.

President Jimmy Carter signs the 1977 Social Security Amendments in a ceremony in the Indian Treaty Room of the Old Executive Office Building.
Source: SSA History Archives.

- A majority of Americans did not believe that their social security benefits would be there when they needed them.

I am happy to be here today to sign legislation which will reassure the 33 million people who are receiving benefits and the 104 million workers now making contributions that the social security system will be financially sound well into the next century.

I congratulate the Members of Congress for the courage and leadership they have shown in enacting this bill this year. The public overwhelmingly supports the purposes of the social security system, and a clear majority feel that the Congress is showing real courage in raising additional taxes to save the system. . . .

Although the final bill differs in some respects from the proposals I submitted last May, it does fulfill all of the campaign promises I made on social security:

- Eliminates the yearly deficits of the social security system and restores the trust funds reserves to healthy levels.
- The delayed retirement credit is increased to reward those who choose to work beyond age 65 before claiming benefits.
- Corrects the flaw in the benefit formula and protects the purchasing power of present and future beneficiaries.
- Raises additional money primarily through increases in the taxable wage base making the system more progressive and minimizing the added burden for low and moderate income workers.
- Eases the earnings test, permitting recipients to earn as much as $6,000 without losing any benefits and those over 70 to continue with full benefits no matter how much they might earn.
- Several provisions are of great importance to women: It removes from the Social Security Act references to the sex of applicants, permits older persons to remarry with out the fear of losing some of their social security benefits, and it makes homemakers who are divorced after 10 years of marriage eligible for benefits.

• Most importantly, it ensures our senior citizens today that their social security benefits will be protected during their retirement and further assures today's workers that the hard-earned taxes they are paying into the system today will be available upon their retirement.

Taken together, these are tremendous achievements and represent the most important social security legislation since the program was established. . . .

This bill was enacted this year in a spirit of compromise. The taxes are higher than those I proposed, but I believe that much of the increase can be offset by my income tax reduction proposals next month and additional reform in the social security system. I am happy that the Congress accepted my advice and avoided costly benefit increases at this time. . . .

[President's Oral Remarks]

Since the social security system was evolved under the administration of Franklin Roosevelt, it's been a sacred pact between the employees and the employers with the framework established and guaranteed by the Government to be sure that the working people of this Nation had some guarantee of security after they reached the age of retirement or after they were disabled and unable to earn their own livelihood.

In recent years, because of the highest unemployment rate since the Great Depression and the greatest inflation rate since the Civil War, the integrity of the social security system has been in doubt. This was an unanticipated drain on the resources of the reserve funds.

When I campaigned throughout the country for 2 years, one of the most frequent questions asked me by working family members and also by those who had already retired was what can be done to assure us that the integrity of the social security system will be maintained. It's a very difficult issue.

It is never easy for a politically elected person to raise taxes. But the Congress has shown sound judgment and political courage in restoring the social security system to a sound basis.

This legislation is wise. It's been evolved after very careful and long preparation. It focuses the increased tax burdens, which were absolutely mandatory, in a way that is of least burden to the families of this Nation who are most in need of a sound income.

The level of payments were raised for those who are wealthier in our country where they can most easily afford increased payments. In the past they've avoided the rate being applied to their much higher income than the average working family.

At the same time, the Congress has removed the unnecessarily stringent limits on how much a retired person can earn and still draw [from] the social security system for which that person has paid during his or her working years. The limit will now be increased to $6,000 per year income over 2 or 3 years without losing social security benefits.

This legislation also moves to eliminate discrimination because of sex. It removes references to the sex of the recipient.

The most important thing, of course, is that without this legislation, the social security reserve funds would have begun to be bankrupt in just a year or two, by 1979. Now this legislation will guarantee that from 1980 to the year 2030, the social security funds will be sound. . . .

Source: Public Papers of the Presidents of the United States: Jimmy Carter, 1977, vol. II (Washington, D.C.: Government Printing Office, 1978), 2153–2157.

Document 6.17
Key Provisions of the 1977 Amendments, December 16, 1977
This excerpt from an internal legislative report produced by the Social Security Administration was used as an informational training document to explain the new 1977 amendments to SSA staff.

I. Social Security Cash Benefits Provisions

A. Decoupling

The "decoupling" provision of H.R. 9346 would assure that, in the future, social security benefits at the time a worker becomes disabled or reaches age 62 (and survivors benefits, at the time the worker dies) would fully reflect changes in wage levels over the person's working lifetime and would bear a relatively constant relationship to preretirement wages. . . . Under current economic projections, future replacement rates—benefits as a percentage of preretirement earnings—under present law are expected to rise substantially faster than average wages in the future.

In order to assure that future social security benefit levels would be stabilized in relation to future wage levels, the bill would provide for basic changes in the way average earnings and social security benefit amounts would be figured in the future. A major feature of the plan is that the worker's earnings (and the benefit formula) would be indexed to reflect the change in wage levels that has occurred during his working lifetime. As a result, benefits would be based on the worker's relative earnings position over his working lifetime. After a worker becomes eligible for benefits, as under present law, the benefits would be kept up to date with increases in prices. These changes would reduce the long-range financial deficit by more than half. . . .

2. Computation Period
Under the bill, as under present law, benefits would be based on a worker's earnings averaged over the number of years after 1950 (or age 21, if later) up to the year he reaches age 62, becomes disabled, or dies, whichever occurs first (excluding 5 years of lowest indexed earnings or no earnings). The computation period would expand from 23 years for those reaching age 62 in 1979, up to 35 years for those reaching age 62 in 1991 or later. . . .

3. Benefit Formula and Maximum Family Benefit Formula
The bill would establish a benefit formula for relating the worker's indexed earnings to a primary insurance amount (PIA). The benefit formula would reproduce roughly the same relative weighting as the present-law formula but would result in benefit levels that are approximately 5 percent lower than the present-law level when the new system becomes effective (January 1979). (Of course, transitional provisions, as discussed below, would protect those then reaching age 62.) The benefit formula would be adjusted automatically in the future as earnings levels rise to maintain the relative weighting in the formula. . . .

4. Transition
In order to provide a degree of protection for workers nearing retirement when decoupling is implemented a worker who reaches age 62 after 1978 and before 1984 would be

guaranteed a retirement benefit no lower than he would have received under present law as of January 1979. . . . *[Authors' note: This transition provision created the phenomenon of the "notch."]*

6. Three Percent Delayed-Retirement Credit
A closely related provision, to strengthen work incentives under the decoupled system, would increase the delayed retirement credit. For workers reaching age 62 after 1978, the delayed retirement credit, now 1-percent per year . . . for months from age 65 up to age 72 for which benefits are not paid would be increased to 3-percent per year. . . .

C. Retirement Test

1. Raise Annual Exempt Amount
The annual exempt amount ($3,000 in 1977) would be increased for beneficiaries age 65 and over to $4,000 in 1978, $4,500 in 1979, $5,000 in 1980, $5,500 in 1981, and to $6,000 in 1982. After 1982, the $6,000 level would be increased automatically as wage levels rise. . . .

The age at which the retirement test no longer applies would be lowered from 72 to 70. . . .

F. Other Cash Benefit Provisions

1. Reduced Benefits for Spouses Receiving Government Pensions
Social security benefits payable to spouses . . . would be reduced by the amount of any governmental (Federal, State, or local) retirement benefit payable to the spouse based on his or her own earnings, in noncovered employment. . . . *[Authors' note: This provision, known as the Government Pension Offset, decreed that some government employees cannot reap the full benefits of their Social Security contributions—a source of continuing discontent among government workers.]*

4. Duration-of-Marriage Requirement
The duration-of-marriage requirement for entitlement to benefits as an older divorced wife or surviving divorced wife would be decreased from 20 years to 10 years. . . .

5. Remarriage of Widows and Widowers
Remarriage of a surviving spouse after age 60 would not reduce the amount of widows or widowers benefits. . . .

II. Financing

H.R. 9346 would substantially reduce the projected 1978 and 1979 annual deficits in the cash benefit program and provide for excesses of income over expenditures starting in 1980. During the remainder of this century, the trust funds would grow relative to annual expenditures, and the program would be soundly financed until well into the next century. Over the long range, the bill would reduce the long-range deficit of more than 8 percent of taxable payroll to less than 1.5 percent of taxable payroll. All of this remaining long-range deficit would occur in the next century. . . . *[Authors' note: This reveals that the long-range deficit in Social Security financing was not fully closed by the 1977 legislation—necessitating future financing legislation.]*

III. Councils, Comissions, and Studies

[Sections A and B omitted.]

C. Study of Proposals to Eliminate Dependency and Sex Discrimination under, the Social Security Program

The Secretary of Health, Education, and Welfare, in consultation with the Justice Department Task Force on Sex Discrimination, would be required to study and report on proposals to eliminate dependency as a factor in the determination of entitlement to spouse's benefits under the social security program, and proposals to bring about equal treatment of men and women under the program. . . . *[Authors' note: This was the compromise position on the elimination of gender distinctions in the law. The remaining gender distinctions would be eliminated in the 1983 legislation.]*

D. Study of Mandatory Coverage

The Secretary of Health, Education, and Welfare would be required to undertake a study and report on mandatory coverage of employees of Federal, State, and local governments and of nonprofit organizations. . . . *[Authors' note: Coverage of government employees under Social Security would be enacted in the 1983 amendments.]*

Source: "Social Security Amendments of 1977," Legislative Report no. 17, December 16, 1977, internal SSA report. Copy in SSA History Archives.

Document 6.18
Final Report of the Commission on the "Notch," December 31, 1994

With the decoupling of benefits in the 1977 amendments, Congress faced a classic policy dilemma: how to implement the decoupling in a manner that would be minimally adverse to those affected. To this end, Congress provided a five-year transition period during which new applicants could have their benefits figured under the new decoupled formula or under a special transition formula (but not under the old coupled formula). The transition period was 1979–1983, with the new formula applied to all new claims beginning in 1984. The transition period affected people who turned sixty-two during the transition years (i.e., were born in the years 1917–1921). But trouble soon appeared, as those retiring in the transition years felt they had fallen into a "notch" and were being treated unfairly compared to those outside the transition cohort.

Consider the real-life case of Edith and Audrey. These sisters started work on the same day in the same southern California factory, where they earned essentially identical wages for nearly thirty years. Upon retiring in 1982 Audrey, who was born in 1916 and was thus not in the notch, *received a monthly benefit of $624.40, while Edith, who was born in 1917 and was thus a "notch baby" received a monthly benefit of $512.60. In a sense you could say this was the intended result of the change in the law—Audrey's benefit was too generous and the 1977 amendments wanted to make sure that Edith did not receive a similar windfall. And yet, personalized in this way, it seemed unfair.*

Advice columnist Abigail Van Buren (who wrote the "Dear Abby" column in hundreds of newspapers) received several letters from "notch babies" among her readers. Moved by the apparent injustice of stories like that of Edith and Audrey, Abby wrote a series of columns in 1983 that brought the issue to the attention of millions of Americans and made it a higly visible political issue.

Proposals to change the law to compensate the notch babies became common. During the 98th Congress (1983–1984) at least twenty-seven bills were introduced to eliminate or ameliorate the notch. In 1992 Congress appointed an independent bipartisan commission to study the issue—with the expectation that the report of the commission would settle the matter. While the commission concluded that the law was functioning as intended and that no remedial legislation was merited, this hardly settled the matter politically as persons affected the notch (the so-called notch babies) have continued to protest what they see as an injustice.

Preface

Since the early 1980s, the federal government has been aware of the concerns of several million older Americans who believe they are being paid less than their fair share of Social Security benefits as a result of Congressional actions taken in the 1970s.

The "Notch" issue—so named because of a v-shaped dip in a graph representing these seniors' benefit levels—has been the focus of Congressional hearings, study panels, and oversight groups. Volumes of detailed analyses have been written about it, and more than 100 legislative bills addressing it have been introduced in both houses of Congress. Yet despite all the attention and interest, no action has been taken, and much of the proposed legislation involves significant costs.

Some national organizations representing older citizens (the National Committee to Preserve Social Security and Medicare, for instance) have strongly supported legislation to raise benefits for those born in the "Notch" years; other such groups (the American Association of Retired Persons, for example) have argued that those born in the "Notch" years received intended and appropriate benefits, and that no corrective legislation is needed.

In 1992, Congress established the bipartisan Commission on the Social Security "Notch" Issue, charging it with examining the question of whether those born in the "Notch" years had been treated unfairly and recommending, if necessary, remedial legislation and the means to pay for it.

At the outset of its work, the Commission arrived at two basic understandings. First, it realized that, despite the current size of its reserve fund, the Social Security system faces serious long-range fiscal issues. Second, it was keenly aware of the size of the Federal budget deficit. The Commission, therefore, approached its mandate with an explicit understanding that, if it were to recommend remedial action regarding the "Notch" issue, it would not recommend financing it through an invasion of the Social Security trust funds or any use of general revenues. The Commission concluded that it would have to recommend financing any changes with an increase in Social Security taxes or a reduction in some benefits—and it was fully prepared to do so if a remedy was justified. . . .

Executive Summary

For more than a decade, many older Americans born between 1917 and 1921 have been expressing concern that they have been denied the benefits they deserve as a result of changes Congress made to Social Security in the 1970s. As evidence, they point to the fact that, after taking inflation into account, their benefits are lower than those for persons born both before and after them. Indeed, when displayed on a vertical bar graph, those benefit levels form a kind of v-shaped "notch," dropping sharply from the left then rising again to the right. . . .

This so-called "Notch issue" has its origins in 1972, when Congress decided to create automatic cost-of-living adjustments to help Social Security benefits keep pace with inflation. Previously, each adjustment had to await legislation, causing beneficiaries' monthly payments to lag behind inflation.

Unfortunately, this new benefit adjustment method was flawed. To function properly, it required that the economy behave in much the same fashion that it had in the 1950s and 1960s, with annual wage increases outpacing prices, and inflation remaining relatively low.

A Revised Computation

That didn't happen. The rapid inflation and high unemployment of the 1970s generated sharp increases in benefits, and millions of seniors born after 1910 began receiving payments far in excess of what Congress had envisioned. Meanwhile, the sluggish economy failed to generate the tax dollars needed to fund those benefit payments, causing experts to express grave concerns about the fiscal stability of Social Security, since the rising benefit levels could not be sustained.

In an effort to end this problem, Congress revised the way that benefits were computed. In making its revisions, Congress decided that it was not proper to reduce benefits for persons already receiving them; it did, however, decide that benefits for all future retirees should be reduced. As a result, those born after January 1, 1917 would, by design, receive benefits that were, in many cases, far less generous.

In an attempt to ease the transition to the new, lower benefit levels, Congress designed a special "transitional computation method" for use by beneficiaries born between 1917 and 1921.

The "Notch" Issue Appears

Some born in the "Notch" years received benefits that were equal to or higher than those paid to beneficiaries born before them, while others received benefits that were higher than those generated by the new (1977) method. Typically, these people retired at 62, which is common under the Social Security program.

However, some of those in the "Notch" years—particularly those who continued to work well beyond age 62—received benefits that were significantly lower than they would have been if calculated under the old law. After comparing their benefit checks against the larger checks of their pre-"Notch" colleagues, neighbors, and friends with similar employment records, they began expressing their dissatisfaction to public officials—and the "Notch" issue was born.

"Notch" year beneficiaries' principal argument is that they have been singled out to receive lower benefits. But the Commission found no evidence to support that position; indeed, the purpose of the 1977 legislation was to reduce benefits for all future beneficiaries, and it has generally done that.

In fact, considering the value of their benefits relative to the Social Security taxes which they paid, those born in the "Notch" years are, in general, receiving a greater return from Social Security than will subsequent generations of beneficiaries. In addition, their "replacement rate"—the percentage of pre-retirement earnings replaced by benefit payments—is equal to that of retirees who follow them, which was also the intent of the 1977 amendments. In this sense they are "doing well" as beneficiaries of the system, although not as "well" as those who came before them, especially those who worked well beyond 62.

To the extent that disparities in benefit levels do exist, they exist not because those born in the "Notch" years received less than their due; they exist because those born before the "Notch" years (who were "grandfathered" under the old law's more generous computational method) continue to receive substantially inflated benefits. This disparity has created an understandable perception of unfairness.

The Commission's Work

In its work, the Commission has heard from hundreds of people who sincerely believe they are adversely affected by the "Notch" issue, and who understandably believe that they are entitled to legislative relief.

Regretfully for them, the facts suggest otherwise. The Commission's principal conclusion, therefore, is that the "Notch" is a necessary and appropriate result of the 1977 legislation which was designed to substantially reduce the growth of future benefit costs and to restore fiscal balance to Social Security, and no legislative remedy is in order. The Commission does not believe that benefit increases for people born after January 1, 1917 are appropriate, or that they can be justified. . . .

Source: Commission on the Social Security 'Notch' Issue, "Final Report on the Social Security 'Notch' Issue," December 31, 1994. Full report available on the Social Security Administration Web site: www.ssa.gov/history/notchfile1.html#executive (accessed November 11, 2006).

Document 6.19
Weinberger v. Wiesenfeld, March 19, 1975

Weinberger v. Wiesenfeld *was the first of five significant gender-bias cases decided by the Supreme Court in the 1970s. In the 1939 amendments women were granted widow's benefits on the earnings records of their deceased husbands. Men were not allowed to claim widower's benefits until a 1950 change in the law. When this benefit was provided to men, it was provided under restrictions not imposed on widows. In particular, if a widow had minor children in her care she could qualify for a benefit for herself and her children under a category known as "young mother's" benefits. There were no equivalent "young father's" benefits.*

In this case, Stephen Wiensenfeld had been denied benefits for himself on his deceased wife's earnings record, even though he was awarded benefits for their young son, on the grounds that there was no such benefit for men. Wiensenfeld argued that he was being discriminated against on the basis of his gender, and the appeals court agreed and ruled he should be granted benefits under the same requirements as women receiving young mother's benefits. The federal government appealed the decision, arguing for the continuance of the existing policy.

In a seeming flip of logic, the Supreme Court ruled that this gender distinction was indeed unconstitutional, but not on grounds that it discriminated against the men who were being denied a benefit; rather, it discriminated against the women on whose record the benefits were being claimed. Thus it was not Mr. Wiesenfeld, but his dead wife, who was the victim of gender bias here. Their reasoning was that the law precluded women from getting a benefit for their families (widower's benefit's for their surviving husbands) that males could receive for their families (widow's benefits for their surviving wives). Despite the unexpected logic, the result was the elimination of this particular form of gender discrimination—the first such gendered provision of the law to be struck down by the Court.

Weinberger v. Wiesenfeld, 420 U.S. 636

Mr. Justice BRENNAN delivered the opinion of the Court.

Social Security Act benefits based on the earnings of a deceased husband and father covered by the Act are payable, with some limitations, both to the widow and to the couple's minor children in her care. . . . Such benefits are payable on the basis of the earnings of a deceased wife and mother covered by the Act, however, only to the minor children and not to the widower. The question in this case is whether this gender-based distinction violates the Due Process Clause of the Fifth Amendment. . . .

Section 402 (g) was added to the Social Security Act in 1939 as one of a large number of amendments designed to "afford more adequate protection to the family as a unit.". . . Monthly benefits were provided to wives, children, widows, orphans, and surviving dependent parents of covered workers. However, children of covered female workers were eligible for survivors' benefits only in limited circumstances . . . and no benefits . . . whatever were made available to husbands or widowers on the basis of their wives' covered employment. . . .

Underlying the 1939 scheme was the principle that "[u]nder a social-insurance plan the primary purpose is to pay benefits in accordance with the probable needs of the beneficiaries rather than to make payments to the estate of a deceased person regardless of whether or not he leaves dependents.". . . It was felt that "[t]he payment of these survivorship benefits and supplements for the wife of an annuitant are . . . in keeping with the principle of social insurance. . . . "Thus, the framers of the Act legislated on the "then generally accepted presumption that a man is responsible for the support of his wife and children.". . .

Obviously, the notion that men are more likely than women to be the primary supporters of their spouses and children is not entirely without empirical support. . . . But such a gender-based generalization cannot suffice to justify the denigration of the efforts of women who do work and whose earnings contribute significantly to their families' support.

Section 402 (g) clearly operates . . . to deprive women of protection for their families which men receive as a result of their employment. Indeed, the classification here is in some ways more pernicious. . . . Here, Stephen Wiesenfeld was not given the opportunity to show, as may well have been the case, that he was dependent upon his wife for his support, or that, had his wife lived, she would have remained at work while he took over care of the child. Second, in this case social security taxes were deducted from Paula's salary during the years in which she worked. Thus, she not only failed to receive for her family the same protection which a similarly situated male worker would have received, but she also was deprived of a portion of her own earnings in order to contribute to the fund out of which benefits would be paid to others. Since the Constitution forbids the gender-based differentiation premised upon assumptions as to dependency . . . the Constitution also forbids the gender-based differentiation that results in the efforts of female workers required to pay social security taxes producing less protection for their families than is produced by the efforts of men. . . .

We held in *Flemming* that the interest of a covered employee in future social security benefits is "noncontractual," because "each worker's benefits, though flowing from the contributions he made to the national economy while actively employed, are not dependent on the degree to which he was called upon to support the system by taxation." Appellant apparently contends that since benefits derived from the social security program do not correlate necessarily with contributions made to the program, a covered employee has no right whatever to be treated equally with other employees as regards the benefits which flow from his or her employment.

We do not see how the fact that social security benefits are "noncontractual" can sanction differential protection for covered employees which is solely gender based. From the outset, social security old age, survivors', and disability (OASDI) benefits have been "afforded as a matter of right, related to past participation in the productive processes of the country.". . . It is true that social security benefits are not necessarily related directly to tax contributions, since the OASDI system is structured to provide benefits in part according to presumed need. For this reason, *Flemming* held that the position of a covered employee "cannot be soundly analogized to that of the holder of an annuity, whose right to benefits is bottomed on his contractual premium payments.". . . But the fact remains that the statutory right to benefits is directly related to years worked and amount earned by a covered employee and not to the need of the beneficiaries directly. Since OASDI benefits do depend significantly upon the participation in the work force of a covered employee, and since only covered employees and not others are required to pay taxes toward the system, benefits must be distributed according to classifications which do not without sufficient justification differentiate among covered employees solely on the basis of sex. . . .

Here, it is apparent both from the statutory scheme itself and from the legislative history . . . that Congress' purpose in providing benefits to young widows with children was not to provide an income to women who were, because of economic discrimination, unable to provide for themselves. Rather, 402 (g), linked as it is directly to responsibility for minor children, was intended to permit women to elect not to work and to devote themselves to the care of children. Since this purpose in no way is premised upon any special disadvantages of women, it cannot serve to justify a gender-based distinction which diminishes the protection afforded to women who do work. . . .

Thus, Congress decided not to provide benefits to all widows even though it was recognized that some of them would have serious problems in the job market. Instead, it provided benefits only to those women who had responsibility for minor children, because it believed that they should not be required to work.

The whole structure of survivors' benefits conforms to this articulated purpose. . . . If Congress were concerned with providing women with benefits because of economic discrimination, it would be entirely irrational to except those women who had spent many years at home rearing children, since those women are most likely to be without the skills required to succeed in the job market. . . .

Given the purpose of enabling the surviving parent to remain at home to care for a child, the gender-based distinction of 402 (g) is entirely irrational. The classification discriminates among surviving children solely on the basis of the sex of the surviving parent. Even in the typical family hypothesized by the Act, in which the husband is supporting the family and the mother is caring for the children, this result makes no sense. . . . It is no less important for a child to be cared for by its sole surviving parent when that parent is male rather than female. . . . Further, to the extent that women who work when they have sole responsibility for children encounter special problems, it would seem that men with sole responsibility for children will encounter the same child-care related problems. . . .

Finally, to the extent that Congress legislated on the presumption that women as a group would choose to forgo work to care for children while men would not, the statutory structure, independent of the gender-based classification, would deny or reduce benefits to those men who conform to the presumed norm and are not hampered by their child-care responsibilities. . . . Thus, the gender-based distinction is gratuitous; without it, the statutory scheme would only provide benefits to those men who are in fact similarly situated to the women the statute aids.

Since the gender-based classification of 402 (g) cannot be explained as an attempt to provide for the special problems of women, it is indistinguishable from the classification held invalid in Frontiero. Like the statutes there, "[b]y providing dissimilar treatment for men and women who are . . . similarly situated, the challenged section violates the [Due Process] Clause.". . .

Affirmed.

Source: United States Supreme Court Reports, October Term, 1974, Lawyers' Edition, vol. 43 (New York: Lawyers Co-Operative Publishing Co.; San Francisco: Bancroft-Whitney, 1976), 518–528.

Document 6.20
Califano v. Goldfarb, March 2, 1977

Another restriction on widower's benefits was that a widower had to prove that he was financially dependent upon his wife prior to her death. There was no equivalent burden on widows— their dependency was granted by presumption.

In the Goldfarb *case, Leon Goldfarb was a retired federal employee who was manifestly not financially dependent on his wife, but he desired to receive widower's benefits on her Social Security record. He claimed that the dependency requirement was gender discrimination. The Appeals Court agreed, as did the Supreme Court.*

Again, the government was the appellant in this case, having lost in the lower courts. The government argued that the case should be viewed as one alleging gender discrimination against Mr. Goldfarb, not against his late wife (because it had already lost on the contrary analysis in

Weinberger v. Wiesenfeld *(Document 6.19) and was hoping to convince the Court that such discrimination was a valid exercise of its legislative discretion). So, the government was advancing Mr. Goldfarb's claim of gender discrimination against him in the hopes of rebutting it.*

Once again, the Court used the Wiesenfeld *logic, finding that the rules for widower's benefits discriminated against Mr. Goldfarb's deceased wife. The result was the elimination of another gender-based distinction in Social Security policy.*

Califano v. Goldfarb, 430 U.S. 199

Mr. Justice BRENNAN announced the judgment of the Court. . . .

. . . [T]he gender-based distinction . . . burdening a widower but not a widow with the task of proving dependency upon the deceased spouse presents an equal protection question indistinguishable from that decided in *Weinberger v. Wiesenfeld, supra.* That decision . . . plainly require[s] affirmance of the judgment of the District Court. . . .

Weinberger v. Wiesenfeld, like the instant case, presented the question in the context of the OASDI program. There the Court held unconstitutional a provision that denied father's insurance benefits to surviving widowers with children in their care, while authorizing similar mother's benefits to similarly situated widows. . . .

Precisely the same reasoning condemns the gender-based distinction made . . . in this case. For that distinction, too, operates "to deprive women of protection for their families which men receive as a result of their employment." . . .

Appellant, however, would focus equal protection analysis not upon the discrimination against the covered wage earning female, but rather upon whether her surviving widower was unconstitutionally discriminated against by burdening him, but not a surviving widow, with proof of dependency. The gist of the argument is that, analyzed from the perspective of the widower,

> the denial of benefits reflected the congressional judgment that aged widowers, as a class, were sufficiently likely not to be dependent upon their wives that it was appropriate to deny them benefits unless they were, in fact, dependent. . . .

But *Weinberger v. Wiesenfeld* rejected the virtually identical argument when appellant's predecessor argued that the statutory classification there attacked should be regarded from the perspective of the prospective beneficiary, and not from that of the covered wage earner. . . .

The Court, however, analyzed the classification from the perspective of the wage earner, and concluded that the classification was unconstitutional because

> benefits must be distributed according to classifications which do not, without sufficient justification, differentiate among covered employees solely on the basis of sex. . . .

From its inception, the social security system has been a program of social insurance. Covered employees and their employers pay taxes into a fund administered distinct from the general federal revenues to purchase protection against the economic consequences of old age, disability, and death. But . . . female insureds received less protection for their spouses solely because of their sex. Mrs. Goldfarb worked and paid social security taxes for 25 years at the same rate as her male colleagues, but . . . the insurance protection received by the males was broader than hers. . . . The section then impermissibly discriminates against a female wage earner because it provides her family less protection than it provides that of a male wage earner, even though the family needs may be identical. . . .

In a sense, of course, both the female wage earner and her surviving spouse are disadvantaged by operation of the statute, but this is because "Social Security is designed . . . for the protection of the *family*" . . . and the section discriminates against one particular category of family—that in which the female spouse is a wage earner covered by social security. Therefore, decision of the equal protection challenge in this case cannot focus solely on the distinction drawn between widowers and widows, but, as Wiesenfeld held, upon the gender-based discrimination against covered female wage earners as well. . . .

Source: United States Supreme Court Reports, October Term, 1976, Lawyers' Edition, vol. 51 (New York: Lawyers Co-Operative Publishing Co.; San Francisco: Bancroft-Whitney, 1978), 273–283.

Document 6.21
Califano v. Webster and the Memorandum Cases, March 21, 1977

The Supreme Court's decision in this quartet of Social Security gender discrimination was announced on March 21, 1977. All raised issues involving gender-based distinctions in Social Security policy.

The main case was Califano v. Webster, *which was decided without arguments and issued as a per curiam decision. In this case Will Webster was appealing another gendered policy. Under the law prior to 1972, women were given more favorable benefit computations than men with the same earnings histories. This policy was instituted in the 1956 amendments and repealed in the 1972 amendments, with an effective date of 1975 and later. Webster's benefit was computed under the old pre-1975 formula, and he sued alleging gender bias against males in the old policy. The district court ruled in Webster's favor, but the direct appeal to the Supreme Court reversed this judgment. The Supreme Court concluded that gender bias in favor of women was under certain circumstances permissible public policy. This case was, therefore, the flip-side of the other cases that found gender bias against women unacceptable. This had the potential to make for ongoing disparities between the genders in Social Security policy, except that Congress has already mooted the question by repealing the prior policy.*

On the same day, the Court announced a bundle of three additional cases, which it issued only as memorandum decisions (meaning there was only a brief announcement of the Court's decision, with no formal supporting opinion). The three memorandum cases were Califano v. Silbowitz, Califano v. Jablon, *and* Califano v. Abbott. *In this trio of cases, the same dependency policy was at issue that the Court had ruled on in* Califano v. Goldfarb *(Document 6.20), although in this instance it was spouse's benefits rather than widower's benefits that were at issue. Like widower's benefits, the existing policy for spouse's benefits required men to demonstrate financial dependency upon their wives before they could collect husband's benefits, whereas women had no such restriction in their eligibility for wive's benefits. The plaintiffs argued that this was gender bias against the male applicants, but the lower courts found the policy unconstitutional on the grounds that it was bias against the women, using the* Wiesenfeld *logic. The government appealed, and the Supreme Court summarily affirmed the lower court's rulings.*

Following this group of decisions, the Social Security Administration began adjudicating benefit claims in a more gender-neutral manner, using the authority of these rulings, even though they had not been codified in subsequent changes in the statutes. As part of its recommendations, the Greenspan Commission—a bipartisan commission studying the problem of Social Security's financing—consolidated all the outstanding gender-based distinctions still in the law and recommended Congress eliminate them, which it did in the 1983 Amendments (see **Document 7.8**).

Califano v. Webster, 430 U.S. 313

Per Curiam

Under 215 of the Social Security Act . . . old-age insurance benefits are computed on the basis of the wage earner's "average monthly wage" earned during his "benefit computation years" which are the "elapsed years" (reduced by five) during which the wage earner's covered wages were highest. Until a 1972 amendment, "elapsed years" depended upon the sex of the wage earner. . . . "[E]lapsed years" for a male wage earner would be three higher than for an otherwise similarly situated female wage earner. . . . Accordingly, a female wage earner could exclude from the computation . . . of her "average monthly wage" three more lower earning years than a similarly situated male wage earner could exclude. This would result in a slightly higher "average monthly wage" and a correspondingly higher level of monthly old-age benefits for the retired female wage earner. . . . A single-judge District Court for the Eastern District of New York . . . held that, on two grounds, the statutory scheme violated the equal protection component of the Due Process Clause of the Fifth Amendment: (1) that to give women who reached age 62 before 1975 greater benefits than men of the same age and earnings record was irrational . . . and (2) that in any event the 1972 amendment was to be construed to apply retroactively, because construing the amendment to give men who reach age 62 in 1975 or later the benefit of the 1972 amendments but to deny older men the same benefit would render the amendment irrational, and therefore unconstitutional. . . . *We reverse.*

To withstand scrutiny under the equal protection component of the Fifth Amendment's Due Process Clause, "classifications . . . by gender must serve important governmental objectives and must be substantially related to achievement of those objectives.". . . Reduction of the disparity in economic condition between men and women caused by the long history of discrimination against women has been recognized as such an important governmental objective. . . . But "the mere recitation of a benign, compensatory purpose is not an automatic shield which protects against any inquiry into the actual purposes underlying a statutory scheme.". . . Accordingly, we have rejected attempts to justify gender classifications as compensation for past discrimination against women when the classifications in fact penalized women wage earners . . . or when the statutory structure and its legislative history revealed that the classification was not enacted as compensation for past discrimination. . . .

. . . The more favorable treatment of the female wage earner enacted here was not a result of "archaic and overbroad generalizations" about women . . . or of "the role-typing society has long imposed" upon women . . . such as casual assumptions that women are "the weaker sex" or are more likely to be child-rearers or dependents. . . . Rather, "the only discernible purpose . . . [is] the permissible one of redressing our society's longstanding disparate treatment of women.". . .

The challenged statute operated directly to compensate women for past economic discrimination. Retirement benefits under the Act are based on past earnings. But as we have recognized: "Whether from overt discrimination or from the socialization process of a male-dominated culture, the job market is inhospitable to the woman seeking any but the lowest paid jobs.". . . Thus, allowing women, who as such have been unfairly hindered from earning as much as men, to eliminate additional low-earning years from the calculation of their retirement benefits works directly to remedy some part of the effect of past discrimination. . . .

The legislative history . . . also reveals that Congress directly addressed the justification for differing treatment of men and women . . . and purposely enacted the more favorable treatment for female wage earners to compensate for past employment discrimination against women. . . .

[T]he legislative history is clear that the differing treatment of men and women was not "the accidental byproduct of a traditional way of thinking about females" . . . but rather was deliberately enacted to compensate for particular economic disabilities suffered by women.

That Congress changed its mind in 1972 and equalized the treatment of men and women does not, as the District Court concluded, constitute an admission by Congress that its previous policy was invidiously discriminatory. . . . Congress has in recent years legislated directly upon the subject of unequal treatment of women in the job market. . . . Congress may well have decided that "[t]hese congressional reforms . . . have lessened the economic justification for the more favorable benefit computation formula.". . . Moreover, elimination of the more favorable benefit computation for women wage earners, even in the remedial context, is wholly consistent with those reforms, which require equal treatment of men and women in preference to the attitudes of "romantic paternalism" that have contributed to the "long and unfortunate history of sex discrimination.". . .

Finally, there is no merit in appellee's argument that the failure to make the 1972 amendment retroactive constitutes discrimination on the basis of date of birth. Old-age benefit payments are not constitutionally immunized against alterations of this kind. . . . It follows that Congress may replace one constitutional computation formula with another and make the new formula prospective only. . . .

Reversed.

Source: United States Supreme Court Reports, October Term, 1976, Lawyers' Edition, vol. 51 (New York: Lawyers Co-Operative Publishing Co.; San Francisco: Bancroft-Whitney, 1978), 362–367.

Document 6.22
House Ways and Means Committee on Gender Bias in Social Security Law, October 12, 1977

The House Ways and Means Committee in its report on the 1977 legislation made a point of expressing the view that the time had come to remove all remaining gender distinctions in the law—equalizing the treatment of men and women. Their view was motivated in no small measure by recent Supreme Court decisions to this effect. Despite those decisions, there were still in 1977 many small, largely unnoticed, provisions of Social Security law that contained gender distinctions—generally to the disadvantage of men.

The House report is notable for the degree to which it exhibits a rather fully developed sense of engagement on the issue of gender discrimination in Social Security law. The House report is useful because it provides a fairly complete list of the remaining gender distinctions, as well as estimates in many cases of the costs involved and the size of the effected populations. In the process, the House report defined an agenda that would sooner or later have to be addressed.

D. Equal Treatment of Men and Women

1. Equal rights

The social security law contains a number of relatively minor provisions that are different for men and women. Your committee believes that these provisions should be changed to eliminate the gender-based distinctions and terminology and provide the same rights for men and women. To accomplish this it has included in its bill the following provisions. . . .

a. Father's Benefits

Benefits are provided by the present statute for a woman who has in her care a minor or disabled child (entitled to child's benefits) of her retired, disabled, or deceased husband, or deceased former husband. By virtue of a 1975 Supreme Court decision in *Weinberger v. Wiesenfeld* benefits are also provided for a similarly situated widowed father. . . . Also under the law, benefits are not provided for a father who has in his care an entitled child of his retired or disabled wife or deceased former wife.

Your committee's bill would provide benefits for men who were not covered by the Supreme Court decision—young husbands of retired or disabled workers, and surviving divorced husbands with an entitled minor or disabled child of the retired, disabled, or deceased worker in their care. . . .

It is estimated that 2,000 husbands or surviving divorced husbands would become newly eligible for benefits or eligible for larger benefits on the effective date. An estimated $2 million in additional benefits would be paid in the first full year of operation.

b. Benefits for Divorced Men

Present law provides benefits based on a former spouse's social security earnings record for an aged divorced wife and an aged or disabled surviving divorced wife but not for divorced men in like circumstances. The committee bill would provide such benefits for aged divorced husbands and aged or disabled surviving divorced husbands.

It is estimated that 2,000 people would become newly eligible for benefits or eligible for larger benefits on the effective date. An estimated $3 million in additional benefits would be paid in the first full year of operation.

c. Remarriage of Widowers before Age 60

Present law provides that an aged or disabled widow (or surviving divorced wife) may qualify for widow's benefits if she "is not married" when she applies for benefits. For a widower (or surviving divorced husband), on the other hand, the requirement specifies that he may qualify for widower's benefits if he "has not remarried." As a result of this difference, a widower (or surviving divorced husband) cannot ever become entitled to widower's benefits based on his deceased wife's (or deceased former wife's) earnings if he has remarried before age 60 even if he is not married at age 60.

The committee bill would permit a widower (or surviving divorced husband) to obtain benefits based on his deceased wife's (or deceased former wife's) social security if he is not married at the time he applies for widower's benefits, as widows now can. . . .

d. Transitional Insured Status

A 1965 amendment to the social security law made certain people who attained age 72 before 1969 eligible for benefits based on a shorter time in covered employment than would otherwise be required. Benefits were also provided for certain wives and widows who attained age 72 before 1969, but similar benefits were not provided for husbands or widowers.

Your committee's bill would provide such benefits for husbands and widowers under the same conditions as for wives and widows.

e. Benefits at Age 72 for Certain Uninsured Individuals

An amendment to the social security law enacted in 1966 made it possible for certain people who reach age 72 before 1968 to get special monthly cash payments (financed from general revenues) even though they have not worked in jobs covered by social security. The special payments can also be made to people who reach age 72 after 1967 and before 1972 if they have a specified amount of work under social security but not enough to qualify for regular retirement benefits.

When both members of a couple are receiving such payments, the husband receives a full benefit (now $78.50) and the wife gets a benefit equal to one-half the husband's benefit (now $39.30).

The committee bill would provide that when both members of a couple are receiving special age-72 payments, the total amount of the payments ($117.80) to the couple would be divided equally between the two.

f. Benefits of Spouses of Childhood Disability or Disabled Worker Beneficiaries

When a childhood disability beneficiary . . . marries another person getting dependent's or survivor's benefits, and when a disabled worker marries a childhood disability beneficiary or a mother, surviving divorced mother, or father, neither's benefits are terminated by reason of the marriage. Subsequent treatment of the spouse's benefits . . . varies depending on the sex of the disability beneficiary. If the disability beneficiary is a male, the benefits of his spouse end when his benefits end. If, on the other hand, the disability beneficiary is a female, the benefits of her spouse do not end when her benefits end.

Your committee has approved a change in the law under which this disparity in the rights of men and women would be removed. Specifically, the committee-approved bill provides that the benefits of the spouse of a female disability beneficiary would be terminated if she ceases to be disabled, as is now the case if the disability beneficiary is a male. . . .

g. Benefit Rights of Illegitimate Children

Present law provides that a man's illegitimate child who cannot inherit from him under applicable State law . . . may nevertheless be deemed to be his child for purposes of receiving social security benefits under certain conditions. Certain of these provisions may also apply with respect to such a child of a woman, but certain others do not. . . .

. . . [Y]our committee believes that the law should be changed to avoid such a gender-based distinction. Accordingly, the committee bill would provide that an illegitimate child's status for purposes of entitlement to child's insurance benefits will be determined with respect to the child's mother in the same way as it is now determined with respect to the child's father. . . .

h. Waiver of Civil Service Survivors Annuities

Generally, present law provides that if a civil service annuity based in part of military service performed before 1957 is payable to an individual, such service may not be used in determining eligibility for or the amount of such individual's social security benefit. An exception applies to a widow . . . but not a widower, entitled to a civil service survivor's annuity based in whole or in part on pre-1957 military service. . . .

The committee believes that a widower, as well as a widow, should be permitted to waive payment of a civil service annuity attributable to credit for military service performed before 1957 in order to have the military service credited toward eligibility for or the amount of a social security benefit, and has made provision for such in the bill.

i. Crediting of Self-Employment Income in Community Property States

Present law provides that all income from self-employment in a trade or business owned or operated by a married couple in a State in which community property statutes are in effect be deemed to be the husband's for social security purposes unless the wife exercises substantially all the management and control of the business, in which case all the self-employment income is treated as the wife's. In noncommunity property States, self-employment income of married couples is credited to the spouse who owns or is predominantly active in the business.

The committee bill would permit self-employment income of a married couple in a community property State to be credited for social security purposes to the spouse who exercises more management and control over the trade or business, with respect to taxable years after 1977. Where the husband and wife exercised the same amount of management and control the self-employment income would be divided equally between both the husband and wife.

2. Elimination of Marriage or Remarriage as a Factor Terminating or Reducing Benefits of Certain Beneficiaries

Present law provides, in general, that the marriage (or remarriage) of a worker's divorced or surviving spouse, parent, or child prevents or terminates entitlement to benefits based on the worker's social security earnings record. . . .

Your committee is especially concerned about the effect of these provisions on older surviving spouses (and divorced spouses). Accordingly, your committee has recommended changes in the law which would eliminate marriage or remarriage as a factor affecting entitlement to benefits or benefit amounts. . . .

In the first full year of operation an estimated 670,000 people would be eligible for benefits that they would not get because of the provisions of present law. An estimated $1.3 billion in additional benefits would be paid in the first full year.

3. Duration-of-Marriage Requirement for Divorced Women (and Men)

In 1965, the Congress provided benefits for aged divorced wives and aged surviving divorced wives of retired, disabled, or deceased insured workers, subject to a 20-year duration-of-marriage requirement. In providing these benefits, your committee stated that the purpose of doing so was to:

> . . . provide protection mainly for women who have spent their lives in marriages that are dissolved when they are far along in years—especially housewives who have not been able to work and earn social security benefit protection of their own—from loss of benefit rights through divorce.

Generally speaking, with a period of marriage considerably shorter than 20 years there is a greater likelihood that a divorced person will either qualify for benefits as a spouse in a second marriage or have earnings and qualify for benefits as a worker under social security. Your committee is concerned, however, that older divorced people married less than 20 years may nevertheless reach old age without any social security protection. Accordingly, your committee's bill would reduce from 20 years to 5 years the length of time a person must have been married to a worker in order for benefits to be payable to an aged divorced spouse or surviving divorced spouse. . . .

It is estimated that 70,000 people would become newly eligible for benefits or eligible for larger benefits on the effective date. An estimated $160 million in additional benefits would be paid in the first full calendar year, 1980.

4. Study of Proposals to Eliminate Dependency and Sex Discrimination

As discussed previously, your committee's bill contains amendments which would make a number of relatively minor social security provisions the same for men and women. However, there are a number of more broad-scale proposals for changing the social security program to take into account the changing role of women in society. Your committee is concerned that the social security program provide adequate protection in terms of the needs of today's society and that women, as well as men, be treated equitably under the program.

Therefore, your committee has directed the Secretary of Health, Education, and Welfare, in consultation with the Task Force on Sex Discrimination in the Department of Justice, to carry out a detailed study of proposals : (1) to eliminate dependency as a requirement for entitlement to social security spouse's benefits, and (2) to bring about the equal treatment of men and women in any and all respects. In conducting this study the Secretary shall take into account the effects of the changing role of women in today's society including such things as : (1) changes in the nature and extent of women's participation in the labor force, (2) the increasing divorce rate, and (3) the economic value of women's work in the home. The study shall include appropriate cost analyses. A full and complete report shall be submitted by the Secretary to the Congress within 6 months after enactment of the bill. . . .

Source: House Committee on Ways and Means, Report and Dissent, Social Security Financing Amendments of 1977, Report no. 95–702 on H.R. 9346 (Washington, D.C.: Government Printing Office, October 12, 1977), 44–49.

Document 6.23
**Senate Finance Committee on Gender Bias in Social Security Law,
November 1, 1977**

*The view of the House Ways and Means Committee on the issue of gender bias in the proposed
Social Security amendments was not shared by the members of the Senate Finance Committee.
While the House report had a six-page discussion of the issue of gender bias, the Senate report contained no such section. Instead, it addressed the issue only obliquely and used its discussion as an
opportunity to urge a vaguely related provision affecting government employees, with the aim
of reducing the Social Security benefits available to them. In the end, this was the only gender-
related provision of either version of the bill that became law (apart from a study of the issue).*

*Given this divergence of views between the two houses of Congress on the gender bias issue, it
is not surprising that the final version the 1977 legislation contained none of the provisions advocated by the House. Instead, the matter was kicked back to the federal courts, leaving it to the
subsequent legislation in 1983 to bring federal statutes in conformance with the legal rulings
and the growing social and political consensus on gender equality.*

Offset of Benefits of Spouses Receiving Public Pensions

Under present law, a woman can become entitled to spouse's or surviving spouse's benefits
without proving dependency on her husband. As a result of a March 1977 Supreme Court
decision, a man can also become entitled to spouse's or surviving spouse's benefits without
proving his dependency on his wife. (In *Califano v. Goldfarb*, the Court ruled that men
should be treated equally with women in determining entitlement for surviving spouse's
benefits. Subsequently, other court decisions extended this ruling to husband's benefits. Previously, a man had been required to prove his dependency on his wife to become entitled
to spouse's or surviving spouse's benefits, although women were presumed dependent).
Under the social security program, an individual who is entitled to two benefits does not
receive the full amount of both benefits. For example, if one is entitled to both a worker's
benefit and a spouse's benefit, the full worker's benefit is paid first and then the amount (if
any) by which the spouse's benefits exceed the worker's benefit. This "dual-entitlement"
provision prevents payment of dependents benefits to some persons not truly dependent.
However, persons who receive civil service pensions based on their work in noncovered
employment and are entitled to social security spouses' benefits, receive their dependent
spouses' benefits in full, regardless of their dependency on the worker. This results in "windfall" benefits to some retired government employees.

The committee recommends that social security benefits payable to spouses and surviving spouses be reduced by the amount of any public (Federal, State, or local) retirement
benefit payable to the spouse. The offset would apply only to pension payments based on
the spouse's own work in public employment which is not covered under social security. In
general, this should assure that dependents' social security benefits will not be paid to persons not dependent on the worker.

Consideration was given to requiring claimants to prove their dependency on the worker
before entitling them to spouses' benefits. However, a dependency test would be subject to
manipulation. For example, a government employee with earnings higher than those of his

wife could qualify for a social security spouse's benefit by allowing a few months to intervene between the date of his retirement and the effective date of his pension. Also, a dependency test could deny spouses' benefits in situations where it would seem undesirable to deny such benefits. For example, a woman might, in fact, be dependent upon her husband for most of her life and might have earned little or nothing in the way of retirement income protection in her own right and yet be denied benefits if a dependency test were implemented. This could occur if her husband became ill shortly before reaching retirement age, thus forcing a temporary reversal of their usual dependency situation. Additionally, a dependency test would require substantial numbers of persons to provide information with regard to their total income in order to establish entitlement, a significant departure from present practice where income is not generally a factor in entitlement. Making such determinations would also create administrative difficulties. For these reasons, the committee believes an offset is preferable to a dependency test. The provision would be applicable only to future beneficiaries.

Costs and number of people affected.—About 85,000 people would be affected by the provision during the first year. The provision is estimated to save $190 million in 1979. . . .

Source: Senate Committee on Finance, Social Security Amendments of 1977, Report No. 95–572 on H.R. 5322 (Washington, D.C.: Government Printing Office, November 1, 1977), 27–28.

CHAPTER 7

The Third Controversy over Financing and the Social Security Amendments of 1983

Initially, the 1977 effort seemed successful. The 1978 and 1979 trustees reports indicated that solvency had been extended for nearly fifty years and the long-range deficit dramatically reduced (see table in **Appendix C**). But the economics of stagflation continued to batter the Social Security system. In 1980 price inflation hit 13.5 percent, while wage growth declined 4.9 percent, adversely affecting Social Security financing. By 1980 the trustees reports indicated a dramatic and immediate financing crisis that was worse than the one addressed in 1977.

During a press conference announcing the final report of the Greenspan Commission, Rep. Claude Pepper (D-Fla.) held forth with his views on the commission's work. Also shown, left to right: chairman Alan Greenspan (hand to chin), Senator Daniel Patrick Moynihan (D-N.Y.), Rep. Pepper, Sen. William Armstrong (R-Col.), Mary Falvey Fuller, Rep. Barber Conable (R-N.Y.), and Robert J. Myers. Source: Courtesy of Robert Ball.

The three trustees reports issued in 1980, 1981, and 1982 were the policy drivers of the legislation that emerged in 1983. The financing crisis certified in these reports forced policymakers to revisit Social Security financing so soon after the major amendments of 1977 and to come together in a bipartisan compromise on a massive new set of legislation.

Propelled by a serious short-term financing crisis, the 1983 amendments shaped the contemporary program in important ways. The taxation of Social Security benefits, the first significant use of general revenues to finance Social Security (from the taxation of benefits), the first coverage of federal employees under Social Security, and the first increase in the retirement age were all adopted in the 1983 amendments. In addition, the 1983 amendments made an important decision regarding the long-range financing of the program by putting in place a tax rate schedule that produced a huge short-term build-up in the size of the trust fund reserves—a decision that continues to drive much of the debate about the future solvency of the program.

The 1983 amendments were the last major Social Security legislation of the twentieth century. Following these amendments, the annual reports projected the program had been restored to long-range solvency—a condition maintained for the next five years. But by 1988 the program was again declared out of long-range financial balance—a condition that has continued ever since.

Document 7.1
1980 Trustees Report, June 19, 1980

The 1980 trustees report was the first to call specifically for "policy action" in the face of the rapidly deteriorating financial situation confronting Social Security. This policy-trigger began the legislative process. This report recommended interfund borrowing between the Social Security and Medicare trust funds as a stop-gap measure, because at the time it was thought that the combined trust funds had enough money to get the Social Security program through its short-range financing problems.

Conclusion

The actuarial estimates presented in this report are based upon economic and demographic assumptions which are inevitably subject to considerable uncertainty. The assumptions and estimates that appear in this report were necessarily prepared before the most recent changes in the economy were known. Current evidence indicates that the economy has moved into a recession and is weakening rapidly. Therefore, revised short-range projections will probably be necessary in the near future as more information becomes available about the intensity of the changes in the economy. Over the longer term, uncertainty is of course an even more difficult factor. However, the Board believes that the long-range estimates presented in this report will remain useful for a longer period of time because they are less sensitive to changes in the short-range economic conditions.

Over the short term the OASI [Old Age and Survivors Insurance] trust fund will face financial strains requiring policy actions. Without such actions, the OASI fund would be depleted in late 1981 or early 1982, depending on the course of the economy. Reallocation of the tax rates between OASI and DI [disability insurance] would postpone depletion until the latter half of 1982 or early in 1983. . . .

Due in part to tax increases in 1985 and 1990, the combined assets of the OASI and DI trust funds should begin rising in 1985 and continue increasing into the 21st century based on the intermediate assumptions. However, largely because of demographic factors, estimated revenues are inadequate to meet demands on the OASI trust fund in the 21st century. . . .

The medium-range and long-range actuarial soundness of the OASDI [Old Age, Survivors, and Disability Insurance] program is usually measured in terms of the difference between expenditures and tax revenues. For the next 25 years, the average annual tax income exceeds the average annual expenditure by 1.19 percent of taxable payroll under the intermediate assumptions. . . .

For the entire 75-year projection period, however, the average annual tax income falls below the average annual expenditure by 1.52 percent of taxable payroll under the intermediate assumptions. . . .

Last January, the Administration proposed legislation which would allow any of [the] trust funds to borrow from another of the funds, with any such loans to be repaid with interest. If this legislation is enacted, the assets in each of the three funds will be available to meet the benefit obligations of any of the funds. . . .

The Board emphasizes that the projected depletion of the OASI trust fund is an immediate problem which requires early attention by the Congress. Therefore, the Board recommends that the problem be addressed in part by the adoption of the Administration's interfund borrowing proposal. In addition, because the tax rates scheduled under present law result in significant overfinancing of the DI program, the Board recommends that the OASDI tax rates be reallocated between the OASI and DI trust funds to more closely reflect the projected future costs of each program. The provision of interfund borrowing authority may be sufficient to adequately finance all three programs throughout the 1980's, thus avoiding the need to provide additional financing. At the very least, it will give the Administration and the Congress sufficient time to assess economic conditions and to address any further measures which may be necessary in order to strengthen the financing of the social security programs.

The Board also notes, as it did last year, that even under optimistic assumptions the balance between aggregate revenues and aggregate expenditures of the three trust funds is quite fragile in the immediate future. Under the pessimistic assumptions, the trust funds require revenues in addition to what is provided under present law. Thus, the Board repeats its recommendation of last year that no reduction be made in the present law payroll tax schedule of the trust funds without a general restructuring of social security financing to assure the integrity of the trust funds over the short-range and medium range period.

The long-range financial difficulties are not projected to occur for several decades into the future. However, the Board recommends that extensive studies continue to be conducted so that possible long-range solutions may be implemented in an orderly manner.

Source: 1980 Annual Report of the Board of Trustees of the Federal Old-Age and Survivors Insurance and Disability Insurance Trust Funds (Washington, D.C.: Government Printing Office, 1980), 56–58.

Document 7.2
1981 Trustees Report, July 8, 1981

In this report the trustees included a brief discussion concerning the macroeconomic impacts of the Social Security program on the larger economy, and they introduced a second set of intermediate actuarial estimates. Traditionally, the actuaries produce three estimates: an optimistic one, a pessimistic one, and an intermediate one that is crafted to be closest to historical experience. Policymakers typically used the intermediate estimate as the basis for legislative proposals. In the 1981 report the trustees provided two intermediate estimates, the second of which was based on slightly more optimistic economic assumptions than the standard estimate. This was done to provide a set of actuarial estimates more in keeping with the economic assumptions in the Reagan administration's general budget estimates. Thus the standard intermediate set of estimates was known as the II-B estimates and the more optimistic set was II-A.

Also of interest here is the combination of the Social Security trust funds (OASDI) with the Medicare Hospital Insurance (HI) trust fund, as OASDI-HI, to make a point about the inadequacy of interfund borrowing as a technique to improve the financial condition of the Social Security system. Comparisons of various kinds between the actuarial status of the Social Security and Medicare trust funds are often made in the annual reports, even though they are published as separate reports.

Five months after the 1981 trustees report appeared, President Ronald Reagan appointed a bipartisan commission to study the financing crisis and make legislative recommendations to Congress (see **Document 7.6**).

Conclusion

The actuarial cost estimates presented in this report are based upon economic assumptions which are subject to considerable uncertainty. Nevertheless, it is virtually certain that, unless legislation to strengthen the financial status of the OASI Trust Fund is enacted soon, that fund will be exhausted in the latter half of 1982. The DI Trust Fund, on the other hand, is projected to increase rapidly. The enactment of legislation to reallocate tax rates from the DI Trust Fund to the OASI Trust Fund or to permit interfund borrowing between the two funds would not, however, postpone the latter's exhaustion by more than a few months. Furthermore . . . there is a strong likelihood that, if additional financing were provided to the OASI Trust Fund by legislation reallocating tax rates from both the DI and Hospital Insurance Trust Funds, or by legislation permitting interfund borrowing among the three funds, the OASI Trust Fund would still become exhausted at some time during the 1980's—perhaps as early as 1984 under alternative III or even 1983 under "worst-case" assumptions. . . .

The economic and demographic assumptions which underlie the projections traditionally have been treated as outside factors acting upon the OASDI system while being largely unaffected by it. We have continued to follow that procedure. However, because of the size and nature of the OASDI system, it is becoming increasingly apparent that interaction of OASDI and the economy as a whole deserves attention. As has been shown earlier in the report, higher real growth, real wages, and labor-force participation increase tax revenues, thereby reducing the relative burden on workers to support OASDI benefits. OASDI may well impact labor force participation, savings and investment, and growth, which, in turn, affect the economy's performance. The Board therefore recommends that attention be given to the long-run interaction of the OASDI system and the economy in future research and policy deliberations on the role and structure of the system. . . .

The long-run projections show that the immediate short-run financing crisis is followed by a period of rising trust fund balances during the remainder of the first 25-year period. For this period as a whole, the average annual income from OASDI taxes is estimated to exceed the average annual outgo by 1.27 percent of taxable payroll. . . .

Although the average financial status of the OASDI program is favorable for the next 25 years, the estimated average annual tax income for the entire 75-year projection period falls below the estimated average annual outgo for the period under both sets of intermediate assumptions—by 0.93 percent of taxable payroll under alternative II-A and 1.82 percent under alternative II-B. This is due to tax receipts falling below outgo at an increasing rate in the second and third 25-year periods. . . .

When the expected net outflows of the HI Trust Fund beginning in the late 1980's are considered in conjunction with the OASDI Trust Funds, the situation of the combined-OASDI-HI Trust Fund looks even worse. The initial 25-year net inflow of the OASDI Trust Funds is then turned into a net outflow under both sets of intermediate assumptions. This emphasizes the need to do more than rely on interfund borrowing to restore the financial strength of the combined system.

The Board strongly urges prompt action by the Congress to prevent the exhaustion of the OASI Trust Fund in the short range and thus permit the timely payment of the current financial obligations of the OASDI program, to build the balances of the OASI and DI Trust Funds to satisfactory levels, and to restore the OASDI system to financial health over the long range. Decisions on actions to strengthen the short-range financing of the system should be made on a basis which minimizes the risk that a possible downturn in economic conditions will require additional action in the short term, thereby further weakening public confidence in the Social Security system.

The Administration has recommended a package of financing proposals that would restore soundness to the OASDI program in the short range and well into the next century. The Board recommends the enactment of these proposals or of similar ones which will accomplish the same objectives within the basic principles set forth by the Administration.

Source: 1981 Annual Report of the Board of Trustees of the Federal Old-Age and Survivors Insurance and Disability Insurance Trust Funds (Washington, D.C.: Government Printing Office, 1981), 70–71.

Document 7.3
Secretary Schweiker's Press Conference, May 12, 1981

As one of its first policy priorities, the incoming Reagan administration was anxious to balance the federal budget and, in particular, to cut the costs of entitlement programs. To this end, in February 1981 the new administration offered a set of budget reconciliation proposals that contained some minor Social Security reductions. At the same time, a highly confidential effort, headed by David Stockman, the director of the Office of Management and Budget, was under way to develop more far-reaching reductions in Social Security costs.

Ultimately, the Reagan administration proposed a package of eight Social Security reforms. The most controversial proposal called for a 38 percent cut in benefits for early retirees, and it was anticipated that this provision would become effective immediately to achieve the maximum in budget savings. On May 12, 1981, Richard S. Schweiker, the secretary of Health and Human Services, held a press conference to announce the administration's Social Security proposals.

The cost estimates presented by Secretary Schweiker asserted that in the five years from 1982 to 1986 the proposed reforms would replace an $11 billion Social Security shortfall with a $35.5 billion surplus, and that over the long-range estimation period the deficit would decline from 1.52 percent of payroll to 1.32 percent. The tables also showed that the vast bulk of the short-term savings ($17.6 billion) came from the immediate implementation of the benefit reduction for early retirement, while the bulk of the long-term savings (86 percent of the savings) came from the proposal to change the benefit formula (the "bend points"). The effect of this second proposal would have been to reset Social Security benefits to their 1972 replacement-rate levels and then start the annual automatic wage indexing from that reduced level.

I am today announcing social security reform proposals which will keep the system from going broke, protect the basic benefit structure, and reduce the tax burden of American workers.

- We will stand by the traditional retirement age of 65; we will not raise it.
- We will not propose raising social security taxes for the 114 million working men and women now contributing to the system. In fact we propose future tax reductions.
- We will phase out the retirement earnings test, thus ending the penalty now in law which discourages senior citizens from remaining in the labor force to supplement their social security income.
- These proposals do not remove from the rolls, or cut benefits for, those currently receiving benefits. . . .

The crisis is inescapable. It is here. It is now. It is serious. And it must be faced. Today we move to face it head-on and solve it. If we do nothing, the system would go broke as early as Fall, 1982, breaking faith with the 36 million Americans depending on social security.

Our package consists of major changes to restore equity to social security benefits and to restrain the growth of non-retirement portions of the program which are out of control.

Some of the changes will be difficult. But as things now stand, without changes, the social security trust fund deficit could climb as high as $111 billion in the next five years and have a long-term deficit of 1.52% of total payroll over the next 75 years. . . .

The sole impact today's proposals would have on the 36 million beneficiaries now on the rolls would be a three-month delay in the automatic cost-of-living increase scheduled for July, 1982. This change would end the anomaly of social security, the largest single federal program, still operating on the pre-1976 fiscal year calendar.

If these proposals are enacted, we will not only put social security back on sound financial ground indefinitely, but also we will be able to significantly lessen the taxes of those currently supporting the system.

We will be able to reduce the social security tax rate increase now scheduled for 1985, and to actually decrease social security tax rates by 1990 below what they are today.

This means that the young person entering the labor force next year would pay an average of $33,600 less in social security taxes over his/her lifetime, a reduction of over 10%. . . .

It is vital that we make these hard choices—and make them now. We cannot postpone any longer the day of reckoning for social security.

[Authors' note: The following fact sheet was released by HHS officials at the secretary's press conference.]

Provisions of the Social Security Proposal

I. Changes to Encourage Work Between 62–65

- Change Benefit Computation Point from Age 62 to 65

Proposal would discourage early retirement by assigning zero value to the age 62–64 period, thus reducing benefits in such cases while rewarding those who elect to work until age 65. This returns the program to the formula used before the age of retirement for women was lowered to 62 in 1956.

- Reduce Benefits for Early Retirement

Workers electing early retirement at 62 now receive benefits equal to 80 percent of what they would receive if they delayed retirement to age 65.

Proposal would reduce early retirement benefits to 55 percent of the maximum, thus strongly encouraging workers to remain in the work force until age 65.

II. Change to Reduce Opportunity for "Windfall" Benefits

- Eliminate "Windfall" Benefits for Non-Covered Employment

The benefit formula now makes it possible for a person, such as a retired Federal employee, who enters Social Security-covered employment for only a few years to receive disproportionately high benefits, in some cases exceeding those paid to low-wage earners who have spent a lifetime in covered employment.

Proposal would have formula take pension resources from non-covered employment into account in such cases, thus sharply lowering the Social Security benefit in such cases.

III. Changes to Relate Disability Insurance Closer to Work History and Medical Condition

- Require "Medical Only" Determination of Disability

Workers can now qualify for disability benefits on combinations of medical and non-medical factors, such as age, education and work experience. More than one-third of disability cases age 60 to 65 involve non-medical factors.

Proposal would limit qualification to medical factors alone, thus restoring program to original purposes.

- Increase Waiting Period to Six Months

Under a 1972 liberalization of the program, the waiting period for disability benefits was reduced from six to five months on the assumption that ample funds would be available.

Proposal would restore the six-month waiting period previously in law. This conforms to the terms of most private disability insurance programs.

- Require Prognosis of 24-Plus Months of Disability

Workers now seeking disability benefits must show only that disability claimed will exceed 12 months or will result in death. The 12-month test; enacted in 1965, replaced a test of "long-continued and indefinite duration" in prior law.

Proposal would restore the original intent of the law, requiring that the prognosis of disability be of long duration, at least 24 months, a more reasonable definition of disability.

- Increase Requirement for Insured Status to 30 Quarters

Workers may now qualify for disability benefits even if they have been in the work force only 20 out of the past 40 quarters. Therefore a person could be out of covered employment for 5 years and still qualify.

Proposal would set the minimum at 30 out of the past 40 quarters, thus more closely tying benefits to the principle that they are replacement for wages recently lost.

IV. Changes to Reduce Welfare Elements

- Eliminate Children's Benefits in Early-Retirement Cases

Children under 18 or under 22 if in school are now eligible for benefits on the basis of a retired parent's wage record. Thus a retiree with a child receives a dependent's benefit, whereas a retiree with no children gets only his own benefit.

Proposal would end this inequity in early-retirement cases and thus encourage the worker to continue work until 65.

- Extend Disability Maximum Family Benefit to Retirement and Survivors Cases

Benefits for families of retired and deceased workers can now actually exceed that worker's net take-home pay.

Proposal would extend the maximum limitation on benefits to families in disability cases enacted in 1980 to retirement and survivor cases. This would return the program closer to its original purpose as a "floor" of protection.

V. Other Amendments for Short-Term

- Increase Bend Points by 50% instead of 100% of Wage Increases for 1982–87

In 1977, the "bend points" (dollar amounts referred to in the weighted benefit formula) were made subject to automatic wage indexing. This change was adopted in legislation intended in part to offset the cost impact of earlier legislation and the faulty benefit computation procedure adopted in the 1972 amendments. However, benefit levels today remain disproportionately high (by about 10 percent) compared with the pre-1972 levels.

Proposal would restore the traditional relative benefit levels for future beneficiaries by increasing the "bend points" by 50% (instead of 100%) of increases in average wage earnings for the years 1982–87, after which the 100% factor would be restored to the formula.

- Move Date for Automatic Benefit Increases from June to September and Use 12-Month CPI [Consumer Price Index] Average

Under the 1972 amendments (as modified in 1974), annual Social Security benefit increases have been automatic each June (payable beginning in July). The increase is based on changes in the Consumer Price Index as measured between the first quarter of the current calendar year and the corresponding quarter of the preceding year, a provision which can unduly inflate or deflate the increase, depending on economic conditions in those quarters.

Proposal would correct the anomaly of having benefit increases initiated on the pre-1976 Federal Fiscal Year basis and change the CPI computation to cover a full year (July-June) period, thus making the measurement a more accurate reflection of economic trends and measuring living costs in a period ending closer to the initiation of benefit increases.

VI. Change in Coverage

• Extend Coverage to First Six Months of Sick Pay

Most sick pay is not taxed due to complex exclusion which forces employers to track sick pay on daily, even hourly basis, and leads some to unwittingly break the law.

Proposal would extend tax to all sick pay during first six months of an employee's illness. This would eliminate the administrative burden and would treat sick pay in the same way as vacation pay.

VII. Phase Out Retirement Earnings Test by 1986

Under current law, 1981 Social Security benefits payable to persons aged 65 through 71 are reduced by $1 for each $2 of annual earnings in excess of $5,500, a level which rises each year in relation to average wage earnings. However, benefits are not reduced for those aged 72 and over (70 and over beginning in 1982).

Proposal would phase out the retirement test over a three-year period, permitting $10,000 in earnings in 1983, $15,000 in 1984, $20,000 in 1985 and unlimited earnings thereafter.

VIII. Reduce Long-Range Social Security Taxes

Assuming enactment of these proposals, and those introduced in the Administration's Budget proposals, it will be possible to lessen the Social Security tax increase now scheduled for 1985 and to actually decrease Social Security taxes below the current level in 1990. . . . Note that while an increase will again become necessary in 2020 due to the aging of the population, the rate will still be lower than the 1990-and-after rate scheduled under current law. . . .

Source: SSA History Archives, Mary Ross Papers, Box MR 73.

Document 7.4
"Sense of the Senate" Resolution, May 20, 1981

The Senate, during its May 20, 1981, session, spent much of its time criticizing the Reagan administration's Social Security proposals and debating how best to express its displeasure. Sen. Daniel Patrick Moynihan (D-N.Y.) introduced a "Sense of the Senate" resolution roundly condemning the Reagan administration and putting the Senate on the record as opposing central features of the administration's proposal. The Republicans resisted the Moynihan language since it specifically criticized the president and the administration. After defeating Moynihan's amendment by a single vote, the Senate then went on to consider an amendment by Finance Committee Chairman Robert Dole (R-Kan.) that contained virtually the identical language to Moynihan's as far as what the Senate objected to, but without any direct attribution to the administration's proposals as the source of their objections. This version of the motion passed 96–0 and was widely understood as an explicit rejection of key aspects of the Reagan proposal. This meant that the administration's proposals were, for all intents and purposes, "dead on arrival" in Congress.

The Senator from Kansas (Mr. DOLE) . . . proposes an unprinted amendment number 113.
. . . At the end of the bill add the following insert:

The Social Security system is vital to the well-being of the Nation's elderly and disabled citizens and
currently provides benefits to about 35 million Americans; and

The Social Security system faces serious short-term and long-term financing problems that jeopardize the payment of benefits; and

   It is essential that Congress act forthrightly to address the Social Security financing problem and
to restore the American people's confidence in the system; and

   Any resolution to this problem will have come as a result of a bipartisan effort; and

   It is the sense of the Congress that Congress should carefully study all options in order to find
the most equitable solution to insuring the fiscal integrity of the system; and

   That Congress shall not precipitously and unfairly reduce early retirees' benefits; and

   That Congress will enact reforms necessary to ensure the short-term and long-term solvency of
the Social Security system but will not support reductions in benefits which exceed those necessary
to achieve a financially sound system and the well being of all retired Americans. . . .

Source: Congressional Record, Senate, May 20, 1981, 10422.

Document 7.5
President Reagan's Letter to Congressional Leaders on Social Security, May 21, 1981

The day following this public rebuke in the Senate, the president tried to salvage matters with this open letter to congressional leaders in the House and Senate, calling for flexibility and a bipartisan compromise on Social Security reform. Although Congress would hold hearings on the administration proposals, they never came close to being enacted.

Over the past several weeks, all Americans have been proud of the bipartisan spirit that we have created in working on the nation's economic recovery. Today I am writing to you to ask that we now bring that same spirit to bear on another issue threatening our public welfare.

   As you know, the Social Security System is teetering on the edge of bankruptcy. Over the next five years, the Social Security trust fund could encounter deficits of up to $111 billion, and in the decades ahead its unfunded obligations could run well into the trillions. Unless we in government are willing to act, a sword of Damocles will soon hang over the welfare of millions of our citizens.

   Last week, Secretary Richard Schweiker presented a series of Administration proposals that we believe are sound, sensible solutions, both in the short and long term. We recognize that Members of Congress on both sides of the aisle have alternative answers. This diver-sity is healthy—so long as it leads to constructive debate and then to an honest legislative response.

   As Secretary Schweiker has pointed out on several occasions, we believe that all of us owe an obligation to our senior citizens to work together on this issue. This Administration is not wedded to any single solution; this Administration welcomes the opportunity to consult with Congress and with private groups on this matter. Our sole commitment—and it is a commitment we will steadfastly maintain—is to three basic principles:

- First, this nation must preserve the integrity of the Social Security trust fund and the basic benefit structure that protects older Americans.
- Second, we must hold down the tax burden on the workers who support Social Security.
- Finally, we must eliminate all abuses in the system that can rob the elderly of their rightful legacy.

It is clear that the half-actions of the past are no longer sufficient for the future. It is equally clear that we must not let partisan differences or political posturing prevent us from working together.

Therefore, I have today asked Secretary Schweiker to meet with you and other leaders of the Congress as soon as possible to launch a bipartisan effort to save Social Security. I have also asked him to make the full resources of his department available for this undertaking. And of course, you can count on my active support of this effort.

None of us can afford to underestimate the seriousness of the problems facing Social Security. For generations of Americans, the future literally rests upon our actions. This should be a time for statesmanship of the highest order, and I know that no one shares that desire more strongly than you.

With every good wish,

Sincerely,

RONALD REAGAN

Source: Public Papers of the President: Ronald Reagan, 1981 (Washington, D.C.: Government Printing Office, 1981), 450.

Document 7.6
Executive Order Creating the Greenspan Commission, December 16, 1981
President Reagan by the end of 1981 hit upon an alternative strategy—a bipartisan commission to study the problem of Social Security's financing and formulate recommendations for Congress and the president that might gain bipartisan political consensus. The chairman was Alan Greenspan, who would later serve as chairman of the Federal Reserve, hence the commission is commonly referred to as the "Greenspan Commission."

Executive Order 12335

By the authority vested in me as President by the Constitution of the United States of America, and to establish, in accordance with the provisions of the Federal Advisory Committee Act, as amended (5 U.S.C. App. I), the National Commission on Social Security Reform, it is hereby ordered as follows:

The fifteen members of the Greenspan Commission were tasked with reviewing the financial condition of Social Security. Seated, left to right: Executive Staff Director Robert Myers, Rep. Claude Pepper (D-Fla.), Martha Keys, Chairman Alan Greenspan, Mary Falvey Fuller, Rep. Bill Archer (R-Texas), and Lane Kirkland. Standing, left to right: Robert Beck, Robert Ball, Alexander Trowbridge, Rep. Barber Conable (R-N.Y.), Sen. John Heinz (R-Pa.), Sen. Daniel Patrick Moynihan (D-N.Y.), Sen. Robert Dole (R-Kan.), and Joe Waggonner Jr.
Source: SSA History Archives.

Section 1. Establishment

(a) There is established the National Commission on Social Security Reform. The Commission shall be composed of fifteen members appointed or designated by the President and selected as follows:

(1) Five members selected by the President from among officers or employees of the Executive Branch, private citizens of the United States, or both. Not more than three of the members selected by the President shall be members of the same political party;

(2) Five members selected by the Majority Leader of the Senate from among members of the Senate, private citizens of the United States, or both. Not more than three of the members selected by the Majority Leader shall be members of the same political party;

(3) Five members selected by the Speaker of the House of Representatives from among members of the House, private citizens of the United States, or both. Not more than three of the members selected by the Speaker shall be members of the same political party.

(b) The President shall designate a Chairman from among the members of the Commission.

Sec. 2. Functions

(a) The Commission shall review relevant analyses of the current and long-term financial condition of the Social Security trust funds; identify problems that may threaten the long-term solvency of such funds; analyze potential solutions to such problems that will both assure the financial integrity of the Social Security System and the provision of appropriate benefits; and provide appropriate recommendations to the Secretary of Health and Human Services, the President, and the Congress.

(b) The Commission shall make its report to the President by December 31, 1982. . . .

Source: Public Papers of the President: Ronald Reagan, 1981 (Washington, D.C.: Government Printing Office, 1981), 1157–1158.

Document 7.7
1982 Trustees Report, April 1, 1982

Between the issuance of the 1981 and 1982 trustees reports, the Social Security program was sustained by a few modest cuts in certain types of benefits (principally the elimination of student benefits) and by the use of interfund borrowing. This report pointed to a worsening of the program's financial condition and indicated that the interfund borrowing strategy could no longer be relied upon to see the program through the crisis. The implication of the report was that immediate policy changes were necessary. This report appeared during the deliberations of the Greenspan Commission, putting additional pressure on policymakers to find a quick solution to the program's financial problems.

Conclusion

The cost estimates in this report are presented on the basis of four sets of economic and demographic assumptions, which are characterized as optimistic (alternative I), intermediate (alternatives II-A and II-B), and pessimistic (alternative III). Of the two intermediate sets, alternative II-A assumes future economic performance resembling that of more robust recent economic expansions which result from policies to stimulate growth and lower inflation. Alternative II-B assumes the adoption of policies which would result in an economic performance resembling less robust recent economic expansions.

The actuarial cost estimates presented in this report confirm the warning in last year's report that, without legislation, the OASI Trust Fund would be exhausted in the latter half of 1982. After last year's report was published, amendments were enacted that reduce the amount of benefits payable under the program. However, most of the reduction in benefit payments occurs after 1982, and the OASI Trust Fund would still be exhausted in the latter half of 1982 were it not for the temporary authority for interfund borrowing that was enacted in December 1981. Full use of this authority would permit the OASI Trust Fund to continue timely payment of benefits through June 1983. The timely payment of benefits past June 1983 is not assured because the authority for interfund borrowing ends on December 31, 1982, and any loans made under such authority can be no larger than the amount required to ensure timely payment of benefits for the 6-month period following the date of the loan. Thus, based on the estimates in this report, it is clear that the OASI Trust Fund will be exhausted no later than July 1983 unless remedial legislation is enacted.

The DI Trust Fund, on the other hand, is expected to increase rapidly after 1982. The expected future growth in the assets of the DI Trust Fund, however, is generally much lower than the expected decline in the assets of the OASI Trust Fund. Thus, the enactment of new legislation to reallocate tax rates from the DI Trust Fund to the OASI Trust Fund, or to permit continued interfund borrowing solely between OASI and DI (that is, excluding HI), would only postpone exhaustion of the OASI Trust Fund until sometime later than July, but before the end of 1983.

Furthermore, even if the authority for interfund borrowing among all three trust funds (including HI) were extended beyond 1982, it is very likely that the OASI Trust Fund would still become exhausted during the 1980's, when the combined assets of the three trust funds become insufficient to pay the combined expenditures on a timely basis. This is in spite of the Social Security tax rate increases that occurred in 1981 and 1982 and the increases sched-uled for 1985 and 1986. . . . Thus, interfund borrowing by itself is not a satisfactory solu-tion to the short-range financing problem. . . .

Source: 1982 Annual Report of the Board of Trustees of the Federal Old-Age and Survivors Insurance and Disability Insurance Trust Funds (Washington, D.C.: Government Printing Office, 1982), 74–76.

Document 7.8
Greenspan Commission Report, January 20, 1983

The official report of the National Commission on Social Security Reform, issued in January 1983, became the blueprint for the 1983 Social Security amendments. Only a few provisions were changed during congressional consideration.

Findings and Recommendations

The National Commission was assigned the critical job of assessing whether the OASDI pro-gram has financing problems in the short run and over the long-range future (as represented by the 75-year valuation period) and, if so, recommending how such problems could be resolved.

The National Commission has agreed that there is a financing problem for the OASDI program for both the short run, 1983–89 (as measured using pessimistic economic assump-tions) and the long range, 1983–2056 (as measured by an intermediate cost estimate) and that action should be taken to strengthen the financial status of the program. . . .

[Authors' note: Even though the first three recommendations that follow were agreed to unan-imously, there were separate dissenting views expressed on several of the recommendations by individual commission members. These dissents appeared in a concluding section of the full report.]

The National Commission makes the following recommendations unanimously:

(1) *The members of the National Commission believe that the Congress, in its deliberations on financing proposals, should not alter the fundamental structure of the Social Security pro-gram or undermine its fundamental principles. . . . The National Commission considered, but rejected, proposals to make the Social Security program a voluntary one or to transform it into a program under which benefits are a product exclusively of the contributions paid, or to con-vert it into a fully-funded program, or to change it to a program under which benefits are con-ditioned on the showing of financial need. . . .*

(2) *The National Commission recommends that, for purposes of considering the short-range financial status of the OASDI Trust Funds, $150–200 billion in either additional income or in decreased outgo (or a combination of both) should be provided for the OASDI Trust Funds in calendar years 1983–89.*

(3) *The National Commission finds that, for purposes of considering the long-range finan-cial status of the OASDI Trust Funds, its actuarial imbalance for the 75-year valuation period is an average of 1.80% of taxable payroll. . . .*

The 12 members of the National Commission voting in favor of the "consensus" pack-age agreed to a single set of proposals to meet the short-range deficit. . . . They further

The political negotiation within the Greenspan Commission was between the House Democrats, on the one hand, and the Senate Republicans and the Reagan White House on the other. House Speaker O'Neill's de facto representative on the commission was former Social Security Administration commissioner Robert Ball. (O'Neill is on the left and Ball on the right.)
Source: Courtesy of Robert Ball.

agreed that the long-range deficit should be reduced to approximately zero. The single set of recommendations would meet about two-thirds of the long-range financial requirements. Seven of the 12 members agreed that the remaining one-third of the long-range financial requirements should be met by a deferred, gradual increase in the normal retirement age, while the other 5 members agreed to an increase in the contribution rates in 2010 of slightly less than one-half percent (0.46%) of covered earnings on the employer and the same amount on the employee, with the employee's share of the increase offset by a refundable income-tax credit. . . .

Provisions of "Consensus" Package

. . . Table A presents the actuarial cost data for this package for both the short range (1983–89 in the aggregate) and the long range (the 75-year valuation period, ending with 2056). . . .

Table A Short-Range and Long-Range Cost Analysis of OASDI Proposals

Proposal	Short-Term Savings, 1983–89 (billions)	Long-Range Savings (percentage of payroll)
Cover nonprofit and new Federal employees	+$20	+.30%
Prohibit withdrawal of State and local government employees	+3	—
Taxation of benefits for higher-income persons	+30	+.60
Shift COLAs to calendar-year basis	+40	+.27
Eliminate windfall benefits for persons with pensions from noncovered employment	+.2	+.01
Continue benefits on remarriage for disabled widow(er)s and for divorced widow(er)s	−.1	—
Index deferred widow(er)'s benefits based on wages (instead of CPI)	−.2	−.05
Permit divorced aged spouse to receive benefits when husband is eligible to receive benefits	−.1	−.01
Increase benefit rate for disabled widow(er)s aged 50–59 to 71½% of primary benefit	−1	−.01

Table A (continued)

Proposal	Short-Term Savings, 1983–89 (billions)	Long-Range Savings (percentage of payroll)
Revise tax-rate schedule	+40	+.02
Revise tax basis for self-employed	+18	+.19
Reallocate OASDI tax rate between OASI and DI	—	—
Allow inter-fund borrowing from HI by OASDI	—	—
Credit the OASDI Trust Funds, by a lump-sum payment for cost of gratuitous military service wage credits and past unnegotiated checks	+18	—
Base automatic benefit increases on lower of CPI or wage increases after 1987 if fund ratio is under 20%, with catch-up if fund ratio exceeds 32%	—	—
Increase delayed retirement credit from 3% per year to 8%, beginning in 1990 and reaching 8% in 2010	—	−.10
Additional long-range changes	—	+.58
Total Effect	**+168**	**+1.80**

Authors' note: Footnotes deleted. Where no values are shown, the figure was assumed to be too small to be of significance.

. . . (4) *The National Commission recommends that coverage under the OASDI program should be extended on a mandatory basis, as of January 1, 1984, to all newly hired civilian employees of the Federal Government. . . . The National Commission also recommends that OASDI-HI coverage should be extended on a mandatory basis, as of January 1, 1984, to all employees of nonprofit organizations.*

It is important to note that covering additional groups of workers such as those specified in this recommendation not only results in a favorable cash-flow situation in the short run, but also has a favorable long-range effect. The additional OASDI taxes paid on behalf of the newly-covered workers over the long run will exceed, on the average, the additional benefits which result from such employment, assuming that the program is in long-range actuarial balance. . . .

(5) *The National Commission recommends that State and local governments which have elected coverage for their employees under the OASDI-HI program should not be permitted to terminate such coverage in the future. . . .*

(6) *The National Commission is concerned about the relatively large OASDI benefits that can accrue to individuals who spend most of their working careers in non-covered employment from which they derive pension rights, but who also become eligible for OASDI benefits as a result of relatively short periods in covered employment with other employers. Accordingly, the National Commission recommends that the method of computing benefits should be revised for persons who first become eligible for pensions from non-covered employment, after 1983, so as to eliminate "windfall" benefits. . . .*

(7) *The National Commission recommends that, beginning with 1984, 50% of OASDI benefits should be considered as taxable income for income-tax purposes for persons with Adjusted Gross Income (before including therein any OASDI benefits) of $20,000 if single and $25,000 if married. The proceeds from such taxation, as estimated by the Treasury Department, would be credited to the OASDI Trust Funds under a permanent appropriation. . . .*

It is estimated that about 10% of OASDI beneficiaries would be affected by this provision. . . .

(8) *The National Commission recommends that the automatic cost-of-living adjustments of OASDI benefits should, beginning in 1983, be made applicable to the December benefit checks (payable early in January), rather than being first applicable to the June payments. . . .*

(9) *The National Commission recommends that the following changes in benefit provisions which affect mainly women should be made:*

(a) *Present law permits the continuation of benefits for surviving spouses who remarry after age 60. This would also be done for (1) disabled surviving spouses aged 50–59, (2) disabled divorced surviving spouses aged 50–59, and (3) divorced surviving spouses aged 60 or over.*

(b) *Spouse benefits for divorced spouses would be payable at age 62 or over (subject to the requirement that the divorce has lasted for a significant period) if the former spouse is eligible for retirement benefits, whether or not they have been claimed (or they have been suspended because of substantial employment). . . .*

(10) *The National Commission recommends that the OASDI tax schedule should be revised so that the 1985 rate would be moved to 1984, the 1985–87 rates would remain as scheduled under present law, part of the 1990 rate would be moved to 1988, and the rate for 1990 and after would remain unchanged. The HI tax rates for all years would remain unchanged. The resulting tax schedule would be as follows:*

Employer and Employee Rate (each)

Year	OASDI Present Law	OASDI Proposal	OASDI-HI Present Law	OASDI-HI Proposal
1983	5.4%	5.4%	6.7%	6.7%
1984	5.4	5.7	6.7	7.0
1985	5.7	5.7	7.05	7.05
1986	5.7	5.7	7.15	7.15
1987	5.7	5.7	7.15	7.15
1988–89	5.7	6.06	7.15	7.51
1990 and after	6.2	6.2	7.65	7.65

For 1984, a refundable income tax credit would be provided against the individual's Federal income-tax liability in the amount of the increase in the employee taxes over what would have been payable under present law. . . .

(11) *The National Commission recommends that the OASDI tax rates for self-employed persons should, beginning in 1984, be equal to the combined employer-employee rates. One-half of the OASDI taxes paid by self-employed persons should then be considered as a business expense for income-tax purposes (but not for purposes of determining the OASDI-HI tax). . . .*

(15) *The National Commission recommends that, beginning with 1988, if the fund ratio . . . of the combined OASDI Trust Funds as of the beginning of a year is less than 20.0% . . . the automatic cost-of-living (COLA) adjustments of OASDI benefits should be based on the lower of the CPI increase or the increase in wages. . . .*

This provision will serve as a stabilizer against the possibility of exceptionally poor economic performance over a period of time. . . .

(16) *The National Commission recommends that the Delayed-Retirement Credit should be increased from the present 3% (for persons who attained age 65 after 1981) to 8%, to be phased in over the period 1990–2010. . . .*

(18) *The National Commission believes that, in addition to the stabilizing mechanism of Recommendation (15), a fail-safe mechanism is necessary so that benefits could continue to be paid on time despite unexpectedly adverse conditions which occur with little advance notice. . . . Several types of fail-safe mechanisms are possible other than the one currently being used—interfund borrowing; there is strong disagreement among the members as to which type of mechanism should be used. A combination of these types of mechanisms would, of course, be possible. . . .*

Investment Procedures

. . . The National Commission believes that the investment procedures followed by the trust funds in the past generally have been proper and appropriate. The monies available have generally been invested appropriately in Government obligations at interest rates which are equitable to both the trust funds and the General Fund of the Treasury and have not—as is sometimes alleged—been spent for other purposes outside of the Social Security program. . . .

(20) *The National Commission recommends that two public members be added to the Board of Trustees of the OASDI Trust Funds. The public members would be nominated by the President and confirmed by the Senate. No more than one public member could be from any particular political party. . . .*

(21) *A majority of the members of the National Commission recommends that the operations of the OASI, DI, HI, and SMI Trust Funds should be removed from the unified budget. Some of those who do not support this recommendation believe that the situation would be adequately handled if the operations of the Social Security program were displayed within the present unified Federal budget as a separate budget function, apart from other income security programs. . . .*

The National Commission believes that changes in the Social Security program should be made only for programmatic reasons, and not for purposes of balancing the budget. Those who support the removal of the operations of the trust funds from the budget believe that this policy of making changes only for programmatic reasons would be more likely to be carried out if the Social Security program were not in the unified budget. Some members also believe that such a procedure will make clear the effect and presence of any payments from the General Fund of the Treasury to the Social Security program. . . .

Those who oppose this recommendation believe that it is essential that the operations of the Social Security program should remain in the unified Federal budget because the program involves such a large proportion of all Federal outlays. Thus, to omit its operations would misrepresent the activities of the Federal Government and their economic impact. . . .

Coverage of State and Local Government Employees

Although the National Commission believes that coverage of all persons who are in paid employment is desirable, some members do not favor mandatory coverage of employees of State and local governments. . . .

Benefit Provisions Primarily Affecting Women

In recent years, there has been widespread discussion as to whether the basic structure of the Social Security program should be altered in view of the changes in the role of women in our society and economy. . . .

Some members of the National Commission believe that there should be a comprehensive change in the program to reflect the changing role of women, for example, by instituting some form of earnings sharing for purposes of the Social Security earnings record. Simply stated, earnings sharing means that all covered earnings received by a couple during the period of marriage would be pooled and half would be credited to each of their earnings records. Some other members believed that such comprehensive changes were outside of the scope of the charge of the National Commission. . . .

Source: National Commission on Social Security Reform. Full text of report available on the Social Security Administration Web site: www.ssa.gov/history/reports/gspan.html (accessed November 10, 2006).

Document 7.9
House Floor Debates on the Greenspan Commission Report, March 9, 1983

Probably the most contentious issue taken up by Congress during its consideration of the recommendations of the Greenspan Commission was the issue of raising the retirement age. This was a key area of disagreement within the commission. Although a bipartisan majority of the commission believed an increase in the retirement age was appropriate, the labor representatives on the commission were adamantly opposed. The Democrats on the commission—in order not to alienate their labor colleagues—declined to vote for the increase, and it was left out of the final version of the commission's consensus recommendations. The end result was that the recommendations did not fully close the funding shortfall facing the program. The remaining deficit would have to be addressed by a congressional initiative—which many commission members expected would come in the form of a proposal regarding the retirement age.

The real debate on the matter occurred in the House of Representatives, where two Democratic members argued the alternative views. Rep. J. J. "Jake" Pickle (D-Texas) debated the issue with the long-time champion of the elderly, Rep. Claude Pepper (D-Fla.). (Also featured in this excerpt are Democrats Bill Richardson of New Mexico, James Shannon of Massachusetts, and Bryon Dorgan of North Dakota.)

Pickle introduced an amendment raising the retirement age in phased steps beginning in the year 2000, and Pepper introduced a counteramendment raising taxes by 0.53 percent in order to accomplish the same effect on the financial balance as raising the retirement age. Their debate illustrates the political dynamics around this issue.

Ultimately Pickle's amendment was adopted on a close vote: 228–202 (with 3 abstentions); the Pickle provision was eventually enacted into law as part of the 1983 amendments.

Mr. PICKLE. Mr. Chairman, we have reached the point now in the consideration of our social security reform bill where the House will be asked to work its will to determine what route we take to correct the long-term deficit of 0.68 percent of payroll. Two amendments have been made in order, and I present the amendment that, in effect, would raise the normal retirement age in the future, starting at the year 2000 and completing in the year 2027.

First, I think it would be best if I would state to the Members what the amendment does. The amendment I have offered raises the normal retirement age in two steps.

First it raises the normal retirement age to 66 by increasing the age for benefits by 2 months per year for 6 years, so that the proposal would be fully effective beginning with those attaining the age 66 in the year 2009.

In other words, the change in age would not be fully completed for some 26 years.

The phase-in would begin at age 62. We retain that 62 level of early retirement. It saves 0.42 percent of taxable payroll. Keep in mind that we must save or raise 0.68.

The second stage does this: It raises normal retirement age from 66 to 67 by increasing the age for full benefits by 2 months a year for 6 years so that the proposal would be fully effective beginning with those attaining age 67 in the year 2027.

The phase-in would begin with those at age 62 which commenced in 2017. This second step saves 0.26 percent of payroll.

Another part of the amendment is that the age 62 benefits would be maintained at an ultimate rate of 70 percent of full benefits fully effective after the age for full retirement is changed to 67. . . .

Now, let me repeat, I would raise the retirement age way in the future by 2 months per year starting in the year 2000. The first stage would be completed by the year 2009. In other words, with 17 years in this century and 9 years later, it would not be fully effective for some 26 years in the future.

Thus anybody 45 years or above would not be affected by this amendment.

The second part of the amendment raises the age from 66 to 67, and that would not start until 2017 and it is not made fully effective until the year 2027. Now with the 17 years in this century and the 27 years that would 44 years. Thus, my second stage would affect a very small percent of the present workforce.

Now why should the Congress take this step and why should the Congress take this step in 1983? Let me mention some of the points that I think should be made today.

First, the social security program faces a long-term deficit after the turn the century that is largely demographic in nature. . . . The deficit is over 26 percent of program costs in the outyears and it begins sooner than most of us think, as income to the trust funds will begin to fall below the outgo somewhere in the years 2010 to 2015.

Now . . . this shortage is a demographic shortfall. Overall program costs will remain fairly steady as a percent of GNP. This long-time deficit arises in spite . . . of the projection of real wage growth of 1.5 percent, of low unemployment of 5.5 percent, of low inflation of 4 percent, and an increase in the birth rate over current levels.

The trustees of the social security program are very clear about the reason for this deficit, and I hope the Members listen to this point: This is the reason they cite for the deficit: The number of beneficiaries will be increasing faster than the number of workers; it is demographic and we should remember that. . . .

Second, the demographic impact on the social security trust funds comes not just from baby booms or from a drop in fertility rates. Longevity has increased dramatically in this century, with most of the increases in the last half occurring among the adult population and not through lower infant mortality or other factors. More people are living longer, and these increases have occurred already across the board among men and women and among all races. . . .

Three, the combination of demographic circumstances facing us means that an increase in the retirement age is inevitable. This Congress has already gone on record many times fighting age discrimination in employment. Once the baby boom is fully adult there will be a slowdown in the growth of the labor force, and it will become even more important to encourage individuals to work longer in order to maintain overall national growth.

Given the inevitability, and I say it is the inevitability, the only fair route, the only reasonable, responsible route, is to make the change now so that individuals have full notice of what to expect.

Now four. Mr. Chairman, any measure which seeks to address the long-term needs of social security are going to make some changes that have unfavorable side effects. Raising taxes hits hardest on the low income and consequently on minorities and women, who are often lower paid. Raising taxes causes inflation. It hurts the little worker more than anything that we could do. Reducing the growth of benefits by any measure or any formula also cuts benefits which hit these same groups just as hard. Only by raising the age are we making it clear that we want individuals who can to stay in the work force longer. And if they do that then they will suffer no reduction. My colleagues are going to hear arguments later that our people who retire early will have to suffer from a reduction in their benefits and they will impart to you the harshness of that. I want to challenge those figures, but I want to say to my colleagues at the very beginning, those people who stay on the work force will not suffer reductions and thus that will not apply.

. . . [T]here is nothing sacrosanct about the age 65. I think we would probably all agree it was a proper age when it was started back in 1935. But it does not mean that automatically you can never tamper with it or change that age. . . .

Mr. Chairman, we do not have the option of not making changes, the House must make changes. The former National Commission on Social Security recommended raising the age. The President's Commission on Pension Policy recommended raising the age. A majority of the most recent National Commission on Social Security Reform recommended raising the age. A clear majority of the Ways and Means Committee, both Democrat and Republican, have recommended raising the age. This is not a partisan matter. It is not a Republican or Democratic matter. . . .

The bill we brought before you makes many changes and it does solve two-thirds of the long-term deficit.

Now . . . we must choose which route will we take. Your choices are simple. You can vote for the measure that is in the bill that reduces benefits and raises taxes. Or, you can vote for the Pepper amendment that raises taxes entirely. Or, you can go the Pickle route which raises age in the future and does not raise taxes. I think my proposal is the preferable one. It is the time to do it. . . .

Mr. RICHARDSON. Mr. Chairman, I strongly oppose Congressman Pickle's proposed amendment to H.R. 1900, the Social Security Act Amendments of 1983, which would increase the age at which a person could retire with full benefits, from age 65 to 67. The hard, cold fact is, this amendment calls for a cut in benefits for future retirees. Although supporters of the Pickle amendment claim that it is only logical to increase the retirement age due to the increased life expectancy of the average American, they ignore some important facts.

Longer life does not necessarily mean better health during later years. Due to rising costs of health care, the health of the elderly may actually worsen. Raising the retirement age would devastate those individuals who are unable to work beyond age 65 due to a lifetime of work in hard physical jobs. Additionally, it is the blue collar worker who already receives the smallest benefit. To further reduce their benefits would be unconscionable. A worker who had lost his job or is unable to work beyond age 65 due to poor health, will be extremely unlikely to find employment at an advanced age.

This amendment would also have an extremely adverse effect on women and minorities. Although women are living longer, their disability rates are on the rise. Older women would find it especially difficult to find employment due to the double burden of sex and age discrimination.

Minorities account for 60 percent of the population of my district in New Mexico. An unfortunate fact is that minorities have a substantially shorter life expectancy than other Americans do. In essence, this amendment asks minorities to pay into the social security system their entire life, with the likelihood that they may never receive benefits.

Mr. Chairman, I urge you and the Members of this body to vote against the Pickle amendment as a violation of the promises that have been made to the American public. Let us make sure, that Americans will be able to retire with security and dignity at a reasonable age. Although Congressman Pepper's amendment will require a small tax increase in the year 2020 should the economy remain weak, it is a compassionate alternative to the Pickle amendment for solving the long-term deficit of social security. . . .

Mr. SHANNON. . . . Mr. Chairman, I rise today in strong opposition to the Pickle amendment.

The idea of increasing the retirement age has some superficial appeal.

But I hope today we can strip away the mythology and look at who is affected by such a change. . . .

Increasing the retirement age would be a major benefit cut for America's most vulnerable senior citizens.

The Pickle amendment would end up cutting benefits by 12 to 14 percent compared to current law.

The Pickle amendment is designed to force people to stay in the work force longer—regardless of whether they are able to continue working, and regardless of whether there are any jobs.

This amendment assumes that most people are able to work longer than they do now.

This is not the case.

Survey after survey shows that a great many people, perhaps 2 out of 3, retire—not because they want to—but because of: First, poor health; second, mandatory retirement; third, lack of skills; and fourth, job loss.

According to the National Center for Health Statistics, as many as 30 percent of early retirees retire due to ill health and have no choice in their retirement decision.

Increasing the retirement age for these people would not keep them in the work force longer. It will simply cut their benefits. And what will they be able to do about it? Nothing.

Look at the numbers.

Two-thirds of the savings from the Pickle amendment come from cutting benefits for early retirees—not from workers staying on the job longer.

Instead of spreading the burden of the long-term solution evenly over all social security beneficiaries, the Pickle amendment heaps it onto the backs of those least able to carry it.

Those affected most harshly by the Pickle amendment include low-skilled blue collar workers, minorities, and women.

Low-skilled and manual workers perform more physically demanding work.

If manual and blue collar workers have health problems, they are more likely than other workers to retire early. A lot of these people cannot keep working up to age 67. Do you want to vote to cut retirement benefits for these people who are already hurting? Then vote for the Pickle amendment. But if you agree these people already have enough problems, vote "no.". . .

And under the proposal, women would get the same bad deal. Women have a higher incidence of chronic illness than men. Do we want to penalize them for this? If we do, the Pickle amendment is a good way to do it.

Mr. PEPPER. Now here is our dilemma, if some regard it as such: If we will pass this package as, of course, we must do and then if you will adopt my amendment, we can go proudly from this Chamber and say to the 26 million senior citizens of America and to their children, and we can say to those who will be the ancestors of those yet to be born, whether it is 10 or 15 or 25 or 75 years from now, "The Congress of the United States of America has said your social security package is secure and we have not cut social security benefits and we made it solvent and sound for 75 years."

Why would we want to violate the principle of maintaining benefits at the end when the rest of the package preserves the current benefit structure? The Commission agreement leaves only the slightest bit of imbalance in the period 50 to 75 years away. It is hardly necessary to adopt the approach of benefit cuts in order to meet the exigencies of that problem.

They say, "Oh, well, but are not people living longer?" Thank God they are. But we had two witnesses before our commission who testified on that subject: Dr. Jacob Feldman of the National Center for Health Statistics and Dr. Robert Butler of the National Institute on Aging. They testified that during the last 10 years the rate of longevity has increased by 10 percent, but, they added, during the same period of time the disability incidence rate of the elderly working people had increased by 26 percent. In other words, what assurance have we that we are not reducing the benefits of people who are going to need it as bad as they do now?

Mr. Dorgan of North Dakota and I were making a TV taping to be broadcast back in his state. During that taping he told me, "The other day in my State of North Dakota a lady approached me and said, 'Mr. Congressman, please do not cut benefits for those who retire at 62 years of age.' She said, 'I am just praying that I can last a few months longer because I have arthritis so bad I can hardly get out of bed in the morning.'"

My dear friend, under Mr. Pickle's amendment, that lady's benefits would be cut 12.5 percent from the amount of benefits she would be entitled to under the present law of this land.

The truth is that about half of the people who retire at 62 do so for reasons of ill health. An additional 20 percent are forced out of the labor market because they have been discriminated against an account of their age.

I suggest that we just don't know whether or not the need may be just as great out there in the future as it is today. The other day when I was testifying before the Ways and Means Committee on this matter, I looked around the room and I said, "I do not see any of these people that we are voting on to cut their benefit out there in the year 2008, 2017." I do not see any of them here today. Somehow I do not feel just right about exerting the privilege of relying on the law of the present and retiring at 65, but saying a man in the year 2000 or 2022 cannot retire when he is 65, he has to wait until he is 67. Why do I need to do that? Is that quite fair to him that I pre-judge his eligibility for these receipts and the desirability of giving them to him?

So, what I am proposing is we simply increase the payroll tax by 0.53 percent. Even if the worker had a salary of $36,000 a year my amendment would add only $190 in a year to the taxes that man would have to pay. Only 20 percent of the American people in their work make over $20,000 a year. So my amendment would not cause the expenditure of very much more. . . .

Mr. PICKLE. Mr. Chairman, first and foremost, I want to pay my respects to my dear friend, Senator Pepper. He and I do have a difference on the approach we should take in the long term. Mine is as sincere as I know his is. I have advocated this for 2 years. I think it is the proper approach. *[Authors' note: Earlier in his career Claude Pepper was a U.S. senator and so some of his colleagues still addressed him by this honorific title.]*

I have asked for this time simply to say to my colleagues that a great many statements have been made in the well now that are not factually correct, and I would hope that we would not be so worked up emotionally that we lose sight of the fact of exactly what we have done.

Let me respond first by saying that if we go with Senator Pepper's amendment now, we are saying in effect that from now on the only way we will correct long-term deficits in the social security program is to raise taxes. There must be some other way than just to keep raising taxes, because eventually that is going to get so onerous the American people will rebel. We know that under the committee bill it is over 15 percent, and within a short time, by Senator Pepper's amendment, it would be 16.3 percent. There just simply must be some way to correct the social security problem other than by just raising taxes. I would think that the approach we have taken will do that.

Let us keep in mind that the amendment we have just passed does not raise taxes. The bill has a reduction of the 0.68 percent deficit by making 60 percent of that deficit in reductions in benefits and an increase of 0.24 percent in taxes. It does both.

There has been criticism, as I said, that the Pickle amendment clobbers the ladies, that it hurts the coal miners, and that it prevents the young from being able to retire on time. What we can do today we can still do under the amendment we just passed. My amendment does not change any of that. It does not change the right to claim benefits at 62, nor does it affect medicare at 65, nor does it affect SSI. We simply do not touch that.

Now, it is true that if one did not stay in the work force 1 more year, in the year 2009 approximately, then there would be some slowing in the growth of benefits. I am of the opinion that the American people would expect us to make some structural change in the social security program. That is not being harsh. If we leave our hearts to control what we do, we would then raise benefits and raise taxes, and then everybody could retire with all the money in the world they need.

Social security is not a full retirement program. It is a floor. It is a supplement, and it can be supported only as long as the American people will support it. I say to the Members that if we keep going in the direction of Senator Pepper, then there will be a generation gap, there will be generation conflict, and our young people simply will not continue to support it. . . .

Source: Congressional Record, House, March 9, 1983, H1046–H1048, H1067–H1068, H1076.

Document 7.10
President Reagan's Remarks on Signing the Social Security Amendments of 1983, April 20, 1983

During the large open-air signing ceremony, President Reagan stressed both the renewal of the nation's commitment to the Social Security system and the bipartisan nature of the deal that led to the enactment of the 1983 amendments. At many points along the way to passage of the bill, its fate was uncertain, and it was not obvious that a bipartisan compromise could be achieved. There was therefore a definite sense of both accomplishment and relief on the part of policymakers when the amendments were signed.

. . . This bill demonstrates for all time our nation's ironclad commitment to social security. It assures the elderly that America will always keep the promises made in troubled times a half a century ago. It assures those who are still working that they, too, have a pact with the future. From this day forward, they have one pledge that they will get their fair share of benefits when they retire.

And this bill assures us of one more thing that is equally important. It's a clear and dramatic demonstration that our system can still work when men and women of good will join together to make it work.

Just a few months ago, there was legitimate alarm that social security would soon run out of money. On both sides of the political aisle, there were dark suspicions that opponents from the other party were more interested in playing politics than in solving the problem. But in the eleventh hour, a distinguished bipartisan commission appointed by House Speaker [Thomas P.] O'Neill, by Senate Majority Leader [Howard] Baker, and by me began to find a solution that could be enacted into law.

Political leaders of both parties set aside their passions and joined in that search. The result of these labors in the Commission and the Congress are now before us, ready to be signed into law, a monument to the spirit of compassion and commitment that unites us as a people.

Today, all of us can look each other square in the eye and say, "We kept our promises." We promised that we would protect the financial integrity of social security. We have. We promised that we would protect beneficiaries against any loss in current benefits. We have. And we promised to attend to the needs of those still working, not only those Americans nearing retirement but young people just entering the labor force. And we've done that, too. . . .

A tumultuous debate about social security has raged for more than two decades in this country; but there has been one point that has won universal agreement: The social security system must be preserved. And rescuing the system has meant reexamining its original intent, purposes, and practical limits.

President Ronald Reagan signing the 1983 Amendments. Looking on from left to right: Sen. Robert Dole (R-Kan.), Rep. J. J. "Jake" Pickle (D-Texas), Rep. Claude Pepper (D-Fla.), Rep. Bob Michel (R-Ill.), Sen. Daniel Patrick Moyni-han (D-N.Y.), Rep. Thomas P. "Tip" O'Neill (D-Mass.), Rep. Barber Conable (R-N.Y.), and Sen. Howard Baker (R-Tenn.). Source: SSA History Archives.

The amendments embodied in this legislation recognize that social security cannot do as much for us as we might have hoped when the trust funds were overflowing. Time and again, benefits were increased far beyond the taxes and wages that were supposed to support them. In this compromise we have struck the best possible balance between the taxes we pay and the benefits paid back. Any more in taxes would be an unfair burden on working Americans and could seriously weaken our economy. Any less would threaten the commitment already made to this generation of retirees and to their children.

We're entering an age when average Americans will live longer and live more productive lives. And these amendments adjust to that progress. The changes in this legislation will allow social security to age as gracefully as all of us hope to do ourselves, without becoming an overwhelming burden on generations still to come.

So, today we see an issue that once divided and frightened so many people now uniting us. Our elderly need no longer fear that the checks they depend on will be stopped or reduced. These amendments protect them. Americans of middle age need no longer worry whether their career-long investment will pay off. These amendments guarantee it. And younger people can feel confident that social security will still be around when they need it to cushion their retirement.

These amendments reaffirm the commitment of our government to the performance and stability of social security. It was nearly 50 years ago when, under the leadership of Franklin Delano Roosevelt, the American people reached a great turning point, setting up the social security system. F.D.R. spoke then of an era of startling industrial changes that tended more and more to make life insecure. It was his belief that the system can furnish only a base upon which each one of our citizens may build his individual security through his own individual efforts. Today we reaffirm Franklin Roosevelt's commitment that social security must always provide a secure and stable base so that older Americans may live in dignity. . . .

Source: Public Papers of the President of the United States: Ronald Reagan, 1983, vol. 1 (Washington, D.C.: Government Printing Office, 1984), 560–563.

Document 7.11
Summary of the Provisions of the 1983 Amendments, April 20, 1983
This White House press release was issued upon the signing of the 1983 amendments. Note that the administration believed—as did almost everyone at the time—that the 1983 legislation resolved both the short-range and long-range financing problems facing the system.

Although not mentioned in the White House statement, the 1983 legislation also eliminated the residual gender distinctions remaining in the Social Security statutes—about a dozen provisions in the law.

Highlights of Major Provisions

Today, President Reagan signed into law the historic Social security Amendments of 1983. Based on recommendations by the bipartisan Commission on Social Security Reform established on December 16, 1981, the new law resolves both short- and long-term threats to the Social Security system.

Social Security Changes

Taken together, the provisions assure a balance of revenues and expenditures that will eliminate the crisis that had been facing the Social Security system in this decade and make structural reforms which will bring the long-range costs of the program into line with program revenues. The law provides for a total of $166 billion during 1983–1989 in additional taxes and income, and reduced expenditures. The law also makes reforms that address the serious long-range financing problems that the program had faced early in the next century because of changing demographic factors.

Retirement Age/Reduction for Early Retirement.   Gradually increases normal retirement age to 66 by 2005 and 67 by 2022. The retirement-age would increase by 2 months a year from 2000 to 2005 and from 2017 to 2022. Does not change age of eligibility for Medicare or the availability of reduced benefits at 62 (60 for widows).

Coverage of Newly Hired Federal Employees.   Covers Federal employees hired on or after January 1, 1984, plus all Members of Congress and the President, the Vice President, Federal judges, and other executive level political appointees of the Federal government effective January 1, 1984.

Coverage of Employees of Nonprofit Organizations.   Covers current and future employees of private tax-exempt nonprofit organizations effective January 1, 1984.

Prohibit Termination of Coverage of State and Local Government Employees.   Prohibits States from terminating coverage of State and local government employees if the termination has not gone into effect by the date of enactment. Also, permits State and local groups whose coverage has been terminated to be covered again.

Shift Cost-of-Living Adjustments to Calendar Year Basis.   Delays the July 1983 cost-of-living adjustment (COLA) to January 1984 and provides for future automatic COLAs on a calendar year basis, with the increase payable in January, rather than in July of each year. . . .

Cost-of-Living Increases to Be Based on Either Wages or Prices (Whichever Is Lower) When Balance in OASDI Trust Funds Falls Below Specified Level—"Stabilizer."   Limits future automatic increases to the lesser of the increase in wages or prices when the ratio of the combined

OASDI trust fund assets to estimated outgo falls below a given percentage. The "triggering" trust fund percentage is 15 percent through 1988 and 20 percent for 1980 and later.

The legislation also includes a catch-up provision for making up for any benefit increases that are based on the lower wage increases, when the trust fund ratio reaches 32 percent.

Eliminate Windfall Benefits for Persons Receiving Pensions from Noncovered Employment. For many workers who are first eligible after 1985 for both a pension based on noncovered employment, and Social Security benefits, applies a different benefit computational method. Specifically, the 90-percent factor now applied to average earnings in the first band of the benefit formula would be replaced by a factor of 40 percent, after a 5-year phase-in. This reduction in Social Security benefits would not exceed one-half of the amount of the pension.

Lower the Withholding Rate under the Earning Test for Individuals Who Have Attained Full Retirement Age.   Beginning in 1990, decreases the earning test benefit withholding rate from $1 for each $2 of earnings over the annual exempt amount to $1 for each $3 of excess earnings, for individuals who attain full retirement age (age 65 in 1990).

Increase Delayed Retirement Credit.   Beginning in 1990, gradually increases from 3 to 8 percent the delayed retirement credit payable to workers who delay retirement past age 65.

Amend the Government Pension Offset to Allow Spouses with Low Government Annuities to Retain a Portion of Their Social Security Spouse's Benefits.   Provides that for spouses and surviving spouses who become eligible after June 1983 for their public pension based on noncovered employment the amount of the public pension used for purposes of the offset against Social Security benefits will be reduced to two-thirds of the public pension.

Taxation of Social Security and Railroad Retirement Tier 1 Benefits.   Beginning in 1984 subjects up to one-half of Social Security (and railroad retirement tier 1) benefits to the Federal income tax if income exceeds $25,000 for a single taxpayer, or $32,000 for married taxpayers filing jointly.

Employee-Employer Tax Rate Schedule and 1984 Employee Tax Credit.   Advances previously scheduled FICA tax-rate increases for OASDI from 1985 to 1984, and advances part of the scheduled 1990 increase to 1988. The new law also provides, for 1984 only, a credit for employees against their FICA tax liability of 0.3 percent of their wages.

Self-Employment [Contribution Act] Tax-Rate (SECA) Schedule and Credit.   Increases tax rates on self-employment income for OASDI and HI to equal the combined employee-employer rates. Provides credits against SECA tax liability for 1984–89 equal to a percentage of self-employment income. After 1989, the credit will be replaced with special provisions designed to treat the self-employed in much the same manner as employees and employers are treated for Social Security and income tax purposes under present law.

Allocations to the OADI and DI Trust Funds.   Provides a new allocation schedule of OASDI taxes for employees and employers, each, and the self-employed. The provision does not raise any new revenue but shifts revenue from the DI trust fund to the OASI trust fund. The effect of this reallocation is to put the two parts of the program in roughly comparable financial condition, with the DI program being in slightly more favorable circumstances than OASI.

Interfund Borrowing.   Reauthorizes interfund borrowing among the OASI, DI and HI funds for calendar years 1983–1987. . . .

Source: SSA History Archives, Downey Books, Social Security Amendments of 1983, vol. 3.

CHAPTER 8

Disability Benefits in the 1980s

The decade of the 1980s in Social Security featured two big policy issues: financing (discussed in Chapter 7) and disability benefits. These issues ran on separate but chronologically overlapping tracks.

In broad terms, the 1980 amendments would tighten eligibility rules and increase adminstrative oversight of the program, with the aim of reducing costs; the 1984 Disability Benefits Reform Act would conclude that the 1980 changes had gone too far and would mandate a move back in the opposite direction.

During the early 1970s the disability incidence rate began to rise, substantially increasing the cost of the disability program and leading to concerns about the need to restrain those costs. This specific concern with the disability program was over and above the general solvency problems addressed in the 1977 amendments. At the time of the passage of

Secretary of Health and Human Services Margaret Heckler and her predecessor, Richard Schweiker, both implemented limited administrative reforms in the disability review process in the hopes of heading off a legislative remedy. Their efforts would prove to be in vain as the Disability Benefits Reform Act passed both houses of Congress overwhelmingly in 1984. Source: SSA History Archives.

the 1977 law, a decision was made to consider the disability program separately at a later time. The House Ways and Means Committee in its report on the 1977 bill warned: "Attention must still be focused on why the costs of the program have risen so rapidly to a level far greater than anticipated. The possibility of not only reducing the cost of the program but also making it more susceptible to administrative control must be thoroughly explored."

Several disability reform bills made it partway through the congressional process in the 94th and 95th Congresses, but none ultimately made it to passage. Late in the Jimmy Carter presidency the administration advanced a bill (the Disability Insurance Reform Act of 1979) that started the process toward what would become the 1980 amendments. The net effect of the administration's proposals was intended to be a long-range reduction in program costs.

The two key provisions in the administration's bill that would figure in the 1980 debates were a "cap" on the family maximum in disability cases and a change in the number of "dropout years" used in the disability benefit computation formula. The cap would place a limit on the total benefits payable to a family with a disabled worker, and the dropout years proposal would require more years of nonearning to be used in the calculation of the benefit amount. Both provisions were fairly technical—and somewhat indirect—forms of benefit cuts.

The Ways and Means Committee rewrote the administration's Social Security bill by adopting most of the administration's provisions (with slight modifications) but adding two crucial new requirements: (1) the Social Security Administration (SSA) would be required to do a preview of a portion of approved claims (that is, get a second opinion from within the organization) so as to make certain that the approvals were correct, but denied claims would not be reviewed; and (2) everyone on the benefit rolls who was not permanently disabled would have their status reviewed and recertified at least once every three years. These reviews—known as continuing disability investigations (CDIs)—were a traditional administrative practice, although they were at the discretion of the SSA. By the late 1970s fewer than 4 percent of the beneficiaries on the rolls had ever had their cases reviewed. These CDIs would become the central issue driving the adoption of the 1984 reforms.

The Senate made various modifications to the House bill (H.R. 3236), the most significant of which turned out to be a floor amendment introduced by Sen. Henry Bellmon (R-Okla.) to mandate that SSA conduct sample reviews of decisions by the administrative law judges (ALJs). Claimants who had their benefits denied or ceased could appeal, and the SSA maintained a quasi-independent corps of administrative judges to hear those appeals. The concern in this area was that the ALJs were too lenient and approved too many claims that the agency thought should be denied.

THE 1984 DISABILITY BENEFITS REFORM ACT

The CDIs mandated by the 1980 amendments would prove to be the cause of the biggest crisis in the history of the disability program. There were both procedural and policy issues involved in the disputes over the CDIs.

Among the procedural issues were:

- The review was a paper review with no contact with the beneficiaries, hence some obviously disabled persons were terminated.
- The initial rate of terminations was more than twice what Congress had been led to expect.
- SSA adopted a highly controversial policy of "non-acquiescence" in court rulings with which it disagreed.

Among the policy issues, were two particularly controversial ones: the problem of multiple impairments and the issue of medical improvement.

Disability claimants sometimes present with multiple impairments. SSA's position was that each impairment would be individually subjected to a severity test, and if they failed to have any single severe impairment, the claim would be denied. In other words, SSA refused to add multiple nonsevere impairments together to see if the net effect was a severe impairment.

Under the CDI process, a new determination was made in each review, only asking the question: "Does the person presently qualify under the rules?" This allowed the possibility of a person whose medical condition had not changed being approved for benefits initially but having those benefits cancelled during a CDI. This issue became focused on the question of the need for a finding of medical improvement before terminating someone's benefits.

Ultimately, the CDIs would lead to unprecedented levels of political and policy turmoil. State disability agencies (who process disability claims under contract to the federal government) in at least half the nation refused to conduct the CDIs under federal rules; some states refused to process the cases at all. The federal courts were overwhelmed with lawsuits. In a typical year, the federal courts would receive about 10,000 Social Security related cases. In fiscal year 1983 there were 23,690 new cases filed; by 1984 there were more than 44,000 cases pending. Several U.S. Attorneys served notice that they would no longer defend every Social Security case brought in their jurisdictions. SSA's own ALJs brought a lawsuit against the agency in federal court, claiming they were being pressured to lower their reversal rates on appealed cases. The newspapers were full of "horror stories"—involving even deaths and suicides—associated with SSA's CDI process. Prominent members of Congress complained in vivid terms about the problems in the disability reviews. The administration tried a series of progressively more accommodating administrative reforms, in an effort to head-off pressure for legislation. But ultimately, Congress would impose a resolution of the issues by passing the Disability Benefits Reform Act of 1984—by a unanimous vote in both houses of Congress.

Document 8.1
GAO Letter to Secretary Califano on the SSI Disability Program, April 18, 1978

In 1978 the General Accounting Office (GAO) did a very small study of certain disability recipients on the Supplemental Security Income (SSI) program. This brief report, in the form of a letter from GAO director Gregory J. Ahart to Joseph Califano Jr., the secretary of Health, Education, and Welfare (HEW), was the first document suggesting that the continuing disability investigation process was ineffective and that large numbers of ineligible beneficiaries were being kept on the rolls.

Even though this study involved only SSI disability beneficiaries, and it had severe methodological limitations (including the use of a sample of only 175 cases for a population of over 2 million disability beneficiaries), it was clearly viewed as having implications for the Social Security disability rolls as well. Its political impact was much larger than its limited parameters might suggest.

Dear Mr. Secretary:

This letter is to inform you of the results of our review on the Social Security Administration's (SSA's) activities related to assessing the continued medical eligibility of over 2 million disabled Supplemental Security Income (SSI) recipients. We selected two samples of SSI disabled recipients and asked SSA to evaluate the recipients' continued eligibility. One sample required an evaluation of the medical evidence supporting the disability determination of 402 recipients who were converted to the SSI program from State disability programs. The other sample required SSA to obtain and evaluate more recent medical evidence on 175 recipients.

Of the 402 converted recipients, SSA found that only 152, or 38 percent, had sufficient medical evidence in their files to support a disability decision. Furthermore, of the 152 cases, 36 cases, or 24 percent, were not disabled as defined by the appropriate State disability criteria. SSA found that of the 175 recipients for whom current medical evidence was obtained, about 10 percent were no longer disabled.

It is important to note that under present operating procedures, SSA would not have reviewed the continued medical eligibility of many of the recipients in our samples. We believe that there is a serious weakness in the administration of the disability aspects of the SSI program which allows medically ineligible recipients, such as those identified in our samples, to go undetected.

While we did not review the 2.6 million disabled beneficiaries receiving benefits under the Social Security Disability Insurance program, the procedures for monitoring this program are similar to those used for the SSI program. Therefore, payments to beneficiaries who are no longer disabled could also occur under the Disability Insurance program and go undetected. . . .

Need for a Systematic Medical Review of the Disabled Caseload

SSA lacks an adequate system for reviewing its SSI disability caseload to insure that only medically eligible persons continue to receive disability payments. . . . SSA estimates show that in 1976, 2.1 million disabled SSI recipients were paid $2.6 billion. However, only about 70,000 are scheduled for a medical reexamination. . . .

In our opinion, ineligible persons will continue to receive disability payments because SSA lacks an appropriate mechanism for systematically monitoring the disabled caseload so that persons who are no longer disabled can be removed from the rolls. . . .

Conclusions and Recommendations

The vast majority of SSI disabled recipients, once they are approved for the program, are not subject to medical reexaminations. SSA assumes that these recipients have impairments which will not improve. The results of our samples indicate that many recipients were no longer disabled or were not disabled at the time they entered the SSI program. Payments to beneficiaries who are no longer disabled could also occur under the Disability Insurance program and go undetected. . . .

Accordingly, we recommend that you direct the Commissioner of SSA to act immediately to establish appropriate mechanisms for systematically reviewing the disabled recipients' caseload so that persons no longer disabled can be removed from the rolls. . . .

Source: GAO Letter Report, HRD–78–97, April 18, 1978. Copy in SSA History Archives, Revolving Files, Folder: 1980 Amendments.

Document 8.2
SSA Disability Pilot Study, 1979

In 1979—in part in response to the 1978 GAO report (Document 8.1)—SSA began developing a quality assurance system for its disability insurance (DI) program similar to those it already had in place for the SSI program and for the retirement and survivors programs under Social Security. One result of the initial pilot test of this new system was the discovery that a significant percentage of the sampled cases (18 percent) were no longer disabled. Although the findings were not published prior to the 1980 legislation, the general result was known to Congress at the time the 1980 legislation was being considered.

(This version of the pilot study report was reprinted for a 1981 congressional hearing. It thus makes reference both to the original study data and to developments subsequent to the passage of the 1980 law.)

Overview: Disability Insurance National Pilot Study I

. . . The Agency is now in the process of developing a payment quality system for the Disability Insurance (DI) program. The first step in the process involved a pilot review of 3,154 DI cases selected from the entire DI payment rolls for April 1979. Both the non-medical and medical aspects of the case were thoroughly reviewed to determine the accuracy of the payment received in the sample month. . . .

The findings from the pilot study showed that 18.2 percent of all dollars paid in the sample month were paid to beneficiaries who were determined by a review not to be entitled to benefits because they were not disabled. These findings also are in accord with the results of studies by the General Accounting Office and other studies by the Social Security Administration. *[Authors' note: The figure cited in this paragraph (18.2%) is not identical to the value shown in the table below, which is 18.7%. The document contains no explanation of this discrepancy.]*

The data from the pilot have been useful in implementing the provision in the 1980 disability admendments that requires that continuing disability in all DI cases be reviewed every 3 years, except for cases involving a permanent disability. SSA has in effect implemented this provision in April 1981 (rather than January 1982) by increasing the number of cases to be reviewed from 135,000 to 274,000 for FY 1981.

By using a "profile" system . . . characteristics of the most error prone cases in the DI pilot were determined. The cases in the DI population with these characteristics were then targeted for review by SSA operational components in 1981. Concentrating on these high error cases will result in the largest amount of error reduction per case reviewed. In one group, as shown by DI pilot Phase I data, over 44 percent of the cases contained payment errors. The error cases in this group averaged in excess of $700 in payment error. . . .

Preliminary Disability Insurance Pilot I Findings, April 1979

I. General

. . . The DI Pilot Study I was conducted in 1979 and 1980 and consisted of a review of 3,154 cases randomly selected from the entire universe of primary beneficiaries in current payment status for April 1979. . . .

In each case, a redetermination was made with respect to the beneficiary's disability status in the sample month, April 1979. . . .

. . . [A] consideration to keep in mind when examining the results of the DI Pilot I data is that the judgments made in this pilot study as to nondisability do not mean that the individual so judged will be taken off the rolls. The true number of beneficiaries who will be removed from the rolls can only be found operationally after the beneficiaries, whose disabilities were judged questionable by the Pilot reviews, have exhausted all their appeal opportunities and are in fact taken off the rolls. The DI Pilot I has identified, as a minimum, a significant number of beneficiaries whose disabilities are questionable. . . .

The table below shows the final case and payment discrepancy rates for the first phase of the DI pilot. . . .

Case Discrepancy Rates

	Number of Cases	Percent of Cases
Sample Universe (Cases)	3,154	100%
Error Cases	640	20.3%
Medical and Vocational	567	18.0%
Non-Medical	73	2.3%

[Authors' note: The significant point in the above table is that in 567 cases out of the 3,154 reviewed (or 18% of the total cases) the person was found to not be disabled. This would be the suggested rate in the general DI population, from this study.]

Payment Discrepancy Rates

	Amount of Dollars	Percent of Dollars
Sample Universe (Dollars)	$1,100,023	100%
Error Dollars	$210,684	19.2%
Payments to Ineligibles	$205,853	18.7%
Overpayments to Eligibles	$4,831	0.4%

Source: "Disability Insurance National Pilot Study I," reprinted in *Social Security Appeals and Case Review Process*, Hearings before the Subcommittee on Social Security of the Committee on Ways and Means, House of Representatives, October 23 and 28, 1981 (Washington, D.C.: Government Printing Office, 1981), 31–111.

Document 8.3
Wilbur Cohen's Testimony at House Hearing, March 16, 1979

Although the 1980 amendments would enjoy strong bipartisan support from the congressional leadership and the administration, various advocacy groups and prominent individuals were strongly opposed. The opposition never seriously threatened passage of the legislation, but it did serve as ballast slowing down the movement for bigger changes.

This excerpt from the House hearings on H.R. 3236 features testimony in opposition to the bill from Wilbur J. Cohen, a former secretary of HEW and the cofounder, with Arthur Flemming, of an advocacy group called SOS—Save Our Security. SOS was a coalition of more than 100 advocacy groups that had as its honorary cochairs former Ways and Means Committee

chairman Wilbur Mills, former Speaker of the House John McCormack, and former HEW sec-
retary Arthur Flemming.

Mr. COHEN: . . . I must frankly say that I am deeply disappointed that the Department of Health, Education, and Welfare has not recommended important additional improvements in the program which I would like to discuss and which I urge the subcommittee to include in any bill it reports to the full committee and to the floor.

I wish to point out, first, that there is presently no crisis in the financing or the administration of disability insurance, as has been alleged. Consequently, I think there are no grounds for haste in acting on this bill, and I think the committee should take additional time to consider various other improvements not included in the chairman's bill.

I particularly note that this concludes the hearings, and there is going to be a markup shortly. I find that very unfortunate, and I believe the subcommittee should take additional time to consider other improvements which have not yet been considered, and that there ought to be a broader consideration of the entire disability insurance program.

As you may know, the volume of disability claims has declined. What we thought was a crisis in the financing of disability insurance couple of years ago has not continued.

You have now more time to consider constructive proposals, and I sincerely recommend that you begin to hear disabled witnesses on the whole problems of rehabilitation and work incentives, which I don't think you have done, and I think that is a fatal error in the procedure that this subcommittee has followed in not actually hearing from disabled people about the problems of rehabilitation and motivation and incentives which are very necessary to find a solution to the problems that the bill represents.

As I said, we recommend that you broaden your inquiry. Your present bill before the subcommittee is in my opinion too narrow and too restrictive.

In addition, you should also await recommendations of the National Committee [Commission] on Social Security of which I am a member by appointment of the Speaker. . . .

Congress, as you know, in the 1977 amendments created a statutory commission on social security. . . . [B]ut you have not asked the National Commission on Social Security for their views, and I believe before you have a markup on this bill, you should ask the National Commission for its views, and if the committee reports out a bill without asking for them, I think that the only recourse we have is to go to the full committee or the Rules Committee and protest the procedure by which the Congress itself appoints a commission and then proposes to take action without asking the Commission for its views on this important matter.

. . . I support some of the proposals in the bill before you, and I oppose others, and we would like to work out with the subcommittee a bill we could support, but we cannot support wholeheartedly the present bill.

We do not want to have to go to the full committee or the Rules Committee to work out the bill. If the subcommittee reports out the present bill in substantially its present form, we respectfully would have to object and oppose it both in the full committee and on the floor of the House.

For instance, we vigorously oppose the proposal to cut back on the dropout years for young disabled workers. This is an unjust, unwise, and unfair proposal. It is discriminatory against young persons. . . .

I am in favor of revised dropout of half of the number of years of coverage. At the least, at the very least, what you ought to do in this bill is to give 1 additional dropout year for each 5 years of coverage for all disabled persons and, if necessary, for other persons as well.

We also recommended that any disabled person who leaves the disability insurance rolls to go to work should have medicare available for the entire period until retirement. This is an important incentive for a disabled person to remain at work when they know, as a disabled person, they will at least have the medicare coverage, both part A and part B, should their work incentive not prove to be successful.

We also support coverage of medicare from the very beginning of the offset of disability. We urge you to include these above provisions in your bill. . . .

We also object to the unclear way in which the Secretary of HEW has proposed to limit court review of disability appeals. Quite frankly, we do not understand what the Secretary is proposing, and we would object to any inclusion of a limitation on court review in the bill unless we could see what the language is because it would be very important.

We urge consultation with distinguished lawyers before you take action on his recommendation, and we specifically request an opportunity to review any changes in the statute on the matter of court review before the subcommittee takes action in this vitally important area.

Mr. Chairman, we are also distressed at the effective dates in your bill. We believe you are not allowing sufficient time to implement effectively and intelligently these complex and somewhat confusing amendments. . . .

We need delay, also, because we do not believe that the Social Security Administration is in good enough shape today to undertake new or changed responsibilities without adequate time. . . .

. . . The disability insurance program requires additional staff to reduce these tremendous backlogs which have existed. . . .

There are two basic flaws in the way Social Security, including disability insurance, presently operates, Mr. Chairman.

First, the Social Security Administration in recent years, and presently, is under great pressures from the Office of Management and Budget and the Secretary's Office to get reductions that will affect the general budget.

I believe, and I say this only reluctantly as a former Secretary, Social Security should be taken out of the Department of Health, Education, and Welfare and made a board or a commission as it was in the original law of 1935. . . .

Second, inclusion of disability insurance contributions and benefit disbursements in the unified budget leads to misunderstanding and confusion of contributors, beneficiaries, and the general public.

We strongly urge exclusion of the social security trust funds from the unified budget, because it is the unified budget that makes it look like what you are doing in the Social Security is only to make the unified budget look better. . . .

So . . . I support the Pepper bill which is before your committee, to take Social Security out of HEW and out of the unified budget, and in my opinion, if you do not do those two things, you are not meeting what I hope you want, which is a much more efficient system of administration and a more intelligent cooperation of the entire program from the contributor. . . .

Finally, Mr. Chairman, in conclusion, we wish to object to the manner in which the changes in social security and disability insurance have been proposed and handled this year by the administration on the grounds that I have just outlined.

As you know, I have spent 45 years in working in this system. I don't want to see it destroyed. It is too important to the American people, and I am sure [to] the Ways and Means Committee, which has the honor of having constructed this, the most successful system of social benefits and transfer income in the history of the United States of America.

But the administration is tampering with the delicacy of a system which you may ruin by thoughtless, hasteful, ineffective action.

In my opinion, social security and disability insurance should be considered completely and separately from the budget deficit, and any surplus problem of the unified budget. . . .

The administration and the Congress make a tragic mistake if they proceed on the basis that the outcome or outgo or income of the social security system should be decided on the basis of the unified budget.

We shall oppose this approach, in a paraphrase of Sir Winston Churchill's immortal language, "on the beaches, in the streets, and in every congressional district. We shall oppose the administration, the Secretary, and the advocates of this approach."

We want persons of compassion and understanding to run the social security system. We appeal to you to reverse the rush which we believe may adversely affect the contributory social security system.

It is too important for the people I represent for us to continue on this confrontation course. And quite respectfully, Mr. Chairman, before you mark up this bill on Tuesday, I hope you will consider other alternatives in order that we may be able to work with you on a bill which will improve this system. . . .

Source: Disability Insurance Legislation, Hearings before the Subcommittee on Social Security of the Committee on Ways and Means, House of Representatives (Washington, D.C.: Government Printing Office, 1979), 406–412.

Document 8.4
House Floor Debates on H.R. 3236, September 6, 1979

H.R. 3236 passed out of the Ways and Means Committee on a unanimous vote and was adopted on the House floor by a vote of 235–162 (with 37 not voting). During the House debates in September 1979 there was some significant opposition to the legislation, primarily from rank-and-file Democrats. These excepts feature the chairman of the Social Security Subcommittee, Rep. James "Jake" Pickle (D-Texas), and two members of the Ways and Means Committee, Rep. Andy Jacobs (D-Ind.) and Rep. Bill Archer (R-Texas), defending the bill, along with Rep. Leon Panetta (D-Calif.), who as a member of the Budget Committee focuses attention on the cost savings in the disability program. Among those speaking out against the bill were Rep. Shirley Chisholm (D-N.Y.), Rep. Mario Biaggi (D-N.Y.), Rep. Claude Pepper (D-Fla.), and Rep. Pete Stark (D-Calif.).

Mr. PICKLE: . . . [T]his bill was passed in essence last year by the Subcommittee on Social Security. Earlier we were concerned then that there was a "run" on the disability program. It looked like the disability program was going to go broke, so in 1977 we passed a social security bill, and we raised taxes so that we would be certain that the American people would have the guarantee that there would be money there for their monthly checks.

. . . I think we corrected four-fifths of the problem on social security when we passed that bill.

Some people will say, "Well, you don't really need now to do anything about the disability program, because we have money in the disability program."

Yes, the disability fund is in much better shape today. We should all know that and be glad about it; but we should also remember that in the last 3 years we have transferred some $3 billion per year from the other trust funds over to the disability fund, so that the disability fund would not go broke. . . .

Second, we know that if there is a recession or a depression and if unemployment goes up . . . then we know what is going to happen under the disability program. Applications are going to go up as they have in the past. . . .

May I repeat that the objective of this bill was to give work incentive to these people to go back to work. . . .

In addition, we have tried to speed up the judicial process so that these cases would not just go on and on and on. . . . We found that they were not having reviews of State decisions. It had degenerated to less than 5 percent of the review by the Federal Government of these cases.

Now this bill says that there would be review in 1980 there would be a 15-percent review; in 1981,15 percent, and 1982, 65 percent.

We also closed the record at the administrative law judge level.

More importantly, we put a provision in there that says that every 3 years each person not determined permanently disabled will be reviewed again to see whether they are disabled and should they be continued.

Now, we are taking nobody off the disabled rolls now. Everybody has been grandfathered, so those people who say we are going to "cut benefits," they are not correct, because we are not actually taking away any funds. We are simply making basic corrections.

We did not set about in this bill to "save money."

Some seem to think, well, we were trying to balance the Federal Government by virtue of savings under the disability program. Well, this would actually affect less than 2 percent of the outlays in this whole program. We would make a savings, perhaps, by virtue of these corrections of, oh, upward of a billion dollars in the next 5 years; but the fifth year from now we will be paying out $175 billion; so obviously, we are not trying to correct the Federal budget by this bill. . . .

If we do not pass the bill today, these thousands, some 2 million people who deserve protection under these work incentives will not get them this year or next year and we do not know when. That would be grossly unfair if we did not pass a bill which we think has good balance. I recognize there has been some opposition, some under the cap, some under the dropout.

The intent was good. We had no idea that we would run into this kind of opposition, because some groups say you simply cannot cut any kind of benefit. We think we can do it and show the public that they can have confidence in the social security program and that is the purpose of this bill. . . .

Mr. JACOBS: . . . This legislation before the House now . . . is not really complicated at all. If you want to do commonsense, if you want to help the people who are severely disabled and you want to make sure that nobody is doing better on disability than he or she did on the job financially, then this is the right bill for you.

I might add that if you sat on that committee through the years and listened to the testimony and examined the data, you would conclude that on the reform side this is a very, very mild, very weak cup of tea. There are other reforms that can be argued logically in the social security disability system that were not brought to the floor because they were perceived by some in the Committee on Ways and Means to be too controversial. What was brought here, apart from the propaganda, and I must say knee-jerk propaganda against this bill, is a very weak reform. If the House of Representatives and this committee cannot even achieve that weak reform, then I think that we have no cause for pride in the work we have done this day.

Mr. ARCHER: . . . Mr. Chairman, I want at the outset to compliment the chairman of the subcommittee . . . and all the members of the subcommittee . . . because as was mentioned earlier, this bill was unanimously approved by the subcommittee which represents, I believe, a cross-section of the philosophies in this entire House. . . .

The bill has succeeded . . . because it represents a workable compromise, an appropriate blending of shared objectives. H.R. 3236 does not make as many changes as some of us would like; it makes more than others want. But, it is realistic, it is feasible, and it does include a number of significant and long-needed improvements in one of the two programs comprising our Nation's basic social insurance system.

First, the bill provides for disability benefit levels that are more reasonable and more equitable. Second, and equally as important, H.R. 3236 makes it easier and more attractive for a disabled beneficiary to return to work, if at all possible.

Actuaries have estimated that the bill would reduce outgo from the social security trust funds by $184 million in 1981. The "savings" would escalate annually, reaching a yearly level of more than $1 billion by 1984. The long-range deficit in the combined old age survivors and disability insurance trust funds would be cut 14 percent, from 1.4 to 1.2 of taxable payroll.

Although these "savings" are significant, I think they will be further enhanced if the added work incentives which the bill provides are fully taken into account. I believe that H.R. 3236 will help more people return to the labor force, thus producing more income for both the Treasury and the social security trust funds.

I also am convinced that these same provisions will bring about an even more important "savings" in human terms. Too many persons who are deemed to be disabled wind up on the shelves of our society. Through its improved work incentives and related provisions, H.R. 3236 should help many of these people to get back into productive pursuits, to rejoin the mainstream, and to enhance their own personal self-respect, a major key to happiness. . . .

The bill also toughens review procedures in the disability determination process. It requires Federal review of an increasing number of initial decisions by state agencies . . . and demands that each disabled beneficiary be reviewed at least once every 3 years as long as there is a possibility of recovery and a return to work.

Perhaps the two most controversial provisions of H.R. 3236 have the net effect of lowering total benefits paid to, and on behalf of future disabled beneficiaries. One provision reduces the number of "dropout" years for benefit computation purposes. Under current law, all beneficiaries may exclude the 5 years of lowest earnings when their benefits are computed. For younger workers who become disabled, this can create disproportionately higher benefit payments. Because maximum covered earnings have risen dramatically in relatively recent years, younger workers who become disabled can have their benefits computed on a much higher average earnings base than older workers, who have to take into account more years of lower covered earnings. H.R. 3236 cuts this benefit disparity between older and younger workers by phasing out the so-called dropout years for workers aged 47 and younger. . . .

Another controversial provision would place a new limit on the dollar benefits that could be paid to a disabled beneficiary and family. Studies by the administration, committee staff, and actuarial experts, have shown that many disabled beneficiaries and their dependents are receiving benefits which, when combined, make them better off financially than they were before the primary workers became disabled. This obviously has constituted a serious disincentive to return to work, and the Committee on Ways and Means Subcommittee on Social Security has endeavored, on a bipartisan basis, to find an equitable way to alleviate this problem.

I think it is clear that a substantial majority of members, at both committee and subcommittee levels, have favored limiting benefits so that the disabled are not better off financially than they would be if they were working. There has been some disagreement, however, as to what the limit should be. . . .

It is also important to note that the limit on benefits is just one element among many in the bill before us. Taken as a whole, H.R. 3236 offers major improvements, without radical restructuring. . . .

Mrs. Chisholm: Mr. Chairman, I rise in opposition to this legislation. Rather than being a "reform" of the social security system, as its proponents claim, H.R. 3236 will have a devastating effect on those Americans who find themselves disabled and unable to find employment in a labor market already contracting under the pressures of our economy. . . .

H.R. 3236 would limit total benefits for future disabled workers to 80 percent of their average monthly earnings or 150 percent of the primary social security benefit they would have received upon normal retirement, whichever is less. This provision could reduce current benefit levels by up to 20 percent. . . . Disabled workers usually lose valuable benefits, such as health care provided by their previous employer and, in addition, they often need to pay others to provide services they can no longer perform for themselves, such as home maintenance, transportation, and additional medical expenses caused by the disability. These increased costs dictate that more income than disabled workers now receive would be far more appropriate than the reducton which would occur under this bill.

While the negative effects of this legislation would apply to all disabled persons. I would like to turn for a moment to the effects that the two most damaging provisions of this bill will have on particular segments of the disabled population. The "cap" on the family benefit level in section 2 of the bill and the reduction in the number of "dropout years" for disabled beneficiaries under the age of 47 in section 3 will work the greatest hardship on younger disabled persons and their families.

Earnings, for most people, tend to rise in the early years of employment and reach a peak in the middle years. Thus, young disabled workers and their families are denied higher real earnings in the future. The ability to exclude low-earning years in computing benefits compensates in part for this loss. Since workers aged 26 or less "would not be allowed to exclude any years," under this legislation, these workers would be particularly penalized, because of the irregular work pattern of many young people.

The American Council of the Blind has indicated to me that the impact of this bill on blind Americans will be particularly startling. According to Social Security Administration statistics, one-third of the total 2.8 million disabled benefieiaries are under the age of 50. However, within the total number of blind beneficiaries, some 116,000, fully 71 percent are under 50 years of age. Thus, the detrimental impact upon the blind would he more than twice as great as upon disabled persons generally.

Blacks and other minorities would also be disproportionately harmed by the provisions in H.R. 3236. A recent review by the study group on social security indicates that "more blacks than whites become disabled and are more apt to have dependents." The 150-percent limitation of earnings on family benefits would be particularly hard on black and other minority workers with greater numbers of young children in their families. The alternative benefit limitation of 80 percent of a worker's average indexed monthly earnings would bear heavily on blacks because of their relatively low earnings records, especially during their younger years. The likelihood of low earnings records in the early years of a minority person's employment makes the current dropout years allowance an important compensation measure for minorities as well as younger workers. Black and other minorities also tend to have greater representation amongst younger disabled workers. Coupled with the high unemployment rate in minority communities, these workers would not only suffer the greatest cuts in benefits, as proposed by H.R. 3236, but they would also have the least hope of finding employment to replace their loss in benefit support.

Another group hit especially hard by these amendments is the Vietnam era veterans who are also in this younger age bracket. We have yet to deal compassionately and effectively with the legacy of our involvement in Southeast Asia, the plight of the Vietnam veteran. Now we are asking that they share a disproportionate burden in the name of "reforming" the social security system.

Public concern for fiscal responsibility cannot be misinterpreted as a license to assault social security benefits. If your constituents were faced with a choice between the type of "reforms" contained in this legislation and continuing to protect those Americans who find themselves disabled and without employment, I cannot believe that they would prefer to strip disabled Americans of what little support they currently receive. I strongly urge you to defeat this legislation. . . .

Mr. PANETTA: Mr. Chairman, I rise to make some comments on the legislative savings which would be achieved through the Disability Insurance Amendments of 1979 (H.R. 3236). . . .

Primarily because the administrative costs of this bill are higher than the estimates . . . the legislative savings in fiscal year 1980 will be less than the target of $62 million recommended by the Committee on Ways and Means in its . . . report to the Budget Committee and assumed in the first budget resolution. The savings in the disability trust fund will be $17 million and there will be a small net cost of $24 million in the overall budget for the first year of operation under this bill.

The significance of legislative savings in a benefit program such as this, however, is not in the first year of implementation but in succeeding years. This occurs because the basic entitlement of current beneficiaries is normally not affected so that savings occur when people first become eligible for benefits. Typically with entitlement legislation, as the proportion of the beneficiaries who enter the program after enactment of reforms increases over time, the savings from reforms also increases. The Disability Insurance Amendments of 1979 are not an exception to the pattern. By fiscal year 1984, the legislative savings from this bill will be $1.1 billion in outlays. Total savings over the next 5 years will be $2.7 billion.

. . . The report accompanying this bill cites testimony by former HEW Secretary Joseph Califano that benefits in about 6 percent of the cases are actually higher than the disabled person's previous net earnings, and in 16 percent of cases, the benefits are more than 80 percent of net earnings before disability. Because of the impact of taxes and work expenses, a replacement rate of 80 percent of net earnings before disability is generally considered adequate to replace predisability income. . . .

While achieving outlay savings of $2.7 billion over the next 5 years, the benefit reforms included in this bill will not jeopardize the benefits available to the needy.

The Congressional Budget Office has estimated that disability benefits allow families with one wage earner who becomes disabled to have on the average 95 percent of disposable family income before disability. This bill would reduce this percentage to an average of 89 percent.

For families with two wage earners, the Congressional Budget Office estimates that if one of the wage earners becomes disabled, disability benefits and other family income enable these families on the average to have disposable family income which is 5 percent above the income before disability. This bill would reduce this percentage to an average of 95 percent.

I would further note that protection against an income loss is provided to the low-income disabled. To the extent that disability benefits decline, low-income individuals will automatically be eligible for higher benefits under food stamps, the supplemental security income program, and in some cases aid to families with dependent children. . . .

It is not desirable public policy to provide financial incentives for people not to work. The Social Security Administration has found that as the percentage of previous income which is replaced by disability benefits has increased over the past decade, the recovery rate has decreased dramatically. Between 1967 and 1976, the average replacement of previous wages increased by 50 percent. Over the same period, the recovery rate decreased by 50 percent.

In considering this bill, we should be aware that the most important budget problem which we will face over the next half century is the financing and benefit structure of programs which replace the earnings of retired and disabled Americans. The largest program in this category is social security with estimated outlays of $116.8 billion in fiscal year 1980. . . .

Ultimately, these programs will be financed through the taxes of workers. . . . Thus, our major budgetary dilemma will be how to finance retirement and disability programs in a way which is fair to both recipients and to workers whose taxes finance the benefits. . . .

Mr. BIAGGI: Mr. Chairman, I rise in strong opposition to H.R. 3236 which some have referred to as the disability insurance reform amendments of 1979. To consider this bill as a "reform" measure is a hoax when in fact its real impact would be to drive millions of disabled Americans deeper into the perils of poverty. . . .

The bill's faults are many and can be traced in large measure to two false premises which proponents base this legislation on. The first is that the disability insurance program trust fund is in serious trouble and therefore benefits must be reduced. The 1979 report by the trustees of the social security trust fund predict a surplus in the disability program for the next 75 years. The second premise is that by reducing benefits you will be somehow providing a work incentive for those on disability. The facts are that many of those on disability are not capable of rehabilitation and in fact more than 70 percent of disability recipients are over age 50 and have chronic disabilities which make rehabilitation impossible. . . .

Much of my objection to this bill stems from section 2 of which imposes a ceiling on family benefits calculated at 80 percent of averaged indexed monthly earnings or 50 percent of the benefit amount whichever is lower. . . .

Perhaps the most fundamental objection I have to this bill is that it is premature. Here we are expected to vote on legislation making major changes in the disability insurance fund before even evaluating major reports which we mandated in 1977 legislation. These include reports by the National Commission on Social Security and the Advisory Council on Social Security.

The list of those opposing this legislation is impressive and should be persuasive. As mentioned earlier, the AFL-CIO is strongly opposed. The leading senior citizen organizations—the American Association of Retired Persons, the National Council of Senior Citizens, the National Council on Aging are all opposed. The Disabled Veterans of America and the Multiple Sclerosis Society and the National Organization of Women are opposed. Perhaps the most germane of all opponents are those who make up the SOS Coalition to protect social security. This group is led by former HEW Secretary Wilbur Cohen who has spoken out repeatedly in opposition to this legislation. Also on the SOS Coalition is Robert Ball, former Social Security Administrator under President Kennedy, Johnson, and Nixon. His two predecessors in that job, Mr. Charles Schottland and William Mitchell, are also part of the SOS Coalition opposed to the bill. These are men who administered the programs who feel these so-called reforms are not good for the program and the disabled of this Nation.

One other note about a distinguished opponent of this legislation. Our revered colleague Wilbur Mills who as chairman of the House Ways and Means Committee had a truly outstanding knowledge of the workings of the social security system in a letter dated June 18 indicated his opposition to H.R. 3236 until Congress may have an opportunity to further examine the situation. . . .

Mr. PEPPER: Mr. Chairman, as chairman of the Committee on Aging, I join several million individuals in over 100 organizations across the Nation in expressing my strong opposition to H.R. 3236. . . .

. . . I have the figures here from HEW, that 30 percent of the people who are affected by this legislation are 60 years of age and over, and the average age of the people who are covered by this disability insurance, the amount of which is attempted to be reduced, is 55-6/10ths. So this affects elderly workers as well as the average workers.

Of particular concern to the tens of millions of elderly and disabled persons are the so-called benefits cap and drop-out provisions. . . .

As it is presented on the floor today, H.R. 3236 represent an alarming lack of mature and intelligent deliberation. The intent of the bill appears to be quite clear. The committee report defends the benefits cap and dropout provisions in terms of "the need for work incentives." It would seem that the supporters of these two provisions do not believe that recipients are in fact disabled. . . .

The authors of the report language, with their continual references to work disincentives, would have us believe that beneficiaries are living off the fat of the land at the expense of the American taxpayer. H.R. 3236, they claim, will end this alleged extravagance by lowering benefit levels to the point where these "freeloaders" will have an incentive to return to work. . . .

. . . The fact is . . . that most disability beneficiaries cannot return to work. In almost all cases the disability is chronic and progressive in nature, and in many the ailment is expected to terminate in death.

We are told, nevertheless, that these cutbacks are necessary to keep the trust fund intact. . . . All too often, however, the fiscal knife has been wielded most enthusiastically on those tied to the stake of poverty and misfortune. H.R. 3236 is a tragic example of moral irresponsibility in the name of fiscal austerity. . . .

Mr. Chairman, to those of us who were around almost 45 years ago when the social security system was in its infancy and have seen it evolve into an ironclad intergenerational compact that has served America well for three generations, this bill is an abomination. . . . I cannot help but believe that the sharp reduction in the level of social security protection will make the over 110 minion current contributors to the program and the 35 million current beneficiaries alarmed about the Government's intention to honor its commitments to them.

Finally . . . I have the figures here . . . showing the total amount proposed to be saved in the next 5 years from 1980 through 1984, which is $1,700 million.

Now . . . from whom is that $1,700 million to be saved? From the crippled people of this country. A cap is to be put on the amount of income under the legislation that is now current that may be received by a family. That includes the children of disabled people who might be the head of a family.

Are we so destitute in America, are we so hard pressed that we have to turn to the cripple as the course of the purchase saving of revenue for the next 5 years?

Is this the leakage that is causing concern to our fiscal structure, the amount we are paying the handicapped of America?

I just hope that I will not be associated in an endeavor that has that purpose. . . .

Mr. Stark: . . . [T]he guts of H.R. 3236 is an average 15 percent reduction in benefits for the families of workers who became disabled after 1978. The question before the House today is not whether social security benefits can ever be cut. It is whether or not the cuts in this bill are fair and necessary.

According to the committee report the cut in family benefits is designed "primarily to strengthen work incentives for disabled beneficiaries." Is cutting family benefits a fair and effective way to get individuals who would otherwise meet the eligibility requirements of the disability program to stay off the program?

Current law states that an applicant for disability insurance must be unable, because of his or her impairment, to do any work that exists in the national economy. . . .

. . . [I]f the law is not being enforced—if there are people on the disability rolls who are able to "do any work that exists in the national economy" then does it not make more sense to improve on the eligibility determination process than to cut benefits across the board?

The benefit cuts in this bill will hit 84 percent of newly disabled workers with dependents receiving benefits. That is reneging on promises we have made to U.S. workers over the years who have paid taxes year after year. . . .

Mr. Chairman, the disability insurance trust fund is in good shape financially. The committee report states that the 1977 amendments assured the solvency of the trust fund well into the 21st century.

It has been alleged that "special interest groups" have mounted an intensive campaign to defeat this bill. The allegation is correct. Organizations of the disabled, labor, women and church groups, civil rights groups, and senior citizens' organizations, and veterans organizations have banded together to protect the public—and I believe, to protect us, from a mistake—a grave mistake. . . .

Source: Congressional Record, House, September 6, 1979, H7400–H7410.

Document 8.5
Senate Finance Committee Report, November 8, 1979

This excerpt from the Senate Finance Committee report on H.R. 3236 gives a clear indication of the nature of the legislative interest in 1980—program costs and the growth of the disability rolls. The range of factors discussed in the report indicates the breadth of the legislative concerns motivating policymakers in the 1980 legislation.

Table 4 in this excerpt compares the cost estimates for the program associated with various legislative expansions and the actual costs as experienced. This table was an effort by the committee to separate the growth in costs from legislative changes from growth due to other factors.

The disability insurance program has grown in caseload size and cost well beyond what was originally estimated. In part, the growth of the program reflects legislative changes which have expanded coverage and benefits. Much of the growth, however, must be ascribed to other causes such as de facto liberalization as a result of court decisions, weaknesses in administration, and greater than anticipated incentives to become or remain dependent upon benefits.

At the time the disability insurance program was enacted in 1956, its long-range cost was estimated to be 0.42 percent of taxable payroll. The "high cost" short-range estimate indicated that benefit outlays would reach a level of $1.3 billion by 1975. Under the 1979 social security trustees' report, the long-range cost of the program is now estimated to be 1.92 percent of taxable payroll. Benefit payments for 1975 totalled $7.6 billion, and benefit payments for 1979 are expected to total approximately $14 billion. (Note: at present payroll levels, 1 percent of taxable payroll is roughly $10 billion.)

Table 4 shows the changes in the estimated costs of the program over the years since it was first enacted. Many of the cost increases in the earlier years are attributable to changes in the law, broadening eligibility. The last major change of this type was enacted in 1967. The reductions in long-range costs after 1977 are partly a result of the new benefit computation for all social security benefits adopted in the 1977 amendments and of the increase in the tax base under those amendments. . . .

There are now about 2.9 million disabled workers receiving DI benefits, increased from 1.3 million in 1969. This represents a 123 percent increase over a 10-year period during which there was no major legislative expansion of eligibility requirements. Currently, in addition to the disabled workers who are receiving benefits, there are benefits being paid to about 2 million dependents of disabled workers. . . .

Table 4 Growth in Estimated Cost of DI Program

Year of estimate	Estimated cost		
	Long-range (as percent of payroll)	Short-range[a] (millions)	1980 projection (millions)
1956	.42	$ 379	[b]
1958	.49	492	$ 1,380
1960	.56	864	1,550
1965	.67	1,827	2,211
1967	.95	2,068	3,351
1973	1.54	6,295	NA
1975	2.97	9,640	NA
1976	3.51	12,715	16,197
1977	3.68	14,822	16,817
1978	2.26	16,532	16,532
1979	1.92	17,212	15,600

[a]Short-range represents intermediate estimate of cost for second year after the year of estimate.
[b]No 1980 projection made; 1975 costs were projected to be $949,000,000.
Note: NA = not available.

Causes for Growth

. . . [T]he experts have had very great difficulty estimating how the disability programs would develop, and they have frequently been wrong. They have found it equally difficult to pinpoint the reasons for growth in the disability programs, particularly in the disability insurance program. The growth that took place, primarily in the first half of the 1970's, would seem to have leveled off. But there is still no consensus on exactly why it happened, the weight to be given to various factors, or even on whether the period of rapid growth is over.

1. Increases in Disability Incidence Rates
The table below shows standardized disability incidence rates under the disability insurance program for the period 1968–75. As can be seen, the rates show an almost steadily increasing trend from 1968, although appearing to level off in 1973–75.

Table 11 Standardized Disability Incidence Rates under DI, 1968–1975 (Rates per 1,000 Insured)

Year	Standardized Rate	Percentage increase over 1968
1968	4.46	—
1969	4.29	–4
1970	4.77	+7
1971	5.25	+18
1972	6.00	+35
1973	7.20	+61
1974	7.14	+60
1975	6.85	+54

Social Security Administration actuaries attempted to assess the reasons for the increase in incidence rates. . . . Their analysis points to a variety of factors, including increases in benefit levels, high unemployment rates, changes in attitude of the population, and administrative factors. . . .

The actuaries believe that another factor in the increase in incidence rates is the high unemployment rate that the country experienced after 1970. They argue that physically impaired individuals are more likely to apply for benefits if they lose their jobs in a recession than during an economic expansion when they can retain their jobs.

According to the actuaries, another factor influencing increases in incidence rates is changes in attitude. Elaborating on this theme, they state that "It is possible that the impaired . . . of today do not feel the same social pressure to remain productive as did their counterparts as recently as the late 1960's.". . .

The authors were unwilling to attribute the increase in disability incidence rates to these factors to any specific degree, and observed only that they were responsible for "a large part" of the increases. Beyond that they state: "We feel that some administrative factors must have also played an important part in the recent increases, but we cannot offer a definite proof to that effect."

One administrative factor mentioned is the multi-step appeals process, which enables the claimant to pursue his case to what the actuaries term as the "weak link" in the hierarchy of disability determination. Under the multi-step appeals process, a claimant who has been denied benefits may request first a reconsideration, then a hearing before an Administrative Law Judge, appeal his hearing denial to the Appeals Council, and, if his case is still denied, take his claim to the U.S. district court. The actuaries claim that by the very nature of the claims process, the cases which progress through the appeals process are likely to be borderline cases where vocational factors play an important role in the determination of disability. . . . To the extent that vocational factors are given higher weight as a claim progresses through the appeals process, the chances of reversal of a former denial is increased.

The actuaries also cite the "massive nature" of the disability determination process as one of the administrative factors which may be responsible for the growth in rolls. There has been an enormous increase in the number of claims required to be processed by the system. In fiscal year 1969, the Social Security Administration took in over 700,000 claims for disability insurance benefits. By 1974 the number of DI claims per year had grown to 1.2 million. In addition, over 500,000 disability claims under the black lung program, which started during 1970, had been taken in. And the number of SSI disability claims being taken in approached another million. As the actuaries point out, all this was happening at a time when the administration was making a determined effort to hold down administrative costs.

During this period it would appear that there was an inevitable conflict within the administrative process between quality and quantity. The winner, it would appear, was quantity. . . .

A final factor given for the increase in the incidence rates is "the difficulty of maintaining a proper balance between sympathy for the claimant and respect for the trust funds in a large public system." The actuaries maintain that they do not mean that disability adjudicators consciously circumvent the law in order to benefit an unfortunate claimant. They mean rather that in a program designed specifically to help people, whose operations are an open concern to millions of individuals, and where any one decision has an insignificant effect on the overall cost of the program, there is a natural tendency to find in favor of the claimant in close decisions. . . .

Decrease in Terminations

At the same time that there have been increases in disability incidence rates, there have also been decreases in disability termination rates. . . . death termination rates have decreased gradually over the years from about 80 per thousand in 1968 to about 50 per thousand in 1977. . . .

. . . [They cite] several reasons for the decline in the death termination rate: legislative changes which brought in younger workers, maturation of the program, the liberalized definition of disability in the 1965 amendments from permanent disability to one that is expected to last at least 12 months, and improved medical procedures that have also contributed to the decline in death rates in the general population.

However, the actuaries state that although all of these reasons contributed to the decline, "it is doubtful that they can fully account for the rather rapid decrease that has been observed." Rather, they say, they believe that healthier applicants are being awarded disability benefits and consequently there is a tendency for the overall mortality rates to decline. . . .

Examining the other significant factor in termination rates, recovery rates, the actuaries come to essentially the same conclusion. . . .

The actuaries also cite administrative changes as a possible reason for a decline in recoveries due to a determination of improvements in the beneficiary's physical condition. Pinpointing "administrative expediency," they note that the high workload pressures of past years forced SSA to curtail some of its policing activities. The Social Security Administration made continuing disability investigations of about 10 percent of the DI beneficiaries on the rolls in years prior to 1970. During fiscal years 1971 to 1974, when the administrative crunch of the black lung and SSI programs were at their peak, there was an investigation of just over 4 percent of the DI beneficiaries in a year.

A final factor which is mentioned in the actuaries analysis is high benefit levels, or high replacement ratios. Defining the replacement ratio as the annual amount of benefits received by the disabled worker and his dependents divided by his after tax earnings in the year before onset of disability, the actuaries claim that the average replacement ratio of disabled workers with median earnings has increased from about 60 percent in 1967 to over 90 percent in 1976. During this period the gross recovery rate decreased to only one-half of what it was in 1967. . . .

Problems Addressed by the Committee Bill

The disability programs administered by the Social Security Administration have been the subject of intensive study and review in recent years. The Congress and the Administration have both participated in this process. In summary, problems which have been identified include unpredicted and extraordinary growth in costs and caseloads, disincentives for beneficiaries to return to work, and inadequate and sometimes inequitable administrative procedures.

The committee bill has as its primary purpose the strengthening of the integrity of the disability programs by placing a limit on disability insurance benefits in those cases where benefits tend to exceed the net predisability earnings on which the benefits are based;

providing positive incentives, as well as removing disincentives, for . . . beneficiaries to return to work; and improving accountability and uniformity in the administration of the programs. . . .

Source: Committee on Finance, U.S. Senate, Social Security Disability Amendments of 1979 (Washington, D.C.: Government Printing Office, November 8, 1979), 19–20, 22, 27–32, 34.

Document 8.6
Senate Floor Debates on H.R. 3236, January 31, 1980

Although there was general support in the Senate for the bill, some amendments were adopted that had the effect of reducing the planned savings from the bill—a fact the Senate sponsor of the bill, Russell Long (D-La.), laments in his comments.

One important amendment that stayed in the final bill was offered by Senator Bellmon, to authorize reviews of administrative law judge decisions. This amendment's importance was not seen at the time, but it would play a role in the ensuing controversies over the CDI process.

Ultimately, the bill, as amended, passed by 87–1 (with 12 not voting). When the conference report eventually returned to the two bodies, the final version of the 1980 amendments passed the House with only two "no" votes and passed the Senate unanimously.

Mr. LONG: . . . I hope everybody is listening . . . because the word should go out . . . that the Senate has embarked on a spending orgy. The Senate has completely disregarded its previous commitment to try to balance the budget, and it has gone wild to try to take these out-of-control spending programs and make them still further out of control.

. . . [W]e on the Committee on Finance were assigned our share of the burden of trying to balance the budget, trying to stop some of the needless spending in Government so that we could keep this Government from going so deeply into debt, because we know that is one of the big items contributing to inflation that the people of this Nation are suffering, namely the great big Federal deficit we have been sustaining.

Then we reported this bill to the calendar . . . on disability insurance. The House . . . has sent us a bill. Imagine; those courageous members of the House brought a bill before that body, and sent it here, this very bill, to reduce the spending in this disability area by $2.7 billion over at 5-year period; a saving of about $600 million a year on the average over that period.

They did that because . . . of all the big spending programs, the very big spending programs, this is the one that is most out of control. Secretary Califano courageously faced up to it and did what he could administratively. Secretary Harris is doing what she can do to limit the unintended spending in this area.

. . . [T]his program was supposed to cost one-half of 1 percent of payroll and it is costing 2 percent of payroll. It is costing almost $16 billion a year. . . . Well-intentioned people, their humanitarian instincts coming to the fore, have seen fit to find a lot of people disabled on a total and permanent basis when, actually, those are handicapped and partially disabled, but not disabled in the sense that Congress originally intended when it passed the program. So we are trying to get this matter under control.

Yesterday, the Senate voted to over rule its Presiding officer, to run roughshod over its Parliamentarian, to break through a unanimous-consent agreement, to vote on an amendment so that some people need have no waiting period any longer to get on the disability rolls.

. . . That will cost $3 billion when fully implemented. . . .

It was only by a tie vote . . . that we succeeded in keeping the Senate from voting to say that the paymeats under disability would be every bit as much as 100 percent of what the person was making when working. . . .

I hope . . . that the time is beginning to arrive when Senators will have a return of fiscal conscience and begin to think in terms of fighting inflation and balancing the budget, because the people in this Nation are interested in that, even if Senators are not.

Mr. BELLMON: . . . [T]his amendment requires the Secretary of Health and Human Services [HHS] to implement a procedure for reviewing a sample of decisions made by administrative law judges. The decisions to be reviewed under this mandate are ones in which administrative law judges have reversed State denials. My amendment will strengthen one of the weakest links in the disability adjudication process, and also help insure the equitable treatment of claimants.

. . . [T]here is almost no disagreement that the appeals process in the disability program is costly and time consuming. Disability cases that go up through the whole appeals ladder take more than 1 year to process. This has led to serious complaints that the social security hearing process is slow and inefficient. This is partly due to the increased number of appeals cases filed each year which lead to backlogging in the appeals process.

The number of disabilty cases appealed has dramatically risen over the years. . . . [T]here were only 43,000 hearing requests in 1970. But in the first 8 months of 1979, 206,000 cases had been received for a hearing.

While much of the increase in the number of appeals can be attributed to the overall growth of the disability program, there is considerable evidence that there are other factors involved as well. Cases that are appealed to the administrative law judge level have a very high probability of being reversed in favor of the claimant.

. . . [T]he reversal rate has increased from 39 percent of all cases heard by the administrative law judges in 1969 to better than half, or 52 percent of all cases heard in 1978.

What concerns me . . . is that if a claimant knows he or she has nothing to lose by appealing a case all the way through the appeals process, and has in fact better than a 50 to 50 chance of having his or her case reversed favorably, then this will undoubtedly add to the number of cases appealed. It may be that, instead of insuring justice, the hearing process may be rewarding persistence.

Much of the problem has to do with the administrative law judge decision-making process itself, which is highly individualized. The judges are independent and differ in their procedural methods on hearings. . . . [T]he judges develop and decide cases in very different ways, some relying heavily on consultative medical examinations and others not, and some using vocational specialists a great deal in deciding cases while others do not. This has led to a great degree of variation in reversal rates among judges. . . . There seem to be more "easy" judges than "hanging" judges, however. . . . 87 percent of the judges reversed 46 percent or more of the cases they heard. This seems to be an exceptionally high number of judges who reverse, on the average, almost half the cases that come before them.

These data indicate why the judges are considered by many experts to be the weakest part of the process. When you consider the individualized and independent style of the judges, combined with the highly subjective nature of many disability cases, there is the great potential for widely varying decisions and high reversal rates. Contributing to this are the factors which the judges must take into consideration when deciding a case. The use of vocational factors in considering a case makes the decision very subjective and heavily dependent on the individual judge's views. This has led to variations in reversal rates among judges and has brought concern that claimants are being treated differently.

The Social Security Administration has attempted to improve the situation by issuing a set of "vocational regulations" as guidelines for deciding cases. As yet, this has not had any effect on slowing the increase in reversal rates. Indeed, the rate has continued its upward climb. More regulations are not going to do the job. We need a method to review the decisions made by the judges so that there is greater consistency among different judges and better assurance that disability awards are not being granted inappropriately in a large number of cases. . . .

The Secretary already has authority to review and reverse both determinations made at the State level and decisions by Federal administrative law judges. . . . Until 1975, the appeals council also reviewed a selection of ALJ decisions that were not appealed. In other words, the council selected and reviewed some decisions in which ALJs reversed State denials. . . .

The appeals council stopped making these so-called "own motion" reviews in 1975, apparently because of workload problems.

Nearly a year ago former Social Security Commissioner Stanford Ross testified that HEW intended to reinitiate these "own motion" reviews of ALJ decisions. Unfortunately, our checks with HEW indicate that there has been no real movement on getting these reviews going. This amendment will require them to get on with the reviews. . . .

Source: Congressional Record, Senate, January 31, 1980. S701–S720.

Document 8.7
President Carter's Statement on Signing the 1980 Disability Amendments, June 9, 1980

In signing the disability legislation, President Carter chose to emphasize the provisions of the bill aimed at helping disability recipients find employment without losing their benefits. As it put it, "H.R. 3236 is designed to help disabled beneficiaries return to work." Implicitly, this meant a hoped-for reduction in the disability rolls and a consequent reduction in program costs, which was the real policy concern behind the legislation. President Carter avoided any mention of what would become by far the most controversial aspect of the legislation: the requirement that the disability rolls be reviewed and that those found to be no longer disabled be removed from the rolls. This enforcement aspect of the new law would, in fact, become the dominant focus of the legislation as it was implemented.

Today I have signed H.R. 3236, the Social Security Disability Amendments of 1980. This bill is the product of several years of intensive study and review conducted by this administration and the Congress. It forms a balanced package, with amendments to strengthen the integrity of the disability programs, increase equity among beneficiaries, offer greater assistance to those who are trying to work, and improve program administration.

Since the mid-1950's the social security disability insurance (DI) program has offered protection to insured workers who have lost wages because of unexpected and often catastrophic disabilities. . . .

Despite their medical impairments, most disabled DI . . . beneficiaries would like to work. Often they are able to find employment either in their previous occupations or in new jobs. But returning to work can now cause a recipient to lose all his cash and medical benefits, and this formidable financial risk deters many beneficiaries from seeking or accepting serious job offers.

H.R. 3236 is designed to help disabled beneficiaries return to work by minimizing the risks involved in accepting paid employment. It does this in several ways:

- by providing automatic re-entitlement to benefits if an attempt to return to work fails within 1 year;
- by continuing medical protection for up to 3 years after a person returns to work, and by providing immediate re-entitlement to medical benefits if the individual subsequently returns to the disability rolls;
- by taking account of an individual's disability-related work expenses in determining eligibility for benefits. . . .

H.R. 3236 adjusts the maximum limitation on disability insurance dependents' benefits. The adjustment addresses problems that exist because some disabled workers can receive cash disability benefits that are greater than their previous employment income. The adjusted benefit limitation will not apply to people currently receiving benefits. In fact, no person now receiving benefits will have his or her benefits reduced as a result of any provision in this bill. . . .

Source: Public Papers of the Presidents: Jimmy Carter, 1980–81, vol. II (Washington, D.C.: Government Printing Office, 1982), 1062–1063.

Document 8.8
Summary of the 1980 Disability Amendments, April 1981

This document is a summary of the final provisions of the 1980 amendments. As this SSA-prepared summary suggests, the 1980 amendments contained a laundry list of seemingly small policy changes. The focus was the disability program, and the aim was to reduce the cost of that program.

The two changes listed under "Provisions Increasing Equity"—maximum family benefit and dropout years—are the main benefit cuts. While all the provisions listed under "Strengthening Work Incentives" were program liberalizations, they were all in the service of removing people from the disability rolls. The various administrative changes under the "Improving DI and SSI Program Administration" heading were procedural changes that would make it less likely that a disability applicant's claim would be successful—hence their implicit purpose was to reduce the disability rolls.

Provisions Increasing Equity

Maximum Family Benefit

The new law sets the maximum family benefit in disability cases at 85 percent of the average indexed monthly earnings or 150 percent of the primary insurance amount, whichever is less, but no less than 100 percent of the primary insurance amount. . . .

One concern that led to this change was that high benefit amounts and replacement rates for some disabled worker families had contributed to growth in the DI program by encouraging persons with serious medical conditions to stop working and apply for benefits and by discouraging those receiving benefits from returning to work. Another concern involved the appropriateness of situations where DI benefits exceed predisability take-home pay, regardless of the effect that such situations might have in encouraging applications for benefits or discouraging rehabilitation. Under the previous law, for example, about 6 percent of newly entitled DI beneficiaries and their families would receive benefits that would he higher than the worker's predisability *net* earnings.

Dropout Years

. . .The number of years that can be dropped from the computation (averaging) period is proportional to the age of the disabled worker. . . .

Provisions Strengthening Work Incentives

Exclusion of Extraordinary Work Expenses Due to Severe Disability

This provision states that for purposes of determining whether the level of earnings received by a disabled beneficiary demonstrates ability to engage in substantial gainful activity . . . the costs to the beneficiary of attendant care services, medical devices, equipment prostheses, and similar items and services needed to enable the beneficiary to work will be excluded from income. . . .

This change reflects the view that a worker's gross earnings are not a fair measure of a worker's ability to engage in substantial gainful activity when a very substantial part of those earnings must be used to pay for extraordinary impairment-related work expenses. . . .

Automatic Reentitlement to Benefits

Extends . . . a person's status as a disabled individual for 15 months after the completion of a 9-month trial work period, as long as there is no medical recovery. Although under the DI program cash benefits are not payable for more than 3 months of this period if the individual engages in SGA [substantial gainful activity], the individual can automatically be reinstated to active benefit status if the work attempt subsequently fails and he or she stops substantial gainful activity. Thus, when earnings exceed SGA cash benefits will be stopped, but the individual is offered the new assurance of automatic reentitlement in the first year after the trial work period ends. . . .

Extension of Medicare Coverage

Medicare coverage under the DI program is extended for an additional 24 months after the end of the automatic reentitlement period. Thus, Medicare benefits can remain available for 3 years after cash benefits end and 2 years after the reentitlement period. . . .

It is often argued that the loss of medical coverage is frequently more of a disincentive than is the loss of cash benefits because medical needs are more uncertain and unpredictable than are cash needs and it may be difficult for a disabled person to obtain private medical insurance. It is hoped that by extending Medicare coverage for up to 4 years after the return to work, the individual has had ample opportunity to adjust to working, to feel secure working and to make the necessary arrangements for medical coverage either individually or through an employer's group plan.

Waiver of Second Medicare Waiting Period

The requirement is eliminated that a person who was previously receiving DI benefits and entitled to Medicare (and who, within a specified period of time, becomes disabled a second time) must undergo another 24-month waiting period before Medicare is available. . . .

This provision assures those who go back to work that the fact that they have attempted to work will not cause a delay in becoming eligible for Medicare should their work attempt fail and they return to the DI rolls. . . .

Trial Work Period for Disabled Widow(er)s

The trial work period, previously applicable only to disabled workers and adults disabled in childhood, is extended to disabled widows and widowers under DI. This change will allow these beneficiaries an opportunity to attempt to work and become self-sufficient. . . .

Continuing Benefits in VR Plans

Special DI and SSI benefits (and, therefore, vocational rehabilitation services) will continue after medical recovery for persons in approved VR programs if (1) the medical recovery was not anticipated and (2) the continuance of such benefits will increase the likelihood that the persons will go off the benefit rolls permanently.

Improving DI and SSI Program Administration

Periodic Review of Disability Determinations

A review is required at least once every 3 years of the status of disabled beneficiaries whose disabilities may not be permanent. Where a finding is made that an individual's disability is permanent, review of the beneficiary's condition may be made at such times as the Secretary considers appropriate. This provision reflects a congressional concern that too little has been done to assure that DI and SSI benefits are not being paid to persons who have medically recovered from their disability. The change is effective January 1, 1982.

Federal Review of State Agency Determinations

A Federal review is required of State disability allowance and continuation determinations on a preeffectuation basis, in order to assure greater uniformity and consistency of the decisions made by various adjudicators within a State agency and of decisions made by the various States. A review of 15 percent of such DI determinations is required in fiscal year 1981, increasing to 35 percent in fiscal year 1982, and 65 percent in fiscal year 1983 and thereafter. . . .

Review of Administrative Law Judge Decisions

The Secretary is required to institute a program of own-motion review of disability decisions rendered by ALJ's and submit a report on the progress of this program to the Congress. . . .

Closed Evidentiary Record

The introduction of new evidence is prohibited in OASDI and SSI claims after a decision on the claim is made at the hearings level, in order to stabilize the record on a claim prior to Appeals Council or Federal Court review. . . .

Source: SSA Office of Legislative and Regulatory Policy, "Social Security Disability Amendments of 1980: Legislative History and Summary of Provisions," *Social Security Bulletin,* vol. 44, no. 4, April 1981, 13–18.

Document 8.9
Reagan Administration Economic Recovery Plan, February 18, 1981

At the start of Ronald Reagan's first administration, a long report was published detailing the administration's plans to cut federal spending in order to produce "A Program for Economic Recovery." One section of that plan concerned the Social Security disability program. This document is the beginning of the post-1980 amendments policy debates. The administration's economic recovery plan proposed to achieve general budget savings by accelerating the implementation of the continuing disability investigation process from the 1980 amendments and by making two additional changes in Social Security law.

The original effective date of the CDI provision in the 1980 law was January 1982, with the first net savings to be achieved in fiscal year 1984. The Reagan administration accelerated the start of the CDIs to July 1981 and forecasted dramatically higher budget savings than previously estimated. The original budget projections for the CDIs showed a net savings of only $10 million for the first four years of the reviews, because the short-term administrative costs of the process had to be offset against any savings. The Reagan budget plan, by contrast, projected $1.45 billion in savings in the first four years and a total of $3.45 billion in the first six years.

Tightening Eligibility for Disability Insurance

The Administration will reduce rapidly growing disability insurance costs by tightening administration and ending misdirected benefits. A new management team will take action to eliminate ineligible payments, and the Administration will propose legislation to relate disability benefits more closely to a disabled worker's prior earnings.

Disability insurance benefits replace lost earnings for disabled workers and their families, allowing recipients to maintain an adequate living standard despite their inability to work to support their families. This is the purpose of social insurance.

In January of 1981, however, the General Accounting Office (GAO) reported that:

"there may be as many as 584,000 beneficiaries not currently disabled but still receiving disability benefits. These beneficiaries represent over $2 billion annually in Trust Fund costs."

Social Security Administration (SSA) studies confirm that huge sums are paid incorrectly to individuals misclassified as disabled. As a result, DI caseloads have risen by 80% since 1970, and costs have climbed by 500%. Under the direction of this Administration, the SSA will begin to intensively review cases to insure that only the truly disabled receive disability benefits.

Overly-generous benefit levels induce some individuals to remain on disability insurance long after any true disability has been overcome. This frequently occurs when a recipient's DI benefits exceed the wage level of his customary work, especially now that indexing in recent years has driven up the value of DI benefits. In addition, DI beneficiaries may receive both disability and workers' compensation from plans sponsored by employers or the States. To remove this work disincentive, a "megacap" will be established on benefits that DI beneficiaries receive to ensure that disability income from all sources never exceeds the worker's prior earnings, adjusted for inflation. This proposal will prevent DI recipients with multiple sources of disability payments from receiving overly-generous benefits.

The Administration will also propose legislation to more closely tie eligibility for DI to those who have paid their fair share of contributions to the social security system. Under current law, people who have not paid social security taxes in the past 5 years are eligible for disability benefits. Requiring disability insurance beneficiaries to have had a more recent attachment to the workforce—measured by working 6 out of the last 13 quarters—would more closely link benefits to the replacement of lost (covered) earnings.

The net effect of these proposals will be to ensure that only those who are truly deserving of support are added to the benefit rolls, and to eventually eliminate those who are capable of self-support. These reforms will reduce the drain on the disability insurance trust fund as follows.

	Outlays (in millions dollars)					
	1981	1982	1983	1984	1985	1986
Current Base	17,400	19,173	20,621	21,884	23,233	24,734
Policy reduction:						
Improve administration	−50	−200	−500	−700	−900	−1,100
Institute a "megagap"	−5	−50	−75	−100	−125	−150
Tighten recency-of-work test	−10	−300	−600	−900	−1,200	−1,500
Proposed Budget	17,335	18,623	19,446	20,184	21,008	21,984

Note: Savings assume the changes will be effective July 1, 1981, take into account associated increases in other Federal assistance programs, and are sensitive to economic assumptions.

Source: America's New Beginning: A Program for Economic Recovery (Washington, D.C.: Government Printing Office, February 18, 1981), 1–9, 1–10.

Document 8.10
GAO Report on the Disability Program, March 3, 1981

This GAO report served to confirm the Reagan administration's claims of the potential for large dollar savings from the CDI process. Indeed, it added pressure on SSA to implement the CDI reviews from the 1980 law, and perhaps rationalized the administration's decision to accelerate those reviews.

One item that would come to assume an unexpected importance is the reference in this document to SSA's efforts to identify the most likely candidates for termination, based on case characteristics. This up-front targeting of likely recovery cases would lead to much higher than expected initial termination rates and this would become yet another source of controversy in the CDI process.

The Continuing Disability Investigation Process

The Continuing Disability Investigation (CDI) process is SSA's way of identifying beneficiaries who may have medically recovered or regained the ability to work and assessing their continuing eligibility for disability benefits. . . .

In 1978 SSA did CDIs on about 141,256 of the 2.9 million disabled workers on the DI rolls and terminated benefits in 72,606 (51.4 percent) of the cases reviewed. . . .

Based on a nationwide sample case review recently conducted by SSA, we estimate that the Trust Fund could be losing over $2 billion a year because as many as 584,000 persons currently collecting disability benefits—20 percent of the 2.9 million primary beneficiaries on the DI rolls—may not meet SSA's current eligibility criteria. Most of them would not be subject to any followup reexamination or reevaluation and can, if they choose, continue to collect benefits until they voluntarily return to work, die, or reach retirement age. This condition exists because, annually, SSA investigates the eligibility of only a small percentage of DI beneficiaries. The majority of beneficiaries on the rolls (about 80 percent) are never reevaluated.

Because of concern expressed by congressional committees and us, SSA now recognizes that its followup on DI beneficiaries has been inadequate. . . . SSA must give more priority to identifying the nondisabled currently on the rolls and terminating their benefits.

SSA Has Not Adequately Reviewed the DI Caseload

SSA has placed little emphasis on reviewing the eligibility of beneficiaries once they are on DI rolls. . . . [O]nly a small percentage of the disabled workers on the rolls are given a medical reexamination each year. This percentage ranged from 3.0 in 1973 to 3.6 in 1978, except in 1974 when SSA reexamined only 1.5 percent on the rolls. . . .

Most beneficiaries never have their impairments reevaluated after initial eligibility is established. . . . From 1973 to 1977, only 18 to 26 percent of initial awards were scheduled for medical reexaminations. This means from 74 to 82 percent of the workers who came on the rolls during that period would probably never have been reevaluated—unless they returned to work and SSA became aware of the work activity.

According to SSA officials, this limited followup activity is due, in part, to the philosophy that has existed in SSA. When the DI program authorized benefits in 1956, the definition of disability was very restrictive and specified that the impairment had to be total and permanent or expected to result in death. Therefore, the DI program was patterned similar to SSA's retirement program and the emphasis was on paying benefits. In 1965 the definition of disability was liberalized to include persons with less permanent impairments—expected to last at least 12 months. However, SSA management did not put added emphasis on followup activity. . . .

Our April [1978] report to the Secretary of HEW was the first to show that a serious problem existed. We found that at least 24 percent of 402 SSI cases converted from the State disability programs and 10 percent of another 175 SSI cases were not disabled. The important point about these cases was that most (77 percent) of those found to be ineligible were not scheduled for a medical reexamination and probauly would never have been detected by SSA.

Prompted by our report, in 1979 SSA reviewed a 5-percent sample of SSI conversion cases in the State of Washington and terminated benefits in 11.8 percent of the cases reviewed. . . . In addition, SSA took a nationwide sample of 13,000 conversion cases in March 1979 to determine which other States warrant a complete review. SSA expects the termination rate from this sample to be about 12.4 percent. SSA plans to review about 310,000 more conversion cases through fiscal year 1983. . . .

Our April 1978 report did not address the DI program, but it did conclude that

> "the procedures for monitoring this program are similar to those used for the SSI program. Therefore, payments to beneficiaries who are no longer disabled could also occur under the DI program and go undetected."

. . . In July 1978 SSA began a review of DI cases which were not scheduled for a medical reexamination. Although this study was suspended after about 6 months to concentrate on the SSI conversion cases, SSA found that 11 percent of about 1,000 cases reviewed before the study's suspension were no longer eligible for DI benefits.

SSA has recently completed a comprehensive study of the DI rolls. This study—the Disability Insurance Pilot—was designed to test methods that SSA could use in an ongoing program for measuring DI payment accuracy. Through the Pilot, SSA also intended to develop indications of the major types and causes of payment error in the DI program.

SSA randomly selected 3,000 sample cases that were representative of the DI population, collected medical evidence, and in some cases visited beneficiaries in their homes to interview them about their impairments. Using this evidence, SSA examiners and physicians determined that about 20 percent of the sample did not meet SSA's current eligibility criteria in the sample month, April 1979.

Based on this ineligibility rate, there could be about 584,000 persons on the DI rolls who may not meet the program's eligibility criteria. Since the Pilot study showed that the average monthly payment was about $350, SSA could be paying over $2 billion a year to persons not eligible for the program. . . .

Although the Pilot study showed that 20 percent of the beneficiaries on the DI rolls are not disabled, the actual termination rate probably would not be that high. In some cases, while the State agencies might determine that the beneficiary is no longer disabled, the decision could be overturned through the appeals process. However, we believe the Pilot study is a good indicator—probably the best one available—that ineligibility in the DI program is a costly problem that must be corrected. For example, even if 10 percent of those on the rolls were ineligible and could be removed, the annual savings to the Trust Fund would amount to about $1 billion.

Several factors have contributed to the large number of nondisabled on the DI rolls. First, SSA believes that because of heavy workloads brought about by the SSI program and limited SSA quality assurance in 1974 and 1975, ineligible persons were erroneously placed on the rolls in these years. In addition, SSA had a policy in effect from 1969 until 1976 called the LaBonte principle (named after an administrative law judge's hearing decision) which stated that terminations had to be based on documentation which supported medical improvement. Under this principle, all initial disability decisions were presumed to be correct—even though this was not always true. As a result, when SSA discovered through medical reexamination that a person had been erroneously awarded DI benefits and was never disabled, the individual was allowed to remain on the rolls because there was no evidence of medical improvement. Finally, because SSA did not have an effective information system to enable it to manage the CDI process, many beneficiaries who met the diary criteria were never scheduled for a medical reexamination and many scheduled medical reexaminations were never done. . . .

In fiscal year 1980, SSA began a review of 25,000 DI cases not currently scheduled for medical reexamination. Through this study, SSA intends to identify the characteristics of individuals most likely to be found ineligible. Such characteristics include the year of initial disability determination, the worker's age, impairment, and geographic location. The complete results of this study will not be available until spring 1981. . . .

The Congress, also concerned about SSA's review of the DI caseload, passed legislation in 1980 that will result in SSA doing more continuing eligibility reviews. Unless the State agency examiner determines that the worker is permanently disabled, SSA must review the status of every beneficiary at least once every 3 years. . . .

While SSA has taken steps to better manage the DI caseload, the question remains—can SSA move faster to identify the nondisabled currently on the DI rolls and prevent the annual loss of billions in Trust Fund money? . . .

We recommend that the Secretary of HHS direct the Commissioner of Social Security to expedite efforts to reevaluate the DI rolls and to provide the necessary resources to support such efforts because of the potential savings. . . .

Source: "More Diligent Followup Needed To Weed Out Ineligible SSA Disability Beneficiaries," GAO Report HRD–81–48, March 3, 1981, 3–11.

Document 8.11
SSA Ruling on Medical Improvement, 1981

Periodically, the SSA issues Social Security Rulings, which are instructions to its adjudicators on various policy matters. This ruling concerns the issue of whether a finding of medical improvement is necessary to cease the benefits of a current recipient. It states the policy under which the CDI process was carried out beginning in 1981. This was probably the single most contested policy involved in the CDIs. By the time the 1984 law was enacted, the SSA was faced with eighteen different federal class-action lawsuits and thousands of individual lawsuits on this issue alone.

Titles II and XVI: Continuance or Cessation of Disability or Blindness

Purpose

To state the policy for determining whether disability or blindness under titles II and XVI continues or ceases. . . .

Pertinent History

Under operating guides which have been in effect for approximately 3 years, disability or blindness is found to have ceased when current evidence shows that the individual does not meet the definition of disability or blindness under which his or her claim was allowed; it is not necessary to show that the individual's medical condition has "improved" since the prior determination. However, prior regulations had been interpreted by some to mean that before cessation of disability or blindness could be found, there must have been a positive showing of medical improvement. Such an interpretation precluded a finding of cessation in cases where current evidence showed that the individual was not disabled or blind, but it could not be shown that actual "improvement" had taken place. The regulations have now been revised to clarify this issue.

Policy Statement

Where the evidence obtained at the time of a continuing disability investigation (CDI) establishes that the individual is not currently disabled or blind, a finding of cessation is appropriate. It will not be necessary to determine whether or how much the individual's condition has medically improved since the prior favorable determination.

Effective Date

Final regulations covering this policy were effective August 20, 1980, the date of publication in the *Federal Register* (45 FR 55566). . . .

Source: Social Security Rulings, Cumulative Edition 1981, SSA Publication no. 65–002 (Washington D.C.: Government Printing Office, 1981), 74.

Document 8.12
SSA Ruling on Severity of Impairments, 1982

Two of the contested policies are actually stated in this ruling: the idea that vocational factors do not have to be considered in the case of nonsevere impairments; and the more important policy that multiple nonsevere impairments may not be added in judging disability. (Although this ruling was formally published in the 1982 volume of Social Security Rulings, *its effective date was August 1980, and the CDI process was implemented in 1981 using this policy.)*

Titles II and XVI: Medical Impairments That Are Not Severe

Purpose

To enunciate the policy regarding nonsevere impairments and to provide examples of impairments that are not severe in order to more clearly illustrate the level of severity required before the concept of "nonsevere impairment" can be applied in the sequential evaluation of disability.

Pertinent History

Regulations No. 4, section 404.1502(a), published in 1960, introduced the principle that a denial determination may be made on the basis of medical considerations alone. It stated that . . . "medical considerations alone may justify a finding that the individual is not under a disability where the only impairment is a slight neurosis, slight impairment of sight or hearing, or other slight abnormality or combination of slight abnormalities."

Sections 404.1504 and 416.904 of the regulations published in 1978 revised the 1960 statement and included a statement on work-related functions as follows . . . "medical considerations alone can justify a finding that an individual is not under a disability where the medically determinable impairment is not severe. A medically determinable impairment is not severe if it does not significantly limit an individual's physical or mental capacity to perform basic work-related functions.". . .

Policy Statement

In determining whether an individual is disabled, we follow a sequential evaluation process whereby current work activity, severity and duration of impairment, residual functional capacity (RFC), and vocational factors (age, education and work experience) are considered in that order.

Built into this process is the statutory requirement that to be found disabled, an individual must have a severe medically determinable impairment. For an impairment to be considered severe, it must significantly limit the individual's physical or mental capacity to perform one or more basic work-related functions such as standing, walking, lifting, handling, seeing, hearing, speaking, and understanding and following simple instructions. An impairment that does not significantly limit the capacity to perform work-related functions, as they are required in most jobs, is not severe.

At that stage in the sequential evaluation process, when we may decide that an impairment is not severe, we do not consider the effects of age, education, and work experience (i.e., the vocational factors) since in such cases the determination is based on medical considerations alone. Similarly, the individual's RFC is not assessed in cases in which the individual's impairment is determined to be not severe. In such cases, the RFC assessment is not relevant because it is based upon functional limitations which result from a severe impairment, and, thus, it only comes into play at a later stage in the sequential evaluation process. . . .

Inasmuch as a nonsevere impairment is one which does not significantly limit basic work-related functions, neither will a combination of two or more such impairments significantly restrict the basic work-related functions needed to do most jobs. However, when a nonsevere impairment(s) is imposed upon a severe impairment(s), the combined effect of all impairments must be considered in assessing RFC. . . .

Effective Date

The policy explained herein was effective on August 20, 1980, the date the regulations covering the basic policy in the subject area were effective (45 FR 55566). . . .

Source: Social Security Rulings, Cumulative Edition 1982, SSA Publication no. 65–002 (Washington D.C.: Government Printing Office, 1982), 102–106.

Document 8.13
SSA's Non-acquiescence Policy, 1982

One of the features of the CDI process was the SSA's defiance of federal court rulings on key aspects of its CDI policies. SSA promulgated a doctrine that it called "non-acquiescence," which meant that it would selectively ignore certain court rulings if those rulings mandated policies that the administration was unwilling to adopt. Essentially, the idea was to restrict the application of a court's ruling to the individual litigants in the case and decline to treat the ruling as precedential for other similar cases.

This policy was used in this June 1981 case from the Ninth Judicial Circuit (one of several instances during this period) and promulgated as a Social Security Ruling in early 1982. (In a similar SSI case in June 1982, Patti v. Schweiker, the SSA also issued a ruling of non-acquiescence.)

The non-acquiescence policy became so untenable that by the time the SSA published its 1986 book of rulings, there was a separate section entitled "Acquiescence Rulings," in which the agency explained how it would apply recent court decisions. The 1986 edition listed twenty-four separate cases in which it acquiesced, and none in which it did not.

Supplemental Security Income—Continuance or Cessation of a Grandfatheree's Disability—A Ruling of Non-acquiescence

Finnegan v. Matthews, 641 F. 2d 1340 (1981)

The Social Security Administration (SSA) does not acquiesce in the court's decision.

. . . SSA determined that the claimant's SSI benefits would terminate because he did not meet the requirements for entitlement at the time of the continuing disability investigation. This determination was affirmed by the district court.

The court of appeals, however, reversed SSA's determination. It found that SSI disability benefits to a grandfatheree may not be terminated unless SSA shows that there was either a material improvement in the grandfatheree's medical condition or a clear and specific error in the prior State determination. Because neither of those conditions was shown by SSA to be met, the court held that SSA's termination of the claimant's SSI benefits was improper.

SSA believes that the court's standard for determining whether SSI disability benefits to a grandfatheree should terminate would be impossible to administer and that the correct standard for making such a determination is . . . that [the] disability of a grandfatheree terminates when his or her "disability as shown by current medical or other evidence does not meet the criteria of the appropriate State plan" and does not meet the Federal criteria. Many grandfatherees were on State disability rolls for years before conversion, and the evidence on which they were originally allowed may not be available, or may not even exist. Therefore, in those cases, SSA could not possibly prove either "material improvement" or "clear and specific error" in the prior State determination. Thus . . . the grandfatheree properly remains in SSI benefit status only until it is found that the grandfatheree's disability, as shown by current medical or other evidence, meets neither the State nor Federal definition of disability. . . .

Consequently, SSA holds that the standard in 20 CFR 416.994(e), and not the one set forth by the court, should apply in determining whether the disability of a title XVI grandfatheree has ceased.

Source: Social Security Rulings, Cumulative Edition 1982, SSA Publication no. 65–002 (Washington D.C.: Government Printing Office, 1982), 303–310.

Document 8.14
Secretary Schweiker's Report to Congress on the Bellmon Reviews under the Disability Amendments of 1980, January 1982

During consideration of the 1980 amendments Senator Bellmon introduced an amendment requiring the SSA to institute a system of reviews of decisions on disability cases by administrative law judges (ALJs) (Document 8.6). His concern was with the high rate of reversals (i.e., approved claims) characteristically seen at the ALJ level of the process. In 1977 the ALJs reversed about 50 percent of the new cases that came before them. (In the CDI process, the reversal rate was about 66 percent.)

These "Bellmon Reviews" became highly contested by the ALJs, who perceived them as an implicit form of pressure to disapprove disability claims—including CDI cases. This perception was aided by the fact that the administration initially targeted the reviews to those ALJs with the highest reversal rates.

The professional organization representing the ALJs lobbied against the reviews and ultimately filed a federal lawsuit seeking to halt them. Ultimately, the lawsuit was settled when the SSA agreed to drop the targeting and select ALJs for review at random.

The 1980 law required the secretary of HHS, Richard Schweiker, to report to Congress on the outcomes of the mandated Bellmon Reviews. This is his report.

(The document makes reference to the Appeals Council. In the administrative process the Appeals Council was a higher authority than the ALJs and had the power to reverse an ALJ decision.)

Executive Summary

Section 304(g) of P.L. 96–265, the "Social Security Disability Amendments of 1980," requires that the Social Security Administration (SSA) institute a program of ongoing review of administrative law judge (ALJ) decisions on claims for Social Security disability benefits. This section—commonly referred to as the Bellmon amendment—is intended to ensure that hearings decisions by ALJs conform to statute, regulations, and binding policy. Decisions which do not meet these criteria are to be administratively reversed. . . .

Initial decisions on applications for disability benefits and reconsiderations of those decisions are made by SSA district offices and State disability determination services (DDSs). Denials may be appealed sequentially to an ALJ, to the Appeals Council in SSA's Office of Hearings and Appeals (OHA), then to Federal district courts. The requirement for this report arose from congressional concern with the increasing number of denials being appealed to ALJs and the high percentage of DDS denials that were being overturned by ALJs. . . .

Findings of the Initial Review

The initial review was based on a sample of 3,600 recent ALJ decisions on disability cases. The case folders were reviewed by two different units within SSA: the Office of Assessment (OA), which operated under the standards governing the DDSs, and the Appeals Council, which applied the standards and procedures governing ALJ decisions. Each unit made new decisions on each case without being aware of the original ALJ decision or the decision of the other reviewing organization. These new decisions were used only for analytical purposes; they were not used to actually alter the original ALJ determination.

The major finding of the initial review was that significant differences in decision results were produced when these different decisionmakers were presented with the same evidence on the same cases. The ALJs allowed 64 percent of the cases. The Appeals Council, applying ALJ standards, allowed 48 percent. OA, applying DDS standards, allowed only 13 percent.

An examination of the standards and procedures governing the ALJs and DDSs indicates distinct differences. In certain instances, operational definitions are not identical. In other instances, ALJ procedures permit a finding of disability that is not possible under the DDS standards. Finally, in some areas the definitions contained in the standards are the same, but procedures differ for evaluating evidence of impairment.

Initial review data also indicated that, even when decisionmakers were applying the same standards, they were not applying them consistently. The Appeals Council denied 37 percent of the cases which ALJs allowed, and allowed 21 percent of the cases which ALJs denied. A detailed examination of the cases on which both the ALJs and the Appeals Council agreed shows that the Council agreed with the ALJs as to the *basis* for an allowance or denial much less frequently than it agreed on whether the case should be allowed or denied. Moreover, if the Appeals Council decision is taken as the "correct" decision under the rules governing ALJs, the review indicates that decisions to allow cases by ALJs with high allowance rates are more often "incorrect" than the decisions of ALJs with lower allowance rates.

There are also indications that varying quality control procedures and management emphases, in combination with the subjective element in the disability determination process, may contribute to the distinct differences and trends in disability decisions made at the different organizational levels.

Results from the review suggest that the in-person appearance of claimants at ALJ hearings may make a difference. The ALJ hearing is the first time that the claimant appears before a decisionmaker. As part of the review, all information related to the claimant's in-person appearance was removed from a special sub-sample of case folders and these folders were then distributed to other ALJs for readjudication based on the case record. The original ALJ allowance rate of more than 60 percent dropped to 46 percent when the in-person information was removed from the case.

Data from this special sub-sample also show that additional medical evidence submitted after the DDS decision significantly affects ALJ allowance rates. The ALJ allowance rate dropped from 46 percent to 31 percent when all evidence added after the final DDS decision was deleted from folders in the sample. . . .

Other Initiatives at the Hearing Level

To address the problem of different adjudicative standards and procedures being used by DDSs and ALJs, the Social Security Administration will disseminate a single set of standards to be followed at all levels of adjudication. These standards will be based on those currently governing the DDSs. . . .

Further, an experiment will be undertaken later this year to determine whether participation of an SSA representative at ALJ hearings in which the claimant is represented will improve the quality and timeliness of hearing decisions.

Initiatives to Improve DDS Performance

As required by the 1980 Disability Amendments, SSA has begun a preeffectuation review of DDS disability allowances. This preeffectuation review, in which incorrect decisions made by the DDSs are reversed prior to notification of the claimant or payment of any benefits, is intended to promote the uniformity and accuracy of disability allowances made by the DDSs.

SSA is also conducting three experiments that test various changes in the DDS reconsideration process. These changes may result in more consistent decisions when cases move on to ALJ hearings.

In summary, SSA has undertaken a number of activities designed to respond to the problems identified in the initial review. The most significant are probably the ongoing review of ALJ decisions required by P.L. 96–265, and the initiation of changes required to ensure that all SSA disability decisionmakers are governed by the same standards. These actions, in conjunction with the other initiatives discussed in this report, should greatly improve the accuracy and consistency of disability decisions made throughout the SSA adjudicative system.

Source: Implementation of Section 304(g) of Public Law 96–265, "Social Security Disability Amendments of 1980," Report to the Congress by the Secretary of Health and Human Services. Copy in SSA History Archives, Mary Ross Papers, Box MR 29.

Document 8.15
Letter from the Association of Administrative Law Judges on the Bellmon Study, 1982

In this letter Paul Rosenthal, president of the Association of Administrative Law Judges, responded to Secretary Schweiker's report to Congress on the Bellmon Reviews.

A Critique of the Bellmon Study

The Bellmon Amendment required the Secretary of the Department of Health and Human Services (DHHS) to review decisions of Administrative Law Judges in claims for disability benefits under the Social Security Act, and to issue a report to Congress. The Secretary has issued his report, and the purpose of this paper is to clarify and amplify certain points covered by that report.

It would be in order, at this point, to look at the rates of denials at the initial, reconsideration and judge levels for the 5-year period from 1975 through 1980. A review of this data . . . indicates the following:

(1) Initial level—1975 through 1980 went from 60% denials to 67% denials. . . .
(2) Reconsideration level—1975 through 1980 went from 67% denials to 85% denials. . . .
(3) ALJ level—1975 through 1980 went from 51% denials to 42% denials. . . .

As can be seen from the above, as both the initial and reconsideration denials increased, the judge's denial rate decreased. Two reasons can be identified for such a decrease in judge's denials. In the first place, it seems clear from the Secretary's Report that the State agencies began to apply more stringent standards for determining "disability" than previously applied and more strict than the disability standards set forth in the Social Security Act. . . . Although the statute had not changed with regard to the definition of disability, the State agencies at the lower level (i.e., initial and reconsideration stages) apparently found only those persons meeting the Listings set forth in the Regulations to be disabled. . . . Thus, other individuals who did not have impairments meeting the Listings, but who nonetheless were "disabled" within the meaning of the Act, were denied benefits at the initial and reconsideration stages. Is it any wonder that requests for hearings and judge allowance rates increased substantially during the period from 1975 through 1980? . . .

Another reason for further increase in judge allowance rates from 1979 through the present was the introduction of the so-called "grid Regulations" in 1979. The most simple illustration of the problems associated with the new regulations is in the area of the claimant's burden of proof. The State agencies have, for whatever reason, probably unwittingly, used the new sequence, as it appears in the new regulations, to create a new, more strict test for the making of a prima facie case than has heretofore been understood by all levels since the 1967 amendments. The State agencies, by using the Program Operations Manual (POMs), provided by the Office of Disability Operations, Social Security Administration, treats the burden of proof as follows:

> "When there is no significant limitation in the ability to perform these work-related functions, an impairment will not be considered to be severe even though it may prevent the individual from doing a highly selective group of jobs, including work that the individual has done in the past."

The judge, following the well-established burden of proof, as enunciated in the regulations and in *all* court cases, finds that the claimant has made a prima facie case when he cannot return to his former job. Put more simply, once the judge finds that a claimant has a "severe" impairment that keeps him from doing his former work, the burden of going forward with the evidence shifts to the Secretary.

The different interpretation applied by the State agencies, as directed in the POMs, has permitted them to find claimants' impairments to be "not severe" even when they cannot return to their former work. In practice, the tendency seems to be to make a finding of "not severe" in most cases where a finding of "severe" would cause a payment of benefits by use of the "grid." The judge, on the other hand, is constrained to find that claimants, who cannot return to their former jobs and who fall into a certain "pigeon hole" in the grid, are "conclusively disabled." *If there is one primary reason for the decline in the State agencies' allowance rate in the last few years, we submit that the above constitutes that reason.*

Moreover . . . the State agencies do not follow "ALJ practice" in finding residual functional capacity less than sedentary. The reference to judges finding residual functional capacity less than sedentary as being "ALJ practice" is a misnomer since the Secretary's published Regulations state that a finding can be made of residual functional capacity less than sedentary. It is the State agencies that are in error here because they are ignoring the Secretary's published Regulations in that regard, probably because of erroneous guidelines imposed on them by either the Office of Assessment or Office of Disability Operations of SSA. Another example of State agencies' failure to follow the Secretary's published Regulations . . . is the refusal to recognize pain (resulting from a significant impairment) as being a disabling impairment. Such failure on the part of the State agencies ignores not only the Secretary's published Regulations, but also all court precedents holding that pain resulting from a significant impairment must be considered in determining whether a person is "disabled."

A third example of State agencies' failure to follow the Secretary's published Regulations is . . . the State agencies do not consider the combined effect of a nonsevere mental impairment together with a significant physical impairment in assessing whether a person is "disabled" *despite the fact that the Act and Regulations require such consideration.*

. . . Aside from the above, it is important to note that, at the judge level, the claimant appears in person to present his case. At the hearing, credibility of his or her complaints are tested by cross-examination. Claimants often submit up-to-date medical evidence at the hearing level. Accordingly, evidence before the judge, in many cases, is different from the evidence reviewed by State agencies.

Therefore, from the above, it must be concluded that the differences between the lower-level and judge-level allowance rates are fully within reasonable expectations, and there should not be expressions of alarm because of variances between judge and State agency allowance rates. Our analysis of the Secretary's Report and our experience in the field, handling thousands of disability cases, lead us to the following conclusions:

1. The differences in judge allowance rates from those at the initial and reconsideration levels are due in great part to 1) State agencies ignoring the mandates of the Act and the Secretary's published Regulations; 2) different interpretations of the various provisions of the grid Regulations; and, most importantly; 3) the different type of review afforded by ALJ hearings (i.e., full due process *de novo* hearings with face-to-face contact with claimants to

assess credibility, as opposed to a mere "paper review" by State agencies). This latter conclusion is important and should indicate that there will always be a difference in allowance rates between results obtained in a "paper review" by a non-independent personnel at lower levels from those obtained by a full "due process" hearing before an impartial and independent judge. Of course, it goes without saying that the only fair way for determining disability or nondisability is by utilization of a full "due process" hearing procedure.

2. Additional uniformity between State agencies and judges is probably not useful; it would either make the State agencies consider facts unavailable to them, thus leading to speculative findings, or it would have the judges ignore the statutory responsibility of perfecting a "de novo" hearing record and considering all pertinent evidence, eventually becoming a bureaucratic "rubber stamp" for lesser qualified, lesser educated individuals.

3. The grid regulations should be closely reviewed to determine whether, as it seems to appear, they have made the State agencies appear too conservative and the judges seem too liberal, thus, being unfair to all the dedicated individuals who work at both levels, and perhaps subtly redefining the definition of disability into something Congress never intended.

In summary, the Association has no problem with ongoing review of judge decisions, as long as it is undertaken by individuals at least as professionally qualified as the judges. Casting no aspersions on the hard-working people in the Office of the Assessment, SSA, and those hard-working paralegals in the Appeals Council, Office of Hearings and Appeals (OHA), SSA, we submit that it is unfair, unproductive and even a little silly to make non-lawyers responsible for reviewing the decisions of Federal Administrative Law Judges. We would suggest that the Office of Personnel Management be asked to become involved in determining qualifications for individuals who make such assessments. To assess results, qualified attorneys more "independent" of the Agency involved should be utilized. . . .

We point out that, as long as OHA is not separated from SSA, it is likely that the types of conflicts indicated in the Secretary's Report will continue, and it is the public that will continue to suffer. The current public uproar concerning the "cessation" cases . . . is solid proof of the natural result of two functionally different governmental entities, both components of DHHS, trying to carry out their responsibilities with all the integrity they can muster. Uniformity and consistency will likely only be meaningful when applied to SSA without OHA, and to OHA without SSA, since both must operate differently in order to carry out their respective responsibilities. When the new grid regulations referred to above are superimposed on this complex mosaic, is it any wonder that the public is confused?

As to all SSA decision makers being governed by the same standards, we strenuously object to the idea of judges being "lumped" in with other SSA decision makers, whose qualifications can never be and, indeed, should never be as stringent as those required of Administrative Law Judges. SSA initiatives at the lower levels may prove useful at the lower levels, but, to the extent that they "flow upward" to the judge level, they are premised fallaciously as stated above, and therefore, would achieve incorrect results.

We urge that serious consideration be given to separating OHA from SSA, either as an independent forum or a review commission, under the umbrella of DHHS, or a separate commission, and that Congress require each entity to achieve a standard of consistency and uniformity within its own separate context, but within a broad framework.

Source: Open letter from Paul Rosenthal, president, Association of Administrative Law Judges. Copy in SSA History Archives, Mary Ross Papers, Box MR 29.

Document 8.16
Secretary Schweiker's Reforms of the Continuing Disability Investigation Process, September 8, 1982

By the late summer of 1982 the controversies surrounding the disability reviews were so great that the secretary of HHS ordered a set of administrative reforms in an effort to quell the conflict. This is the HHS press release announcing those reforms.

HHS Secretary Richard S. Schweiker and Commissioner of Social Security John A. Svahn today announced further administrative reforms of the Continuing Disability Investigation (CDI) review process which is being carried out under a 1980 Congressional mandate.

Secretary Schweiker and Commissioner Svahn also renewed their endorsement, first announced last April, of several legislative proposals designed to further ease the impact of the CDI program on persons whose cases are selected for review.

The administrative reforms announced today include:

- Face-to-face interviews in the Social Security Administration's 1,350 local offices for all CDI cases chosen for review beginning Oct. 1;
- A 20 percent reduction in the number of CDI cases to be reviewed by State Disability Determination agencies during the 1983 Fiscal Year beginning Oct. 1, dropping the number from about 806,000 to about 640,000, a move designed to ease the workload burden and allow states more time to develop medical evidence in each case; and,
- Continuation through September of a selective moratorium on referral of cases to a number of states with unusually large CDI case backlogs under which 56,000 case files have been held in Baltimore since August pending state action to clear up overdue reviews.

Commissioner Svahn said that under the new procedure, persons selected for CDI reviews will first be interviewed by Social Security personnel before their cases are sent on to state agencies for intensive review.

"This is a major new responsibility for our local offices," Svahn said, "but it is one we believe we must take on for the good of the beneficiary and the integrity of the program.

"We want to make sure, up front, that each recipient is fully aware of what the process is all about, why it's being done, how important it is to provide all available medical evidence to the state agencies, and that each person is fully aware of his or her rights and responsibilities.

"We also want to make sure to the extent possible short of a medical examination that each case sent to a state agency is indeed an appropriate case for review," Svahn said.

"This is, however, only a first step. We still need Congressional action to help us take a necessary second step," Svahn said.

Schweiker and Svahn repeated the administration's April 28 endorsement of certain provisions of CDI reform legislation now pending in Congress which, Svahn said, "would go far toward improving the process and lessening its impact on individuals."

Chief among the endorsed reforms are:

- A mandate, beginning Oct. 1, 1983, for a face-to-face evidentiary hearing at the "reconsideration" or first-level appeal of state agency decision, a process which is now conducted entirely via examination of submitted evidence.
- Provision for disability benefits to be continued for up to six months during the initial appeals process. Benefits are now terminated 60 days after the original state agency decision.

"The 1980 Congress mandated that all disability cases be reviewed periodically," Svahn said. "Both the General Accounting Office and our own auditors have found that an alarmingly high number of ineligible persons—as many as one in four—are receiving disability benefits. We simply cannot afford to give away as much as $4 billion each year to ineligible people.

"But we must proceed with the CDI review program in a responsible, responsive manner which at once gets ineligible people off the rolls and at the same time takes great pains to protect the rights and benefits of those who truly belong in the program.

"These reforms—along with Congressional action to let us do even more—will be crucial to our ability to accomplish both of those goals," Svahn said.

Source: HHS press release, September 8, 1982. Copy in SSA History Archives, Mary Ross Papers, Box MR 60.

Document 8.17
Senator Heinz's Remarks on the CDI Controversy, September 17, 1982

These brief remarks by Sen. John Heinz (R-Pa.) raised some of the issues that fueled the controversy over the CDIs—including the personalization of the suffering the process sometimes produced.

Mr. HEINZ: Mr. President, the problems surrounding the current social security disability review system have been well documented. The Senate Finance Committee recently held hearings on this subject. And just this week, a number of our colleagues in the House communicated to our distinguished chairman of the Finance Committee, Bob Dole, their conviction, which I and other Senators share, that Congress must take urgent action to alleviate these problems.

The goal of reviewing the disability status of individuals on the social security rolls is a sound and necessary principle. But when Congress mandated, in 1980, a 3-year review of individuals on the disability rolls, no one foresaw the high rates of termination and the poor quality of reviews that we are witnessing today. The Social Security Administration has been terminating 45 percent of the beneficiaries it reviews. When Congress passed the Disability

Amendments of 1980, the periodic disability reviews were not expected to produce any net savings during the first 3 years of operation; fiscal years 1982 through 1984. And, during the 4-year period fiscal year 1982 through fiscal year 1985, the periodic reviews were projected to save only $10 million. Yet, the President's fiscal year 1983 budget indicates that the program of periodic reviews will now save $3.25 billion in fiscal year 1982–84—or 325 times the original estimate.

On the front page of today's *Los Angeles Times*, there appears a troubling story relating the tales of 11 individuals who have died from disabilities which the Social Security Administration denied their having. I submit this article for the *Record* and urge my colleagues to read it with care. It emphasizes the need to continue working with the administration to enact legislation at the earliest opportunity to redress this sorry situation.

Source: Congressional Record, Senate, September 17, 1982, S11765.

Document 8.18
Senator Heinz's Letter to Secretary Schweiker, October 5, 1982

This letter from Senator Heinz to HHS secretary Richard Schweiker highlights the tensions existing between some Republican members of Congress and the Reagan administration over the CDIs. Notice, in particular, that Senator Heinz stresses the necessity for a medical improvement standard.

Dear Mr. Secretary:

As one directly involved in efforts to reform the Social Security continuing disability investigation process, I believe that recent news accounts of deaths among disability beneficiaries deserve scrutiny.

I refer to the account carried in the *Los Angeles Times* on September 17, and in the *Philadelphia Inquirer* on September 18, of eleven deaths among those whose disability benefits had either been discontinued or denied. These people appear to have died of the very disabilities which SSA believed were not sufficiently serious to keep these people from working.

As Chairman of the Special Committee on Aging, a Member of the Senate Finance Committee, and an author of continuing disability review reform legislation, I request a full accounting by the Social Security Administration of all eleven cases. Further, I request a complete compilation of all deaths which have occurred among disability recipients during the period in which their appeals of termination decisions are pending. What were the disabilities being disputed? What rationale had been developed in each case for terminating or denying benefits? What was the status of the pending appeal where one had been filed?

I am distressed that these horror stories continue to surface. The goal of reviewing beneficiaries is sound and necessary, but the entitlement rights of individuals must not be abridged by a process which is often thoughtless and inhumane. I regret that emergency legislative relief became stalled in the Senate during the final days of the session. According to my calculations, delaying until January the reforms contained in H.R. 7093 will adversely effect 160,000 disability recipients who are candidates for review and as many as 100,000 others terminated before October 1. Beyond the emergency legislation, these eleven deaths demonstrate that comprehensive reform of the process is urgently needed—and that reform must include language to require a showing by the Social Security Administration of medical or vocational improvement in the beneficiary substantial enough to enable a return to work.

I urge the Social Security Administration to come forward with concrete, mutually acceptable reform language, including medical improvement provisions, which Congress may begin to review immediately. In the meantime, I look forward to receipt of the information outlined in this request.

Sincerely,

John Heinz, Chairman

Source: Copy of letter in SSA History Archives, Mary Ross Papers, Box MR 60.

Document 8.19
SSA Commissioner's Letter to Governor Clements, October 20, 1982

Following enactment of the initial disability legislation in 1954, the federal government had delegated to the states the task of making the initial finding of medical disability. The CDI process put serious strains in federal/state relations over the administration of the reviews. Despite the fact that the states were under contract to perform their services according to federal specifications, by March 1983 eighteen states were refusing to follow federal regulations in the CDI process (imposing their own medical improvement standard, among other things). By January 1984, nine states (containing 28 percent of the total workload) had stopped processing CDIs altogether, often under orders from their state governor.

This letter from SSA commissioner John Svahn to Gov. William Clements Jr. (R-Texas), the head of the Southern Governors' Association, was written relatively early in the process and was one of many attempts by the administration to head off pressure for sweeping congressional legislation. In the letter, Svahn gives a good summary of the various administrative reforms the administration had introduced by that point in an effort to reform the process and lessen the controversy.

Dear Governor Clements:

The administration shares the concern of the Southern Governors' Association with regard to the fair and equitable carrying out of the provisions of the 1980 amendments for the periodic review of the continuing disability status of people receiving disability benefits. This process of continuing disability investigations—the so-called CDI process—has been a source of major concern to us, as well as to the Congress and the public generally, and we have been moving in both legislative and administrative areas to deal with problems that have arisen in this area.

Secretary Schweiker and I have been strongly supportive of major elements of a Ways and Means Social Security Subcommittee bill, H.R. 6181, now awaiting action in the House, that would lead to improvements in the quality and fairness of the CDI process. Chief among the provisions of H.R. 6181 which we support are the requirements that: (1) a face-to-face evidentiary hearing be held at the reconsideration level of appeal of State agency disability determinations, and (2) disability benefits be continued for up to 6 months during the reconsideration process (or until the reconsideration decision, if earlier). These provisions would enable us to proceed with the CDI review program in a responsible, responsive manner so that we can remove ineligibles from the disability rolls and yet adequately protect the rights of those who are disabled under the law.

However, pending such legislative action, we have given the very highest priority to those actions which we can take administratively—in close concert with the States—to implement a fundamental reform of the CDI program. These reforms will, I believe, go a long way toward solving many of the problems and resolving many of the issues that have led to the current concern about the CDI process. Indeed, these reforms will take us about as far as we can go towards those ends without substantive legislation.

Twelve major steps SSA is taking to reform the CDI process are as follows:

1. In March, SSA initiated a policy of determining that, in general, a person's disability ceases as of the time the beneficiary is notified of the cessation. This change reduces situations where the beneficiary is faced with the need to pay back past benefits because of a retroactive determination.
2. Since May, SSA has mandated that States review all medical evidence available for the past year—a directive which ensures that every State is looking at every piece of evidence that might be pertinent to a case.
3. SSA has underway, in two States, a study to test the value of obtaining more than one special mental status examination in cases where evidence from the beneficiary's treating source is incomplete or inadequate. This is intended to determine whether a person's mental condition can drastically change from one day to another. One criticism of SSA's practice of getting only one mental status examination is that it gives a misleading "snapshot" of a person.
4. SSA is in the process of issuing Social Security rulings, binding at all levels of adjudication, to assure that disability determinations are made in a more uniform manner.
5. Since March, SSA has required State agencies to furnish detailed explanations of their decisions in all cases in which a person's disability has ceased.
6. To insure quality in CDI cases, SSA conducts a quality review of a sample of cases before benefits are stopped. In June 1982, SSA doubled the number of quality reviews of termination cases. The quality has been holding very high at 97.5 percent. In addition, to demonstrate the importance of quality in the CDI process, SSA established an interim accuracy goal for the State agencies without waiting for publication of regulations.
7. SSA has consistently monitored State agency resources and workloads closely and adjusts the flow of cases to the individual States to avoid backlogs when problems have arisen in their acquiring adequate resources. The selective moratoriums on new CDI cases that SSA has implemented for August and September (and even earlier in some States) has been easing problems in specific States that have had unusually large backlogs.
8. Starting in October, SSA is using a new procedure for beginning a CDI review: each beneficiary has a face-to-face interview with an interviewer in the local Social Security office. . . .

    This corrects the single most glaring anomaly in the CDI process. Recipients whose cases are selected for review under the 1980 congressional mandate rarely, if ever, come face-to-face with a decisionmaker until and unless the case is pursued to the third level of review and appeal—a process which may drag on as much as 6 months to a year after benefits have been stopped. This one flaw in the program is perhaps more to blame than any other factor for the seemingly senseless "horror stories" we have all seen from time-to-time of people being dropped from the rolls despite glaringly obvious disabilities.

9. SSA has taken many actions to improve the quality of consultative examinations purchased by the Government in cases where medical evidence from a person's physician is unavailable or incomplete.

10. SSA has been very sensitive to the need for special handling of cases involving psychiatric impairments. SSA has met with mental health groups to obtain their recommendations for improvements and is reevaluating all guidelines for evaluation of mental impairments. SSA has also encouraged the States to increase the number of psychiatrists on their staffs in order to enhance their ability to review cases involving mental impairments. Secretary Schweiker has asked the American Psychiatric Association for assistance in recruiting psychiatrists for the States.

11. SSA has added more than 140 Administrative Law Judges to what is already perhaps the largest single adjudicative system in the world, bringing their total number to more than 800 and providing them with significantly more support staff to help reduce the backlog of cases that has been a chronic problem in past years.

12. Based on our findings in the first year of the CDI program, SSA has broadened the definition of the permanently disabled who need not be subject to the every 3-year CDI process mandated under the law. SSA expects to exempt an additional 165,000 beneficiaries from the CDI process during the next fiscal year—which will mean reducing the total from about 800,000 to about 640,000, a major reduction in workloads for the State agencies.

In summary, we believe that with the implementation of these administrative steps, we can very substantially improve the quality and the fairness of the CDI process, prevent the kinds of mistakes that have led to horror stories and given rise to some exaggerated concerns, and move toward guaranteeing the integrity of the disability rolls in a way that is equitable and humane as well as effective and efficient.

Sincerely,

John A. Svahn

Source: Copy of letter in SSA History Archives, Mary Ross Papers, Box MR 60.

Document 8.20
Secretary Schweiker's Letter to Senator Heinz, November 15, 1982

Secretary Schweiker's response to Senator Heinz reveals the administration's initial position on the pending reform legislation.

Three sections of H.R. 6181 were referred to in this letter. The section 3 proposal would have continued benefits for four additional months after termination (as opposed to the three months then in the law). The section 9 provision would have raised substantial gainful activity levels each year as average wages grew. Various liberalizations in the vocational rehabilitation process were addressed in section 12. All three sections were opposed because of objections from the Office of Management and Budget.

Dear Mr. Chairman:

Thank you for your letter concerning the continuing disability investigation (CDI) process on Social Security disability claims. I share your concern about the inpact of the CDI process on disability beneficiaries. This Administration supports legislation which, if enacted, will ease the impact of CDIs on beneficiaries and, together with administrative reforms the Social Security Administration (SSA) is making, lead to improvements in the quality and fairness of the CDI process.

Both Commissioner Svahn and myself have strongly supported major elements of H.R. 6181, the Disability Amendments of 1982, that would provide the means necessary to improve the CDI process. Specifically, we support all of the provisions of H.R. 6181 except sections 3, 9 and 12. Chief among the provisions of H.R. 6181 which we support are the requirements that (1) a face-to-face evidentiary hearing be held at the reconsideration level of appeal of State agency disability determinations, and (2) disability benefits be continued for up to six months during the reconsideration process (or until the reconsideration decision, if earlier). These provisions would enable SSA to proceed with the CDI review program in a responsible and responsive manner so that ineligible beneficiaries can be removed from the disability rolls and, at the same time, those who are truly disabled will be adequately protected.

Pending completion of congressional action on the legislation we support, SSA has given the very highest priority to administrative actions to implement a fundamental reform of the CDI process. We believe these actions will substantially improve the quality and fairness of the CDI process and help prevent the kind of mistakes that lead to the "horror stories" you mentioned. . . . One improvement which started on October 1, involves a face-to-face interview in the social Security office at the beginning of each CDI review. This interview corrects a flaw in the program which is perhaps more to blame for people being dropped from the disability rolls despite glaringly obvious disabilities. Under the new procedure, the interviewer curtails the CDI when the beneficiary's current medical condition clearly warrants curtailment.

I have asked Social Security Commissioner John Svahn to review the cases of those beneficiaries you mentioned in your letter who died after their disability benefits had been stopped and to provide you with a report. . . .

Sincerely,

Richard S. Schweiker, Secretary

Source: Copy of letter in SSA History Archives, Mary Ross Papers, Box MR 60.

Document 8.21
SSA's Internal Reform Proposals, May 25, 1983

As political pressure mounted on the CDI process, John Svahn, the commissioner of Social Security, developed a package of potential administrative reforms. This internal memo was sent by Svahn to Margaret Heckler, the secretary of Health and Human Services, proposing ways that the disability program might be modified, short of legislation.

Disability Reform Plan

Background

In 1980 the Congress mandated an eligibility review of all Social Security disability beneficiaries to be conducted at least every three years, except for individuals considered to be permanently disabled, beginning in 1982. . . . The Congress acted in response to the large growth of the disability program in the 1970's, and information that large numbers of ineligible individuals were on the rolls. The General Accounting Office had found that approximately 20 percent of the disability recipients at that time were actually ineligible.

The Social Security Administration (SSA) began the review . . . in March of 1981. (SSA has been criticized for "accelerating" the review process as a budget saving device, although in fact this has allowed for a greater period of time in which to review the required number of cases.) Approximately 45 percent of the cases reviewed have been terminated (340,000 out of 750,000 cases). Approximately 60 percent of the individuals *who have appealed* to administrative law judges (ALJs) have had their benefits restored.

The very high termination rate and ALJ reversal rate, coupled with "horror stories" involving people taken off the rolls who were obviously still disabled, have generated substantial media and Congressional interest in the disability program. There have been countless newspaper and television stories and over a dozen Congressional hearings on the subject, all very unfavorable to SSA and the Administration. There has also been substantial litigation prompted by the reviews.

As a consequence of media attention and intensive lobbying from advocacy groups, there is a growing effort in the Congress to pass radical legislation that would either halt the review process outright or impose so many limitations as to make the removal of an unquestionably ineligible recipient from the rolls virtually impossible. For example, Senator Heinz has introduced a bill establishing a "moratorium" on reviewing mental disability cases, a category which has been particularly difficult to adjudicate and that has produced a number of "horror stories." Every day brings yet another bill that could have very unfortunate effects. . . .

Nature of the Problem

Cutting through the political rhetoric and media blitz, many of the "problems" are beyond our control. For example:

- The law is very strict and most people, including Congressmen, do not understand it. People who look disabled are frequently precluded from eligibility by the express terms of the law, not by regulations or other policy or interpretation.

- Many people on the rolls never expected to be reviewed, let alone terminated. Their shock in learning that their benefits could and would be cut off has generated much of the problem, regardless of their genuine ineligibility.

Nonetheless, certain real problems do exist. Generally, they fall into one of these two categories:

- The strong reaction from the GAO and the Congress in 1980 to the excessive looseness in the disability program during the 1970's produced a natural reaction in the bureaucracy to tighten up the program. The pendulum swung completely to the other direction, creating an "adjudicative climate" interpreted by frontline eligibility workers as encouraging denial and termination of disability benefits.
- Certain problems may have existed with disability policies and procedures for many years. These problems went largely unnoticed until the large review program began. Generally, the problems involve an overly bureaucratic, insensitive and paper oriented eligibility determination process.

Reforms Already Implemented

In the past several months, SSA has instituted several steps to respond to the problems in the disability program. . . .
    . . . Further changes have now been identified which should be made. Carrying out these other measures will complete the task of reforming disability. They should respond to much of the criticism that has been generated about disability, but more importantly, will produce a balanced, sound program that will be fair and have integrity.

Initiatives to Complete the Reform of Disability

1. *Nationwide Implementation of Evidentiary Hearings.* . . .
2. *Continued Benefits Through the Evidentiary Hearing.* . . .
3. *Change the "Cessation" Policy*
    - Under current policy, a disability beneficiary can be terminated even though his or her medical condition might be the same as, or worse than, when he or she went on the rolls. The only question looked at is whether the person meets the current definition of disability.
    - This policy has generated considerable controversy, both in the Congress and the courts. SSA is losing court cases on this issue, and legislation is pending which would mandate the use of a medical improvement standard.
    - We are studying the possibility of adopting a standard that would consider such factors as whether the beneficiary has improved medically or in ability to work, or whether the initial decision to grant benefits was erroneous. If the person has been on the rolls for a long period and consequently out of the workforce, this would be taken into account in determining the ability to work.

4. *Change the Policy for Mental Disability*

  • Mental disability has caused perhaps the greatest number of "horror stories" and is the most difficult type of disability to adjudicate. Fundamental changes are necessary. *Immediate Changes:*

    ○ We have identified characteristics of those mental cases that are most likely to be terminated incorrectly. . . . These cases will be screened out and exempted from review. . . .

    ○ We will conduct a national re-review of all mental cases that have been terminated over the past two years and reinstate any cases that were incorrectly ceased. This should also have the effect of avoiding further litigation in this area.

    Longer Range Changes:

    ○ The eligibility criteria for cases involving psychiatric impairments are being completely reviewed and evaluated . . . and

    ○ We will develop new requirements that States will use to evaluate mental cases. . . .

5. *Revise the "Medical Listings"*

  • SSA regulations contain detailed descriptions of the medical criteria that must be met in order to be eligible for disability. They have not been examined and revised for a long period of time.

  • We will work with appropriate professionals to insure that our medical standards are reasonable, comprehensive, and up-to-date. . . .

6. *Re-Examine the Concept of Non-Severe Impairments*

  • Current policy allows many cases to be denied or terminated on the basis of a "non-severe impairment." This means that the normal disability evaluation process which considers the effect of age, education, and work experience on eligibility is not followed. These cases are more prone to being incorrectly decided and later reversed at the ALJ level.

  • We will issue instructions prohibiting the use of this device to determine eligibility. Decisions should be made on the basis of evaluating the total person, including age, education, work experience, and emotional stability in addition to clinical medical evidence. . . .

8. *Prepare a Development Guide for Adjudicators*

  • Disability adjudicators must "develop" a case before deciding on eligibility. . . .

  • There is great disparity as to how disability cases are developed. State agencies may do too little development before deciding a case, ALJs may do too much.

  • We will prepare a guide that will set standards for developing cases to be used by all disability adjudicators. . . .

11. *Further Refine the Definition of Permanent Disability*

  • . . . The expansion of cases defined as permanently disabled will increase the percentage of the caseload exempted from the three year review to approximately 37 percent. . . .

12. *Select Cases for Review on a Random Basis*

  • SSA has used a profile to select cases for the three year review that was designed to select first those cases that had a higher than average probability of being ineligible. In theory, as the three year review period progressed, the cases selected for review would become less likely to be ineligible.

- We will now select all further cases on a random basis. This will accomplish two results. We will no longer have to defend and explain our profile, which has repeatedly been attacked in the Congress and by advocacy groups as unfairly targetting certain types of cases for review. Furthermore, the termination rate will drop somewhat upon instituting a random selection process.

13. *Improve the "Curtailment" of Disability Reviews*

- . . . We are developing additional curtailment criteria that will allow more cases to be screened out at the field office level. . . .

Summary

Taken together, these actions promise a revolutionary impact on the CDI program and should lead to a marked reduction in the "horror stories" flowing from it.

From the viewpoint of individual cases, the principal impact would be as follows:

- About 37 percent of all ongoing cases would be exempt from the three year review cycle, up from the 27 percent exempt under current rules.
- About two-thirds of all mental impairment cases, the most difficult to review, would be exempted.
- All cases would get faster access to a face-to-face appearance before a decisionmaker and, accordingly, get a better chance at winning their appeals.

The sole negative side-effect would be the potential budget impact. Depending on how quickly and completely these reforms are implemented, the reduction in projected savings to the Disability Insurance Trust Fund could range from one-third to one-half of those projected, or from $200 million to $300 million cumulatively over Fiscal Years 84–86.

Source: Memorandum from John A. Svahn to the Secretary, May 25, 1983. Copy in SSA History Archives, Mary Ross Papers, Box MR 60.

Document 8.22
Announcement of Secretary Heckler's Reforms, June 7, 1983

In June 1983 the secretary of HHS, Margaret Heckler, issued a moratorium on the most contested forms of CDIs and implemented certain ancillary reforms in the process—basically adopting the recommendations put to her by the SSA. Again, the hope was that these administrative reforms would eliminate the need for legislation.

I announce today a specific series of steps—a package of major reforms in the process of reviewing the eligibility of Social Security Disability beneficiaries. That review was long ago mandated by the 1980 Congress.

The contents of this package—and especially its fairness have been a prime priority of mine since I took command of this Department in March.

President Reagan fully shares my concern. He has personally approved the reforms I am announcing today. He is as committed as I am to making these reforms work—and to making sure that this program is as fair and humane and compassionate as humanly possible. He is also concerned, as I am, that this program be responsive to the mandate placed on us by the Congress. . . .

Like most of my colleagues in the 96th Congress, I was appalled when the Carter Administration and GAO audit findings documented the fact that as many as one-in-five of the 2.8 million workers then on the Disability rolls were ineligible to receive benefits.

There was an immediate rush to find a remedy:—to protect the truly eligible recipients (and the taxpayers!) but also to staunch the $2 billion dollars in annual losses to the hard-pressed Social Security Trust Fund.

But, like most of my colleagues, I had no idea that the sudden, three-year review of millions of cases we then mandated might result in hardships and heartbreaks for innocent and worthy disability recipients who would fall through the cracks of the existing long-time, paper-oriented review process that had never before had to cope with such an overwhelming workload.

It is clear to me now from my own review of our experience to date with this program, that the old, paper-oriented review process we inherited was too insensitive, too bureaucratic. Mistakes were too easy to make—and too hard to rectify.

The reforms which Social Security instituted last year—which introduced a face-to-face human contact at the very beginning of the review process and set the stage for a face-to-face hearing at the very first level of appeal—represented a giant step toward humanizing this program.

But we need to go further. . . .

These reforms respond to the concerns expressed by leaders of the Congress. These reforms respond to concerns raised by medical and mental health professional groups. These reforms respond to the concerns of the State agencies which administer much of the program for us. And, most importantly, these reforms respond to the demands of beneficiaries, that the review system be as fair and humane and error-free as possible. . . .

First, I am authorizing an expansion of the number of those exempted from the Continuing Disability Investigation process by 200,000, bringing the total so exempted to more than 1 million, or 37 percent of the disabled workers now on the rolls.

This action will ease the workload on State agencies, giving them more time to review each case.

Second, I am authorizing a temporary exemption from review of two-thirds of all mental impairment cases, or 135,000 of those still to be reviewed.

This exemption, involving those diagnosed as having "functional psychotic disorders," will last until we and appropriate, compassionate outside experts have thoroughly reviewed the standards we use in this most controversial area.

Once we have acceptable standards, I will authorize going back to re-review those who may have been dropped from the rolls in the past under existing standards.

Third, I am authorizing a major change in the way the Social Security Administration selects cases for review by State agencies.

This change, which will mean moving from a selection of cases by means of a "profile" to selection on a more random basis, should sharply reduce the number of initial decisions to stop benefits. This will mean a major reduction in the growing backlog of cases being appealed, freeing staff resources for closer review of the most difficult cases.

Fourth, I am proposing legislation to remove a built-in bias against recipients now in the law that forces the Social Security Administration to review fully two-thirds of all State decisions to allow benefits—but does not mandate a review of decisions to deny benefits.

I believe that any audit system we use should be absolutely neutral—which would be the case under my proposal that we review an appropriate mix of both allowance and denial decisions.

Fifth, I am proposing legislation to make permanent the practice of paying benefits to individuals through their first opportunity for a face-to-face evidentiary hearing.

This would replace the temporary legislation passed last December—with Administration support—which provided payment through the Administrative Law Judge level, the first chance anyone now has to take his or her case personally to a decision-maker.

Beginning in January we will have a new face-to-face hearing process in place Nationwide.

We have tested that process—and it works, just as we predicted. It produces far more favorable decisions very early on in the review process—and far fewer appeals to the Administrative Law Judge level.

If we could get this new system fully in place tomorrow, I would order it done. I have ordered the Social Security Administration to move as rapidly as humanly possible.

Sixth, I have ordered the Social Security Administration to accelerate its top-to-bottom review, in consultation with appropriate experts and the States, of any other policies and procedures which have any affect on both the decisions on cases that are made and on the adjudicatory climate in which they are made. . . .

Taken together, these reforms will mean the loss of one-third to one-half of the savings projected for this program over the next three years, or $200 million dollars to $300 million dollars. The exact number will depend in part on the outcome of our further review of our policy and procedures.

There is a broad, non-partisan consensus in this Nation that when any American woman or man is truly disabled—mentally or physically—our Social Security system should respond by extending a prompt, humane helping hand. Almost all Americans are agreed: the trauma of disability is enough. It should not be compounded by a loss of independence and dignity.

At the same time, we have a delicate balance to strike.

The Congress acted in 1980 out of concern that the traditional and instinctive generosity of working Americans was being abused—that too many other than the truly disabled were benefitting from the Social Security program.

I believe these reforms will help us better maintain that delicate balance.

Source: Copy of HHS press release in SSA History Archives, Downey Books, Social Security Disability Benefits Reform Act of 1984 and Related Amendments.

Document 8.23
Department of Justice Letter Concerning Non-acquiescence,
September 19, 1983

This confidential "eyes only" letter was sent to Juan A. del Real, the general counsel of HHS, from J. Paul McGrath, the assistant attorney general in the Department of Justice (DOJ), expressing the DOJ's discomfort with the SSA's policy of non-acquiescence.

As you know, it has been the policy of the Social Security Administration to deem itself not bound by court of appeals decisions even within the circuit issuing the decision. As your office has recognized, this policy raises sensitive concerns regarding the relationship between the executive and judicial branches, and is a matter on which close coordination between your office and the Justice Department is essential. . . . The purpose of this letter is to set forth a method for improving that cooperation.

As we understand it, there are two elements which comprise the agency's non-acquiescence policy. First, in a limited number of instances, the agency announces formally that it does not intend to apply legal principles announced in a particular court of appeals decision. In *Lopez v. Heckler* . . . the district court, in response to two such announcements regarding Ninth Circuit decisions, imposed extraordinarily broad and burdensome obligations on the agency, obligations that probably would not have been imposed but for the court's obvious negative reaction to the agency policy. Second, even where the agency does not formally announce a non-acquiescence, its standing instructions require agency employees not to follow lower court interpretations of law or regulation that conflict with the Secretary's interpretation unless and until instructed otherwise. This policy has recently been criticized by the Eighth Circuit in *Hillhouse v. Harris* . . . in which a concurring judge indicated that he would seek to bring contempt proceedings against the Secretary in her official and individual capacities if the non-acquiescence policy persists.

These and other similar cases—which result in burdens on SSA and which tend to erode the litigating credibility of the executive branch—underscore the need for a more searching scrutiny of non-acquiescence decisions. In addition to those practical concerns, considerations of comity and respect for the courts of appeals also mandate a reform in the procedure by which, to borrow Mr. Gonya's phrase, "the blessing of the Justice Department," is obtained for non-acquiescences. . . .

Accordingly, we believe that the following procedures should be adopted. Henceforth the Department of Health and Human Services should acquiesce in all court of appeals decisions within the deciding circuit unless this Department has approved in advance the non-acquiescence in writing. . . .

A policy of "acquiescence" does not, of course, require the agency to follow the broadest possible readings of decisional law. The agency can continue to urge reasonably arguable distinctions, or to follow the more favorable interpretation where the "law of the circuit" is unclear. But the new policy would preclude deliberate refusal to follow the law of a particular circuit within that circuit. . . .

Sincerely,

J. Paul McGrath, Assistant Attorney General

Source: Letter, dated September 19, 1983, to Mr. Juan A. del Real, General Counsel, Department of Health and Human Services, from J. Paul McGrath, Assistant Attorney General, DOJ. Copy in SSA History Archives, Mary Ross Papers, MR Box 60.

Document 8.24
Statement of Senator Cohen on Disability Insurance Reform,
January 25, 1984

In late January 1984 the Senate Finance Committee held a hearing on the disability program and the legislation then advancing in the House and Senate to change the procedures and rules governing the CDI process. In his statement, Sen. William S. Cohen (R-Maine) summed up where he thought matters stood at this point in the controversy.

. . . We have waited far too long to remedy a clearly inhumane, inefficient, and inflexible system for deciding who should continue to receive disability payments. Perhaps we are numbed by the statistics and have forgotten the injustice inflicted on thousands of disabled people. As a result of a flawed review process, severe hardships have been imposed on the disabled. A man with a shattered spine in a full body cast, a woman involuntarily committed to a mental institution, individuals with advanced multiple sclerosis, and a man in an iron lung are among individuals who have received notices from our government informing them that they are well enough to return to work.

In desperation, people have committed suicide after losing their benefits, and men and women have died of the ailments that the Social Security Administration had decided were no longer disabling. Even severely disabled individuals whose medical conditions had actually deteriorated since they were awarded benefits decades ago have been dropped from the program.

The problem is a review process that strives for efficiency at the expense of equity. Witnesses at hearings held by the Oversight of Government Management Subcommittee recounted case after case in which a truly disabled person lost benefits due to a paper oriented review process characterized by misinformation, incomplete medical examinations, inadequately documented files, conflicting standards, and erroneous decisions. The General Accounting Office has testified that the message perceived by the state agencies, swamped with cases, is to "deny, deny, deny," and, I might add, to process cases faster and faster and faster. In the name of efficiency, we have scanned our computer terminals, rounded up the disabled workers in the country, pushed the discharge button, and let them go into a free-fall toward economic chaos.

The need for fundamental change in the disability reviews has been evident for some time. Our failure to remedy this problem has fostered contempt for the rule of the law and has permitted injustice to flourish unchallenged.

In response to congressional inaction, the states have taken matters into their own hands. Half of the states no longer follow the flawed procedures and criteria mandated by the Social Security Administration. In a dozen states, including Maine, the Governors have imposed moratoriums on further disability reviews, while other states have devised their own standards for determining eligibility or are following court decisions that require medical improvement in a beneficiary's condition before benefits can be curtailed.

Legislation such as S. 476 is required to end this chaos and to ensure an equitable review process. . . .

. . . S. 476 would require that the claimant be given a clear and complete notice of what the review process entails. Although the SSA has taken steps to improve its notices, this basic safeguard should be incorporated into the disability statute. Considerable confusion in the disability process resulted from the agency's early notices, which simply told the beneficiary: "Your case is due for review" to see if you "continue to meet all requirements." This notice was misleading because it did not inform disability recipients that they would have to prove all over again with new medical evidence that they qualified for benefits.

Second, our legislation would require that the standards for determining disability be issued as regulations subject to public notice and comment. This provision would accomplish three essential objectives: It would promote uniformity in decision-making by requiring all adjudicators to use the same criteria; it would improve the quality and consistency of the standards by involving the public, including the medical profession, in their development; and it would ensure that everyone involved has ready access to the standards. An attorney in Maine who represents the disabled recently described the current criteria as "secret" because the internal agency guidelines used by state claims examiners are not available for public scrutiny and are so difficult for her to obtain.

Third, S. 476 would institute a face-to-face meeting between the claimant and the state adjudicator to humanize the process and to permit a more complete understanding of the individual's capabilities.

Fourth, the cornerstone of our bill is the section which would establish clear criteria for terminating benefits. The specific criteria in S. 476 would clear the confusion that shrouds the current review process and, for the first time, would provide beneficiaries, attorneys, state claims examiners, and administrative law judges with a clear understanding of the grounds for terminating benefits. The bill would establish a general rule requiring the Social Security Administration show medical improvement in the claimant's condition before benefits can be ended. . . .

Another provision of our bill would make permanent the continuation of benefits pending appeal to an administrative law judge. . . .

To streamline the appeals process S. 476 proposes that the reconsideration step be eliminated so that claimants could appeal directly to an administrative law judge. . . .

S. 476 also would include language on pain in the statute. The Social Security Administration's regulations require consideration of a claimant's pain in reaching a disability determination. However, for a time, the agency eliminated the evaluation of pain section from the POMS, the internal guidelines which set forth the standards for disability decisions, saying there had been an "improper emphasis" on the role of pain. I would point out that Federal courts have recognized the importance of pain in disability determinations for more than 20 years. Although new guidance on pain has been reinserted into the POMS, our bill would provide statutory guidance on evaluating a claimant's pain to prevent future confusion or arbitrary deletions by the agency.

Finally, I urge the Committee to carefully examine the provisions of the bill affecting the SSA's policy of issuing rulings on nonacquiescence when it disagrees with a federal court decision but chooses not to appeal it. The implications of the agency's current approach are troubling. When the SSA issues a ruling of nonacquiescence, it, in effect, forces an identically situated claimant to go to court in order to obtain relief. This renders the administrative proceedings pointless as the disabled individual knows he will have to file a district court action if the administrative law judge follows the agency's policy and ignores the court ruling. Moreover, the circuit court opinions in which the SSA has a nonacquiesced have involved major issues, such as medical improvement, which would have significantly altered disability determinations had they been followed.

Mr. Chairman, I want to emphasize that I support periodic reviews of individuals receiving disability. Since a worker does not have to be permanently disabled in order to receive benefits, it makes sense to recheck beneficiaries from time to time to ensure that only those who remain disabled continue to collect disability checks. Workers who have recovered should go back to work. Periodic reviews also provide a useful check against the fraud that plagues virtually every Federal program.

But what we have now is a 40 percent solution to a 20 percent problem. The percentage of ineligibles was estimated to be about 20 percent when Congress passed the 1980 amendments, but benefits are being terminated for twice that number. Based on the administrative law judges' reversals of state termination decisions, more than 160,000 mistakes have already been made, and that doesn't include those severely disabled people who didn't pursue an appeal because they lacked the resources, willpower, or understanding.

Government has a duty to be just as well as efficient, and right now, the disability review process is neither. . . .

. . . While Secretary Heckler deserves praise for the administrative reforms she has implemented, it is clear that legislation is still needed to rectify the fundamental flaws in the disability program. . . .

Source: Social Security Disability Insurance Program, Hearing before the Committee on Finance, Senate, January 25, 1984 (Washington, D.C.: Government Printing Office, 1984), 4143.

Document 8.25
Statement of Senator Levin on Disability Insurance Reform, January 25, 1984

This opening statement by Sen. Carl Levin (D-Mich.) at the January hearing on the Social Security disability insurance program is very much along the same lines as Senator Cohen's (Document 8.24) and indicates the wide unanimity on the core issues, across party lines. Senator Levin's remarks are a summary of the problems encountered with the CDI process from its inception until the point in early 1984 when Congress was on the verge of enacting major reforms.

Mr. Chairman, I have mixed feelings as I testify before this committee today. While I am, of course, pleased that the committee is taking up S. 476 for consideration, I can only recall that it was in August, 1982—almost a year and a half ago—that Senator Cohen and I appeared before this committee on the same subject. In that period of time, tens of thousands of severely disabled persons have suffered through the anxiety inherent in the disability appeals process—where they have been terminated by the state disability services only to be reinstated by an administrative law judge or a federal district court.

The comments of one person who experienced this process are rather telling and sound more like the words of a prisoner of war than of a disabled American worker:

"I pray that no one has to experience the grief, pain, and humiliation I've felt."

Mr. Chairman, S. 476, which I introduced along with Senator Cohen now has a total of 35 cosponsors representing a broad spectrum of support. . . .

As my colleagues well know—from the reports they have been receiving through their caseworkers back home—something is seriously wrong with the administration of the Social Security disability program. Severely disabled persons who should be protected by the benefits of this program have been terminated in unexpected numbers. The horror stories have proven to be not isolated examples but to reflect the experience of tens of thousands of disabled people. . . .

Let me briefly explain how we got into the shameful situation we are in today with this program.

In 1980, Congress enacted into law an amendment to the Social Security Act which required the SSA to review every three years the eligibility of persons receiving Social Security disability benefits. This was based on a growing concern that large numbers of persons were receiving benefits who were really ineligible to do so. This was a reasonable management initiative and one I endorse. It is the implementation of that provision that has created the chaos and hardship we have been hearing so much about.

To begin with, the reviews themselves were begun prematurely—before adequate planning, training, and hiring of staff. Persons who had never been reviewed before were not given adequate notice about what was expected of them and the type of evidence they were required to produce to retain their eligibility. But most important, a signal was being sent from the national Social Security office that the people being reviewed were to be held to very strict standards, and that any error should favor the SSA as opposed to the disabled worker. More weight was given to a one-time exam by a SSA-paid consultative physician than the beneficiary's long-term treating physician. The combination of these factors led to the unanticipated termination of 45–47 percent of the persons who were being reviewed—this was over double the number of terminations the SSA itself estimated would occur at the time the 1980 amendment was considered and passed.

In 1982, support for the reviews began to erode as there were increasingly dramatic press accounts of the effects these reviews were having on severely disabled persons. Numerous congressional committees in early 1982 began oversight hearings on the disability review process. House Aging held a hearing in May of 1982. The Subcommittee on Oversight of Government Management, which Senator Cohen chairs and on which I serve as ranking minority member, convened a hearing on May 25, 1982, and heard testimony that should have embarrassed us all as public officials. We heard the moving account of Mrs. Richard Kage, who described how the disability review process forced her severely disabled husband to try to go back to work, intensified the degree of his disability and finally was a causal factor in his untimely death at the age of 49. We had documentation from Mr. Kage's doctor that it was his medical opinion that the emotional anxiety surrounding the review process contributed to Mr. Kage's death. That is a stunning accusation. And it is not the only such accusation that has been made about this process.

There were also hearings by the Social Security Subcommittee of the House Ways and Means Committee, the Senate Aging Committee, and, of course, the hearing in August of 1982 by this committee. Throughout all these hearings the testimony has been the same. Something has to be done to improve the way in which these reviews are being conducted to restore order and fairness to the disability program.

The congressional concern was complimented by a growing number of cases in the federal courts. Numerous lawsuits have been filed challenging the standards used by Social Security for terminating someone from the program and to date some half dozen federal courts have held that Social Security should have to prove that the person's condition has changed or medically improved before the person can be terminated. But the Social Security Administration has a policy of nonacquiescence which means it picks and chooses those Circuit Court decisions with which it will agree and refuses to follow those court decisions with which it disagrees. This means that although litigants were winning in the courts on the question of showing medical improvements before termination, these court decisions were not being applied to other disability beneficiaries.

Two major class action cases have forced Social Security to change its procedures. In the Ninth Circuit, in a case entitled *Lopez v. Schweicker,* the federal district judge ordered Social Security to follow prior decisions by the Circuit Court and require a showing of medical improvement prior to termination. The judge has ordered the SSA not only to apply such a standard prospectively, but also to review those persons who have been terminated over the past two years and apply the standard retroactively. The SSA is complying with that court order, but it is also on appeal to the Ninth Circuit. That medical improvement standard, however, is being applied by the SSA only to persons within the six states covered by the Ninth Circuit.

In the Eighth Circuit, a federal district court ruled that the SSA had used an erroneous process in reviewing the eligibility of persons with mental impairments and has ordered the SSA to review all persons with mental impairments within the jurisdiction of the Chicago regional office who have been terminated without completing the full sequential evaluation process. That involves some 32,000 persons in my state of Michigan alone.

In an effort to protect their own constituents, and to abide by the authority of the federal courts, many states have taken action on their own to address the problems in the disability program. At my last count, 17 states have imposed moratoriums on the reviews of disability beneficiaries until Congress passes a reform bill or the SSA straightens the system out administratively or they have imposed their own standard for terminations, which include a showing of medical improvement or change in the beneficiary's condition. Nine other states are under court order to follow a medical improvement standard.

On June 8, 1983, Secretary Heckler attempted to bring some administrative reforms to the disability program. She instituted, among other actions, a partial moratorium on reviews of those with mental impairments and initiated a study of the disability program. While her efforts were in the right direction, they were far from solving the real problems which only comprehensive reform legislation can do.

When these reviews started in March of 1981, there was no statutory protection for the payment of benefits for these individuals while they were appealing their termination decisions. This was particularly troubling in light of the fact that over two-thirds of the persons who appealed their benefit terminations to administrative law judges were being reinstated. The latest SSA statistics show that since March of 1981, of some 470,000 persons who have been terminated initially, 160,000 have been reinstated on appeal and 120,000 appeals are pending. Seeing the human tragedy that was resulting from this process—persons were losing their homes, their ability to purchase basic necessities, and even their will to live while the appeals process dragged on—Congress passed last year an emergency provision which continues the payment of benefits through appeal to an administrative law judge. That provision expired on October 1, 1983, and we extended it to December 7, 1983, but unexpectedly failed to renew the extension before the close of the last session. The assumption has always been that that provision was merely a stopgap measure until Congress could pass comprehensive reform legislation. Now we don't even have that. But, because the SSA pays benefits for two months beyond the month of termination, and because the SSA has imposed its own nationwide temporary moratorium on terminations, no one has been affected by our failure to renew the aid-paid-pending provision. However, soon it will be a different story once terminations are again processed by the SSA. That is the deadline we now face on this legislation.

We introduced S. 476 on February 15, 1983. We offered an amendment to S. 476 on June 29. . . .

(1) The bill requires that before a person receiving disability benefits can be terminated, the SSA must be able to show medical improvement. . . .

The weight of court opinion supports—on the basis of procedural fairness—the concept of medical improvement. Some courts have ruled that the burden in termination cases shifts from the beneficiary to the SSA to show a change in the person's condition or a reason why the person is no longer found to be eligible; others simply state that the SSA should show medical improvement. The SSA has refused to follow these decisions.

Applying a standard of medical improvement as that contained in S. 476 is only reasonable and fair. When a disability beneficiary was initially allowed benefits, Social Security was concluding, by its own standards and tests, that that person was so severely disabled as to not be able to do any job in the national economy. Now Social Security has "tightened" the administration of the program and may judge that same person, who has not experienced any change or improvement in his or her condition, as no longer being eligible. Basically, the SSA is saying it changed its mind; no other reason is necessary. I think that's wrong and terribly unfair. Now if the SSA can prove that the person was fraudulent in his initial application, or the SSA committed an error in processing that initial claim, then the SSA should be able to terminate that person even though the person's condition has not changed. Likewise, the SSA should be able to take advantage of recent developments in the medical field. Thus, if there is a new device that can better assess the extent of disability or that can lessen the effects of the disability, then the SSA should be able to require its use and take advantage of the changes, regardless of whether or not the beneficiary's condition has in fact improved. . . . S. 476 allows for these exceptions. But where these factors are not present and where the individual's condition has not changed, then the SSA should be required to stand by its previous judgment of eligibility. Frankly, I cannot see how a person can legitimately be terminated unless one of these exceptions applies.

(2) The bill requires the SSA to consider multiple impairments in determining whether or not a disability is severe or meets or equals the listings. . . . SSA has restricted its interpretation of severity and has precluded consideration of multiple impairments. . . . That is simply unfair and unjustifiably restrictive.

(3) The bill requires certain improvements in the administration of the reviews—better, more complete notice to the individual, the opportunity for a personal appearance with the

state disability examiners before actual termination, and a thorough documentation of the beneficiary's preceding twelve-month medical history with foremost reliance on the comments of the treatment physician as opposed to the SSA ordered and bought consultative examiners.

(4) The bill establishes by statute a standard for consideration of pain. Earlier hearings brought to light gross inconsistencies in the treatment of pain between the state disability examiners and the administrative law judges—largely a result of the SSA's use of internal guidelines (the POMs) which were different from the regulations. The standard contained in S. 476 would allow for pain to be considered disabling without proof of a medical cause (as the SSA now requires) if there are medical findings of the presence of the pain. . . .

(5) The bill would make the payment of benefits through the administrative law judge stage permanent law. Since these benefits are frequently the only object that stands between subsistence and poverty for many of these beneficiaries, they should only be terminated when the administrative appeals process has been completed and the decision of the SSA is final. Not only does a beneficiary lose his or her benefits, he or she also loses the important Medicare coverage which helps the beneficiary obtain needed medical treatment. The termination of benefits is, therefore, a very serious consequence and should only be done when the SSA prevails at the ALJ level.

(6) The bill requires the Secretary to either appeal or acquiesce in decisions of federal circuit courts. This is a very difficult issue. Absent a direct court order involving an entire class of people, the SSA feels free to ignore as to subsequent beneficiaries' decisions of federal district and circuit courts interpreting substantive law except as they apply in the specific case being decided. Some believe that is violative of the fundamental principle of the separation of powers as interpreted by the Supreme Court in *Marbury v. Madison*. The SSA replies that it has the responsibility to administer a national program and can't respond to decisions with which it disagrees in less than a national way. Were it to follow a Circuit Court decision on a national basis, it would be thereby elevating the Circuit Court of Appeals to the level of the Supreme Court. Because of the SSA's arguments . . . [t]he change I would propose would be to require the Secretary of HHS to report all acquiescence and nonacquiescence decisions and the reasoning for those decisions to Congress. This is a very important policy question—the extent to which a federal agency can ignore federal district and circuit court interpretations of law—and one that has implications governmentwide. I can understand if this Committee does not feel it can fully respond to the problem in just the SSA context.

(7) The bill requires that any standard for determining disability to be followed or used by the SSA be made subject to public notice and comment and applied at all levels of the administrative process, from the state disability examiners to the Appeals Council. I was shocked to discover that many of the most important determinative standards and factors used by state disability examiners at the insistence of the SSA are not published as regulations. . . . There really is no acceptable justification for allowing standards of disability which so clearly affect the final outcome of the eligibility decision to be promulgated and made effective without public notice and comment.

Mr. Chairman, at last count 41,000 of the 44,000 lawsuits pending against HHS involved disability claimants. In Detroit the figures are equally staggering and the percentages are growing. . . .

By failing to enact comprehensive reform legislation to clean up this chaotic system, Congress is unnecessarily burdening our already overburdened federal courts.

The actions by the states, the enormous growth in federal district court disability cases, the tens of thousands of persons who are terminated only to be reinstated on appeal—these are facts which compel your Committee's action on this legislation. . . .

Source: Social Security Disability Insurance Program, Hearing before the Committee on Finance, Senate, January 25, 1984 (Washington, D.C.: Government Printing Office, 1984), 54–58.

Document 8.26
Commissioner McSteen's Testimony at the Hearing on Disability Insurance Reform, January 25, 1984

This excerpt is from testimony given to the Senate Finance Committee hearing by the SSA's acting commissioner, Martha McSteen. Her statement clearly indicates that even at this late date in the process, the administration was still resisting the legislation.

. . . I would like to make clear at the outset that the administration opposes enactment of disability legislation. As I will discuss . . . we believe that the administrative and legislative reforms already accomplished make further reforms unnecessary. . . .

Medical Improvement

The Administration strongly opposes . . . a separate standard of disability for those already on the rolls. About three-quarters of the cost of the House bill is attributable to this provision alone. . . .

Both H.R. 4170 and the disability amendments introduced by Senators Cohen and Levin . . . would provide a medical improvement standard for terminating disability benefits. . . . [W]e have concluded that we must strongly oppose a medical improvement standard.

A basic problem with a medical improvement standard is that it would create different standards of eligibility for initial claims and for continuing disability reviews. . . .

Also, a medical improvement standard is unworkable because of the difficulties with comparing a person's current condition with history or her condition at the time benefits were awarded. . . .

In addition to these serious concerns, we believe that reforms in the disability program now under way make such a standard unnecessary. . . .

For all of these reasons we believe that a medical improvement standard is not in the best interest of the disability program, and we strongly oppose enactment of such a provision even if applied prospectively only. . . .

Compliance with Court Orders

This proposal . . . would require us either to recommend appeal of Circuit Court decisions with which we disagree or to acquiesce in the decision and apply it within the jurisdiction of the Circuit Court.

We strongly oppose this provision. HHS has always complied with the terms of court orders as they relate to individuals or classes of individuals named in a particular suit. However, our policy of nonacquiescence is essential to ensure that the Agency follows its statutory mandate to administer the Social Security program nationwide in a uniform and consistent manner. . . .

Conclusion

In conclusion, we think the legislative and administrative steps that have been taken to date have improved and strengthened the disability process, and the proposed legislative changes discussed earlier are not needed.

Source: Social Security Disability Insurance Program, Hearing before the Committee on Finance, Senate, January 25, 1984 (Washington, D.C.: Government Printing Office, 1984), 93–107.

Document 8.27
Senators' "Dear Colleague" Letter, March 16, 1984

In this letter to their Senate colleagues, Senators Levin, Cohen, and Heinz reiterated their bipartisan complaints about the administration's conduct of the CDIs and offered their legislation, which would in fact initially serve as the main legislative vehicle in the Senate.

Dear Colleague:

Within the next several weeks we will be offering an amendment, to a suitable bill on the floor, that will significantly revise the way in which the Social Security Disability Program is administered. The amendment will correct many of the injustices and abuses that have occured and are occuring in SSA's continuing disability reviews of persons receiving disability benefits.

The amendment will be a revised version of S. 476, introduced by Senators Levin and Cohen on February 15, 1983, which now has 35 cosponsors. . . . CBO's latest estimate of the cost of the amendment is $1.1 million over five years. . . . We have worked hard to pare down the costs of this bill without affecting the significant, substantive reforms, and we believe we have accomplished that goal.

The reason we feel compelled to take this bill to the floor as an amendment to a possibly unrelated bill now is the reinstitution of the continuing disability reviews and the sizeable number of wrongful terminations that will result from those reviews. In December, 1983, when Congress failed to reenact the provision requiring the payment of benefits through appeal, SSA, on its own initiative, imposed a moritorium on all terminations. For the last three months no one has been terminated from the disability program. But that hiatus has now come to an end, and SSA has notified all the states that processing of the terminations should begin immediately. That means shortly thousands of persons—and there will be many because of the accumulated backlog of terminations over the past three months—will be terminated. Using past statistics as a guide, almost half of those severely disabled people who will be terminated will eventually be reinstated. And, with the provision requiring the payment of benefits through appeal having expired, people will be without benefits for which they are really eligible for 9–18 months (the average length of the appeal process). There are thousands of horror stories out there waiting to happen, and we in the Congress can prevent them by acting on this legislation now. The need is urgent.

The Social Security Disability Program is in a shambles.

- Severely disabled persons are being unjustly terminated. Since March, 1981, more than 470,000 beneficiaries have been terminated; 160,000 of those persons were reinstated after a lengthy appeals process.
- The states and the courts which bear the administrative brunt of this tragedy are rebelling. More than half of the states have either refused to process terminations or are under court order to do so or are applying standards other than SSA's. The courts, which are fast becoming overwhelmed with disability cases—41,000 of the 44,000 lawsuits pending against HHS involve disability claimants—are reinstating terminated beneficiaries and castigating SSA for its refusal to follow court opinions.

In all of this, it is the disabled worker of this country who suffers the most. Social Security Disability is an insurance program; it is not welfare. Employees contribute to this program for protection against unexpected illness or injury. We are violating their trust and our promise when we allow this program to be administered so unjustly.

We ask you to join us in support of this amendment. . . .

Source: Copy of letter in SSA History Archives, Mary Ross Papers, Box MR 60.

Document 8.28
Summary of the 1984 Disability Benefits Reform Legislation, September 21, 1984

This internal SSA report summarized the provisions of H.R. 3755—the Social Security Disability Benefits Reform Act of 1984.

Summary of Provisions

Section 2: Standard of Review for Termination of Disability Benefits and Periods of Disability

Permits the Secretary to terminate a beneficiary's entitlement to Social Security disability . . . only if there is substantial evidence of at least one of the following:

(1) That the individual has medically improved . . . and is now able to engage in substantial gainful activity (SGA);

(2) That . . . new medical evidence and a new assessment of the individual's residual functional capacity demonstrate that, although the individual has not improved medically, (a) he is a beneficiary of advances in medical or vocational therapy or technology, related to his ability to work, and is now able to perform SGA, or (b) he has undergone vocational therapy, related to his ability to work, and is now able to perform SGA;

(3) That . . . on the basis of new or improved diagnostic techniques or evaluations, the individual's impairment is not as disabling as it was considered to be . . . and that therefore the individual is able to engage in SGA; or

(4) That . . . a prior determination was in error.

. . . Provides that any determination under this standard should be made neutrally—without any initial inference as to the presence or absence of disability—on the basis of all evidence (both prior and new) available in the case file concerning the individual's prior or current condition.

Applies similar provisions . . . to widows, widowers, and surviving divorced spouses. . . .

The provision is intended to promote administration of the program in a uniform manner nationwide by making explicit to the State agencies administering the program and to the courts the standards to be applied in determining continuing eligibility for benefits—the standards as set forth in national policy by the Congress. The provision also represents a response to broad-based concerns that the continuing disability review requirements of the 1980 amendments resulted in unforeseen hardships to beneficiaries whose benefits were terminated even though their conditions were unchanged from the time they were awarded benefits. . . .

The conference report noted that the agreement reached was an attempt "to strike a balance between the concern that a medical improvement standard could be interpreted to grant claimants a presumption of eligibility, which might make it extremely difficult to remove ineligible individuals from the benefit rolls, and the concern that the absence of an explicit standard of review . . . could be interpreted to imply a presumption of ineligibility or to allow arbitrary termination decisions, which might lead to many individuals being improperly removed from the rolls."

Section 3: Evaluation of Pain

Provides a temporary statutory standard (through December 31, 1986) for using subjective and objective evidence in evaluating cases involving pain or other symptoms. . . .

Also requires the Secretary to appoint a Commission on the Evaluation of Pain to conduct a study, in consultation with the National Academy of Sciences, concerning the evaluation of pain in determining whether a person is disabled under the Social Security Act. . . .

The study is intended to address concerns about the use of evidence of pain, particularly subjective evidence, in making disability determinations. The interim statutory standard is to assure that SSA's current policy for evaluating pain is adhered to until the study report can be completed and evaluated; some courts have used their own standards in evaluating pain.

Section 4: Multiple Impairments

Requires the Secretary . . . to consider the combined effect of all impairments without regard to whether any one impairment, if considered separately, would be severe. . . .

This provision is intended to ensure that the combined effect of multiple impairments is considered in determining whether a person's impairment(s) is severe and that when the combined effect is found to be severe, the full sequential evaluation process (including, if appropriate, the consideration of vocational factors) will be followed.

Section 5: Moratorium on Mental Impairment Reviews

Delays periodic review of mentally impaired individuals until criteria for evaluating mental disorders are revised to realistically evaluate the ability of a mentally impaired person to engage in SGA in a competitive workplace. . . .

The provision reflects the concern of the Congress that some claims involving mental impairments were not adjudicated properly in the last few years and that the criteria for evaluating mental impairments require updating to make them consistent with present-day diagnosis, treatment, and evaluation of mental impairments.

Section 6: Notice of Reconsideration; Preview Notice; Demonstration Projects

Requires the Secretary to notify a Social Security . . . disability beneficiary whose case is selected for periodic review as to the nature of the review, the possibility that the review could result in the termination of benefits and his right to provide medical evidence to be used in the review.

Also requires the Secretary to implement demonstration projects in at least five States in which an opportunity for a personal appearance by the claimant prior to a Social Security . . . disability cessation decision will be substituted for the reconsideration evidentiary hearing that is now applicable when disability benefits are terminated for medical reasons. . . .

Section 7: Continuation of Benefits During Appeal

Extends the temporary provision . . . for Social Security disability insurance benefit continuation up to the ALJ decision to disability cessation determinations made prior to January 1, 1988. . . . Benefits cannot be continued for months after June 1988. . . .

Also, requires the Secretary to conduct a study on the effect of this provision on the Social Security trust funds and on the rate of appeals to the ALJ level and to report the results of this study to the House Ways and Means Committee and the Senate Committee on Finance by July 1, 1986.

The intent of the provision is to prevent undue hardship to beneficiaries who are found on appeal to be still disabled. The Social Security provision is temporary because other reforms in this bill should improve the quality and accuracy of determinations made at adjudicatory levels below the ALJ level, enhance the uniformity of decisions at different levels of appeal, and reduce the number of appeals and the rate of reversals by ALJs.

Section 8: Qualifications of Medical Professionals Evaluating Mental Impairments

Requires the Secretary to make every reasonable effort to ensure that a qualified psychiatrist or psychologist complete the medical portion of the case review and any residual functional capacity assessment, if evidence indicates the existence of a mental impairment, before determining that an individual is not disabled. . . .

The purpose of the provision is to have qualified medical specialists evaluate mental impairment cases to help to assure accurate decisions.

Section 9: Consultative Examinations; Medical Evidence

Requires the Secretary to prescribe within 6 months after enactment regulations covering: (1) standards for deciding when a consultative examination should be obtained, (2) standards for the type of referral to be made, and (3) monitoring procedures for the consultative examinations and the referral process.

Also requires that the Secretary make every reasonable effort to obtain evidence from a treating physician before evaluating medical evidence obtained on a consultative basis. . . .

Requiring the standards for consultative examinations to be included in regulations is intended to provide greater direction on the use of consultative examinations by State agencies. . . . Requiring reasonable efforts to obtain evidence from a treating physician is intended to underscore the importance of such evidence, since the treating physician is likely to be the medical professional most able to provide a detailed, longitudinal picture of the individual's medical condition.

Section 10: Uniform Standards

Requires publication of regulations setting forth uniform standards for Social Security . . . disability determinations under the Administrative Procedure Act (APA) rulemaking procedure, which would be binding at all levels of adjudication. . . .

In the conference report, the conferees urge but do not require that all Social Security . . . regulations relating to benefits be published under APA notice and comment rulemaking procedures.

The provision is intended to ensure public participation in the disability policymaking process. . . .

Section 11: Payment of Costs of Rehabilitation Services

Provides several additional circumstances under which States are reimbursed for vocational rehabilitation (VR) services provided to Social Security . . . disability beneficiaries. . . .

Section 12: Advisory Council Study

Requires the next Advisory Council on Social Security to study and make recommendations on the medical and vocational aspects of disability. . . .

Section 13: Qualifying Experience For Appointment of Certain Staff Attorneys to Administrative Law Judge Positions

Requires the Secretary to submit a report . . . on actions taken by the Secretary to establish positions to enable SSA staff attorneys to acquire sufficient qualifying experience to compete for ALJ positions. . . .

Section 15: Frequency of Continuing Eligibility Reviews

Requires that the Secretary promulgate regulations . . . which establish the standards to be used in determining the frequency of periodic eligibility reviews. Until final regulations are issued, no individual's eligibility may be reviewed under periodic review more than once. . . .

Section 16: Determination and Monitoring of Need for Representative Payee

Requires the Secretary to (1) evaluate the qualifications of prospective representative payees. . . .

Also, increases the penalties for misuse of benefits by representative payees. . . .

The purpose of the provision is to protect beneficiaries with representative payees by requiring payees who are not close relatives or who do not live with the beneficiaries to account annually for the use made of the benefits. . . .

Section 17: Measures to Improve Compliance with Federal Law

Requires the Secretary to assume the functions of a State Disability Determination Service (DDS) within 6 months of finding that the State is failing to follow Federal law and agency guidelines in making disability determinations. . . .

Non-acquiescence: Statement of Managers

. . . Although there is no provision in the bill, the conferees included a statement in the conference report dealing with the issue of non-acquiescence. First, the conferees stated that the absence of a provision in the bill is not to be interpreted as approval of non-acquiescence as a general policy. The conferees noted that by refusing to apply circuit court interpretations and by not promptly seeking review by the Supreme Court, the Secretary forces beneficiaries to relitigate the same issue over and over again in the circuit, at substantial expense to both beneficiaries and the Federal government. The conferees urged that the policy of non-acquiescence be followed only where the administration intends to take the steps necessary to get the issue reviewed by the Supreme Court. Alternatively, the administration could seek a legislative remedy from the Congress. The conferees also said that the legal and constitutional issues raised by non-acquiescence can only be settled by the Supreme Court and urged the administration to seek a resolution of this issue.

Source: John Trout, director, Office of Legislative and Regulatory Policy, SSA Legislative Report, "Social Security Disability Benefits Reform Act of 1984," September 21, 1984. Copy in SSA History Archives, Revolving Files, Folder: Amendments, 1984.

Document 8.29
President Reagan's Statement on Signing the Disability Benefits Reform Act of 1984, October 9, 1984
Despite the continued opposition of the administration, Congress eventually passed the Disability Benefits Reform Act of 1984 by unanimous votes in both houses of Congress and President Reagan signed the bill.

I am pleased to sign into law H.R. 3755, the Social Security Disability Benefits Reform Act of 1984. This legislation, which has been formulated with the support of the administration and passed by unanimous vote in both Houses of Congress, should restore order, uniformity and consensus in the disability program. It maintains our commitment to treat disabled American citizens fairly and humanely while fulfilling our obligation to the Congress and the American taxpayers to administer the disability program effectively.

When I took office on January 20, 1981, my administration inherited the task of implementing the continuing disability investigations required by the 1980 Disability Amendments which had been enacted and signed into law during the previous administration. Soon after the Department of Health and Human Services began the mandatory reviews, we found that trying to implement the new law's requirements within the framework of the old, paper-oriented review process was causing hardships for beneficiaries. Accordingly, back in 1982, the Department began a long series of administrative reforms designed to make the disability review process more humane and people-oriented. These reforms included providing face-to-face meetings between beneficiaries and Social Security Administration (SSA) claims representatives at the very start of the review process.

These initial steps were followed by further important reforms announced by Secretary Heckler in June of 1983, including:

- classifying additional beneficiaries as permanently disabled, thus exempting them from the 3-year review;
- temporarily exempting from review two-thirds of cases of individuals with mental impairments while the decisionmaking standards were being revised; and
- accelerating a top-to-bottom review of disability policies by SSA and appropriate outside experts.

While those June 1983 reforms went a long way towards humanizing the process, by the spring of 1984, it became apparent that legislation was needed to end the debate and confusion over what standard should be used in conducting continuing disability investigations. The administration worked with the Congress to develop this consensus legislation and, in the interim, took the additional step of suspending the periodic disability reviews pending implementation of new disability legislation.

One indication of the complexity of the issues involved is the fact that Congress held more than 40 hearings on the disability review process over a 3-year period before arriving at a consensus on this legislation.

One significant provision of H.R. 3755 is the so-called medical improvement standard that sets forth the criteria SSA must apply when deciding whether a disability beneficiary is still disabled. The standard this new legislation would establish for future determinations will restore the uniformity that is so essential to a nationwide program.

Another provision in H.R. 3755 would extend temporarily the ability of a Social Security disability beneficiary who has decided to appeal a decision that his disability has ended to have benefits continued up to the decision of an administrative law judge. This will prevent undue hardship to beneficiaries who are found on appeal to be still disabled while the new law is being put in place.

In addition, the legislation places a desirable moratorium on reviews to determine whether individuals with mental impairments are still disabled until revised criteria for evaluating these impairments are published. The Department of Health and Human Services has been working with mental health experts on these criteria.

Several other changes are written into this new law that will clarify and expedite the administration of the disability program.

I have asked Secretary Heckler to implement the provisions of this legislation as speedily and as fairly as possible. The Department of Health and Human Services will act promptly in reviewing individual cases so that no disabled beneficiary has to wait any longer than necessary for the proper decision on his or her case.

Source: Public Papers of the Presidents: Ronald Reagan, 1984, vol. II (Washington, D.C.: Government Printing Office, 1987), 1477–1478.

CHAPTER 9

The Fourth Controversy over Financing and the Battle over Privatization, 1983–2006

Since the adoption of the 1983 amendments, no major Social Security cash-benefits legislation has been enacted in the United States. The 1983 legislation, while successful in solving the short-term financing problems of the system, did not fully address the long-range financing challenges facing the program. Thus, the system is presently facing its fourth financing controversy, in the form of a long-range financing shortfall.

At the start of his presidency, George W. Bush appointed a commission to study Social Security reform. He intended this to be a major initiative of his first term. Source: White House.

The financing challenges confronting the Social Security system are defined and measured by the annual reports of the Social Security trustees. There are several measures used in the annual reports, one common one being the shortfall expressed as a percentage of taxable payroll. (One can think of this measure as being equivalent to the tax rate for the program. So, for example, a shortfall of 2 percent of payroll would mean that if benefits were held constant, then taxes would have to be raised by 2 percent to restore fiscal balance.)

Since 1988, each of the annual reports of the Social Security trustees has indicated that the program has a long-range financing problem (see **Appendix C**). The 2007 trustees report shows a shortfall of 1.95 percent of payroll. Sometime around the year 2041 the system will no longer have sufficient income/assets to pay all its promised benefits. Indeed—in dollars and cents terms—the actuaries suggest that at that point the program could only pay about 75 cents of each dollar of promised benefits.

For those who seek to move Social Security away from the existing social insurance model, fears about the fiscal future of the program represent an opportunity to convince citizens and policymakers to support a transformation of it along the lines of savings plans like 401(k)s.

In the Republican primary for the 1964 presidential election, Barry Goldwater suggested in his early speeches that he thought participation in Social Security should be voluntary. This call by Goldwater to make Social Security voluntary—in the context of a major-party candidacy for president—was a symbolic beginning to the stream of political thought that would in time become the Social Security privatization movement.

During the 1970s, free-market economists such as Milton Friedman, and later Martin Feldstein, suggested that Social Security either should be made voluntary or be replaced by some form of market-based investment system.

In 1980 the Cato Institute published the first book suggesting privatization through the mechanism of private accounts carved out of the existing payroll tax. In the 1988 presidential primaries, minor Republican candidate Gov. Pete DuPont of Delaware endorsed the private accounts idea. Organizations like Cato, the Heritage Foundation, and the American Enterprise Institute all housed scholars who were advocating some form of privatization, often using the mechanism of private accounts.

On Capitol Hill, interest in addressing the resurgent financing problems of the system was voiced most prominently by Sen. Daniel Patrick Moynihan (D-N.Y.), who began in 1989 introducing a recurring series of bills aimed at addressing the fiscal shortfall—although not initially through the use of private accounts.

It was not until the Bill Clinton presidency that the idea of private accounts became part of the mainstream of policy debates. An important milestone in this transformation was the report of the 1994–1996 Advisory Council on Social Security—as one proposal put forward by that council was for partial privatization of the system.

The Clinton Administration itself addressed the long-range solvency challenge outside the context of privatization—although it never presented any fully developed proposals for dealing with the problem.

The issue was briefly engaged in the 2000 presidential campaign, and when George W. Bush came to office in 2001, partial privatization became an item on the presidential agenda for the first time since the program's inception (**Documents 2.1–2.3**).

Over the years, dozens of bills have been introduced in the Congress to address the post-1983 financing problems, and numerous think tanks and independent scholars have offered Social Security reform plans. This chapter contains a representative sample of some of the more prominent of those proposals.

Document 9.1
Cato Institute on "Achieving a 'Leninist Strategy,' " 1983

As privatization began to occur in Latin American nations such as Chile (in 1981), scholars at the Cato Institute had hopes and expectations that the Reagan administration might introduce similar privatized schemes in the United States. In particular, Cato had some expectation that the financing crisis of the early 1980s would led to a Chilean-style alternative to the traditional Social Security system. When this did not occur—and the 1983 amendments adopted a traditional approach to the problems in the program's finances—Cato decided that it needed to engage in an extended campaign both to undermine support for the Social Security system and build support for private alternatives. This document, published in 1983 in the aftermath of the

1983 amendments, was Cato's statement of its goals and objectives, and the document foretells, to a remarkable degree, subsequent developments in the debate around privatization.

Introduction

. . . As we contemplate basic reform of the Social Security system, we would do well to draw a few lessons from the Leninist strategy. Many critics of the present system believe, as Marx and Lenin did of capitalism, that the system's days are numbered because of its contradictory objectives of attempting to provide both welfare and insurance. All that really needs to be done, they contend, is to point out these inherent flaws to the taxpayers and to show them that Social Security would be vastly improved if it were restructured into a predominantly private system. . . .

While this may indeed happen, the public's reaction last year against politicians who simply noted the deep problems of the system, and the absence of even a recognition of the underlying problems during this spring's Social Security "reform," suggest that it will be a long time before citizen indignation will cause radical change to take place. Therefore, if we are to achieve basic changes in the system, we must first prepare the political ground so that the fiasco of the last 18 months is not repeated.

First, we must recognize that there is a firm coalition behind the present Social Security system, and that this coalition has been very effective in winning political concessions for many years. Before Social Security can be reformed, we must begin to divide this coalition and cast doubt on the picture of reality it presents to the general public.

Second, we must recognize that we need more than a manifesto—even one as cogent and persuasive as that provided by Peter Ferrara. What we must do is construct a coalition around the Ferrara plan, a coalition that will gain directly from its implementation. . . .

Framework for Reform

Peter Ferrara's "family security plan" provides a sound framework for reform. The Ferrara plan resolves the contradiction within the existing system and provides a realistic phase-in process for a private pension plan. . . .

In an effort to identify a broad framework for Social Security reform, the Heritage Foundation (1982) gathered various experts, who discussed the essential ingredients of reform. The principles and observations that emerged from that gathering can now be summarized.

Calming Existing Beneficiaries

The sine qua non of any successful Social Security reform strategy must be an assurance to those already retired or nearing retirement that their benefits will be paid in full. It was irresponsible in the first place for the federal government to promise unrealistic benefits. But it would be even more irresponsible now to break faith with the millions of people who have based their retirement plans on these expected benefits. Instead of spreading widespread panic among our elderly, which will only undermine our efforts to reform the system, we should acknowledge the system's liabilities as a total writeoff. . . .

. . . By accepting this principle, we may succeed in neutralizing the most powerful element of the coalition that opposes structural reform.

Educating the Public

. . . During the recent financing crisis, there was only a vague awareness among the general population that the system was in serious trouble; the true nature of the problem and the proposed reforms were understood by very few Americans.

. . . The many myths surrounding the system must be dispelled, especially the popular belief that Social Security is an "insurance" program financed by "contributions" that provide an "earned annuity.". . .

Recognizing Successful Alternatives

Despite the unwillingness of Congress to undertake or even consider real reform, the public has shown a great deal of interest in private alternatives to Social Security. In a poll conducted . . . for the Heritage Foundation, for instance, a majority of people surveyed said that they would favor a voluntary system. Even more people expressed the view that the private sector would be a more efficient vehicle than Social Security for providing pension benefits. . . .

A restricted private option is now being tried in Great Britain. . . .

The British system indicates that many employees are willing to choose a private retirement option in preference to a government guaranteed plan. It also indicates that workers are willing to pay a price to leave Social Security. . . .

. . . It does seem that the price people are willing to pay to leave Social Security is substantial. Perhaps in the United States it is large enough that those wishing to leave the system can cover a large part of its current obligations to beneficiaries while it still enables a high proportion of workers to opt out, thus reducing the system's future obligations.

A Plan of Action

The background issues discussed above suggest a political strategy to achieve basic reform of the Social Security system in the fashion suggested by Peter Ferrara. There are two main elements to this strategy.

The first element consists of a campaign to achieve small legislative changes that embellish the present IRA system. . . . If these objectives are achieved, we will meet the next financial crisis in Social Security with a private alternative ready in the wings—an alternative with which the public is familiar and comfortable, and one that has the backing of a powerful political force.

The second main element in our reform strategy involves what one might crudely call guerrilla warfare against both the current Social Security system and the coalition that supports it. An economic education campaign, assisted by modest changes in the law, must be undertaken to demonstrate the weaknesses of the existing system and to allow it to be compared accurately (and therefore unfavorably) with the private alternative. In addition, methods of neutralizing, buying out, or winning over key segments of the Social Security coalition must be explored and formulated into legislative initiatives. . . . The aim is to weaken political support for the present system when the next financial crisis appears. . . .

Creating a Private Model

Expanding IRAs

IRAs are a powerful vehicle for introducing a private Social Security system. . . .

The reason for designing a "super IRA" law . . . is purely political. Expanding the IRA system . . . would make it a private prototype of Social Security. . . . The public would gradually become more familiar with the private option, and would no doubt view it as a parallel system. If that did happen, it would be far easier than it is now to persuade people to adopt the private plan as their principal source of old-age insurance and retirement income.

Coalition Building

Building a constituency for Social Security reform requires mobilizing the various coalitions that stand to benefit from the change. Such a constituency is already extensive, but mobilizing it could become a self-generating process. . . .

The business community, and financial institutions in particular, would be an obvious element in the constituency. . . .

. . . [T]he young are the most obvious constituency for reform and a natural ally for the private alternative. The overwhelming majority of people in this group have stated repeatedly that they have little or no confidence in the present Social Security system. . . .

Despite misgivings about Social Security, however, the young have yet to have a significant impact on the political process as it relates to reform measures. It is imperative, therefore, that they be informed about the problems inherent in the current system and that they be organized behind the private alternative. . . .

Weakening the Opposition

Individual Accounts

To emphasize how unfavorably Social Security compares with the private alternative, the Social Security Administration should be required to establish an individual account for each person participating in the program. Furthermore, each person should be provided with an annual statement showing how much he has paid into the system and what benefits he can expect to receive. Individuals could then compare their returns from private investment with their returns under Social Security. Such a scheme would illustrate in cold numbers just what the program means for different individuals, and would help reveal the inter- and intra-generational distribution that occurs under the current system. The retired population might then come to realize that they have not purchased an earned annuity but instead are receiving a tremendous welfare subsidy. Younger workers, on the other hand, would see just how much of a loss they are taking by participating in the program. This mechanism for demonstrating the individual gains and losses that occur under Social Security is a key step in weakening public support for the present system. . . .

Detaching Supporters of Social Security

The final element of the strategy must be to propose moving to a private Social Security system in such a way as to detach, or at least neutralize, segments of the coalition that supports the existing system. A necessary step toward this objective is to honor all outstanding claims on the current system. Without such a commitment, we can never overcome the political opposition to reform. . . . Retaining the obligation to fund existing liabilities, however, will necessarily place constraints on the mechanisms that can be used to move the country towards a private system.

. . . We should consider, therefore, modifying Peter Ferrara's phase-in plan.

Under Ferrara's plan, workers would be allowed to invest part, and eventually all, of the money they now pay into Social Security in expanded IRAs, in return for a corresponding reduction in their future Social Security benefits. Under our proposed modification, workers who choose to opt out of the system would not only lose their corresponding future benefits but would even have them reduced somewhat further for the privilege of getting out of Social Security. This added reduction in benefits could be viewed as a tax that would be used to pay off the system's remaining obligations.

An interim "opting-out tax" hardly conforms with the principles of fairness; yet it makes good political sense. . . . But the opting-out tax would have important political advantages. It would serve to calm the fears of the elderly, because the net phase out losses to the Social Security fund would be smaller under opting out than under the Ferrara plan, for virtually the same reduction in future liabilities. Hence, under an opting-out plan the support needed from general revenues would be smaller, and the threat to the trust funds would be reduced.

This modification would slightly dampen the enthusiasm of young workers. . . . But on the other hand, this modification would help to meet the concerns of the elderly and of the taxpayers and beneficiaries of federal programs who might resist the use of general revenues to cover the phase-in period. . . .

Conclusion

The last two years have demonstrated beyond a doubt that Social Security can be reformed only by treating the issue primarily as a political problem. There is little point in arguing over the nuances of theoretical plans if the political dynamics are not altered; no amount of logic will overcome an unfavorable coalition of interest groups. . . .

Finally, we must be prepared for a long campaign. The next Social Security crisis may be further away than many people believe. Or perhaps it will occur before the reform coalition is strong enough to achieve a political breakthrough. In either case, it could be many years before the conditions are such that a radical reform of Social Security is possible. But then, as Lenin well knew, to be a successful revolutionary, one must also be patient and consistently plan for real reform.

Source: Cato Journal, 3 (2) (Fall 1983): 547–556; www.cato.org/pubs/journal/cj3n2/cj3n2-11.pdf (accessed September 21, 2006). Used by permission.

Document 9.2
1983 Trustees Report, June 27, 1983

This is the first trustees report prepared by the actuaries following the enactment of the 1983 amendments. It clearly indicates that the amendments had restored the program's finances, and it projects that the system will have sufficient funding to fully meet its benefit obligations throughout the entire seventy-five-year estimating period. This document, then, is the official statement of the presumed success of the 1983 law.

This report contained four sets of actuarial estimates. The one labeled II-B corresponds to the traditional "intermediate" set of estimates and was the one most commonly used in assessing the program's finances.

II. Highlights. . . .

Financial Status of the Trust Funds

As a result of the enactment of the Social Security Amendments of 1983, the estimates in this report indicate that the Old-Age, Survivors, and Disability Insurance [OASDI] program will be able to pay benefits on time for the next 75 years under all but the most pessimistic of the various sets of assumptions for which estimates are shown. . . . The financial outlook shown in this report for the OASDI program is therefore dramatically improved as compared to that shown in the last annual report. The 1982 Annual Report indicated that interfund loans to the Old-Age and Survivors Insurance [OASI] Trust Fund from the Disability Insurance [DI] and Hospital Insurance [HI] Trust Funds would be required in the second half of 1982, and that by July 1983 OASI benefits could not be paid on time, in the absence of corrective legislation. The 1982 Annual Report also showed a long-range actuarial deficit of 1.82 percent of taxable payroll under the intermediate II-B set of assumptions over 75 years. That average deficit consisted of an average surplus of 0.64 percent of taxable payroll over the first 25-year subperiod, and average deficits of 1.68, and 4.41 percent over the second and third 25-year subperiods, respectively.

In November 1982, the first interfund loan was made to the OASI Trust Fund under the limited authority granted by Public Law 97–123. In December, more interfund loans were made. In total, $17.5 billion was borrowed—$5.1 billion from the DI Trust Fund, and $12.4 billion from the HI Trust Fund. As stated by the Trustees in the 1982 Annual Report, without such loans, OASI benefits could not have been paid on time beginning in November 1982. Even with such loans, benefits could not have been paid on time after June 1983, without corrective legislation.

The National Commission on Social Security Reform, which had been established by the President on December 16, 1981, issued its report on January 20, 1983. The Commission's recommendations formed the basis of two similar bills that were introduced in the Congress as H.R. 1900 in the House of Representatives and S. 1 in the Senate. The Conference Committee agreement on the House and Senate bills was passed by both Houses of the Congress on March 24. President Reagan signed the Social Security Amendments of 1983 into law (Public Law 98–21) on April 20, 1983.

The improved financial status of the OASDI program is achieved through the increases in income and decreases in outgo that will result from the 1983 amendments. For the first time in 3 years, the short-range projections in the annual report indicate that OASI and DI benefits will be paid on time in the short range and for many years thereafter. For the first time in a decade, the current intermediate projections indicate a 75-year actuarial balance between income and outgo, on the basis of the alternative II-B assumptions. This average balance consists of average surpluses of 1.83 and 0.32 percent of taxable payroll over the first and second 25-year subperiods, respectively, and an average deficit of 2.08 percent over the third 25-year subperiod. Thus, the actuarial balance is a moving average, and continuing review of the financing of the OASDI program is necessary. . . .

The operating deficits that began in 1975 reduced the assets of the OASI and DI Trust Funds to very low levels at the beginning of 1983. Certain provisions of the 1983 amendments will result in substantial immediate increases in those assets, but the rate of growth in 1984–87 is expected to be relatively small. As a result, the estimated trust-fund levels shown in this report are relatively low through 1987. Thus, although the OASDI program is estimated to be financially sound for many years into the future based on the assumptions in this report, the solvency of the program cannot be guaranteed under all circumstances. If actual economic conditions in 1984–87 are, on the average, worse (in regard to the effect on OASDI financing) than those assumed under alternative III, the OASDI program could again experience financial difficulties. . . .

The financial projections are described in detail for three time periods . . . summarized as follows:

(a) Short range (1983–87)—. . . Under all four sets of assumptions, the OASI Trust Fund would have sufficient assets to permit timely payment of benefits throughout this period. The level of assets relative to annual expenditures, however, would remain relatively low through about 1987, making the fund vulnerable to any severe economic downturn during this period. The short-range financial status of the DI Trust Fund is generally similar to that of the OASI Trust Fund. This represents a marked decline as compared with the status shown for the DI Trust Fund in the 1982 Annual Report. The change is attributable primarily to a reallocation of the OASDI payroll-tax rate between the two trust funds. This reallocation was included in the 1983 amendments in order to place the two funds in a similar financial position. . . .

(b) Medium range (1983–2007)—Under the four alternative sets of assumptions, average annual costs for the OASDI program during the 25-year projection period range from 9.22 to 11.44 percent of taxable payroll, while average income ranges from 12.45 to 12.53 percent. Thus, the projected medium-range actuarial balance is a surplus varying from 3.23 to 1.08 percent of taxable payroll. . . .

(c) Long range (1983–2057)—Over the 75-year period, annual costs for the OASDI program are projected to average from 9.81 to 16.56 percent of taxable payroll, depending on the assumptions. During this period, average income ranges from 12.73 to 13.04 percent of taxable payroll. Thus, the projected long-range actuarial balance varies from a surplus of 2.92 percent of taxable payroll under the optimistic alternative I assumptions to a deficit of 3.51 percent of taxable payroll under the pessimistic alternative III assumptions. Under alternatives II-A and II-B, respectively, average surpluses of 0.84 and 0.02 percent of taxable payroll are projected. . . .

Such 75-year projections are subject to considerable uncertainty and should be interpreted, not as precise forecasts of expected program operations, but as indications of how the trust funds would operate under present law if the assumed economic and demographic conditions actually materialize. Despite their inherent uncertainty, these projections, and the patterns of surpluses and deficits that they reveal in the various subperiods, provide a valuable picture of the long-range financial obligations of the Social Security program and information on how program costs would respond to changing conditions. . . .

VIII. Conclusion

The Social Security Amendments of 1983 have restored the financial soundness of the OASDI program for many years into the future. This is the case in the short range, on the basis of all four alternative sets of assumptions shown in this report, and in the long range, on the basis of all but the most pessimistic of the four sets.

The short-range projections shown in this report are in marked contrast to those shown in the last three annual reports, all of which indicated that the assets of the OASI Trust Fund would soon become insufficient to permit the timely payment of benefits. As discussed in earlier sections of this report, the assets of the OASI Trust Fund were sufficient to permit benefits to be paid on time through June 1983 only because of temporary legislative changes, including the interfund borrowing authority under which loans were made from the DI and HI Trust Funds to the OASI Trust Fund in the latter part of 1982. On the basis of the economic and demographic assumptions presented in this report, the 1983 amendments would enable OASI and DI benefits to be paid on time in the short range and for many years thereafter. . . .

While the OASDI program is expected to be able to pay benefits on time for many years into the future, the trust-fund levels are estimated to be relatively low through 1987. If economic conditions in 1984–87 are worse than those assumed, under the pessimistic alternative III assumptions, the OASDI program could again experience financial difficulties in the near future. After 1987, the program's ability to withstand economic downturns is projected to steadily improve. . . .

Source: 1983 Annual Report—Federal Old-Age and Survivors Insurance and Disability Insurance Trust Fund (Washington, D.C.: Government Printing Office, June 27, 1983), 2–6, 84.

Document 9.3
1988 Trustees Report, May 5, 1988

Barely five years after the passage of the 1983 amendments, the actuaries reported that the program had long-range financing problems. This 1988 report was the first official statement of this fact.

Technically, the actuaries concluded that the program was still in "close actuarial balance" because the amount of its deficit was small enough to be considered within the margin of error of such long-range estimates. However, this was the first post-1983 report to show a trust fund depletion date before the end of the seventy-five-year estimating period. Thus, the report projects that the program will exhaust its trust funds—and hence be unable to meet all its financial commitments—in the year 2048. This would be the first report in an unbroken series of annual reports that continue to show the program to be in long-range financial difficulty.

Summary

Highlights

As shown in the 1988 Annual Report, the assets of the Old-Age and Survivors Insurance (OASI) Trust Fund increased by $23.1 billion in calendar year 1987, reflecting the continuing growth in the economy. Although the Disability Insurance (DI) Trust Fund declined by $1.1 billion, the growth in the combined trust funds, at $21.9 billion, was larger than the growth estimated in the 1987 Annual Report on the basis of intermediate assumptions.

The trust funds are expected to continue growing for many years into the future. However, if experience is very adverse, the assets of the DI Trust Fund could decline to such a low level that financial problems could occur within the next 10 years.

The long-range 75-year estimates indicate that, under the intermediate assumptions, the OASDI program will experience about three decades of positive annual balances, with continuing annual deficits thereafter. The positive balances in the first part of the 75-year projection period nearly offset the later deficits, so that the program, as a whole, is in close actuarial balance. Over the long-range 75-year projection period, the OASDI program has an actuarial deficit of 0.58 percent of taxable payroll, based on the intermediate alternative II-B assumptions and calculated on a level-financing basis.

The combined trust funds are expected to accumulate to a maximum fund ratio of 531 percent of annual outgo in the year 2015, based on the alternative II-B assumptions. Thereafter, the fund ratio is estimated to decline until the funds are exhausted in 2048. Therefore, according to the alternative Il-B projections, the OASDI program will have enough funds to cover expenditures for about 60 years into the future.

For OASI and DI, separately, the long-range actuarial deficits, based on the alternative 11-B assumptions, are 0.45 percent and 0.13 percent of taxable payroll, respectively. The deficit for DI represents about 8.3 percent of the cost rate over the 75-year period, and the DI program is therefore not in close actuarial balance. However, the DI program could be brought into close actuarial balance by a small reallocation of the contribution rate from OASI to DI in such a way that the OASI program would still remain in close actuarial balance. Such reallocation is not being recommended by the Board of Trustees, but the DI program needs careful monitoring in both the short-range and the long-range periods. . . .

5. Long-Range Financing (1988–2062)

Long-range 75-year estimates for OASDI, although sensitive to variations in the assumptions, indicate the trend and general range of the program's future financial status. During this long-range period, income and outgo are greatly affected by demographic, as well as economic, conditions. Most of the beneficiaries during the next 75 years have already been born, so that their numbers are projected mainly from the present population. The numbers of workers involved in these projections, however, depend on future birth rates, which are subject to more variability.

Several important demographic trends are anticipated to raise the proportion of the aged in the population during the next 75 years. First, because of the large number of persons born in the two decades after World War II, rapid growth is expected in the aged population after the turn of the century. Second, assumed declines in death rates also would increase the numbers of aged persons. At the same time, birth rates, which began to decline in the 1960s and are assumed to remain relatively low in the future, would hold down the numbers of young people. . . .

The long-range OASDI actuarial deficit of 0.58 percent of taxable payroll, based on the intermediate Il-B assumptions, results from a level-financing income rate of 12.94 percent of taxable payroll over the 75-year period and a level-financing cost rate of 13.52 percent over the period. The level-financing rates reflect the full effects of the assumed interest earnings of the trust funds. In the absence of other changes, the long-range actuarial balance will tend to decline slowly in future annual reports, as the valuation period moves forward and additional distant years of deficit are included in the valuation. The actuarial deficits in the later years of the 75-year projection period are caused primarily by the demographic trends described above. . . .

VI. Conclusion

The economy continued to grow in 1987, and the combined assets of the OASI and DI Trust Funds also grew. The growth of the combined trust funds in calendar year 1987 was larger than estimated in the 1987 Annual Report on the basis of both sets of intermediate assumptions, alternatives II-A and II-B. As a result, the ability of the OASDI program to withstand temporary economic downturns improved significantly during the year.

The long-range actuarial estimates in this report show that the OASDI program as a whole is in close actuarial balance, on a level-financing basis. Over the 75-year projection period, the OASDI program has an estimated level-financing deficit of 0.58 percent of taxable payroll, based on the intermediate alternative II-B assumptions. This deficit represents about 4.3 percent of the level-financing cost rate. In other words, the long-range income rate (including the funds on hand at the beginning of the valuation period) represents about 95.7 percent of the long-range cost rate.

However, while the program is in close actuarial balance, deficits appear after the first three decades. . . . The OASDI long-range estimates . . . show a pattern of recurring annual positive balances in the first three decades and recurring annual deficits thereafter. These annual balances do not reflect interest earnings, which, when taken into account, result in trust fund growth, in dollars, continuing for another 10 to 15 years after the first annual deficit occurs.

The estimates therefore show that the assets of the OASI and DI Trust Funds, on a combined basis, will be sufficient to enable the timely payment of OASDI benefits for many years into the future, on the basis of all four sets of economic and demographic assumptions. . . . The combined funds are estimated to build up, then decline, and then become exhausted in 2048, or 60 years from now, based on alternative II-B. . . .

For several years, the single figure representing the long-range actuarial balance over the 75-year projection period, as well as the figure for each of the 25-year subperiods, has been calculated on an "average-cost" basis. For comparability with the 1987 report, the OASDI average actuarial balance over the 75-year projection period is a deficit of 0.87 percent of taxable payroll, based on the alternative II-B assumptions. During the first 25 years, the average balance is a positive balance of 2.15 percent of taxable payroll. However, the average balances in the second and third 25-year subperiods are deficits of 1.45 percent and 3.32 percent, respectively. On a level-financing basis, the corresponding balances for the first, second, and third 25-year subperiods are a positive balance of 2.07 percent and deficits of 1.44 percent and 3.39 percent, respectively. . . .

Thus, in the absence of other changes, the long-range actuarial balance will tend to decline slowly in future annual reports, as the valuation period moves forward and additional distant years of deficit are included in the valuation. The actuarial deficits in the later years of the 75-year projection period are caused primarily by the demographic trends, which will result in a lower ratio of workers to beneficiaries in the distant future.

Under the average-cost basis, the balance for each period is determined by calculating the arithmetic mean of the annual balances over the period. The average-cost calculation does not correctly reflect the full effects of the interest earnings of the accumulated trust funds. On the other hand, the level-financing calculations shown in this report properly reflect the full effect of interest earnings. Thus, the 75-year actuarial deficit of 0.58 percent of taxable payroll, on a level-financing basis, is a more accurate measure because it takes account of all the interest earnings of the trust funds, as well as the funds on hand at the beginning of the projection period. . . .

Source: 1988 Annual Report of the Board of Trustees of the Federal Old-Age and Survivors Insurance and Disability Insurance Trust Funds (Washington, D.C.: Government Printing Office, May 5, 1988), 1–8, 89.

Document 9.4
Report of the Kerrey-Danforth Commission, January 1995

On November 5, 1993, President Bill Clinton issued Executive Order 12878, creating the Bipartisan Commission on Entitlement and Tax Reform. The commission, which began work in February 1994, was cochaired by Sen. Robert Kerrey (D-Neb.) and Sen. John Danforth (R-Mo.). The commission was comprised of ten U.S. senators, ten House members, and twelve members of the public, along with a professional staff of twenty-seven.

The commission went well beyond the topics of Social Security and Medicare and lumped together everything that might be considered an "entitlement"—from welfare programs, to the home mortgage interest tax deduction, to the cost of federal civilian and military retirement. Its goal was to devise a package of proposals that would reduce the overall cost of all these programs.

The commission made little progress on its task and was only able to release an "interim report" in August 1994 that merely defined the size of the problem, without containing any suggested policies to address it. Even without any policy recommendations, unanimous agreement could not be reached as only thirty of the thirty-two members signed off on the report.

One of the commission's more noticeable products was a computer game that allowed members of the public to try to balance the federal budget through various policy options.

The two cochairs of the commission developed their own Social Security proposal, which featured raising the retirement age to seventy, a cut in the Social Security payroll tax with the money redirected into mandatory private accounts, and adopting price-indexing (among other changes). This was perhaps the first advocacy of "carve-out" private accounts, and of price indexing, by a prominent mainstream group.

Kerrey and Danforth had hoped to make their overall proposal the basis for the commission's report, but there was insufficient support for their proposal. In all, the commission's members proposed fifteen specific potential Social Security policy changes (many with several variations), but none of the proposals could win the support of a majority of the members.

Ultimately, the commission failed to achieve consensus on any entitlement reforms and went out of business without issuing any recommendations. Instead, its final report was a compilation of competing proposals. The two cochairs pushed their own proposal, and another six members advocated four competing plans, while eight members inserted into the report their critical remarks on the plans of the other members. Although the group was not able to agree on any policy recommendations, the commission put the future of the nation's entitlement programs on the policy agenda.

The final report contained—in lieu of any actual agreed-upon recommendations—two sets of introductory letters: one by the two cochairs and one signed by twenty-four of the thirty-two members; eight members refused to sign even the generic statement. Those two introductory statements are excerpted here.

Dear Mr. President:

When you created the Bipartisan Commission on Entitlement and Tax Reform, you charged us with addressing perhaps the most challenging fiscal issues facing this country. Left unchecked, the Federal government's long-term spending commitments on entitlement programs will lead to excessively high deficit and debt levels, unfairly burdening America's children and stifling standards of living for this and future generations of Americans. . . .

The Commission was not formed to "sugar coat" the issues or provide easy but dishonest answers. Rather, it was created to frame the long term issue, educate the American people and policy leaders about the problem and potential choices, and make specific recommendations on how to bring our future entitlement commitments and revenues into balance.

On August 8, 1994, the Commission adopted by a 30–to–1 vote an Interim Report that graphically lays out the economic and social future the country faces if action is not taken. It is a stark call to action, alerting Americans about the burden that is being shifted to future generations . . . and the impending insolvency of both the Social Security and Medicare Trust Funds. . . .

The Commission Staff created "Budget Shadows," a user-friendly interactive computer model that lets the American people see the fiscal future and design different policies to alter it. . . . While the computer model is not meant to be an exhaustive list of policy options, it provides the user with more than 50 choices and lets him or her see the range of potential solutions and the tradeoffs that must be evaluated. . . .

In the end, the Commission was unable to settle on a specific set of recommendations on how to combat the issue it framed in the Interim Report. That should not be surprising in an environment where political leaders in both parties are focusing more on short-term initiatives than the long-term, politically sensitive economic and social issues that sit on the horizon. . . .

J. Robert Kerrey, Chairman
John C. Danforth, Vice-Chairman

Dear Mr. President:

The Bipartisan Commission on Entitlement and Tax Reform concluded in its Interim Report that:

> . . . *the government must act now. A bipartisan coalition of Congress, led by the President, must resolve the long-term imbalance between the government's entitlement promises and the funds it will have available to pay for them.*

According to our Report, we acquire false optimism when we look only five years ahead, as we do with our traditional budgeting process. Only when we look at the next 30 years . . . does the problem and its size come into full view.

. . . [T]he next 30 years is a period of significant increases in entitlement costs plus net interest. Two crucial moments conspire to make our lives miserable.

The first moment is the year 2001 when the Medicare Hospital Insurance program . . . becomes insolvent. . . .

This condition becomes painfully evident when we arrive at the second crucial moment. In 2008, the first of the Baby Boom generation . . . will begin to retire. In a single decade, while our overall population increases by 2 percent, our retired population will increase nearly 30 percent. Thus, in a single decade, the ratio of the number of Americans working versus Americans retired will be cut by 40 percent, from 5:1 to 3:1.

While this situation may have relatively little impact on Americans over the age of 48, it may have considerable impact on younger Americans. Specifically, if we delay action now, the choices will be higher taxes for Americans still in the workforce or larger benefit reductions for retirees.

Thus, the first and most important of our recommendations is that our major spending and tax decisions should be made with reference to a time period longer than the traditional five-year budget window, such as the 30-year timeframe . . . so that appropriate planning is incorporated in budget decisions. When discretionary spending was the largest share of our budget, short-term planning may have been appropriate. However, today we are in the business of operating the world's largest social insurance programs, and their costs are expected to exceed their revenues substantially over coming decades.

The Commission's Interim Report has established that the projected imbalance between spending and revenues—particularly with regard to health care and retirement entitlement programs—will, together with interest on the Federal debt, undermine America's capacity to make appropriate investments in the well-being of our citizens and undertake other essential government functions, such as national defense.

Our second recommendation is that we change our current laws to create a future in which we balance our entitlement commitments and the funds available to honor those promises. We must restore balance to our Social Security Trust Fund and strengthen the confidence of all Americans that Social Security will endure on a sound footing.

To be clear, this Commission could not reach agreement on the details of a plan to achieve our objective. Nonetheless, those of us who are prepared to recommend partial or complete solutions have included our proposals in this Report.

Our third recommendation is that we empower the American people to participate in developing satisfactory solutions. . . .

This Report contains the numerous policy options which the Commission staff has developed, none of which have been specifically endorsed by the Commission as a whole. While the list is by no means all inclusive, it makes clear that few easy and popular decisions are available to the American people. That is where leadership is so urgently needed. We must describe the future that current law dictates so that Americans will know why tough action is needed sooner rather than later. And, we must describe the alternative future as well as the benefits that will accrue to all Americans. . . .

The Commission believes there is a window of opportunity for policymakers to enact reforms now. Acting sooner rather than later enables us to protect current beneficiaries from financial hardship and allows future beneficiaries to take steps to offset the effects of any changes.

On the question of tax reform, the Commission heard criticism of the structure of the current tax system. This is a topic that has been getting increased attention. The Commission recommends that the Administration and Congress consider reform of the tax system.

While this Commission does not endorse detailed recommendations—our most ambitious goal—this Final Report forwards many solutions to be considered in addressing the problem and underscores the need for immediate action.

Source: Bipartisan Commission on Entitlement and Tax Reform, "Final Report to the President," January 1995, ii–iv; 1–3.

Document 9.5
Report of the Advisory Council on Social Security, January 7, 1997

When the Social Security Administration (SSA) became an independent agency in March 1995, a permanent body—the Social Security Advisory Board—replaced the traditional advisory councils. The following excerpts are from the final report of the last advisory council on Social Security. Particularly important is the lack of consensus among the last advisory council's members, which led to the preparation of three separate sets of recommendations. In effect, the council split into three groups: one offering a traditional package of benefit cuts and tax increases to restore long range solvency (six of the thirteen members); one advocating private accounts as additions to the existing Social Security system (two of the members); and one advocating partial privatization of the system by "carving out" a portion of the Social Security payroll tax and diverting it into private accounts (five of the members).

Although the council was unable to agree on a consensus approach to Social Security reform, its report helped move the idea of Social Security reform in general, and privatization in particular, onto the federal policy agenda.

Findings, Recommendations and Statements

. . . While the Council has not found any short-term financing problems with the Old-Age, Survivors, and Disability (OASDI) program, there are serious problems in the long run. Because of the time required for workers to prepare for their retirement, and the greater fairness of gradual changes, even long-run problems require attention in the near term. . . .

The Council identified four major areas of concern.

Long-Term Balance

Under their intermediate assumptions, the Trustees of the Social Security Funds estimated that income . . . will exceed expenses each year until 2020. . . . The trust fund balances will then start to decline as investments are cashed in to meet the payments coming due. The

Trustees estimated that although 75 percent of costs would continue to be met from current payroll and income taxes, in the absence of any changes full benefits could not be paid on time beginning in 2030.

The deficit over the traditional 75-year projection period was 2.17 percent of taxable payroll. This means that if payroll tax rates had been increased in 1995 by just over 1 percentage point each on employers and employees—from their present level . . . the system would be in balance over this 75-year period. . . .

. . . [O]ne of the three major tasks the Council set for itself in the area of financing was to make recommendations that would eliminate the 2.17 percent of taxable payroll deficit. All members of the Council agree that this should be done, though there are differences of opinion on how the goal should be met.

Long-Term Balance Beyond the 75-Year Horizon

The second major problem with Social Security financing is the deterioration in the program's long-range balance that occurs solely because of the passage of time. Because of the aging of the U.S. population, whenever the program is brought into 75-year balance under a stable tax rate, it can be reasonably forecast that, without any changes in assumptions or experience, the simple passage of time will put the system into deficit. The reason is that expensive years previously beyond the forecasting horizon, with more beneficiaries getting higher real benefits, are then brought into the forecast period. There is no simple answer to the question of how much higher the long-term actuarial deficit is above the 2.17 percent to bring Social Security into balance beyond the 75-year horizon, but there could be a significant increase. . . . All members of the Council agree that it is an unsatisfactory situation to have the passage of time alone put the system into long-run actuarial deficit, though there are again differences on how the problem should be corrected.

Contribution/Benefit Ratios

The third area of concern for the Council arises from the fact that from now on many young workers and workers of future generations under present law will be paying over their working lifetimes employee and employer taxes that add to considerably more than the present value of their anticipated benefits. This is the inevitable result of a pay-as-you-go system such as the United States has had, and an aging population. Although the money's worth that workers get from Social Security is only one of many criteria for judging the value of the Social Security system, the Council believes that the system should meet a test of providing a reasonable money's worth return on the contributions of younger workers and future generations, while taking account of the redistributive nature of the Social Security system.

The Council is breaking new ground by dealing so explicitly with money's worth issues. It does so because of concerns about equity from one generation to another. The Council feels that equity among generations is a serious issue and that it is important to improve the return on retirement saving for young people.

All members of the Council favor the objective of improving the money's worth given by Social Security to younger generations. There are again differences on how this objective should be achieved. . . .

. . . But despite its best efforts, the Council was not able to agree on one single plan for dealing with Social Security's financial difficulties. Rather, Council members expressed interest in three different approaches to restoring financial solvency and improving money's worth returns. One group of members favors an approach, labeled the Maintenance of Benefits (MB) plan, that involves an increase in income taxes on Social Security benefits, a redirection to the OASDI funds beginning in 2010 of the part of the revenue from taxes on OASDI benefits now going to the Hospital Insurance (HI) Trust Fund, coverage of newly hired State and local government workers not currently covered by Social Security, a payroll tax increase in 2045, and serious consideration of a plan allowing the Government to begin investing a portion of trust fund assets directly in common stocks indexed to the broad market. . . .

Another group of members supports an approach, labeled the Individual Accounts (IA) plan that creates individual accounts alongside the Social Security system. This plan involves an increase in the income taxation of benefits (though not the redirection of HI funds), State and local coverage, an acceleration of the already-scheduled increase in the age of eligibility for full benefits up to year 2011 and then an automatic increase in that age tied to longevity, a reduction in the growth of future Social Security benefits is structured to affect middle- and high-wage workers the most, and an increase in employees' mandatory contribution to Social Security of 1.6 percent of covered payroll, which would be allocated to individual defined contribution accounts. . . . [T]he combination of the annuity income attributable to their individual accounts and their scaled-back Social Security benefits would on average yield essentially the same benefits as promised under the current system for all income groups.

A third group of members favors an approach, labeled the Personal Security Accounts (PSA) plan, that creates even larger, fully-funded individual accounts which would replace a portion of Social Security. Under this plan, workers would direct 5 percentage points of the current payroll tax into a PSA, which would be managed privately and could be invested in a range of financial instruments. The balance of the payroll tax would go to fund a modified retirement program and modified disability and survivor benefits. When fully phased in, the modified retirement program would offer all full-career workers a flat dollar benefit (the equivalent of $410 monthly in 1996, the amount being automatically increased to reflect increases in national average wages prior to retirement) plus the proceeds of their PSAs. This plan also would involve a change in benefit taxation, State and local coverage, an acceleration of the already-scheduled increase from 65 to 67 in the age of eligibility for full retirement benefits, with the age increased in future years to reflect increases in longevity, a gradual increase from 62 to 65 in the age of eligibility for early retirement benefits (although workers could begin withdrawing the proceeds of their PSAs at 62), a reduction in future benefits for disabled workers, a reduction in benefits for women who never worked outside the home, and an increase in benefits for many elderly widows.

. . . [T]he combination of the flat benefit payment and the income from their PSAs would, on average, exceed the benefits promised under the current system for all income groups. There would be a cost associated with the transition to this new system equivalent to 1.52 percent of payroll for 72 years. This transition cost would be met through a combination of increased tax revenues and additional borrowing from the public.

Findings, Principles and Recommendations Regarding the Overall Social Security System

The Social Security system is part of a four-tier system of retirement income arrangements in which each tier is important and complementary to the others: Social Security, employer-sponsored pensions, individual savings, and a safety-net program, called Supplemental Security Income (SSI).

Social Security is the universal system that forms a base for the other three tiers, but all are important and need to be improved. . . .

Social Security's replacement rates—that is, the ratio of retirement benefits to final wages—are relatively high for low-wage earners because it is expected that they will have less help from private pensions and individual saving. Replacement rates are lower for higher paid workers who are more likely to be covered by employer pensions and who are better able to save on their own. . . .

The Council believes that Social Security should continue to take responsibility for paying benefits to low-wage, full-time, regular workers that are sufficient to keep them from having to turn to means-tested assistance for support in old age. . . .

It is of great importance to the nation that this four-tier retirement system, based on a compulsory Social Security system, be continued.

. . . The Council rejects the proposition that Social Security will "not be there" for future generations. Indeed, the Council proposes steps to improve the money's worth ratios for these younger workers. . . .

Social Security requires that all workers—provident and improvident alike—contribute to their future security. A compulsory program ensures that these contributions take place. Compulsion also makes it possible to provide for redistribution of protection from the higher to the lower paid and to avoid the problem of adverse selection that could occur if individuals were allowed to decide when and to what extent they wished to participate. Compulsion reduces the need for public assistance. In contrast, a voluntary plan would allow the improvident to escape their share of paying for their own future retirement needs—leaving the community as a whole to pay for them through some safety net program like SSI.

The Council favors partial advance funding for Social Security.

Historically, Social Security has been financed on a current pay-as-you-go basis, with tax inflows barely covering benefit outflows. As a result of the 1977 and 1983 Social Security Amendments, the Social Security Trust Funds began to accumulate some reserves, now about $500 billion (140 percent of next year's outflow), in advance of the sharply rising retirement costs of the baby boom generation.

All three plans favored by Council members endorse the practice of partial advance funding. The MB approach would increase the taxation of Social Security benefits, extend coverage to more State and local government workers, cut benefits by extending the computation period (or alternatively, slightly increase the contribution rate), slow down future benefit increases from changes in the CPI, and redirect some revenues now going to the HI Trust Fund to build up OASDI reserves. The two approaches involving individual accounts would build up reserves both in the central system and in the individual accounts. . . . Whatever the approach, the Council feels it is desirable to build up these reserves soon.

Early action should be taken to reform Social Security.

While OASDI revenues are projected to exceed expenditures for another two decades, the Council urges that early action be taken to reduce the actuarial imbalance in the system. . . . Actions taken now to trim the growth of benefits, raise taxes, or raise income in other ways could generate additional assets immediately. These additional assets could be invested (whether directly or through individual accounts), and these investments could raise money's worth ratios for younger workers.

The more notice provided to individuals, the more time they would have to replace any reduction in benefits. If the nation delays making any changes in Social Security for another 10 years, it would require a 25 percent reduction in benefits to rebalance the system without tax increases. By that time the baby boom generation will be on the cusp of its own retirement. The sooner the nation adopts changes and puts people on notice, the less disruptive the changes will be.

Moreover, early action also ensures that the widest possible array of options is available to policymakers. For example, any increase in retirement ages must be phased in gradually over time. . . .

The long-term actuarial balance of Social Security should not be adversely affected solely by the passage of time.

The Council believes that all factors known at the time of the 75-year projections should be considered and reported on by the Trustees. The fact that the 75-year projection period changes as the years pass creates a problem in this regard. Because of the financing scheduled in present law, even as the Trustees are reporting that the system is in balance over the next 75 years, they know that if everything else stays the same, they will not be able to report actuarial balance in, say, another 10 years because demographic trends make the additional 10 years more expensive.

The Council therefore urges that any legislative action be designed to assure financial solvency for the 75-year horizon, but that instead of just arriving at actuarial balance for 75 years, in addition assure that the ratio of fund assets to annual expenditures, known as the trust fund ratio, be stable over the final years of the forecast horizon. . . .

Social Security should provide benefits to each generation of workers that bear a reasonable relationship to total taxes paid, plus interest.

Many important values served by a Social Security system are not fully captured by looking solely at money's worth or rates of return. Nevertheless, the Council believes that it is important that young workers perceive that the system is fair. This perception in turn suggests that the younger generation should be well treated in terms of the issue of money's worth, taking into account the fact that within each generation there will be a redistribution toward the lower paid.

In the Council's opinion, this goal cannot be reached unless Social Security, in one way or another, is allowed to receive a greater return on accumulated funds than low-yielding Government bonds. Thus, plans put forth by the Council would, in one way or another, involve investment in private equities of part of the retirement funds. . . .

Ways to achieve the higher money's worth ratios differ greatly from one plan to another. In fact, these differences are so great that the Council found no basis for compromise, and indeed these differences, in some cases, are so great as to be much more important than the single similarity of investing in equities.

Any sacrifices in bringing the system into balance should be widely shared and not borne entirely by current and future workers and their employers.

Although reductions in the growth of future benefits and/or increased payroll and income taxes may be involved in bringing the system into long-range balance, the Council believes that present beneficiaries should also share in any sacrifices that might be required. While the details differ, the Council believes that the fairest way to bring these sacrifices about is to apply appropriate income taxation to Social Security benefits. The incomes of low-wage earners would still be protected—about 30 percent of Social Security beneficiaries would not pay any taxes under any of the Council's proposals—and the degree of sacrifice involved would depend upon standard income tax principles.

Maintaining full cost-of-living-adjustments (COLAs) throughout the period of benefit receipt is one of Social Security's most important contributions to individual security.

Inflation-proof benefits are generally available only in Federal retirement plans. Most State and local plans offer only partial protection against inflation, and private pension plans usually do not offer automatic adjustments, although they may provide ad hoc benefit increases to recipients from time to time.

In the case of Social Security, the goal of keeping up with wages and prices has been part of the program for decades. Before an explicit provision was added to the law in 1972, the financing of the program allowed for such periodic updating, and this was accomplished, although with some lag. Since the mid-1970s, benefits have been updated on an annual basis.

Inflation protection makes Social Security benefits increasingly valuable to people as they grow older. The longer people live, the more likely they are to have depleted whatever personal savings they may have accumulated, but expenses continue and, particularly in the case of health care and other services, are likely to increase with age.

The Consumer Price Index (CPI) is the basis for calculating inflation adjustment rates. Because the CPI is so important to Social Security, the Council urges that the market basket on which the CPI depends be updated much more frequently than at present. The Council also supports current efforts to remove bias from the CPI and believes that the Social Security cost-of-living adjustment (COLA) should follow the changes in the CPI made by the Bureau of Labor Statistics (BLS) wherever they may lead. . . .

To evaluate the financial effects of different policy approaches favored by various members, the Council has assumed that there will be a downward adjustment in the inflation assumption due to a change in the way the CPI is calculated. For these comparative purposes, all of the plans were analyzed assuming a downward adjustment in inflation rates of 0.21 percent per year, announced by the BLS in March, 1996. In addition, it was assumed that all real variables in the forecast (such as real wage growth and real interest rates) are 0.21 percent per year higher than was assumed by the Trustees. Were these same assumptions to have been adopted by the Trustees, the long-term actuarial deficit would be lowered by 0.31 percent of taxable payroll, or by 14 percent.

Conventional means-testing of Social Security is unwise.

The amount of Social Security benefits depends on lifetime earnings—a key component of lifetime income. Whether one is eligible at all for Social Security depends on having had earnings in covered employment, or on being a dependent family member of someone who has. . . .

The Council rejects the further proposition that Social Security should also condition benefits on assets or other income at retirement—conventionally known as "means-testing." The fact that benefits are paid without regard to a beneficiary's current income and assets is the crucial principle that allows—in fact encourages—people to add savings to their Social Security benefits and makes it feasible for employers and employees to establish supplementary pension plans. . . .

Social Security should be financed by taxes on worker's earnings, along with taxes paid by employers, earmarked taxes on benefits, and interest earnings on accumulated reserves, without other payments from the general revenue of the Treasury. . . .

. . . .The fiscal discipline in Social Security arises from the need to ensure that income earmarked for Social Security is sufficient to meet the entire cost of the program, both in the short run and long run, rather than from competition with other programs in the general budget. . . .

. . . Social Security . . . is a very long-range program—people pay dedicated taxes today toward benefits that may not be received for 30 or 40 years—and should not be part of an annual budgetary allocation process. . . .

Benefits for low-wage retirees should be protected.

The Council is mindful of numerous statistical data that report very high rates of poverty among certain groups of older beneficiaries. . . . To the extent that projected future benefit growth needs to be reduced under any of the proposed plans, the Council prefers to protect benefits for low-wage workers. Council members differ on the protection that ought to be afforded higher wage workers from the OASDI Trust Fund itself. . . .

The long-standing goal of universal coverage under Social Security can be obtained by extending mandatory coverage to all State and local government employees hired after 1997.

To the extent feasible, everyone who works for pay should be covered by the Social Security program. Every occupational group contains substantial numbers of people who at one time or another will need the protection of the program. . . .

Basically the issue of covering the last sizable group of workers not under Social Security is an issue of fairness. Newly-hired State and local government employees, like everyone else, should be part of this important national program. . . .

For Social Security, this extension of coverage saves money over both the short- and long-term. Partly this is because contributions will be received for many years before the benefit payments must be made, partly because under present law a high proportion of these State and local government employees will get Social Security benefits anyway. Including all State and local government workers hired after 1997 saves 0.22 percent of taxable payroll, 10 percent of the present long-term actuarial deficit. . . .

There should be improved incentives for people to extend their working careers.

One natural solution to the future problem of increasing numbers of retirees per worker is to improve the incentives for workers to extend their working careers. Present law already includes measures to bring Social Security's delayed retirement credit to the full actuarial equivalent so that the same expected amount of benefits will be paid no matter when the worker retires between ages 62 and 70. . . . The Council favors extending the benefit computation period so that those who work steadily through age 67 get higher benefits than those who do not. . . . Those plans featuring individual accounts also increase retirement work incentives as compared to the present system, because contributions to the individual accounts continue as long as workers work.

The period over which the indexed average wage is computed should be extended to 38 years.

Average indexed earnings, on which Social Security retirement benefits are now based, are computed over an averaging period of the 35 years of highest earnings. With the age of eligibility for full retirement benefits rising to 67 under present law, and as a means to increase retirement work incentives, it seems reasonable and consistent to increase the working lifetime period to 38 years for purposes of calculating the average earnings on which retirement benefits are based. . . .

The income taxation of Social Security benefits should be revised.

Many Council members feel that the fairest way to ask present retirees to share in the cost of bringing Social Security into balance is by revising the taxation of Social Security benefits. In 1993, when the income tax provisions applying to Social Security beneficiaries were broadened, the goal was to tax Social Security recipients in a way similar to the recipients of other contributory defined benefit pension plans—that is, including as taxable income recipients' benefits to the extent that they exceed what workers had paid in. However, Congress chose a proxy of 85 percent of benefits as representing amounts not attributable to employee contributions rather than having taxes on benefits computed individually. . . .

There are three other aspects of the present taxation of Social Security benefits that should be recognized to understand the various benefit taxation options. One is that in 1983 the policy was established of having the revenue from the taxation of Social Security benefits dedicated to the OASDI Trust Funds. The second is that the additional revenue from the 1993 introduction of the 85 percent rule goes to the Hospital Insurance (HI) program under Medicare rather than to OASDI. The third is that the tax on Social Security benefits does not apply to those who have adjusted gross incomes below $25,000 if single and $32,000 for couples.

All three plans proposed by various Council members would drop this last provision by phasing out the low-income thresholds by year 2007. . . .

Both the MB plan and the IA plan would, in addition, replace the 85 percent rule with a scheme whereby benefit taxes are computed individual-by-individual. . . . Then the MB plan would, in addition, shift revenues now going to HI to OASDI between 2010–2020. . . . The PSA plan, on the other hand, would move to a system of full taxation of employer-paid benefits (paid for with tax deductible contributions) and no taxation of employee-paid benefits (paid for with already taxable contributions), implying an immediate elimination of the taxes that now go to the HI program.

The change in the age of eligibility for full retirement benefits from age 66 to age 67 should be accelerated, and this age should later rise in line with overall longevity.

. . . A majority of Council members favor speeding up this schedule, so that the age of eligibility for full retirement benefits increases to 67 by the year 2011. . . .

Source: Advisory Council on Social Security, "Report of the 1994–1996 Advisory Council on Social Security," vol. 1: *Findings and Recommendations, January 1997.* Available on Social Security Administration Web site: www.ssa.gov/history/reports/adcouncil/report/toc.htm (accessed September 21, 2006).

Document 9.6

President Clinton's Call to "Save Social Security First" in the 1998 State of the Union Address, January 27, 1998

In both the 1988 and 1992 presidential campaigns, the future of the Social Security program was not a major issue. The topic was briefly raised in both campaigns, but neither of the major-party candidates advocated doing anything beyond what had already been done in 1983. By the 1996 campaign, the issue was being raised more frequently, but again neither candidate was suggesting major changes were ahead for Social Security.

The debate over Social Security's future became increasingly prominent in the public arena following the 1996 advisory council report—which appeared after the election—but it was only in his 1998 State of the Union address that President Clinton put the issue on the presidential agenda. In this speech, President Clinton argued that Congress should not undertake any increases in spending or any cuts in taxes—and thus cause any reduction in the surplus—until the government had dealt with the issue of Social Security's solvency. His call was to "save Social Security first." This speech can thus be viewed as a milestone toward putting the issue of Social Security reform atop the policy agenda.

(In the absence of specific programmatic or structural reforms in the Social Security program itself, the commitment to saving the surplus would result in the surplus being used to buy-down the outstanding federal debt held by the public, thereby reducing the government's overall indebtedness and making it easier to afford the future costs of Social Security benefits. Initially, the administration was making no commitments to anything beyond this idea of saving the surplus so that it might be used in this way. In the spring of 1999 President Clinton would propose the idea of crediting the interest savings from the retired debt to the Social Security trust funds, as a more specific way to use the debt reduction to bolster Social Security.)

. . . When I took office, the deficit for 1998 was projected to be $357 billion, and heading higher. This year, our deficit is projected to be $10 billion, and heading lower. For three decades, six Presidents have come before you to warn of the damage deficits pose to our nation. Tonight, I come before you to announce that the federal deficit—once so incomprehensibly large that it had 11 zeroes—will be, simply, zero. I will submit to Congress for 1999 the first balanced budget in 30 years. And if we hold fast to fiscal discipline, we may balance the budget this year—four years ahead of schedule.

You can all be proud of that, because turning a sea of red ink into black is no miracle. It is the product of hard work by the American people, and of two visionary actions in Congress—the courageous vote in 1993 that led to a cut in the deficit of 90 percent—and the truly historic bipartisan balanced budget agreement passed by this Congress. Here's the really good news: If we maintain our resolve, we will produce balanced budgets as far as the eye can see.

We must not go back to unwise spending or untargeted tax cuts that risk reopening the deficit. Last year, together we enacted targeted tax cuts so that the typical middle class family will now have the lowest tax rates in 20 years. My plan to balance the budget next year includes both new investments and new tax cuts targeted to the needs of working families: for education, for child care, for the environment.

This 1999 poster announces the Social Security Administration's willingness to provide services to non-English-speaking customers who might be eligible for benefits.
Source: SSA History Archives.

But whether the issue is tax cuts or spending, I ask all of you to meet this test: Approve only those priorities that can actually be accomplished without adding a dime to the deficit.

Now, if we balance the budget for next year, it is projected that we'll then have a sizeable surplus in the years that immediately follow. What should we do with this projected surplus? I have a simple four-word answer: Save Social Security first. . . .

Tonight, I propose that we reserve 100 percent of the surplus—that's every penny of any surplus—until we have taken all the necessary measures to strengthen the Social Security system for the 21st century. Let us say to all Americans watching tonight—whether you're 70 or 50, or whether you just started paying into the system—Social Security will be there when you need it. Let us make this commitment: Social Security first. Let's do that together.

I also want to say that all the American people who are watching us tonight should be invited to join in this discussion, in facing these issues squarely, and forming a true consensus on how we should proceed. We'll start by conducting nonpartisan forums in every region of the country—and I hope that lawmakers of both parties will participate. We'll hold a White House Conference on Social Security in December. And one year from now I will convene the leaders of Congress to craft historic, bipartisan legislation to achieve a landmark for our generation—a Social Security system that is strong in the 21st century. . . .

Source: Public Papers of the Presidents of the United States: William J. Clinton, 1998 (Washington, D.C.: Government Printing Office, 1999), 113.

Document 9.7
President Clinton's Remarks on Social Security at Georgetown University,
February 9, 1998

Following his 1998 State of the Union address, President Clinton spoke at Georgetown University in a speech dedicated to the topic of Social Security. In this speech he wanted to explain his views on Social Security reform in more detail.

During this speech the president announced the beginning of a year-long national campaign of town-hall type forums around the country to discuss Social Security reform.

. . . It may seem a long way away from the time where you are until you will need retirement. It may seem a long way away before most of your parents need retirement—but it isn't. And great societies plan over long periods of time so that individual lives can flower and take root and take form. And that is what we have to do today.

Social Security is a lot more than a line in the budget. It reflects some of our deepest values—the duties we owe to our parents, the duties we owe to each other when we're differently situated in life, the duties we owe to our children and our grandchildren. Indeed, it reflects our determination to move forward across the generations and across the income divides in our country, as one America.

Social Security has been there for America's parents in the 20th century, and I am determined that we will have that kind of security for the American people in the 21st century. . . .

For five years we have reduced the size of the deficit, reduced the size of government, dramatically reduced the budget deficit by over 90 percent, but continued to invest in your future. . . .

. . . I've submitted to Congress for 1999 the first balanced budget in 30 years. All that is a remarkable achievement. But, as I said, we have to be thinking about the future. And all of you know to a greater or lesser degree of specificity, every one of you know that the Social Security system is not sound for the long-term, so that all of these achievements . . . are threatened by the looming fiscal crisis in Social Security.

Today I want to talk about what it is and how we propose to deal with it. . . .

. . . [W]e have eliminated the deficit, so that over time we should have a balanced budget, and over time, most times we should be running a surplus now if we stay with the discipline we have now over the next couple of decades.

Now, if that's so, it is now estimated that with normal ups and downs in economic growth, over the next 10 years, after 30 years of deficits, that the United States will have a budget surplus in somewhere in the range of a trillion dollars in the aggregate over the next 10 years. I have said before we spend a penny of that on new programs or tax cuts, we should save Social Security first. I think it should be the driving principle of this year's work in the United States Congress: Do not have a tax cut; do not have a spending program that deals with that surplus—save Social Security first.

That is our obligation to you and, frankly, to ourselves. . . .

Let me back up just a minute, mostly for the benefit of the young people in the audience, to talk a little bit about the importance of this effort. It's hard for even people in my generation to understand this, much less yours, but early in this century, to be old meant to be poor—to be old meant to be poor. The vast majority of people over 65 in America early in this century were living in poverty. Their reward for a lifetime of work, for doing right by their children, for helping with their grandchildren, unless their kids could take care of them, was living in poverty.

If you ever have a chance you ought to read some of the books that have thousands of letters that older people sent to President Roosevelt, begging him, in the words of one typical letter writer, to eliminate—and I quote—"the stark terror of penniless, helpless old age." That's what prompted President Roosevelt to launch the Social Security system in 1935, to create what he called the cornerstone of a civilized society.

Now, for more than half a century Social Security has been a dramatic success. If you just look at the first chart over here on the right, you will see that in 1959 . . . the poverty rate among seniors was still 35 percent. As recently as 1959, still over a third of seniors lived in poverty. By 1979, it had dropped to 15.2 percent. By 1996, it had dropped to 10.8 percent. . . .

. . . [I]f you don't do anything, one of two things will happen—Either it will go broke and you won't ever get it; or if we wait too long to fix it, the burden on society of taking care of our generation's Social Security obligations will lower your income and lower your ability to take care of your children to a degree most of us who are your parents think would be horribly wrong and unfair to you and unfair to the future prospects of the United States.

So what's the bottom line? You can see it. Today, we're actually taking in a lot more money from Social Security taxes enacted in 1983 than we're spending out. Because we've run deficits, none of that money has been saved for Social Security. . . .

. . . And if nothing is done by 2029, there will be a deficit in the Social Security trust fund, which will either require . . . a huge tax increase in the payroll tax, or just about a 25 percent cut in Social Security benefits. . . .

Now, again I say, if we act soon, less is more. If we can develop a consensus as a country to act soon we can take relatively modest steps in any number of directions to run this 2029 number well out into the future in ways that will keep Social Security's role in providing some retirement security to people without unfairly burdening your generation and your ability to raise your children to do that. And I can tell you, I have had countless talks with baby boomers of all income groups and I haven't found a single person in my generation who is not absolutely determined to fix this in a way that does not unfairly burden your generation. But we have to start now.

We have to join together and face the facts. We have to rise above partisanship, just the way we did when we forced the historic balanced budget agreement. This is—as you can well see, this is reducible to stark mathematical terms. This need not become a partisan debate. Oh, there ought to be a debate, a good debate on what the best way to invest the funds are; there ought to be a good debate on what the best tradeoffs are between the changes that will have to be made. But it ought to be done with a view toward making America stronger and, again, preserving the ties that bind us across the generations.

I have asked the America Association of Retired Persons, the AARP, a leading voice for older Americans, and the Concord Coalition, a leading voice for fiscal discipline, to organize a series of four nonpartisan regional forums this year. The Vice President and I will participate. I hope the Republican and Democratic leadership will also participate. I was encouraged that Speaker [Newt] Gingrich said the other day that he felt we should save the surplus until we had fixed the Social Security first.

The first forum, which will set out before the American people the full nature of the problem—essentially, what I'm doing with you today with a few more details—will be in Kansas City on April 7th. Then in subsequent ones we will hear from a variety of experts and average citizens across all ages. It is very important to me that this debate involve young people—very important—because you have a huge stake in it, and you need to imagine where you will be and what kind of investment patterns you think are fair for you and how you think this is going to play out over the next 20, 30, 40 years. We want people of all ages involved in this.

This national call also will spread to every corner of the country, to every member of Congress. There are other private groups which have to play a role. The Pew Charitable Trust has launched a vital public information campaign—Americans Discuss Social Security. On March 21st, I will help kick off the first of many of their town hall meetings and teleconferences.

Now, when we go out across the country and share the information and get people's ideas, then, at the end of the year in December, I will convene a historic White House Conference on Social Security. And then, in a year, I will call together the Republican and Democratic leaders of the House and Senate to begin drafting comprehensive, bipartisan landmark legislation to save the Social Security system. . . .

We can do this. President Roosevelt often called us to the spirit of bold, persistent experimentation. We will have to do that. But he also reminded us that our greatest challenges we can only meet as one Nation. . . .

Acting today for the future is in some ways the oldest of American traditions. It's what Thomas Jefferson did when he purchased the Louisiana Territory and sent Lewis and Clark on their famous expedition. It's what Abraham Lincoln did when at the height of the Civil War, he and the Congress took the time to establish a system of land grant colleges, which revolutionized the future of America. It's what we Americans did when, in the depths of the Depression, when people were only concerned about the moment, and 25 percent of the American people were out of work, our Congress and our President still took the time to establish a Social Security system, that could only take flower and have full impact long after they were gone.

. . . What I prefer is a future in which my generation can retire, those who are not as fortunate as me can retire in dignity, but we can do it in a way that does not burden you and your ability to raise our grandchildren. . . .

Source: Public Papers of the Presidents of the United States: William J. Clinton, 1998 (Washington, D.C.: Government Printing Office, 1999), 196–201.

Document 9.8
"Social Security Saved!" Address by Senator Moynihan, March 16, 1998

Frustrated with what he saw as the government's inability to save the system's annual surpluses properly by using them to reduce federal indebtedness, and convinced that the large build up in the trust funds had become a political liability for the program, in 1989 Senator Moynihan began proposing a restoration of the pay-as-you-go financing that had been replaced by the partial prefunding introduced by the 1983 amendments. A return to pay-as-you-go financing would permit an immediate cut in payroll tax rates. Moynihan thus began proposing cuts in the payroll tax, in combination with longer-term benefit reductions and future tax increases.

By 1998 Moynihan had added to his plan an optional personal account provision. Privatization advocates saw this proposal as evidence of Moynihan's support of partial privatization. In 2001 President Bush appointed Senator Moynihan to cochair a commission charged with proposing just that.

The following is a speech from Senator Moynihan, making the case for his 1998 plan. (Footnotes have been deleted from the text.)

Let me begin with a proposition appropriate to our setting. Social Security in the United States is very much the work of academicians. It came about in an exceptional 14 months in the first Roosevelt administration, but economists had been planning it for a third of a century.

A second proposition. As with much social policy that originates with academic experts, the level of informed political support for Social Security within the electorate has always been low, and just now is getting lower.

This history goes back to the progressive era at the beginning of the century. It is to be associated, for example, with John R. Commons of the University of Wisconsin who helped found the American Association for Labor Legislation in 1906. The German government had created a workman's compensation system, a form of insurance against industrial injuries, and a sickness insurance program in 1884. In the academic manner, these ideas crossed the Atlantic. . . .

In a fairly short order workman's compensation became near universal among the states, and the reformers now looked to universal health insurance, a logical follow-on. In a mode we have experienced in our time, this proved too much. . . .

And so it came about that on August 14, 1935 . . . FDR signed the bill. . . .

Over the years, the original excitement surrounding Social Security faded; and few noticed. When a time came that a majority of non-retired young adults had concluded they themselves would never get Social Security, few showed any great concern. . . . Then in the late 1970s a combination of high inflation and over-indexing did indeed move the Trust Funds perilously close to insolvency. There was no great danger. At worst, checks might have been delayed a few days. But this did not prevent President Reagan's budget director from stating in the spring of 1981 that "Unless both the House and the Senate pass a bill in the Congress which can be signed by the President within the next 15 months, the most devastating bankruptcy in history will occur on or about November 3, 1982." A Presidential Commission was set up, chaired by the redoubtable Alan Greenspan. . . . But no agreement could be reached by the time the commission expired at the end of 1982.

. . . On January 3, 1983, Robert J. Dole, Senate Majority Leader, published an article on the op-ed page of *The New York Times,* entitled "Reagan's Faithful Allies." It seemed that many people thought Congressional Republicans weren't giving the President the support he needed and deserved. Not so, Senator Dole said, we are with the President and there are great things still to be done. Then this:

> Social Security is a case in point. With 116 million workers supporting it and 36 million beneficiaries relying on it, Social Security overwhelms every other domestic priority. Through a combination of relatively modest steps including some acceleration of already scheduled taxes and some reduction in the rate of future benefit increases, the system can be saved. When it is, much of the credit, rightfully, will belong to this President and his party.

That day I was being sworn in for a second term in the Senate. I had read the article and went up to Senator Dole on the Senate Floor and asked if he really thought that, why not try one last time? And he did think it. . . . We met the next day. The day after that Barber Conable was brought in, a Republican who both understood and believed in Social Security. On January 15th, 13 days from our first exchange, agreement was reached at Blair House and the crisis passed. (In a November 2, 1997 interview on "Meet The Press," Senator Dole cited this as his greatest accomplishment in his Senate career. And well he might.)

Social Security was secure for the time being. Indeed, the payroll tax generated a considerable surplus which we have lived off ever since, and will continue to enjoy for yet a few years. But the loss of confidence was grievous. Had we, indeed, just barely escaped bankruptcy? What then did the future hold but more such crises? In the meanwhile the academic world had changed. Energetic and innovative minds . . . had turned away from government programs—"the nanny state"—toward individual enterprise, self-reliance, free markets. As the 1990s arrived, and the long stock market boom, the call for privatization of Social Security all but drowned out the more traditional views. . . .

Will the Old Age pensions and survivors benefits disappear as well? What might once have seemed inconceivable is now somewhere between possible and probable. I, for one, hope that this will not happen. A minimum retirement guarantee, along with survivors benefits, is surely something we ought to keep, even as we augment retirement income in other ways. What is more, this can readily be done. Let me outline a solution.

I have a bill entitled "The Social Security Solvency Act of 1998." Senator Robert Kerrey and I will introduce it in the Senate this week. Here are the specifics:

I. Reduce Payroll Taxes and Return to Pay-As-You-Go System with Optional Personal Accounts

A. Reduce Payroll Taxes and Return to Pay-As-You-Go
As I first proposed in 1989, this bill would return Social Security to a pay-as-you-go system. That is, payroll tax rates would be adjusted so that annual revenues from taxes closely match annual outlays. This makes possible an immediate payroll tax cut amounting to about $800 billion over the next decade, with the lower rates remaining in place for the next 30 years. We would cut the payroll tax from 12.4 to 10.4 percent between 2001 and 2024, and the rate would stay at or below 12.4 percent until 2045. Even in the out-years, as we say, the pay-as-you-go rate under this plan will increase only slightly above the current rate of 12.4 percent. It would top out at 13.4 percent in 2060. And in order to ensure continued

solvency, the Board of Trustees of the Social Security Trust Funds will make recommendations for a new pay-as-you-go tax rate schedule if the Trust Funds fall out of close actuarial balance. Such a new tax rate schedule would be considered by the Congress under fast track procedures.

There is a matter of fairness here. Of families that have payroll tax liability, 80 percent pay more in payroll taxes than in income taxes.

B. *Voluntary Personal Savings Accounts*

Beginning in 2001, the bill would permit voluntary personal savings accounts, which workers could finance with the proceeds of the two percent cut in the payroll tax. Alternatively, a worker could simply take the employee share of the tax cut in the form of an increase in take-home pay equal to one percent of wages. (Economists will argue that workers who do not opt for voluntary personal savings accounts will also, eventually, receive the employer share in the form of higher wages. But that's a discussion for another time.)

The magic of compound interest will enable workers who contribute two percent of their wages to these personal savings accounts for 45 years (2000–2045) to amass a considerable estate, which they can leave to their heirs. . . .

C. *Increase in Amount of Wages Subject to Tax*

Under current law, the Social Security payroll tax applies only to the first $68,400 of wages in 1998, indexed to the annual growth in average wages. At that level, we are taxing about 85 percent of wages in covered employment. That percentage has been drifting down because wages of persons above the taxable maximum have been growing faster than wages of persons below it.

Historically, about 90 percent of wages have been subject to tax. Under this bill, we propose to increase the taxable maximum to $97,500 (thereby taxing about 87 percent of wages) by 2003. We then resume automatic changes in the base, tied to increases in wages, as under current law. (The taxable maximum is projected to increase to $82,800 in 2003 under current law.)

II. Indexation Provisions

As students of the Congress, you know by now that every tax cut requires an offset. So how do we offset the payroll tax cut in this bill? By two indexation procedures, and some other changes that most observers agree are needed.

A. *Correct Cost of Living Adjustments by One Percentage Point*

We propose to correct cost of living adjustments by one percentage point. This adjustment would apply to all indexed programs (outlays and revenues) except Supplemental Security Income.

This is an issue that has been with us for a long while now. Some 35 years ago in the Kennedy Administration I was Assistant Secretary of Labor for Policy Planning and Research, with nominal responsibility for the Bureau of Labor Statistics. The then-Commissioner of the Bureau of Labor Statistics, Ewan Clague, could not have been more friendly and supportive; he and his staff undertook to teach me, to the extent I was teachable. Although the BLS statisticians were increasingly confident of the accuracy with which they measured unemployment, business and labor were still distrustful. By contrast, the Consumer Price Index, begun in 1918 (monthly unemployment numbers only begin in 1948) was quite a different matter. It was beginning to be used as a measure of inflation in labor contracts and such like. Our BLS economists knew that the CPI overstated inflation, but no one seemed to mind. Business could make that calculation in collective bargaining contracts. And if they failed to, well, it was good for the workers. Indeed, on taking office in 1961, the Kennedy Administration had waiting for it a report by a distinguished National Bureau of Economic Research committee headed by George Stigler, who would go on to win the Nobel Prize in economics. The Stigler report, "The Price Statistics of the Federal Government," concluded that the CPI and other indexes overstated the cost of living.

That theme was picked up again by Professor Robert J. Gordon in an article in the Public Interest in 1981. Gordon wrote "It is discouraging that so little has been done [by the BLS] . . . for so long." The bias identified by Stigler was still present in the CPI, which Gordon pointed out was "the single most quoted economic statistic in the world."

In 1994, in a celebrated memorandum entitled "Big Choices," then-OMB Director Alice Rivlin noted that "CPI may be overstated by 0.4% to 1.5%." It then fell to the Senate Finance Committee to pursue the issue. We held three hearings and in short order found that the BLS itself acknowledges that the CPI is not a cost of living index. In the BLS pamphlet "Understanding the Consumer Price Index: Answers to Some Questions" there is the following Q & A:

Is the CPI a cost of living index? No, although it frequently (and mistakenly) is called a cost-of-living index.

In 1995, the Finance Committee appointed the Advisory Commission to Study the Consumer Price Index. Chaired by Professor Michael J. Boskin of Stanford, who had been Chairman of the Council of Economic Advisers under President [George H. W.] Bush. Also on the Commission were two eminent members of the Economics Department here at Harvard: Zvi Griliches and Dale Jorgenson. Their final report concluded that the CPI overstates changes in the cost of living by 1.1 percentage points.

It is true that recently the Bureau of Labor Statistics has made some improvements, a routine of some 80 years now, but most of these were already anticipated when the Boskin Commission issued its final report. That bias has not been corrected. It is not in the nature of this beast. Speaking before the annual meetings of the American Economic Association and the American Finance Association in Chicago in January of this year, Alan Greenspan said:

Despite the advances in price measurement that have been made over the years, there remains considerable room for improvement.

So our legislation includes the one percentage point correction, but it also establishes a Cost of Living Board to determine on an annual basis if some further refinement is necessary.

B. Increase in Retirement Age

In our 1983 agreement, the retirement age was increased, over time, to age 67 for those turning 62 in the year 2022. This legislation would make gradual increases in the retirement age by two months per year between 2000–2017, and by one month every two years between years 2018 and 2065. This increase is a form of indexation which results in retirement ages of 68 in 2017 (for workers reaching age 62 in that year), and 70 in 2065 (for workers reaching age 62 in that year.)

I refer to the increase as a form of indexation because it is related to the increase in life expectancy. Persons retiring in 1960 at age 65 had a life expectancy, at age 65, of 15 years and spent about 25 percent of their adult life in retirement. Persons retiring in 2073, at age 70, are projected to have a life expectancy at age 70 of about 17 years, and would also spend about 25 percent of their adult life in retirement. These are persons not yet born today. And they can expect, on average, to live almost to age 90. And that may be a conservative estimate as we don't know where medical technology will take us.

III. Program Simplification—Repeal of Earnings Test

The so-called earnings test would be eliminated for all beneficiaries age 62 and over, beginning in 2003. (Under current law, the test increases to $30,000 in 2002.) The earnings test is a relic of the Depression years. When Social Security was enacted in 1935, the Federal government was trying to discourage elderly workers from remaining in the labor force because there were not enough jobs. Today, the unemployment rate is down to 4.6 percent, and we should do everything possible to encourage workers to remain in the labor force. The earnings test is also an administrative burden with about one million beneficiaries submitting forms to the Social Security Administration so that benefits can be withheld—reduced—if the beneficiary has wages in excess of the earnings test. All for naught because higher benefits—roughly offsetting the loss in benefits—are paid in the future for each month for which benefits are withheld.

IV. Other Changes

All three factions of the 1994–1996 Social Security Advisory Council supported some variation of the following three provisions.

A. Normal Taxation of Benefits,

We propose to tax Social Security benefits to the same extent private pensions are taxed. That is, Social Security benefits would be taxed to the extent that the worker's benefits exceed his or her contributions to the system. Consequently, about 95 percent of Social Security benefits would be taxed. (For private pensions, the percentage taxed varies according to how much of the plan is funded by employee contributions. In many private pensions, the employee makes no contribution, so 100 percent of the pension benefits are taxed.)

B. Coverage of Newly Hired State and Local Employees

Effective in 2001, we would extend Social Security coverage to newly hired employees in currently excluded State and local positions. In 1935, State and local employees were not included in Social Security because it was believed that the Federal government did not have the power to tax State governments. However, subsequent actions by Congress providing for mandatory Medicare coverage of State and local employees have not been challenged.

Then a unanimous Supreme Court decision in 1986 put the issue to rest. In *Bowen v. Public Agencies Opposed to Social Security Entrapment,* the Court upheld a provision in the Social Security Amendments of 1983 that prevented States from withdrawing from Social Security. Including State and local workers is not only constitutional, it is fair, since most of the five million State and local employees (about a quarter of all State and local employees) not covered by Social Security in their government jobs do receive Social Security benefits as a result of working at other jobs—part-time or otherwise—that are covered by Social Security. Relative to their contributions these workers receive generous benefits. Our bill will bring these employees into the system, preventing them from getting a windfall.

C. Increase in Length of Computation Period

We would increase the length of the computation period from 35 to 38 years. Consistent with the increase in life expectancy and the increase in the retirement age, we expect workers to have more years with earnings. Computation of their benefits should be based on these additional years of earnings.

Budget Effects

Not only does this proposal provide for long-run solvency of Social Security, financed with payroll tax rates not much higher than current rates in the out-years, but it is also fully paid for in the short-run. The Congressional Budget Office's (CBO) preliminary estimate indicates that for the 10-year period FY 1999–2008, the bill would increase the projected cumulative budget surplus by more than $100 billion, from $671 billion to $803 billion. For the five year period FY 1999–2003, CBO projects that, under this plan, the cumulative surplus would be reduced by just $6 billion. In no year is there a deficit. And, to repeat, all of this is accomplished while reducing payroll taxes by almost $800 billion.

Will this happen? I just do not know. In a manner that the late Mancur Olson would recognize, over time Social Security has acquired a goodly number of veto groups which prevent changes, howsoever necessary. There are exceptions as in 1983 when we did our work in 13 days and behind closed doors. But otherwise, stasis is the norm. Thus for the past three or four years almost all the major players in the Administration have recognized that we had to employ a better measure of price inflation. But repeatedly action was vetoed by the, well, veto groups.

They can go on in this manner if they choose. But if they do, in 30 years time Social Security as we have known it since 1935 will have vanished. . . . It is time then for courage as well as policy analysis.

Source: Daniel Patrick Moynihan, "Social Security Saved!" Speech to John F. Kennedy School of Government at Harvard University, March 16, 1998. Copy in SSA History Archives, Revolving Files, Folder: Social Security Reform II.

Document 9.9
President Clinton's Remarks on Social Security in the 1999 State of the Union Address, January 19, 1999

On December 8–9, 1998, the promised First White House Conference on Social Security was held in Washington, D.C. Top administration officials, key members of Congress, and representatives of major organizations all convened for two days of discussion and debate. No real agreements—or discernible progress toward consensus—was evident in the conference report.

The following month, in his 1999 State of the Union address, President Clinton explicitly rejected the idea of private accounts carved out of the Social Security revenue stream. He also added a little more detail to his own plan to "Save Social Security first." This plan included government investment of Social Security surpluses in equities, as well as the creation of new personal savings accounts ("universal savings accounts") alongside the existing pay-as-you-go program.

. . . Early in this century, being old meant being poor. When President Roosevelt created Social Security, thousands wrote to thank him for eliminating what one woman called the "stark terror of penniless, helpless old age." Even today, without Social Security, half our nation's elderly would be forced into poverty.

Today, Social Security is strong. But by 2013, payroll taxes will no longer be sufficient to cover monthly payments. By 2032, the trust fund will be exhausted and Social Security will be unable to pay the full benefits older Americans have been promised.

The best way to keep Social Security a rock-solid guarantee is not to make drastic cuts in benefits, not to raise payroll tax rates, and not to drain resources from Social Security in the name of saving it.

Instead, I propose that we make an historic decision to invest the surplus to save Social Security.

Specifically, I propose that we commit 60 percent of the budget surplus for the next 15 years to Social Security, investing a small portion in the private sector, just as any private or state government pension would do. This will earn a higher return and keep Social Security sound for 55 years.

But we must aim higher. We should put Social Security on a sound footing for the next 75 years. We should reduce poverty among elderly women, who are nearly twice as likely to be poor as our other seniors. And we should eliminate the limits on what seniors on Social Security can earn.

Now, these changes will require difficult but fully achievable choices over and above the dedication of the surplus. They must be made on a bipartisan basis. They should be made this year. So let me say to you tonight, I reach out my hand to all of you in both Houses, in both parties, and ask that we join together in saying to the American people: We will save Social Security now.

Now, last year we wisely reserved all of the surplus until we knew what it would take to save Social Security. Again, I say, we shouldn't spend any of it—not any of it—until after Social Security is truly saved. First things first.

Second, once we have saved Social Security, we must fulfill our obligation to save and improve Medicare. Already, we have extended the life of the Medicare trust fund by

10 years—but we should extend it for at least another decade. Tonight, I propose that we use one out of every $6 in the surplus for the next 15 years to guarantee the soundness of Medicare until the year 2020.

But again, we should aim higher. We must be willing to work in a bipartisan way and look at new ideas, including the upcoming report of the bipartisan Medicare Commission. If we work together, we can secure Medicare for the next two decades and cover the greatest growing need of seniors—affordable prescription drugs.

Third, we must help all Americans, from their first day on the job—to save, to invest, to create wealth. From its beginning, Americans have supplemented Social Security with private pensions and savings. Yet, today, millions of people retire with little to live on other than Social Security. Americans living longer than ever simply must save more than ever.

Therefore, in addition to saving Social Security and Medicare, I propose a new pension initiative for retirement security in the 21st century. I propose that we use a little over 11 percent of the surplus to establish universal savings accounts—USA accounts—to give all Americans the means to save. With these new accounts Americans can invest as they choose and receive funds to match a portion of their savings, with extra help for those least able to save.

USA accounts will help all Americans to share in our nation's wealth and to enjoy a more secure retirement. I ask you to support them.

Fourth, we must invest in long-term care. I propose a tax credit of $1,000 for the aged, ailing or disabled, and the families who care for them. Long-term care will become a bigger and bigger challenge with the aging of America, and we must do more to help our families deal with it.

I was born in 1946, the first year of the baby boom. I can tell you that one of the greatest concerns of our generation is our absolute determination not to let our growing old place an intolerable burden on our children and their ability to raise our grandchildren. Our economic success and our fiscal discipline now give us an opportunity to lift that burden from their shoulders, and we should take it.

Saving Social Security, Medicare, creating USA accounts—this is the right way to use the surplus. If we do so—if we do so—we will still have resources to meet critical needs in education and defense. And I want to point out that this proposal is fiscally sound. Listen to this: If we set aside 60 percent of the surplus for Social Security and 16 percent for Medicare, over the next 15 years, that saving will achieve the lowest level of publicly held debt since right before World War I, in 1917.

So with these four measures—saving Social Security, strengthening Medicare, establishing the USA accounts, supporting long-term care—we can begin to meet our generation's historic responsibility to establish true security for 21st century seniors. . . .

Source: Public Papers of the Presidents of the United States: William J. Clinton, 1999 (Washington, D.C.: Government Printing Office, 2000), 62–64.

Document 9.10

Report of the National Commission on Retirement Policy, March 1, 1999

By 1998 partial privatization had become a mainstream idea. In response to President Clinton's call for a "year of discussion," the Center for Strategic and International Studies (CSIS) created the National Commission on Retirement Policy (NCRP). Cochaired by Sen. Judd Gregg (R-N.H.), Sen. John Breaux (D-La.), Rep. Jim Kolbe (R-Ariz.), Rep. Charles W. Stenholm (D-Texas), and business leaders Donald B. Marron and Charles A. Sanders, this bipartisan commission, which included twelve Democrats and twelve Republicans, proposed a number of changes to restore solvency to the Social Security trust fund, while carving out a private account from 2 percent of payroll. Their final plan, frequently referred to Gregg-Breaux-Kolbe-Stenholm (GBKS) plan, was proposed to both houses of Congress in 1998, although the formal report was not released until 1999. In the Senate, by the summer of 1998 the proposal had attracted more cosponsors than any other solvency plan to that point. Though never passed, the GBKS plan is considered the predecessor of partial-privatization proposals thereafter.

Dear Fellow Americans:

The National Commission on Retirement Policy (NCRP) is issuing the final report of its recommendations at a particularly critical time. The President and Congress have each publicly committed themselves not only to strengthening the Social Security program, but also to increasing retirement income for all Americans in the twenty-first century. Improved revenue projections for the federal budget provide a unique opportunity to set aside the necessary funds to ensure that future benefit promises are met. The question before us is whether there exists a true spirit of bipartisan cooperation and compromise needed to complete the job.

The attached report can serve as a road map for such reform. We commend this proposal to you not only for the policy goals it achieves, but also for the spirit of compromise it embodies. Our Commission included 24 experts on retirement policy from both the public and private sectors. . . . After 15 months of work, last May the Commission voted unanimously to report the enclosed recommendations. Our success came about not because 24 members, or even one member, felt persuaded that every element of our proposal was the best one. It was, rather, that each of the 24 members of the Commission worked together in the spirit of cooperation and compromise to develop this plan.

Similar cooperation will be necessary if Congress and the president are to make the necessary choices to expand and solidify all sources of retirement income in the twenty-first century. We hope that, like the members of our Commission, members of Congress, and the administration will follow the model of compromise established by the NCRP and eschew rigid perspectives toward policy in the interest of completing this most important task—enhancing the retirement security for all Americans.

Naturally, any cooperative agreement on a comprehensive proposal to strengthen retirement security will require trade-offs and tough choices. Our proposal is no different. Although you may not agree with every part of this plan, we ask that you consider it in its entirety, including all it achieves, before making a judgment. Moreover, we encourage you to ask, "What other plan achieves as much?". . .

The National Commission on Retirement Policy

The Center for Strategic and International Studies (CSIS) established the bipartisan National Commission on Retirement Policy (the "Commission") at the beginning of 1997 to highlight the looming retirement security challenge and recommend comprehensive and politically viable solutions to meet it. . . .

In its mission statement, the Commission outlined three primary objectives:

- to educate the American public about the scope and magnitude of the retirement financing challenge;
- to provide the foundation for nonpartisan and informed policy debate; and
- to build a national consensus for the changes necessary to place the country on a sound, long-term fiscal footing and ensure a secure retirement for all Americans.

The Commission also established three guiding principles in the beginning of its deliberative process:

- National retirement policy should be designed to enable Americans to enjoy a reasonable standard of living in their retirement years. National retirement policy should encompass government programs that require a floor of financial support for elderly retirees and initiatives that encourage and facilitate group (that is, employer) and individual savings to provide additional retirement income above the floor of support;
- National retirement policy should contribute to long-term growth and economic prosperity; and
- Government programs for elderly retirees should be financially sound and economically sustainable. The costs of financing these programs and other initiatives that encourage and facilitate national saving should be borne equitably between and among generations. . . .

The 21st Century Retirement Security Plan

The result of the Commission's 18-month deliberative effort is the 21st Century Retirement Security Plan. The Plan is unique in its bipartisan, comprehensive approach to retirement security, which encompasses improvements and reforms to all three principal sources of retirement savings: Social Security, private pensions, and personal savings. The interdependence of these areas cannot be ignored. The more Americans save and invest through private pensions and personal savings, the more capital will be available to fuel growth and to provide the government with more options to ensure the stability of the Social Security system.

The 21st Century Retirement Security Plan meets the goals established by the NCRP for Social Security. The Plan would:

- restore the long-term solvency of Social Security (OASDI);
- provide the traditional OASDI program with a stable Trust Fund at the end of the actuarial valuation period, so that the passage of time will not affect adversely measures of solvency;

- increase the retirement income provided through Social Security relative to traditional means of restoring the program to solvency;
- reduce significantly long-term debt and liabilities of the federal government to Social Security;
- enable Social Security to lift more of the elderly out of poverty than current law does;
- add incentives for individuals to remain in the workforce longer, thereby improving worker-to-beneficiary ratios;
- create individual savings accounts within Social Security that provide individuals with ownership and control over the investment of a portion of their Federal Insurance Contributions Act (FICA) taxes;
- enhance opportunities for providing retirement security through private pension plans and personal savings; and
- accomplish all the above objectives without a tax increase and without placing an additional mandatory savings requirement on employers or employees. . . .

Social Security: Recommendations

Individual Security Accounts

Refund two percentage points of the current 12.4-percent payroll tax into individual accounts. . . .

Increase Minimum Benefits

The Commission recommends. . . . All Social Security beneficiaries with 20 years of covered earnings would be guaranteed a benefit of at least 60 percent of the poverty level, phasing upward at 2 percent with each year of covered earnings until it reaches 100 percent of the poverty level after 40 years of work. . . .

Conform Eligibility Age for Benefits to Increased Life Span

The Commission recommends indexing the eligibility age for benefits to increased life spans. . . .

Include State and Local Government Employees in the Social Security System

The Commission recommends covering all state and local government employees hired after 1999. . . .

Address Inequities between Two-earner and One-earner Couples

The Commission recommends a reduction in the percentage of Primary Insurance Amount (PIA) payable to aged spouse beneficiaries from 50 percent to 33 percent, phased in from 2000 to 2016. . . .

Increase Earnings Years Covered in the AIME Formula to Reflect Longer Working Lives

The Commission recommends that, beginning in 2000, all years of earnings should be counted in the numerator of the Average Indexed Monthly Earnings (AIME) formula, and that the number of computation years in the AIME formula should be increased gradually from 35 to 40 years by adding 1 additional year every 2 years from 2001 to 2010. . . .

Eliminate the Earnings Test Above the Normal Retirement Age

The Commission recommends eliminating the "earnings test," partly because of the inducement it gives individuals to retire in order to collect some Social Security once they hit an eligible age. . . .

Redirect Social Security Benefit Taxation toward the Social Security Trust Fund

The most recent increase in Social Security benefit taxation was allocated to the Medicare Hospital Insurance (HI) Trust Fund. The Commission recommends gradually returning the income from this benefit taxation back to Social Security, phased in from 2010 to 2019. . . .

Adjust Early Retirement Benefits to Reflect Extra Taxes Paid Prior to Retirement

The Commission recommends adjustments to the early retirement benefit level and the delayed retirement credit to reflect more accurately the value of extra taxes paid prior to retirement. . . .

Add a "Fail-Safe" Mechanism

The Commission recommends that a "fail-safe" provision be included to prevent unexpected deterioration of Social Security's projected soundness. . . .

Adjust Bend Points

The Commission recommends that bend-point factors of 32 percent and 15 percent would be multiplied by a factor of 0.98 each year from 2001 to 2020. . . .

Source: National Commission on Retirement Policy, "The 21st Century Retirement Security Plan," March 1, 1999, viii, 4–6, 31–40. Full report available on the Cornell University Digital Commons Web site: http://digitalcommons.ilr.cornell.edu/institutes/7/.

Document 9.11
Excerpts on Social Security from the 2000 Presidential Debates, October 3, 2000

During the 2000 presidential campaign, Texas governor George W. Bush became the first presidential candidate of either major party ever to support openly Social Security partial privatization via carve-out private accounts. In contrast with Bush's stance, Vice President Al Gore criticized the private accounts plan of Governor Bush and offered his own alternative plan: "Social Security Plus."

Although the explanation of Gore's plan is very brief in this debate, it actually had four parts: (1) use the existing Social Security surplus exclusively to retire outstanding federal debt; (2) credit the interest savings from the retired debt to the trust funds to extend their life; (3) increase certain benefits for widows, widowers and mothers; and (4) encourage the creation of private-equity retirement savings plus accounts outside of the Social Security system by providing a tax credit to match individual contributions to such accounts.

MODERATOR: . . . New question on Social Security. Both of you have Social Security reform plans, so we could spend the rest of the evening and two or three other evenings talking about them in detail. . . .

Many experts, including Federal Reserve Chairman [Alan] Greenspan, Vice President Gore, say that it will be impossible for either of you, essentially, to keep the system viable on its own during the coming baby boomer retirement onslaught without either reducing benefits or increasing taxes. You disagree?

GORE: I do disagree. Because if we can keep our prosperity going, if we can continue balancing the budget and paying down the debt, then the strong economy keeps generating surpluses. Here is my plan. I will keep Social Security in a lockbox and that pays down the national debt. And the interest savings I would put right back into Social Security. That extends the life of Social Security for 55 years.

Now, I think that it's very important to understand that cutting benefits under Social Security means that people like Winifred Skinner from Des Moines, Iowa, who is here, would really have a much harder time. Because there are millions of seniors who are living almost hand to mouth. And you talk about cutting benefits. I don't go along with it. I am opposed to it.

I'm also opposed to a plan that diverts 1 out of every $6 away from the Social Security Trust Fund. Social Security is a trust fund that pays the checks this year with the money that is paid into Social Security this year. The governor wants to divert 1 out of every $6 off into the stock market, which means that he would drain a trillion dollars out of the Social Security Trust Fund in this generation over the next ten years, and Social Security under that approach would go bankrupt within this generation. His leading advisor on this plan actually said that would be okay, because then the Social Security Trust Fund could start borrowing. It would borrow up to $3 trillion. Now, Social Security has never done that. And I don't think it should do that. I think it should stay in a lockbox, and I'll tell you this. I will veto anything that takes money out of Social Security for privatization or anything else other than Social Security.

BUSH: I thought it was interesting that on the two minutes he spent about a million-and-a-half on my plan, which means he doesn't want you to know what he's doing is loading up IOUs for future generations. He puts no real assets into the Social Security system. The revenues exceed the expenses in Social Security until the year 2015 which means all retirees are going to get the promises made. For those of you who he wants to scare into the voting booth to vote for him, hear me loud and clear. A promise made will be a promise kept.

You bet we want to allow younger workers to take some of their own money. That's the difference of opinion. The vice president thinks it's the government's money. The payroll taxes are your money. You ought to put it in prudent, safe investments so that $1 trillion over the next ten years grows to be $3 trillion. The money stays within the Social Security system. It's a part of the Social Security system. He claims it will be out of Social Security. It's your money, it's a part of your retirement benefit. It's a fundamental difference between what we believe. I want you to have your own asset that you can call your own. That you can pass on from one generation to the next. I want to get a better rate of return for your own money than the paltry 2% that the current Social Security Trust gets today.

Mr. Greenspan, I thought, missed an opportunity to say there's a third way, and that is to get a better rate of return on the Social Security monies coming into the trust. There is $2.3 trillion of surplus that we can use to make sure that younger workers have a Social Security plan in the future. If we're smart and if we trust workers and if we understand the power of the compounding rate of interest.

GORE: Here is the difference. I give a new incentive for younger workers to save their own money and invest their own money, but not at the expense of Social Security, on top of Social Security. My plan is Social Security plus. The governor's plan is Social Security minus. Your future benefits would be cut by the amount that's diverted into the stock market. If you make bad investments, that's too bad. But even before then the problem hits because the money contributed to Social Security this year is an entitlement. That's how it works. And the money is used to pay the benefits for seniors this year. If you cut the amount going in 1 out of every $6, then you have to cut the value of each check by 1 out of every $6 unless you come up with the money from somewhere else. I would like to know from the governor—I know we're not supposed to ask each other questions—but I'd be interested in knowing, does that trillion dollars come from the trust fund, or does it come from the rest of the budget?

BUSH: No. There's enough money to pay seniors today in the current affairs of Social Security. The trillion comes from the surplus. Surplus is money—more money than needed.

Let me tell you what your plan is. It's not Social Security plus, it's Social Security plus huge debt. That is what it is. You leave future generations with tremendous IOUs. It's time to have a leader that doesn't put off tomorrow what we should do today. It's time to have somebody to step up and say look, let's let younger workers take some of their own money and under certain guidelines invest it in the private markets. The safest of federal investments yields 4%. That's twice the amount of rate of return than the current Social Security Trust. It's a fundamental difference of opinion here, folks. Younger worker after younger worker hears my call that says I trust you. And you know what, the issue is changing. Seniors now understand that the promise made will be a promise kept, but younger workers now understand we better have a government that trusts them and that's exactly what I'm going to do.

GORE: Could I respond to that, Jim? This is a big issue. Could we do another round on it?

MODERATOR: We're almost out of time.

GORE: Just briefly. When FDR established Social Security, they didn't call them IOUs, they called it the full faith and credit of the United States. If you don't have trust in that, I do. If you take it out of the surplus in the trust fund, that means the trust fund goes bankrupt in this generation within 20 years.

BUSH: This is a government that thinks a 2% rate of return on your money is satisfactory. It's not. This is a government that says younger workers can't possibly have their own assets. We need to think differently about the issue. We need to make sure our seniors get the promise made. If we don't trust younger workers to manage some of their own money with the Social Security surplus, to grow from $1 trillion to $3 trillion, it will be impossible to bridge the gap without it. What Mr. Gore's plan will do is cause huge payroll taxes or major benefit reductions. . . .

Source: Commission on Presidential Debates, "The First Gore-Bush Presidential Debate," unofficial debate transcript, October 3, 2000. Available at: www.debates.org/pages/trans2000a.html (accessed September 21, 2006).

Document 9.12
President G. W. Bush Introduces His Social Security Commission, May 2, 2001

In the spring of 2001 President Bush launched the President's Commission to Strengthen Social Security. Although membership in the commission was bipartisan, the president appointed all the members, and participation was contingent upon support of the idea of introducing private accounts into the Social Security system.

THE PRESIDENT: . . . Social Security is one of the greatest achievements of the American government, and one of the deepest commitments to the American people. For more than six decades it has protected our elderly against poverty and assured young people of a more secure future. It must continue to do this important work for decades to come.

Yet, it has been apparent for many years that Social Security, itself, is becoming insecure. Social Security was designed for an era when few Americans lived much past the age of 65, and when families of three or four children were more than the exception. When Social Security was created there were about 40 workers paying Social Security taxes for every one retiree receiving benefits. Today, there are three workers for every retiree; soon, there will be two. Long life is a blessing. Smaller families are an individual choice. But the consequence of this blessing and this choice is that the Social Security payroll tax, which was once 2 percent, has now passed 12 percent.

Economists calculate that it will have to rise past 18 percent if the baby boomers are to receive the same benefits that Social Security has promised, unless we take steps soon to reform the way Social Security is financed.

The threat to the stability of Social Security has been apparent for decades. For years, political leaders have agreed that something must be done. But nothing has been done. We can postpone action no longer. Social Security is a challenge now; if we fail to act, it will become a crisis. We must save Social Security and we now have the opportunity to do so. Our government will run large budget surpluses over the next 10 years. These surpluses provide an opportunity to move to a stronger Social Security system.

Two months ago, in my address to Congress, I described the principles that must guide any reform of Social Security. First, Social Security reform must preserve the benefits of all current retirees and those nearing retirement. Second, Social Security reform must return the Social Security system to sound financial footing. Third, Social Security reform must offer personal savings accounts to younger workers who want them. Today, young workers who pay into Social Security might as well be saving their money in their mattresses. That's how low the return is on their contributions. And the return will only decline further—maybe even below zero—if we do not proceed with reform.

Personal savings accounts will transform Social Security from a government IOU into personal property and real assets; property that workers will own in their own names and that they can pass along to their children. Ownership, independence, access to wealth should not be the privilege of a few; they're the hope of every American, and we must make them the foundation of Social Security.

Today, I am naming a Presidential Commission to turn these principles into concrete reforms. This task is not easy, but the mandate is clear: strengthen Social Security and make its promise more certain and valuable for generations to come. I have asked the Commission to deliver its report later this fall.

Social Security does not belong to any one political party, so the Commission is drawn from both parties. Social Security does not belong to the government or to the politicians, and so my Commission has members from many different walks of life. It will be chaired by two outstanding Americans: Senator Daniel Patrick Moynihan and Richard Parsons, of AOL/Time Warner.

Senator Moynihan has been aptly described as the Nation's best thinker among politicians since Lincoln, and its best politician among thinkers since Jefferson. A profound mind, a compassionate heart, and a far-seeing imagination have distinguished him throughout his career.

Our task today is to preserve what is the best in Social Security, while updating it, and for a new time. And nobody will do that job better than this great student of Social Security's history, and stalwart champion of Social Security's principles.

As cochief operating officer of AOL/Time Warner, Richard Parsons is one of the leaders of this Nation's Information Age economy. Few people have served more tours of duty in the American government and business; a senior aide in the Ford administration; managing partner of a distinguished law firm; CEO of a major savings bank, before becoming president of Time Warner. . . .

Fourteen other fine Americans have joined the Moynihan-Parsons Commission; seven of them are Republicans and seven are Democrats. They include a former aide to Robert Kennedy and a former aide to Ronald Reagan, political leaders, entrepreneurs, eminent experts on the Social Security system. Every one of these fine men and women is passionately committed to the safety, success and long-term security of Social Security.

I'm giving this Commission a great task and its members have my full faith. When it makes its report, the Congress and I will face some serious decisions, but we must be inspired by the example of the founder of Social Security, President Franklin Delano Roosevelt. In his Fireside Chat of September 1934, shortly before Congress enacted Social Security, he warned that there will always be those "frightened by boldness and cowed by the necessity for making decisions." They will complain, he said, "that all we have done is unnecessary and subject to great risks."

But now, as then, bold action and serious decisions are necessary and we in our time must rededicate ourselves to the great ideal Roosevelt defined 67 years ago: greater freedom and greater security for the average man than he has ever known before in the history of America. That's our charge and we must keep it. . . .

Source: "Remarks on Establishing the President's Commission to Strengthen Social Security," *Public Papers of the Presidents of the United States: George W. Bush, 2001* (Washington, D.C.: Government Printing Office, 2003), 477–479.

Document 9.13
Executive Order 13210 Establishing the President's Commission to Strengthen Social Security, May 2, 2001

This executive order officially created the President's Commission to Strengthen Social Security. Executive Order 13210 set the principles the commission's report had to follow.

By the authority vested in me as President by the Constitution and the laws of the United States of America . . . and to preserve Social Security for senior Americans while building wealth for younger Americans, it is hereby ordered as follows:

Section 1. Establishment. There is established the President's Commission to Strengthen Social Security (Commission).

Sec. 2. Membership. The Commission shall be composed of sixteen members appointed by the President, of which no more than eight shall be members of the same political party. The President shall also designate two members of the Commission to act as co-chairs. The two co-chairs shall not be members of the same political party.

Sec. 3. Mission. The mission of the Commission shall be to submit to the President bipartisan recommendations to modernize and restore fiscal soundness to the Social Security system according to the following principles:

(a) Modernization must not change Social Security benefits for retirees or near-retirees;
(b) The entire Social Security surplus must be dedicated to Social Security only;
(c) Social Security payroll taxes must not be increased;
(d) Government must not invest Social Security funds in the stock market;
(e) Modernization must preserve Social Security's disability and survivors components; and
(f) Modernization must include individually controlled, voluntary personal retirement accounts, which will augment the Social Security safety net. . . .

Source: George W. Bush, *Executive Order 13210: President's Commission to Strengthen Social Security,* May 2, 2001. Available at: www.whitehouse.gov/news/releases/2001/05/20010502-5.html (accessed September 21, 2006).

Document 9.14
Report of the President's Commission to Strengthen Social Security, December 21, 2001

The report of the President's Commission to Strengthen Social Security offered three reform models, all to include the creation of voluntary personal savings accounts as part of a reshaped social security system. The administration would eventually indicate that its policy preference was for a plan along the lines of Reform Model 2.

*All three plans involved substantial "transition costs" (see **Glossary**). The issue of transition costs would become a major stumbling block in the initial efforts of the Bush administration to push its private accounts plan.*

Introduction by the Co-Chairs

. . . The Social Security tax . . . began at two percent and has been raised more than twenty times, reaching the present 12.4 percent. This is a regressive tax that is paid on the first dollar of income by rich and poor alike. In fact, as of 1997, 79 percent of American households paid more in payroll taxes than in income taxes.

One egregious failing of the present system is its effect on minorities with shorter life spans than the white majority. . . . And because Social Security provides no property rights to its contributors . . . a worker could easily work forty years then die and own not a penny of the contributions he has made for retirement benefits he will never collect. There are, to be sure, survivors and dependents benefits, but many workers die before eligibility for these is established. Disability insurance was added during the Eisenhower Administration. . . . But far too many never receive any retirement benefits and leave no estate.

Similarly, the present Social Security program can prove unjust to women, especially divorced women who too often share nothing of the benefits acquired by a previous spouse. It is time we addressed this matter. There are a number of legitimate approaches that simply need to be worked out, with the plain objective of equal treatment. . . .

As the early administrators of Social Security anticipated . . . the program steadily evolved. . . . By the 1990s, the time had come for Personal Retirement Accounts. . . . In the mode of earlier innovations, the subject was first broached in academic circles, notably by economists such as Harvard's Martin Feldstein. In the fall of 1997, the Clinton Administration began to analyze proposals to create a system of individual retirement accounts, either as part of Social Security or outside of it. By early 1998, working groups were formed within Treasury and other departments to study issues related to such proposals.

A primary issue was how a feasible system of accounts could be administered and what would be the associated costs. In the spring of 1999 the Treasury had contracted a study by the State Street Bank entitled, "Administrative Challenges Confronting Social Security Reform." The sum of it was that the task was feasible—the Thrift Savings Accounts were already in place—and the cost modest. . . . In 1998 and 1999 a range of similar measures were introduced in Congress. None were enacted, but there was now a striking new item on the national agenda.

In the course of the Republican presidential primary campaign of 2000, then Governor George W. Bush gave a major address on Social Security, proclaiming it "the single most successful government program in American history . . . a defining American promise." He went on to discuss Personal Retirement Accounts. . . .

Governor Bush then added:

> Ownership in our society should not be an exclusive club. Independence should not be a gated community. Everyone should be a part owner in the American dream.

In his address, then-Governor Bush insisted that "personal accounts are not a substitute for Social Security," but a supplement, a logical completion. He proposed several measures necessary to ensure the long-term fiscal viability of Social Security itself. Among them was the following:

> Reform should include personal retirement accounts for young people—an element of all the major bipartisan plans. The idea works very simply. A young worker can take some portion of his or her payroll tax and put it in a fund that invests in stocks and bonds. . . .

Personal retirement accounts within Social Security could be designed and financed in a number of ways, some of which are analyzed by the Commission in detail in the pages that follow. . . .

As the Commission's interim report has shown, Social Security is in need of an overhaul. The system is not sustainable as currently structured. The final report demonstrates that there are several different approaches that national policymakers could take to address the problem, and we hope the pages that follow will provide sufficient analysis and suggestion to prompt a reasoned debate concerning how best to strengthen Social Security.

In the accompanying report, the Commission recommends that there be a period of discussion, lasting for at least one year, before legislative action is taken to strengthen and restore sustainability to Social Security. Regardless of how policymakers come to terms with the underlying sustainability issues, however, one thing is clear to us: the time to include personal accounts in such action has, indeed, arrived. The details of such accounts are negotiable, but their need is clear. The time for our elected officials to begin that discussion, informed by the findings in this report, is now.

Carpe diem! . . .

Executive Summary

Findings

. . . Social Security will be strengthened if modernized to include a system of voluntary personal accounts. Personal accounts improve retirement security by facilitating wealth creation and providing participants with assets that they own and that can be inherited, rather than providing only claims to benefits that remain subject to political negotiation. . . .

Partial advance funding of Social Security should be a goal of any effort to strengthen the system. Advance funding within Social Security can best be accomplished through personal accounts rather than direct government investment. Personal accounts offer numerous economic benefits, including a likely increase in national saving. . . .

Personal accounts can be administered in an efficient and cost effective manner. . . .

Personal accounts can also contribute towards the fiscal sustainability of the Social Security system. While there are multiple paths to fiscal sustainability that are consistent with the President's principles for Social Security reform, we have chosen to include three reform models in the report that improve the fiscal sustainability of the current system . . . and are preferable to the current Social Security system.

Under the current system, benefits to future retirees are scheduled to grow significantly above the level received by today's retirees, even after adjusting for inflation. The cost of paying these benefits will substantially exceed the amount of payroll taxes collected. To bring the Social Security system to a path of fiscal sustainability—an essential task for any reform plan—there are differing approaches. The Commission believes that no matter which approach is taken, personal accounts can increase expected benefits to future participants in the Social Security system.

Each of the three reform plans abides by the President's Principles for reform. . . .

Unifying Elements of the Three Reform Plans

- The Commission has developed three alternative models for Social Security reform that feature personal accounts as a central component. Under all three reform plans, future retirees can expect to receive benefits that are at least as high as those received by today's retirees, even after adjusting for inflation.

- All three models include a voluntary personal retirement account that would permit participants to build substantial wealth and receive higher expected benefits than those paid to today's retirees. . . .

- Because the Commission believes that the benefits currently paid to low-wage workers are too low, it has included a provision in two of the three plans that would enhance the existing Social Security system's progressivity by *significantly increasing benefits for low-income workers above what the system currently pays*. . . . Two of the three models also boost survivor benefits for below-average income widows and widowers.

- The Commission set a goal of moving the Social Security system toward a fiscally sustainable course that reduces pressure on the remainder of the federal budget and can respond to economic and demographic changes in the future. . . .

- All three reform models improve the fiscal sustainability of the program, though some move farther than others. Model 1 would require additional revenues in perpetuity in order to pay scheduled Social Security benefits under the plan. Model 3 prescribes an amount of additional revenues needed to pay scheduled benefits under the plan, an amount smaller than that required under Model 1. Model 2 does not require permanent additional funding.

- All three models also require transitional investments to move to a system that includes Personal Accounts. These transitional investments advance fund future benefits, thus substantially reducing the cost on future generations.

- All three models reduce the long-term need for general revenues as compared to the current, unsustainable system. . . .

- All three of the models are expected to increase national saving, though some would do so more than others.

- The Commission concludes that building substantial wealth in personal accounts can be and should be a viable component of strengthening Social Security. . . .

Three Reform Models

Reform Model 1 establishes a voluntary personal account option but does not specify other changes in Social Security's benefit and revenue structure to achieve full long-term sustainability.

- Workers can voluntarily invest 2 percent of their taxable wages in a personal account.
- In exchange, traditional Social Security benefits are offset by the worker's personal account contributions compounded at an interest rate of 3.5 percent above inflation.
- No other changes are made to traditional Social Security.
- Expected benefits to retirees rise while the annual cash deficit of Social Security falls by the end of the valuation period.
- Workers, retirees, and taxpayers continue to face uncertainty because a large financing gap remains requiring future benefit changes or substantial new revenues.
- Additional revenues are needed to keep the trust fund solvent starting in the 2030s.

Reform Model 2 enables future retirees to receive Social Security benefits that are at least as great as today's retirees, even after adjusting for inflation, and increases

Social Security benefits paid to low-income workers. Model 2 establishes a voluntary personal account without raising taxes or requiring additional worker contributions. It achieves solvency and balances Social Security revenues and costs.

- Workers can voluntarily redirect 4 percent of their payroll taxes up to $1000 annually to a personal account. . . . No additional contribution from the worker would be required.
- In exchange for the account, traditional Social Security benefits are offset by the worker's personal account contributions compounded at an interest rate of 2 percent above inflation.
- Workers opting for personal accounts can reasonably expect combined benefits greater than those paid to current retirees; greater than those paid to workers without accounts; and greater than the future benefits payable under the current system should it not be reformed.
- The plan makes Social Security more progressive by establishing a minimum benefit payable to 30-year minimum wage workers of 120 percent of the poverty line. Additional protections against poverty are provided for survivors as well.
- Benefits under the traditional component of Social Security would be price indexed, beginning in 2009.
- Expected benefits payable to a medium earner choosing a personal account and retiring in 2052 would be 59 percent above benefits currently paid to today's retirees. At the end of the 75-year valuation period, the personal account system would hold $12.3 trillion (in today's dollars; $1.3 trillion in present value), much of which would be new saving. This accomplishment would need neither increased taxes nor increased worker contributions over the long term.
- Temporary transfers from general revenue would be needed to keep the Trust Fund solvent between 2025 and 2054.
- This model achieves a positive system cash flow at the end of the 75-year valuation period under all participation rates.

Reform Model 3 establishes a voluntary personal account option that generally enables workers to reach or exceed current-law scheduled benefits and wage replacement ratios. It achieves solvency by adding revenues and by slowing benefit growth less than price indexing.

- Personal accounts are created by a match of part of the payroll tax—2.5 percent up to $1000 annually (indexed annually for wage growth)—for any worker who contributes an additional 1 percent of wages subject to Social Security payroll taxes.
- The add-on contribution is partially subsidized for workers in a progressive manner by a refundable tax credit.
- In exchange, traditional Social Security benefits are offset by the worker's personal account contributions compounded at an interest rate of 2.5 percent above inflation.
- The plan makes the traditional Social Security system more progressive by establishing a minimum benefit payable to 30-year minimum wage workers of 100 percent of the poverty line (111 percent for a 40-year worker). This minimum benefit would be indexed to wage growth. Additional protections against poverty are provided for survivors as well.

- Benefits under the traditional component of Social Security would be modified by:
  - adjusting the growth rate in benefits for actual future changes in life expectancy,
  - increasing work incentives by decreasing the benefits for early retirement and increasing the benefits for late retirement, and
  - flattening out the benefit formula (reducing the third bend point factor from 15 to 10 percent).
- Benefits payable to workers who opt for personal accounts would be expected to exceed scheduled benefit levels and current replacement rates.
- Benefits payable to workers who do not opt for personal accounts would be over 50 percent higher than those currently paid to today's retirees.
- New sources of dedicated revenue are added in the equivalent amount of 0.6 percent of payroll over the 75-year period, and continuing thereafter.
- Additional temporary transfers from general revenues would be needed to keep the Trust Fund solvent between 2034 and 2063. . . .

Transition Financing

For Reform Model 1, no new "transition" cash would be needed before 2012 when the investment in personal accounts for the first time exceeds current-law surpluses. The "transition" financing requirements begin comparatively small—$12 billion annually in 2012—and they would grow to a maximum of $64 billion annually from 2016–2018. Thereafter the amount of new cash requirements for the new system would diminish, until in 2043, the new system would be permanently less expensive than the old.

These figures presume that only Social Security cash surpluses are available to provide transition financing. Through 2043, a total of $1.1 trillion in transition investments would be required, in present value terms. Assuming that Social Security cash surpluses are available to provide such financing, the remaining transition investment required would be approximately $700 billion in present value terms. Were Congress to "lockbox" both cash and interest surpluses as previously intended, transition financing needs would be postponed by additional years. . . .

Reform Model 2 would significantly reduce fiscal pressures on the rest of the federal government relative to current law.

For Reform Model 2, no new "transition" cash would be needed before 2010 when the investment in personal accounts for the first time exceeds current-law surpluses. The "transition" financing requirements begin comparatively small—$4 billion in real dollars as of 2010—and they would grow to a maximum of $73 billion (in 2001 dollars) in the years 2015–2016. Thereafter the amount of new cash requirements for the new system would diminish, until in 2029, the new system would be permanently less expensive than the old.

In sum, the total transition investments under Reform Model 2 would be approximately $900 billion in present-value terms. The amount required beyond that which is already accounted for by projected Social Security cash surpluses under Model 2 is approximately $400 billion in present-value terms.

Again, all of the figures above presume that only Social Security cash surpluses are available to provide transition financing. Were Congress to "lockbox" both cash and interest surpluses as previously intended, transition financing needs would be postponed by additional years. . . .

Reform Model 3 employs infusions of general revenues, with effects on the unified federal budget. . . . Beyond these infusions, no new "transition" cash would be needed before 2012, assuming 67 percent participation, when the investment in personal accounts for the first time exceeds current-law surpluses. The "transition" financing requirements begin comparatively small—$12 billion in real dollars 2012—and would grow to a maximum of $54 billion in real dollars in 2015–2016. Thereafter the amount of new cash requirements for the new system would diminish, until in 2028, the new system would be no longer requires additional temporary transition financing. The system, however, would continue to rely on permanent infusions of general revenues throughout the valuation period, and the model's net impact on the federal budget would turn positive in 2029. . . .

In all, Reform Model 3 would require approximately $400 billion (present-value) in total transition financing. Beyond that which would be available from projected Social Security cash surpluses under the plan, the figure would be approximately $100 billion (in present value.)

Again, all of the figures above presume that only Social Security cash surpluses are available to provide transition financing. Were Congress to "lockbox" both cash and interest surpluses as previously intended, transition financing needs would be postponed by additional years. . . .

Source: President's Commission to Strengthen Social Security, "Strengthening Social Security and Creating Personal Wealth for All Americans," December 2001. Available on the Social Security Administration Web site: www.ssa.gov/history/reports/pcsss/Final_report.pdf (accessed September 21, 2006).

Document 9.15
Senator Graham's "Social Security Solvency and Modernization" Proposal, November 18, 2003

One prominent member of Congress—Sen. Lindsey Graham (R-S.C.)—in 2003 introduced in Congress his Social Security Solvency and Modernization Act (one among many such plans). This is an excerpt from his press release announcing his legislation.

The innovation in Senator Graham's proposal is the idea that those who choose not to participate in his private accounts option would be required to accept a 2 percent payroll tax increase as the premium for staying in the existing system—that is, as the cost to make that system solvent.

Social Security is the most popular government program in American history. . . .

Unfortunately, Social Security as it's currently structured is not sustainable. The program must be reformed. . . .

It's time for Republicans and Democrats to work together to modernize Social Security in a responsible way and bring the political blame game to an end.

To keep Social Security solvent in the future, we have three choices. We can raise payroll taxes by 50 percent or cut benefits by 30 percent. The first choice will devastate the economy. The second choice will devastate those relying on Social Security. Some have suggested putting Social Security in a "lockbox" will save the system. However, the Social Security Administration says even with a lockbox, the system will still go bankrupt.

Fortunately for us there is a third choice—modernize the system through innovative reforms that include personal accounts.

The plan I introduce today combines the best of traditional Social Security system with the opportunity for younger workers at all income levels to build a retirement nest egg through personal accounts. Personal accounts would provide safe investment options similar to those now available to federal employees and improve on a system that will provide low—if not negative—growth rates for younger workers. It also provides stronger anti-poverty protections than are present in today's system.

Current retirees, workers 55 and older, and persons with disabilities would remain in today's system with no changes to benefits, taxes, or annual cost of living adjustments.

For workers 54 and younger, my plan gives workers the choice to join a modernized system that provides future retirees an inflation-indexed traditional benefit from Social Security that is at least as high as the benefits received by retirees today plus a personal retirement account. Workers would have the opportunity to set aside 4 percentage points of the social security taxes . . . in a personal retirement account that they would own and control.

Workers would be permitted to invest their contributions in stock and bond index funds. These investments would build value over time. At retirement, workers could draw on their account assets to help pay their monthly Social Security benefits or pass their account onto their heirs.

For the first time, workers of all income levels would be given ownership and control over part of their Social Security contributions. With greater returns, there will be more at stake. The key is to minimize any risk through diversification, long holding periods, and investor education.

A modernized Social Security system would also keep the majority of Social Security funds in the traditional system to provide a safety net.

Those who don't want to take part in a modernized system could choose to keep all their Social Security money in the traditional system and receive today's benefit levels if they are willing to pay more to maintain that system. Initially, workers selecting this option would pay an additional 2 percent of their wages into Social Security. Unfortunately, the cost of maintaining Social Security into the future will continue to increase. So, workers would pay increasingly higher tax rates over time.

My plan makes no false promises—each option leads to solvency for the system and will substantially reduce the cost of Social Security sparing future generations from being buried under a mountain of debt. . . .

If people don't like the idea of modernizing Social Security with personal accounts, they should come up with something else. Let's debate all of the options and examine what different plans would mean for putting Social Security back on solid footing. . . .

Social Security is going broke. No matter how hard we try to ignore the warnings or how far we stick our heads in the sand, we won't fix the problem until we roll up our sleeves and get to work. . . .

When it comes to Social Security, the most devastating option we could choose is to do nothing. That would doom the system to bankruptcy and in my opinion, is simply not acceptable.

Source: Press release, "Statement from Senator Lindsey Graham," November 18, 2003. Available at: www.senate.gov/~lgraham/index.cfm?mode=presspage&id=219419 (accessed February 11, 2007).

Document 9.16
The Diamond/Orszag Plan for Reforming Social Security, December 2003
In late 2003, MIT economist Peter Diamond and Brookings Institution economist Peter Orszag coauthored an alternative Social Security reform plan that did not rely on private accounts but attempted to restore Social Security's solvency through tax and benefit changes.

A Balanced Reform Plan

Our plan for restoring actuarial balance has three components, each of which addresses a factor that contributes to the long-term deficit. Each component includes a balanced package of adjustments to both benefits and revenue to help close the long-term deficit:

Life Expectancy

Life expectancy at age sixty-five has risen by four years for men and five years for women since 1940, and is expected to continue rising. Increasing life expectancy raises the value of Social Security benefits to workers, because benefits last as long as the recipient is alive. By the same token, however, improving life expectancy raises Social Security's cost, because beneficiaries then collect benefits over a longer period.

Many observers have recognized that adjusting Social Security automatically for increasing life expectancy makes sense. Previous proposals have taken the extreme approach of doing all of the adjustment through reductions in benefits. Instead, we propose a balanced approach with roughly half the life expectancy adjustment occurring through changes to benefits and the rest through changes to payroll taxes. . . .

Earnings Inequality

Over the past two decades, earnings have risen most rapidly among workers with the highest earnings. This affects Social Security's financing, since the Social Security payroll tax is imposed only up to a maximum taxable level ($87,000 in 2003). . . .

Our plan again includes a balance of revenue and benefit adjustments. First, the maximum taxable earnings base rises gradually until the share of total earnings that is above the base—and hence escapes the payroll tax—has declined to 13 percent, roughly its average level over the past twenty years. Second, to offset the effects of disproportionately rapid gains in life expectancy among higher earners, benefits are reduced for the highest earners (about 15 percent of workers). Lifetime earnings that fall in the top tier of the benefit formula (above about $44,000 in 2003) add less to benefits than under current law. Instead of the current 15 cents in benefits for each dollar of lifetime earnings in the top tier, our plan gradually reduces the benefit rate to 10 cents of benefits for each dollar of lifetime earnings in the top tier.

Legacy Debt

The third component of our plan recognizes the legacy debt stemming from Social Security's history. . . .

First, we introduce mandatory Social Security coverage for newly hired state and local government workers to ensure that eventually all workers bear a portion of the cost of the benefits paid out to earlier generations. While most state and local workers are covered by Social Security, about 4 million of them are not. Their nonparticipation means that those workers escape any contribution to financing the legacy debt.

Second, we impose a legacy tax on earnings above the maximum taxable earnings base, thereby ensuring that very high earners contribute to financing the legacy debt in proportion to their full earnings. The legacy tax above the maximum taxable earnings base starts at 3 percent and gradually rises along with the charge for everyone described in the next paragraph, reaching 3.5 percent by 2080.

Third, we impose a universal legacy charge on future workers and beneficiaries, roughly half in the form of benefit reductions for all beneficiaries becoming eligible in or after 2023, and the rest in the form of very modest increases in the payroll tax from 2023 onward. These changes begin right after the last of the benefit reductions that Congress passed in 1983. This universal legacy charge gradually increases over time, so as to help stabilize the ratio of the legacy debt to taxable payroll. . . .

Our three-part proposal would restore long-term balance to Social Security: revenues would be projected to be sufficient for expenditures over the next seventy-five years, and the system would be expected to remain in balance thereafter. In addition, our plan provides some resources for the improvements to benefits. . . .

Implications for Benefits and Revenue

Taken together, these changes are sufficient to restore actuarial balance. . . . Moreover, the life of the Social Security trust fund is not only extended throughout the projection period, but the trust fund is slowly rising (relative to annual benefits) at the end of the seventy-five-year period. . . .

What effect will these changes have on individual workers' taxes and benefits? Workers who are fifty-five years old or older in 2004 will experience no change in their benefits from those scheduled under current law. For younger workers with average earnings, our proposal does lower benefits relative to those scheduled under current law, with the reductions smaller for older cohorts than for younger ones. For example, a forty-five-year-old average earner (in 2004) is projected to experience less than a 1 percent reduction in benefits under our plan. And a twenty-five-year-old with average earnings experiences less than a 9 percent reduction in benefits. . . . Higher earners experience somewhat larger reductions in benefits than the average, and lower earners experience smaller reductions. . . .

To increase revenue under our plan, the employee share of the payroll tax is projected to gradually increase from 6.2 percent in 2005 to 7.1 percent in 2055. Because employees and their employers each pay half of the payroll tax, the combined employer-employee payroll tax rate is projected to rise from 12.4 percent today to 12.45 percent in 2015, 13.2 percent in 2035, and 14.2 percent in 2055. This gradual increase in the payroll tax rate . . . helps ensure that Social Security continues to provide an adequate level of benefits that are protected against inflation and financial market fluctuations, and that last as long as the beneficiary lives.

Individual Accounts

Unlike many other proposals for Social Security reform, our plan does not call for the creation of individual accounts within Social Security. Individual accounts, which include tax-favored private sector accounts such as 401(k)s and IRAs, already provide an extremely useful supplement to Social Security, and they can be improved and expanded. But they are simply inappropriate for a social insurance system that provides the basic tier of income during retirement, disability, and other times of need.

Conclusion

Social Security plays a critical role in the lives of millions of Americans and in the federal budget, so reform is naturally controversial.

Our plan represents the most auspicious way of reforming the program because it: balances benefit and revenue adjustments; restores long-term balance and sustainable solvency to Social Security; does not assume any transfers from general revenue; does not rely on substantial reductions in disability and young survivor benefits to help restore long-term balance; strengthens the program's protections for low earners and widows; does not divert Social Security revenue into individual accounts; and preserves Social Security's core social insurance role, providing a base income in time of need that is protected against financial market fluctuations and unexpected inflation.

Source: Peter A. Diamond and Peter R. Orszag, "Reforming Social Security: A Balanced Plan," Policy Brief no. 126, December 2003, available on the Brookings Institution Web site: www.brook.edu/comm/policybriefs/pb126.htm (accessed February 11, 2007). Reprinted with permission of the Brookings Institution.

Document 9.17
Cato Institute's "6.2% Solution" Reform Plan, February 17, 2004
In early 2004, the director of the Cato Institute's Project on Social Security Choice, Michael Tanner, began advocating what he called the "6.2% solution." The essence of the idea was that the employee's share of the Social Security payroll tax (6.2%) would be diverted into private accounts and the employer's share (the matching 6.2%) would be retained in the Social Security system to fund the very much reduced program that would remain behind after the partial privatization of the system.

This document makes reference to the figure of $26 trillion as the "unfunded liabilities" of the Social Security system and cites in reference the "2003 Trustees Report," but no such figure actually appears in the 2003 report. The 2003 report provided three alternative ways to estimate the program's unfunded liability: the seventy-five-year open-group estimate of $3.5 trillion, the one hundred-year closed group figure of $11.9 trillion, and the open group infinite horizon figure of $10.5 trillion.

(Footnotes in the original have been deleted from the excerpt.)

Introduction

For the past several years . . . the Cato Institute has provided studies and other information on the problems facing Social Security and the advantages of individual accounts as a way to reform the system. But until now we have not suggested a specific plan for reform. . . .

. . . The Cato Project on Social Security Choice, therefore, has developed a proposal to give workers ownership of and control over their retirement funds.

This plan would establish voluntary personal accounts for workers born on or after January 1, 1950. Workers would have the option of (a) depositing their half of the current payroll tax (6.2 percentage points) in an individual account and forgoing future accrual of Social Security retirement benefits or (b) remaining in the traditional Social Security system and receiving the level of retirement benefits payable on a sustainable basis given current revenue and expenditure projections.

. . . Workers choosing the individual account option would also receive bonds recognizing their past contributions to Social Security.

At retirement, workers would be able to choose an annuity, a programmed withdrawal option, or the combination of an annuity and a lump-sum payment. The government would maintain a safety net to insure that no senior would retire with income less than 120 percent of the poverty level.

We expect this proposal to restore Social Security to long-term and sustainable solvency and to do so at a cost less than the cost of simply continuing the existing program. And it would do far more than that.

Workers who chose the individual account option could accumulate retirement resources substantially greater than those that are currently payable under traditional Social Security. They would own and control those assets. At the same time, women and minorities would be treated fairly, and low-income workers could accumulate real wealth.

Most important, this proposal would reduce Americans' reliance on government and give individuals greater responsibility for and control over their own lives. It would provide a profound and significant increase in individual liberty. . . .

Principles for Reform

In developing a proposal for Social Security reform, we relied on five basic principles:

Solvency Is Not Enough

The goal of Social Security reform should be to provide workers with the best possible retirement option, not simply to find ways to preserve the current Social Security system. After all, if solvency were the only goal, that could be accomplished with tax increases or benefit cuts. . . . A successful Social Security reform will of course result in a solvent system, not just in the short run, but sustainable over time as well. And it will also improve Social Security's rate of return; provide better retirement benefits; treat women, minorities, and low-income workers more fairly; and give workers real ownership of and control over their retirement funds.

Don't Touch Grandma's Check

Although there is no legal right to Social Security benefits, workers who have relied on the program in good faith should not become scapegoats for the government's failures. Workers who are retired today or who are nearing retirement should not have their benefits reduced or threatened in any way.

More Investment Is Better Than Less

You don't cut out half a cancer. Many proposals for Social Security reform would allow workers to privately invest only a small portion of their payroll taxes; they would continue to rely on the existing PAYGO [pay-as-you-go] Social Security system for the majority of Social Security benefits.

But small account proposals will not allow low- and middle-income workers to accumulate real wealth or achieve other objectives of reform. Individual accounts should be as large as feasible.

Individuals, Not Government, Should Invest

The only way to increase Social Security's rate of return is to invest in private capital assets. This should be done through the creation of individually owned accounts, not by allowing the government to directly invest Social Security surpluses. Individual accounts would give workers ownership of and control over their retirement funds, allowing them to accumulate wealth and pass that wealth on to their heirs; it would also give them a stake in the American economic system. Government investment would allow the federal government to become the largest shareholder in every American company, posing a potential threat to corporate governance and raising the possibility of social investing. And government, not workers, would still own and control retirement benefits.

Be Honest

The American people can handle an open and honest debate about Social Security reform. Individual accounts will create a better, fairer, and more secure retirement system. But they cannot create miracles. They will provide higher retirement benefits than Social Security can pay. But they will not make everyone a millionaire. They will help solve Social Security's financial crisis and save taxpayers trillions of dollars over the long run. But there is no free lunch. There are short-term costs that will require the president and Congress to make tough choices.

Promised vs. Payable Benefits

Opponents of individual accounts frequently suggest that the creation of such accounts would result in cuts in the promised level of Social Security benefits. Those critics are confusing changes necessary to restore the system to balance with changes resulting from individual accounts. As noted above, Social Security faces unfunded liabilities of nearly $26 trillion. Quite simply, unless there is a substantial increase in taxes, the program cannot pay the promised level of benefits. . . .

. . . The Social Security Administration is legally authorized to issue benefit checks only as long as there are sufficient funds available in the Social Security Trust Fund to pay those benefits. Once those funds are exhausted, in 2042 by current estimates, Social Security benefits will automatically be reduced to a level payable with existing tax revenues, approximately 73 percent of the current benefit levels.

This, then, is the proper baseline to use when discussing Social Security reform. Social Security must be restored to a sustainable level regardless of whether individual accounts are created. . . .

Because one goal of this reform plan is to bring the Social Security system into balance and eliminate the system's unfunded liabilities, changes are made to bring the system's finances into balance in a sustainable PAYGO system. Those changes are separate from the creation of individual accounts. . . .

A Proposal for Individual Accounts

Current workers should be given a choice. Beginning January 1, 2005, workers born on or after January 1, 1950, would have two options: Those who wish to remain in the traditional Social Security system would be free to do so, accepting a level of benefits payable with existing levels of revenue. Those workers would continue to pay the full 12.4 percent payroll tax and would continue to receive Social Security benefits as under current law. However, beginning in 2012, the formula used to calculate the accrual of benefits would be adjusted to index them to price inflation rather than national wage growth.

That change would have no impact on people who are already retired. . . . Nor would it reduce benefits for those nearing retirement. However, for younger workers, benefits would gradually be adjusted to a level sustainable under the current level of payroll taxation.

At the same time, those workers who wished to enter the new market-based system would be allowed to divert their half of the payroll tax (6.2 percentage points) to individually owned, privately invested accounts. Those choosing to do so would agree to forgo all future accrual of retirement benefits under traditional Social Security. The remaining 6.2 percentage points of payroll taxes would be used to pay transition costs and to fund disability and survivors' benefits. Once transition costs were fully paid, this portion of the payroll tax would be reduced to the level necessary to pay survivors' and disability benefits.

Although they would forgo future benefits under traditional Social Security, workers who chose the individual account option would receive a bond in recognition of their past contributions to Social Security. That bond would be a zero-coupon bond calculated to provide a benefit based on accrued benefits under the current Social Security system as of the date that the individual chose an individual account.

The bonds would be fully tradable on secondary markets, but all proceeds would have to be fully redeposited in the worker's individual account until the worker became eligible to make withdrawals.

The recognition bonds may be valued at something less than the full present value of accrued benefits because we believe that workers will attach a value to receiving a tangible asset, making them willing to accept a discount in the face value of the bond. . . .

Finally, the federal government provides a safety net insuring that no worker's retirement income falls below 120 percent of the poverty level. Workers whose accumulations under the private investment option fall below the amount required to purchase an annuity at that level receive a supplement sufficient to enable them to purchase such an annuity. This safety net is funded from general revenues rather than from the Social Security payroll tax. . . .

Paying for the Transition

Although moving to a system of individual accounts will save money in the long run, there will almost certainly be a short-term requirement for additional revenues. That is because, to the degree that workers choose the individual account option, payroll tax revenues are redirected from the payment of current benefits to personal accounts. But because most of the workers who choose accounts are likely to be young, it will be many years before the accounts result in significant savings to the traditional system.

Where, then, will the transitional financing come from? Ultimately, this is a decision for Congress, which will have to weigh the utility of various financing mechanisms, including debt, taxes, and reductions in current government spending.

However, three sources are worth special note. First, the portion of taxes on Social Security benefits currently used to fund Medicare should be redirected back to Social Security. That would provide an estimated $8.3 billion annually in additional revenue.

Second, the Cato Institute has identified more than $87 billion annually in corporate welfare, roughly defined as "any government spending program that provides payments or unique benefits and advantages for specific companies or industries.". . .

Third, to the degree that they actually represent an increase in national savings, contributions to individual accounts may, in themselves, prove to be a source of additional revenue for the federal government, revenue that could be used to help finance the transition.

It works in this way: The return on investment received by individuals is not the actual return earned by a given investment. A portion of the returns is actually taxed away through corporate taxes before returns are realized at the level of the individual investor. Therefore, a portion of the funds diverted to individual accounts is actually "recaptured" and available to help fund the transition. . . .

After using the three financing sources discussed above, we believe that any remaining transition could be financed through reductions in other wasteful government spending. . . .

We recognize that it may be necessary to issue some new debt to cover short-term year-to-year cash shortfalls. . . . At the same time, we should understand that this would not really be new debt; it would simply be making explicit an already existing implicit debt.

It is also important to remember that the financing of the transition is a one-time event that actually serves to reduce the government's future liabilities. The transition moves the government's need for additional revenue forward in time, but—depending on the transition's ultimate design—it does not necessarily increase the amount of spending necessary. In fact, it will likely reduce the total cost of Social Security. In effect, it is a case of pay a little now or pay a lot later. . . .

Why 6.2 Percent Accounts?

. . . Of course, one might ask, if big accounts are better than small, then why not allow workers to privately invest the full 12.4 percent payroll tax, or at least the roughly 10 percentage points used for OASI benefits? . . .

. . . [W]e believe that 6.2 percent accounts are a very easy concept to explain to the average worker. The worker can privately invest his half of the 12.4 percent payroll tax, while the employer's half is used to finance the transition (and fund survivors' and disability benefits). Of course we recognize that, from an economic point of view, there is no difference between the employer and the employee share of the tax. The employee ultimately bears the full cost, but most workers make the distinction in their own minds. A 6.2 percent account proposal, then, becomes clear, concise, and easy to understand in an age of eight-second sound bites. . . .

Source: Michael Tanner, "The 6.2 Percent Solution: A Plan for Reforming Social Security," Cato Institute, February 17, 2004, available on the Cato Institute Web site: www.socialsecurity.org/pubs/ssps/ssp32.pdf (accessed February 13, 2007). Used by permission.

Document 9.18
Excerpts on Social Security from the 2004 Presidential Debates, October 13, 2004

The 2004 presidential campaign witnessed a return of Social Security to the center of federal political debates. President Bush pushed this issue onto the agenda during the last weeks of the presidential campaign. The president continued to advocate his personal accounts idea for young workers, while the Democratic candidate, Sen. John Kerry (D-Mass.), depicted the president's plan as a threat to the program's survival.

Moderator BOB SCHIEFFER: Mr. President, the next question is to you. We all know that Social Security is running out of money, and it has to be fixed. You have proposed to fix it by letting people put some of the money collected to pay benefits into private savings accounts. But the critics are saying that's going to mean finding $1 trillion over the next 10 years to continue paying benefits as those accounts are being set up.

So where do you get the money? Are you going to have to increase the deficit by that much over 10 years?

BUSH: First, let me make sure that every senior listening today understands that when we're talking about reforming Social Security, that they'll still get their checks.

I remember the 2000 campaign, people said if George W. gets elected, your check will be taken away. Well, people got their checks, and they'll continue to get their checks.

There is a problem for our youngsters, a real problem. And if we don't act today, the problem will be valued in the trillions. And so I think we need to think differently. We'll honor our commitment to our seniors. But for our children and our grandchildren, we need to have a different strategy.

And recognizing that, I called together a group of our fellow citizens to study the issue. It was a committee chaired by the late Senator Daniel Patrick Moynihan of New York, a Democrat. And they came up with a variety of ideas for people to look at.

I believe that younger workers ought to be allowed to take some of their own money and put it in a personal savings account, because I understand that they need to get better rates of return than the rates of return being given in the current Social Security trust.

And the compounding rate of interest effect will make it more likely that the Social Security system is solvent for our children and our grandchildren. I will work with Republicans and Democrats. It'll be a vital issue in my second term. It is an issue that I am willing to take on, and so I'll bring Republicans and Democrats together.

And we're of course going to have to consider the costs. But I want to warn my fellow citizens: The cost of doing nothing, the cost of saying the current system is OK, far exceeds the costs of trying to make sure we save the system for our children.

SCHIEFFER: Senator Kerry?

KERRY: You just heard the president say that young people ought to be able to take money out of Social Security and put it in their own accounts.

Now, my fellow Americans, that's an invitation to disaster.

The CBO said very clearly that if you were to adopt the president's plan, there would be a $2 trillion hole in Social Security, because today's workers pay in to the system for today's retirees. And the CBO said—that's the Congressional Budget Office; it's bipartisan—they said that there would have to be a cut in benefits of 25 percent to 40 percent.

Now, the president has never explained to America, ever, hasn't done it tonight, where does the transitional money, that $2 trillion, come from?

He's already got $3 trillion, according to the *Washington Post,* of expenses that he's put on the line from his convention and the promises of this campaign, none of which are paid for. Not one of them are paid for.

The fact is that the president is driving the largest deficits in American history. He's broken the pay-as-you-go rules.

I have a record of fighting for fiscal responsibility. In 1985, I was one of the first Democrats—broke with my party. We balanced the budget in the '90s. We paid down the debt for two years.

And that's what we're going to do. We're going to protect Social Security. I will not privatize it. I will not cut the benefits. And we're going to be fiscally responsible. And we will take care of Social Security.

SCHIEFFER: Let me just stay on Social Security with a new question for Senator Kerry, because, Senator Kerry, you have just said you will not cut benefits.

Alan Greenspan, the chairman of the Federal Reserve, says there's no way that Social Security can pay retirees what we have promised them unless we recalibrate.

What he's suggesting, we're going to cut benefits or we're going to have to raise the retirement age. We may have to take some other reform. But if you've just said, you've promised no changes, does that mean you're just going to leave this as a problem, another problem for our children to solve?

KERRY: Not at all. Absolutely not, Bob. This is the same thing we heard—remember, I appeared on "Meet the Press" with Tim Russert in 1990–something. We heard the same thing. We fixed it.

In fact, we put together a $5.6 trillion surplus in the '90s that was for the purpose of saving Social Security. If you take the tax cut that the president of the United States has given—President Bush gave to Americans in the top 1 percent of America—just that tax cut that went to the top 1 percent of America would have saved Social Security until the year 2075.

The president decided to give it to the wealthiest Americans in a tax cut. Now, Alan Greenspan, who I think has done a terrific job in monetary policy, supports the president's tax cut. I don't. I support it for the middle class, not that part of it that goes to people earning more than $200,000 a year.

And when I roll it back and we invest in the things that I have talked about to move our economy, we're going to grow sufficiently, it would begin to cut the deficit in half, and we get back to where we were at the end of the 1990s when we balanced the budget and paid down the debt of this country.

Now, we can do that.

Now, if later on after a period of time we find that Social Security is in trouble, we'll pull together the top experts of the country. We'll do exactly what we did in the 1990s. And we'll make whatever adjustment is necessary.

But the first and most important thing is to start creating jobs in America. The jobs the president is creating pay $9,000 less than the jobs that we're losing. And this is the first president in 72 years to preside over an economy in America that has lost jobs, 1.6 million jobs.

Eleven other presidents—six Democrats and five Republicans—had wars, had recessions, had great difficulties; none of them lost jobs the way this president has.

I have a plan to put America back to work. And if we're fiscally responsible and put America back to work, we're going to fix Social Security.

SCHIEFFER: Mr. President?

BUSH: He forgot to tell you he voted to tax Social Security benefits more than one time. I didn't hear any plan to fix Social Security. I heard more of the same.

Source: Commission on Presidential Debates, "The Third Bush-Kerry Presidential Debate," debate transcript, October 13, 2004. Available at: www.debates.org/pages/trans2004d.html (accessed September 21, 2006).

Document 9.19
President George W. Bush's Social Security Reform Proposal in the 2005 State of the Union Address, February 2, 2005

After his reelection, President Bush launched a major campaign for his Social Security reform proposal. The year 2005 was to be decisive in the debate over the president's plan, and the campaign was symbolically launched in this State of the Union message.

. . . One of America's most important institutions—a symbol of the trust between generations—is also in need of wise and effective reform. Social Security was a great moral success of the 20th century, and we must honor its great purposes in this new century. The system, however, on its current path, is headed toward bankruptcy. And so we must join together to strengthen and save Social Security.

Today, more than 45 million Americans receive Social Security benefits, and millions more are nearing retirement—and for them the system is sound and fiscally strong. I have a message for every American who is 55 or older: Do not let anyone mislead you; for you, the Social Security system will not change in any way. For younger workers, the Social Security system has serious problems that will grow worse with time. Social Security was created decades ago, for a very different era. In those days, people did not live as long. Benefits were much lower than they are today. And a half-century ago, about sixteen workers paid into the system for each person drawing benefits.

Our society has changed in ways the founders of Social Security could not have foreseen. In today's world, people are living longer and, therefore, drawing benefits longer. And those benefits are scheduled to rise dramatically over the next few decades. And instead of sixteen workers paying in for every beneficiary, right now it's only about three workers. And over the next few decades that number will fall to just two workers per beneficiary. With each passing year, fewer workers are paying ever-higher benefits to an ever-larger number of retirees.

So here is the result: Thirteen years from now, in 2018, Social Security will be paying out more than it takes in. And every year afterward will bring a new shortfall, bigger than the year before. For example, in the year 2027, the government will somehow have to come up with an extra $200 billion to keep the system afloat—and by 2033, the annual shortfall would be more than $300 billion. By the year 2042, the entire system would be exhausted and bankrupt. If steps are not taken to avert that outcome, the only solutions would be dramatically higher taxes, massive new borrowing, or sudden and severe cuts in Social Security benefits or other government programs.

I recognize that 2018 and 2042 may seem a long way off. But those dates are not so distant, as any parent will tell you. If you have a five-year-old, you're already concerned about how you'll pay for college tuition 13 years down the road. If you've got children in their 20s, as some of us do, the idea of Social Security collapsing before they retire does not seem like a small matter. And it should not be a small matter to the United States Congress. You and I share a responsibility. We must pass reforms that solve the financial problems of Social Security once and for all.

Fixing Social Security permanently will require an open, candid review of the options. Some have suggested limiting benefits for wealthy retirees. Former Congressman Tim Penny has raised the possibility of indexing benefits to prices rather than wages. During the 1990s, my predecessor, President Clinton, spoke of increasing the retirement age. Former Senator John Breaux suggested discouraging early collection of Social Security benefits. The late Senator Daniel Patrick Moynihan recommended changing the way benefits are calculated. All these ideas are on the table.

I know that none of these reforms would be easy. But we have to move ahead with courage and honesty, because our children's retirement security is more important than partisan politics. I will work with members of Congress to find the most effective combination of reforms. I will listen to anyone who has a good idea to offer. We must, however, be guided by some basic principles. We must make Social Security permanently sound, not leave that task for another day. We must not jeopardize our economic strength by increasing payroll taxes. We must ensure that lower-income Americans get the help they need to have dignity and peace of mind in their retirement. We must guarantee there is no change for those now retired or nearing retirement. And we must take care that any changes in the system are gradual, so younger workers have years to prepare and plan for their future.

As we fix Social Security, we also have the responsibility to make the system a better deal for younger workers. And the best way to reach that goal is through voluntary personal retirement accounts. Here is how the idea works. Right now, a set portion of the money you earn is taken out of your paycheck to pay for the Social Security benefits of today's retirees. If you're a younger worker, I believe you should be able to set aside part of that money in your own retirement account, so you can build a nest egg for your own future.

Here's why the personal accounts are a better deal. Your money will grow, over time, at a greater rate than anything the current system can deliver—and your account will provide money for retirement over and above the check you will receive from Social Security. In addition, you'll be able to pass along the money that accumulates in your personal account, if you wish, to your children and—or grandchildren. And best of all, the money in the account is yours, and the government can never take it away.

The goal here is greater security in retirement, so we will set careful guidelines for personal accounts. We'll make sure the money can only go into a conservative mix of bonds and stock funds. We'll make sure that your earnings are not eaten up by hidden Wall Street fees. We'll make sure there are good options to protect your investments from sudden market swings on the eve of your retirement. We'll make sure a personal account cannot be emptied out all at once, but rather paid out over time, as an addition to traditional Social Security benefits. And we'll make sure this plan is fiscally responsible, by starting personal retirement accounts gradually, and raising the yearly limits on contributions over time, eventually permitting all workers to set aside four percentage points of their payroll taxes in their accounts.

Personal retirement accounts should be familiar to federal employees, because you already have something similar, called the Thrift Savings Plan, which lets workers deposit a portion of their paychecks into any of five different broadly-based investment funds. It's time to extend the same security, and choice, and ownership to young Americans. . . .

Source: George W. Bush, *State of the Union Address,* February 2, 2005. Available at: www.whitehouse .gov/news/releases/2005/02/20050202-11.html (accessed September 21, 2006).

Document 9.20
NCPSSM on Myths and Reality about Social Security Privatization, March 2005

Some advocacy groups strongly opposed President Bush's plan for private accounts. This document, from the National Committee to Preserve Social Security and Medicare (NCPSSM), sought to argue the case against Social Security privatization.

For 70 years the Social Security program has been protecting Americans against the loss of income due to retirement, death or disability. . . .

Social Security is an enormously successful program which is essential to the retirement security of the vast majority of Americans. Social Security is the single largest source of retirement income. Two-thirds of Social Security beneficiaries receive over half their income from Social Security. For nearly 20 percent of retirees, Social Security is their only source of income. Without Social Security, nearly half of the elderly would fall into poverty. Social Security provides a sound, basic income that lasts as long as you live.

Despite Social Security's continuing successes, the program is under attack by those who would like to privatize it. President Bush has said that he wishes to divert money away from Social Security into private investment accounts. Young workers are intrigued by the idea of diverting their payroll taxes into Wall Street accounts. Proponents of privatization promise ownership of accounts and big investment returns.

They argue that Social Security is in a deep and immediate financial crisis that cannot be resolved without dismantling Social Security and converting it into a system of market-based individual investment. To support their arguments, proponents of privatization have used misleading arguments about the nature of Social Security, the crisis facing it, and the value of converting Social Security to private investment accounts. Here are some of the myths and realities surrounding the Social Security debate.

Myths and Realities

Myth 1: Privatization is a plan to save Social Security.

Reality: Privatization isn't a plan to save Social Security. It is a plan to dismantle Social Security. Private accounts do nothing to address Social Security solvency. In fact, because private accounts are financed by taking money out of Social Security, privatization actually increases Social Security's funding gap and moves forward the date of its insolvency from 2040 to 2030. The plan proposed by President Bush, which would divert two-thirds of the current employee-paid Social Security tax into private accounts, would cause an almost immediate cash-flow problem for Social Security.

Myth 2: Returns from private accounts will make up for the cuts in Social Security benefits.

Reality: Privatization results in huge cuts in Social Security benefits with no guarantee that private investment can replace lost benefits. The privatization plan favored by President Bush, known as the "price-indexing" plan, would reduce guaranteed Social Security benefits over time by nearly 50 percent, *even for those people who do not choose a private account.* For those who opt for a private account, benefits would be reduced even further. Under the President's plan, an individual's already-reduced Social Security benefit would be cut by one dollar for every dollar that he or she has saved in the private account up to a limit specified in law. The Center on Budget and Policy Priorities has calculated that an average-earning individual, who chooses to keep his or her private account assets in a safe investment, earning the same return as U.S. Treasury Securities, will find that his or her Social Security benefit has been reduced to nearly zero. As a consequence, that individual will have almost none of the special protections afforded by traditional benefits. Moreover, his or her total income, consisting almost entirely of proceeds from the private account, would be 50 percent below currently-scheduled Social Security benefits.

Myth 3: Private account assets can be passed along to one's heirs.

Reality: Privatization leaves little to be passed on to one's heirs. The President's plan would force account holders, upon retirement, to use the assets in their private accounts to purchase an annuity sufficient to raise their total remaining Social Security benefits and monthly annuity payments to a poverty level income. The remaining assets in the account could then be used during retirement to make up for the plan's huge cuts in Social Security benefits. Only the excess after required annuitization and after expenses of retirement would be available to pass on to one's heirs. This is likely to amount to very little.

Myth 4: Private accounts are voluntary.

Reality: Private accounts may be voluntary, but the cuts are not. Even for those people who choose not to participate in a private account, Social Security benefits would be cut nearly in half. Under the plan favored by the President, known as the "price-indexing" plan, cuts in benefits would be considerably larger than necessary to solve Social Security's financing problem. Those cuts would effectively transfer money from those who opt out of accounts to those who opt in, forcing workers who decide against exposing themselves to the risks of Wall Street to subsidize those who are more willing to gamble with their retirement.

Myth 5: Privatization will exempt retirees and near retirees.

Reality: Retirees and near retirees should not count on being exempt. Because privatization diverts two-thirds of the employee-paid Social Security tax away from Social Security and into private accounts, Social Security's financial status is worsened and benefits for every retiree are threatened. In order to continue to pay benefits to retirees, privatization plans must borrow trillions of dollars over several decades from the general fund of the Treasury, causing an already huge federal deficit to balloon. This will increase the debt burden on all Americans, forcing policy makers to consider cuts in all federal programs, including Social Security.

Myth 6: Younger workers will receive a higher rate of return under a privatized system.

Reality: Younger workers will receive a lower rate of return under privatization than they will under Social Security. That is because younger workers will have to pay twice—once to fund the benefits of current retirees under Social Security's pay-as-you go system and a second time to fund their own individual accounts. The Congressional Budget Office concluded in a recent study that the costs of the transition to a privatized, prefunded system would reduce the rate of return on today's young people, the transitional generation, to a level lower than the rate of return on Social Security.

Myth 7: Private accounts will cost only about $750 billion in the first 10 years.

Reality: Private accounts will increase the national debt by nearly $5 trillion in the first 20 years after full implementation, and costs will continue to grow thereafter. The 10-year costs of the President's private accounts are misleading because those accounts are not fully phased in until 2011. According to the Center on Budget and Policy Priorities, private accounts will increase the national debt by nearly $5 trillion in the first 20 years after full implementation. In about 50 years, costs will reach nearly 30 percent of GDP and will remain at that level for the full 75-year projection period.

Myth 8: The cost of fixing Social Security is over $11 trillion.

Reality: According to the Social Security actuaries, the 75-year cost of fixing Social Security is estimated to be $4.6 trillion (in present value). Some proponents of privatization set the cost of financing Social Security at $13.4 trillion. However, this figure is the liability of the system into infinity. It includes the costs of not just the baby boom generation, but everyone alive today and people not yet born.

The Realities about Social Security's Solvency

Social Security is a successful program that will be able to pay benefits for decades to come. This year Social Security has an accumulated surplus of over $1.9 trillion. By 2015, that surplus will be over $3.9 trillion or more than four times the amount needed to pay benefits in that year. While payments from Social Security will begin to exceed Social Security tax revenues in about 2017, Social Security will have sufficient reserves to pay benefits until 2040. Even after 2040, Social Security will have enough money to pay nearly 74 percent of the benefits owed, according to the Social Security actuaries.

The Congressional Budget Office has concluded that Social Security will be solvent even longer, through 2052, and will be able to pay nearly 80 percent of benefits thereafter. Moreover, Social Security money is held in the safest investment available—U.S. government securities. Those securities are legal obligations of the U.S. to pay principal and interest to the holder of the bonds. The securities have the same status as U.S. government bonds held by any other investor, including individual Americans and pension funds, and the Social Security Trust Fund has a legal obligation to pay full benefits as long as it has the funds to do so.

Conclusion

Many myths and misconceptions have contributed to the belief that Social Security is in imminent danger and that Social Security privatization is the answer. Nothing could be further from the truth. The reality is that Social Security will continue to provide millions of retirees a sound, stable retirement. It may require some modest adjustments over a period of time, but it does not face an insurmountable crisis requiring major structural changes. Privatization, on the other hand, will unravel Social Security's important insurance protections, force huge cuts in benefits, increase risks to retirees, and cost trillions of dollars. Social Security has been providing Americans a secure retirement for nearly three quarters of a century. With sensible action it can continue to provide that security for decades to come.

Source: National Committee to Preserve Social Security and Medicare, "Myths and Reality about Social Security Privatization," March 2005. Available at NCPSSM Web site: www.ncpssm.org/news/archive/myths/ (accessed September 21, 2006). Used by permission.

Document 9.21
Representative Wexler's Plan, May 16, 2005

During the height of the 2005 debates, Rep. Robert Wexler (D-Fla.) introduced a Social Security reform plan that rejected both private accounts and benefit cuts. Wexler's plan would address solvency by eliminating the cap on the taxable wage base and reducing the payroll tax rate from 12.4% to 6% on wages over $90,000 per year.

(This document makes reference to a trust fund exhaustion date of 2052. This is not a date from the annual trustees reports, but is an estimate performed by the Congressional Budget Office, which used slightly more optimistic economic assumptions than those used by the Social Security actuaries, which resulted in a longer period of program solvency.)

President Bush has been traveling all over the country to sell his plan to privatize Social Security using the term "crisis." With all due respect to the President, there is no Social Security crisis. If we do absolutely nothing—if Congress goes home and doesn't come back until the year 2052. . . . Social Security will continue to pay full benefits.

When the Greenspan Commission fixed Social Security in 1983 it planned for the aging of the baby boomers by building a surplus. Social Security now holds 1.7 trillion dollars in US Treasury bonds that earn interest. That is why Social Security is able to pay full benefits for 40 plus years. And even then, if we do nothing, Social Security would pay 80% of scheduled benefits. To put this "supposed crisis" in perspective, let's remember back to the Greenspan Commission in 1983. Does anyone remember how far off insolvency was for Social Security then? 3 months—not 40 years. That was a crisis. . . .

Which brings me to President Bush's ideas. He proposes creating private accounts—allowing workers to divert one third of payroll taxes into a personal account. By gutting one third of Social Security's revenue, he actually moves up the insolvency by more than 20 years. And worse, the accounts do nothing to shore up Social Security. They do, however, cost almost 5 trillion dollars in the first 20 years.

The President also suggests we change the benefit formula to make up for the shortfall and the money taken out of Social Security for his personal accounts.

Translation: A huge cut in benefits for 70 percent of Social Security beneficiaries, even those not opting for personal accounts.

The President's plan would—for the first time—means test social security benefits. For example: A worker who earned $37,000 per year would receive a 28 percent benefit cut, a worker who earned $58,000 per year would receive a 42 percent cut and someone who earned $90,000 per year would lose almost half of his or her benefits. Only low-income workers who earned $20,000 or less per year would be exempt from benefit cuts. By means testing Social Security, President Bush effectively ensures the gradual loss of support among higher and middle-income Americans and begins the process of dismantling the Social Security System by turning it into a welfare program.

Under President Bush's proposal, benefits for over two-thirds of Social Security beneficiaries would actually be smaller in 2052 than if we do absolutely nothing and the system is only able to pay 80% of current benefits.

This is a classic example of the cure being worse than the disease.

Now with all that said, changes do need to be made to fix the long term solvency of Social Security. And doing it right will take political courage and lots of support from people like you in this room today. That's because there are only two real options that close the Social Security shortfall without gimmicks or huge amounts of borrowing: Cut benefits or raise revenue.

I refuse to support any plan that cuts benefits. Social Security is an irreplaceable part of America's retirement system and the most successful government program in history. It has saved generations of seniors from falling below the poverty line. And now with medical and prescription drug costs soaring much faster than the growth of Social Security COLAs, I cannot imagine a majority of seniors living on anything less.

That leaves revenue. . . .

I vehemently disagree with President Bush on creating private accounts and cutting benefits but I do agree with him that the cap should be raised. And that is why I am pleased to announce here today that I am filing legislation this week that lifts the earnings cap on Social Security. My plan, the Social Security Forever Act of 2005, will lift the cap on taxable earnings requiring workers to pay a three percent payroll tax on wages above $90,000. This will be matched by the employer. . . .

Using the non-partisan Congressional Budget Office projections, my plan will close the entire funding gap in Social Security. And here is the good part:

No Benefit cuts.
No raising of the retirement age.
No borrowing.
No Privatization.
No market risk.
And no gimmicks.

This idea is not revolutionary. It is not even original. For years, the AARP has supported lifting the cap on taxable wages. . . .

But now Democrats must move beyond criticizing the President's plan and start offering alternatives that are true to our Democratic values.

The Democrat Party gave birth to the Social Security program and it is now time we seize the moment and provide a plan that guarantees hard working Americans 100% of their promised benefits.

Not all of my Democratic colleagues agree this is the right thing to do—and their opinions have my respect. . . .

The President has been challenging Democrats to offer a plan for months. Today, that challenge is answered. Mr. President: Social Security can be fixed and strengthened without privatizing or destroying the foundation of the system. . . .

Source: Representative Wexler's Web site: http://wexler.house.gov/pages.php?ID=8 (accessed February 11, 2007).

Document 9.22
Senator Bennett's Social Security Plan, June 2005

In June 2005 Republican senator Robert F. Bennett of Utah introduced a comprehensive Social Security reform proposal that attempted to separate the solvency issue from the private accounts issue by placing them in separate pieces of legislation. His hope was that Congress might be able to enact his solvency proposals even if it did not immediately adopt his private accounts proposal.

This document is a press release Senator Bennett's office published in advance of the introduction of his bill.

. . . The president exhibited tremendous leadership in calling upon Congress to address these important issues. Unfortunately, the debate has become too polarized by centering almost exclusively on the merits of the president's proposal to allow workers to create and contribute to Personal Accounts with a portion of their Social Security taxes.

Personal Accounts alone cannot fix Social Security's solvency problem. At the same time, addressing the long-term retirement security needs of future retirees cannot be met without Personal Accounts and stronger incentives to increase personal savings.

The current lack of consensus in Congress concerning Personal Accounts should not be allowed to stand in the way of essential legislation to address Social Security's chronic solvency problem, which will only become more acute and intractable in the absence of timely action. Therefore, in an attempt to move the political process forward to start dealing today with what will be unavoidable tomorrow, Senator Bennett has announced that he will be introducing two separate pieces of legislation. He is seeking both Democratic and Republican senators to join him in all or part of this effort.

Specifically, Senator Bennett will introduce one bill that addresses only the solvency problem and does not increase the payroll tax rate or expand the base of earnings subject to Social Security taxes. The senator will also introduce a second bill to enhance the income security of future retirees by allowing the creation of "Carve In" Personal Accounts and revising existing pension laws to encourage higher levels of personal retirement savings in employer-sponsored pension plans.

The following provides a brief summary of the two separate pieces of legislation that Senator Bennett plans to introduce. . . .

Solvency Legislation

1. *Progressive Indexing*—In 2012, begin the phase in of "progressive indexing" to determine initial retirement benefits under Social Security for new retirees. Under current law, retirement benefits are calculated under a "wage indexing" formula that will help propel benefits to levels significantly higher than the payroll tax revenue available to pay for them. The formula uses the average rate of growth of wages within the economy, rather than changes in the cost of living, to adjust (or "index") the past earnings of a worker that are used to determine their initial benefit level at retirement. Because average wages generally grow faster than prices over time, the current benefit formula essentially guarantees that future retirement benefit levels will grow faster in "real" dollar value from generation to generation.

Under Bennett's proposal, the individuals in the lowest 30 percent of all wage earners retiring in a given year would continue to have their past wages, and resulting benefit levels, indexed according to wage growth, while those at the top of the wage distribution would have their past wages indexed for changes in prices. Those falling in between would have their past wages indexed based upon a "progressive blend" of wage and price changes. In short, future benefit levels for workers who earned higher wages over their working career would not rise as much as benefit levels for workers with lower lifetime earnings, but those workers most dependent on social security for retirement income would be protected from such changes.

2. *Longevity Indexing and Acceleration of Present Law Normal Retirement Age Changes*— Under present law, the retirement age is scheduled to increase incrementally to age 67 beginning in 2022 (the normal retirement age gradually increases for workers born in 1960 and later years, by two months each year starting in 2022 until it reaches age 67 in 2027). Under Senator Bennett's proposal, the move from age 66 to age 67 would begin in 2012. The Normal Retirement Age or NRA would be increased by two months each year until the NRA reached age 67 in 2017. After that date, initial benefits for future retirees would be periodically adjusted by the Social Security Administration to account for changes in the expected average lifetimes of future retirees.

3. *Protection of Disabled Workers*—This proposal would exempt those receiving disability benefits under the Social Security system from the application of changes in the benefit formulas while they are disabled. Upon reaching retirement age, their benefits are no longer paid by the Disability Insurance Trust Fund and they become eligible for retiree benefits financed by the Old Age and Survivor Trust Fund. At that point, their retirement benefits would be calculated using a blend of the two formulas that would account for the relative periods of time when they were disabled and when they were able to engage in covered employment.

Carve In Accounts and Enhanced Retirement Savings Opportunity

1. "Carve In" Personal Accounts—Beginning four years following enactment, workers would have the opportunity to create voluntary "carve in" personal accounts. Under this proposal, workers who elected to contribute an additional 2% of their wages into a TSP [Thrift Savings Plan] style personal account would also be allowed to have Social Security tax contributions equal to 2% of their covered wages moved into that account as well. Investment options would be similar to those offered Members of Congress and federal employees in their TSP plan. For workers choosing carve-in accounts, their future retirement benefits from the core Social Security program would be adjusted to reflect the lower level of tax contributions of these workers allocated to the traditional Social Security retirement fund. . . .

Senator Bennett believes that the enactment of both legislative proposals will restore the solvency of the Social Security system and provide for increased retirement income for America's workers. It will do so in a fair and equitable manner and without increasing the tax burden on working Americans. The inability to reach a comprehensive agreement incorporating the elements of both proposals should not be allowed to stand in the way of beginning meaningful progress through passage of solvency legislation.

Source: Senator Bob Bennett's Web site: http://bennett.senate.gov/issues/topissues2.html#social security (accessed February 11, 2007).

Document 9.23
President George W. Bush on Strengthening Social Security, June 8, 2005
During the late spring of 2005, President Bush pursued his efforts to convince Americans that in order to "save" Social Security, it was urgent to restructure it. One aspect of the campaign was that the president participated in a series of town-hall type meetings around the country, in very much the same manner as President Clinton had in his 1998 "year of education" initiative. President Bush's campaign was called the "60 stops in 60 days" campaign, and it went on throughout much of 2005. He was especially active in this way during February, March, and April. He also gave more traditional political speeches on the issue. This document—from a June 2005 speech in Washington, D.C., before a meeting of a trade association—illustrates the arguments used by the president during the active phase of his national campaign.

(In this speech the president advocates a shift to what he called "progressive indexing" of initial benefit amounts. Recall from Chapter 7 that initial benefits are inflated by the increase in wage levels and subsequent benefits are inflated by the rise in prices. Because wages tend to rise

about 2 percent more than prices, a shift in the basis of the initial benefit indexation from wages to prices would reduce those initial benefits, and hence reduce the cost of the program. "Progressive indexing" means making the shift on a sliding scale, dependent upon the beneficiary's income level.)

. . . There's one other issue I want to talk about, that's Social Security. First, Social Security worked great for a lot of folks for a long period of time. My predecessor, Franklin D. Roosevelt, did a smart thing in setting up the Social Security system. Social Security provided a safety net for a lot of seniors, and it was an important safety net. . . . I'm traveling a lot talking about Social Security. I'm meeting people that say, I'm dependent upon my Social Security check. I'm confident you know folks that say, I need my check; it's a part of my life.

And so the system has worked fine for a lot of folks. As a matter of fact, it's going to work fine for everybody born prior to 1950. So if you're a senior getting your Social Security check out there, you have nothing to worry about, the system is solvent for you. You're in good shape—I don't care what the politicians say, I don't care what the ads say, the pamphlets say. Don't let them scare you; you're going to get your check. And that's important for people to understand.

But if you're a younger citizen, you'd better be paying attention to this issue. And here's the reason why: There's a lot of people like me—we're called the baby boomers—who are getting ready to retire. . . .

Do you realize that there's about 40 million Americans retired today; by the time the baby boomer generation fully retires, there will be 72 million Americans, more or less. There is a lot of us. . . . And a lot of politicians have run in prior years, and said, vote for me, I'll increase the benefits for a generation coming up. And you know what? They did. And so, therefore, my generation, our generation, which will be living longer—and more of us—have been promised greater benefits, which is okay until you realize this aspect of the problem: fewer people are now paying into the system.

In 1950, there were about 15 workers per every retiree. In other words, the load was pretty well spread across a group of people paying payroll taxes. Today, there's 3.3 workers per retiree. Soon there's going to be two workers per retiree, trying to take care of a generation which is going to be living longer with greater benefits and a lot of us. So that's the problem. That's the math. That's the beginning of your understanding—or the country's understanding of why we have a problem.

Let me put it in terms of dollars for you. In 2017, the system goes into the red. In other words, more benefits going out than payroll taxes coming in. In about 2027, it's about $200 billion short. In other words, every year from 2017, the red—the deficit—gets larger and larger and larger. In 2027, it's $200 billion. In the 2030's, it's about $300 billion. In 2041, the system is bust.

Now, think about that for a minute. We're fine, by the way, those of us born before 1950. All seniors are getting their check. You're in good shape. But you need to start asking people who have been elected to office what we intend to do about this problem for your children and grandchildren, because we're asking young Americans to come up in a system and pay a pretty sizeable payroll tax into a system where those of us in Washington who look at the facts understand it's going broke. That doesn't seem to make sense to me. That doesn't seem like good stewardship of the people's money, nor does it seem like good leadership.

See, my job as the President of the United States is confront a problem if I see one, and not pass it on to future Presidents and future Congresses.

I see a problem. I've just defined it to you. And it's clear. This is a—these are solid numbers that I'm talking about. You can't—people in Washington can't say baby boomers aren't getting ready to retire and there's a lot of us who have been promised more benefits and we're living longer. That's a fact. And it's a fact that fewer people are paying into the system. And it's a fact this system is going bankrupt. I'm—and so I'm going to keep talking about it. . . .

Here are some principles by which I am conducting discussions. One, the reform system must say to future generations you'll get benefits equal to or greater than the current generation. I think that's a wise principle to be able to say to somebody putting money into the system—remember, you've got these youngsters now putting money into the system to pay for us, and they're wondering where the system is going to be for them. And the answer is a reform system for people coming up ought to be—you ought to get benefits equal or greater than the current benefit structure.

Secondly, I think this principle is very important. And that is if you've worked all your life, you've worked hard at a job, and you've contributed into Social Security, you shouldn't retire into poverty. I mean, the safety net is more than just providing a check. The safety net is to provide, you know, peace of mind in retirement. So I like the idea of sending this principle to Congress. You can work hard, but you're not going to retire into poverty.

And there's a way to make the system do that, and here it is—it's called progressive indexing, an idea that I embraced in a press conference the other day, in the East Room of the White House. . . . [R]ight now, benefits increase . . . at the rate of wage increases, not price increases. Wages go up faster than prices. And so the benefits are going up faster than the cost of living.

And so what I think Congress ought to consider doing is saying that for the poorest of Americans, your benefits, future benefits will go up based upon wage increases, and for the wealthier of Americans, your benefits go up based upon price increases. . . . Again, we're talking about a younger generation of Americans coming. Those of us born in 1950—prior to 1950, nothing changes. It's really important for Americans to understand that. It's for the new generation coming up, as we calculate a reformed plan that permanently fixes Social Security.

One idea is to say, for the poor Americans, your benefits—calculated benefits over time go up with the rate of wage increases. For wealthy Americans, it goes up at the rate of inflation, cost of living. And in between, there's a scale. Now, that's a system where we can say, poor Americans won't retire into poverty. But interestingly enough, if that were to be passed by Congress that alone would permanently fix a majority, a significant portion, of the Social Security problem. Isn't that interesting? Just that alone, just that change alone would go a long way, a significant way for doing our duty to permanently fix the Social Security problem for a younger generation of Americans. . . .

I want to talk about another idea that Congress needs to seriously consider. As we permanently fix the system, we ought to make the system a better deal for younger workers, as well. You see, here's the issue with—another issue with Social Security, it's called a pay-as-you-go system. You pay your payroll tax and we go ahead and spend it. You see, some people think that the Social Security system is a system where you pay in your Social Security tax and we hold it for you, and then when you retire, we give it back to you. That's not the way it works.

The way it works is this: you pay your payroll tax, we pay out to current retirees, and then we spend your money on other government programs. That's the way it works. And that's been going on for quite awhile. I happen to believe there's a better way to do this than to say there's a Social Security system where we're guarding your money and not spending it on other programs.

And here it is: I think the best way to make sure that people have got real assets in the Social Security system, not just IOUs in a file cabinet, is to let younger workers take some of their own money, if they so choose, a voluntary program, and set up a personal savings account. In other words, the proposal I made to Congress says you can take a third of your payroll tax and set it aside as part of your Social Security retirement system.

And here's why I believe that it makes a lot of sense. First, I like the idea of people owning their own assets in America; I like the idea of people having ownership in something. And I also understand the power of compound interest. In other words, when you set aside money, it grows, it compounds over time. That's how money works. Right now, in the Social Security system, we get about 1.8 percent on your money for you, which is really low. A conservative mix of bonds and stocks is expected to pay about 4.6 percent annually over time. It's been the historical average. . . .

It seems like to me that that makes sense to let younger workers take advantage of the compound rate of interest. It makes sense to give people a better rate of return on their own money. After all, when we're talking about payroll taxes, we're not talking about the government's money. That's your money. It's the money that you put into the Treasury.

. . . This isn't . . . the government . . . saying, you must do this. See, some people won't be comfortable about putting money aside in a voluntary personal account, and you won't have to. There will be a Social Security—reformed Social Security system available for you. This just says you can put some of it, if you so choose to do so. . . .

Let me tell you something else wrong with the current Social Security system. If you both work, in your family, husband and wife work, and one of you dies before 62 years old, the Social Security system will pay for your burial benefits. And then, upon retirement, the surviving spouse gets a choice between the deceased's benefit structure or the survivor's benefit structure from Social Security, but not both.

See, in other words, the system today says, you get to work all your life, and if you die early, the money you put in the system just goes away. I don't think that's fair. I don't think it's fair to say to a citizen in this country who has been working hard to make a living that the money you've earned through the payroll taxes isn't around anymore, if you go on. Your spouse gets the greater of your benefits or her benefits, but not both.

So think about what a personal account would mean: A voluntary personal savings account would mean that there would be an asset base from both the husband and wife. And if one of them unfortunately died early, that asset base, that group of assets that had grown over time, could be passed on to the husband or wife, whoever the spouse is, the surviving spouse. That's fair, that makes sense. It means the money that you have worked for just won't go away. It will be available to help in times of need. . . .

I like the idea of saying you can take some of your own money if you so choose and set up a personal savings account as a part of your retirement plan. You know who else liked it?

Members of the United States Congress. They've got what they call the Thrift Savings Plan here in America. It's a plan that says it's okay if you're a member of the United States Senate to take some of your own money and set it aside and watch your money grow at a better rate of return than government would get for you. It's called a Thrift Savings Plan.

And here's my attitude: If a Thrift Savings Plan, if a personal savings account is good enough for a member of the United States Senate, it is good enough for working people all across America.

Now is the time for Congress to come to the table and get something done. It's important, because we've got unfunded liabilities out there that can serve as a drag on our economy, and we've got a young generation of Americans coming up that are going to be contributing to a system that's broke. And that's not fair. I believe those of us who've been elected have got a solemn obligation to tackle tough problems. I know that's what the American people expect.

I'm confident we can get something done. I really am. I don't care what all the naysayers say, or the people that are so political they can't—they can't get out of their current mind set here in Washington. See, I believe when it's all said and done, the American people are going to start speaking. And louder and louder, they're going to say, we got the problem with Social Security folks—now we expect you in Washington to do something about it. And I'm ready to take the lead on it, and continue to take the lead on it. There's no doubt in my mind I'm doing the right thing addressing this issue, and there's no doubt in my mind when Republicans and Democrats come together to solve this problem, a lot of good people are going to be saying, you know what, I've done my duty for the American people. . . .

Source: George W. Bush, "President Discusses Strengthening Social Security," speech before a meeting of the Associated Builders and Contractors organization, Washington, D.C., June 8, 2005. Available at: www.whitehouse.gov/news/releases/2005/06/20050608-3.html (accessed September 21, 2006).

Document 9.24
The Robert Ball Plan, December 2006

*Former Social Security commissioner Robert M. Ball has long offered various plans to restore Social Security's long-range solvency, while maintaining the basic principles of the traditional program. Ball was also the principal author of the Maintain Benefits Plan from the 1994–1996 Advisory Council (see **Document 9.5**). This is the December 2006 version of Ball's plan.*

We can close the projected shortfall and build up the trust funds with just three modifications of present law that are, as noted, desirable in themselves—and, very importantly, we can do the job without more benefit cuts.

1. Restore The Maximum Earnings Base to 90 Percent of Earnings

We should start by restoring the practice of collecting the Social Security tax on 90 percent of earnings in covered employment, the traditional goal reaffirmed by Congress in 1983.

Present law contains a provision that was intended to maintain the coverage level at 90 percent: an automatic annual increase in the maximum annual earnings base (now $95,000) by the same percentage as the increase in average wages. But this adjustment mechanism has not worked as planned, because over the past 20 years earnings at the top of the economic ladder have risen much more than average wages—so an increasing proportion of earnings exceeds the maximum earnings base and thus escapes Social Security taxation. Today, only about 83 percent of earnings is being taxed. That seemingly small slippage translates into billions of dollars in lost revenues each year.

We should get back to 90 percent, but I propose to get there very gradually, so that the 6 percent of earners with salaries above the cap would be required to pay only slightly more from year to year. . . .

With this approach we would get back to the 90-percent level in about 36 years. Such a gradual adjustment would be virtually painless—but this seemingly small change would reduce the projected 2 percent of payroll deficit by nearly a third, to about 1.3 percent of payroll. . . .

2. Earmark the Estate Tax for Social Security

In addition to restoring the taxable earnings base, we should establish a new source of funding by changing the estate tax into a dedicated Social Security tax beginning in 2010.

Present law gradually reduces the estate tax so that by 2009 only estates valued above $3.5 million ($7 million for a couple) will be taxed. . . . we should freeze the tax at the 2009 level and earmark the proceeds for Social Security from 2010 on, thereby converting the residual estate tax into a dedicated Social Security tax just like the tax on employers' payrolls. . . .

Such a tax would be a fair way to partially offset the deficit of contributions that was created in Social Security's early years. At that time the sensible decision was made to pay higher benefits to workers reaching retirement age than would have been possible had their benefits depended entirely on the relatively small contributions that they and their employers would have had time to make. But this decision created a "legacy cost" that future generations would have to address.

Like most of the founders of Social Security, I once assumed that general revenues would eventually be used to make up for this initial deficit of contributions. In principle that idea still makes sense, since there is no good reason why the cost of getting the system started should be met solely by the contributions of workers and their employers in the future. But there are no general revenues available for this purpose today because we now face deficits rather than surpluses as far as the eye can see. So it makes sense to substitute for general revenues this new dedicated Social Security tax based on a residual estate tax that might otherwise be dropped altogether. . . .

Carving a modest tax on large estates out of general revenues to help pay off part of the cost of establishing a universal system of basic economic security would be a highly progressive way to partially offset the legacy cost. Moreover, to allow the transfer of huge estates from one generation to another without requiring a contribution to the common good is undemocratic in principle (as Tom Paine, among other early advocates of an inheritance tax, recognized). . . .

Changing the estate tax to a Social Security tax reduces Social Security's projected long-term deficit by about 0.5 percent of payroll. When combined with restoration of the earnings base, it cuts the projected deficit slightly more than in half, to 0.9 percent of payroll.

These two changes bring the deficit within sight of "close actuarial balance"—the point where income and costs are projected to be within 5 percent of each other over 75 years. . . .

Although I favor judging the adequacy of long-range financing according to the trustees' projections, it should be noted that the Congressional Budget Office anticipates a much smaller long-term deficit than the trustees estimate. Thus, according to CBO's assumptions, these two changes alone might well be sufficient to eliminate the 75-year deficit.

3. Invest in Equities

Even though the two changes described above would bring the system near or within close actuarial balance, we should further strengthen Social Security's financing by diversifying trust fund investments. Some of the accumulated funds should be invested in equities, as is done by just about all other public and private pension plans. Several other government programs . . . already make such direct investments in stocks, as does Canada's social insurance system. There is no good reason to continue to require Social Security to invest only in low-yield government bonds.

Investment of a portion of Social Security's assets in stocks should be done gradually. I would propose starting with 1 percent in 2007, 2 percent in 2008, and so on, up to 20 percent in 2026 and capped at that percentage of assets thereafter. Investments should be limited to a very broad index fund (such as the Wilshire 5000) that reflects virtually the entire American economy. . . .

Investment by the trust funds has a major advantage over investment by individual accounts. For an individual it is very risky to invest one's basic retirement funds in stocks because, among other reasons, he or she will ordinarily need the money upon retirement, and in order to be sure of making the income last until death will need to promptly buy an annuity with the proceeds. But that could mean having to sell stocks and buy an annuity during a market downturn. . . . A variation of even a few months in the time of buying an annuity can make a huge difference in its value. In contrast, investment by the trust funds carries no such risk because Social Security could ride out market fluctuations.

As with the investments of a private retirement plan, the goal of trust fund investing would be to build up and maintain a reserve whose earnings would help meet future costs. This proposal is estimated to save about 0.4 percent of payroll. When combined with the other two changes outlined above, it brings the 75-year deficit anticipated by the trustees to an estimated 0.5 percent of payroll, well within close actuarial balance.

Fail-Safe Funding

It bears repeating that all three of these proposals are desirable in themselves regardless of their importance in reducing the long-range deficit. And even if their adoption were to result in overfinancing the program, it would still be desirable to enact them and then provide for an increase in benefits or a reduction in Social Security tax rates when it becomes clear that the system is overfinanced.

Similarly, it would be a good idea to provide for a contingency contribution-rate increase. As noted, a major objective in strengthening Social Security's financing is to ensure that the build-up of the trust funds is maintained so that earnings on the funds continue to contribute to future financial stability beyond the current 75-year estimating period. Thus it makes sense to provide for a contingency contribution-rate increase that may or may not be needed, depending on how closely experience follows the estimates.

If, despite adoption of the three changes outlined above, the trustees were at some point to project that the trust funds would begin to decline within the next five years, the contingency rate increase would go into effect automatically to prevent such a decline. . . .

It should be noted that there are other financing changes that could address the long-term shortfall, making it less likely that the contingent tax increase would be triggered. For example, adoption of the more accurate Consumer Price Index recently developed by the Bureau of Labor Statistics would result in slight reductions in Social Security's annual Cost of Living Adjustment, thereby saving an additional 0.5 percent of payroll and bringing the system into full actuarial balance according to the trustees' current projections. And if Social Security coverage were to be extended, as it should be, to all newly hired state and local government employees, the 75-year deficit anticipated under the middle-range estimates would become a surplus of 0.1 percent of payroll.

It is also possible, of course, that because of productivity increases greater than previously assumed and other favorable factors, the trustees' middle-range estimates may prove to be too pessimistic and actual experience may be closer to their low-cost estimates. In that case just the three changes that I propose to make immediately effective . . . might well be sufficient to maintain the trust funds at the highest point achieved and produce a surplus beyond the next 75 years. . . .

A Balanced Approach

The three-point plan outlined here addresses Social Security's long-term shortfall solely by increasing income to the system. Why not cut benefits too?

There are two important reasons why benefit cuts should be firmly ruled out. First, benefits are already being cut as a result of gradually increasing the retirement age, which has the same effect as an across-the-board benefit cut. So a truly balanced approach to meeting the long-term shortfall must call for more income, not more benefit cuts.

Second, and more fundamentally, we simply cannot afford to reduce the protection that Social Security currently provides. Social Security benefits are the principal source of support for two out of every three beneficiaries—and are vitally important to nearly all the rest. At the very least, benefit levels need to be maintained. Ideally, they should be improved, particularly in light of the increasingly uncertain future faced by private pension plans—with traditional defined-benefit plans (many of them underfunded) now covering only about 20 percent of the private-sector workforce, and with the 401(k) individual savings plans that are to some extent replacing the traditional plans subject to the vagaries of individual investment experience and vulnerable to being cashed out before retirement.

It is within this context that we must assess Social Security's long-term financing shortfall. I believe that an accurate assessment can lead to only one conclusion: changes are needed but radical changes are unwarranted. And the changes outlined here are anything but radical.

They are vastly preferable to the drastic benefit cuts that would accompany privatization or the drastic tax rate increases that would be required to cover the system's obligations in a strictly pay-as-you-go (no reserves) system. They are, in fact, not just necessary changes but desirable improvements that will strengthen the system now and for the long run.

It can be said of Social Security's future, as was once memorably said of the nation's, that the only thing we have to fear is fear itself. Social Security does not face bankruptcy. It is not going broke. The system faces only a long-term shortfall and needs only a few sensible changes such as those outlined here.

Source: Robert M. Ball's Web site: www.robertmball.org (accessed February 11, 2007). Used by permission.

Document 9.25
President Bush's Fiscal Year 2008 Budget Plan, February 5, 2007
In its fiscal year (FY) 2008 budget plan, presented to Congress in early February 2007, the George W. Bush administration reiterated its support for its previous Social Security reform proposals, including the introduction of private accounts and the use of "progressive indexing" in computing benefit amounts.

(In this excerpt, reference is made to the "unfunded obligations" of the Social Security system being $15.3 trillion "over the indefinite future." This figure does not appear as such in the 2006 trustees report, although it can be constructed by declining to credit the system for the $1.9 trillion current balance in the trust funds shown in that report.)

Social Security: Promised Benefits Outpacing Resources

Social Security was designed as a pay-as-you-go, self-financing program whereby current workers pay taxes directly and indirectly, through their employers, to support the benefit payments for current retirees, disabled persons, and survivors (collectively, beneficiaries). Such a system can only be sustained if the number of workers and the taxes they pay align with the number of beneficiaries and the benefits they receive. In 1950, when there were 16 workers for every program beneficiary, the combined payroll tax rate was very low at 3 percent of taxable wages. Currently, there are 3.3 workers for every beneficiary and the tax rate is 12.4 percent. The ratio of workers to beneficiaries is expected to decline further as the first of the baby boom generation becomes eligible for Social Security in 2008, and will fall to 2.2 workers per beneficiary in 2030.

Even after the baby boom generation is fully retired, the ratio of workers to beneficiaries will continue to fall, reaching 1.9 in 2080 primarily because of the growing difference between projected life expectancy and the age at which seniors become eligible for Social Security benefits. The increase in longevity, coupled with the fact that Americans are spending fewer years in the workforce, means that Americans are spending a greater proportion of their lives in retirement than ever before. Since 1940, life expectancy at age 65 has increased by approximately 40 percent and is projected to increase by an additional 20 percent by 2080.

The growth in retirees resulting from the retirement of the baby boom generation and increases in life expectancy will create a large and rapidly growing mismatch between scheduled Social Security benefits and the resources available to the program under current law. Through 2016, Social Security is projected to collect more in cash receipts than it pays in benefits. Beginning in 2017, however, Social Security benefit payments are projected to exceed the cash income dedicated to the trust funds. From this point forward, the Federal Government must borrow, tax, or cut other spending to pay excess Social Security benefits. Receipts are projected to continue falling to 70 percent of promised benefits by 2080.

There are many ways to summarize the extent of the mismatch between expected Social Security receipts and benefits. One such summary is the discounted present value of all future scheduled benefits net of receipts, or unfunded obligations under Social Security. The concept is to compare scheduled benefits and receipts under current law into the indefinite future, and to recognize through discounting that a dollar tomorrow is worth less than a dollar today. Based on the 2006 Social Security Trustees' Report, the unfunded obligation of Social Security totals $15.3 trillion over the indefinite future. To put this figure into perspective, this is about three times the amount of Federal debt currently held by the public.

The President is committed to strengthening Social Security through a bipartisan reform process in which participants are encouraged to bring different options for strengthening Social Security to the table. The President has identified three goals for reform: to strengthen permanently the safety net for future generations without raising payroll tax rates; to protect those who depend on Social Security the most; and to offer every American a chance to experience ownership through voluntary personal retirement accounts.

The 2008 Budget again reflects the President's proposal to allow workers to use a portion of the Social Security payroll tax to fund voluntary personal retirement accounts. These accounts will permit Americans to have greater control over their retirement planning, giving them an opportunity to obtain a higher return on their payroll taxes than is possible in the current Social Security system. The result will be to shift Social Security from an entirely pay-as-you-go system of financing toward a system that is less dependent on current workers. Beginning in 2012, workers will be allowed to use up to four percent of their Social Security taxable earnings, up to a $1,300 annual limit, to fund their personal retirement accounts; the $1,300 cap will be increased by $100 each year through 2017.

As one component of reforms to make the system sustainable, the President has embraced the idea of indexing future benefits of the highest-wage workers to inflation while continuing to index the wages of lower-wage workers to wage growth. Over time, wages tend to rise faster than prices, and so "progressive indexing" provides a higher rate of indexing for lower-wage workers than for higher-wage workers. This proposal would help restore the solvency of Social Security, while protecting those who most depend on Social Security. Comprehensive Social Security reform including personal retirement accounts, changes in the indexation of wages, and other modest changes will ensure the sustainability of the program for future generations, and help slow the unsustainable growth in total entitlement spending. . . .

Source: Budget of the United States Government, Fiscal Year 2008 (Washington, D.C.: Government Printing Office, February 2007), 17–18.

Document 9.26
2007 Trustees Report, April 23, 2007

The 2007 report of the board of trustees continued to show that the program faces a long-range financial shortfall, now estimated to be 1.95 percent of payroll, and the trust funds are projected to be exhausted in 2041. The unfunded liability of the system under the traditional seventy-five-year estimating period is now $4.7 trillion. Two other alternative measures of the unfunded liability are also shown: under one method (open group, infinite horizon) the unfunded liability is estimated to be $13.6 trillion; under the other way of measuring the shortfall (closed group) the unfunded liability is put at $14.4 trillion.

This financial problem continues to frame debates about the future of Social Security.

II. Overview

A. Highlights

. . . At the end of 2006, 49 million people were receiving benefits: 34 million retired workers and their dependents, 7 million survivors of deceased workers, and 9 million disabled workers and their dependents. During the year an estimated 162 million people had earnings covered by Social Security and paid payroll taxes. Total benefits paid in 2006 were $546 billion. Income was $745 billion, and assets held in special issue U.S. Treasury securities grew to $2.0 trillion.

Short-Range Results
The OASI and DI Trust Funds, individually and combined, are adequately financed over the next 10 years under the intermediate assumptions. The combined assets of the OASI and DI Trust Funds are projected to increase from $2,048 billion at the beginning of 2007, or 345 percent of annual expenditures, to $4,210 billion at the beginning of 2016, or 407 percent of annual expenditures in that year. Combined assets were projected in last year's report to rise to 344 percent of annual expenditures at the beginning of 2007, and 407 percent at the beginning of 2016.

Long-Range Results
. . . OASDI cost will increase more rapidly than tax income between about 2010 and 2030, due to the retirement of the large baby-boom generation. After 2030, increases in life expectancy and relatively low fertility rates will continue to increase Social Security system costs relative to tax income, but more slowly. Annual cost will exceed tax income starting in 2017 at which time the annual gap will be covered with cash from redemptions of special obligations of the Treasury that make up the trust fund assets, until these assets are exhausted in 2041. Separately, the DI fund is projected to be exhausted in 2026 and the OASI fund in 2042. For the 75-year projection period, the actuarial deficit is 1.95 percent of taxable payroll, 0.06 percentage point smaller than in last year's report. The open group unfunded obligation for OASDI over the 75-year period is $4.7 trillion in present value, and is $0.1 trillion above the measured level of a year ago. . . .

. . . Expressed in relation to the projected gross domestic product (GDP), OASDI cost is estimated to rise from the current level of 4.3 percent of GDP, to 6.2 percent in 2030, and to 6.3 percent in 2081.

Conclusion

Annual cost will begin to exceed tax income in 2017 for the combined OASDI Trust Funds, which are projected to become exhausted and thus unable to pay scheduled benefits in full on a timely basis in 2041 under the long-range intermediate assumptions. For the trust funds to remain solvent throughout the 75-year projection period, the combined payroll tax rate could be increased during the period in a manner equivalent to an immediate and permanent increase of 1.95 percentage points, benefits could be reduced during the period in a manner equivalent to an immediate and permanent reduction of 13.0 percent, general revenue transfers equivalent to $4.7 trillion in present value could be made during the period, or some combination of approaches could be adopted. Significantly larger changes would be required to maintain solvency beyond 75 years.

The projected trust fund deficits should be addressed in a timely way to allow for a gradual phasing in of the necessary changes and to provide advance notice to workers. Making adjustments sooner will allow them to be spread over more generations. . . .

IV. Actuarial Estimates

This chapter presents actuarial estimates of the future financial condition of the Social Security program. . . .

5. Additional Measures of OASDI Unfunded Obligations

. . . [A] negative actuarial balance (or an actuarial deficit) provides one measure of the unfunded obligation of the program over a period of time. Two additional measures of OASDI unfunded obligations under the intermediate assumptions are presented below.

a. Open Group Unfunded Obligations

Consistent with practice since 1965, this report focuses on the 75-year period (from 2007 to 2081 for this report) for the evaluation of the long-run financial status of the OASDI program on an open group basis (i.e., including taxes and cost for past, current and future participants through the year 2081). . . . [T]he present value of the open group unfunded obligation for the program over that period is $4.7 trillion. The open group measure indicates the adequacy of financing over the period as a whole for a program financed on a pay-as-you-go basis. On this basis, payroll taxes and scheduled benefits of all participants are included through 2081. . . .

However, there are limitations on what can be conveyed using summarized measures alone. . . .

. . . [One] limitation is that continued, and possibly increasing, annual shortfalls after the period are not reflected in the 75-year summarized measures. In order to address this limitation, this section presents estimates of unfunded obligations that extend to the infinite horizon. The extension assumes that the current-law OASDI program and the demographic and most economic trends used for the 75-year projection continue indefinitely. . . . [E]xtending the calculations beyond 2081 adds $8.9 ($13.6–$4.7) trillion in present value to the amount of the unfunded obligation estimated through 2081. That is, over the infinite horizon, the OASDI open group unfunded obligation is projected to be $13.6 trillion. The $8.9 trillion increment reflects a significant financing gap projected for OASDI after 2081. Of course, the degree of uncertainty associated with estimates beyond 2081 is substantial. . . .

b. Unfunded Obligations for Past, Current, and Future Participants
The future unfunded obligation of the OASDI program may also be viewed from a generational perspective. This perspective is generally associated with assessment of the financial condition of a program that is intended or required to be financed on a fully-advance-funded basis. However, analysis from this perspective can also provide insights into the implications of pay-as-you-go financing, the basis that has been used for the OASDI program.

The . . . present value of future cost less future taxes over the next 100 years for all current participants equals $16.5 trillion. For this purpose, current participants are defined as individuals who attain age 15 or older in 2007. Subtracting the current value of the trust fund (the accumulated value of past OASDI taxes less cost) gives a closed group (excluding all future participants) unfunded obligation of $14.4 trillion. This value represents the shortfall of lifetime contributions for all past and current participants relative to the lifetime costs associated with their generations. For a fully-advance-funded program this value would be equal to zero. . . .

Source: 2007 Annual Report of the Board of Trustees of the Federal Old-Age and Survivors Insurance Trust and the Federal Disability Insurance Trust Funds (Washington, D.C.: Government Printing Office, April 23, 2007), 2–3, 30, 58–60.

Appendix A: Legislation Affecting Social Security and Medicare Programs

This table is a listing of legislation enacted since the passage of the Social Security Act that contained some provisions related to Social Security and Medicare.* Appropriation bills that did not contain policy changes and bills that only made changes in administrative procedures are not included. Legislation considered to be of major importance is in **boldface** type and is also included in **Appendix B: Vote Totals by Party for Selected Social Security Legislation,** which lists the percentage of the Democratic and Republican support in Congress for that legislation.

*Although the document collection does not include Medicare, major Medicare legislation is included in this list.

Date enacted	P.L.	Title of the law
Aug. 14, 1935	**74–271**	**Social Security Act**
Aug. 10, 1939	**76–379**	**Social Security Act Amendments of 1939**
Oct. 21, 1942	77–753	Revenue Act of 1942
March 24, 1943	78–17	War Shipping Administration
Dec. 22, 1943	78–211	Joint Resolution Regarding Tariff Act
Feb. 25, 1944	78–235	Revenue Act of 1943
April 4, 1944	78–285	War Shipping Administration
Dec. 16, 1944	78–495	Federal Insurance Contributions Act of 1945
Oct. 23, 1945	79–201	Bonneville Project Act—Amendment
Nov. 8, 1945	79–214	Revenue Act of 1945
Dec. 29, 1945	79–291	International Organizations Immunities Act
July 31, 1946	79–572	Railroad Retirement and Unemployment Insurance
Aug. 10, 1946	79–719	Social Security Act Amendments of 1946
Aug. 6, 1947	80–379	Social Security Act Amendments of 1947
April 20, 1948	80–492	Employment Taxes—Newspaper Vendors
June 14, 1948	80–642	Maintain Status Quo Concept of Employee
Aug. 28, 1950	**81–734**	**Social Security Act Amendments of 1950**
Sept. 23, 1950	81–814	Revenue Act of 1950
July 12, 1951	82–78	Agricultural Workers—Republic of Mexico Amendments
Oct. 30, 1951	82–234	Railroad Retirement and Unemployment Insurance
June 28, 1952	82–420	State and Local Employees—Retroactive Old-Age and Survivors Insurance Coverage
July 18, 1952	**82–590**	**Social Security Act Amendments of 1952**
Aug. 14, 1953	83–269	Social Security—Wage Credits for Military Service

Date enacted	P.L.	Title of the law
Aug. 15, 1953	83–279	Wisconsin Retirement Fund—Coordination with Federal Old-Age and Survivors Insurance System
Sept. 1, 1954	**83–761**	**Social Security Act Amendments of 1954**
Aug. 9, 1955	84–325	Military Service Wage Credits—Social Security
Aug. 1, 1956	**84–880**	**Social Security Act Amendments of 1956**
Aug. 1, 1956	84–881	Servicemen's and Veterans' Survivor Benefits Act
July 17, 1957	85–109	Social Security Act—Disability Determination
Aug. 30, 1957	85–226	Social Security—State and Local Employees
Aug. 30, 1957	85–227	Social Security—State and Local Employees
Aug. 30, 1957	85–229	Social Security—State and Local Employees
Aug. 30, 1957	85–238	Social Security Act—Alien Survivors of Members of Armed Forces
Aug. 30, 1957	85–239	Internal Revenue—Self Employment Income—Ministers
Aug. 27, 1958	85–786	Social Security Act—Definition of "Wages"
Aug. 27, 1958	85–787	Massachusetts and Vermont Retirement Systems— Division for Social Security Purposes
Aug. 28, 1958	85–798	Social Security—Mother's Insurance Benefits
Aug. 28, 1958	**85–840**	**Social Security Amendments of 1958**
Sept. 2, 1958	85–857	Title 38 "Veterans Benefits"
Sept. 6, 1958	85–927	Railroad Retirement Act—Amendment
June 25, 1959	86–70	Alaska Omnibus Act
Aug. 18, 1959	86–168	Farm Credit Act of 1959
Sept. 16, 1959	86–284	Social Security—Non Professional School Employees
Sept. 22, 1959	86–346	Savings Bonds—Interest Rates
April 8, 1960	86–415	Public Health Service Commissioned Corps Personnel Act of 1960
April 22, 1960	86–442	Government Employees—Unemployment Compensation
June 11, 1960	86–507	Mail—Certified and Registered
July 12, 1960	86–624	Hawaii Omnibus Act
Sept. 13, 1960	**86–778**	**Social Security Amendments of 1960**
June 30, 1961	**87–64**	**Social Security Amendments of 1961**
Sept. 21, 1961	87–256	Mutual Educational and Cultural Exchange Act of 1961
Sept. 22, 1961	87–293	Peace Corps Act
Oct. 24, 1962	87–878	Social Security—State and Local—Arkansas
Feb. 26, 1964	88–272	Revenue Act of 1964
July 2, 1964	88–350	Social Security—Retirement Systems
July 23, 1964	88–382	Social Security Coverage—Nevada State Employees
Oct. 13, 1964	88–650	Social Security—Amendments
July 30, 1965	89–97	Social Security Amendments of 1965
March 15, 1966	89–368	Tax Adjustment Act of 1966

Date enacted	P.L.	Title of the law
April 8, 1966	89–384	Internal Revenue—Foreign Expropriation Losses—Social Security
Nov. 2, 1966	89–713	Internal Revenue—Data Processing
Sept. 30, 1967	90–97	Medical Enrollment Act of 1967
Jan. 2, 1968	90–248	Social Security Amendments of 1967
Aug. 13, 1968	90–486	National Guard Technicians Act of 1968
Dec. 30, 1969	91–172	Social Security Amendments of 1969
Oct. 15, 1970	91–452	Organized Crime Control Act of 1970
Jan. 12, 1971	91–690	Social Security—Hospital-Nursing Service Requirement
March 17, 1971	92–5	Public Debt Limit—Interest Rate—Social Security Wage Base
Dec. 28, 1971	92–223	Social Security—Lump-Sum Death Payment
July 1, 1972	**92–336**	**Public Debt Limit—Extension**
Oct. 30, 1972	92–603	Social Security Amendments of 1972
July 6, 1973	93–58	Railroad Retirement—Employees—Medical Coverage
July 9, 1973	93–66	Renegotiation Amendments of 1973
Dec. 31, 1973	93–233	Social Security Benefits—Increase
Aug. 7, 1974	93–368	Vessels—Equipment and Repairs—Exemption From Duty
Oct. 16, 1974	93–445	Railroad Retirement Act of 1974
Oct. 26, 1974	93–484	Tariffs—Horses
Dec. 31, 1975	94–182	Social Security Act
Jan. 2, 1976	94–202	Social Security Act—Hearings and Review Procedures
March 23, 1976	94–241	Commonwealth—Covenant to Establish—Northern Mariana Islands
April 21, 1976	94–273	Fiscal Year Adjustment Act
April 21, 1976	94–274	Fiscal Year Transition Act
July 16, 1976	94–368	Social Security Act—Medicare Improvements
Sept. 30, 1976	94–437	Indian Health Care Improvement Act
Oct. 4, 1976	94–455	Tax Reform Act of 1976
Oct. 8, 1976	94–460	Health Maintenance Organization Amendments of 1976
Oct. 19, 1976	94–563	Internal Revenue Code of 1954—Social Security Act
Oct. 25, 1977	95–142	Medicare—Medicaid Anti-Fraud and Abuse Amendments
Nov. 23, 1977	95–202	GI Bill Improvement Act of 1977
Dec. 13, 1977	95–210	Social Security Act—Rural Health Clinic Services
Dec. 20, 1977	**95–216**	**Social Security Amendments of 1977**
June 13, 1978	95–292	Social Security Act—End Stage Renal Disease Program—Improvements
Oct. 17, 1978	95–472	Internal Revenue Code of 1954—Tax Court—Retired Pay
Nov. 6, 1978	95–600	Revenue Act of 1978
Oct. 17, 1979	96–88	Department of Education Organization Act

Date enacted	P.L.	Title of the law
June 9, 1980	**96–265**	**Social Security Disability Amendments of 1980**
June 17, 1980	96–272	Adoption Assistance and Child Welfare Act of 1980
Oct. 9, 1980	96–403	Federal Old-Age and Survivors Insurance Trust Fund and the Federal Disability Insurance Trust Fund—Allocation of Social Security Tax
Oct. 19, 1980	96–473	Social Security Act—Retirement Test
Dec. 5, 1980	96–499	Omnibus Reconciliation Act of 1980
Dec. 28, 1980	96–611	Parental Kidnapping Prevention Act of 1980
Aug. 13, 1981	97–34	Economic Recovery Tax Act of 1981
Aug. 13, 1981	97–35	Omnibus Budget Reconciliation Act of 1981
Dec. 29, 1981	97–123	Omnibus Reconciliation Act of 1981—Social Security Act Benefits
Sept. 3, 1982	97–248	Tax Equity and Fiscal Responsibility Act of 1982
Dec. 21, 1982	97–377	Further Continuing Appropriations, 1983
Jan. 12, 1983	97–448	Technical Corrections Act of 1982
Jan. 12, 1983	97–455	Virgin Island Source Income—Social Security Disability Benefit Appeals
March 11, 1983	98–4	Payment-in-Kind Tax Treatment Act of 1983
April 20, 1983	**98–21**	**Social Security Amendments of 1983**
July 30, 1983	98–63	Supplemental Appropriations Act, 1983
Aug. 12, 1983	98–76	Railroad Retirement Solvency Act of 1983
Aug. 29, 1983	98–90	Medicare Hospice Reimbursement
Oct. 11, 1983	98–118	Unemployment and Social Security Benefits, Extension
Nov. 29, 1983	98–168	Federal Physicians Comparability Allowance Amendments of 1983—Federal Employees' Retirement Contribution Temporary Adjustment Act of 1983
Nov. 8, 1983	98–213	Insular Affairs
July 18, 1984	98–369	Deficit Reduction Act of 1984
Oct. 9, 1984	**98–460**	**Social Security Disability Benefits Reform Act of 1984**
Oct. 30, 1984	98–604	Social Security, Cost-of-Living Increases
Nov. 8, 1984	98–617	Payment Rates for Hospice Care Under Medicare
June 17, 1985	99–53	Federal Employee Health Benefit
Sept. 30, 1985	99–107	Emergency Extension Act of 1985
Nov. 14, 1985	99–155	Public Debt Limit, Temporary Increase
Dec. 12, 1985	99–177	Public Debt Limit—Balanced Budget and Emergency Deficit Control Act of 1985
Dec. 13, 1985	99–181	Temporary Extension of Miscellaneous Provisions
Dec. 18, 1985	99–189	Temporary Extension of Certain Tax Authorities
Dec. 23, 1985	99–201	Temporary Extension of Various Authorities
Dec. 26, 1985	99–221	Cherokee Leasing Act
April 7, 1986	99–272	Consolidated Omnibus Budget Reconciliation Act of 1985
June 6, 1986	99–335	Federal Employees' Retirement System Act of 1986

Date enacted	P.L.	Title of the law
July 2, 1986	99–349	Urgent Supplemental Appropriations Act, 1986
Oct. 21, 1986	99–509	Omnibus Budget Reconciliation Act of 1986
Oct. 22, 1986	99–514	Tax Reform Act of 1986
Oct. 27, 1986	99–556	Federal Employees' Retirement System Technical Corrections Act of 1986
Oct. 28, 1986	99–576	Veterans' Benefits Improvement and Health-Care Authorization Act of 1986
Nov. 6, 1986	99–603	Immigration Reform and Control Act of 1986
Nov. 10, 1986	99–643	Employment Opportunities for Disabled Americans Act
Aug. 18, 1987	100–93	Medicare and Medicaid Patient and Program Protection Act of 1987
Sept. 29, 1987	100–119	Public Debt Limit Increase; Deficit Reduction Procedures; Budget Process Reform
Dec. 22, 1987	100–203	Omnibus Budget Reconciliation Act of 1987
July 1, 1988	100–360	Medicare Catastrophic Coverage Act of 1988
Oct. 13, 1988	100–485	Family Support Act of 1988
Nov. 10, 1988	100–647	Technical and Miscellaneous Revenue Act of 1988
Nov. 18, 1988	100–690	Anti-Drug Abuse Act of 1988
Dec. 13, 1989	101–234	Medicare Catastrophic Coverage Repeal Act of 1989
Dec. 19, 1989	101–239	Omnibus Budget Reconciliation Act of 1989
Oct. 1, 1990	101–403	Continuing Appropriations, 1991
Nov. 5, 1990	101–508	Omnibus Budget Reconciliation Act of 1990
Nov. 16, 1990	101–597	National Health Service Corps Revitalization Amendments of 1990
Nov. 28, 1990	101–624	Food, Agriculture, Conservation, and Trade Act of 1990
Nov. 29, 1990	101–649	Immigration Act of 1990
May 7, 1991	102–40	Department of Veterans Affairs Health-Care Personnel Act of 1991
June 13, 1991	102–54	Veterans Programs for Housing and Memorial Affairs
Aug. 6, 1991	102–83	Department of Veterans Affairs Codification Act
Sept. 30, 1992	102–375	Older Americans Act Amendments of 1992
Oct. 24, 1992	102–496	Intelligence Authorization Act for Fiscal Year 1993
Oct. 29, 1992	102–572	Federal Courts Administration Act of 1992
Aug. 10, 1993	103–66	Omnibus Budget Reconciliation Act of 1993
Dec. 3, 1993	103–178	Intelligence Authorization Act for Fiscal Year 1994
Aug. 15, 1994	103–296	Social Security Independence and Program Improvements Act of 1994
Oct. 22, 1994	103–387	Social Security Domestic Employment Reform Act of 1994
Oct. 31, 1994	103–432	Social Security Act Amendments of 1994
March 29, 1996	104–121	Contract With America Advancement Act of 1996
April 26, 1996	104–134	Omnibus Consolidation Rescissions and Appropriations Act of 1996

Date enacted	P.L.	Title of the law
Aug. 20, 1996	104–188	Small Business Job Protection Act of 1996
Aug. 21, 1996	104–191	Health Insurance Portability and Accountability Act of 1996
Aug. 22, 1996	104–193	Personal Responsibility and Work Opportunity Reconciliation Act of 1996
Sept. 30, 1996	104–208	Omnibus Consolidated Appropriations Act, 1997
Oct. 2, 1996	104–224	Medical Device Reporting Requirement, Repeal
Oct. 2, 1996	104–226	Medicare and Medicaid Coverage Data Bank, Repeal
Oct. 11, 1996	104–299	Health Centers Consolidation Act of 1996
Aug. 5, 1997	105–33	Balanced Budget Act of 1997
Aug. 5, 1997	105–34	Taxpayer Relief Act of 1997
Oct. 21, 1998	105–277	Omnibus Consolidated and Emergency Supplemental Appropriations Act, 1999
Dec. 14, 1999	106–169	Foster Care Independence Act of 1999
Dec. 17, 1999	**106–170**	**Ticket to Work and Work Incentives Improvement Act of 1999**
April 7, 2000	**106–182**	**Senior Citizens' Freedom to Work Act of 2000**
Dec. 21, 2000	106–554	Consolidated Appropriations Act of 2001
Jan. 10, 2002	107–117	DOD and Emergency Supplemental Appropriations for Recovery from and Response to Terrorist Attacks on the United States Act of 2002
Jan. 23, 2002	107–134	Victims of Terrorism Relief Act of 2001
Dec. 8, 2003	108–173	The Medicare Prescription Drug, Improvement, and Modernization Act of 2003
March 2, 2004	108–203	Social Security Protection Act of 2004

Source: Authors' compilation.

Appendix B: Vote Totals by Party for Selected Social Security Legislation

This table lists the percentage of each of the two major political parties supporting final passage of sixteen major Social Security bills. (See explanations below.)

Public law	Democrats (%)	Republicans (%)
EXPANSIONARY PERIOD IN POLICYMAKING		
74–271: Social Security Act of 1935	House: 89.03 Senate: 86.96	House: 79.41 Senate: 64.00
76–379: Social Security Act Amendments of 1939	House: 84.82 Senate: 60.87	House: 84.02 Senate: 60.87
81–734: Social Security Act Amendments of 1950	House: 89.32 Senate: 85.45	House: 81.55 Senate: 83.33
82–590: Social Security Act Amendments of 1952	House: 84.78 Senate: n/a	House: 83.00 Senate: n/a
83–761: Social Security Act Amendments of 1954	House: 80.93 Senate: n/a	House: 83.03 Senate: n/a
84–880: Social Security Act Amendments of 1956	House: 87.88 Senate: 93.75	House: 83.25 Senate: 93.62
85–840: Social Security Amendments of 1958	House: 85.71 Senate: 85.71	House: 88.44 Senate: 78.72
86–778: Social Security Amendments of 1960	House: 84.95 Senate: 65.15	House: 86.84 Senate: 91.18
87–64: Social Security Amendments of 1961	House: 96.91 Senate: 87.50	House: 86.63 Senate: 91.67
92–336: Public Debt Limit-Extension	House: 76.28 Senate: 75.93	House: 60.89 Senate: 79.55
CONTRACTIONARY PERIOD IN POLICYMAKING		
95–216: Social Security Amendments of 1977	House: 60.42 Senate: 62.30	House: 10.27 Senate: 44.74
96–265: Social Security Disability Amendments of 1980	House: 88.36 Senate: 87.93	House: 92.41 Senate: 85.37
98–21: Social Security Amendments of 1983	House: 61.05 Senate: 56.52	House: 48.19 Senate: 59.26
98–460: Social Security Disability Benefits Reform Act of 1984	House: 94.01 Senate: 97.79	House: 90.96 Senate: 100.00
106–170: Ticket to Work and Work Incentives Improvement Act of 1999	House: 96.70 Senate: 97.78	House: 95.50 Senate: 92.73
106–182: Senior Citizens' Freedom to Work Act of 2000	House: 97.16 Senate: 100.00	House: 96.85 Senate: 100.00

Totals for the Sixteen Bills Listed	Democrats (%)		Republicans (%)	
	House	Senate	House	Senate
Vote all bills	84.89	81.69	78.20	80.36
Vote on expansions	86.06	80.16	81.70	80.36
Vote on contractions	82.95	83.72	72.36	80.35

Explanations of Tabular Data

Selected Bills

The table includes only sixteen bills, which the authors view as major pieces of Social Security legislation. (One likely additional candidate for inclusion is the Social Security Amendments of 1965, which primarily involved Medicare. As Medicare is not treated in detail in this work, this bill has been left out of the calculations.) Inclusion of additional legislation would slightly alter the party totals, although the general pattern of support for most of the bills has been observed even with the inclusion of additional legislation.

Counting of "Aye" Votes Only

The table counts "aye" votes only; a vote of "present" or a member "not voting" is the functional equivalent of a "no" vote. Where an entry shows "n/a," this means no recorded vote was taken on final passage.

Votes on Final Passage

Legislation is typically amended multiple times before final enactment. The votes in this table are the *last recorded votes closest to final passage*. This measure is used as it is the closest to the final enacted version of the legislation. In some instances, this means that the votes in the two houses of Congress may not be on identical versions of the bill.

Expansion versus Contraction

The identification of a bill as expansionary or contractionary is a judgment by the authors. Most bills are in fact mixed, with some of both types of effects, but an effort has been made to identify the overall policy direction of the bills in this regard. Here, expansion means the adoption of policies that make benefits more generous, add additional types of benefits, liberalize conditions for receipt of benefits, and the like. Contraction means the adoption of policies that make benefits less generous, eliminate benefits, scale back benefits, tighten eligibility requirements, or raise payroll taxes. (Expansions are shown in plain typeface and contractions in **boldface** type.) As a handy dividing line, most legislation up through 1972 was expansionary, while much legislation since that time has been contractionary.

Sources of the Data

Roll-call votes on all legislation are available back to 1990 on the Library of Congress's Web site: http://thomas.loc.gov/home/rollcallvotes.html. For legislation prior to 1990, the printed *Congressional Record* is the only source of roll-call vote tallies. For legislation prior to 1990, the authors have made the party identifications and computed the vote totals from the reported votes in the *Congressional Record*. All percentage calculations are by the authors.

Appendix C: Key Indicators from the Annual Trustees Reports, 1941–2007

Annual reports on the status of the trust funds have been prepared by the actuaries and issued by the Social Security trustees since 1941. The reports are complex, with many tables of actuarial data. This table summarizes four main indices from the reports:

1. The length of the estimation period, which has varied from as few as thirty-five years to as many as eighty, and which is currently seventy-five years.
2. A general assessment of whether the funds are in long-range actuarial balance over the entire estimation period.
3. A measure of the balance in the trust funds over the estimation period, expressed as a percentage of taxable payroll.
4. The projected date of trust fund exhaustion, if appropriate.

There are several points of interest to note in the table. The current estimation period of seventy-five years has been in practice only since 1965. The 1973 report was the first to unambiguously indicate that the trust funds were not in long-range balance. The funds were restored to balance for five years by the 1983 amendments, but they have been continuously out of balance since 1988. By comparing the projected date of trust fund exhaustion (where shown) with the date the report was issued, one can get a measure of how near in time the event of trust fund exhaustion was.

Year of report	Long-range estimation period	In long-range actuarial balance?	Trust fund balance as a percentage of payroll[a]	Date of trust fund exhaustion[b]
1941	50 years	uncertain[c]	—	—
1942	40 years	uncertain	—	—
1943	40 years	uncertain	—	—
1944	45 years	uncertain	—	—
1945	45 years	uncertain	—	—
1946	none[d]	not shown	—	—
1947	45 years	uncertain	—	—
1948	45 years	uncertain	—	—
1949	45 years	uncertain	—	—
1950	40 years	uncertain	—	—
1951	40 years	yes	—	—
1952	40 years	yes	—	—
1953	40 years	yes	—	—
1954	40 years	uncertain	—	—
1955	40 years	yes	—	—
1956	35 years	yes	—	—
1957	35 years	yes	(0.13)	—
1958	80 years	yes	(0.42)	—

Year of report	Long-range estimation period	In long-range actuarial balance?	Trust fund balance as a percentage of payroll[a]	Date of trust fund exhaustion[b]
1959	60 years	yes	(0.24)	—
1960	55 years	yes	(0.05)	—
1961	55 years	yes	(0.30)	—
1962	55 years	yes	(0.30)	—
1963	55 years	yes	(0.31)	—
1964	55 years	yes	(0.24)	—
1965	75 years	yes	0.01	—
1966	75 years	yes	(0.07)	—
1967	75 years	yes	0.74	—
1968	75 years	yes	0.01	—
1969	75 years	yes	0.53	—
1970	75 years	yes	(0.08)	—
1971	75 years	yes	(0.10)	—
1972	75 years	yes	0.05	—
1973	75 years	no	(0.32)	—
1974	75 years	no	(2.98)	—
1975	75 years	no	(5.32)	—
1976	75 years	no	(7.96)	—
1977	75 years	no	(8.20)	—
1978	75 years	no	(1.40)	2028
1979	75 years	no	(1.20)	2032
1980	75 years	no	(1.52)	1983
1981	75 years	no	(1.82)	1982
1982	75 years	no	(1.82)	1983
1983	75 years	yes	0.02	—
1984	75 years	yes	(0.06)	—
1985	75 years	yes	(0.41)	—
1986	75 years	yes	(0.44)	—
1987	75 years	yes	(0.62)	—
1988	75 years	yes[e]	(0.58)	2048
1989	75 years	no	(0.70)	2046
1990	75 years	no	(0.91)	2043
1991	75 years	no	(1.08)	2041
1992	75 years	no	(1.46)	2036
1993	75 years	no	(1.46)	2036
1994	75 years	no	(2.13)	2029
1995	75 years	no	(2.17)	2030
1996	75 years	no	(2.19)	2031
1997	75 years	no	(2.23)	2029
1998	75 years	no	(2.19)	2032
1999	75 years	no	(2.07)	2034
2000	75 years	no	(1.89)	2037
2001	75 years	no	(1.86)	2038
2002	75 years	no	(1.87)	2041
2003	75 years[f]	no	(1.92)	2042
2004	75 years	no	(1.89)	2042
2005	75 years	no	(1.92)	2041
2006	75 years	no	(2.02)	2040
2007	75 years	no	(1.95)	2041

Source: Authors' compilation from *Annual Reports of the Social Security Trustees.*

[a] Figures in parentheses indicate negative values. A negative value is not always an indication of trust fund insolvency. The test deployed by the actuaries is "close actuarial balance," which allows for a small varia-

tion from strict numerical balance to still count as in balance (this is done because of the inherent measure of uncertainty in such long-range estimates). A negative number in this column must be associated with a "no" value in the prior column in order to indicate a financing shortfall.

[b] The actuaries began reporting the date of trust fund exhaustion in 1978.

[c] Some of the early reports did not indicate a definitive assessment of whether the trust funds were in long-range balance.

[d] This report contained no long-range cost estimation, so actuarial balance cannot be assessed.

[e] Although the long-range deficit in this report was small enough that the system could still be said to be in "close actuarial balance," this was the first post–1983 report to indicate a trust fund depletion date before the end of the seventy-five-year estimating period, and thus is the first to indicate continuing financing difficulties facing the system. Note also that in this report the actuaries changed their estimating methodology. Previously, they had assessed actuarial balance using the "average cost" basis. Starting with this report, they shifted to a "level financing" basis. Under the prior methodology, the actuarial deficit in 1988 would have been 0.87 percent of payroll rather than the 0.58 percent reported. Under the old measure the system would already have been judged out of long range actuarial balance.

[f] Starting with the 2003 report, the actuaries began including—in addition to the traditional seventy-five-year estimates—a set of estimates designed to project the financing of the program to the "infinite horizon" (see the **Glossary** for an explanation of this concept). This was not a replacement of the standard seventy-five-year estimates, but rather an additional measure of financial adequacy.

Appendix D: Social Security Trust Fund Finances, 1937–2006

This table presents a streamlined version of the annual reporting data regarding the financial transactions to the Social Security Old-Age and Survivors and Disability Insurance Trust Funds.

Noteworthy is the fact that in ten calendar years thus far the Social Security program has run an annual deficit and has expended a portion of the assets in the trust funds to make up the shortfall. (See the negative values in the "Annual net change" column, starting in 1959.)

The table also shows quite vividly the effects of the financing crisis of the mid-1970s and the effects on program financing from the 1977 and 1983 amendments.

Year	Total receipts ($ millions)	Total expenditures ($ millions)	Annual net change ($ millions)	Balance at end of year ($ millions)
1937	767	1	766	766
1938	375	10	366	1,132
1939	607	14	592	1,724
1940	368	62	306	2,031
1941	845	114	731	2,762
1942	1,085	159	926	3,688
1943	1,328	195	1,132	4,820
1944	1,422	238	1,184	6,005
1945	1,420	304	1,116	7,121
1946	1,447	418	1,029	8,150
1947	1,722	512	1,210	9,360
1948	1,969	607	1,362	10,722
1949	1,816	721	1,094	11,816
1950	2,928	1,022	1,905	13,721
1951	3,784	1,966	1,818	15,540
1952	4,184	2,282	1,902	17,442
1953	4,359	3,094	1,265	18,707
1954	5,610	3,741	1,869	20,576
1955	6,167	5,079	1,087	21,663
1956	6,697	5,841	856	22,519
1957	8,090	7,567	523	23,042
1958	9,108	8,907	201	23,243
1959	9,516	10,793	(1,277)	21,966
1960	12,445	11,798	647	22,613
1961	12,937	13,388	(451)	22,162
1962	13,699	15,156	(1,457)	20,705
1963	16,227	16,217	10	20,715
1964	17,476	17,020	456	21,172
1965	17,857	19,187	(1,331)	19,841
1966	23,381	20,913	2,467	22,308
1967	26,413	22,471	3,942	26,250
1968	28,493	26,015	2,479	28,729
1969	33,346	27,892	5,453	34,182

Year	Total receipts ($ millions)	Total expenditures ($ millions)	Annual net change ($ millions)	Balance at end of year ($ millions)
1970	36,993	33,108	3,886	38,068
1971	40,908	38,542	2,366	40,434
1972	45,622	43,281	2,341	42,775
1973	54,787	53,148	1,639	44,414
1974	62,066	60,593	1,472	45,886
1975	67,640	69,184	(1,544)	44,342
1976	75,034	78,242	(3,209)	41,133
1977	81,982	87,254	(5,272)	35,861
1978	91,903	96,018	(4,115)	31,746
1979	105,864	107,320	(1,456)	30,291
1980	119,712	123,550	(3,838)	26,453
1981	142,438	144,352	(1,914)	24,539
1982	147,913	160,111	239	24,778
1983	171,266	171,177	89	24,867
1984	186,637	180,429	6,208	31,075
1985	203,540	190,628	11,088	42,163
1986	216,833	201,522	4,698	46,861
1987	231,039	209,093	21,946	68,807
1988	263,469	222,514	40,955	109,762
1989	289,448	236,242	53,206	162,968
1990	315,443	253,135	62,309	225,277
1991	329,676	274,205	55,471	280,747
1992	342,591	291,865	50,726	331,473
1993	355,578	308,766	46,812	378,285
1994	381,111	323,011	58,100	436,385
1995	399,497	339,815	59,683	496,068
1996	424,451	353,569	70,883	566,950
1997	457,668	369,108	88,560	655,510
1998	489,204	382,255	106,950	762,460
1999	526,582	392,908	133,673	896,133
2000	568,433	415,121	153,312	1,049,445
2001	602,003	438,916	163,088	1,212,533
2002	627,085	461,653	165,432	1,377,965
2003	631,886	479,086	152,799	1,530,764
2004	657,718	501,644	156,075	1,686,839
2005	701,758	529,938	171,821	1,858,660
2006	744,900	555,400	189,500	2,048,100

Source: Authors' compilation based on Table 4.A3 from the Social Security Administration, *Annual Statistical Supplement to the Social Security Bulletin,* various years. Figures for 2006 from 2007 Annual Trustees Report, Table IV. A3.

Note: "Total receipts" include: payroll taxes, interest income, income from the taxation of benefits, and general reimbursements from the Treasury. "Total expenditures" include: benefit payments, administrative expenses, and transfers to the Railroad Retirement Program. "Annual net change" is the difference between annual receipts and expenditures. Negative annual balances are shown in parentheses. For the period 1937–1956, table includes only the Old-Age and Survivors Trust Fund. For 1957–2005, table includes Old-Age and Survivors and Disability Trust Funds combined. Table does not include transactions to the Medicare Trust Fund.

Appendix E: Social Security Beneficiaries, 1937–2005

This table compiles the growth in the number of Social Security beneficiaries since benefits were first paid in 1937. It distinguishes between adults and children, and between adults receiving retirement benefits and those receiving disability benefits. The number of beneficiaries is as of December each year.

What is most apparent about this table is the steady growth in the overall number of beneficiaries. Within this overall trend, there are other interesting variations. For example, the number of disabled workers has increased fairly dramatically since 1990, while the number of other adults has been declining since its peak in 1992 and the number of children receiving Social Security benefits reached its highpoint in 1977.

Calendar year	Retired workers	Disabled workers	Other adults	Children	Total
1937	53,236	none	none	none	53,236
1938	213,670	none	none	none	213,670
1939	174,839	none	none	none	174,839
1940	112,331	none	55,509	54,648	222,488
1941	199,966	none	116,346	117,410	433,722
1942	260,129	none	165,708	172,505	598,342
1943	306,161	none	212,425	229,230	747,816
1944	378,471	none	278,302	298,108	954,881
1945	518,234	none	379,739	390,134	1,288,107
1946	701,705	none	478,838	461,756	1,642,299
1947	874,724	none	578,738	524,783	1,978,245
1948	1,047,985	none	685,307	581,265	2,314,557
1949	1,285,893	none	817,478	639,437	2,742,808
1950	1,770,984	none	1,006,556	699,703	3,477,243
1951	2,278,470	none	1,254,268	846,247	4,378,985
1952	2,643,932	none	1,442,866	938,751	5,025,549
1953	3,222,348	none	1,705,877	1,053,195	5,981,420
1954	3,775,134	none	1,950,576	1,160,770	6,886,480
1955	4,473,971	none	2,210,405	1,276,240	7,960,616
1956	5,112,430	none	2,674,696	1,340,995	9,128,121
1957	6,197,532	149,850	3,279,438	1,502,077	11,128,897
1958	6,920,677	237,719	3,647,703	1,624,135	12,430,234
1959	7,525,628	334,443	4,012,299	1,831,548	13,703,918
1960	8,061,469	455,371	4,327,298	2,000,451	14,844,589
1961	8,924,849	618,075	4,672,376	2,279,462	16,494,762
1962	9,738,500	740,867	5,026,971	2,547,057	18,053,395
1963	10,263,331	827,014	5,258,185	2,686,959	19,035,489
1964	10,668,731	894,173	5,449,182	2,787,453	19,799,539
1965	11,100,584	988,074	5,685,450	3,092,659	20,866,767
1966	12,292,756	1,097,190	5,984,336	3,392,970	22,767,252
1967	12,019,175	1,193,120	6,907,483	3,585,209	23,704,987

Calendar year	Retired workers	Disabled workers	Other adults	Children	Total
1968	12,420,742	1,295,300	7,048,663	3,795,669	24,560,374
1969	12,822,201	1,394,291	7,145,212	3,952,358	25,314,062
1970	13,349,995	1,492,948	7,263,381	4,122,305	26,228,629
1971	13,926,939	1,647,684	7,409,841	4,307,044	27,291,508
1972	14,555,475	1,832,916	7,572,004	4,515,633	28,476,028
1973	15,364,562	2,016,626	7,800,209	4,687,378	29,868,775
1974	15,958,521	2,236,882	7,881,905	4,775,509	30,852,817
1975	16,811,425	2,488,774	7,812,304	4,972,008	32,084,511
1976	17,352,515	2,670,208	7,963,078	5,035,145	33,020,946
1977	17,979,236	2,837,432	8,177,649	5,082,825	34,077,142
1978	18,491,498	2,879,774	8,276,699	4,938,372	34,586,343
1979	19,081,694	2,870,590	8,378,048	4,794,163	35,124,495
1980	19,654,721	2,858,680	8,465,037	4,606,517	35,584,955
1981	20,271,685	2,776,519	8,528,188	4,429,979	36,006,371
1982	20,825,842	2,603,599	8,527,386	3,882,511	35,839,338
1983	21,469,594	2,569,029	8,452,748	3,593,377	36,084,748
1984	21,946,858	2,596,516	8,526,852	3,408,457	36,478,683
1985	22,463,585	2,656,638	8,618,604	3,319,490	37,058,317
1986	23,005,718	2,728,463	8,674,208	3,294,587	37,702,976
1987	23,458,691	2,785,859	8,701,430	3,243,939	38,189,919
1988	23,872,342	2,830,284	8,720,571	3,203,822	38,627,019
1989	24,336,894	2,895,364	8,753,999	3,165,113	39,151,370
1990	24,845,533	3,011,294	8,788,288	3,187,010	39,832,125
1991	25,294,018	3,194,938	8,834,965	3,268,252	40,592,173
1992	25,761,409	3,467,783	8,886,823	3,391,173	41,507,188
1993	26,106,762	3,725,966	8,885,508	3,527,483	42,245,719
1994	26,409,376	3,962,954	8,857,253	3,653,887	42,883,470
1995	26,672,806	4,185,263	8,795,093	3,734,097	43,387,259
1996	26,898,072	4,385,623	8,650,350	3,802,791	43,736,836
1997	27,274,572	4,508,134	8,416,606	3,771,774	43,971,086
1998	27,510,535	4,698,319	8,267,949	3,768,928	44,245,731
1999	27,774,677	4,879,455	8,146,697	3,794,795	44,595,624
2000	28,498,945	5,042,334	8,070,652	3,802,863	45,414,794
2001	28,836,774	5,274,183	7,927,168	3,839,381	45,877,506
2002	29,190,137	5,543,981	7,799,943	3,910,256	46,444,317
2003	29,531,611	5,873,673	7,672,303	3,960,909	47,038,486
2004	29,952,465	6,198,271	7,550,638	3,986,319	47,687,693
2005	30,474,930	6,510,420	7,428,240	4,032,310	48,445,900

Source: Authors' compilation based on Table 5.A1 from the Social Security Administration's *Annual Statistical Supplement to the Social Security Bulletin,* various years.

Note: The category "Other adults" combines the figures for the remaining adult categories listed separately in Table 5.A1.

Glossary

"Add on" personal accounts: Individual equity-based investment accounts that would supplement a person's Social Security benefits. They are called "add on" accounts because they typically would leave existing Social Security benefits and taxes in place and would be an addition to the Social Security system. The funding for these personal accounts would thus comes from an increase in the payroll tax or from other federal tax sources or changes in tax policy. *See* **"Carve out" personal accounts.**

Average indexed monthly earnings (AIME): The method of computing benefit amounts in effect since 1978. First, the person's annual average monthly earnings are computed, then these annual figures are indexed to wage inflation, and, finally, the average of these indexed annual values is computed and this becomes the person's AIME. The final step in the benefit calculation is to then use the AIME to determine a person's primary insurance amount. *See* **Primary insurance amount (PIA).**

Average monthly earnings (AME): The method of computing benefit amounts in effect prior to 1978. Under this method, the person's average monthly earnings over the base years period were first computed, and this served as the basis for determining the primary insurance amount. *See* **Base years; Primary insurance amount (PIA).**

Base years: The years included in the calculation of a person's Social Security benefit amount. Generally, the base years are the highest thirty-five years of earnings (with some exceptions). Since the base years are part of the benefit calculation, changes in the base years, or in a person's earnings during a base year, will affect the benefit amount.

"Carve out" personal accounts: Individual equity-based investment accounts in lieu of some or all of a person's Social Security benefits. They are called "carve out" accounts because the money to establish them would come from diverting some portion of the Social Security payroll tax into the personal accounts; that is, the funding would be "carved out" of Social Security revenues.

"Closed group" actuarial estimates: A method of performing long-range actuarial estimates that assumes the system will be "closed" at the time of the estimate and no future participants will enter the system. This allows an estimate to be made of the full future costs to the system for all current participants. To construct such a closed group estimate, the actuaries project income/outgo for 100 years into the future—on the assumption that everyone currently in the system will be dead by the end of that period. The advantage of this type of estimate is that it captures the full future cost obligations of the system. The disadvantage is that it is an entirely artificial construct, as the Social Security system will continue to have new participants with each passing year. Estimates constructed on a closed group basis typically show higher long-term costs than estimates performed on an open group basis, other things being equal. *See* **"Open group" actuarial estimates.**

Consumer Price Index (CPI): The index calculated by the Bureau of Labor Statistics that is used in computing the annual Social Security cost of living adjustment. It is a measure of the increase in prices from one year to the next. Social Security presently uses a measure known as the CPI-W, which is the CPI for urban wage earners and clerical workers.

Continuing disability investigation (CDI): The procedure by which the Social Security Administration periodically reassesses the eligibility of persons receiving Social Security disability benefits. Following the controversies over these reviews in the early 1980s, SSA renamed them continuing disability reviews (CDRs), which is the term currently used.

Continuing disability review (CDR): *See* **Continuing disability investigation (CDI).**

Cost of living adjustment (COLA): The annual increase in Social Security benefits to keep pace with increases in the cost of living (inflation).

Delayed retirement credits (DRC): An increase in Social Security benefits if retirement is delayed beyond the full retirement age. Increases based on delaying retirement no longer apply when people reach age seventy, even if they continue to delay taking benefits.

Disability insurance (DI): *See* **Old Age, Survivors and Disability Insurance (OASDI).**

Early retirement: Taking Social Security retirement benefits at any age prior to the full retirement age. Early retirement subjects the retiree to a benefit reduction. Social Security benefits are payable starting at age sixty-two, but the full retirement age is higher.

Earnings base: *See* **Wage base.**

Earnings record: The complete history of a worker's annual earnings subject to Social Security payroll taxes. This is the record used to compute a Social Security benefit.

Federal Insurance Contributions Act (FICA): The law under which Social Security taxes are levied. The Social Security payroll tax is sometimes referred to as the FICA tax.

Full retirement age (FRA): The age at which a person first becomes entitled to full or unreduced retirement benefits. Beginning with the year 2000 for workers and spouses born 1938 or later and widows/widowers born 1940 or later, the retirement age increases gradually from age sixty-five until it reaches age sixty-seven in 2022. This increase affects the amount of the reduction for persons who begin receiving reduced benefits.

Health, Education, and Welfare (HEW), Department of: The main cabinet department responsible for the social welfare programs of the federal government. The Social Security program was within HEW jurisdiction from the agency's creation in 1953 until 1980, when it was replaced by the Department of Health and Human Services.

Health and Human Services (HHS), Department of: The main cabinet department responsible for the social welfare programs of the federal government. The Social Security program fell within the jurisdiction of this agency from its creation in 1980 until 1995, when the Social Security Administration became an independent agency within the federal government.

Hospital insurance (HI): Part A of Medicare, which pays a portion of the costs of hospital stays.

Infinite horizon actuarial estimates: Estimates of Social Security costs conducted using a 1,000-year time period. In addition to the traditional seventy-five-year actuarial estimates, recent trust fund reports have sometimes included estimates of the program's costs over the "infinite horizon." These are estimates of the income and outgo of the Social Security system over the next 1,000 years. The advantage of this type of estimate is thought to be that it more fully captures the long-term obligations of the system. The disadvantage is that estimates of this length generate values that are so remote as to be virtually meaningless.

Legacy debt: The level of unfunded debt, carried through time in the form of a long-term unfunded liability, that the Social Security program acquired by giving early cohorts of beneficiaries payments in excess of anything they and their employers contributed to the system. Part of the current obligations the system has to meet is some lingering amount from this source. If there were no legacy debt, the unfunded liabilities of the system would be lower.

Level premium rate: The tax rate that would have to be charged throughout an estimating period in order for the Social Security system to be fully funded. For example, a level-premium rate (or level annual cost) of 5 percent for a fifty-year estimating period means that the tax rate would have to be at 5 percent throughout the fifty years in order for the taxes to equal the expenditures.

Maximum earnings: The maximum amount of earnings the federal government can count in any calendar year when computing a person's Social Security benefit. This is also the maximum amount subject to the payroll tax. Earnings above the maximum earnings level are untaxed for Social Security purposes. *See* **Wage base**.

Normal retirement age (NRA): *See* **Full retirement age.**

Old Age, Survivors and Disability Insurance (OASDI): The three types of Social Security benefits. OASI refers to the Old-Age (OA) and Survivors (SI) program without the disability component; DI refers to the disability component. For some purposes the acronyms are combined; for other purposes they are sometimes shown separately.

"Open-group" actuarial estimates: A method of doing long-range actuarial estimates over a fixed period of time. If the estimates range for seventy-five years, the open group estimate computes the balance of taxes and benefits for everyone who will be in the system during the next seventy-five years. The estimate is "open" in that it allows for the addition of new entrants into the system each year. The advantage of this type of estimate is that it describes the actual operation of the Social Security system. The shortcoming of this type of estimate is that it does not reflect the full costs of future benefit obligations because some persons in the system at the time the estimate is made will receive benefits beyond the seventy-five-year period. Typically, open group estimates tend to show lower long-term costs than closed group estimates, other things being equal. *See* **"Closed-group" actuarial estimates.**

Present value: A method of making long-range economic or actuarial estimates that attempts to express the value of very long-term and very large figures in terms that are meaningful in the present. The present value of the unfunded liabilities of the Social Security system is the amount of money one would need in the present to pay all those liabilities on into the future. This is related to—but is not precisely the same—as the concept of expressing future costs in constant dollars rather than in nominal dollars. Expressing very long range costs in nominal dollars tends to inflate the values so massively that one can no longer have any intuitive sense of what such numbers mean. A present value calculation is one technique for coping with this problem. (The calculations of Social Security's unfunded liabilities performed by SSA's actuaries are typically expressed in terms of present value.)

Primary insurance amount (PIA): The basic Social Security benefit amount for a given beneficiary. It is derived from the average indexed monthly earnings through an additional calculation to reflect mandatory reductions or increases (such as the reduction for early retirement). Once a PIA is computed, this becomes the basis for the actual benefit amount. The PIA is also the basis for computing benefits for auxiliaries of a primary beneficiary. Thus, for example, the spousal benefit is defined as 50 percent of the primary beneficiary's PIA. *See* **Average indexed monthly earnings (AIME).**

Quarter of coverage (QC): Social Security "credits." As people work and pay taxes, they earn credits that count toward eligibility for future Social Security benefits. One can earn a maximum of four credits each year. Most people need forty credits to qualify for benefits. Younger people need fewer credits to qualify for disability or for a spouse or child to qualify for survivors' benefits.

Replacement rate: The ratio between a person's initial Social Security benefit and their monthly earnings immediately before retirement. It is a customary way to measure the adequacy of the benefit level. (The average earner would typically have a replacement rate somewhere around 40 percent of his or her preretirement wage.)

Retirement earnings test: A test of whether a person receiving Social Security retirement benefits is, in fact, retired. Typically this is a dollar amount test, but it also can be a level of effort test for a self-employed person. Historically, Social Security retirement benefits were not paid to a person who was not substantially retired from gainful work. Although the level of acceptable earnings has been raised many times over the years, persons who receive retirement benefits prior to full retirement age are still subject to this test. Under the test, their benefits can be reduced or even eliminated if their earnings from work are too high. There is no retirement test for persons at or above the full retirement age.

Self-Employment Contributions Act (SECA): The law under which Social Security taxes are levied for the self-employed. This is the analog of FICA.

Substantial gainful activity (SGA): A dollar figure that is the level of earnings above which a disabled beneficiary is judged to be no longer disabled under the law, even if they are still suffering from a medical impairment. Earnings above the SGA level thus are taken as an indication of recovery from disability and, after certain procedures and various timeframes, could lead to the cessation of disability benefits.

Supplementary Medical Insurance (SMI): Part B of Medicare, which helps pay the cost of doctor bills.

Social Security Administration (SSA): The federal agency created in 1946 that has responsibility for the Social Security programs.

Social Security Board (SSB): The federal agency that had responsibility for the Social Security programs from 1935 to 1946.

Transition costs: The costs associated with shifting from a system of Social Security benefits to one consisting of both the Social Security program and a private accounts program. Under the "carve-out" approach to private accounts, money is diverted out of the Social Security income stream to fund the private accounts. Since the plans typically promise to continue the existing Social Security system for all those now retired or "nearing retirement," the existing system would have to continue to be funded for at least a generation. Thus the diverted monies have to be made up in order to keep the Social Security system in operation for this transition generation; the costs of doing so are the transition costs associated with the carve-out private accounts. Carve-out type private accounts thus have additional costs, over and above any costs associated with solving the existing Social Security system funding shortfall. In most plans, these costs will run into the trillions of dollars.

Unfunded liabilities: This is the difference (if any) between projected future costs and projected future revenues, including any current or projected assets. In private pension systems an unfunded liability is generally the shortfall that would exist if the firm were to go out of business at the time of the estimate. In the case of Social Security (since the government can be assumed to continue in business), the calculation is in reference to a given period of time (as in the standard seventy-five-year actuarial estimates). In Social Security's case, an unfunded liability over the next seventy-five years means that projected income/outgo during that time would not be in balance. It is not clear that this concept is as meaningful a measure of Social Security's financial health as it is in the case of a private pension system.

Wage base: The range of earnings subject to Social Security payroll taxes. There is a cap on the wage base, so that in 2007 earnings from $1 per year up to $97,500 per year are subject to the payroll tax. The cap on the wage base is raised automatically each year to keep pace with the growth in average wages. (Also known as the **Earnings base**.)

Annotated Bibliography

The number of books about Social Security is staggering. This bibliography identifies forty-four books that the authors feel are most useful for scholars and informed citizens alike who are looking for additional information about the history of Social Security and the debates over its future.

Aaron, Henry J., Joseph A. Pechman, and Michael K. Taussing. 1968. *Social Security: Perspectives for Reform*. Washington, D.C.: Brookings Institution Press.
Takes a critical look at Social Security, which is not described as a social insurance program but as a tax transfer mechanism. The idea that Social Security is not a social insurance program is a contentious one, and it is still a significant aspect of the contemporary debate over the future of Social Security.

Achenbaum, Andrew W. 1986. *Social Security: Visions and Revisions*. Cambridge: Cambridge University Press.
Two parts comprise this book. The first part briefly explores the history of Social Security and its development up to the enactment of the 1983 amendments. The second part offers a discussion about a number of policy issues related to the future of Social Security.

Altman, Nancy. 2005. *The Battle for Social Security: From FDR's Vision to Bush's Gamble*. Hoboken, N.J.: John Wiley & Sons.
A narrative history of the program from its inception to the present day, with an emphasis on the legislative battles that have defined the program. The author favors preserving the program along the lines suggested by Robert Ball.

Altmeyer, Arthur J. 1966. *The Formative Years of Social Security*. Madison: University of Wisconsin Press.
Traces the development of Social Security from the New Deal to the 1950s. Alongside Edwin Witte's book, *The Development of the Social Security Act*, this is probably the best known "insider look" at the program's early history. Altmeyer was the first chairman of the Social Security Board.

Amenta, Edwin. 2006. *When Movements Matter: The Townsend Plan and the Rise of Social Security*. Princeton: Princeton University Press.
Tells the story of the Townsend Plan and shows how it affected the development of Social Security and state old age assistance programs between 1934 and 1950. Draws upon the sociological literature on social movements to explain how grassroots mobilization can impact policy change.

Arnold, R. Douglas, Michael J. Graetz, and Alicia H. Munnell, eds. 1998. *Framing the Social Security Debate: Values, Politics, and Economics*. Washington, D.C.: Brookings Institution Press.
Offers a good overview of the Social Security privatization debate, which became increasingly intense at the time this edited volume appeared. Interestingly, it gives voice to both supporters and opponents of Social Security privatization.

Baker, Dean, and Mark Weisbrot. 1999. *Social Security: The Phony Crisis*. Chicago: Chicago University Press.
A liberal take on the debate over Social Security privatization. Claims that those supporting privatization have created a false sense of fiscal crisis by exaggerating the demographic challenge the program could face in the decades to come.

Ball, Robert M. (with Thomas N. Bethell). 1998. *Straight Talk about Social Security: An Analysis of the Issues in the Current Debate.* **New York: Century Foundation/Twentieth Century Fund.**
Stresses what former Social Security commissioner Robert Ball describes as the risks associated with Social Security privatization. Offers a complex plan that would improve the long-term fiscal status of Social Security without repudiating its social insurance logic.

Ball, Robert M., 2000. *Insuring the Essentials: Bob Ball on Social Security.* **New York: Century Foundation.**
A collection of essays by a prominent Social Security expert that articulates the traditional view of the value of social insurance in general and Social Security in particular. Provides—by way of essays written between 1942 to 2000—a window into the historical development of Social Security, written by an insider who participated in much of that history.

Béland, Daniel. 2007. *Social Security: History and Politics from the New Deal to the Privatization Debate* **(paperback edition with new afterword). Lawrence: University Press of Kansas.**
A theoretically informed analysis of the historical and political development of Social Security from the 1930s to the mid-2000s. Examines the impact of gender, race, comparative pension policy, and the role of business and labor interests in social policy.

Berkowitz, Edward D. 1989. *Disabled Policy: America's Programs for the Handicapped.* **New York: Cambridge University Press.**
The most comprehensive historical account on the development of federal disability insurance and other programs for the disabled. Covers more than eight decades and "brings order to the labyrinth of disability programs." Suggests that the United States, despite the development of many disability programs, lacks a coherent disability policy.

Berkowitz, Edward D. 1995. *Mr. Social Security: The Life of Wilbur J. Cohen.* **Lawrence: University Press of Kansas.**
Traces the professional life of one of the founders of the American social insurance system. Cohen was a key federal civil servant involved in the creation of Medicare and the postwar expansion of Social Security.

Berkowitz, Edward D. 2003. *Robert Ball and the Politics of Social Security.* **Madison: University of Wisconsin Press.**
Explores the politics of Social Security through the life and work of Robert Ball, who played a major role during the postwar expansion of Social Security. Later, Ball became a prominent member of the Greenspan Commission and the 1994–1996 Advisory Council on Social Security.

Blahous, Charles P., III. 2000. *Reforming Social Security for Ourselves and Our Prosterity.* **Westport, Conn.: Praeger.**
A comprehensive critique of the existing Social Security program by an experienced Capitol Hill staffer and policy advocate. Argues for major changes in Social Security, along the lines of those originally proposed by the National Commission on Retirement Policy of the Center for Strategic and International Studies, of which Blahous was a staff member.

Bonoli, Giuliano, and Toshimitsu Shinkawa, eds. 2005. *Ageing and Pension Reform around the World: Evidence from Eleven Countries.* **Cheltenham, U.K.: Edward Elgar.**
Provides a comparative overview of the international debates about the future of public pension systems like Social Security. Countries analyzed include Britain, Canada, France, Germany, Japan, South Korea, Sweden, Switzerland, Taiwan, and the United States. R. Kent Weaver wrote the chapter on the United States.

Burns, Eveline. 1936. *Toward Social Security. An Explanation of the Social Security Act and a Survey of the Larger Issues.* **New York: Whittlesey House.**
Takes a critical look at the initial Social Security Act, which is seen as largely inadequate. Authored by a member of the technical staff of the Committee on Economic Security who would later serve as professor of economics at Columbia University for nearly four decades.

Cates, Jerry R. 1983. *Insuring Inequality: Administrative Leadership in Social Security, 1935–1954.* Ann Arbor: University of Michigan Press.
Stresses the key role of top civil servants like Arthur Altmeyer in the early debates over the development of old age insurance. Argues that these actors successfully prevented the enactment of what Cates describes as a more egalitarian and fairer alternative to Social Security: the flat pension.

Derthick, Martha. 1979. *Policymaking for Social Security.* Washington, D.C.: Brookings Institution Press.
For many years the definitive account of the politics that characterized the program from 1950 to 1972. Particularly known for its look at the bureaucrats who ran the program with little interference from the White House.

Diamond, Peter A., and Peter R. Orszag. 2004. *Saving Social Security: A Balanced Approach.* Washington, D.C.: Brookings Institution Press.
Formulates a reform plan dealing directly with the demographic and fiscal challenges that should affect Social Security over the next few decades. Rejects both privatization and the status quo.

Epstein, Abraham. 1936 (1933). *Insecurity: A Challenge to America,* 3d ed. New York: Random House.
Offers historical and international background on social insurance as well as a critical overview of the 1935 Social Security Act. Describes this legislation as grossly inadequate. Written by a prominent social reformer who helped organize the American pension movement during the 1920s and early 1930s.

Favreault, Melissa M., Frank J. Sammartino, and C. Eugene Steuerle, eds. 2001. *Social Security and the Family: Addressing Unmet Needs in an Underfunded System.* Washington, D.C.: Urban Institute.
Examines the history and the current structure of spousal and family benefits for Social Security. Assesses a number of reform proposals dealing with this policy area.

Ferrara, Peter J. 1998. *A New Deal for Social Security.* Washington, D.C.: Cato Institute National Book Network.
Makes a systematic case for Social Security privatization. A fine example of the individualistic discourse against social insurance that is a central aspect of the debate over Social Security's future.

Ferrara, Peter J., and Michael D. Tanner. 1998. *Common Cents, Common Dreams: A Layman's Guide to Social Security Privatization.* Washington, D.C.: Cato Institute.
An accessible overview of the arguments traditionally formulated in order to convince ordinary citizens to support Social Security privatization. These arguments include the unsustainable nature of Social Security and the higher return rates of personal savings accounts at the center of most privatization proposals.

Haber, William, and Wilbur Cohen, eds. 1960. *Social Security: Programs, Problems, and Policies.* Homewood, Ill.: Richard D. Irwin.
Draws on a variety of sources to document major social policy debates taking place during the 1940s and 1950s. Updates and supplements Haber and Cohen's social policy reader published twelve years earlier (*Readings in Social Security,* Prentice-Hall, 1948). The words "Social Security" in the title of both books refers to federal social policy at large, but they each feature major documents dealing with the early development of old age insurance.

Hacker, Jacob S. 2002. *The Divided Welfare State: The Battle over Public and Private Social Benefits in the United States.* New York: Cambridge University Press.
Compares the changing relationship between public and private benefits in two policy areas: health care and old age pensions. Focuses mainly on the period of the mid-1930s to the mid-1970s.

Kingson, Eric R., and Edward D. Berkowitz. 1993. *Social Security and Medicare: A Policy Primer.* Westport, Conn.: Auburn House.
An accessible introduction to the key policy issues in the Social Security and Medicare programs.

Kingson, Eric R., and James H. Schulz, eds. 1997. *Social Security in the 21st Century.* **New York and Oxford: Oxford University Press.**
An anthology of essays that provides a comprehensive examination of Social Security's history and contemporary policy debates.

Klein, Jennifer. 2003. *For All These Rights: Business, Labor, and the Shaping of America's Public-Private Welfare State.* **Princeton: Princeton University Press.**
Offers a detailed exploration of the interaction between public and private benefits in health care and old age pensions. Provides original insight about issues like gender and the ideology of protection related to the development of Social Security during and after the New Deal.

Lieberman, Robert C. 1998. *Shifting the Color Line: Race and the American Welfare State.* **Cambridge, Mass.: Harvard University Press.**
Explores the relationship between race and federal social policy development (i.e., old age pensions, unemployment insurance, and welfare) in the United States from the New Deal to the postwar era. Uses both qualitative and quantitative methods; devotes one full chapter to old age pensions and Social Security.

Light, Paul. 1995. *Still Artful Work: The Continuing Politics of Social Security Reform.* **New York: McGraw-Hill.**
The most detailed account available on the political debates and strategies leading to the enactment of the 1983 amendments. Focuses primarily on the role of political actors like the AARP, Congress, the White House, and key members of the Greenspan Commission.

Meriam, Lewis. 1946. *Relief and Social Security.* **Washington, D.C.: Brookings Institution Press.**
A systematic assessment of the Social Security Act published barely eleven years after its enactment. Takes a critical look at old age insurance and proposes the abolition of the payroll tax and the creation of a universal social security system similar to the one adopted in New Zealand during the 1930s.

Mettler, Suzanne. 1998. *Dividing Citizens: Gender and Federalism in New Deal Public Policy.* **Cornell: Cornell University Press.**
Provides a feminist perspective on welfare state development, with a focus on the relationship between citizenship, gender, and federalism during the New Deal. Features in-depth discussions about the enactment of Social Security and the structuring role of gender in the adoption of the 1939 amendments.

Moss, David A. 1996. *Socializing Security: Progressive-Era Economists and the Origins of American Social Policy.* **Cambridge, Mass.: Harvard University Press.**
Traces the history of the American Association for Labor Legislation, which played an instrumental role in popularizing the idea of social insurance during the Progressive Era. Explores early debates over social insurance in the United States.

Myers, Robert J. 1993. *Social Security, Fourth Edition.* **Philadelphia, PA.: University of Pennsylvania Press.**
The definitive expert explanation of the provisions of the Social Security and Medicare programs.

Orloff, Ann Shola. *The Politics of Pensions: A Comparative Analysis of Britain, Canada and the United States, 1880s–1940.* **Madison: University of Wisconsin Press.**
Explores the early development of old age pensions from a comparative and sociological perspective.

Poole, Mary. 2006. *The Segregated Origins of Social Security: African Americans and the Welfare State.* **Chapel Hill: University of North Carolina Press.**
Analyzes the impact of race on the enactment of the Social Security Act. In contrast to Robert Lieberman's *Shifting the Color Line,* rejects the idea that Southern Democrats in Congress are largely responsible for the 1935 exclusion of agrarian and domestic workers from Social Security. Argues that the hidden racial beliefs of top federal officials like Edwin Witte explain this exclusion, which disproportionately affected African Americans.

Quadagno, Jill. 1988. *The Transformation of Old Age Security: Class and Politics in the American Welfare State.* Chicago: University of Chicago Press.
Discusses the changing relationship between Social Security and two other key aspects of American old age policy: social assistance and private pensions. Stresses the role of race and labor politics in American pension reform from the 1930s to the 1960s.

Rubinow, Isaac M. 1913. *Social Insurance: With Special Reference to American Conditions.* New York: Henry Holt and Company, 1913.
Supports the implementation of social insurance programs in the United States. A discussion of recent European reforms supplements the analysis of economic and social transformations that, according to this prominent social reformer, exacerbate the economic insecurity of workers. Social insurance is described as the best way to fight this growing insecurity related to industrialization and urbanization.

Schieber, Sylvester J., and John B. Shoven. 1999. *The Real Deal: The History and Future of Social Security.* New Haven: Yale University Press.
A perspective on the history and future of Social Security grounded in the idea that this program is a "bad deal" for Americans. An example of the contemporary scholarship explicitly supporting Social Security privatization. Surveys the history of the program from the mid-1930s before making a case for privatization.

Shaviro, Daniel. 2000. *Making Sense of Social Security Reform.* Chicago: University of Chicago Press.
An attempt by a law school professor to explain in a balanced way what the issues and options are in the debate over Social Security reform.

Steuerle, C. Eugene, and Jon M. Bakija. 1994. *Retooling Social Security.* Washington, D.C.: Urban Institute Press.
A comprehensive review of the way the Social Security works today, along with the authors' prescriptions for how to reform the program—whether or not it faces long-range financing problems—to make it better reflect the health, longevity, and work patterns of contemporary America.

Tynes, Sheryl R. 1996. *Turning Points in Social Security: From "Cruel Hoax" to "Sacred Entitlement."* Stanford: Stanford University Press.
A sociological analysis of the emergence and the postwar expansion of Social Security. Features systematic theoretical discussions that frame the historical narration.

Weaver, Carolyn L. 1982. *The Crisis of Social Security: Economic and Political Origins.* Durham, N.C.: Duke Press Policy Studies, 1982.
Covers the enactment and the post-war development of Social Security. Describes this development—especially the reforms enacted during the Nixon presidency—as unreasonable. Stresses the central role of Congress and federal civil servants in what is described as an overly generous expansion of Social Security.

Weaver, R. Kent. 1988. *Automatic Government: The Politics of Indexation.* Washington, D.C.: Brookings Institution Press.
Offers a systematic analysis of the advent and expansion of automatic indexation schemes in federal public policy. The chapter on Social Security explores the politics of indexation in Social Security during the Nixon administration.

White, Joseph. 2001. *False Alarm: Why the Greatest Threat to Social Security and Medicare Is the Campaign to "Save" Them.* Baltimore, Md.: Johns Hopkins University Press.
Argues that dramatic reforms are not needed to address the challenges facing Social Security and Medicare, and that incremental reforms in keeping the traditions of these programs is the appropriate policy response. Attempts to "debunk" the notion that the nation faces a massive crisis in its entitlement programs.

Witte, Edwin, E. 1962. *The Development of the Social Security Act.* Madison: University of Wisconsin Press.
A personal recollection of the debates surrounding the formulation and enactment of the Social Security Act. The author served as executive director and secretary of the Committee on Economic Security.

Index

547